The Basics of Sociology

Bassim Hamadeh, CEO and Publisher
Angela Schultz, Senior Field Acquisitions Editor
Michelle Piehl, Project Editor
Alia Bales, Production Editor
Miguel Macias, Senior Graphic Designer
Stephanie Kohl, Licensing Coordinator
Don Kesner, Interior Designer
Natalie Piccotti, Director of Marketing
Kassie Graves, Vice President of Editorial
Jamie Giganti, Director of Academic Publishing

ISBN: 978-1-5165-1353-6 (pbk) / 978-1-5165-1354-3(br)

The Basics of Sociology

DEVELOPING AND APPLYING THE SOCIOLOGICAL IMAGINATION

FIRST EDITION

Edited by Christina Ryder
Missouri State University

Contents

Foundations of the Discipline

1 | An Introduction to Sociology and Public Sociology

CHAPTER SUMMARY

- This chapter defines society and provides the history and foundations of sociology.

- This chapter discusses the "sociological imagination" and how to think sociologically and invites readers to begin developing their sociological imagination.

- This chapter defines "public sociology" and asks readers to contemplate the role of sociology in everyday life and in the discussion of social problems.

PRELIMINARY QUESTIONS FOR READERS

- How does our environment (the social context and time in history in which we live) impact our attitudes and behavior? This can include things like what we wear, eat, and watch but can also include things like how we interact in public spaces as compared to other societies around the world.

- What is the value in understanding how our environment impacts individual or collective behavior?

- How might an understanding of the influence of our environment impact discussion about problems that impact the larger society or environment in which we live?

CHAPTER INTRODUCTION

The Origins of Society and the Definition of Sociology

Every discipline, including religious theologies and others, has a unique way of understanding the origins of human behavior, the purpose of society, why humans gravitate to one another (or form groups), and the reasons behind why we have developed elaborate structures for organizing ourselves (such as forming countries, laws for behavior, etc.). Sociology, clearly, also provides some insights into such phenomena. A **society** is traditionally defined as a group that exists within specific and identifiable geographic boundaries and a group that shares some common laws and a common popular culture.

In his book, *Unraveling Social Policy* (1981), David G. Gil sees societies as forming as a direct result for the need of humankind to survive. He sees society as a means by which basic needs (such as food, shelter, the need for friendship and belonging) are distributed and maintained. Out of this, **roles** are given to individuals (such as farmer, trash collector, homemaker, and so forth) in order to ensure that the necessary functions for the survival of a society are performed. These roles, according to Gil, contain various rights and privileges in a society depending on the level of prestige and value assigned to them. These roles then also assign **status** to individuals and groups, or give individuals and groups a certain level of access to specific and/or necessary goods, resources, and power in a society. We will explore this process, called social differentiation and social stratification, in further chapters. **Social policies** that emerge from discourse, debate, and competition (otherwise defined as **politics**), according to Gil, exist to either protect these processes as they are (what might be defined as the "status quo") or seek to alleviate disparities and inequalities that result from these structures.

As explored in the first article in this chapter, **sociology** is simply defined as the scientific study of society or the study of societies. This includes social behavior, how environments impact individual behavior, the study of groups, culture (or the ways of life, including traditions, artifacts, values, and the belief systems of various groups and subgroups in a society), social issues, social phenomena, roles and status, social problems that are a result of how a society and its institutions are organized, and social policies. While sociology is considered to be a part of the social sciences, it differs from other disciplines included within this broad category, such as psychology (the study of human personality), anthropology (the study of culture), and political science (the study of government and politics). The social sciences utilize a specific set of research techniques and theoretical frameworks to research, discuss, and explain social occurrences and social behaviors. An introduction to these research techniques and theories is provided in the second and third chapters of this book.

THE HISTORY OF SOCIOLOGY

The first article in this chapter, "Sociology and the Social Sciences," explores some of the philosophical underpinnings of the discipline. In doing so, it is first important to also understand the historical context in which it emerged. Sociology was formalized as a scientific discipline in Europe as a direct result of the changes brought about due to the Industrial Revolution. As explored briefly in the second article in the chapter, this time period brought about changes in population and social organization—including the movement to cities (otherwise known as "urbanization," and current sociological approaches to studying population and urbanization are explored in further depth in the final section of this book), the formalization of what became defined as a "working class" (class structures and the institution of work are further discussed in the fifth chapter of this book), changes to the family and changes in gender relations (gender and the institution of family is explored in Chapter 6 in this book), and socio-structural inequalities (as well as social differentiation) that characterize much of our conversation around modern social inequality. The significance and influence of various institutions, such as religion, for example, were also being questioned in the face of such rapid change (the institution of religion is explored in Chapter 7 as is the study of social change) (Collingwood, 1946). While these are not the only topics that the discipline of sociology explores, the trajectory of this book and its topics is intentional and couched within these topics, not only because of their historical significance to the discipline, but also because these topics have ongoing significance in understanding and analyzing society.

HOW TO THINK SOCIOLOGICALLY

C. Wright Mills (1916–1962) wrote about how to think sociologically in his book *The Sociological Imagination*. Mills defined the **"sociological imagination"** as the ability to see the social patterns that influence the individual as well as groups of individuals (or the way in which society impacts our interpersonal and collective lives) (Mills, 1960). In his work, he defines "troubles" as those concerns that impact the individual specifically (such as falling down a flight of stairs and breaking one's leg). He defines "issues" as those concerns that were a direct result of social structures and concerns that impacted a wide range of individuals (such as having to file bankruptcy as a result of not having medical insurance or not being able to pay the medical bills associated with a broken leg). This difference between "troubles" and "issues" is imperative as we explore social concerns, problems, and constructs (and the overt policies or subtle social behavior that are a result of these constructs) in a society. The second article in this chapter, "How to Think Sociologically," explores the underpinnings of the discipline and fundamental concepts for developing one's sociological imagination. It discusses how we can incorporate the sociological imagination in our observations of the everyday social world.

SOCIOLOGY OUTSIDE OF THE UNIVERSITY

"Sociology is something you do, not something you read."

—Erving Goffman

This book is divided into three sections: (1) The Foundations of the Discipline of Sociology; (2) Social Inequality and Social Problems; (3) Social Change and Applying Sociology. This book also focuses specifically on the institutions of family, religion, education, work and economy (or the systems that distribute resources, particularly within the increasing influence of capitalism in the modern world), as well as the structures and constructs of age, gender, race, and sexuality among a variety of potential social institutions and structures given that these have not only held prominence in the study of the discipline historically, but also because these are prominent institutions and structures that socialize new members into society, influence identity, and often regulate social and individual opportunity for achievement. The institutions and structures discussed in this text are intended to be examples that serve as a basis for analyzing the arrangements, challenges, and benefits of other institutions and structures. For example, while the institution of media is not discussed in detail, the importance of media as an institution and its impact on the dissemination and absorption of social and cultural values is not intended to be understated but rather understood as a medium in which popular cultural beliefs and values are both impacted and expressed upon the social stage (Muchlan & Lapham, 1964).

Each chapter includes an introduction, a compilation of key historical, contemporary, or applied readings that relate to the concepts being explored, review and discussion questions, as well as case studies and secondary data exercises designed to assist in developing the sociological imagination and provide the opportunity for you to engage directly in the work of "public sociology."

Public sociology, as defined by Michael Burawoy (2004), "endeavors to bring sociology into dialogue with audiences beyond the academy, an open dialogue in which both sides deepen their understanding of public issues." This is not simply the application of sociological principles to solve social problems or issues but rather exposing the foundations and structures on which such problems are built upon or are a result of. There are many ways in which sociology over the course of its tenure as a scientific discipline has been applied to various spheres of social, political, and institutional life outside the study of society in a university setting. This book places particular emphasis on how the concepts being explored can, or have been, put to use.

WORKS CITED

Burawoy, M. (2004). *For public sociology. 2004 presidential address.* Berkeley, CA: University of California, Berkeley Press.

Collingwood, R.G. (1946). *The idea of history.* London: Oxford University Press (Reprint Edition, September 22, 1994).

Gil, D.G. (1981). *Unraveling social policy*. Cambridge, MA: Schenkman Publishing Company, Inc.

McLuhan, M. and Lapham, L.H. (1964). *Understanding media: The extensions of man*. Cambridge, MA: The MIT Press (Reprint Edition, October 20, 1994).

Mills, C.W. (1960). *The sociological imagination*. London: Oxford University Press (Reprint Edition, April 13, 2000).

Peters, S.I. (2008). World migration in the age of globalization: Policy implications and challenges. *New Zealand Population Review, 33/34*: 1–22.

Sociology and the Social Sciences

by Émile Durkheim; ed. Mark Traugott

When dealing with a new science such as sociology, which, born only yesterday, is merely in the process of being constituted, the best way to understand its nature, object, and method is to retrace its genesis in a summary fashion.

The word *sociology* was created by Auguste Comte to designate the science of societies.[1] If the word was new, it was because the thing itself was new; a neologism was necessary. To be sure, one could say in a very broad sense that speculation about political and social matters began before the nineteenth century: Plato's *Republic,* Aristotle's *Politics,* and the innumerable treatises for which these two works served as models—those of Campanella, of Hobbes, of Rousseau and of so many others—already dealt with these questions. But these various studies differed in one fundamental respect from those which are designated by the word *sociology.* They took as their object not the description or explanation of societies as they exist or as they have existed, but the investigation of what societies *should be, how they should be organized* in order to be as perfect as possible. The aim of the sociologist is entirely different; he studies societies simply *to know them* and *to understand them,* just as the

physicist, the chemist, and the biologist do for physical, chemical, and biological phenomena. His sole task is properly to determine the facts which he undertakes to study, to discover the laws according to which they occur, leaving it to others to find, if there is need, the possible applications of the propositions which he establishes.

That is to say that sociology could not appear until men had acquired the sense that societies, like the rest of the world, are subject to laws which of necessity derive from and express their nature. Now this conception was very slow to take form. For centuries, men believed that even minerals were not ruled by definite laws but could take on all possible forms and properties if only a sufficiently powerful will applied itself to them. They believed that certain expressions or certain gestures had the ability to transform an inert mass into a living being, a man into an animal or a plant, and vice versa. This illusion, for which we have a sort of instinctive inclination, naturally persisted much longer in the realm of social phenomena.

In effect, since they are far more complex, the order which inheres in social phenomena is far more difficult to perceive and, consequently, one is led to believe that they occur in a contingent and more or less disordered way. At first sight, what a contrast exists between the simple, rigorous sequence with which the phenomena of the physical universe unfold and the chaotic, capricious, disconcerting aspect of the events which history records! From another viewpoint, the very part which we play therein disposes us to think that, since they are done by us, they depend exclusively on us and can be what we want them to be. In such circumstances, there was no reason to observe them, since they were nothing by themselves but derived any reality they had from our will alone. From this point of view, the only question which could come up was to know not what they were and according to what laws they operated but what we could and must desire them to be.

It was only at the end of the eighteenth century that people first began to perceive that the social realm, like the other realms of nature, had its own laws. When Montesquieu declared that "The laws are the necessary relationships which derive from the nature of things," he well understood that this excellent definition of natural law applied to social as well as to other phenomena; his book, *The Spirit of Laws,* attempts to show precisely how legal institutions are grounded in man's nature and his milieu. Soon thereafter, Condorcet undertook to reconstruct the order according to which mankind achieved its progress.[2] This was the best way to demonstrate that there was nothing fortuitous or capricious about it but that it depended on determinate causes. At the same time, the economists taught that the phenomena of industrial and commercial life are governed by laws, which they thought they had discovered.

Although these different thinkers had prepared the way for the conception on which sociology rests, they had as yet only a rather ambiguous and irresolute notion of what the laws of social life might be. They did not wish to say, in effect, that social facts link up according to definite and invariable relations which the scholar seeks to observe by procedures analogous to those which are employed in the natural sciences. They simply meant that, given the nature of man, a course was layed out which was the only natural one, the one mankind should follow *if it wished to be in harmony with itself and to fulfill its destiny;* but it was still possible that it had strayed from that path.

And in fact, they judged that mankind had ceaselessly strayed as the result of deplorable aberrations which, moreover, they did not take much trouble to explain. For the economists, for example, the true economic organization, the only one which science should undertake to know, has, so to speak, never existed; it is more ideal than real. For men, under the influence of their rulers and as a result of a veritable blindness, have always let themselves be led astray. That is to say that the economists far more often constructed it deductively than observed it; and in this way they returned, though in an indirect way, to the ideas which were the basis of the political theories of Plato and Aristotle.

It is only at the beginning of the nineteenth century, with Saint-Simon at first, and especially with his disciple, Auguste Comte, that a new conception was definitively brought to light.[3]

Proceeding to the synthetic view of all the constituted sciences of his time in his *Cours de philosophie positive,* Comte stated that they all rested on the axiom that the phenomena with which they dealt are linked according to necessary relationships, that is to say, on the determinist principle. From this fact, he concluded that this principle, which had thus been verified in all the other realms of nature from the realm of mathematical splendors to that of life, must be equally true of the social realm. The resistances which today are opposed to this new extension of the determinist idea must not stop the philosopher. They have arisen with regularity each time that it has been a question of extending to a new realm this fundamental postulate and they always have been overcome. There was a time when people refused to accept that this principle applied even in the world of inanimate objects; it was established there. Next it was denied for living and thinking beings; now it is undisputed there as well.

One can therefore rest assured that these same prejudices which this principle encountered in the attempt to apply it to the social world will last only for a time. Moreover, since Comte postulated as a self-evident truth—a truth which is, moreover, now undisputed—that the individual's mental life is subject to necessary laws, how could the actions and reactions which are exchanged among individual consciousnesses in association not be subjected to the same necessity?

Viewed in this way, societies ceased to appear as a sort of indefinitely malleable and plastic matter that men could mold, so to speak, at will; thenceforth, it was necessary to see them as realities whose nature is imposed upon us and which, like all natural things, can only be modified in conformity with the laws which regulate them. Human institutions could be considered no longer as the product of the more or less enlightened will of princes, statesmen, and legislators, but as the necessary result of determinate causes that

physically imply them. Given the composition of a nation at a given moment in its history, and the state of its civilization at this same period, a social organization results which is characterized in this or that manner, just as the properties of a physical body result from its molecular constitution. We are thus faced with a stable, immutable order of things, and pure science becomes at once possible and necessary for describing and explaining it, for saying what its characteristics are and on what causes they depend. This purely speculative science is sociology. In order better to suggest the relationship in which it stands to the other positive sciences, Comte often calls it social physics.

It has sometimes been said that this conception implies a sort of fatalism. If the network of social facts is so solid and so resistant a web, does it not follow that men are incapable of modifying it and that, consequently, they cannot act upon their own history? But the example of what has happened in the other realms of nature demonstrates to what extent this reproach is unjustified. As we were saying a moment ago, there was a time when the human mind did not know that the physical universe had its laws. Was it then that man held greatest sway over things? No doubt, the sorcerer or the magician believed that he could transmute at will various bodies one into another; but the powers which he thus attributed to himself were, we know today, purely imaginary. On the contrary, since the positive natural sciences were established (and they too were established by taking the determinist postulate as a foundation), what changes we have introduced into the universe! It will be the same way in the social realm. Until yesterday we believed that all this was arbitrary and contingent, that legislators or kings could, just like the alchemists of yore, at their pleasure change the aspect of societies, make them change from one type to another. In reality, these supposed miracles were illusory; and how many grave errors have resulted from this yet too widespread illusion! On the contrary, it is sociology which by discovering the laws of social reality will permit us to direct historical evolution with greater reflection than in the past; for we can change nature, whether moral or physical, only by conforming to its laws. Progress in political arts will follow those in social science, just as the discoveries of physiology and anatomy helped perfect medical arts, just as the power of industry has increased a hundredfold since mechanics and the physico-chemical sciences have sprung to life. At the same time that they proclaim the necessity of things, the sciences place in our hands the means to dominate that necessity.[4] Comte even remarks with insistence that of all the natural phenomena, social phenomena are the most malleable, the most accessible to variations and to changes, because they are the most complex. Therefore, sociology in no way imposes upon man a passively conservative attitude; on the contrary, it extends the field of our action by the simple fact that it extends the field of our science. It only turns us away from ill-conceived and sterile enterprises inspired by the belief that we are able to change the social order as we wish, without taking into account customs, traditions, and the mental constitution of man and of societies.

But, as essential as this principle may be, it was not a sufficient basis on which to found sociology. For there to be substance to a new science called by this name, it was yet necessary that the subject matter which it undertakes to study not be confused with those which the other sciences treat. Now on first consideration,

sociology might appear indistinguishable from psychology; and this thesis has in fact been maintained, by Tarde, among others.[5] Society, they say, is nothing but the individuals of whom it is composed. They are its only reality. How, then, can the science of societies be distinguished from the science of individuals, that is to say, from psychology?

If one reasons in this way, one could equally well maintain that biology is but a chapter of physics and chemistry, for the living cell is composed exclusively of atoms of carbon, nitrogen, and so on, which the physico-chemical sciences undertake to study. But that is to forget that a whole very often has very different properties from those which its constituent parts possess. Though a cell contains nothing but mineral elements, these reveal, by being combined in a certain way, properties which they do not have when they are not thus combined and which are characteristic of life (properties of sustenance and of reproduction); they thus form, through their synthesis, a reality of an entirely new sort, which is living reality and which constitutes the subject matter of biology. In the same way, individual consciousnesses, by associating themselves in a stable way, reveal, through their interrelationships, a new life very different from that which would have developed had they remained uncombined; this is social life. Religious institutions and beliefs, political, legal, moral, and economic institutions—in a word, all of what constitutes civilization—would not exist if there were no society.

In effect, civilization presupposes cooperation not only among all the members of a single society, but also among all the societies which interact with one another. Moreover, it is possible only if the results obtained by one generation are transmitted to the following generation in such a way that they can be added to the results which the latter will obtain. But for that to happen, the successive generations must not be separated from one another as they arrive at adulthood but must remain in close contact, that is to say, they must be associated in a permanent fashion. Thus, this entire, vast assembly of things exists only because there are human associations; moreover, they vary according to what these associations are, and how they are organized. These things find their immediate explanation in the nature of societies, not of individuals, and constitute, therefore, the subject matter of a new science distinct from, though related to, individual psychology: this is sociology.[6]

Comte was not content to establish these two principles theoretically; he undertook to put them into practice, and, for the first time, he attempted to create a sociological discipline. It is for this purpose that he uses the three final volumes of the *Cours de philosophie positive*. Little remains today of the details of his work. Historical and especially ethnographic knowledge was still too rudimentary in his time to offer a sufficiently solid basis for sociological inductions. Moreover, as we shall see below, Comte did not recognize the multiplicity of the problems posed by the new science: he thought that he could create it all at once, as one would create a system of metaphysics; sociology, however, like any science, can be constituted only progressively, by approaching questions one after another. But the idea was infinitely fertile and outlived the founder of positivism.

It was taken up again first by Herbert Spencer.[7] Then, in the last thirty years, a whole legion of workers arose—to some extent in all countries, but particularly in France—and applied themselves to these studies. Sociology has now left behind the heroic age. The principles on which it rests and which were originally proclaimed in a very philosophical and dialectical way have now received factual confirmation. It assumes that social phenomena are in no way contingent or arbitrary. Sociologists have shown that certain moral and legal institutions and certain religious beliefs are identical everywhere that the conditions of social life are identical. They have even been able to establish similarities in the details of the customs of countries very distant from each other and between which there has never been any sort of communication. This remarkable uniformity is the best proof that the social realm does not escape the law of universal determinism.[8]

II. THE DIVISIONS OF SOCIOLOGY: THE INDIVIDUAL SOCIAL SCIENCES

But if, in a sense, sociology is a unified science, still it includes a multiplicity of questions and, consequently, a multiplicity of individual sciences. Therefore, let us examine these sciences of which sociology is the corpus.

Comte already felt the need to divide it up; he distinguished two parts: social statics and social dynamics. Statics studies societies by considering them as fixed at a given point in their development; it seeks the laws of their equilibrium. At each moment in time, the individuals and the groups which shape them are joined to one another by bonds of a certain type, which assure social cohesion; and the various estates of a single civilization maintain definite relations with one another. To a given degree of elaboration of science, for example, corresponds a specific development of religion, morality, art, industry, and so forth. Statics tries to determine what these bonds of solidarity and these connections are. Dynamics, on the contrary, considers societies in their evolution and attempts to discover the law of their development. But the object of statics as Comte understood it is very indeterminate, since it arises from the definition which we have just given; moreover, he devotes only a few pages to it in the *Cours de philosophie*. Dynamics take up all the rest. Now the problem with which dynamics deals is unique: according to Comte, a single and invariable law dominates the course of evolution; this is the famous Law of Three Stages.[9] The sole object of social dynamics is to investigate this law. Thus understood, sociology is reduced to a single question; so much so that once this single question has been resolved—and Comte believed he had found the definitive solution—the science will be complete. Now it is in the very nature of the positive sciences that they are never complete. The realities with which they deal are far too complex ever to be exhausted. If sociology is a positive science, we can be assured that it does not consist in a single problem but includes, on the contrary, different parts, many distinct sciences which correspond to the various aspects of social life.

There are, in reality, as many branches of sociology, as many individual social sciences, as there are different types of social facts. A methodical classification of social facts would be premature and, in any case, will not be attempted here. But it is possible to indicate its principal categories.

First of all, there is reason to study society in its external aspect. From this angle, it appears to be formed by a mass of population of a certain density, disposed on the face of the earth in a certain fashion, dispersed in the countryside or concentrated in cities, and so on. It occupies a more or less extensive territory, situated in a certain way relative to the seas and to the territories of neighboring peoples, more or less furrowed with waterways and paths of communications of all sorts which place the inhabitants in more or less intimate relationship. This territory, its dimensions, its configuration, and the composition of the population which moves upon its surface are naturally important factors of social life; they are its substratum and, just as psychic life in the individual varies with the anatomical composition of the brain which supports it, collective phenomena vary with the constitution of the social substratum. There is, therefore, room for a social science which traces its anatomy; and since this science has as its object the external and material form of society, we propose to call it *social morphology*. Social morphology does not, moreover, have to limit itself to a descriptive analysis; it must also explain. It must look for the reasons why the population is massed at certain points rather than at others, why it is principally urban or principally rural, what are the causes which favor or impede the development of great cities, and so on. We can see that this special science itself has a multitude of problems with which to deal.[10]

But parallel to the substratum of collective life, there is this life itself. Here we run across a distinction analogous to that which we observe in the other natural sciences. Alongside chemistry, which studies the way in which minerals are constituted, there is physics, the subject matter of which is the phenomena of all sorts for which the bodies thus constituted are the theater. In biology, while anatomy (also called morphology) analyzes the structure of living beings and the mode of composition of their tissues and organs, physiology studies the functions of these tissues and organs. In the same way, beside social morphology there is room for a social physiology which studies the vital manifestations of societies.

But social physiology is itself very complex and includes a multiplicity of individual sciences; for the social phenomena of the physiological order are themselves extremely varied.

First there are religious beliefs, practices, and institutions. Religion is, in effect, a social phenomenon, since it has always been a property of a group, namely, a church, and because in the great majority of cases the church and the political society are indistinct. Until very recent times, one was faithful to certain divinities by the very fact that one was the citizen of a certain state. In any case, dogmas and myths have always consisted in systems of beliefs common to an entire collectivity and obligatory for the members of that collectivity. It is the same way with rituals. The study of religion is, therefore, the domain of sociology; it constitutes the subject matter of the *sociology of religion*.

Moral ideas and mores form another category, distinct from the preceding. We shall see in another chapter how the rules of morality are social phenomena; they are the subject matter of the *sociology of morality*.

There is no need to demonstrate the social character of legal institutions. They are to be studied by the *sociology of law*. This field is, moreover, closely related to the sociology of morality, for moral ideas are the spirit of the law. What constitutes the authority of a legal code is the moral idea which it incarnates and which it translates into definite formulations.

Finally, there are the economic institutions: institutions relating to the production of wealth (serfdom, tenant farming, corporate organization, production in factories, in mills, at home, and so on), institutions relating to exchange (commercial organization, markets, stock exchanges, and so on), institutions relating to distribution (rent, interest, salaries, and so on). They form the subject matter of *economic sociology*.

These are the principal branches of sociology. They are not, however, the only ones. Language, which in certain respects depends on organic conditions, is nevertheless a social phenomenon, for it is also the product of a group and it bears its stamp. Even language is, in general, one of the characteristic elements of the physiognomy of societies, and it is not without reason that the relatedness of languages is often used as a means of establishing the relatedness of peoples. There is, therefore, subject matter for a sociological study of language, which has, moreover, already begun.[11] We can say as much of aesthetics, for, despite the fact that each artist (poet, orator, sculptor, painter, and so on) puts his own mark on the works that he creates, all those that are elaborated in the same social milieu and in the same period express in different forms a single ideal which is itself closely related to the temperament of the social groups to which they address themselves.

It is true that certain of these facts are already studied by disciplines long since established; notably, economic facts serve as the subject matter for the assembly of diverse research, analyses, and theories which together are designated as political economy. But just as we said above, political economy has remained to the present a hybrid study, intermediate between art and science; it is much less concerned with observing industrial and commercial life such as it is and has been in order to know it and determine its laws than with reconstructing this life as it should be. The economists have as yet only a quite weak sense that economic reality is imposed upon the observer just like physical realities, that it is subject to the same necessity, and that, consequently, the science which studies it must be created in a quite speculative way before we undertake to reform it. What is more, they study facts, which are dealt with as if they formed an independent whole which is self-sufficient and self-explanatory. In reality, economic functions are social functions and are integrated with the other collective functions; they become inexplicable when they are violently removed from that context. Workers' wages depend not only on the relationships of supply and demand but upon certain moral conceptions. They rise or fall depending on the idea we create for ourselves of the individual. More examples could be cited. By becoming a branch of sociology, economic science will naturally be wrenched from its isolation at the same time that it will become more deeply impregnated with the idea of scientific determinism. As a consequence of thus taking its place in the system of the social sciences, it will not merely undergo a change of name; both the spirit which animates it and the methods which it practices will be transformed.

We see from this analysis how false is the view that sociology is but a very simple science which consists, as Comte thought, in a single problem. As of today, it is impossible for a sociologist to possess encyclopedic knowledge of his science; but each scholar must attach himself to a special order of problems unless he wishes to be content with very general and vague views. These general views may have been useful when sociology was merely trying to explore the limits of its domain and to become aware of itself, but the discipline can no longer dally in such a fashion. This is not to say, however, that there is no place for a synthetic science which will manage to assemble the general conclusions which all these other specific sciences will reveal. As different as the various classes of social facts may be, they are, nonetheless, only species of the same genus; there is, therefore, reason to seek out what makes for the unity of the genus, what characterizes the social fact *in abstracto,* and whether there are very general laws of which the very diverse laws established by the special sciences are only particular forms. This is the object of general sociology, just as general biology has as its object to reveal the most general properties and laws of life. This is the philosophical part of the science. But since the worth of the synthesis depends on the worth of the analyses from which it results, the most urgent task of sociology is to advance this work of analysis.

In summary, table 1.1 represents in a schematic way the principal divisions of sociology.

III. THE SOCIOLOGICAL METHOD

Having determined the domain of sociology and its principal subdivisions, we must now try to characterize the most essential principles of the method employed in this science.

The principal problems of sociology consist in researching the way in which a political, legal, moral, economic, or religious institution, belief, and so on, was established, what causes gave rise to it, and to what useful ends it responds. Comparative history, understood in the sense which we are going to try to specify, is the only instrument of which the sociologist disposes to resolve these kinds of questions.

In effect, to understand an institution, one must know of what it is made. It is a complex whole, comprised of parts; one must know these parts and be able to explain each of them separately as well as the way in which they are

TABLE 1.1 Principal divisions of sociology

SOCIAL MORPHOLOGY	The study of the geographic base of various peoples in terms of its relationships with their social organization.
	The study of population: its volume, its density, and its disposition on the earth.
SOCIAL PHYSIOLOGY	Sociology of Religion
	Sociology of Morality
	Sociology of Law
	Economic Sociology
	Linguistic Sociology
	Aesthetic Sociology
GENERAL SOCIOLOGY	

combined. To discover all this, it is not enough to consider the institution in its completed and recent form, for, being accustomed to it, we find it rather simple. In any case, there is nothing in it which indicates where the various elements of which it is formed begin or end. There is no line of demarcation which separates them from one another in a visible way, any more than we perceive with our naked eyes the cells which form the tissues of the living being or the molecules which compose inert bodies. We need an instrument of analysis to make them appear. It is history which plays this role. In effect, the institution under consideration was established gradually, piece by piece; the parts of which it is formed were born one after another and were added more or less slowly. Therefore, all we need to do to see the various elements from which it results naturally dissociated is to follow its genesis in time, that is, in history. They then present themselves to the observer one after another in the very order in which they were formed and combined. For example, there is nothing simpler, it would seem, than the notion of kinship.

Yet history shows us that it is extremely complicated: the idea of consanguinity plays a role, but many other things enter in, for we find types of families in which consanguinity plays only a very accessory role. Matrilineality and patrilineality are qualitatively distinct phenomena which depend on entirely different causes, consequently requiring that they be studied separately, for we find in history types of families in which only one of the two types of kinship existed. In a word, history plays a role in the order of social realities analogous to that of the microscope in the order of physical realities.

What is more, it alone allows us to create explanations. In effect, to explain an institution is to account for the various elements which served in its formation; it is to show their causes and their raisons d'être. But how are we to discover these causes if not by carrying ourselves back to the moment when they were operative, that is to say, when they gave rise to the facts which we seek to understand? For it is only at that moment that it is possible to grasp the way in which they acted and engendered their effect. But this moment is in the past. The only way to succeed in knowing how each of these elements came into being is to observe it at the very instant when it was born and to be present at its genesis. But this genesis took place in the past and, consequently, can only be known through history. For example, today kinship is bilateral: both the paternal and the maternal lines count. In order to discover the determining causes of this complex organization, one would first observe societies in which kinship is essentially or exclusively uterine and would try to find its cause; then, one would consider peoples among whom agnatic kinship was established.[12] Finally, since the latter, when it appears, often relegates the former to a secondary role, one would investigate civilizations in which both have begun to be placed on an equal footing and would attempt to discover the conditions which determined this equality. It is in this way that sociological questions are graded, so to speak, into different stages of the past, and it is only on condition of situating them in this way, of relating them to the various historical milieux in which they were born, that it is possible to resolve them.

Sociology is, therefore, in large part a form of history which has been extended in a certain way. The historian also deals with social facts; but he considers, above all, the way in which they are peculiar to a determinate people and time. In general, he proposes to study the life of a given nation or of a given collective individuality taken at a given moment in its evolution. His immediate task is to rediscover and to characterize the particular, individual physiognomy of each society and even of each of the periods which comprise the life of a single society. The sociologist sticks solely to discovering the general relationships and verifiable laws of different societies. He does not especially try to find out what religious life or property law was like in France or in England, in Rome or in India, in a particular century; but these specialized studies, which are, moreover, indispensable to him, are but the means of arriving at the discovery of a few of the factors of religious life in general. We have only one way to demonstrate that a logical relationship (for example, a causal relationship) exists between two facts; we would have to compare cases in which they are simultaneously present or absent and to see if the variations which they present in these different combinations of circumstances bear witness to the dependence of one on the other. Experiment is, fundamentally, just a form of comparison; it consists in making a fact vary, of producing it in various forms which are subsequently methodically compared. The sociologist cannot, therefore, limit himself to the consideration of a single people or even of a single era. He must compare societies of the same type and also of different types. Thus, the variations in the institution or the practice for which he wishes to account—once brought together with the parallel variations which are observed in the social milieu, in the state of ideas, and so on—allow him to perceive the relationships which unite these two groups of facts and to establish some causal relationship between them. The comparative method is thus the preeminent instrument of the sociological method. History, in the usual sense, is to sociology what Latin grammar or Greek grammar or French grammar, taken and treated separately from one another, are to the new science which has taken the name "comparative grammar."[13]

There are, however, cases in which the material for sociological comparisons must be requested of a discipline other than history.

One sometimes investigates not how a legal or moral rule or religious belief was formed, but what determines whether it is more or less well observed by the collectivities which practice it. For example, instead of wondering where the rule prohibiting homicide originates, one would undertake to discover the various causes which make peoples and groups of all sorts more or less inclined to violate it. In the same way, one could propose to find some of the factors which make marriages more or less frequent, more or less early, more or less easily dissolved by divorce, and so on. To resolve these kinds of questions, one must essentially address oneself to statistics. One would investigate how the frequency of homicides, marriages, or divorces varies with societies, religious confessions, professions, and so on.[14] Problems related to the various conditions on which peoples' morals depend must notably be dealt with according to this method.[15] With the help of the same procedure one can, in economic sociology, study the causes, in function of which wages, rents, interest rates, the value of monetary exchanges, and so on, vary.

But, whatever the particular technique to which he has recourse, there is a rule of which the sociologist must never lose sight: before beginning the study of a determinate category of social phenomena, he must begin by making *tabula rasa* of the notions of them which he may have formed in the course of his life; he must accept as a matter of principle the fact that he knows nothing about them or about their characteristics or of the causes on which they depend. He must, in a word, place himself in a state of mind like that of physicists, chemists, physiologists, and today even psychologists when

they enter a previously unexplored region of their scientific domain.

Unfortunately, as necessary as this attitude may be, it is not easy to maintain vis-à-vis social reality; inveterate habits lead us astray. Because every day we practice the rules of morality and of law, because we buy, sell, and exchange sums, and so forth, we necessarily have some idea of these various phenomena; without them we could not manage our daily tasks. A quite natural illusion derives from this: we believe that with these ideas we grasp all the essentials of the things to which they may refer. The moralist takes no great pains to explain what the family, kinship, paternal power, contract, or the right of property may be; the economist proceeds in the same way as far as value, exchange, or rent are concerned. It seems that the science of these things is innate; all we need is to be aware as clearly as possible of the notions which are commonly held of these complex realities. But these notions, which are formed without any method in order to answer practical exigencies, are devoid of any scientific value. They express social phenomena no more exactly than the notions which the layman has of physical bodies—of their properties, of light, sound, heat, and so on—represent exactly the nature of these bodies and their objective characteristics. The physicist and the chemist set aside these everyday representations, and reality, as they make us see it, is, in fact, singularly different from what the senses perceive directly. The sociologist must do the same; he must place himself face to face with social facts, forgetting all that he believed he knew about them, as if he faced an unknown. Sociology must not be a simple illustration of ready-made and deceptive truisms; it must fashion discoveries which, moreover, cannot fail often to upset accepted notions. We know nothing at all of these social phenomena amid which we move; the task of progressively revealing them to us belongs to the various social sciences.

NOTES

1 The word, formed by the coupling of one Latin and one Greek root, has a hybrid quality which purists have often reproached. But despite this unfortunate derivation, it has today won acceptance in all European languages. (E. D.)

2 In the *Tableau des progrès de l'esprit humain*. (E. D.)

3 The principal works of Saint-Simon concerning sociology are: *Mémoire sur la science de l'homme,* 1813; *L'Industrie,* 1816–1817; *L'Organisateur,* 1819; *Du Système industriel,* 1821–1822; *Cathéchisme des industriels,* 1822–1824; *De la Physiologie appliquée aux améliorations sociales.* (E. D.)

4 People object that sociological determinism cannot be reconciled with free will. But if the existence of freedom truly implies the negation of any determinate law, it is an insurmountable obstacle not only for the social sciences but for all sciences. For, since human volitions are always bound to some external movements, it renders determinism just as unintelligible outside of us as within. However, no one, even among the partisans of free will, any longer disputes the possibility of physical and natural sciences. Why would it be otherwise with sociology? (E. D.)

5 See in particular his book *L'Imitation.* (E. D.)

6 The nature of societies doubtless depends in part on the nature of man in general; but the direct, immediate explanation of social facts is to be found in the nature of the society, for, otherwise, social life would not have varied more than the constituent attributes of humanity. (E. D.)

7 See his *Principles of Sociology.* (E. D.)

8 A few examples are to be found in my *Rules of the Sociological Method.* (E. D.)

9 This is the law according to which humanity has successively passed through and must necessarily pass through three stages: first, the theological age; then the metaphysical age; and finally, the age of positive science. (E. D.)

10 What the Germans call *Anthropogeographie* is not unrelated to what we call social morphology. (See the works of Ratzel in Germany and of Vidal de la Blache in France). (E. D.)

11 See Meillet's works, especially the memoire which appeared in *L'Année sociologique,* volume 9, under the title "*Comment les mots changent de sens*" (E. D.)

12 The form of kinship which is established exclusively or essentially through women is called uterine; agnatic kinship is that which is essentially or exclusively established through men. (E. D.)

13 We do not intend to explain here what we think the future relationships of sociology and history will be; we are convinced that they are destined to become ever more intimate and that a day will come when the historical spirit and the sociological spirit will differ only in nuances. In effect, the sociologist can proceed in his comparisons and inductions only on the condition of knowing well and from close up the particular facts which he relies upon, just like the historian; and, on the other hand, the concrete reality which the historian studies can be most directly clarified by the results of sociological inductions. If, then, in what precedes we have differentiated history and sociology, it was not in order to raise an impassable barrier between these two disciplines, since they are, on the contrary, called upon to become more and more closely integrated; it was only in order to characterize as exactly as possible what the sociological perspective possesses in its own right. (E. D.)

14 Durkheim published a study of precisely this sort on the subject of divorce in 1906. See "Divorce by Mutual Consent," chapter 15 in this volume. (M. T.)

15 One must not confuse morals and morality. Morals (*la moralité*) are assessed according to the way in which morality (la morale) is applied. The same kind of question could be posed concerning religion. (E. D.)

How to Think Sociologically

by Steven M. Buechler

People have always tried to make sense of the world around them. Myths, fables, and religion provided traditional ways of making sense. More recently, science has provided additional ways of understanding the world. Sociology is part of the rise of science as a means of making sense of the world.

As we know in our own time, there can be tension between religious and scientific views. Contemporary disputes over evolution, sexuality, marriage, and even the age of our planet often pit religious values against scientific interpretations. More broadly speaking, both at home and abroad, religious fundamentalisms rest uneasily alongside modern, secular worldviews. These familiar tensions have a history that takes us back to the origins of sociology itself.

SOCIOLOGY AND MODERNITY

The rise of sociology is part of a much larger story about the emergence of the modern world itself. Modernity emerged in European societies through a long process of social change that unfolded from the sixteenth to the nineteenth centuries. During this time, virtually everything about organized social life in Europe was fundamentally transformed. In our day, we speak of globalization as a force that is changing the world in the most basic ways. But current patterns of globalization can be traced back to the rise of modernity itself; in many respects, they are a continuation of the changes that ushered in the modern world.

Economically, modernity transformed most people from peasants to workers in a complex division of labor. Politically, modernity created distinct nation-states with clear boundaries. Technologically, modernity applied scientific knowledge to producing everything from consumer goods to lethal weapons. Demographically, modernity triggered population growth and massive migration from small, familiar, rural communities to large, urban, anonymous cities.

When social worlds change like this, some people benefit while others are harmed. In addition, most people find rapid change and its inevitable conflict to be unsettling, and they seek to understand what is happening. It was this moment that gave rise to sociology. Explaining modernity became sociology's task at the same time that modernity was making sociology possible in the first place.

The link between modernity and sociology was the Enlightenment. This intellectual revolution accompanied other revolutionary changes occurring throughout Europe. In the broadest terms, the Enlightenment challenged religious belief, dogma, and authority. It sought to replace them with scientific reason, logic, and knowledge.

Four basic themes pervaded Enlightenment thought (Zeitlin 1987). First, human reason was the best guide to knowledge, even if it meant that scientific skepticism displaced religious certainty. Second, reason must be paired with careful, scientific observation. Third, Enlightenment thought insisted that social arrangements be rationally justified; if not, they must be changed until they could be rationally defended. Finally, Enlightenment thought assumed that with the systematic application of reason, the perfectibility of people and the progress of society were all but inevitable.

Enlightenment thought contained some potentially fatal flaws. It was a Eurocentric worldview, created by privileged white men, that made universal pronouncements about all people in all times and places. While applauding Europe's progress, it ignored the colonial domination of the rest of the world that provided the labor, goods, and wealth that underwrote that progress. Generalizations about "humanity" meant "males," to the exclusion of women, and pronouncements on the "human race" meant white Europeans, to the exclusion of darker people, who were viewed as subhuman.

The Enlightenment was much more than a justification of imperialism, sexism, and racism, but it could become that as well. More than two centuries later, the jury is still out on whether Enlightenment biases can be overcome and its promises be fulfilled. Some postmodernists see little hope for this to happen. Others, myself included, think that the critical spirit of the Enlightenment can help uproot its biases. The project is already under way as feminists, people of color, and postcolonial writers find their way into contemporary sociological discourses (Lemert 2013).

In its own day, the Enlightenment provoked a "romantic conservative reaction" (Zeitlin 1987) that rejected the elevation of reason and science over faith and tradition. It defended traditional customs, institutions, and ways of life from the new standard of critical reason. The debate between Enlightenment progress and conservative reaction set the agenda for sociology as the social science of modernity. Progress or order? Change or stability? Reason or tradition? Science or religion? Individual or group? Innovation or authority? Such dichotomies framed the subject matter of the new science of sociology.

The classical era of sociology refers to European thinkers whose ideas brought this new discipline to maturity from the late eighteenth to the early twentieth centuries. The very different sociologies of Auguste Comte, Herbert Spencer, Ferdinand Toennies, Karl Marx, Max Weber, Georg Simmel, Emile Durkheim, and others are variations on sociology's main theme: How do we understand modern society? Given these efforts, we might think of sociology as the ongoing effort of human beings to understand the worlds they are simultaneously inheriting from earlier generations and maintaining and transforming for future generations.

This approach has been described as the "sociological imagination." It arises when people realize that they can only know themselves by understanding their historical period and by examining others in the same situation as themselves. We think sociologically when we grasp how our historical moment differs from previous ones and how the situations of various groups of people differ from each other (Mills 1959).

The sociological imagination is guided by three related questions. The first concerns the social structure of society. How is it organized, what are its major institutions, and how are they linked together? The second concerns the historical location of society. How has it emerged from past social forms, what mechanisms promote change, and what futures are possible based on this historical path? The third concerns individual biography within society. What kinds of character traits are called forth by this society, and what kinds of people come to prevail? The sociological imagination is thus about grasping the relations between history and biography within society.

The sociological imagination sensitizes us to the difference between "personal troubles" and "public issues." A personal trouble is a difficulty in someone's life that is largely a result of individual circumstances. A public issue is a difficulty that is largely owing to social arrangements beyond the individual's control. The distinction is crucial because common sense often interprets events as personal troubles; we explain someone's difficulties as springing from individual shortcomings. The sociological imagination recognizes that such difficulties are rarely unique to one person; they rather happen to many people in similar situations. The underlying causes derive more from social structures and historical developments than the individual alone. If our goal is "diagnosis," the sociological imagination locates problems in a larger social context. If our goal is "treatment," it implies changing the structure of society rather than the behavior of individuals.

This applies to success as well. Common sense often attributes success to individual qualities. The sociological imagination asks what social and historical preconditions were necessary for an individual to become a success. Many successful people, in Jim Hightower's memorable phrase, "were born on third base but thought they hit a triple." The point is that whereas common sense sees the world in individual terms, sociological thinking sees it in structural terms. Only by seeing the connections between structure, history, and biography can we understand the world in a sociological way.

This discussion implies that professional sociologists and ordinary people see the world differently. This is often true, but the issue is more complicated. Modernity has also led ordinary people to develop a practical sociology in their everyday lives. Think about it this way. Sociology sees the world as a social construction that could follow various blueprints. Indeed, social worlds *are* constructed in very different ways in different times and places.

In our time, an awareness of the socially constructed nature of social worlds is no longer the privileged insight of scholars, but has become part of everyday understanding. Whether owing to rapid change, frequent travel, cultural diffusion, or media images, many people understand that we live in socially constructed worlds. Some people are distressed by this fact, and others rejoice in it, but few can escape it. Thus, an idea that was initially associated with professional sociology has become part of the everyday consciousness of ordinary people today.

The result is that many people without formal sociological training understand social processes quite well. Put differently, the objects of sociological analysis are people who are quite capable of becoming the subjects of the sociological knowledge created by that analysis. Although few people can explain how quantum mechanics governs the physical world, many can describe sociological processes that shape the social world.

Certain circumstances prompt people to think sociologically. Perhaps the key stimulant is when familiar ways of doing and thinking no longer work. It is when people are surprised, puzzled, challenged, or damaged that they are most likely to think sociologically (Lemert 2008). People then develop sociological competence as they try to make sense out of specific, individual circumstances by linking them to broader social patterns. In this way, sociological awareness begins to understand bigger things as a by-product of wrestling with the practical challenges of everyday life.

Circumstances do not inevitably provoke sociological consciousness. Some people redouble their faith or retreat into ritualism. So perhaps we can conclude this way. Societies confront people with problems. These problems have always had the potential to promote a sociological awareness. In our times, there is a greater awareness of the socially constructed nature of the world. This makes it even more likely that when people in this society are confronted with practical challenges, they will develop sociological competence as a practical life skill. In late modernity, everyone can become a practical sociologist.

THINKING SOCIOLOGICALLY

The sociological perspective involves several themes. They overlap with one another, and some may be found in other social sciences as well as everyday consciousness. Taken together, they comprise a distinctive lens for viewing the social world. Here are some of those themes.

Society Is a Social Construction

People construct social order. Sociology does not see society as God-given, as biologically determined, or as following any predetermined plan beyond human intervention. At the same time, this does not mean that everyone plays an equal role in the process or that the final product looks like what people intended.

Social construction begins with intentions that motivate people to act in certain ways. When many people have similar goals and act in concert, larger social patterns or institutions are created. Goal-driven action is essential to the creation of institutions, and it remains equally important to their maintenance and transformation over time. Put succinctly, society is a human product (Berger and Luckmann 1966).

Basic human needs ensure some similarities in the goals that people pursue in all times and places. But these pursuits also unfold in specific historical circumstances and cultural contexts that have led to a dazzling variety of social worlds. This variety is itself the best evidence of the socially constructed nature of social worlds. If biology or genetics were the determining force behind social worlds, wouldn't they look a lot more similar than what we actually see around the globe?

Social constructionists thus insist that society arises from the goal-driven action of people. But they also recognize that the institutions created by such actions take on a life of their own. They appear to exist independently of the people who create and sustain them. They are experienced by people as a powerful external force that weighs down on them. When this external force becomes severe enough, people are likely to lose sight of the fact that society is a social product in the first place.

The value of the social constructionist premise is this dual recognition. On one hand, society is a subjective reality originating in the intentions of social actors. On the other hand, it becomes an objective reality that confronts subsequent generations as a social fact that inevitably shapes *their* intentional actions—and so it goes. Understood this way, the idea that society is a social construction is at the heart of the sociological perspective.

Society Is an Emergent Reality

Another premise of sociology is emergentism. This reveals sociology's distinctive level of analysis. For psychology, the level of analysis is the individual, even if it is acknowledged that individuals belong to groups. For sociology, the level of analysis is social ties rather than individual elements. Emergentism recognizes that certain realities only appear when individual elements are combined in particular ways. When they are, qualitatively new realities emerge through these combinations.

Take a simple example. Imagine a random pile of ten paper clips. Now imagine linking these paper clips together to form a chain. There are still ten paper clips, but a new emergent reality has appeared that is qualitatively different from the random pile because of how the elements are related to one another. Or consider human reproduction. Neither sperm nor egg is capable of producing human life on its own; in combination, qualitatively new life begins to emerge from a particular combination of elements.

Sociology specializes in the social level of analysis that emerges when elements are combined to create new, larger realities. Emergentism also implies that when we try to understand elements outside of their context, it is at best a simplification and at worst a distortion. The parts derive meaning from their relationship with other parts, and the sociological perspective is fundamentally attuned to such relationships.

Society Is a Historical Product

Thinking historically is a crucial part of the sociological imagination (Mills 1959). Classical sociologists thought historically because they lived in times of rapid social change and it was a major challenge to understand such change. Modern sociology tends to be more static, and modern people tend to be very present-oriented. Both professional and practical sociologists would benefit from a more historical perspective on the social world.

Seeing society as a historical product means recognizing that we cannot understand the present without understanding the past. Historical knowledge of past social conditions provides crucial comparisons. Without such benchmarks, it is impossible to understand what is genuinely new in the present day. Without a historical referent for comparison, sociology is clueless when it comes to understanding social change. Historical knowledge also provides the raw material for categories, comparisons, typologies, and analogies that are crucial to understanding both the present and possible future worlds.

The concept of emergentism applies here because the importance of seeing relationships between elements also works chronologically. If we look at society at only one point in time, we sever it from its past and its potential futures. Its very meaning arises from these relationships; to ignore them is to distort even the static understanding of society at one point in time. Consider the difference between a photograph and a film that presents a succession of images. We can learn something from the still photo, but its meaning often changes dramatically when we see it as one of a series of interrelated images.

Society Consists of Social Structures

Sociologists use the term *structure* to refer to the emergent products of individual elements. Structure implies that the social world has certain patterns or regularities that recur over time. Put differently, sociologists are keenly interested in social organization.

Structures are products of human purposes, but they acquire an objective reality and become a powerful influence on human action. Think about how physical structures like buildings shape action. We almost always enter buildings through doors; in rare cases we might do so through windows, but walking through walls is not an option. Social structures are less visible and more flexible than buildings, but they also channel people's actions, because they make some actions routine and expected, others possible but unlikely, and still others all but impossible.

Like buildings, social structures often have a vertical dimension. Social structures ensure that some people are better off than others and that some are not very well off at all. Some residential buildings have penthouses at the top, premium suites near the top, standard accommodations below them, and housekeeping staff in the basement. Social structures are also stratified, granting power, privilege, and opportunity to some while limiting or denying them to others. Sociologists are especially interested in the hierarchical dimension of social structures.

Sociologists traditionally thought of social structures as powerful forces weighing down upon the individual. In this image, structures constrain freedom of choice and behavior. But this is a one-sided view. Structures are constraining, but they are also enabling. These established patterns of social organization also make many actions possible in the first place or easier in the second place. Without preexisting social structures, we would have to do everything "from scratch," and the challenge of sheer survival might overwhelm us. The trick is thus to see social structures as simultaneously constraining and enabling social action (Giddens 1984).

Society Consists of Reflexive Actors

People in society are aware of themselves, of others, and of their relationships with others. As reflexive actors, we monitor our action and its effects on others. We continue, modify, or halt actions, depending on whether they are achieving their intended effects. According to one school of thought, we are literally actors, because social life is like a theatrical performance in which we try to convince others that we are a certain kind of person (Goffman 1959). To stage effective performances, we must constantly be our own critic, judging and refining our performances. Reflexivity thus means that when we act, we are conscious of our action, we monitor its course, and we make adjustments over time.

To stage such performances, we must undergo socialization. Along the way, we acquire a language that provides us with tools for reflexive thinking. We also acquire a self. Oddly enough, to have a self requires that we first have relationships with others. Through those relationships, we imaginatively see the world from their perspective, which includes seeing ourselves as we imagine we appear to them. It is this ability to see ourselves through the perspective of others—to see ourselves as an object—that defines the self. Reflexive action only becomes possible with a self.

Reflexivity makes ordinary people into practical sociologists. To be a competent person is to be a practical sociologist. We cannot help being sociologists every time we ponder a potential relationship, reconsider a hasty action, or adopt someone else's viewpoint. All such situations call upon and refine the reflexivity that is the hallmark of social action as well as a defining characteristic of the sociological perspective.

Society Is an Interaction of Agency and Structure

Social structures and reflexive actors are intimately connected. Unfortunately, much sociology emphasizes one side of this connection at the expense of the other. Agency-centered views stress the ability of people to make choices out of a range of alternatives in almost any situation. The emphasis on choice implies that people control their own destiny, at least within broad limits. Structure-centered views stress the extent to which people's choices are limited by social structures. The emphasis on structures implies that people's options—if not their lives—are essentially determined by larger social forces over which they have little control. Both approaches have merit, but the challenge is to see structure and agency in a more interconnected way.

Marx once said that people make their own history (acknowledging agency), but under circumstances they do not choose but rather inherit from the past (acknowledging

structure). Here's an analogy from the game of pool. Each time you approach the table, you "inherit" a structure left by your opponent when they missed their last shot. Yet, for every layout of balls on the table, there is always a shot that you can attempt, and that action will alter the structure of the table for subsequent shots. In this analogy, structure (the position of balls on the table) both limits and creates opportunities for agency (taking a shot), which in turn alters the structure for the next round of shooting. If pool is not your game, chess is also a good analogy. The point is that agency and structure are two sides of the same coin; each conditions the possibilities of the other as we make our own history in circumstances we don't choose.

The close connection between structure and agency has led one theorist to reject the notion of structure altogether, because it implies something that exists apart from agency. Anthony Giddens (1984) talks about a *process* of structuration. In this view, actors use preexisting structures to accomplish their goals, but they also re-create them as a by-product of their actions. Consider a wedding ceremony. It is a preexisting cultural ritual people use to accomplish the goal of getting married. The by-product of all these individual marriages is the perpetuation of the cultural ritual itself. Generalize this to any situation in which we draw upon an established part of our social world to achieve a goal; in using this part we also sustain (and perhaps transform) it as a part of social structure.

Society Has Multiple Levels

Although society has multiple levels, sociologists often focus on one level at a time. Think about using Google Maps to locate a destination. You can zoom out to get the big picture at the expense of not seeing some important details. Alternatively, you can zoom in on some key details at the expense of not seeing the big picture. Combining these differing views will orient you to your destination, but we must remember it is ultimately all one interconnected landscape.

Sociologists nevertheless distinguish between macro and micro levels of society. When we look at the macro level, we typically include millions of people organized into large categories, groups, or institutions. The macro level is the "big picture" or "high altitude" perspective in which society's largest patterns are evident and individuals are invisible. When we look at the micro level, we might inspect no more than a dozen people interacting in a small group setting. Here, the role of particular individuals is very prominent, and larger social patterns fade into the background.

Some of the best sociology involves understanding not only structure-agency connections but also micro-macro links. Every macro-structure rests on micro-interaction, and every micro-interaction is shaped by macro-structures. The previous example of a wedding also illustrates this point. On the macro level, weddings are a cultural ritual that inducts people into the institution of marriage and the family. However, weddings, marriage, and the family would not exist on the macro level without countless, micro-level interactions. The macro-level institution depends on micro-level actions to sustain it. At the same time, anyone who has ever gotten married will tell you that macro-level, cultural expectations about weddings impose themselves on people as they plan for this supposedly personal event. Every micro-level wedding depends on a macro-level, cultural blueprint for its social significance. The micro and macro levels of society are one interdependent reality rather than two separate things.

Society Involves Unintended Consequences

One of the more profound insights of the sociological perspective concerns unintended and unanticipated consequences of action. Much human action is purposive or goal-directed. People act because they want to accomplish something. Despite this, they sometimes fail to achieve their goals. But whether people achieve their goals or not, their actions always create other consequences that they don't intend or even anticipate. Shakespeare made a profoundly sociological point when he had Juliet fake her own suicide to dramatize her love for Romeo. Unfortunately, the plan never reached Romeo. Juliet neither intended nor anticipated that Romeo would find her unconscious, believe that she was really dead, and take his own life in response. Nor did he intend (or even realize) that she would awaken, discover his real death, and really take her life in response. Talk about unintended consequences!

This principle acknowledges the complexity of the social world and the limits on our ability to control it. It says that despite our best efforts, the effects of social action cannot be confined to one intended path; they always spill over into unexpected areas. The principle is also a cautionary message for those seeking to solve social problems. Such efforts might succeed, but they often bring other consequences that are neither positive nor intended.

Efforts to control crime provide an example. Consider policies to "get tough" on crime through harsher treatment like capital punishment and mandatory sentencing. Because the human beings who serve as judges and juries are reflexive actors who take these facts into account, they are often less likely to convict suspects without overwhelming evidence because of the harshness of the sentence. Thus, the unintended consequence of an attempt to "get tough" on crime might be the opposite, because fewer suspects are convicted than before.

A related idea is the distinction between manifest and latent functions. A manifest function is an outcome that people intend. A latent function is an outcome that people are not aware of; it can complement, but it often contradicts, the manifest function. Crime and punishment provide yet another example. The manifest function of imprisonment is punishment or rehabilitation. The latent function is to bring criminals together where they can meet one another, exchange crime techniques, and become better criminals upon their return to society.

The concept of latent functions is crucial to sociological analysis. Sometimes we observe behavior or rituals that seem irrational, pointless, or self-defeating. This is the time to begin looking for latent functions. What we will often find is that such "irrational" behavior reinforces the identity and sustains the cohesion of the group that performs it. Thus, before we dismiss the tribal rain dance (because "rain gods" don't exist), we must explore its latent function. Even when people don't (manifestly) know what they are (latently) doing, their behavior can be crucial to group cohesion.

Recognizing unintended consequences and latent functions is not just for professional sociologists. Daily living requires managing risk, and ordinary people in everyday life recognize the tricky nature of goal-directed action. The folk wisdom that "the road to hell is paved with good intentions" acknowledges the potential disconnect between goals and outcomes.

Such recognition, however, never completely prevents outcomes we neither intend nor expect. These principles give social life some of its most surprising twists, and sociology some of its most fascinating challenges.

No attempt to capture the sociological perspective in a small number of themes can be complete. Other sociologists would doubtless modify this list. But most would recognize these themes as central to thinking sociologically. As such, they provide a foundation for the more detailed investigations to follow.

SOCIOLOGY'S DOUBLE CRITIQUE

This final theme deserves special emphasis as the foundation of this book. Last but not least, thinking sociologically means looking at the social world in a critical way.

In everyday language, *critical* implies something negative. Being critical is often seen as being harsh, unfair, or judgmental. When we say someone is "critical," we often mean that their behavior is inappropriately mean-spirited. This is a perfectly reasonable use of everyday language, and the point it makes about how people should treat one another is also perfectly reasonable.

In sociological language, *critical* means something else. Doing sociology in a critical way means looking beyond appearances, understanding root causes, and asking who benefits. Being critical is what links knowledge to action and the potential of building a better society. Being critical in the sociological sense rests on the profoundly *positive* belief that we can use knowledge to understand the flaws of the social world and act to correct them.

The sociological perspective contains a double critique. First, mainstream sociology brings an inherently critical angle of vision to its subject. Second, some particular approaches in sociology carry this critique further by building on values that make sociological analysis especially critical of power and domination.

The critical dimension of mainstream sociology derives from the Enlightenment. Despite the flaws noted earlier, the Enlightenment advocated the use of reason, science, and evidence to critically examine religious truth, established doctrine, and political authority. Given its Enlightenment roots, sociology has always cast a critical eye on all types of claims, forms of knowledge, and exercises of power.

It is this quality that Peter Berger (1963) called the "debunking" tendency of sociological consciousness. Debunking means that the sociological perspective never takes the social world at face value and never assumes that it is what it appears to be. The sociological perspective rather looks at familiar phenomena in new ways to get beyond the immediately obvious, publicly approved, or officially sanctioned view. In this way, sociology sees through the facades of social structures to their unintended consequences and latent functions. Sociologically speaking, the problem might not be crime but laws, not revolution but government. Berger concludes that sociology is not compatible with totalitarianism, because the debunking quality of sociology will always be in tension with authoritarian claims to knowledge and power.

Although the world has changed since Berger wrote, the need for debunking is greater than ever. The political fundamentalisms of Cold War and rival superpowers have been replaced by other fundamentalisms that are logical targets for sociology's debunking insights. A world in which more and more people feel they know things with absolute certainty is a world that drastically needs the sociological perspective.

At the same time that some people embrace fundamentalist beliefs, others become suspicious and cynical about everything. This stance ("debunking on steroids") is too much of a good thing. For the ultra-cynical poser, all ideas, values, and beliefs are suspect, and none deserve support. Against this stance, sociology offers nuance and judgment. The sociological perspective recognizes that some ideas, values, and beliefs have more merit, logic, or evidence than others. Careful sociological thinkers make such distinctions. Indeed, the ultra-cynical mind-set itself needs debunking. Cynicism helps people avoid action or evade responsibility. A sociological perspective suggests that such inaction, or evasion, *is* action that tacitly supports dominant powers by refusing to challenge them in any way.

Mainstream sociology does not take the world for granted. Just when we think we have the answers, it poses another level of questions. For all these reasons, sociology in its most generic form has always included a critical angle of vision.

Although mainstream sociology is inherently critical, some versions of sociology take critique to another level by adopting certain values as the basis for their critique. In contrast to mainstream sociology, these approaches are devoted to a critical analysis of how social structures create relations of domination.

This fully critical sociology is best understood in contrast to mainstream sociology. Although mainstream sociology is critical because of its debunking tendency, it also adopts a scientific posture of detachment. Mainstream sociology seeks to be value-free, value-neutral, or objective. Put differently, mainstream sociology deliberately refrains from taking sides that would jeopardize its scientific neutrality. Mainstream sociology recognizes that *as citizens,* sociologists can be political actors. But it insists that in their role as scientific sociologists, they must maintain their objectivity.

Critical sociology differs from mainstream sociology on these issues. It emphasizes that in social science, humans are both the subjects and the objects of study. Notions of objectivity derived from the natural sciences don't necessarily translate into social science. But even if sociology could approximate objectivity, critical sociologists reject such a stance. It is not desirable, because the quest for objectivity diverts sociologists from asking the most important questions and from taking a more active role in the resolution of social problems.

Think of the contrast in this way. Mainstream sociology is primarily committed to one set of Enlightenment values having to do with science and objectivity. Critical sociology is primarily committed to another set of Enlightenment values having to do with freedom and equality. The latter values demand critical scrutiny of any social order that imposes unnecessary inequalities or restrictions on people's ability to organize their lives as they wish. These values require critical analysis of social arrangements that create conflicting interests between people and allow one group to benefit at the expense of another.

Critical sociologists deliberately focus on relations of domination, oppression, or exploitation, because these actions so obviously violate the values of freedom and equality. Critical sociologists are willing to advocate for groups who are victimized by such arrangements. Good critical sociologists realize they cannot speak for such groups. But they can explore how social arrangements make it difficult for some to speak for themselves, and they can underscore the importance of changing those arrangements.

Other issues distinguish mainstream from critical sociology. Mainstream sociology's commitment to science means it maintains a strict divide between scientific questions of what *is* and normative questions of what *ought* to be. Critical sociology wants to transcend this divide by linking critical analysis of how the world is organized now with normative arguments for how the world should be organized in the future. Behind such arguments are hopeful, or even utopian assumptions about alternative worlds that might be constructed. Critical sociology is simultaneously pessimistic about the current state of the world and optimistic about its possible futures. It examines our potential for living humanely, the social obstacles that block this potential, and the means to change from a problematic present to a preferable future.

The debate between mainstream and critical sociology is important and complex, and it will not be resolved by anything said here. But what can be said is that sociology is better because of the debate. Each side provides a corrective to the faults of the other. At the extreme, mainstream sociology becomes an inhumane, sterile approach that reduces human beings to objects of scientific curiosity; it needs a course correction through the humane values of critical sociology. At the extreme, critical sociology becomes an empty, ideological stance that denies the complexities of its own value commitments; it needs a course correction through the scientific caution of mainstream sociology.

Sociology's double critique thus derives from mainstream and critical sociology, respectively. My primary goal in this book is to illustrate critical sociology, but I also include the critical insights of mainstream sociology. I do so because these approaches sometimes speak to different issues, because neither seems adequate on its own, because they are often complementary, and because this best conveys the richness of our discipline itself. In the end, it is less important which side is "right" than that both sides coexist and continually provoke us to be reflexive about our role as sociologists and as actors in the world.

Sociology's double critique is also crucial to rethinking the flaws of the Enlightenment itself. Mainstream sociology's notion of debunking accepted truths grew out of the Enlightenment struggle against religion, but there is no reason it can't also foster critical examination of the Enlightenment itself. Critical sociology's challenge to domination also seems tailor-made to examining and overturning those forms of domination that the Enlightenment ignored, accepted, or promoted. Thus, for all its flaws, the Enlightenment provides tools for its own examination, critique, and transformation.

1 | Chapter Review

REVIEW QUESTIONS

1. What is the primary purpose of sociology? How can the discipline assist in understanding human behavior?
2. What is the sociological imagination? What are the main components necessary for applying the sociological imagination or how to think sociologically?
3. What is public sociology? According to the articles, what potential does applying the sociological imagination and thinking sociologically have for us as individuals, as a society, and as part of a global community?

CASE STUDY: HOW TO THINK SOCIOLOGICALLY

As noted, the second article in this chapter explores primary concepts for how to approach analyzing social issues and phenomena from a sociological perspective. Our environment (where we live and even the time frame within history) can impact our understandings, beliefs, values, and behaviors. Of course, none of us is immune to this influence 100% of the time. This influence and the extent to which it impacts one's life and behavior can vary. Research suggests some people are more influenced by a social environment, group, or society than others based upon how tied that individual feels to a group, country, or society (and what that society values); how people interpret those values in light of their own individual experiences and journey; one's age and the extent of their diverse experiences; and their personality.

Despite this, as we all agree, none of us lives in a vacuum. We are bombarded every day with messages about what is good and bad, right or wrong, positive or negative. Social influence is simply the reality of living within groups that have laws, structures, and means of organizing members to live in harmony or operate in agreement together. It is how a society or group survives. Of course, this can be very positive. Rules (and the enforcement of rules) that make people think twice about stealing or murder, for example, would likely be considered positive by most people as they contribute to our ability to survive and live productively with one another. Values that praise diversity, freedom of speech, or freedom of religion would also likely be considered extremely valuable to the human experience for many in the United States. We grow up learning and cherishing these things. Of course, sometimes the influence of a group can be negative. As a culture, we hold certain ideas regarding beauty, for example, with studies demonstrating that as a group, most Americans, hold a subconsciousness preference for those who are thin versus those who struggle with their weight. This is not the case when compared to many other countries where a healthy (or even high) level of body fat is considered a sign of health and vitality. This idea or value, many researchers and health experts agree, led to an epidemic of anorexia in our country, particularly among teenage girls, although rates among teenage boys have also been steadily increasing over time.

We can apply some of these concepts to discussions related to social concerns like race and ethnicity, socioeconomic status, disability, age, gender, or sexual orientation. For example, we are all aware that preferences about skin color resulted in part in our country from the unequal treatment bestowed on Native Americans, African-Americans, and others throughout our history. Despite those who stood against such atrocities, why did hundreds of thousands of people go along with it? Why do some people still hold prejudicial or stereotypical attitudes about people of color? While the answer is invariably complex, part of the answer lies in the influence of groups on

our lives and the enforcement of laws and policies in our society that reinforced such ideas and behaviors. In short, the social environment and history shape our current attitudes and behaviors. As this chapter briefly introduces, public sociologists examine and discuss this history and its resulting impact on social life, individual identity, and group and individual behavior.

For this case study, we will utilize the social issue of immigration. Worldwide economic restructuring related to globalization has had significant impacts on immigration to the United States and Europe, generally increasing these levels somewhat over time (Peters, 2008). Many (although not all) immigrants often arrive in the United States to seek a better life than what is available in their own country of origin. Some people also immigrate due to persecution, discriminatory practices, or unstable governments. Some immigrate simply because they believe in the values and systems of government in the United States, and they want their lives to align with and represent those values and belief systems. In short, they want to live in alignment with their understandings, experience, and identity.

Think about the issue of immigration and current debates in the United States and Europe related to immigration, refugee resettlement, and migration (particularly from Muslim countries). Follow each of the steps outlined in the second article in this chapter, "How to Think Sociologically," and write your response to each step in the process outlined to the best of your ability and knowledge regarding the issue and the debates about it. How might a sociologist approach understanding public sentiment toward this social issue? What is happening in society that might be influencing larger public attitudes toward these topics?

DEVELOPING THE SOCIOLOGICAL IMAGINATION:
Performing National Identity

Different countries and societies have different beliefs about who is considered a part of that country and society. These ideas may influence thoughts or values on immigration policies in a given society. Notably, these views can also be influenced by age, gender, nationality, individual values, and individual or collective belief systems. In February 2017, the Pew Research Center conducted a study on such global attitudes. A link to the article can be found here: http://www.pewglobal.org/2017/02/01/what-it-takes-to-truly-be-one-of-us/.

Review the study on global attitudes toward national identity. What are some differences among regions of the world? What dominant cultural values, traditions, and beliefs may be influencing U.S. attitudes toward national identity and belonging? Please note that this article also includes a link to the full dataset, and therefore you are also welcome to compare and contrast countries and regions of your choice if you wish.

2 | Sociological Theories

CHAPTER SUMMARY

- This chapter explores the main theoretical frameworks utilized in the discipline of sociology and asks readers to contemplate the role of cultural context in the development of social theory.

- This chapter also outlines classical theories utilized in the study of society as well as common postmodern theories utilized in the study of society. These theories will provide the framework by which we will examine social institutions and social issues in subsequent chapters.

PRELIMINARY QUESTIONS FOR READERS

- It has been said that "theory is important because theory impacts everything that we do." A theory (or a set of principles on which we often act) about what it takes to be successful in an Introduction to Sociology course, for example, might impact how a student goes about studying the subject and preparing for exams. Identify one or two theories you have upon which you base important life decisions (such as "Work hard, play hard" as an hypothetical example). How has this impacted the choices that you have made?

- From a sociological perspective, how might theory impact how a psychologist versus a sociologist goes about exploring a particular social problem like violence? What might be the difference in approach, method, response, and how these findings might be put to use?

CHAPTER INTRODUCTION

The Sociology of Knowledge and the Development of Social Theory

Even the cultural context in which we live can impact the development of knowledge and theoretical frameworks. This is part of what has been termed **"The Sociology of Knowledge"** or the extent to which our environment impacts what we study, how society impacts how we approach a particular topic (or do not), and as a result what type of information is concluded and how such conclusions are interpreted, disseminated, and applied (Stark, 1991). This has resulted in various theories that have been created and that have evolved since the foundation of the discipline. The first two articles in this chapter look at the concept of classic (historic) theories and newer theories (postmodern theories) that are currently used to explore and approach the scientific study of social life.

MAIN THEORETICAL CONSIDERATIONS RELATED TO THE COURSE

While a variety of theories are utilized, and some that are very specific to concepts such as social inequality, social interaction, and social behavior, according to Anderson and Taylor (2007), in sociology there are three main and broad theories by which sociologists examine and analyze social issues, processes, and phenomena. Theorists may use one or all of these theories to explore a specific component of social life. These three main theories include (1) Structural Functionalism, (2) Conflict Theory, and (3) Symbolic Interactionism. These theories provide a framework for understanding what holds a group or society together and for understanding various social processes and structures within a society.

Throughout the book, we will examine how these three main and broad theories can contribute to our understanding of social phenomena, social institutions, social structures, and social problems. We will also look at various specific theories associated with various sociological topics or subjects. Many of these theories are discussed, in summary, within the two articles in this chapter. These main theories, however, are the foundation on which we develop our sociological imagination. To summarize these theories:

- **Structural Functionalism** is a macro-theory and looks at the relationships between larger social processes and problems such as the relationship between social institutions, economies, or social structures and its impact on the individual or groups. This theory views society as an organism with each part of a society (i.e. an education system, healthcare system, system of laws, etc.) working together to keep society functioning as is. Each part of a society has a particular purpose or function. This theory may also look at various social issues or processes being considered as "functional" or "dysfunctional" for a society. More of a discussion on the concept of social institutions, social structures, and social problems can be found in the case study at the end of this chapter.

- **Conflict Theory** is also a macro-theory that views society as a system that is upheld or maintained through relationships of **power** (or the ability to exercise control over another despite potential resistance). This particular theory is often utilized when discussing issues of inequality or oppression. According to this theory, a society is held together by systems of power, particularly those who have power and those who do not. Those in power are able to design a society (including laws, economic processes, and institutions) according to their interests. The **"power elite" model** (discussed more in Chapter 5) discusses the basis in which it is thought that dominant groups emerge and continue to remain in positions of control over others. Original thinking in the development of conflict theory suggested that those with little power would eventually rise to defeat those in ruling groups or classes as an attempt to regain certain rights and resources. As a result, this theory not only speaks to issues of inequality but also the social conditions under which addressing inequality may occur.

• **Symbolic Interactionism** views society as a complex set of both overt and insinuated meanings and symbols that work together to create a sense of shared identity. This shared identity, according to this theory particularly, is what holds a society together. This is a micro-theory and therefore is focused on smaller social processes (such as one-on-one relationships or between individuals and groups). According to this theory, a country's flag, for example (as a symbol), has profound meaning for its citizens based on the what is associated with the symbol (such as a shared set of values). This theory particularly points to the influence our associations and groups (or the places in which we find our identity) can have over our attitudes, behaviors, and understandings.

WORKS CITED

Andersen, M. L. & Taylor, H.F. (2007). *Sociology: The essentials*. 4th Edition Belmont, CA: Thompson Wadsworth Press.

Jones, R.A. (1986). *Emile Durkheim: An introduction to four major works*. Beverly Hills, CA: Sage Publications, Inc., 1986. Pp. 60–81.

Metzel, J. & MacLeish, K. (February 2015). Mental illness, mass shootings, and the policies of American firearms. *American Journal of Public Health 105*(2): 240–249.

Social institutions. (2008). Stanford Encyclopedia of Philosophy. Available online at: https://plato.stanford.edu/entries/social-institutions/.

Stark, W. (1991). *The sociology of knowledge: Towards a deeper understanding of the history of ideas*. Piscataway, NJ: Transaction Publishers.

Classical Social Theory

by Larry Ray

This chapter introduces the ideas of some major classical social theories—especially the quartet of Karl **Marx**, Émile **Durkheim**, Georg **Simmel** and Max Weber—while highlighting some recurring themes and debates that feature in classical sociology. It explains how classical sociology emerged through a debate with the Enlightenment, in which the concept of the 'social' took shape. This was constructed around various themes emphasizing contrasting components of social life—including material, cultural, rational and moral factors. These divergent theorizations set the scene for the play of theoretical oppositions that characterize much subsequent theoretical dispute. For the particular theorists mentioned this is a brief introduction and my intention is to show how what has been passed on to us as the 'classical tradition' contains diverse attempts to address certain core and abiding themes.

What is loosely contained within the 'classical tradition' is an unfinished enterprise of imagining the social in various ways. Contemporary sociology remains, in important respects, indebted to these categories, which overlap, play against each other and combine in the works of individual theorists. However, this is a claim that some dispute. It is sometimes argued that social life changed so irrevocably during the later twentieth century that the concepts and theories of classical sociology are no longer of value for understanding the contemporary world. For example, Ulrich **Beck** writes of an 'epochal break' brought by globalization that renders empty previously central sociological concepts such as those of 'nation' and 'class'—they are he says, 'zombie categories' because 'they are dead but somehow go on living, making us blind to the realities of our lives' (Beck 2000). This catchy phrase 'zombie categories' is often quoted but actually avoids the difficult task of working through what really has been transformed and what purchase existing analysis might still have on social life. The theories and concepts of classical sociology are crucial to this exercise. It is true, of course, that many social developments of the twentieth and twenty-first centuries were unanticipated by classical sociology—for example, the consequences of world wars, the rise and fall of communism and the consequent reconfiguration of the world system, the expansion of the modern state into capillaries of everyday life, the digital technological revolution, new forms of computer mediated networking and lifestyle niches, not to mention globalization and a 24/7 society. Classical analytical frameworks, however, continue to provide ways of understanding contemporary issues.

RECURRENT THEMES AND DEBATES

Sociology emerged with the conditions of **modernity**, that is, the modes of social life and organization that emerged in Europe from about the seventeenth century, subsequently becoming global. The emergence of the modern world entailed dynamic technological and social transformations, leading to a ruthless break with all preceding historical conditions, and a 'never-ending process of internal ruptures and fragmentation within itself' (Harvey 1994: 12). I have argued (Ray 1999) that the circumstances of its emergence have inscribed into sociology a set of antinomies on which sociological theories will tend, implicitly or explicitly, to take a position. By contrast with much earlier philosophy, sociology was historical in the sense that it was concerned less with timeless attributes of human life and more with their historical emergence. The following broad themes can be identified, which appear in different ways in a great deal of social theory.

First, there is the interplay of nature and gender. The growth of capitalism transformed gender relations, something of which classical sociologists were aware, even if their understandings of this were very different from those of contemporary sociologists. It is sometimes suggested that classical sociology ignored gender but this is not so and actually, in some cases, it was an organizing principle in their work. Durkheim (1984), for example, begins with a discussion of 'conjugal solidarity' (the domestic division of labour), which he then takes to be fundamental to social organization and a model for differentiated sociality in

general. Theories of gender were often constructed around a dichotomy of nature and society in which the 'natural' was characteristically coded as feminine—thus, for Simmel, the emergence of an 'objective' instrumental culture entailed an irrevocable loss of a 'subjective' feminine one. He does, however, invest his analysis with a romantically loaded and essentialized concept of 'femininity'.

Second, there is a central debate about science and methods. The development of natural science combined with the Enlightenment vision of progress through reason together suggested the possibility of a scientific analysis of society, which occurred in the context of a decline in religious belief and observance and, more generally, the 'crisis of industrial society'. Sociology promised to provide not only a scientific analysis of society that would guide future practice, but also to offer a scientifically based morality and thus resolve problems of social disorganization and conflict. However, this scientistic vision was challenged by a hermeneutic conception, emphasizing essential differences between scientific and cultural knowledge. The debate between naturalism and hermeneutics became a major issue in subsequent sociological theory and this tension is particularly evident in Weber's work.

Third, there is the theme of the duality of social system and social action. We perceive ourselves as agents whose actions have effects. Yet, viewed as a whole, society appears to be a system of interrelated institutions and practices that have unintended consequences. A central rationale for sociology was that the increasing complexity of social organization, combined with markets and bureaucratic organizations, meant that social processes escaped everyday understanding and became susceptible to the specialist understanding of the social sciences. Sociology claimed to be capable of guiding rational (and therefore willed) interventions in the social system. Thus, the duality of action and system became one of the central problems of sociological theory, with some theories opting for action *or* system (e.g. **structuralism**, symbolic interactionism), and others attempting to reconcile the dilemma. All classical sociologists attempted, in some way, to resolve the problem of structure and agency and this debate continues into contemporary sociology—for example, through Giddens's early work on 'structuration' (e.g. Giddens 1984: 25–6).

A fourth sociological debate has centred on the conditions for social solidarity in the midst of often deep and multiple conflicts and social divisions. With the emergence of a market economy it was possible to imagine a self-equilibrating society based on individual rational calculations, although some classical advocates of the market, such as Adam Smith, insisted on the importance of moral sentiments in regulating human conduct. In opposition to *laissez faire* political economists, early theorists such as Saint-Simon, Comte and Durkheim, emphasized the moral, rather than purely instrumental, foundations of social integration. They did not accept the claim of political economists, that 'the pursuit of individual interests produces the greatest good of all'. The uneasy relations between these schools of thought in nineteenth century social theory erupted in the 1880s in the *Methodenstreit* (dispute over method), which resulted in the split between economics and sociology. The ramifications of this dispute continued well into the twentieth century and the sociology of economic life generally situates and embeds market structures within supportive and constraining cultural and institutional systems.

Finally, the development of modern systems of social and economic organization were, from their beginning, accompanied by a Romantic critique of lost communal authentic social relations. This ambivalence within the modern worldview was reproduced within sociology and informed debates about destiny and value of modern industrial society. Many classical sociological theories sought to rediscover community as a counterbalance to mass society. Disenchantment with the consequences of modernity also underlay the growth of hermeneutic methods and wider resistance to **positivism**, which was viewed as an inappropriate application of scientific methods to cultural phenomena. This view was evident in early twentieth century German sociology; for example, the tension in Tönnies between 'community' and 'society'. In Marx, too, we find the paradoxical combination of an enthusiastic endorsement of modernity (e.g. in the *Manifesto of the Communist Party*) with his expectation that post-capitalist society would overcome alienation and re-establish communal regulation and social solidarity. Some contemporary alternative visions, such as deep ecology or eco-feminism, or post-modernist aesthetics, also perhaps draw on anti-modernist cultural traditions. Part of the culture of industrial society is the notion of a rupture with a traditional, communal past, which remains central to sociological theorizing.

DEBATE WITH THE ENLIGHTENMENT

Sociology arrived with the ambitious promise of resolving the crisis of industrial society through the application of scientific inquiry to social organization. Sociology offered a critical diagnosis of the process of modernization of which it was a part. The role of the diffuse intellectual movement loosely understood as the 'Enlightenment' was significant in complex ways. Sociology was not a *direct* legacy of the Enlightenment but it was an elaboration of some of its themes and gave rise to one of the most persistent debates in sociology—whether, and to what extent, it could be 'scientific'. The Enlightenment was to pose a number of issues that provided a context for subsequent social theory, which included:

- Critique of religious thought in the name of scientific validity. Even though many exponents of the new philosophers were deists rather than atheists, they were critical of institutional religion and Diderot, editor of the *l'Encyclopédie*, to which all leading eighteenth century French intellectuals contributed, claimed that humans would progress in peace only if the idea of God was obliterated (Hazard 1965: 407).
- The idea of progress through reason and a linear historical expansion of reason became popular, as philosophy moved away from cyclical theories of the rise and decline of civilizations, which had roots in classical historiography. Condorcet (1743–94) developed an influential progressive history in *Sketch of a Historical Table of the Progress of the Human Mind* (1794).
- Knowledge would enable practical intervention in the world, rather than speculation and contemplation—as Comte subsequently said, 'Knowledge for foresight, foresight for action'.
- For Montesquieu (1689–1755), for example, society was understood as a system of interrelated elements working for mutual benefit and societies were

subject to a process of social differentiation into sub-systems in which laws regulate subjects, manners regulate private lives and customs regulate external behaviour. It was thus possible to imagine homologies between social and natural organisms.

However, although these themes of the Enlightenment were important for the subsequent development of sociology, the post-Revolutionary counter-Enlightenment of conservatives such as Louis de Bonald (1754–1840) and Joseph de Maistre (1754–1821) for whom the Enlightenment's critical individualism, combined with the Jacobins' violent assault on the *ancien regime*, had destroyed the bases of social order. Opposed to the notion that society might be founded on reason, de Maistre and de Bonald's social order was based on the slow, invisible work of history. Although informed by a deeply conservative and nostalgic desire to re-create a pre-Revolutionary past, they offered reflections on the nature of social order that were to be echoed in later sociology. For example, de Bonald argued that the practice of ritual sacrifice—whether actual or, as in the Catholic Mass, symbolic—is common to all societies. This could be understood only if one regards the social as a sacred order whose bonds are ritually reaffirmed. This idea was to be particularly important in Durkheim's theory of ritual and, more generally, in his understanding of the non-rational bases of social order.

SAINT-SIMON AND COMTE— ORDER AND PROGRESS

Two figures deserving brief mention are Henri Saint-Simon (1760–1825) and his one-time protégé Auguste Comte (1798–1857). Both were part of the post-Revolutionary generation of French intellectuals who had been educated in the Napoleonic Écoles Polytechniques, where they had become imbued with a technical and scientific ethos but were, at the same time, disaffected by limited skilled employment opportunities. Many were drawn to socialist and radical movements in Paris—especially those with technocratic schemes for a new society in which technically trained graduates would find their rightful place. For Saint-Simon, the moral crisis threatening Europe could be resolved by immediate construction of a theoretical system unifying all knowledge. Some of his proposals, such as the application of scientific method to the study of society, the organization of a new scientific age in which the state would assume responsibility for social welfare and institutional co-operation in a unified Europe, were later to become widely shared. Anticipating Marx, on whom he exercised some influence, Saint-Simon understood history in terms of class conflict (class defined in terms of functional-occupational groups) between productive and idle classes (Saint-Simon 1975: 158 and 187). Systemizing many of Saint-Simon's ideas and accumulating historical material to support his view, Comte developed a system of 'positive philosophy' which conceived of society as a natural system, subject to objective forces that could be managed by social scientists. 'Society' (which, used in this sense, was still a novel concept) obeyed law-like principles and passed through three states—the Theological, Metaphysical and Positive. In the Theological stage, magical and supernatural worldviews attributed spiritual powers to the immediate physical environment. In the Metaphysical (transitional) state, worldviews were based on natural philosophy and abstract entities of Spirit, Matter, Force

and Ultimate Causes. Contemporary European society, however, was entering the Positive Age in which people would renounce the search for metaphysical essences and inhabit a world governed by reason and scientific knowledge. However, both Saint Simon and Comte held that, in a secular age, social solidarity would be maintained through the rituals of a secular religion, which Comte developed into his Religion of Humanity. Although little read today, Comte was significant in mapping the conceptual terrain for sociology and particularly for posing, if not resolving the question of the foundations of social bonding in complex, post-traditional societies.

KARL MARX—EMANCIPATION AND REVOLUTION

Karl Marx (1818–83) undertook a critical synthesis that brought together in different measures Hegelian philosophy, French socialism and British political economy. Like Saint-Simon, Marx had a vision of the future towards which analysis of the present was orientated. They differed in other respects, though. A great deal of Saint-Simon's work contains plans for future social organization, including draft constitutions, parliaments, professional and scientific associations and a new religion. Marx eschewed this kind of utopian thinking and preferred not to 'write recipes for the soup kitchen of the future' (Månson 2000: 24). Unlike Saint-Simon, moreover, Marx identified a central class conflict *within* capitalism, rather than one between representatives of the decaying and rising social systems.

Marx was centrally concerned with relationships between economy and politics within a progressive historical movement that constituted (class) actors within a context that was structurally determined. Although the 'history of hitherto existing society is the history of class struggle' (Marx and Engels 1967 [1848]) the organizing theme of Marx's theory is that capitalist society has created a social class, the proletariat, whose struggle to abolish its own exploitation will abolish class rule itself and thereby usher in an age in which genuine human history can begin. The logic of this for Marx was that, unlike all previously existing social classes, the proletariat is propertyless (it has only its labour to sell) and therefore no particular interests to defend. The bourgeoisie, when challenging the rule of the aristocratic landed social order, invoked ideas of (especially economic) freedom, civic liberties, democracy and the rule of law and therefore appeared to invoke the universal interests of humanity as a whole but, once bourgeois rule was established, defended the particular interests of capital. The proletariat, however, was structurally determined by its position within the capitalist system of production, yet embodied the truly universal interests of humanity and therefore made possible a leap from necessity (life governed by objective social forces) to freedom—a life based on unconstrained self-conscious organization.

Marx's critique of the capitalist system had many dimensions. That capitalism was a system of exploitation that 'comes dripping from head to foot, from every pore, with blood and dirt' (Marx 1976: chap. 31) could be witnessed in the conditions of poverty, draconian factory discipline and degradation in which much of the new proletariat lived and which have been documented by Engels' *Condition of the Working Class in England* (1844). However, Marx also understood exploitation through a more technical calculation of the rate of extraction of surplus value. At the core of

capitalist social relations was the wage as a means of exchange between capital and labour. While this *appeared* to be a fair exchange of labour time (the working day) for money (wages) it was actually exploitative since a portion of the value created by labour was withheld by capital in the form of 'surplus value'. When human labour time is bought as a commodity, it has the peculiar property that its consumption *increases* its value for the owner. In the simple exchange of commodities C–M–C (commodities transformed into money which is transformed back into commodities) money is a medium that enables commodities to be circulated—as, for example, when crops are sold and the money received is spent on clothes and improved fencing for the farm, all of which have use value for their purchaser. However, there is a complex form of circulation M–C–M^1 where money (M) is spent on the purchase of labour power (C) with the intention of generating a greater quantity of money than the buyer had initially (M^1). Marx argued that political economy has no explanation of this increase in value although its origin was really quite simple. If the worker works, for example, a ten-hour day and the first eight of these hours are 'necessary' labour, in that the value created is returned to the worker as wages to cover subsistence needs, the remaining two hours create 'surplus value' that is withheld by capital. It is important to note, though, that surplus value does not equal profit but will 'crystallize' in different measure into rent, interest and profit (Marx 1976: chap. 18). This relationship is concealed partly by the appearance of 'free wage labour'—unlike earlier systems of slavery, serfdom and indentured labour, the wage relation *appears* to be a voluntarily entered and therefore equal contract.

This bears on the much-discussed concept of ideology in Marx. His elaborated theory of ideology is rather sparse ('ruling ideas are ideas of the ruling class') and he suggests that, unlike previous societies such as the ancient world and feudalism, capitalism lacked an ideology represented as a systematic body of beliefs. Rather, the dynamic energies of capitalism drowned 'all bonds of sentiment' in the 'icy waters of egotistical calculation'. Thus, unlike earlier systems of production, capitalism did not have time to create a 'halo'—a body of beliefs and ideas that would provide it with stability. Subsequently, in the face of the survival of capitalism, Marxists have given a great deal of attention to ideology as a means of protecting the system from radical assault, both intellectual and political.

Marx believed that, through the critique of existing political economy, he had discovered the secret self-destructive logic of capitalism—that its core achievement was also its undoing. Competition and technical innovation generate continually more efficient replacement of labour by machinery and therefore the 'organic composition of capital'—the proportion of machinery to living labour—rises. This means that, although the mass of surplus value generated in the system rises, the percentage that is classed as profit (as opposed to fixed overheads and investment) declines, resulting in a long-run crisis of profitability. Further, since machinery replaces living labour, there is a growing 'reserve army of unemployed' who provide cheap labour and depress average proletarian wages. This, in turn, creates relative if not absolute immiseration of the proletariat while undermining markets for mass-produced goods. This is not elaborated in detail in Marx, but the implication of his analysis is that recurrent crises of capitalism would create a revolutionary situation as economic crises combined with growing class consciousness, confidence and organization of the working class, who would mobilize a mass social movement to overthrow capitalism and establish socialism. Despite the failure of this prediction and the disastrous experience of Soviet-type societies, Marxism's ability to combine rigorous theoretical social analysis with political activism, and a belief that history would in the end work out well, perhaps accounts for its abiding appeal to many, especially in a period of global capitalist crisis.

ÉMILE DURKHEIM AND MORAL SOCIALITY

Central to the sociology of Émile Durkheim (1858–1917) were questions about the nature of social solidarity. He elaborated the concept of society as an emergent moral entity in itself, *sui generis*, that was not reducible to any other explanatory level. While Marx and Engels developed a material concept of the social, Durkheim insisted not only on the autonomy of the cultural-symbolic realm, but also on its priority in social development. Durkheim saw economic forms and contracts as embedded in cultural and moral systems— so, for example, contracts depend on trust, which presupposes the existence of society as a moral reality. Further, society is a ritual order, a collective conscience founded on the emotional rhythms of human interaction. In common with positivists, Durkheim regarded sociology as a science, albeit with distinctive methods appropriate to the study of society. In the *Rules of Sociological Method* (1893), Durkheim set out to demonstrate the existence of social realities outside the individual; to separate sociology from philosophy; and to define the subject matter of sociology.

The *Rules* began with the famous injunction to 'consider social facts as things' (Durkheim 1964: 2), that is, to regard social norms as objective 'ways of acting, thinking and feeling external to individuals'. This could simply mean that humans acquire social habits that could not have been arrived at spontaneously, but are derived from a pre-existing social world (such as language). But Durkheim gave little attention to peoples' ability to manipulate and distance themselves from social conventions and he tended to write about these with reference to macrosocietal processes. Thus, the persistence (although not origin) of a social form could be explained with reference to the functions it performs for social cohesion and survival (Durkheim 1964: 110). However, a social practice that might be thought of as 'pathological' might not be—for example, contrary to what one might expect, crime is necessary since the collective ritual of punishment serves to reaffirm and strengthen collective sentiments (1964: 81). The three types of social facts identified in the *Rules*—legal codes, social statistics and religious dogmas—correspond to the bases of Durkheim's three major studies: *The Division of Labour* (1895), *Suicide* (1897) and *Elementary Forms of the Religions Life* (1912) respectively.

The *Division of Labour* develops an evolutionary theory based on the transition from 'mechanical' (simple) to 'organic' (complex) forms of the division of labour. In the former, beliefs were common to all members (1964: 129); there was a unified collective conscience that was reinforced through public rituals. Legal and moral rules were 'repressive' and punishments were generally severe (Durkheim 1969a: 250). Kinship was the dominant institution in mechanical societies and domestic production formed the basis of social integration. Organic

solidarity, on the other hand, is heterogeneous, with a complex and differentiated division of labour, based on specialization, diversification and cooperation. While expanding the scope of individual liberty, the organic division of labour also increases the extent of interdependence among its branches, thus individuals are linked more closely to each other than in mechanical societies. The collective conscience weakens as it fragments into moral codes specific to particular occupations and activities, while religion ceases to be a unifying system of belief. Repressive criminal law diminishes proportionately, as the extent of civil, restitutive law increases. However, this notion of a harmoniously integrated organic division of labour had not been realized in nineteenth century industrial societies, which were characterized by an 'anomic' imbalance between individual expectations and the constraints of social reality. Normative regulation (transmitted via socialization, or 'moral education') acts as a constraint on desires that cannot all be satisfied within a given social environment. This analysis is further developed in *Suicide*, where Durkheim argues that 'suicide varies inversely with the degree of integration of social groups of which the individual forms a part'. He developed a scheme of paired concepts in which egoism and altruism lie at opposite poles of social integration. Egoism, on the one hand, refers to weakening of the ties binding people together—forms of solidarity such as religious ritual, marriage and nationalism bind people to collective integration and their weakening results in higher suicide rates. On the other hand, altruistic suicide is conversely a result of excessive social integration—where custom and habit govern individuals who sacrifice their own life because of commandments from a higher source of authority, such as religious or political allegiances. On a second axis of regulation—weak regulation generates anomic suicide resulting from social dislocations such as rapid industrial and commercial changes. Fatalistic suicide (which he suggested was of largely historical significance) results from an excess of social integration that is so oppressive that the certainty of death is preferable.

This question (fuelled by his involvement in the Dreyfus Affair) led Durkheim to attempt to reconcile individualism and republicanism with the need for sacred legitimation of the social order. An organic, differentiated society is no longer integrated by a common value system but, on the contrary, by respect for human rights, which is the only possible basis of legitimation in a democratic society. However, by contrast with Weber's concept of disenchanted formal rationality, in Durkheim's 'cult of individualism' the rights of the individual acquire sacred significance. Respect for individual rights is the shared moral bond offering institutional regulation of an organic society in which people have divergent interests and beliefs. Indeed, whereas in the *Division of Labour* he regarded individualism with some suspicion, as binding people not to society but to themselves (Durkheim 1984: 140), his later account of the cult of individuality is 'neither anti-social nor egoistic', but involves 'sympathy for all that is human, pity for all sufferings, miseries and greater thirst for justice' (1969b). In this way, Durkheim offers perhaps the first *sociological* theory of human rights which regarded these as deriving not from the individual but from society and therefore as evolving with the moral division of labour.

The significance of religion increased in Durkheim's later work, culminating in *Elementary Forms of the Religious Life* (1912), in which the idea of a collective conscience, as the moral regulator of society, gave way to 'collective representations'. These constitute the symbolic order of society and comprise religious doctrine, legal rules, legends, proverbs, customs and traditions; that is, the symbolic constitution of society. This opened up analysis of society as a symbolic order, which, arguably, led through Marcel Mauss and **Lévi-Strauss** to Roland **Barthes**' semiotics and **Foucault**'s discourse analysis (Alexander 1990: 8). In *Elementary Forms*, Durkheim set out to show that the social is indispensable to understanding the formation of all beliefs, institutions and conceptions since, in religion, we find an 'essential and permanent aspect of humanity'. Thus, to show that religious systems were representations of society would show, too, that categories of scientific knowledge were socially constructed.[1] The idea of a 'class', which is fundamental to all cognitive systems, is an instrument of thought that has been socially constructed in the form of a hierarchy. Thus, systems of knowledge construct relations of subordination and co-ordination, which people would never have thought of organizing in this way had they not already known what a hierarchy was (Durkheim 1976: 148). Similarly, an orientation to space comes initially from the spatial relations with which people are familiar, thus, where the camp has circular form, space is conceived in the form of an immense circle and is subdivided in the same way as the camp (1976: 11–12). The concept of time is derived from the rhythmic activities which punctuate social experience, such as rituals, rites and cycles. The concept of cause as an arrangement of sequences is derived from the logical relations of social organization. The mind then constructs the relationships of cause—effect in the world *a priori* derived from the model offered by society (1976: 363ff).

Elementary Forms aimed to develop a theory of religion based on four hypotheses: religion is socially determined; it is cognitive; ritual expresses and dramatizes social roles; religion is conducive to social solidarity. One of the most famous and controversial claims in *Elementary Forms* is that religion and piety are symbolic representations of the relationship between society and individuals. Society is experienced by individuals as superior and transcendent, a force demanding our acquiescence. It not only creates moral obligations that are external, but it is also continuous while individuals die and are replaced. Thus, as a symbolic representation, the sacred too has features of immortality, transcendence and superior power. People have a dual existence, impersonal and personal, both as a member of society and yet also as a particular person and body existing at a moment in time and space. The essence of religion (as for de Bonald) lies in sacred rituals, which reaffirm social solidarity, and the division between the sacred and profane is an evolutionary universal, found in all societies.

Support for these claims came from the study of 'simple' societies, such as the totemic cultures of Australia and North America, which he believed would possess the 'elementary forms' of all religious practice. Here, the totem is a symbol of collective life, but rather than products of pure imagination, these are derived from external reality, from society, and the object of worship is an anonymous and impersonal force independent of individuals. Totemism is the emblem of the group, which represents the collective to itself through myths and legends. Totemic societies are organized around strictly enforced taboos or interdicts, which are the simplest form of veneration of the sacred. These may be either positive or negative. Positive taboos secure bonds between members of the group, such as the spilling of blood at a sacred rock, which reaffirms the common link between the collective and the object. Negative taboos create prohibitions on forms of contact and conduct, as in the case of prohibited foods or sexual taboos. The incest taboo is both the first interdiction, defining relationships within the group and with others, and also paradigmatic for all other taboos (1969c).

Collective solidarity, moreover, is periodically renewed through rituals that serve in different ways to reaffirm the power of the totem. In these assemblies a 'collective effervescence' reaffirms social integration through four kinds of rites: sacrificial, imitative (taking on qualities of the totem), commemorative (such as ancestor worship), and piacular (expiatory) rites that involve mourning, fasting and weeping, with obligations to slash or tear clothing and flesh, thereby renewing the unity of a group following misfortune. Mourning, however, carries the risk of transforming grief from symbolic into actual violence. Although he was often wrongly regarded as a 'conservative', Durkheim developed radical theoretical reflections on the foundations of the social and the interplay between emotions and collective identities.

GEORG SIMMEL—ELUSIVE SOCIALITY

With Georg Simmel (1856–1917) the emphasis of sociology shifted from an exclusively macroscopic concern towards individuals in interactions. Ambivalence is a keynote of Simmel's sociology. He was reluctant to define terms unambiguously and often develops an argument in one direction, only to appear then to argue the contrary. So, having elaborated his central concept of 'form' as opposed to 'content' in sociology, he said, 'of course, what is form in one respect is content in another' (Simmel 1971: 25). Simmel's critique of sociological reason focused on the activity of subjects who internalized but nonetheless constructed and manipulated social types, which were the categorical basis of social life.

Simmel shared with Durkheim an interest in social differentiation, individualism and competitiveness, although these are taken by each in radically different directions. Simmel opposed functional approaches to the social and emphasized the centrality of conflict and competition in social life. Simmel rejected the idea of 'society' as an organic unity, arguing instead that 'society' was a metaphor for forms of association abstracted from everyday life. Simmel attempted to view society simultaneously from the standpoints of the individual and the social. We reveal parts of ourselves in social interaction, but also hold parts of ourselves back. We present different aspects of the self in different interactions (Simmel 1971: 24). His sociology was not generally written in a way that appealed to data for support but, rather, he invoked a kind of shared intuition, inviting us to recognize the ways of the social in his vignettes and descriptions.

This is not to say that Simmel's sociology was entirely intuitive and unsystematic. Indeed, he was sometimes criticized for writing in an overly formalistic and descriptive way. Simmel's 'formal sociology' was to study the forms of association that made generalized and routinized social interactions possible. Experience is inescapably organized in forms. Try, for example, to imagine colour—one cannot imagine 'pure' colour, but only colours appearing in particular shapes, or forms. There are then two components to experience: a formal,

organizing aspect and content, that which is perceived. Another way of understanding this is through Simmel's analogy with geometry. He described sociology as the 'geometry of social life' (Simmel 1971: 28ff) in that, just as geometry was concerned with the abstract relational properties of the material objects, irrespective of their particular content or nature, so sociology would describe the forms through which the content of social life took place.[2] 'Contents' are the materials of sociation—everything that is present in individuals, such as drives, interests, purposes, inclinations and psychic states (Simmel 1971: 24).

To the question, 'How is society possible? Simmel answered that society is an ongoing creation of its subjects and hence, unlike nature, society needs no observer since it is directly realized by its own elements. This occurs through *typification*, the process whereby we construct social categories. In order to interact socially, we must continuously add to and subtract from another's individuality, as Simmel put it. We never encounter anyone as unique (this would be 'formless' experience) but always as 'more and less than they are'. More, because we typify someone as a parent, sister, student, teacher or any such category—attributing characteristics that extend beyond the individual. Less, because we thereby subtract from someone's individuality by relating to them as a bearer of a general category. Society is possible only because of these abstractions that are the basis of formal associations. Forms are relatively stable features of social life—such as superordination and subordination, exchange and competition, inclusion and exclusion— that have regular features irrespective of the particular contexts in which they appear. So conflict and competition, for example, will have a recognizable structure and dynamic whether they appear in the family, in a royal court, or between nations.

Further, there is a balance of individuality and abstraction in different social forms—some are more abstract and impersonal than others. Money exchanges represent a high degree of impersonality and abstraction, whereas love relationships have low typification and higher degrees of individuality. Thus, the affective structure of intimacy is based on what each of the two participants gives or shows only to the one other person and to nobody else. Intimacy then, is based on the exclusive content of a relationship between members, regardless of its specific nature. However, when intimate relations become formalized, as in marriage, their character changes. Marriage is no longer simply an intimate exchange between two people, but is socially regulated and historically transmitted, requiring official recognition by external authorities of law or religion. Nonetheless, modern marriage, Simmel says, seems to have a weaker objective character than unions of the past, allowing a greater degree of individuality, creativity and differentiation (Simmel 1971: 227ff). While relationships of intimacy are becoming less formalized, some public interactions are more relaxed—for example, exchanges between superiors and subordinates become more courteous and apparently egalitarian. Yet sociation is increasingly stylized in that it is pursued playfully as an end in itself. Conversation, for example, becomes an 'art' to be pursued with tact following unspoken rules. Similarly, eroticism as the pursuit of sexual interests is subordinated to coquetry, the play of 'hinted consent and hinted denial', where all participants understand that this is a game not meant to lead to actual seduction (Simmel 1971: 134). Thus, sociability as a play-form becomes an end in itself that mirrors and parodies the serious business of social life.

Yet, the analysis of social forms may reveal a whole world of social relations in apparently unimportant facets of social life. This is illustrated by his concept of the 'senses as forms' (e.g. Simmel 1997: 109–19). A social world may be encapsulated in a glance, revealing mutuality, self-disclosure, concealment and subordination or superordination. The erotic glance contains an 'absorbing moment of playful delight' when two people's eyes meet and both are drawn transiently into an absorbing moment of experience, of 'mutual conspiracy beyond convention'. The glance among lovers constitutes communion and conspiracy beyond social norms. Thus, the eye has a 'uniquely sociological function' of establishing reciprocity and intimacy, a gift to the other, which assumes equality. However, inequality inhibits the glance (it was once considered subversive for a Black in the southern USA to look a White in the eyes) and, where no reciprocity is possible, the eyes are hidden. Thus, we close the eyes of the dead and place a hood over the face of the executed or executioner.

The formation of an objective culture, in which social forms become autonomous and self-sufficient is the outcome of a long developmental process of the human spirit. The instrumentality and calculability of modern life is analysed in Simmel's longest work, *The Philosophy of Money* (1900). Here, he juxtaposes freedom and impersonality with the loss of culture. The development of money, he argues, is an element in a profound cultural trend towards objectification and impersonality. Money is not only evidence of increasing abstraction, but itself becomes more abstract. Once tied to an apparent guarantee of value (gold) it now floats freely and expands into more abstract forms like credit (spending money you have not got, trading on future prices, etc.) imaginary and symbolic worlds that Simmel did not directly anticipate but that his analysis suggested. Money, then, is iconic for the modern age, bringing freedom and depersonalization, proximity and distance. Money and the urban economy reduce spatial distance between people while separating 'nature' from modern life, for which it becomes an object of contemplation. But Simmel saw no possibility of return to pre-capitalist harmony; even if socialism were to replace capitalism it would simply intensify bureaucratic impersonality and the complete calculability of life. This theme of the cultural tragedy of lost wholeness became more explicit in Simmel's last works, such as the 'Crisis of culture' (1916). The tragedy of modern culture arises from the increasing objectivity of life in which world forms (like language, morals and technical and legal systems) lose links with the subject and take on a life of their own. This is a tragedy in the classical sense in that, like the character whose otherwise noble qualities are fatally flawed, the destruction of the unified subject is the necessary result of the very nature of social life. The human being becomes the 'bearer of the compulsion with which this logic rules developments' (Simmel 1997: 72).

Like other 'founding fathers', Simmel was aware that the transformation of gender relationships is one of the core elements of modernization. He went further than most others in regarding the very process of the formation of objective culture as gendered. The separation between subjective and objective culture is also a divide between feminine and masculine culture, in that objective culture was founded on a 'male way of seeing' (Vucht Tijssen 1991). Capitalism intensifies the dominance of male culture, as money creates a division of labour between domestic (female) work and the (paid) work of men, with the consequence that woman's economic value loses substance and she appears to be supported by her husband, a liability which gives rise to dowry (Simmel 1990: 375). Simmel's remedy for the dominance of masculine culture is a reappraisal of the female form of life and the reinforcement of the position of women in society. This could lead towards an independent female culture or to a culture common to men and women that had more female nuances. However, like earlier social theorists, Simmel projected onto women a set of 'natural' attributes. This further illustrates how classical sociology theorized the transformation of gender relations in terms of the nature/society dualism—which was to become a centrally contested division in subsequent sociological theory.

MAX WEBER—THE HUBRIS OF REASON

The debate with the Enlightenment was, in part, about the extent and value of reason in human society and it is with Max Weber (1864–1920) that rationality becomes an unfolding theme in human history. His approach to sociology was framed by the *Methodenstreit*. Weber attempted to define a path for sociology that was both historical and recognized the need for understanding the role of subjective meanings of actors but also met objective standards of evidence. In particular, he developed a method of generalization through the construction of 'ideal types'—intellectual constructs that attempt to abstract from the complexity of actual social life some central defining characteristics that then enable us to compare societies and institutions. One of

Weber's most famous ideal-types was his concept of bureaucracy, in which he attempted to identify the core features of modern bureaucracy as opposed to pre-modern 'patrimonial' institutions. Modern bureaucracies he defined in terms of hierarchical authority: a single command centre, impersonality and separation of office from the salaried office-holder, written rules of conduct, specifically defined spheres of expert competence and promotion through a career structure based on merit. Partrimonial bureaucracies he saw as based on personal loyalty and obligations to the ruler, regarding the office as a locus of benefit for personal gain, the exercise of power as discretionary and personalized, rather than rule-following, and judgements made by viewing each case individually (Weber 1978: 235–6).

His concern with bureaucracy as a system of rational action was driven by an overarching project—which is most clearly defined in his posthumously published *Sociology of Religion*—to understand the tendency in modern societies towards *rationalization*. He developed a typology of action—traditional, affective, value-rational and goal-rational. Traditional action is rooted in customary habits of thought and habitual stimuli. Affective action is an emotional response to stimuli. Value-rational (*wertrational*) action involves calculating the most appropriate means to a substantive end (which might itself be non-rational, such as salvation). Goal-rational (*zweckrational*) action calculates both the means and the rationality of the ends—for example, rational accounting in a market economy. In practice, these types of action will appear together (the model is an ideal-type) and Weber was well aware of the complexities of rationality in social life. His famous Protestant Ethic essays, for example,

were, in part, an attempt to show how the motivational disposition (the 'spirit of capitalism') necessary for the emergence of a modern capitalist system was the unintended outcome of an attempt by early modern Calvinists to resolve theological problems. For sixteenth and seventeenth century Calvinists (Weber argues), the doctrine of predestination (that those elected to be saved had been determined in advance for eternity) combined with the rejection of a route to salvation through holy sacraments or 'good works' left followers with an 'unprecedented inner loneliness' and uncertainty. In pursuit of 'evidence' of salvation some then followed an ascetic but worldly life of hard work, abstinence and the accumulation of wealth. But since a dissolute life of conspicuous consumption would indicate evidence of damnation rather than salvation, believers began to pursue accumulation as an end itself—thereby the religious (substantive) rational goal of salvation became transposed into the (rational) goal of accumulation and capital growth. Weber's thesis has given rise to more than a century of debate (e.g. Ray 1999: 175–80).

Although Weber did not have a **deterministic** theory of history, he suggested that there was a long-run cultural tendency towards increasing 'rationalization', which was developed 'with full force' in Occidental civilization but is evident elsewhere. Rationalization involves features such as extending scientific rationality and calculation to 'the conduct of life itself'; secularization or 'disenchantment' (decline of public religious belief which becomes increasingly private); and especially the growth of bureaucratic systems of action. This is located within worldviews and is not a unilinear process but is subject to interruption and temporary reversal. Indeed, Weber counterpoised charisma to rationalization and it is through charisma that personality forces its way into history and is a 'truly revolutionary force' that disrupts bureaucracy and rationalization (Weber 1978: 1117). Charismatic social movements—often headed by leaders claiming divine inspiration—sweep away conservative bureaucratic procedures but are, in the end, doomed to routinization. Charisma is subject to routinization in that it must eventually face the problem of succession, which requires some principle of selection. At this point, charisma is no longer focused on the qualities of the leader but rather on the legitimacy of the selection procedures, whether these are resemblance to the original leader, revelation, election or personal endorsement of the leader. Since it must always be replaced by some form of procedures, charisma will tend to develop into either traditional or rational-legal authority (Weber 1978: 246–8). Similarly, the Charismatic movement of Puritan asceticism became routinized in the capitalist spirit (Mommsen 1987: 35–51). Weber's view that we are apparently doomed to live in a dull disenchanted world of rationality and bureaucracy (after all, 'the future belongs to bureaucratization') is open to the suggestion of pessimism, as Coser says, 'He is not a prophet of glad tidings to come but a harbinger of doom and disaster' (Coser 1977: 233–4).

This view of Weber the pessimist has been influential and has some foundation. He wrote of a bureaucratic nightmare, in which:

> The performance of each individual worker is mathematically measured, each man becomes a little cog in the machine and aware of this, his one preoccupation is whether he can become a bigger cog ... it is horrible to think that the world could one day be filled with these little cogs, little men clinging to little jobs, and striving towards bigger ones.... this passion for bureaucracy is enough to drive one to despair.

> (Weber 1978: 1402)

This is a view that has less relevance for the contemporary multiplicity of organizational forms and systems that in some respects progress 'beyond the "iron cage"' (Reed 2005). But Weber was, arguably, offering a warning regarding a possible future that was not inevitable. He asked whether we can preserve meaningful existence in a social world dominated by impersonal forces of rationalization. The strengthening of pluralistic democracy and, in particular, the parliamentary committee system that could hold bureaucrats accountable, represented the possibility of at least mitigating the vista of total control. On the other hand, Weber's pessimism was highly influential among a generation of critical social theorists, such as **Adorno** and **Horkheimer**.

CHALLENGES FOR CLASSICAL SOCIOLOGY

Classical sociology was the product of the first Great Transformation of (initially) European societies from largely agrarian to industrial capitalist societies—a period of social change of an extent and intensity probably without precedent in human history. At the moment of its inception, industrial society was already diagnosed as being 'in crisis'— morally, politically, socially and economically. Classical sociology offered systematic critical analysis of its effects, its trajectory and the possibilities for achieving a new equilibrium, which the theorists discussed here envisaged in differing ways. Classical sociology further encapsulated the hopes of the industrial age—the possibilities for a rational, emancipated society of unbounded technological progress and social and individual freedom. It further articulated fears—of atomized individuals in a dull, conformist iron cage of rationality in which a scientific civilization would come to dominate its creators. The twentieth century, then just dawning, was to exceed expectations on both counts but would also post new problems, largely unanticipated by classical theories. Stalinist and Nazi totalitarianism generated, not Weber's dispassionate official, but politicized central bureaucratic control, organizing homicidal mass state terror on a scale previously unimagined. Yet the post-Second World War developed world saw the paradoxical combination of the Damoclean sword of nuclear destruction and the rise of an affluent consumer society in which fundamental contradictions of capitalism appeared, if not resolved, then assuaged within state welfare capitalism. At the same time, the erosion of the imperial, patriarchal and European-centred world of classical sociology gave way to the challenges of anti-colonial movements, second wave feminism and digital technologies that transformed understandings of self and the social. Again, the world after 1989 posed new questions once more—with the collapse of the Soviet 'experiment', the realigned world order and intensifying forces of globalization within a world dominated by issues of global immiseration, renewed capitalist crisis, polarization and environmental catastrophe. The challenge for our understanding of classical social theory is to reveal its relevance to an age in which so much has changed but in which the fundamental dilemmas of social analysis remain.

NOTES

1 Durkheim did, however, try to avoid the possibly relativistic implications of this view by insisting that truth, which requires long and specialist training, embodies the moral authority of the collective (Crook 1991: 47).

2 Simmel did stress that geometry, in contrast to sociology, isolates absolutely pure forms, whereas in sociology abstraction is merely an analytical device. But the analogy is interesting in that it emphasized visual and spatial social relations.

REFERENCES

Alexander, J.C. (ed.) (1990) *Durkheimian Sociology: Cultural Studies*, Cambridge: Cambridge University Press.

Beck, U. (2000) 'The cosmopolitan perspective: the sociology of the second modernity' *Sociology*, 51(1): 79–106.

Coser, L. (1977) *Masters of Sociological Thought*, New York: Harcourt Brace.

Crook, S. (1991) *Modernist Radicalism and Its Aftermath: Foundationalism and Anti-Foundationalism in Radical Social Theory*, London: Routledge.

Durkheim, E. (1964) [1893] *The Division of Labour in Society*, trans. by Wilfred Douglas Halls, London: Macmillan.

——(1969a) 'Individualism and the intellectuals', *Political Studies*, 17: 14–30.

——(1969b) 'Deux lois de 'évolution pénale', *Journal Sociologique*, 244–73.

——(1969c) 'La prohibition de l'inceste et ses origines', *Journal Sociologique*, 37–101.

——(1976) [1912] *The Elementary Forms of Religious Life*, trans. by J.W. Swain (2nd edition), London: Routledge.

——(1984) [1893] *The Division of Labour in Society*, trans. by W.D. Halls, New York: Macmillan.

Giddens, A. (1984) *The Constitution of Society: Outline of the Theory of Structuration*, Berkeley, CA: University of California Press.

Harvey, D. (1994) *The Condition of Postmodernity*, Oxford: Blackwell.

Hazard, P. (1965) *European Social Thought in the Eighteenth Century*, Harmondsworth: Penguin.

Månson, P. (2000) 'Karl Marx', in H. Anderson and L.B. Kaspersen (eds), *Classical and Modern Social Theory*, Oxford: Blackwell, pp. 16–33.

Marx, K. (1976) *Capital: A Critique of Political Economy*, vol. 1, Moscow: Progress Publishers.

Marx, K. and Engels, F. (1967) *Manifesto of the Communist Party*, Moscow: Progress Publishers.

Mommsen, W. (1987) 'Personal conduct and societal change', in S. Lash and S. Whimster (eds), *Max Weber, Rationality and Modernity*, London: Allen & Unwin, pp. 35–51.

Ray, L.J. (1999) *Theorizing Classical Sociology*, Milton Keynes: Open University Press.

Reed, M. (2005) 'Beyond the Iron Cage: bureaucracy and democracy in the knowledge economy and society', in P. Du Gay (ed.), *The Values of Bureaucracy*, Oxford: Oxford University Press, pp. 116–40.

Saint-Simon, H. (1975) *Selected Writings on Science, Industry and Social Organization*, ed. and trans. by K. Taylor, London: Croom Helm.

Simmel, G. (1971) *On Individuality and Social Forms*, D. Levine (ed.), Chicago: Chicago University Press.

——(1990) *The Philosophy of Money*, T. Bottomore and D. Frisby (eds), London: Routledge.

——(1997) *Simmel on Culture*, D. Frisby and M. Featherstone (eds), London: Sage.

Vucht Tijssen, van L. (1991) 'Women and objective culture: Georg Simmel and Marianne Weber', *Theory Culture and Society*, 8(3): 203–18.

Weber, M. (1978) *Economy and Society*, 2 vols, G. Roth and C. Wittich (eds), London: University of California Press.

——(1993) *Sociology of Religion*, trans. by Ephraim Fischoff, Boston, MA: Beacon Press.

Postmodern Social Theory

by Sam Han

Within the nebulous field of contemporary academic discourse, the once hotly-contested debates on 'the postmodern' have all but faded completely. For many, this is a good thing. As those who agree with this sentiment would have it, the debates surrounding 'the postmodern', '**postmodernism**' and 'postmodernity', though they provided some temporary excitement within intellectual circles, ended up confusing a lot more people than helping them to understand anything. For them, this is due to, among other things, the 'obtuse' writing-style of many authors and scholars with postmodern sympathies. And, indeed, for the adherents of the postmodern backlash, the eventual fizzling out of the postmodern wave was well overdue. Likewise, those who were not necessarily stalwart defenders of the postmodern, but had believed there to be something substantive in its philosophy, have equally shied away from the concept. It is very difficult to find, among theorists today, those who would welcome the label of 'postmodernist'.

Nevertheless, the fact that 'postmodernism' no longer pops up as a keyword within journal articles does not mean that its conceptual and political challenges to various disciplines have been wiped clean away. In fact, it can be argued that they have spread unnoticed throughout so many disciplinary traditions that they have now become normalized. For example, the skepticism towards a Universal Truth, an idea associated with postmodernism mostly due to philosopher Jean-François **Lyotard**'s *The Postmodern Condition* (1984), is readily discussed in a positive light among intellectuals who would not, for the life of them, consider themselves to be postmodern. Hence, this 'decline' may be the worst nightmare of the anti-postmoderns; for, despite their disdain, postmodernism has leaked through the crevices of the disciplines and, undoubtedly, also social theory.

In this chapter, I will use 'the postmodern' to encompass 'postmodernism' as well as 'postmodernity'. By using the generalized category, my aim is to draw attention to the variety of ways in which 'postmodern' is tagged onto numerous phenomena and, ultimately, to clarify a clearly baffling topic for many. To do so, it will be important to take seriously one of the ideas most readily attributed to postmodern thought—the attention to language and **discourse**. This is especially daunting today as the word 'postmodern' creeps up every now and then outside of scholarly literature, usually misused horribly by the author. In mainstream public discourse in the United States, the label 'postmodern' continues to be the favorite adjective to tack onto anything considered intellectually 'fuzzy'. Recently, it has even been deployed in the press coverage of the US presidential elections to describe Barack Obama. Jonah Goldberg in an op-ed for the national daily *USA Today* wrote:

> The Obama campaign has a postmodern feel to it because more than anything else, it seems to be about itself. Its relationship to reality is almost theoretical. Sure, the campaign has policy proposals, but they are props to advance the narrative of a grand movement existing in order to be a movement galvanized around the singular ideal of movement-ness. Obama's followers are … hooked on a feeling. 'We are the ones we have been waiting for!' Well, of course you are.

> (Goldberg 2008)

We can see from Goldberg's rather caustic characterization of the postmodern that it remains an empty signifier for self-referentiality ('a grand movement centered around movement') and overt theoretical interest ('reality is almost theoretical'). The intended image of the postmodern is clear for writers like Goldberg and others. It is a catch-all for those who are considered not only 'out-there' but unserious. And, by attaching this term to then candidate Obama, the conservative Goldberg was certainly trying to paint him in a negative light. It is this kind of silly mistake which we want to avoid.

So where did 'postmodern' come from and what does it have to do with social theory?

Many scholars suggest that the term 'postmodern' began in the arts (painting specifically), then moved to the realm of architecture and finally blossomed in full force in high literary theory, through which it finally found its way into the mainstream public discourse in the 1980s. As a result, some of the best works dealing with the postmodern have been written by literary theorists and art historians. Perhaps the most significant and best known among them is Fredric **Jameson**, a literary theorist by training, who has written on numerous topics including **Marxism**, **structuralism** and science fiction. He argues that postmodernism is the cultural reflection of a certain mode of capitalism, which he describes, following Ernest Mandel, as 'late-capitalism'. In his widely-read essay, 'Postmodernism, or the cultural logic of late capitalism,' Jameson outlines a historical **aesthetic** analysis (using a method he calls 'periodization') of the postmodern, rooted in his very unorthodox Marxism.

> The case for its [postmodernism's] existence depends on the hypothesis of some radical break or *coupure*, generally traced back to the end of the 1950s or the early 1960s.

> As the word itself suggests, this break is most often related to notions of the waning or extinction of the hundred-year-old modern movement (or to its ideological or aesthetic repudiation). Thus, abstract expressionism in painting, existentialism in philosophy, the final forms of representation in the novel, the films of the great *auteurs*, or the modernist school of poetry (as institutionalized and canonized in the works of Wallace Stevens): all these are now seen as the final, extraordinary flowering of a

high modernist impulse which is spent and exhausted with them.

(Jameson 1984: 53)

However, postmodernism's impact on social theory, it is believed, was considerably later, and, for the most part, minimal, although it is interesting that Lyotard cites *sociology* as the originator of the term in his famous study (1984: xxiii). Even if he were inaccurate, the question—what is postmodern social theory?—is still a significant one, especially since many studies of the postmodern have only minimally considered the impact of the postmodern on social theory.

One of the recurring themes in the debates on the postmodern, and consequently in this chapter, is that of crisis. 'Postmodern', for many, indicated not only a transformation but a crisis in the values, culture and aesthetics of the modern. This crisis was sometimes articulated as 'the end' of modern life. The Italian philosopher and theologian, Gianni Vattimo, for instance, authored a book called *The End of Modernity* (1991). To approach the question of 'crisis' and 'end' and to figure out what exactly the 'postmodern' means in postmodern social theory, it will be helpful to view just the phrase 'postmodern social theory'. It can be taken to have two meanings. The first is to believe that postmodern social theory is, in effect, postmodern*ist* social theory. That is to say, within this interpretation, postmodern is a modifier that entails a certain theoretical or philosophical disposition, what I will call throughout this chapter the 'positional' approach. The second view would be to see the 'postmodern' in 'postmodern social theory' as a conditional modifier, one which stems from a socio-historical epoch known as 'postmodernity'. This approach is what I will call the 'historicist' approach, and it is favored by mostly

post-Marxist theorists, such as Jameson, but also by geographer David Harvey, whose book *The Conditions of Postmodernity* (1994) takes into consideration changes in the global financial system to produce the social condition of 'postmodernity'. In turn, it is the aim of this chapter to investigate what I earlier referred to as the permeation of 'the postmodern' in social theory, by looking closely at various thinkers, including Jameson but also Jean-François Lyotard, Jürgen **Habermas**, Richard Rorty and Jean **Baudrillard**, who have weighed on the postmodern and exemplify these two approaches.

There is absolutely no guarantee that the reader will come out with the feeling of understanding postmodern social theory *in toto* because, in a sense, 'the postmodern' is, among other things, about smashing totalities. However, what this chapter does attempt to do is to provide the reader with some basic co-ordinates to navigate the murky waters by reading a debate on, not simply accounts of, the postmodern. What reading the debate closely will, hopefully, achieve is not only an explication of the concepts surrounding the postmodern but also what is *at stake*.

THE CRISIS OF CAPITALISM: FREDRIC JAMESON

Jameson utilizes the figure of 'the end' and 'crisis' in his analysis of contemporary culture and capitalism. Beginning with his explosive article on postmodernism that appeared in the *New Left Review* in 1984, and his subsequent book based on the article, he has emerged as perhaps the most learned voice in the 'historicist' approach to the study of the postmodern. There are many reasons for this, but most significant is his allegiance to a certain brand of unorthodox Marxism and his knack for cultural analysis.

Postmodernism, according to Jameson, is the end to the divide between aesthetic production and commodity production which, in turn, is a signal for a new brand of capitalism.

> The frantic economic urgency of producing fresh waves of ever more novel-seeming goods (from clothing to airplanes), at ever greater rates of turnover, now assigns an increasingly essential structural function and position to aesthetic innovation and experimentation.

(Jameson 1984: 56)

Capitalism, long believed by Marxists and neoclassical economists alike to be a fundamentally economic phenomenon requires, for Jameson, not only a cultural aspect but essentially works *through* culture. Yet, as he readily acknowledges, the fact that capitalism requires an ideological component ('superstructure') has long been a vital component of Marxist theory. However, Jameson's argument cannot simply be labeled a rearticulation of Marx's or even **Gramsci**'s conceptions of 'ideology' because Jameson believes there to be a fundamental transformation in the workings of capitalism, effecting a new society as a whole. Hence, he acknowledges some intellectual affinity with the writings of Daniel Bell, the sociologist responsible for the term 'post-industrial society'.

> [I]ndeed, theories of the postmodern—whether celebratory or couched in the language of moral revulsion and denunciation—bear a strong family resemblance to all those more ambitious sociological generalizations which, at much the same time, bring us the news of the arrival and inauguration of a whole new type of society, most famously baptized 'post-industrial society' (Daniel Bell), but often also designated consumer society, media society, information society, electronic society or 'high tech', and the like. Such theories have the obvious ideological mission of demonstrating, to their own relief, that the new social formation in question no longer obeys the laws of classical capitalism, namely the primacy of industrial production and the omnipresence of class struggle. The Marxist tradition has therefore resisted them with vehemence, with the signal exception of the economist Ernest Mandel, whose book *Late Capitalism* sets out not merely to anatomize the historic originality of this new society (which he sees as a third stage or moment in the evolution of capital), but also to demonstrate that it is, if anything, a *purer* stage of capitalism than any of the moments that preceded it.

(Jameson 1984: 55)

Jameson therefore utilizes postmodernism as an intervention within Marxist theory, to haul it into crisis. It has too long either simply ignored aesthetics or seen it as secondary in importance. This intra-Marxist mission of Jameson's is reflected also in the Marxist theorists from whom he draws—Theodor **Adorno** and Herbert **Marcuse**. Culture, or more specifically *aesthetics*, is not a mirror of capitalism, but an essential component. It is this analytical centrality of aesthetics in the analysis of capitalism that differentiates Jameson's 'post-modern' from other approaches that will be considered below.

One aspect of postmodernism is the blurring of the boundaries between high and 'mass' culture. Mass culture is, of course, one of the major concepts utilized not only by Adorno and **Horkheimer** in the famous chapter on 'the culture industry' in The *Dialectic of the Enlightenment* (2002), but also in Marcuse's *One Dimensional Man* (1964). This 'effacement of boundaries' can be seen, argues Jameson, in the rising interest in:

> the whole landscape of advertising and motels, of the Las Vegas strip, of the late show and Grade-B Hollywood film, of so-called paraliterature with its airport paperback categories of the gothic and the romance, the popular biography, the murder mystery and the science fiction or fantasy novel. They no longer 'quote' such 'texts' as a Joyce might have done, or a Mahler; they incorporate them, to the point where the line between high art and commercial forms seems increasingly difficult to draw.
>
> (Jameson 1998: 112)

Here, Jameson identifies a crisis in not only capitalism, but in the space of art and literature, which in the classical-modernist mode was 'oppositional'.

> It emerged with the business society of the gilded age as scandalous and offensive to the middle-class public—ugly, dissonant, bohemian, sexually shocking. It was something to make fun of (when the police were not called in to seize the books or close the exhibitions): an offense to good taste and to common sense, or, as Freud and Marcuse would have put it, a provocative challenge to the reigning reality—and performance-principles of the early 20th-century middle class society.
>
> (Jameson 1998: 124)

Whereas the high modernism of Joyce or Mahler preserved a somewhat autonomous and critical space, removed from the mundane, humdrum of mass or popular culture, figures like Andy Warhol in the visual arts and Robert Venture in architecture not only incorporated it in their work but championed it. Jameson's critique of postmodernism is political—in short, whereas high-modernist culture used to be resistant, it is now wholly subsumed and normalized by bourgeois, capitalist society.

> Not only are Joyce and Picasso no longer weird and repulsive, they have become classics and now look rather realistic to us. Meanwhile, there is very little in either the form or the content of contemporary art that the contemporary society finds intolerable and scandalous. The most offensive forms of this art—punk rock, say, or what is called sexually explicit material—are all taken in stride by society, and they are commercially successful, unlike the productions of the older high modernism … [C]ommodity production and in particular our clothing, furniture, buildings and other artifacts are now intimately tied in with styling changes which derive from artistic experimentation;

our advertising, for example, is fed by postmodernism in all the arts and inconceivable without it.

(Jameson 1998: 124)

Thus, Jameson suggests that not only have changes in middle-class tastes rendered art and literature devoid of political opposition (an argument which Slovenian philosopher Slavoj Žižek has rightly identified as an updated form of Marx's 'commodification') but that postmodernism *needs* commercial art for its existence. Commodity production and artistic production are no longer distinguishable in this sense. It is this sort of 'aesthetic populism' of postmodernism that Jameson believes to be representative of a larger dynamic in the evolution of capitalism. Ultimately, the postmodern in postmodern social theory, according to Jameson, is a 'periodizing concept, whose function is to correlate the emergence of new formal features in culture with the emergence of a new type of social life and a new economic order' (Jameson 1998: 113).

THE CRISIS OF KNOWLEDGE: JEAN-FRANÇOIS LYOTARD

One of the most well-known postmodern pronouncements is Lyotard's oft-quoted definition of the postmodern 'as incredulity toward metanarratives' (Jameson 1998: xxiv). Many sympathetic and unsympathetic interpreters of Lyotard have attributed to him what has widely been cited as the **epistemological** grounding of postmodern theory. Yet, as is the case with many things associated with the postmodern, this interpretation has been riddled with misreading. One of the points of confusion has come from Lyotard's work, especially

The Postmodern Condition, being read as the explication of an intellectual stance, that is, as a postmodern*ist* stance. Though, indeed, Lyotard's own words do have something to do with that, it is not necessarily a fair reading of him since it is not his purpose to argue for a sharp break between the modern and postmodern because, in part, he suggests that the break was already taking place when he was writing in the 1970s.

In giving his report on knowledge, Lyotard outlines which modern tenets he believes to be in critical condition.

I will use the term *modern* to designate any science that legitimates itself with reference to a metadiscourse of this kind making an explicit appeal to some grand narrative, such as the dialectics of Spirit, the hermeneutics of meaning, the emancipation of the rational or working subject, or the creation of wealth. For example, the rule of consensus between the sender and addressee of a statement with truth-value is deemed acceptable if it is cast in terms of a possible unanimity between rational minds: this is the Enlightenment narrative, in which the hero of knowledge works toward a good ethico-political end—universal peace. As can be seen from this example, if a metanarrative implying a philosophy of history is used to legitimate knowledge, questions are raised concerning the validity of the institutions governing the social bond: these must be legitimated as well. Thus justice is consigned to the grand narrative in the same way as truth.

(Jameson 1998: xxiii)

In this paragraph, which precedes the famous declaration of incredulity, Lyotard compiles a list of what he believes to be modern tenets. It is not full of esoteric, strictly philosophical concerns but, rather, the intellectual grounds of modern culture. Indeed, one of the main objects of critique is the process of the legitimation of knowledge itself, which Fredric Jameson notes in his foreword to the English translation is a direct critique of German social theorist Jürgen Habermas. Lyotard asks how the truth-value of any statement is evaluated, believing there to be a metaphysical undergirding—the real significance of the term 'metanarrative'—at work. This he calls the 'rule of consensus,' which relies on the meeting of rational minds. This 'rule of consensus' is nothing other than the law of equivalence that constitutes the conditions of possibility for modern grand narratives, such as 'truth' and 'justice,' to list just two that Lyotard mentions. And, importantly for our purposes, Lyotard brings his critique of legitimate knowledge to the level of the social bond, specifically institutions, which he identifies as the legislators of legitimacy in the realm of knowledge. This 'regime' of legitimate knowledge, Lyotard puts under the heading of 'narrative'.

The crisis of the modern is the crisis of narrative. So what is happening to narrative? 'The narrative function,' he writes, 'is losing its functors, its great hero, its great dangers, its great voyages, its great goal. It is being dispersed in clouds of narrative language elements—narrative, but also denotative, prescriptive, descriptive, and so on'. And the social bond?

Thus the society of the future falls less within the province of a Newtonian anthropology (such as structuralism or systems theory) than a pragmatics of language particles. There are many different language games—a heterogeneity of elements. They only give rise to institutions in patches—local determinism.

(Jameson 1998: xxiv)

While the epistemological critiques of Lyotard have been well commented upon, Lyotard's explicit references and commentary on the 'social bond' have not yet been analyzed to the same extent. This section will connect Lyotard's epistemology to his social theory.

One recurring theme within the scholarly treatment of the postmodern has been the turn to language (sometimes called 'the linguistic turn'), regarding which many analysts have rightly pointed to the work of Ludwig Wittgenstein, the Austrian philosopher, who was one of the first analytic philosophers to look at ordinary language or language in-use. On this point, Lyotard falls in line. Undoubtedly, his references to 'language games' and 'language particles' are direct borrowings from Wittgenstein and it is true that he is one of Lyotard's lasting influences. However, Lyotard does not simply reiterate Wittgenstein's philosophy of ordinary language but extracts from him a critique of consensus in increasingly 'computerized' societies, which is parallel to the kind of methodological move Wittgenstein made in analytic philosophy, which was to look at aspects of everyday life, not solely metaphysics.

According to Lyotard, the status of knowledge has been shifting since the immediate post-Second World War years, during which Western societies experienced a shift from industrial to post-industrial societies.

Additionally, this socioeconomic shift also marked a parallel shift, which he describes as the transition to the postmodern age; thus, for Lyotard, industrial to postindustrial in the socioeconomic roughly correlates to the modern and postmodern in the cultural realm. One of the clearest of indications of the shift to post-industrial society is the increased penetration of media technologies throughout various sectors of society. 'The nature of knowledge cannot survive unchanged within this context of general transformation,' Lyotard argues. The epistemological result of the 'computerization of societies' is the dominance of scientific knowledge, which for Lyotard has an instrumental quality. In other words, scientific knowledge exists in information commodities, thereby undermining any sense of knowledge as an end in itself. One of the main products of the Enlightenment was the pursuit of knowledge for the sake of knowledge, which Immanuel Kant captured in his famous dictum: 'Dare to know'. To be sure, Kant had no small part in the hegemony of 'scientific objectivity', but the kind of power which scientific knowledge has maintained since the nineteenth century has been supported by technology. In other words, the progressive accumulative aspect of science (that it continually builds, gets better and more accurate) has been mostly unchallenged, thus eliding the question of legitimation. In point of fact, Lyotard is suggesting that scientific knowledge is a discourse, involved in language games, not simply truth-incarnate.

The question of the legitimacy of science has been indissociably linked to that of the legitimation of the legislator since the time of Plato. From this point of view, the right to decide what is true is not independent of the right to decide what is just, even if the statements consigned to these two authorities differ in nature. The point is that there is a strict interlinkage between the kind of language called 'science' and the kind called 'ethics and politics': they both stem from the same perspective, the same 'choice' if you will—the choice called 'the Occident' … revealing that knowledge and power are simply two sides of the same question (Jameson 1998: 8).

Lyotard's 'outing' of scientific legitimacy as a largely Eurocentric enterprise brings together the two seemingly separate issues—knowledge and government, which resonates with Michel Foucault's concept of power/knowledge. Ultimately, the point he is trying to make is that truth, which under the modern regime of knowledge, is agreed upon and thus universal, can only be uttered through what Wittgenstein calls a 'language game'. More simply, that all statements or 'utterances' are

defined in terms of rules specifying their properties and the uses to which they can be put—in exactly the same way as the game of chess is defined by a set of rules determining the properties of each of the pieces, in other words, the proper way to move them.

(Jameson 1998: 10)

By suggesting that science participates in a language game, Lyotard challenges the accepted wisdom of science and, in turn, knowledge, as merely a 'mirror of nature,' a phrase Richard Rorty uses in his well-known book *Philosophy and the Mirror of Nature*.

Understood in this way, knowledge is what makes someone capable of forming 'good' denotative utterances, but also 'good' prescriptive and 'good' evaluative utterances…. It is not a competence relative to a particular class of statements (for example, cognitive ones) to the exclusion of all others.

(Jameson 1998: 18)

But, in addition to scientific knowledge, Lyotard also notes that there is still a complementary knowledge that exists alongside it—narrative knowledge. Narrative knowledge takes shape in customs, as customs are another type of knowledge—*savoir-faire* (know-how). Traditional or customary knowledge, what Émile Durkheim and Marcel Mauss may have once called culture or 'collective reality,' frequently comes in the form of narration. In traditional-narrative knowledge, authority comes from the narrator having heard the story themselves. It is assumed that the narratee will, in turn, be able to occupy the position of the narrator after he or she listens to the story. On the other hand, the 'pragmatics' of scientific knowledge differ drastically from those of customary knowledge based on narration. Scientific knowledge is based on the principles of referentiality and validity, which underlie what used to be called 'verification' in the nineteenth century and what is today called 'falsification'. Referentiality and validity ensure that the rules of engagement are followed, acting as the condition for entrance into the language game. Unlike customary knowledge, authority is not so easily transferred but is handed down through education training. But, in the increasingly computerized field of knowledge, science, also trapped by the logic of technology, is forced to lean on narration for legitimation. The dynamics of this appeal to narrative by science are based on the construction of a metasubject—humanity. In turn, this becomes the seedbed for the notion of progress, in which 'the people' become the subject of this progress. Hence, in the narrative of scientific progress, 'the name of the hero is the people, the sign of legitimacy is the people's consensus, and their mode of creating norms is deliberation' (Jameson 1998: 30) and the end is the emancipation of humanity.

In Lyotard's estimation, the compensatory appeal to narrative has been ultimately failing for science, and other grand narratives, since the Second World War due to the technologies that have become so prevalent. As Bernard Stiegler (1998) and others have argued, these technologies, especially digital technologies, are based on discontinuity; this makes it nearly impossible to achieve the mode of unification necessitated by any grand narrative. The emergence of new languages, such as machine languages, game theory, musical notation and non-destructive logic, bears no small burden of responsibility for this. What we have in the postmodern age is a plethora of 'little narratives' which no longer uphold the abstract subject of 'the people', as their hero nor do they hold the promise of emancipation. On the contrary, little narratives do not rely on consensus and unity.

Lyotard's views are in clear contrast to those of Jürgen Habermas, whose work privileges precisely the themes that Lyotard argues as modern, and thus on the decline–consensus and unity. This disagreement, however, is not simply a skirmish between two philosophers at the level of ideas. Their differences have consequences for social theory. One aspect of these differences is precisely on this point regarding unity. Lyotard argues that Habermas, who had been quite critical of another German social theorist Niklas Luhmann, has more in common with systems theory, of which Luhmann was a main proponent, than he would like to admit. Habermas's line of criticism leveled at Luhmann was that systems theory offered no place for emancipation—in short, that it lacked any kind of politics. But Lyotard levels a similar critique at Habermas's insistence on consensus to solve the crisis of legitimation.

It is easy to see what function this recourse plays in Habermas's argument against Luhmann. *Diskurs* is his ultimate weapon against the theory of the stable system. The cause is good, but the argument is not. Consensus has become an outmoded and suspect value. But justice as a value is neither outmoded nor suspect. We must thus arrive at an idea and practice of justice that is not linked to that of consensus (Jameson 1998: 66).

Diskurs, Habermas's word for the search for a universal consensus, troubles Lyotard on two grounds. First, universal consensus would mean that all the speakers must come to an agreement on the rules of engagement. According to Lyotard's reading of Wittgenstein, language games are heteromorphous. In other words, the rules are constantly changing. Second, Habermas assumes that the goal of language is consensus. Lyotard argues that consensus cannot be the end of the language but merely a state of language. Habermas's *Diskurs*, for Lyotard, functions to discourage dissent. If there were going to be consensus, it cannot reach for universality but rather locality.

THE CRISIS OF MODERN CULTURE:

JÜRGEN HABERMAS

It would be unfair simply to read Habermas through Lyotard. Habermas has been one of the most ardent and reasoned critics of the postmodern. As a sociologist and philosopher in the tradition of the **Frankfurt School**, Habermas has maintained a certain hope in the project of Enlightenment. This has already been evidenced in the section on Lyotard, as Lyotard has accused him of inheriting the Enlightenment in an uncritical fashion. But this is not a point which Habermas would contest. His reading of modernity as 'an incomplete project' is one of his most well-known formulations on the subject (Habermas 1998: 3).

In his attempt to recover some aspects of the modern, Habermas delves more deeply than Lyotard into what 'modern' really means.

> With varying content the term 'modern' again and again expresses the consciousness of an epoch that relates itself to the past of antiquity, in order to view itself as the result of a transition from the old to the new.
>
> (Habermas 1998: 3)

There are different aspects to modernity—aesthetic, cultural and societal. The modern, as he says, was not a fixed ideal.

> The most recent modernism simply makes an abstract opposition between tradition and the present; and we are, in a way, still the contemporaries of that kind of aesthetic modernity which first appeared in the midst of the nineteenth century.

(Habermas 1998: 4)

But this is not necessarily the case for all 'modernisms,' Habermas says. Each modernism has its own relation to the past and present. Aesthetic modernity, found in the work of Baudelaire as well as the Dadaists and surrealists, focused on a changed consciousness of time. The value was placed on 'the transitory, the elusive and ephemeral, [and] the very celebration of dynamism' (Habermas 1998: 5), which he interprets as the longing for an immaculate present. This rejection of the historical embodied by so many of the artists associated with aesthetic modernism is thus found in the theory of the modern put forth.

> Modernity revolts against the normalizing functions of tradition; modernity lives on the experience of rebelling against all that is normative. This revolt is one way to neutralize the standards of both morality and utility.

(Habermas 1998: 5)

The waning of this aesthetic tradition is clear; but does this signal the end of modernity itself? There are certainly many that believe so. One whom Habermas mentions is American sociologist Daniel Bell, a neoconservative, who has suggested that the crisis of Western societies is one of cultural modernism. That is to say that the regulative and normative functions of culture have been infected with the surrealist rebellion of aesthetic modernism. 'Because of the forces of modernism, the principle of unlimited self-realization, the demand for authentic self-experience and the subjectivism of hyperstimulated sensitivity have come to be dominant' (Habermas 1998: 6), unleashing

hedonism throughout society. The only way in which norms can be re-established, according to those like Bell, would be through a religious revival that restores faith in tradition, offering clearly defined individual identities.

While he does not agree with the politics of Bell, Habermas does see wisdom in Bell's thesis that there is a divergence between society and culture. As Habermas points out, this divergence has been a gradual process, beginning in the nineteenth century, which Max Weber had already noted. But, for Habermas, neoconservative thinkers like Bell too easily confuse cultural modernity and societal modernization.

The neoconservative doctrine blurs the relationship between the welcomed process of societal modernization on the one hand, and the lamented cultural development on the other. The neoconservative does not uncover the economic and social causes for the altered attitudes towards work, consumption, achievement and leisure. Consequently, he attributes all of the following—hedonism, the lack of social identification, the lack of obedience, narcissism, the withdrawal from status and achievement competition—to the domain of 'culture'. In fact, however, culture is intervening in the creation of all these problems in only a very indirect and mediated fashion (Habermas 1998: 7).

This distinction between Habermas's own position and the neoconservative position is mainly a methodological one, with a slight twist. It is merely a matter of where Habermas locates the root of the 'crisis' of modern values and modern life. Whereas, for Bell, it was the injection of aesthetic modernism into mainstream cultural life, for Habermas, it is the pressures of capitalism—the logic of economic growth and rationality—'colonizing' the life-world, into every form of human existence. This, in Habermas's view, is an effect of societal modernization, not cultural modernism. Hence, we see in his critique of Daniel Bell not so much a political departure as an argumentative quibble. This is not to suggest that Habermas is in any way a neoconservative. Many who are Habermas scholars have already, and correctly in my estimation, labeled Habermas a liberal, though this fact is surely debatable.

But, in point of fact, Habermas too sees a crisis occurring in modern life, one in which he acknowledges the role of the intellectual heritage of the Enlightenment. Although he has been one of the Enlightenment's most noted defenders in recent times, he does so critically, in much the same way as his forebears of the critical theory tradition—Theodor Adorno and Max Horkheimer in their 1944 masterpiece *The Dialectic of the Enlightenment*. One of the ways in which Habermas upholds the Enlightenment tradition is through a rereading of the Weberian notion of rationalization.

The project of modernity, formulated in the eighteenth century by the philosophers of the Enlightenment, consisted in their efforts to develop objective science, universal morality and law and autonomous art according to their inner logic. At the same time, this project intended to release the cognitive potentials of each of these domains from their esoteric forms. The Enlightenment philosophers wanted to utilize this accumulation of specialized culture for the enrichment of everyday life— that is to say, for the rational organization of everyday social life (Habermas 1998: 9).

Habermas's definition of the project of modernity is characterized by an optimistic view of the rationalization of everyday life. Where it went wrong, Habermas says, is the point at which the rationalization process transforms into specialization, thereby separating itself from 'the hermeneutics of everyday communication' (Habermas 1998: 9).

The political question is, do we ultimately jettison the project of modernity or are there bits and pieces worth saving? This might be the critical point of difference between Lyotard and Habermas. Clearly, Habermas believes that the project of modernity, though it should be rationally criticized, should not be discarded altogether. Habermas leaves us an interesting an alternative:

In sum, the project of modernity has not yet been fulfilled…. The project aims at a differentiated relinking of modern culture with an everyday praxis that still depends on vital heritages, but would be impoverished through mere traditionalism. This new connection, however, can only be established under the condition that societal modernization will also be steered in a different direction. The life-world has to become able to develop institutions out of itself which set limits to the internal dynamics and imperatives of an almost autonomous economic system and its administrative complements.

(Habermas 1998: 13)

THE CRISIS OF THE UNIVERSAL: RICHARD RORTY AND JEAN BAUDRILLARD

Thus far we have looked at various perspectives on the postmodern, some of which are clearly sympathetic (Lyotard) and some of which are not (Habermas), while others defy such binaries (Jameson). But, no matter where the authors' sympathies lie, there is surely an identifiable recurrence of the thematic of crisis in the writings dealing with the postmodern. By looking at two additional figures, Richard Rorty and Jean Baudrillard, we continue with the theme of 'crisis' to track a crisis of the largest proportions—a crisis in the universal and of reality. The universal is one of the most fundamental precepts of modern life, in particular modern science. As Alfred North Whitehead argues in *Science and the Modern World* (1925), abstraction, which is the foundation for mathematics, necessitates a notion of the universal. 'Reality' is, indeed, the ultimate universal, since it is constantly used as a transcendent, overarching reference for all. That is to say, it is assumed that we all live in the *same* reality.

Richard Rorty lays out what he believes to be up for grabs in the debate between Habermas and Lyotard in a classic essay 'Habermas and Lyotard on Postmodernity' (1985). Though, at first glance, the disagreement is about metanarratives, according to Rorty, it is, more specifically, about the status of the universal. Even Habermas's largely sympathetic critics, he notes, accuse him of overreaching in his attempt to construct a universal in support of liberal politics. Hence, the French writers that Habermas criticizes are most skeptical of his idea of 'true consensus', which relies precisely on a universal agreement of the rules of conduct as well as what constitutes subjectivity. This is also an area of contention for Lyotard since the subject-formation entailed in Habermas's schema would undoubtedly be equated to the adoption of bourgeois values, within which Habermas believes emancipatory elements of the Enlightenment to remain.

For Rorty, the attempt to reclaim bourgeois ideals is Habermas's weakest defense

of modernity. Bourgeois ideals, according to Habermas, are repositories for Reason that have not been corrupted by the technological knowledge of the system. Although interpreting Lyotard's misgivings about Habermas, Rorty asks a question that does not arise for Lyotard. Rorty sharply inquires: why not just be frankly ethnocentric? That is to say, what constitute bourgeois ideals are, in effect, the political norms of Western democracies. And, if it is the case that Habermas wishes to hold onto bourgeois ideals, then why not simply make the implicit ethnocentrism explicit?

Modern science will appear to be something which a certain group of human beings invented, in the same sense in which these same people can be said to have invented Protestantism, parliamentary government and Romantic poetry. What Habermas calls the 'self-reflection of the sciences' will thus consist not in the attempt to 'ground' scientists' practices (for example, free exchange of information, normal problem-solving and revolutionary paradigm-creation) in something larger or broader, but rather of attempts to show how these practices link up with, or contrast with, other practices of the same group or of other groups (Rorty 1985: 166).

Continuing his evaluation of Lyotard's critique of Habermas's philosophy of science, Rorty highlights the significance of Lyotard's insistence that the 'aims and procedures of scientists and those of politicians' are fundamentally the same (Rorty 1985: 166). Habermas very much maintains some positive 'inner dynamic' to scientific knowledge which he believes aids humanity's trajectory towards emancipation. Today, we do not have scientific knowledge proper, Habermas would say, but rather technoscience, in which scientific knowledge is co-opted by the enslaving logic of technology, trapping human beings in an 'iron cage' that even Max Weber would have had trouble envisaging. Quite simply, Lyotard does not afford science this special privilege, whereas Habermas does. For Rorty, Habermas does so in the service of liberal politics. Without the conception of Progress through Reason, founded on the principle of 'universal consensus,' Habermas sees no grounds for his politics of emancipation. But, as a fellow liberal, Rorty ultimately believes Habermas's unbridled faith in Reason and universality to be misplaced.

So, if science or Reason cannot be seen as grounds for a universal, what about 'reality'? One of the most vehement critics of 'reality' is Jean Baudrillard, the French philosopher and social theorist, who famously declared the First Gulf War not to have taken place. (In fact, he did believe that it took place, but more through informational waves of radar and television than in physical reality.) While never declaring himself postmodern, Baudrillard was perhaps the chief figure whom critics of the postmodern would use as a straw man. There are several reasons for this, one of them being his rather unorthodox writing style, which in his later years began to resemble less and less North American conventions of 'scholarly' writing. Additionally, Baudrillard purposely utilizes hyperbole in order to make his point. Hence, many of his writings have been misused and poorly interpreted.

One of the ideas most closely associated with Baudrillard is that of the 'hyper-real'. It is perhaps one of his most famous ideas (though not necessarily most important in the grand scheme of philosophical writings) due to the purported claim by the Wachowski brothers, the writer-directors of *The Matrix* films that they were inspired by Baudrillard. In fact, Neo, the lead character portrayed by Keanu

Reeves is, at one point, reading a copy of *Simulacra and Simulation* in the film. The hyperreal, Baudrillard explains, is an effect of the crisis in the exchange-relation between meaning and substance. Or, to put it in the terms of Whitehead, it is a fundamental change in the process of abstraction.

Abstraction today is no longer that of the map, the double, the mirror or the concept. Simulation is no longer that of a territory, a referential being or a substance. It is the generation by models of a real without origin or reality: a hyperreal. The territory no longer precedes the map, nor survives it. Henceforth, it is the map that precedes the territory—*precession of simulacra*—it is the map that engenders the territory … It is the real, and not the map, whose vestiges subsist here and there … The desert of the real itself.

(Baudrillard 1988: 166)

As it is usually understood, abstraction is a process by which there must be a referent, an object, a thing. A map, in this instance, is an abstraction of the territory. But, according to Baudrillard, the map *precedes* the territory. That is to say, there is no longer any privilege given to the origin because, as Baudrillard alludes to in referring to 'generation by models,' of the computerized society in which we all live. 'The real,' he writes, 'is produced from miniaturized units, from matrices, memory banks, and command models—and with these it can be reproduced an indefinite number of times' (Baudrillard 1988: 167). And, indeed, a most notoriously famous illustration Baudrillard gives is that of Disneyland as 'the perfect mode of all the entangled orders of simulation'(Baudrillard 1988: 171). According to Baudrillard, one can find the 'objective profile of the United States' throughout Disneyland:

> All its values are exalted here, in miniature and comic-strip form. Embalmed and pacified ... Disneyland is presented as imaginary in order to make us believe that the rest is real, when in fact all of Los Angeles and the America surrounding it are no longer real, but of the order of the hyperreal and of simulation. It is no longer a question of a false representation of reality (ideology), but of concealing the fact that the real is no longer real, and thus of saving the reality principle.

(Baudrillard 1988: 171)

Here, in Baudrillard, we see an analysis of postmodernism which differs slightly from Jameson. Whereas Jameson sees the cultural dominant of late-capitalism in postmodernism, meaning that a certain type of aesthetic regime dominates alongside a new form of capitalism, Baudrillard argues in a more technologically materialist vein that reality itself, not simply capitalism, is altered at its foundation. And yet there is some connection, which makes them both historicist postmodern social theorists. Baudrillard, like Jameson, argues that something has indeed changed; that is to say, there is a clear 'break' from one mode of social life to another. In Baudrillard's words:

> Something has changed, and the Faustian, Promethean (perhaps Oedipal) period of production and consumption gives way to the 'proteinic' era of networks, to the narcissistic and protean era of connections, contact, contiguity, feedback and generalized interface that goes with the universe of communication.

(Baudrillard 1998: 127)

Moreover, what distinguishes Baudrillard's work, along with Lyotard's, on the postmodern from that of others is his keen eye for the shifting landscape of media technologies. Though Jameson does, indeed, come close when mentioning aesthetics, there is no reckoning with the fundamental impact of new media technologies on modern life, which mostly saw technologies in an instrumental (in effect, anthropocentric) mode. It seems that, today, in the era of technomedia, in which the boundary between the virtual and the real are quickly vanishing (see Han 2007), Baudrillard and Lyotard seem not to be as delusional as they once did.

And finally, to conclude on the question of what is at stake in the debates on the postmodern, we should return to the theme of crisis. Despite the clear and abounding differences among Jameson, Lyotard, Habermas, Rorty and Baudrillard, there seems to be no disagreement on the existence of some fundamental transformation in the social order. Hence, one point is clear. Although sociologists such as Bell and Alain Touraine had pointed out an earlier major shift, suggesting that so-called liberal democracies in the West had moved into a stage of 'post-industrial society', it took the debates on the postmodern to bring the shift to the forefront. The crises of capitalism (Jameson), knowledge (Lyotard), modern culture (Habermas) and the universal (Rorty and Baudrillard) challenged social theory to rethink not only the tenets of modernity but also the implicit values of modern social theory since the 'founders' (Marx, Weber and Durkheim), namely, stability and order—two interlocking ideas that modern social theory took as given and good, which Jameson would potentially label as the 'political unconscious' of modern social theory.

If something has indeed ended or changed fundamentally, a premise with which even Habermas and Jameson seem to agree, then it is the task of social theory to take stock and reckon with it, just as the classical social theorists did when modernity was in its nascent stages. Though he so expertly defends the project of the Enlightenment and modernity, Habermas nevertheless acknowledges the *incomplete* nature of modernity, striking a rather unusual resonance with Bruno Latour, a sociologist who has frequently been lumped in with 'postmodernism' and author of a book entitled *We Have Never Been Modern*. If there is a 'lesson' to be learned from the debates on the postmodern, it must be the critical evaluation of what modernity attempted to portray as natural. It is this call to be radical, in the real sense of the term—to get to the root and, in turn, not to fear crisis but to think alongside it, which, I think, makes the postmodern a truly important moment in the history of social theory. Judging from the intellectual stagnation in the field of contemporary social theory, at least in the United States, it seems that it is one that more students of social theory must revisit.

REFERENCES

Baudrillard, Jean (1988) *Jean Baudrillard: Selected Writings*, Mark Poster (ed.), Stanford, CA: Stanford University Press.

—— (1998) 'Ecstasy of communication', in Hal Foster (ed.), *The Anti-Aesthetic: Essays on Postmodern Culture*, New York: The New Press.

Bell, Daniel (1973) *The Coming of Post-Industrial Society*, New York: Basic Books.

Foster, Hal (ed.) (1998) *The Anti-Aesthetic: Essays on Postmodern Culture*, New York: The New Press.

Goldberg, Jonah (2008) 'Obama, the postmodernist', *USA Today*, 5 August.

Habermas, Jürgen (1998) 'Modernity—an incomplete project', in Hal Foster (ed.), *The Anti-Aesthetic: Essays on Postmodern Culture*, New York: The New Press.

Han, Sam (2007) *Navigating Technomedia: Caught in the Web*, Lanham, MD: Rowman & Littlefield.

Jameson, Fredric (1984) 'Postmodernism, or the cultural logic of late capitalism', *New Left Review*, I/146, July–August.

Latour, Bruno (2008) *We Have Never Been Modern*, Cambridge, MA: Harvard University Press.

Lyotard, Jean-François (1984) *The Postmodern Condition: A Report on Knowledge*, trans. by Geoffrey Bennington and Brian Massumi, Minneapolis: University of Minnesota Press.

Rorty, Richard (1979) *Philosophy and the Mirror of Nature*, Princeton, NJ: Princeton University Press.

—— (1985) 'Habermas and Lyotard on Postmodernity', in Richard J. Bernstein (ed.), *Habermas and Modernity*, Cambridge, MA: MIT Press.

Stiegler, B. (1998) [1994] *Technics and Time, 1: The Fault of Epimetheus*, trans. by George Collins and Richard Beardsworth, Stanford, CA: Stanford University Press.

Vattimo, Gianni (1991) *The End of Modernity: Nihilism and Hermeneutics in Postmodern Culture*, Baltimore, MD: Johns Hopkins University Press.

Whitehead, Alfred North (1925) *Science in the Modern World*, New York: Free Press.

2

Chapter Review

REVIEW QUESTIONS

1. What is the primary function of theory in the social sciences?
2. Is there a particular theory (either among the three main sociological theories or among those discussed in the readings) that you might gravitate to in understanding and analyzing your social world? Why or why not? Choose one situation in which you might see this theory at work and explain.
3. What is the difference between what is termed "classical" and what is termed "postmodern" theory? What are the benefits that both can bring to the study of society in the 21st century?

CASE STUDY: CULTURE AND ITS IMPACT ON THE MANIFESTATIONS OF ILLNESS—A CASE STUDY IN SYMBOLIC INTERACTION

As briefly explored above, symbolic interaction theory discusses the meanings we associate with behavior in a society and its popular culture. We learn this meaning and what our behavior communicates to others (verbal or nonverbally) through the **"socialization" process** (explored in Chapter 4). One central idea to the study of society is whether the behavior we observe in the social world originates from biology (defined as **"biological determinism"**) or from the influence of culture (defined as **"social determinism"**)

(Jones, 1986). The sociology of illness has explored to what extent culture or society influences manifestations of illness. For example, in the case of mental or behavioral health concerns, men and women tend to react and respond differently. Research suggests that men statistically tend to be more outward and aggressive in response (such as in the case of mass shootings), and women tend to internalize such feelings, resulting in higher suicide rates historically than men in U.S. society (Metzel and MacLeish, 2015). Many believe that these difference may be a result of social **gender role expectations** (explored more in Chapter 6). The following article outlines one particular phenomena occurring in Sweden and the potential cultural and group influence at work among children whose families are at risk for deportation.

http://www.npr.org/sections/goatsandsoda/2017/03/30/521958505/only-in-sweden-hundreds-of-refugee-children-gave-up-on-life/

What are the potential cultural or group influences involved in the story above? How might this story be an example of the symbolic interaction theory briefly discussed above?

DEVELOPING THE SOCIOLOGICAL IMAGINATION
Understanding the Concept of Social Structures

The study of what is a social structure is imperative in understanding the theory of structural functionalism or structuration.

SOCIAL STRUCTURES

The study of social structures falls under the broad sociological topic of social organization. **Social organization** refers to the ways in which society is organized, including the roles, activities, and functions of individuals, relationships, and groups. A **social structure** can be defined as a system of rules and relationships that is created by groups by which individuals or groups in society access social goods, resources, and have access to social power.

Social structures are considered to be the architecture or framework of a society. Just as a building is comprised of hallways, rooms, and staircases, for example, society is also "built" in a particular way. Depending upon the values, traditions, and culture of a society, different individuals may need to navigate this architecture differently to survive (the ultimate purpose of a society, as we explored in Chapter 1) or to otherwise obtain access the resources of that society. Therefore, for something to be considered a social structure, it must have an institutional component as well as be supported by specific means of interaction (or otherwise also experienced in interpersonal communication and relationships). **Gender** (the social expectations associated with one's understood or ascribed biological sex), for example, could be considered a social structure because gender is an attribute that may be experienced differently within different institutions (consider the concept of the "**glass ceiling effect**") but may also be felt within interpersonal relationships (in the case of familial gender roles, what household tasks are assigned to members of a family). Given that social structures consists of two components (social institutions and social interaction), it is important to briefly define the study of these two components.

THE STUDY OF SOCIAL INSTITUTIONS

While the definition of a **social institution** has changed somewhat over time, most often sociologists use the term to discuss the entities that are established to accomplish social tasks, such as the legal system, the institution of education, the institution of work, and so forth. A society can be comprised of many larger and smaller institutions. One of the primary purposes of a social institution is to provide socialization to society's members. The institutions also assist in distributing resources and accomplishing the tasks necessary for survival in a society. For example, the institution of family serves many functions including meeting our primary needs for intimate relationships and companionship; the institution of education serves the purpose of educating workers in most societies; the institution of work ensures that resources are distributed within a society, and so forth. Throughout the remainder of the chapters in this book we will be exploring various social institutions and challenges or problems experienced within these institutions. This book in particular utilizes the concept of a social institution to explore social inequality and social change.

Within the institutions that we all interact with and within in a society, we occupy various **roles** (the expected behavior associated with a particular title) and typically there is a particular **status** (or value or prestige) associated with this role. As such, our behavior and methods of interaction within different institutions can be different depending on our role in that setting and the value assigned to it. Similarly, the ways others treat us or approach interaction with us can also be different. How we interact in a classroom setting, for example, with other students may be very different from how we interact with members of our family because these relationships serve different purposes and have different expectations. How we interact as a "mother," for example, may also vary from the expected behavior of a "daughter" in the institution of the family as each of these roles has different functions and perceived or common social authority hierarchies.

THE STUDY OF SOCIAL INTERACTION

Social interaction is defined as the particular set of behaviors or actions that individuals use to relate to one another in a group. Included in this definition is language and the use of language (as well as the use of tone, body language, and touch), but also what is defined as appropriate cultural one-to-one interaction in a society. It may explore the concept of "social skills" and how this concept reflects expected behavior in certain social settings, between roles, or within different social institutions. Formally or informally defined and expected modes of social interaction are what upholds social institutions and therefore also social structures.

INTERSECTIONALITY

Of particular interest to many sociologists who study social structures is the concept of how various structures for individuals intersect. According to the concept of **"intersectionality"** it is important to know the pattern or patchwork of structures that individuals operate within in order to obtain a realistic view of their lives, their access to social resources and power, and what challenges they may face. For example, the experience of a white male in U.S. society as compared to a white female may vary, as does the experience for an adult African-American woman as compared to a adolescent Latino male. The structures of age, ethnicity, and gender can impact one's life experience, life chances, and quality of life differently even within the same given society depending upon the value assigned to these categories and labels.

TROUBLES VS. ISSUES

For this particular exercise, we will very briefly look at the issue of **socioeconomic status** and poverty, as this will be discussed in much more depth in subsequent chapters. Poverty often (particularly in capitalist societies) is oftentimes seen a result of individual or personal failings (a "trouble" as C. Wright Mills might define it). While individual behavior is certainly significant in determining life outcomes, poverty is also a larger social concern, and the number of individuals in a specific country that live in poverty can be influenced by a variety of structural and outside factors as well. For example, countries with unstable governments, countries that are experiencing war, countries that are often exploited, countries that are considered to be "less developed," or countries that otherwise do not have the ability to provide an infrastructure of health and economic support are more likely to have large pockets of their population that live in poverty (an "issue" according to C. Wright Mills).

In the United States, we can also see the structural patterns influencing poverty and poverty rates with the assistance of U.S. Census data. For example, in the 1990s poverty rates as a whole dropped dramatically with the introduction of various workforce development programs. This dramatic decrease was not attributed to large groups of individuals who made personal life changes or choices but rather attributed directly to specific supports and policies designed to increase economic self sufficiency (such as incentivized work training programs).

A substantial amount of research suggests that people live in places that they can afford to live. Not all groups in society and not all neighborhoods in a given town, city, state, or country are equal in terms of opportunity, education, safe housing options, or in the type(s) of work that are accessible or available. Many social scientists believe that these conditions (structures) can greatly impact one's life chances and what opportunities are available. If, for example, in certain neighborhoods, schools are underperforming (due to the lack of resources provided by tax funding, typically tied to property taxes in a given area) in the United States, students may be more likely to drop out, and given that education remains one of the most influential factors in social mobility in the United States, that may further perpetuate disadvantage and poverty for those living in under-resourced neighborhoods.

For this exercise, go to the U.S. Census Bureau, American FactFinder website:

https://factfinder.census.gov/faces/nav/jsf/pages/index.xhtml

Search the zip code of where you grew up and another zip code in your community (known either for being home to wealthy or

under-resourced families) and click on the "Education" tab on the left-hand-side tool-bar and click on "Educational Attainment." How does educational attainment vary by age, race, and poverty level between these zip codes? Then approach these differences sociologically. What might account for these differences? What exposure to diversity might one have depending on where they live? How might this ultimately impact life chances and opportunities for individuals living in these neighborhoods?

3 | The Science of Sociology

CHAPTER SUMMARY

- This chapter introduces readers to the methodologies utilized in the scientific study of society.
- This chapter also introduces readers to the ethics involved with social research.
- Readers are prompted to collect data about their social world by utilizing the qualitative research methodology tool "ethnomethodology."

PRELIMINARY QUESTIONS FOR READERS:

- What is the value of science in everyday life? What value might science bring to the study of society?
- What might be the dangers of coming to conclusions based solely upon a singular set of observations when attempting to analyze social life?
- How might researching society and determining social facts through the research process be used to benefit society?

CHAPTER INTRODUCTION

Researchers in sociology and the social sciences utilize a variety of methodologies to go about exploring social reality or to create or test sociological and social science theories or hypothesis based on these theories. There are various considerations to take into account when conducting social research. This chapter provides a brief introduction to the process of social research methodology and research ethics considered central to the study of society.

THE SCIENTIFIC METHOD

Given that sociology is a science, as a general principle, sociologists utilize the scientific method. As with any other person, social scientists are subject to making anecdotal observations about the social world that may or may not be accurate simply based upon our life experiences, our perspectives, and our biases (implicit or those that we identify that we have). The scientific method provides a means and framework by which we can go about suspending these biases. The **scientific method** is a systematic process that can be utilized to inquire about new phenomena in our social worlds, test theories about our social world, and collect empirical evidence to ultimately arrive at conclusions about social realities and social life. The scientific method is traditionally considered to include the following general steps: (1) forming a question; (2) formulating a hypothesis; (3) collecting data; (4) analyzing said data; and (5) forming conclusions or discussing results. A summary of the main research techniques utilized by social scientists is also provided below. It is significant to note that while, in general, social scientists follow this process, in some cases, forming a hypothesis (such as is the case at times in observation or exploration) can influence what we look out for and therefore observe. This can result in, if even unintentionally, arriving at faulty conclusions; therefore, an inductive (vs. deductive) method of science may be utilized. The case study for this chapter deals with some of these potential complexities.

CONDUCTING SOCIAL RESEARCH
Ethics and Methodologies

Social research contains a process that includes various ethical guidelines (that assist in protecting those being studied), guidelines for reporting results (such as reporting results in an unbiased manner), and guidelines for ensuring that a sufficient and representative sample has been obtained to reach reasonable conclusions that can be applied to a majority population (or sample).

According to Earl Babbie (20007), the author of *The Basics of Social Research*, five main scientific research methodologies are utilized in the social sciences. This includes experiments, survey research, qualitative field research, unobtrusive research, and evaluation research. A brief description of these methodologies is provided below. Each methodology contains its own set of benefits and limitations.

- **Experiments:** This particular methodology is much like what is traditionally envisioned by the term "experiment" in the natural sciences. Perhaps you would think of a researcher, with a lab coat and several beakers preparing to test whether or not a particular stimulus once added impacts the way the material in the beaker looks or behaves. In the social sciences, the principle is similar. Essentially, the traditional experiment has an experimental group and a control group. The experimental group receives the stimulus, and the control group does not. Both groups are then tested to determine the relative impact of the stimulus (post-testing). Both groups are also usually tested before the experiment (pre-testing) as well in order to further isolate the impact of the stimulus being applied. An example of this methodology could be a social scientist who created a video that he believed could reduce prejudice among highly prejudicial people. In order to test this hypothesis, he tested two groups of people to determine their relative level of prejudice; then the video was shown to the experimental group, and then the experimental group was tested again to determine each participant's level of prejudice after viewing the film. The results between both groups would then be examined to determine if the video was indeed responsible for any changes in levels of prejudice among the experimental group.
- **Survey Research:** This particular methodology utilizes pre-created questionnaires. These questionnaires can be individual in nature (such as a course evaluation survey that is completed by a student) or can be conducted in an interview format (simply utilizing a pre-planned set of questions that occurs within a discussion with the researcher present). The survey methodology is particularly well-suited for large studies that attempt to gain insights into the attitudes, feelings, behaviors, or characteristics of a particular group of individuals.
- **Qualitative Research:** The classical (and also a bit exaggerated and stereotypical) example of this particular method is an anthropological study in which a researcher might ride up in a canoe to a remote village to observe and document the practices and behaviors of a newly-identified culture or group of people. Essentially, this method utilizes observation, note-taking, and at times, participation, in various subcultures, groups, or social situations to better understand these ways of life, groups, or social situations. Given that this method is highly subjective to the researcher's interpretations, this is a method that has limited ability to reach conclusions that are reflective of a larger society or group but does provide valuable insights into very specific, and at times nuanced, social phenomena. In recent years there has been quite a bit of attention and focus on the use of qualitative methods in sociology specifically. Oftentimes sociology has been considered to rely much more heavily on quantitative data. More and more, public sociologists are being asked to participate in quantitative, qualitative, and "mixed" (both quantitative and qualitative) methods in their work.

- **Unobtrusive Research:** Unobtrusive research is a means of conducting research without in any way manipulating, interjecting, or participating in social life. One popular kind of unobtrusive research is content analysis, such as exploring historical documents over time to examine trends in policy, law, or interaction. Another example of content analysis may be examining changes in political speeches over time. Another example of unobtrusive research is utilizing existing data that has been collected and simply reanalyzing this data with a different set of questions or areas of interest (secondary analysis). For example, the U.S. Census collects demographic (population characteristics) information every ten years. A researcher might look at how a population has changed over 50 years using this existing data.

- **Evaluation Research**: This particular form of research methodology is particularly concerned with determining whether or not a particular social policy, social program, or other form of intervention had its desired effect. Essentially, the policy, social program, or intervention can be considered one big "experiment." Given this, many of the procedures (such as pre and post testing) occur; however, they often occur in conjunction with other methodologies such as survey research or qualitative interviewing. For example, if a non-profit organization would like to know whether or not an after-school program is actually assisting students in raising their GPA, a researcher could utilize this methodology to determine the program's relative success in doing so. Of particular importance in this particular methodology is knowing the goals and objectives of the intervention to determine whether or not the intervention accomplished its desired outcomes. It is also significant to quantify what might be considered a "successful" intervention or a "failure" prior to undertaking an evaluation research project. The article "Evaluative Research" outlines common methodologies utilized in evaluation research. This research method can be an important means of sociological contribution in the public sphere.

The articles in this chapter provide an overview of quantitative (numeric), qualitative (non-numeric), and evaluation methodologies.

RESEARCH ETHICS

As explored in the last chapter, "The Sociology of Knowledge" relates to the extent to which our environment impacts what we study, how society impacts how we approach a particular topic (or do not), and as a result what type of information is concluded and how such conclusions are interpreted, disseminated, and applied. This might also include, for example, the set of guidelines we understand to be current "research ethics" and how ethical guidelines for conducting research are improved or changed over time as we learn more about human emotions and behavior and the impact that certain manufactured situations or methodologies might have on an individual. The main purpose of research ethics is to ensure that no harm is done to those who are engaging in study. Current research ethics include the following (Trochim, 2006):

- **Voluntary Participation/Informed Consent:** It is generally considered that if people are part of a social science research project, they should know that they are a part of the study, they should have agreed to participate in the study, they should be aware of what is required of their participation, and they should be informed of any potential harm.
- **Confidentiality/Anonymity:** In order to protect individual responses and to gain the most honest responses possible, it is also generally considered that participants remain anonymous and, if possible, that the names and identifying details of participants be kept confidential (particularly in the reporting process),
- **Right to Service:** In some cases, there are situations in which one group may receive an intervention or a program that may make an impact on individuals' lives (in the case of medicine or an after-school tutoring program for example). In many situations, it is recommended that every attempt be made to provide an equal alternative in such an event.
- **Review Boards:** Many universities require the approval of a research design and methodology prior to the implementation of any study to insure that the methodology is in compliance with ethical standards and institutional and federal laws. There are also some independent review boards that can provide insight for projects not being run through universities.
- **Research Sampling:** It is also significant that the group being studied (the **sample group** or **sampling frame**) be representative of the population being studied. Typically this means that the sample is selected randomly and that each individual involved in the sampling frame have an equal chance at selection. Computers can randomly select student ID numbers; for example, in a student survey, every fifth person on a list may be selected, or a proportional or disproportional approach may be taken to make sure that members of underrepresented groups are included in selection. This process is quite scientific and includes various methods of calculating **"sampling error"** or the extent to which the sample population reflects the sampling frame.
- **Research Design Considerations:** It is also imperative that the design of a research study does not cause harm or otherwise ask questions or engage in observation that is leading or manipulative. Therefore, there is often an art to survey creation, for example, to make sure that the questions being asked are fair, that they are eliciting honest responses, and not simply requesting socially acceptable responses.

More about the ethics and processes of social research are explored in the articles in this chapter and can be found in the reference section of this chapter.

WORKS CITED

Babbie, E. (2007). *The basics of social research*. 4th Edition. Belmont, CA: Wadsworth Publishing.

Trochim, William K. (n.d.). Research Methods Knowledge Base. Available online at https://www.socialresearchmethods.net/kb/ethics.php,

Quantitative Research

by Paul M. Parobek

The root of quantitative research is that a numeric value can be assigned to the data and it can be measured. Measurement is the correlation or comparison of data that has been collected for each variable, which has been assigned a numeric value. After data is accumulated, the results are interpreted and presented in mathematical forms such as graphs or statistics. Probabilistic designs are also utilized. If there are no variables, then the numeric value is compared to a set scale. Two designs of quantitative research are descriptive and experimental. Quantitative methodology usually utilizes surveys or a series of questions to obtain data from a relatively large representative sample. There can be multiple variables, such as surveying males separately from females so a comparison is established between the two groups. Quantitative research is more deductive and objective than qualitative research, and is a time-consuming process.

The measurement of data in physical science is relatively straightforward since the data collected is compared to standards such as the accepted system of weights and measures. An example is determining the amount of rain that fell last month. A standardized container utilized in meteorology is placed in specific areas. When it rains, water enters the container. When the rain ends, a measurement is recorded. There are daily measurements even if no rain fell. At the end of the month, the daily amounts are added together, the total being the amount of precipitation for the month. This figure can be compared to previous months or years.

Measurement in the social sciences is a more intricate process since it is human behavior that is quantified and is subjected to mathematical correlations or evaluations. The Item Response method is one technique used to collect and evaluate data. An example of the Item Response model in the social sciences would be gathering attitudes of married females to determine their attitudes towards the amount of work their husbands do around the house. Any data collected that does not fit the model (such as data given by single women) is disregarded. A simple yes/no survey is given to those in the sample and the results would be in the form of percentages, such as 85% of married women feel their husbands should be more involved in household chores. In the Rasch method, a form of Item Response, data is usually collected through tests and questionnaires. In psychology, determining a person's intelligence quotient (I.Q.) is based on the subject taking a test where the answers are given a numerical weight. A mathematical formula is then utilized comparing the data to a set standard based on the probability of correct answers. However, a person's I.Q. score may fluctuate. If the person where ill, their score may be lower than if they were in good health.

An example of a quantitative research project would be to establish the hypothesis that there is a direct correlation between a person's body mass index (weight) and risk of getting high blood pressure. Large samples of the population whose weight is within normal range, slightly overweight, obese, and extremely obese are screened for high blood pressure and a mathematical correlation drawn from the results in order to test the hypothesis. Relating to qualitative research the question is not whether the overweight person has high blood pressure, but what are the behavioral and social causes for the person's continued obesity.

Quantitative research can be applied to all areas of social science including, but not limited to, economics, education, and sociology. In the United States, one of the most widely used methods for the collection of data relating to economics is the use of a swipe card given to the customer by various grocery stores. While the stores do advertise that you can get items at a reduced price by using the card, what is not widely known is that after the card is entered into the system, each item they purchase is recorded to determine the shopper's buying habits as well as what items sell well and what does not. By doing this, the grocery store determines what products they will continue to carry.

An example of the Item Response method in education is the standardized tests for various grade levels. Students are tested in the areas of math, science, reading, and social studies. Individual student results are compared to overall class results. The comparison grows to include other classes at the same school, classes at different schools, comparisons of different school systems, ultimately comparing one nation's academic level to another. Through this testing method, a determination can be made as to the effectiveness of an educational system and what, if any, steps are needed to improve education. Basic standardized tests resulted in the "No Child Left Behind Act of 2001" in the United States as an attempt to improve the education of that nation's youth, and make the future generation more competitive in the global job market. However, controversies as to the effectiveness of the act have arisen. Teachers feel the curriculum is determined by what is on a test. They are teaching for the sake of test taking, and not providing the student with a quality education. Further, the information being questioned on the test must be a part of the curriculum or the test result is not valid. In other words, a researcher cannot assess a student's ability in geometry if the student has never been taught geometry. This is an example of how quantitative research changed an entire system of education.

An example of item response in sociology would be the approval rating of an elected official. A simple question is asked, "Do you believe that the mayor is doing a good job?" The answer is either "yes" or "no" and the rating is given in a percentage. Another model that can be used in social studies is the Rasch system. With this system, the researcher can manipulate or disregard data, leaving only that which fits into the parameter of his model to be measured. An example would be that a researcher wants to measure whether the populous of London were satisfied with the handling by the British emergency response teams (police, fire, and medical departments) to the July 7, 2005, railway bombings. However, the researcher is only interested in the responses of male registered voters between the ages of 25 and 60 who reside in the city of London. Any data collected regarding individuals who do not fit this specific model are disregarded, and the final result is measured in terms of percentages.

Quantitative research is an essential part of understanding human behavior and interaction. It is used to determine the demographics of a city, changes in population, the increase or decrease of teen pregnancies, and other aspects of human life. Quantitative research does not minimize man making him only a number. Instead, the statistics it provides leads us to ask "Why do we do what we do?"

There are several forms of quantitative research used to collect data, with surveys being one of the most common. Since the advent of personal computers and the internet, online research has become a popular form of data collection. Online research cannot be used for all quantitative research models but it is effective in the area of marketing. There are no geographical boundaries, and this allows for worldwide research of consumer buying habits and opinions. Online research does have a fast turnaround time for data collection and is more cost effective than other methods. Further, questions on the survey are easily changed if it is found they do not meet the needs of the researcher. In market research, websites, newsletters, and e-mails are commonly used. Warranties can be activated online, usually with a brief survey attached. This survey gives the company information as to household size, income, what store the product was purchased at, and reasons for the purchase. Companies

also use surveys to determine customer satisfaction. An example is Dell Incorporated. Any time customer or technical service departments are contacted by the consumer, Dell will send out an e-mail requesting that the customer complete a satisfaction survey. This is Dell's method to improve customer service.

The main disadvantage to online research is the relatively low response rate. Many surveys come in the form of popup ads, giving consumers the notion that they may receive a gift for the completion of the survey. What does happen is the consumer's e-mail address is sold, resulting in the consumer receiving massive amounts of spam or junk e-mails. This causes the consumer to become reluctant and not complete future surveys. Further, the respondent may give false information leading to incorrect data; and the demographic group is not a true random sample since lower income groups and elderly households usually do not have personal computers, much less the internet.

By using telephone surveys, the researcher is able to prescreen participants. If there were a member of the household who meets the researcher's criteria, the survey would continue with the selected person's permission. An example would be a research group calling on behalf of a radio station seeking information as to the listening habits of people between the ages of 35 and 55. If the criteria are not met, then the call is terminated. However, the length of the interview must be limited, and the researcher cannot use promotional materials. There is also less representation in the lower socioeconomic group since they may not have telephones.

With the use of paper-based surveys, you are able to screen participants and offer incentives. Paper-based surveys should be short and easily understood. Further, questions can be asked that are not included on phone interviews. Many times companies will include trial products or other incentives for the completion of surveys. A common paper-based survey is attached to the warranty card when a product is purchased. Instead of completing the product registration online, the registration card is mailed in. This method is used to collect data and determine the amount and focus of the advertising a company may do. One of the largest paper-based survey projects in the United States is the U.S. Census that takes place every ten years. The census gives detailed information regarding household demographics, including number of people, ages, and race. Further, population shifts based on the data collected are used to determine congressional districts. If a household does not respond, the census taker will follow up with a phone call or home visit. Mass mailings are an advantage; however, they are not as cost-effective as online and telephone surveys due to the cost of printing the surveys and postage. There are disadvantages to paper-based surveys beyond cost. If the surveys are mailed out and then an error was discovered, immediate corrections could not be made and the process would have to start all over again. Another drawback is the lack of response. Unlike telephone surveys, the consumer usually views paper-based surveys as a waste of time. Paper-based surveys are also not representative of the whole population.

Face-to-face surveys are the most expensive and they do not provide a good random sample of the population. If they are done door-to-door, the researcher oftentimes has to return due to no one being home. The number of surveys that can be done within a specific period is also lower than that of online and telephone surveys. With the current presidential race in the United States, a nonprofit group called Working America has been doing door-to-door surveys trying to gain support for their candidate. If the person responds favorably to their candidate, the interview is very short. If not, the interview takes on a qualitative aspect. Face-to-face surveys do have some advantages. First, they can be conducted anywhere. One of the most popular places for marketing surveys is at the local mall. Further, the survey can be longer and more in-depth.

Experimental design is a form of research where a maximum amount of control is exerted over external influences so that accurate measurements can be taken between variables. Manipulation, control, and randomization are the three elements of experimental design. The researcher must be able to manipulate at least one of the factors of at least one of the subject groups in the experiment in order to minimize external influences on the test subjects. Experimental designs can have a control group or not, such as with time series. What is important is that a mathematical correlation can be formed between variables, and that the experiment meets the requirements of manipulation, control, and randomization.

The most widely known form of experimental design is in the area of pharmaceutical testing. Two groups, formed through random designation, are established. One group receives the experimental drug and the other group, known as the control group, receives a placebo (aka sugar pill). Unlike animal testing, the use of placebos is necessary since the subjects are assuming they will be receiving a medication. The only problem in giving a placebo to the control group is what is termed "placebo effect." A person may respond as well to a placebo as they would to the actual medication because of the power of the human mind. Subjects are monitored and data is collected in the form of blood tests, and so forth. This may take years before a medication is approved.

With experimental design of this nature, there are three different types of studies. In a single blind study, only the researcher is aware of which subject is in the test group and who is in the control group. In a double blind study, both the researcher and the subjects are unaware of who was assigned to what group. The advantage of a double blind study is that the researcher cannot inadvertently influence the results of the experiment. Multiple-cross over is the third type of random control trial. This would be the second part in the example of drug testing. When the initial treatment ends, a specific amount of time is allotted before the test is resumed. The previous control group becomes the test group and vice versa. Time between the tests is necessary so that the chemicals contained within the medication can be fully eliminated from the person's system. By using the multiple-cross over additional data is obtained. Further, if the experiment is truly a random test, then the results of the initial experiment and the cross over should be within an acceptable range of variance.

Time series is another form of the experimental design where measurements are taken before and after the introduction of a stimulus or treatment. The problem with this type of research is that changes to the test subject can come from external sources not under the control of the researcher. This can cast doubt on the results.

An example of a time series experiment is whether exposure to sunlight decreases the time it takes for plants to decompose. Two fresh maple leaves of similar size and weight are selected. They are placed in covered vented containers. The vents are necessary so gases released during decomposition can be released into the air rather than being built up within the container and affecting the result of the experiment. Since leaves become lighter during the decomposition process, each container is weighed. This sets the starting point for later measurements. The containers are then placed under an artificial light source, mimicking sunlight. The light source must be far enough away from the containers so the heat being emitted by the lamp will not affect the outcome. For the same reason, room temperature and humidity must remain constant. One container is covered so light cannot affect the decomposition process. At designated intervals of time, each container is weighed and observational notes, such as change in color, are taken. The experiment must continue until both leaves are decomposed. The researcher may stop collecting data on one leaf when it reaches the designated decomposition stage, but he must continue with the other until that same stage is reached. At the end of the experiment, all weight data is analyzed and a mathematical comparison is done as to the effect sunlight has on the rate of decomposition. Observational notes aid in supporting the hypothesis.

There are a multitude of situations where quantitative research is applicable. However, man's behavior cannot always be put into mathematical terms. For this reason, the researcher may wish to utilize qualitative research techniques.

Qualitative Research

by Paul M. Parobek

The intent of qualitative research is to explore the relationship man has with the environment around him. The environment is not limited to the physical geography or climate the subject resides in, but encompasses personal ideologies, socialization, and any other variable man experiences. Unlike its counterpart, quantitative research, the results of qualitative research cannot be described in mathematical terms. Further, the data being collected in qualitative research are more in-depth and covers a wider range of information. The result is understanding the situation or events on a larger scope. Data collection and analysis is subjective and usually based upon the researcher being an observer or participant. However, this subjectivity leads to problems in qualitative research. The reliability of the research results can become questionable because the researcher may inject his own beliefs into the collection and analysis of data. Further, the research must be limited due to the wide range of variables in the environment.

There are ten attributes of qualitative research with the first being purpose. Gaining an understanding of how others experience and view various stimuli is the general purpose of qualitative research. Prior to beginning a research project, the researcher must establish one or two areas of interest to explore. Otherwise, due to the wide scope of variables, it would be impossible to obtain in-depth data and draw an accurate conclusion. As an example, a researcher observes a child being spanked in public and it peaks his curiosity. Is this type of punishment an accepted norm within a specific culture or society? The researcher may explore all forms of punishment but this would not sufficiently answer the question of corporal punishment of children. Further, the researcher must be an impartial observer. The researcher may be an only child given everything he wanted and never disciplined, and feels that spanking is deplorable. This view can skew the results of the study.

The next two attributes of qualitative research deal with reality. First, reality is what a person believes the world around him to be. If a man were raised to believe there is a heaven and a hell, then these concepts become his reality. A man's views and ideologies are a result of all of his experiences from birth on. He is influenced by the views of parents, friends, and teachers, as well as other factors such as the economic status and culture in which he was raised. It is with these experiences that he views and interprets reality. It is his viewpoint, how he views his environment. Secondly, reality is not consistent, which can become a problem in qualitative research. There are constant external forces exerted on man's environment causing some views of reality to change. Utilizing the example of a child being spanked in public, if a law were passed stating that corporal punishment of a child is a crime punishable by fines or jail time, the reality for the parent regarding his right to spank the child suddenly changes. This change in law would affect the outcome of the research project. The researcher's own perception of reality may change as he collects and analyzes data, but the researcher must stay focused on the purpose of his research. Any changes in his perspective are dealt with during the reporting of his results.

The fourth attribute is values. Just as a man's views of reality are based on prior influences and experiences, so too are his values. The values people have are an integral part of qualitative research because they often dictate how man reacts with his environment. Values of the subject group must be taken into account, and the researcher must understand these values in order to give an accurate interpretation of his findings. Further, the values held by the researcher must not influence the subject group or he runs the risk of changing their view of reality. Again, he must remain an impartial observer. As an example, a field research project is exploring the social habits of Amazonian Indian tribes. Scantily clad, living in huts, and hunting with spears is a major part of their environment. If the researcher will not accept the conditions with which these tribal people live and their values, and he sets about to change them,

then the findings of the research project are no longer viable and accurate.

The focus, or what is actually being researched, is the fifth attribute of qualitative research. In order to obtain accurate results, the study must encompass as many variables as possible. A school system funds a study as to why they have a 50% dropout rate. If the researcher only focuses on the school system such as student-teacher ratio, books and computer availability, and building environment, but fails to take into account the sociological and economic factors of the community, the complete picture as to the dropout rate cannot be given and a recommendation may be made based on incomplete data. The impact of as many variables as possible, within the parameter of the study, must be explored to gain a true understanding of the question being explored.

The sixth attribute in quantitative research is that data is collected and analyzed in order to test the validity of the hypothesis. The opposite is true for qualitative research. Instead of a statement being made at the beginning of a study, a question is asked. Hypotheses are formulated as the data is collected and analyzed. This is the orientation attribute of qualitative research. In the study cited above, the researcher would ask "What factors cause the school system to have a 50% dropout rate?" Since qualitative research is subjective, the researcher must avoid making a specific assertion prior to data collection. Otherwise, he may only obtain information supporting his assertion rather than a true representation of what is or has occurred within the environment.

The fact that the data being collected is based on human perception of his environment, and that it is a human who is collecting data either as an observer or participant are two more attributes of qualitative research. This relates directly to the ninth attribute, which is that research must be done under natural conditions since the intent of qualitative research is to explore the relationship man has with the environment around him. Bringing in unnatural conditions negates the research data.

The final attribute of qualitative research is the results. While the result of quantitative analysis is given in mathematical terms, the result of qualitative research does not have this objective quality. The data being collected must be comprehensive, and a true representation of the relationship of man to his environment and the results of their interaction. Failure on the part of the researcher to collect enough data, not understand the perspectives and values of his test subjects, and analyzing data based on his own presuppositions and beliefs may invalidate his final results.

Mathematical data can be used in qualitative research, but its uses are limited since qualitative research focuses more on the causes and effects of human behavior. The sample size would be smaller, information obtained would be based more on social events or interactions, and interpretation of the data is used more to explain why something happened. Qualitative research data is more open to interpretation by the researcher, and therefore tends to be subjective.

In the realm of physical, or natural science, the main method of research is the quantitative method. However, it can be applied to social sciences where a mixed methodology (utilizing both quantitative and qualitative methods) may best serve the needs of the researcher. An example is with political opinion polls. The researchers may utilize focus groups, or observe group interactions at political rallies.

They would then use the information obtained through qualitative methods and establish a series of questions on a survey for their quantitative research. The result of the research is presented in mathematical terms, such as 56% of the females between the ages of 21 and 50 would vote for a particular candidate.

To many people, psychology is the study of man's mind, how man perceives and interacts with the world around him—his behavior. This is a simplified definition, for there are many different branches of psychology and each can be explored through qualitative research. A few branches of psychology are abnormal psychology, comparative psychology, and social psychology.

Abnormal psychology is the study of individuals whose behavior is outside accepted norms. There are varying degrees of abnormality ranging from simple anxieties, which every human experiences, to the narcissistic behavior of a sociopath. Since the researcher is exploring man's mind, the first step in researching moderate to severe abnormal behavior is to rule out the physical variables that can affect the function of the brain. This process starts with simple questions, such as the amount a person drinks or if there is any history of drug use. Further, physiological tests could be done, including the position emission tomography (PET) scan to eliminate that a tumor may be causing the problem.

A case study technique is commonly used by clinical psychologists, whose main function is the diagnosis and treatment of mental illness and social adjustment problems. A person would enter psychotherapy, having in-depth discussions over a period of time. Medications may also be prescribed. Ethnography is also used since the case study must have a holistic approach. In psychotherapy, past events, especially if they were traumatic, impact current behavior. There are cases where a person's past cannot explain their current behavior such as with serial killer Jeffery Dahmer, who cannibalized his victims. He was raised in a loving, two parent, middle-class home, and he was not physically or sexually abused as a youth. What was discovered after his arrest was that he enjoyed torturing and killing small animals as a teenager, unbeknownst to his parents. Had his abnormal behavior been discovered and dealt with at an early age, it is possible that his killing spree many never have happened. The field of forensic psychology has developed to profile criminals and aid in their capture.

Jeffery Dahmer is an extreme example of abnormal behavior. An example of a routine case study would be a man entering counseling due to his frigid response towards his wife's sexual advancements. After a number of sessions, the psychiatrist finds that the man was raised by puritanical parents and sex was considered to be taboo. With this underlying cause, the man is unable to sustain an intimate relationship. The psychiatrist works with him, and at times, his wife, to resolve these issues.

Another branch of psychology for which qualitative research is applicable is comparative psychology. As the name implies, human behavior is compared to the behavior of various other animal species. Field research is most appropriate for this type of study. The researcher remains hidden observing the animal's behavior in their natural environment. They note such things as whether the animals, like beavers, build habitats; how they interact socially, their mating habits, and how they care for their young. Comparisons are then made to human behavior. While most studies have been conducted in the wild, laboratory experiments have been conducted, especially

with chimpanzees. Word, number, and shape recognition are a part of the experiments.

Action research may be used in social psychology, which focuses on human behavior in a group setting. The researcher becomes a part of the group dynamics, oftentimes becoming a stimulus to which the group reacts. However, the researcher must be careful not to pursue a course of action that might have a negative effect. As an example, a researcher attends a soccer match and sits in the home team section of the bleachers. He is observing the fans' reactions to the performance of their team. To test his theory that viewing soccer does not heighten aggressive behavior, he decides to cheer for the opposing team. A fight breaks out in the stands. The researcher did not know the aggressive nature of his test subjects nor understand the impact sporting events have on some people.

Qualitative research was designed to study cultural and social issues at hand. It is more subjective to the researcher's own beliefs about a particular situation. In the social sciences, there is a variety of ways to study a social problem, including surveys and interviews; action research, which is learning from performing; doing a case study; and as a participant observer doing field work, which is usually the last stage.

The first method, performing surveys and doing interviews, allows the researcher to pool information from a select group of people with a common connection to the situation, such as teenage girls who became pregnant in a particular region. The researcher can ask if they were taught about responsible sex, birth control, or none of the above; the researcher can also ask who taught them about sex and at what age. For action research, the researcher may teach a health class and perform a mini-exam on the students to see if they are retaining the material, and the researcher will get firsthand knowledge on sex education. As a participant observer, the researcher may sit in on a sex education class and observe what is being taught, along with participating in the class, making sure the information being taught is clear and straightforward. For the case study, the researcher would perform a study on the modern methods of sex education to verify if the methods are more successful in lowering teenage pregnancies than they were five or ten years ago, or comparing the results against another developed country. The case study is the most widely used method in qualitative research because it is the most in-depth study of a social situation.

Ethnography is another form of qualitative research. Here, the social scientist researches the social situation of a particular ethnicity, and the research is only performed as a participant observer. It is the most inclusive and is based on the idea that properties are best understood by relying on each other. Ethnography is best performed by a social scientist in anthropological research.

Grounded theory is another method used in the social sciences to understand the human condition. The grounded theory proposes to develop a theory that is based on analyzed data that was systematically collected with constant interaction between the collection and analysis of the data. There are four codes to the Grounded Theory, which are: one, the codes that identify the anchors of which the data will be gathered from; two, the concepts that are the groupings of the codes for which the data will be gathered; three, categories that help produce the theory; and four, the theory which is an explanation for the concepts. The Glaser model uses emergence and the researcher's creativity and freedom of thought to produce a theory, while the Strauss model works to validate the research.

The philosophical aspects of qualitative research are that they are symbolic and interactive with the researcher trying to define what constitutes valid research. To make the research valid, the researcher must decide which research methods are most appropriate. The underlying philosophical assumptions deal with the theory and breadth of knowledge that the researcher must use to define the limits of their research. For qualitative research there are three pillars, which are: one, positivism, which states knowledge is derived from experience and based on statistics, which set the boundaries; two, interpretive, which describes a social situation; and three, critical, which sets the boundaries by crosscutting through disciplines. However, the pillars are not always clear-cut and distinctive.

There are several methods of data collection in qualitative research. Most social scientists use interviews, surveys, participant observer, and archival research to collect the data. Most social scientists will also differentiate between firsthand sources, such as letters and memorandums, and secondary sources, such as articles and interpretations. To collect first hand data, the researcher might join a particular group that has a clear interest in a particular field, such as a cancer study, working with cancer patients and families to understand the effects of cancer and the importance of cancer research. For secondary sources, the researcher might read up on other methods of research that have already been produced on cancer research in other geographic areas to corroborate the significance of the research. Data analysis is done after the data is gathered, as after performing a single month's work of research on a particular topic, such as prostate cancer, and reading a variety of sources on the effects of various treatments on prostate cancer. In data collection and analysis, problems arise if you try to separate the two because of various perceptions.

Just as there are many forms of data collection, there are many forms of data analysis. There are three major types of data analysis. The first is hermeneutics, which states that the understanding of texts relies on the researcher's way of interpreting a text or social event. Hermeneutics deals with what has happened before to guide the researcher's ability to interpret the text. The second is semiotics, which is the study of signs and symbols in language, and it can be grouped into broad categories. Semiotics also deals with how meaning is made and understood. Semiotics comes from the philosopher John Locke in his 1690 book, *An Essay Concerning Human Understanding*. There are also several forms of semiotic analysis. The first is content analysis, which states that the researcher searches for patterns and makes an inference from the patterns. The second form is conversation analysis, which states that interactions and exchanges shape the meaning of the signs. The third is discourse analysis, which states that both content analysis and conversation analysis work together to define the meaning of the sign. The narrative works in discourse analysis by telling the story of the signs, while the metaphor works by naming the signs.

There are various approaches to the construction of a qualitative report. Ronald J. Chenail, in his article, "Presenting Qualitative Data," found in *The Qualitative Report,* Volume 2, Number 3, December 1995, lists different presentation methods. Presenting data which goes from simple to most complex is one method. By presenting it in this manner, building upon complexity, the intended reader may gain a better understanding of the research results. Data may also be presented in a time-line fashion. Reports dealing with historical events are often presented in this fashion. Some of the other approaches are listing

the data from most important to least important, dramatic presentation, and theory-guided.

To form a good qualitative report, the researcher might start with Wolcott's book, *Writing Up Qualitative Research*. Wolcott points out that the writing should not be left until the end, but that it should be taking place as the research is being performed as it helps the researcher think about what he is doing. The second point is to treat each section as an individual part, yet also as a part of the whole, so that it may be published as a paper, or in a journal, and then as a book. The benefit of writing it up individually allows for the researcher to write it from many different angles, and allows for it to be published many times in several forms.

The differences between quantitative and qualitative research are very important. Which method would be a more valid study is directly related to what type of information is required and how it will be applied. Are you correlating weight to high blood pressure as in quantitative research, or are you evaluating social events and human behavior to determine the causes of obesity? The research techniques used would differ between these two scenarios. Further, these differences are important in setting up a research project and the implementation of its method, since researchers may want to set up the project beginning with a quantitative methodology to test a theory and evolve into a qualitative project to find the answer.

Qualitative research can be used in many areas, such as educational and developmental psychology in exploring the mind of man. One of the fundamentals of qualitative research is that it provides in-depth data. Although the analysis of this data may be subjective, it does provide researchers with an understanding of how man relates to himself and to his environment.

Evaluative Research

by Paul M. Parobek

Evaluative research is the process by which programs are constantly being evaluated for their effectiveness. There are two elements of evaluative research: 1) did the program have the desired outcome; and 2) is it being delivered as it was constructed to be? The first element, did the program have the desired effects, has two parts. First, a determination is made as to what the impact of the new program or policy is. Secondly, the question of the effectiveness of the new program or policy must be answered. In other words, did the program or policy attain its goal? Together, these two questions will be used to evaluate the process of how a project is planned, and to evaluate each portion individually. They will also be used to explore the outcomes of the project by evaluating the final outcomes compared to the intended outcomes. Before beginning any evaluative research project, it is of paramount importance that the researcher has a clear understanding of the goals of the project or policy being studied. Without this understanding, the validity of the research becomes questionable.

Evaluative research is widely used in exploring social issues, such as on *Sesame Street*, a television program aimed to help preschoolers prepare for Kindergarten by teaching numbers, letters, and colors. A good use of evaluative research would be in the field of education and forming instructional lessons. In the formative phase, an instructor would want to use a lesson-specific audience, such as a fifth-grader for a fifth-grade lesson, to develop the lesson. Next, the instructor would test the lesson by giving the students a mini-exam following the lesson in order to understand it, and to observe if the students learned what they were supposed to learn.

Another example of evaluative research would be testing a vocational training center— did the vocational training center actually help students with planning and training for a career and in obtaining that specific plan? To measure the outcomes, researchers would look at several "types" of people: those who went to college, those who went to a vocational training center, and those who did not have any higher education. Next, the researcher would look at how successful the people were at getting their job—did they have a long wait or were they hired immediately? To test how effective the program is, the researcher examines the operations of the program and examines how it may be improved.

Many perceive scientific research to be limited to the laboratory environment. However, scientific research is another method of evaluation and can be utilized in almost any area of interest or physical setting. It consists of four steps: 1) the observation of the phenomenon and its description; 2) formulating a hypothesis; 3) utilizing the hypothesis in order to predict the outcome of new observations of a phenomena; and 4) the performance of experiments to test the hypothesis.

In order to effectively develop a hypothesis or theory, the researcher must be able to accurately describe the phenomena. This is generally done in the form of a question, such as "How long does it take a caterpillar to turn into a butterfly?" or "What influence does mass media have on elections?" Both of these questions will set the tone for what is being observed and will help formulate the rest of the research project. Describing a phenomenon is generally done through the observational process. However, boundaries need to be established as to what will be observed. In the example of the butterfly, the researcher limits his scope to only the Monarch butterfly. This limitation is necessary because there are too many species of butterflies to conduct an accurate, all-inclusive study.

Once the researcher is able to observe and describe the phenomena, he develops a hypothesis. It is this step where the researcher will make a preliminary attempt at making a deductive answer to the question. In my examples, the hypotheses would be "It takes a Monarch caterpillar a week in a cocoon to turn into a butterfly," and "Mass media has a heavy influence on elections due to political alliances and economic lobbying to sway an electoral group." Robert Dublin believes that theories are developed because men need to

make sense of the world around them—of what they are experiencing or observing—of how things interact. Through a hypothesis, man is trying to establish an order in nature.

Two goals in natural and social science are to be able to understand a phenomenon, and to be able to make predictions relating to new observations of that phenomenon. The ability to make predictions from the hypothesis is the third step in scientific research. In the example of the butterfly, the first step is the researcher's observations and description of a particular caterpillar becoming a Monarch butterfly, posing the question of how long this metamorphosis within the cocoon takes. The hypothesis is that it takes one week in a cocoon for a particular caterpillar to become a Monarch butterfly. The third step is the prediction, which is that the transition takes one week for all Monarch butterflies. This prediction should hold true for all future observations.

The fourth step in scientific research is to conduct experiments to test the hypothesis. Depending on the subject of the research, qualitative or quantitative data is collected and analyzed. Further, experimentation can take place in a laboratory or in the field depending on the research model being employed. With the butterfly example, the researcher may study one hundred Monarch caterpillars in a laboratory, documenting the time of each transition. If the cocoon stage takes a week for all samples, the experiment upholds the hypothesis.

The four steps given for the scientific method can be considered the hypothetico-model developed in the twentieth century. First, try to understand a problem by utilizing your experiences. Secondly, explain the phenomenon. In other words, develop a hypothesis. Thirdly, make predictions and finally, test your theory.

It is the objectivity, the impartiality, and the accuracy of the data being obtained and scrutinized in the scientific method that benefits any research being conducted.

There are several other forms of evaluative research, which are formative and summative evaluation. In formative evaluation, a program is evaluated while being constructed. Feedback and other empirical data are obtained to determine if any alterations must be made prior to final implementation. A simplified example of formative evaluation is the development of a new hamburger by McDonald's. While the hamburger is first developed in the research kitchen, routine taste tests are conducted using volunteers from a random population. Through feedback from these taste tests, adjustments are made to the product. Once the hamburger has reached the completion stage, various franchises offer it on their menu. In this phase of the formative evaluation process, researchers determine the sales potential of the new product.

There are various steps that can be taken in formative evaluation. The first step is meeting with those individuals to determine the goal of the program and to establish effective communication. At this time, a communication plan is developed. The elements of that program include what information is needed, who receives the information and in what format, and the period and setting. For example, the program director needs progress updates and final recommendations. Progress updates may be given in the form of memos or oral reports. These would be given every two weeks in either memo form and/or meetings. Before the research begins, a final deadline is established. By this deadline, a written final recommendation or progress report where changes were either proposed or implemented is given.

Usually the setting is a formal meeting rather than informal conferences, as with updates.

After the initial meeting and a period for communication has been established, the researcher determines the methods of data collection. These include: one, observation; two, informal discussions; three, short tests; four, feedback through group discussions; and five, a short survey with the following questions: 1) were the training needs clearly identified? 2) are there any other areas that need attention? 3) will the training needs be met? 4) revising the objectives, 5) are the training topics being taught? 6) are there additional training topics that need to be taught? and 7) do the training methods need to be adjusted? Group discussions and feedback from line staff, those actually implementing the program, are vitally important. While department heads, program managers, and other high echelon individuals have knowledge relating to the program goals, their knowledge of how it is actually being implemented and the problems being encountered is limited. Without input from those implementing the program, the researcher has very little knowledge as to what changes may be required. Finally, data is then collected, analyzed, recommendations are made, and, at times, changes implemented immediately.

There are various models of formative evaluation. One of these was developed by D. L. Shufflebeam and is called Context-Input-Process-Product model. This model has four sections: the intended goals and intended means; and the actual means and actual ends. The goals, or intended ends, are established. These are usually determined by a series of meetings utilizing continuous context evaluation and needs assessment. The intended process or procedure is the intended means.

Input evaluation is utilized in this step. Here, through meetings and other forms of feedback, alternative methods of implementation can be explored. By acquiring knowledge regarding intended program goals and means, the researcher can conceptualize how the program is to work in order to effectively meet its goal. The last two steps in Shufflebeam's model are determining the actual means of the process and its actual ends. Process evaluation is utilized to assess and monitor the implementation of the program and any changes that are implemented during the process. In other words, the process is being "debugged." Finally, product evaluation is conducted to determine the actual ends of the program. Product evaluation also includes assessing any unintended effects the program may have. Whatever model is utilized, formative evaluation is an effective tool for ensuring that programs meet their goals in an efficient manner.

In formative evaluation, needs assessment studies are conducted to determine the target population of the new program, such as illiterate individuals, as well as what form the program will take to attain its goal. Another formative evaluation type is the evaluability assessment. Its function is to assess the feasibility of evaluating a program. In this type of study, a determination must be made as to how those involved with the policy or program can aid in the formation of the evaluation process. Their input is essential for a successful study. Other types include implementation evaluation, which centers on the integral workings of policy or program, or policy in delivering their service; as well as process evaluation, which evaluates the delivery process.

The findings of formative evaluation studies are not meant to be generalized. Any recommendations and improvements are usually addressed only to those directly involved or who have a "stake" in the outcome. Further, the results of the formative study are limited to the specific area or site being studied.

The purpose of summative evaluation is to determine if the product, policy, or program has been effective in attaining its goal, and is conducted after it has been in effect. Summative evaluation is conducted after the new program or policy is in effect. Here, research is done to assess a program's effectiveness. Since summative evaluation is conducted after the policy or program is in effect, it may take months or even years to determine the program's effectiveness, especially in the areas of new social or educational programs implemented by the government.

In the case of the new McDonald's hamburger, sales figures are analyzed usually within several months after its introduction to determine if the product should continue or not. The length of time prior to beginning a summative evaluation varies depending upon what is being evaluated. If the project or policy involves social issues, such as education or poverty as with the United States' "No Child Left Behind Act" or "Welfare to Work" regulations, it may be years before a summative study can be done in order to determine if the program has met its intended goals.

In summative evaluation, the main type of study is the outcome evaluation. A determination is made as to whether or not the program met its intended goal. With the impact study, researchers analyze the consequences of the policy or program, or the impact they had. As an example, with the "No Child Left Behind Act," while its intent was to improve the education of America's youth, an unintended effect was that many qualified teachers left the field because they were tired of only teaching for the sake of test taking. Another example of an impact study is what occurred on the Penghu Archipelago in Taiwan. Rick Newman of the Universal Press Syndicate reported in the *Cleveland Plain Dealer* on May 30, 2009, that eight wind turbines had been erected. While this is clean energy, the noise from these turbines has caused the deaths of over 400 goats due to terminal insomnia, an unforeseen impact on the environment. The government is now helping the farmers move. Secondary analysis is often utilized to re-address completed studies. With changes in technology and shifts in the social climate, programs and policies require a "second-look" to see if they are viable. What may have worked ten years ago may not work today.

The results of summative evaluations are meant to be generalized and can be applied to other programs that have similar goals. While the findings of formative evaluation are reported to a limited number of people, the findings of summative evaluation are presented to a larger audience. Reports are prepared for those funding the project as well as government policymakers if applicable. These reports may also be published and utilized for future projects. Summative evaluations are utilized in practically all areas from business to education. Many are cost-effective studies, which affect everyday life. Reorganizing companies, the continued production of products we see on the store shelves, as well as social services from medicine to education are all subject to summative evaluation.

Strategies utilized to conduct evaluations vary in approach and are based upon what area is being evaluated. Participant-oriented models, management-oriented system models, and qualitative/anthropological models are three evaluation strategies. Most evaluators do not rely solely on one strategy. Instead, they draw from several in developing their evaluative process.

The participant-oriented approach to evaluation relies heavily on input from the client or stakeholders. Responsive evaluation is one model of this strategy. In responsive evaluation, the researcher utilizes observation, interviews, focus groups, and other face-to-face techniques allowing him to gain personal firsthand knowledge about the intention of the policy or program and the desired effects. By utilizing this method, issues and concerns are readily identifiable. Further, the researcher gains a better understanding of the important elements of the new program or policy and can determine which of these elements require evaluation. According to R. E. Stake, the primary function of responsive evaluation is to make a program more useful, and it does not focus on the program's goals.

There are various steps in conducting responsive evaluation. First, there is input by clients, staff, and others who have a concern or are involved in the program. As previously stated, evaluators do draw on several strategies in developing their process. This part of responsive evaluation is utilized in other strategies. Based upon the input, the researcher establishes limits to the evaluative research project. These limits are necessary since responsive evaluation cannot address all of the concerns or problems. Observations and further informal conversations continue aiding the evaluator in determining what is actually occurring, thereby enabling him to select what data collecting methods he will utilize. Data is collected and a final report issued. This report can take many forms, from formal reports to oral discussions. Responsive evaluation is a very informal approach and the methods are subjective by nature, including conversations and observations. Even with its subjective nature, there are many areas where responsive evaluation is adequate. These areas include literary reviews, assessing the suitability of new textbooks, and addressing conflict management issues within the workplace.

Another evaluation strategy is the management-oriented system. Models classified under this system are often utilized by governments and businesses in order to effectively implement large-scale projects. A unique management model is called Utilized Focus Evaluation developed by Michael Patton. This model focuses heavily on user or stakeholder input, drawing on responsive evaluation. Before any evaluation is conducted, information must be exchanged between the evaluator and the users of the program. The primary focus is on use or functionality. If it is determined that there is no or only a limited potential for the use of the program, then the evaluation process does not even begin and the project is "scrapped."

One of the main models of a management-oriented system is called PERT (Program Evaluation and Review Technique), and was first utilized in the late 1950s when the United States constructed the Polaris submarine. An element of PERT is the Critical Path Method. Here, the overall project is broken down into tasks and arranged in sequence of events. Each event is given a period for completion. Three periods may be used for each task. These are: the optimistic (or best) time; most likely time; and pessimistic (worst) time. A weighted average of the three times is done in order to determine the approximate completion time for each task as well as the entire project. A network diagram is then constructed which allows managers to have a visual representation of the project. Managers

are able to assess if tasks are being completed in a timely fashion. Since the completion of each task impacts the next task, such as the foundation of a building being completed before the walls go up, it is important to stay on schedule.

However, as with any managerial process, the system is only as good as those who monitor it. Many projects are riddled with time delays and cost overruns, especially with the United States' effort to rebuild Iraq. Because of cost overruns and time delays, Stewart Bowen Jr., the United States Special Inspector General for Iraq Reconstruction, issued a March 2007 report entitled "Lessons in Program Management 3." This report states:

An effective monitoring and oversight plan needs to be in place within each agency from the outset of contingency operations. This will allow for early and direct feedback to program managers, who can implement course corrections in operating practices and policies. Early and effective oversight will also deter fraud, waste, and abuse. For construction projects, there should be consistent oversight, including appropriate quality assurance and quality control programs. In Iraq, successful projects were usually those that received good quality assurance and effective quality control.[1]

Many reconstruction projects are being handled by private contractors who are not being adequately monitored by the appropriate

1 "Lessons in Program Management 3." <http://www.sigir.mil/reports/pdf/Lessons_Learned_March21.pdf> p. 19, June 3, 2009. (Government report in public domain.)

government agency. A one-year project initially costing $3 million dollars can easily turn into a three-year project at five times the initial cost. Managers in the private sector who utilize the PERT method are far more diligent in monitoring a project's completion time and cost, such as the construction of a new office tower. This is mainly because money for the project comes out of the company's profits and not from the taxpayers. Further, the private sector is more diligent in applying penalties to contractors for unsubstantiated time delays and cost overruns.

Qualitative data-gathering techniques, such as interviews and focus groups, are utilized in the evaluation process. However, the most important technique is observation. There is a drawback to utilizing observation as an evaluative tool and that drawback is observer bias. A goal-free model for evaluation addresses this drawback. Most techniques require the evaluator to know the goals of the program. However, there is one model that does not—the goal-free model. In the goal-free model, the researcher collects data and makes assessment without knowing the intended goal of the project. One benefit in conducting goal-free evaluation is that researcher bias is eliminated since the researcher has no knowledge of the program's intended goal, thereby maintaining his objectivity. In addition, if there are unexpected effects, these can be objectively reviewed as to importance rather than automatically being negatively assessed.

Qualitative/anthropological evaluation models are well suited for the evaluation of programs addressing social issues, such as methods used to teach autistic children or assessing conditions in hospitals and nursing homes. This holds true not just for their physical environments, but for their level of care as well. Further, qualitative/anthropological models are utilized in individual performance evaluations. Many evaluations include not only the quality and quantity of a person's work, but other aspects that cannot be mathematically measured. These aspects include adaptability, initiative, and cooperation.

Programs such as employment advice centers, educational programs, organ donation programs, and programs dedicated to physical wellness, such as dieting, fitness, and substance abuse reduction, are most likely to benefit from evaluative research. These programs are continually examined for their effectiveness through measures such as pretesting by questioning the participants on their expectations, and post-testing by doing surveys and focus groups.

As with case study research, there are many facets to evaluative research. With today's social and economic climate, the importance of evaluative research cannot be understated. It is vitally important that new programs be evaluated not only for their cost-effectiveness, but for their ability to meet the needs of those individuals they are to service.

Chapter Review

REVIEW QUESTIONS

1. What is the primary function of research in the social sciences?
2. What is the value of quantitative methods as outlined in the article in this section?
3. What is the value of qualitative methods as outlined in the article in this section?
4. Taking into consideration social science research ethics, how might you go about exploring the concept of "empathy" through a quantitative (or a statistical or numerical) tool, such as a survey, versus through a qualitative tool, such as an interview or focus-group method? What benefits could each of these methodologies bring to the exploration of this concept?

CASE STUDY: QUALITATIVE RESEARCH ETHICS IN HEALTHCARE SETTINGS

Qualitative research typically involves much more one-on-one interaction with research subjects, and as such ethics and boundaries in such cases can be somewhat obscure and contextual at times. Take, for example, the idea of **"participant observation."** This type of observation relies on the researcher taking on a fictional role within a group or organization (otherwise becoming a member of this group) for the purpose of understanding the subtle culture of that group and its influence on its members. An example might include pretending to join a cult for the purposes of understanding and studying that cult. Such studies can sometimes create complexities within commonly understood research ethics, such as voluntary participation or informed consent.

Qualitative approaches to research are becoming much more common in the health and social sciences. In healthcare studies, this may be particularly complex as the potential for relationships develops depending on the length of studies or medical trials, as well as the fact that participants are in a vulnerable position and often very hopeful for a positive outcome. Read about some of the challenges of qualitative research in healthcare settings here:

https://www.ncbi.nlm.nih.gov/pmc/articles/PMC4263394/

What are the main challenges presented in the article? How might they also apply to other types of social research, including qualitative research with other vulnerable populations (such as children)? What are your thoughts on how such issues might be mitigated in the behavioral or social sciences?

DEVELOPING THE SOCIOLOGICAL IMAGINATION
Ethnomethodology

Various components and means of interaction in a society are often subconsciously absorbed as we age and learn about our social environment and appropriate means of interaction with others in this environment. Oftentimes this is referred to as just "common sense" views or behavior. Given that language, the use of tone, touch, and other elements of interaction can vary greatly across societies, it is likely that "common sense" is not an ingrained cognitive phenomena but rather a reflection of what we have been taught and have absorbed from or about our social world.

Ethnomethodology is a method of analysis that examines these sometimes "taken for granted" or subconscious means of interaction (conversation or gestures as an example) that we absorb or these "common sense" views or behavior that we use in everyday life to navigate our environment. This research approach purposefully disrupts these social norms in an effort to point out that such a subconscious rule for behavior or interaction exists and then analyzes how social order is restored in such a situation. Evaluator behavior has been used as an example frequently. There are many "rules" that we abide by when riding in an elevator in U.S. society, such as facing the doors, limited interaction or conversation

with others, and maintaining an appropriate amount of space between oneself and a neighbor. A person using an ethnomethodological research approach might purposefully break these rules, observe and record the behavior of others when these rules are broken, and record how order was reestablished in the elevator. *Candid Camera* is famous for "elevator experiments," an example that we will revisit in the next chapter on group influence and conformity. Ethnomethodology would likely fall under the "qualitative field research" broad research methodology as it relies primarily on recorded observation.

Think of a "taken-for-granted" means of interaction that we use in U.S. society and purposefully disrupt this norm by acting in an unexpected way. (Please do so safely and legally.) What was the reaction when this "rule" was broken? How was order reestablished? Record your observations. Using the three main theories in the course, what was the either implicit or observed meaning (symbolic interactionism) of this "rule"? Were there power or authority structures involved or who perhaps had a hand in creating this "rule" (conflict theory)? What purpose does it serve the larger social order (structural functionalism)?

4 | Deviance and Social Control

CHAPTER SUMMARY

- This chapter explores the concept of social control and the definition and purpose of "socialization." This chapter also explores how socialization occurs (through the influence of groups) and how one's behavior can be influenced and may vary depending upon group size and by what authority and power structures are present.

- This chapter explores the concept of deviance (the violation of a social norm) and crime (the violation of a social norm that specifically breaks a law) and the punishment of deviance as a form of social control. This chapter also explores social theory related to informal or formal punishment.

- As a demonstration of the social components of deviance, the chapter also explores the types of crimes often measured and issues related to measurement.

PRELIMINARY QUESTIONS FOR READERS:

- What typically constitutes one's identity or sense of self? Is it possible to have a sense of self outside of our environment or environmental contexts?

- What are the social groups (family, religious congregations, or school, for example) that have had the most influence on your worldview thus far?

- We often take on new roles and responsibilities as we age, and as we reach retirement age, we begin to step out of various roles and responsibilities. What are the roles and responsibilities that you are currently acquiring or letting go of? How are you learning to either step into or out of those roles?

- From a sociological perspective, what would be a primary reason for punishing (either formally or informally) those who break established social norms?

- What are some ways U.S. society has attempted to deter crime? Are these methods effective in your opinion?

CHAPTER INTRODUCTION
Socialization

As we have been exploring, the society in which we were raised and live and the groups that we identify with can have an enormous impact on our lives. A central area of interest for sociologists is how one's environment impacts who they understand themselves to be (or how one's environment comes to impact one's sense of self or identity), what is expected of them by other groups and by society at large, and how groups and societies continue to assert this influence over time and throughout the life course. This is traditionally referred to as "social control" or the process by which groups and individuals within those groups are swayed to conform to the expectations of society. **Social control** can be formal (such as imprisonment if one breaks an established law) or informal (such as rejection by peers or colleagues). In most societies, dominant social expectations are often the values and traditions of a dominant (or majority) group in society as dominant groups (for example, historically dominant class, gender, age, or ethnic groups) in most societies have the power and means to determine to define "popular culture" and disseminate those beliefs over time.

Socialization is defined as the lifelong process by which individuals learn the values and beliefs of their society and the expectations that society and the groups with which an individual may identify have of them and the roles they occupy. We learn who we are in light of how others and our society views us, our place in that society or group, and as a result the role(s) we are also expected to play. As you can imagine, these expectations differ greatly based on various factors, including sub-cultures, gender, age, class standing, race/ethnicity, and religious background, among other attributes. We also learn these expectations through a variety of social institutions. Among the most powerful agents of socialization are the family, the media, peers, religion, sports, and schools. The article "Theories on Socialization and Social Development" discusses how socialization assists in enabling people to act in socially accepted ways, how it impacts our identity, and how it assists in informing and reaffirming personal and collective values. As also explored in these articles, socialization is considered a lifelong process.

TYPES OF GROUPS

In addition to the larger groups (like society or various social institutions), the smaller groups that we belong to also can have a tremendous amount of influence on our lives, behaviors, and sense of self. No individual is a member of only one group. As you know and as evidenced by your own life, an individual can belong to a variety of macro and micro groups and social networks. A **group** can be defined as two or more individuals brought together for a specific purpose. Research has demonstrated that different groups have different influences on our behavior. According to David Myers (2002), author of *Social Psychology* (a discipline that studies group dynamics), those groups that are more long lasting, intimate, and fulfill emotional needs are likely to have a greater degree of influence on our attitudes and behavior than temporary groups that we are affiliated with for shorter periods of time.

Research has also demonstrated that the size of groups can sometimes vary in their influence on us; for example, a dyad (a group consisting of exactly two people) is considered to be the most influential type of group, likely because there is little room for disagreement (particularly if someone has social or relational power or authority over the other), and typically compromise is needed. Conversely, a triad (a group of three) or a group of any variation of three is considered to hold the weakest amount of influence, likely because there is the possibility of two dissenting or agreeing opinions that stand in the face of another. The study of group size and its influence on the individual is known as the **study of group size effect.**

DEVIANCE AND CRIME

Groups can have tremendous influence on our behavior in both tangible and subtle ways over time or in specific events. As explored, even the number of those in a group may impact our behavior in a given setting. For a society to define what is **deviant** (or what violates an expected social rule or norm) in and of itself communicates expected modes of interaction and behavior with one another in a group. Punishing deviance (either formally or informally), therefore, reinforces these initial expectations. The second article in this chapter reflects on various theories and the purpose of punishment in a society.

While deviance is not always a **crime** (a type of deviance that violates a law), the study of crime (otherwise defined as **criminology**) can provide some significant insights into the study of social order and control. The third article provided in this chapter discusses crime, the concept of social order, and traditional means of crime control. This chapter also explores the concept of **stigma** (the assignment of either a formal or inferred deviant label in society) and its potential impact on one's perception of self and social experience.

Of course, what is defined as "criminal" or "deviant" can change significantly over time in any given society and can also change in various social contexts. For example, while murder and killing someone in self-defense both involve the taking of a life, self-defense in the eyes of the law carries much less (if any) culpability in the United States depending upon the circumstances, for example, compared to what may be considered the unprovoked act of doing so in most societies. Similarly, as we learn about different types of behavior that are defined as "deviant" by society, classifications of certain behavior as "deviant" can also change. Social movements that seek to decriminalize or destigmatize certain types of behavior, for example, can assist in the reclassification of such behavior.

There is often quite a bit of social debate, not only in determining or defining what is both deviant and a crime but also as to the means in which a society seeks to correct deviance and the extent to which such methods are effective in **resocializing** individuals to current or preferred social expectations and to the larger social order.

WORKS CITED

Myers, D. (2002,) *Social psychology*. 7th Edition. New York, New York: McGraw Hill.

Theories of Socialization and Social Development

by Olivia N. Saracho and Bernard Spodek

Right from their moment of birth, children are unique in their rate of growth and development, as well as in their social awareness and ability to interact socially. Characteristics for each age group have been identified, but these are only norms that indicate expected developmental sequences. However, there is a range of individual differences among children.

Newborn infants are aware of their needs and use their activity level to make these needs known. As they mature, they develop other ways to make their needs known. They also become aware of both their physical and social environment. Interactions between mothers and children are important for social development as adequate mothering satisfies children's social and emotional needs.

SOCIALIZATION FORCES

Children's socialization is influenced by several important social forces such as those found in the family, the peer group, and among significant others. Each is discussed separately here.

The Family Context

Children are first influenced by their early exposure at home with their family. Each family reflects an ethnic background, a series of relationships, educational attitude, and a social status. Each family also establishes definite rituals, habits, and attitudes. The family is the child's first and most important socializing agency. An emotional attachment to family is essential in the development of all relationships in life. Within the family environment, children begin to understand and build relationships and interactions among all the family members.

Children's experiences within the family ultimately give them a feeling that the primary group accepts or rejects them. Children may develop an unhealthy personality when they experience feelings of rejection. They may become aggressive, attention-getting, hostile, hyperactive, jealous, or rebellious. If this happens, the children can use one or many attention-getting mechanisms, not all of which are positive. Parents can help children acquire a healthy personality by creating an environment of acceptance through love and encouragement. The family can establish a set of standards and provide security for the emerging child. Children need to have opportunities to assume responsibilities and make choices as early as they can handle these. They may experience the natural consequences of bad choices and learn from them as long as the family provides them with support. If the children are independent from adults and experience the consequences of their behavior, they will ultimately be able to deal with the realities of their social world.

Peer Group Affiliates

Achieving the highest level of social development depends on the children's ability to meet their social needs to have more intense social contacts with friends. As they mature, children make a transition from affiliation with family members to affiliations with peers. Peers assume an increasingly important role in the children's social development. The children's peer groups represent a unique society that helps them make the transition to adult status. Becoming an equal member of the peer group becomes a basic need.

Peer groups are important disciplinary agents who monitor how the children conform to the social expectations of the group. When children interact within peer groups, they experience workshops of human relationships. In these situations, children first encounter children from different backgrounds. They learn to accept, work with, and cooperate with those who possess different opinions and beliefs. They also feel a new kind of security and belonging. The children's transfer of loyalty from the family to the peer group contributes to a later development of loyalty to society. Peers also contribute to the children's self-concept when they provide them with feedback about who they are and the type of behavior that will be accepted or rejected in their peer group.

Originally the peer groups may emerge from the children's immediate neighborhood. As children have contact with the world outside their family, various larger, more remote peer groups appear. At this time, children select their peer group based on their interests and social status needs. The peer groups' contribution is crucial, because it prepares the children to succeed in several give-and-take relationships. If children want to belong to a peer group, they need to conform to the peer group's expectations, follow its standards, maintain its secrets, and meet its expectations.

The Role of Significant Others

Children identify and have contact with many individuals who are important to them. These individuals differ based on the range of the children's experiences. They may be the parents, siblings, older children in the neighborhood, or leaders of a child's group. Initially, children learn social behavior from the family constellation. Later they meet individuals outside their family and encounter a variety of experiences and learn different social behaviors. As others approve, accept, or reject them, children identify and learn different social roles. For example, when children play, they attach specific meaning to their experiences. As the children mature, they usually identify and imitate those individuals who are important to the children. This is another way that children identify and formulate social values and attitudes.

Acculturation Thrusts

Socializing forces (e.g., family, family constellation, peer group, significant others) influence the children's social development. These social forces help them develop their ability to give or receive attention and affection. The similarity in expectations in the family, family constellation, and peer groups can facilitate the children's socialization process. In contrast, different expectations among these socialization forces can create a conflict in values and standards and the socialization process can become unpredictable. In any case, the children's perceptions and experiences are the guiding force in the children's socialization process. Children develop their social behaviors based on their perceptions, beliefs, and convictions.

SOCIALIZATION THEORIES

Several developmental theories have influenced our understanding of the socialization process. These include maturationist theory (developed by Arnold Gesell), constructivist theories (developed by such theorists as Jean Piaget, Lev S. Vygotsky, and Jerome Bruner) and psychodynamic theories (developed by such theorists as Sigmund Freud, Erik Erikson, Harry Stack Sullivan, and Alfred Adler), and ecological theory (developed by Urie Bronfenbrenner). Each theory provides interpretations on the meaning of the children's social development.

Maturationist Theory

Maturation theory suggests that human development is mainly genetically determined with the environment having a minimum influence. Although negative environmental conditions can prevent the emergence of natural developmental patterns, this theory indicates that the patterns continue their course. Thus, children's maturation is an unfolding process. Specific attempts to create desired behaviors before their natural manifestation should be avoided, because such forcing may be detrimental. Children who are coerced to function at a higher level than their natural stage may develop inadequately and may have a negative effect on their sense of worth and self-confidence. Intervention, however, may take place if the children's expected maturation patterns fail to develop. According to Murray Thomas (2004), an intervention can occur if (1) the characteristic is unacceptable, (2) the children's maturational ability allows movement to an advanced stage, and (3) the constituents in the children's environment neglect to "naturally" modify the unaccepted characteristic.

Arnold Gesell (1880–1961) was the psychologist who contributed most to the maturationist view of children's social development. He observed and described in detail infants and children from birth through age ten in different domains, including social development. He generated norms according to ages for these children, which he considered to be representative of their normal development. Gesell posited that forces within the organism that unfold with age determine children's development. He felt that the environment was a less important element in modifying their development. Gesell recognized that children have their own developmental pattern and need to develop at their own pace. He believed that educational environments need to support the children's development, needs, and interests, following the individual children's developmental patterns.

Psychodynamic Theories

Psychodynamic theory focuses on personality, which is a major aspect of children's social development. Although psychoanalysis relates to the adults' personality problems, it helps one understand how childhood experiences contributed to adult personalities. Since it provides important insights concerning childhood, it was added to the study of child development. The theorists that contributed to the children's personality include Sigmund Freud, Erik Erikson, Harry Stack Sullivan, and Alfred Adler.

Sigmund Freud (1856–1939) was the pioneer of psychoanalysis, where patients explore their past history and their present situation. He used a variety of techniques to help patients face their fears and struggles. Freud's theory of development identifies a series of psychosexual stages. Freud considered these stages of psychosexual development to be universal. He believed that they reflect developmental human needs that are embedded in all cultures. Individuals need to successfully evolve through these stages to develop a healthy personality. However, if individuals become fixated at a certain stage, they would have to cope with needs from an earlier developmental period even though they are mature adults, possibly making their behavior seem irrational.

Freud's psychoanalytic theory extensively influenced the thinking of psychologists, psychiatrist, and psychoanalysts. Though he focused on the adults' childhood experiences, his theory stressed the importance of early childhood experiences in the individual's personality development. Freud's contribution to child development has motivated several psychologists and social workers to accept several elements of Freudian theory, even though they might not accept the entire psychoanalytic theory. Freud influenced others throughout Europe and the United States. Other psychoanalysts studied psychoanalytic theory, modified it, and searched for cultural influences. Eric Erikson was one of these psychoanalysts.

Erik Erikson (1902–1994) broadened Freud's thoughts on personality development, altering Freud's psychosexual stages into a set of psychosocial stages, where each stage is associated to the ego's effectiveness initiating its form at birth and continues throughout development (Erikson, 1963). He assumed that individuals evolve throughout their lives through interactions within their social environment. Each of Erikson's stages develops throughout an individual's life (Erikson, 1968) and each has a distinguishing critical conflict related to it. Individuals need to resolve the conflict before proceeding to the next stage.

One major difference between Freud's and Erikson's stages of development is that Freud believed that development terminates by the end of adolescence, whereas Erikson believed that development continues throughout the individuals' life. He based his stages (Table 4.1) on a series of social conflicts in which all individuals need to become successfully proficient to reach maturity (Erikson, 1982). The individuals' culture and historical reference point affects those conflicts.

Harry Stack Sullivan's (1892–1949) stages of development also differed from Freud's. His stages were based on the interpersonal relationships in which individuals experience as they strive for confidence (Sullivan, 1953). These stages are presented in Table 4.2.

Many views on social development are based on Sullivan's (1953) theory of friendship. He suggested that individuals experience different developmental stages where they have precise interpersonal needs and have different

TABLE 4.1. Erikson's Stages of Psychosocial Development

Age	Stage	Characteristics
0-1½ years	trust vs. mistrust	Reliance on caregiver, predictability leads to trust in environment, or lack of care leads to basic mistrust.
1½-3 years	autonomy vs. shame and doubt	Environment encourages independence, pride and sense of self-worth, or doubt and lack of self-esteem result from overt-control.
3-6 years	initiative vs. guilt	Ability to learn and to enjoy mastery; or fear of failure and of punishment leads to guilt.
6 years–puberty	industry vs. inferiority	Valuing work, skill, and competence; or feelings of inadequacy and inferiority.
Adolescence	identity vs. role confusion	Development of individuality; or confusion related to self.
Young adulthood	intimacy vs. isolation	Commitment to personal reactions; or withdrawal from others and self-absorption.
Middle age	generativity vs. stagnation	Care of next generation, widening interests; or self-indulgence.
Old age ego	identity vs. despair	Gaining the meaning of one's existence or disappointment with life and fear of death.

From Spodek, B., & Saracho, O. N. (1994). *Right from the start: Teaching children ages three to eight.* Boston: Allyn & Bacon.

kinds of relationships with different needs at each stage. Individuals must acquire the social skills and competencies for successful social interactions within the context of these relationships. Researchers have identified several approaches as they examined different populations, cultural groups, and age groups. The concern for social interest in Sullivan's theory is similar to the development of social interest in Adlerian psychology (Savage, & Nicholl, 2003; Seligman, 2006).

Alfred Adler's (1870–1937) observation that "human beings live in the realm of meanings" reflects the social constructivist view of human behavior. Alfred Adler strongly advocated the importance of understanding individuals within their social context. He believed that everybody has the basic desire and goal to belong and feel important. Adlerian theory has been important in the children's growth and development. Adlerians assume that "a misbehaving child is a discouraged child" and that the most effective strategy in coping with difficult children's behaviors is to help them feel valued, significant, and competent. They are interested in understanding the specific and private beliefs and strategies that each individual produces in childhood. This cognitive schema and personal life style become the individuals' reference for attitudes, behaviors, and one's private view of self, others, and the world. For healing, growth, and change to

TABLE 4.2. Sullivan's Stages of Social Development

Age	Stage	Characteristics
Infancy	Empathetic relationship with "mothering" individuals	Infants respond to the significant adults about them. They reflect the parents' mood. For example, an anxious parent may have an anxious, crying infant. Infants are in a state of equilibrium and need their parents' approval. When infants can distinguish between the others and their own bodily limitations, they also develop the need for confidence.
Childhood	Relationship with peers	Children develop the need for playmates, especially their own age group. They have the motor and language skills to move and interact more freely. They also learn that language is a means of communication and become aware about the dimensions of their culture.
Juvenile Era	Determine their own status and identify the self	This stage relates to the children's entry into school and continues through most of their grammar-school years. Children are beginning to separate themselves from other entities and identify the self. They are surrounded by peers and meet significant adults other than their parents. They begin to objectively analyze themselves, becoming internal critics who test their impulses. Since the internal critic reflects the assessments by significant adults, it may be compared to the superego. Attitudes of competition, rivalry, and ultimately a realistic compromise start to emerge.
Preadolescence	Strong interest toward another person	An extremely essential but chronologically condensed interval that psychologically or psychiatrically terminates with the individuals' strong interest for another individual. Thus, the preadolescents make a transition from egocentric achievements and begin to need approval and satisfactions of significant others. They become capable of a more mature love that goes beyond the pursuit of their own security. Their concern for others may be conveyed toward a friend of the same sex with a similar pattern of behavior as their own.
Adolescence	Interest toward a person of the opposite sex	Adolescents transfer their interest from an individual of the same sex to one of the opposite sex. Thus, they need to must come to terms with the sex drive. Society's attitudes toward sex usually forces adolescents to encounter new difficulties in integrating their personality.
Late Adolescence	Personality development	The individual's personality continues to develop into their appropriate relationship.
Adulthood	Intimacy with another person	Individuals establish a love relationship with a significant person. This may be a very intimate relationship with another individual, which becomes their major source of satisfaction in life.

occur, individuals need to examine their early life experiences, the continuous behavior patterns, and the methods that individuals use to acquire significance and belonging (Savage & Nicholl, 2003; Seligman, 2006).

As articulated by noted Adlerian psychotherapist Henry Stein, the theory and application of Adlerian Psychology have as their lynchpins seven critical ideas. According to Stein (2003), in psychotherapy the progressive development of the feeling of community usually involves the organization of cognitive, affective, and behavioral strategies. Henry T. Stein (2003), of the Alfred Adler Institute of Northwestern Washington, developed the following *Developmental Sequence of The Feeling of Community* (See Table 4.3), which was based on concepts originally developed by Heinz Ansbacher, who was one of the world's leading experts on Adlerian psychology.

Children's personality development begins in infancy. Infants become conscious of inadequacies in everyday tasks as compared to older children and adults. Adler attributed this consciousness to inferiority feelings, where children become aware of their limitations. However, these feelings motivate individuals to strive in a direction where they develop, strive, achieve, and seek for success to compensate for their defeats. According to Adler, individuals sometimes use both reality and fiction to guide their actions, which they believe are true. Therefore, Adler established a final goal: a fictional perception of individuals in which they visualized an idealistic situation of perfection, completion, or overcoming. Individuals strive toward the final goal to overcome their feelings of inferiority. While this final goal symbolizes a subjective, fictional perception of the future; it motivates the individuals toward the future.

Constructivist Theory

Constructivist theory offers a philosophical resolution to the confrontation between rationalism and empiricism. Both of these perspectives provide an understanding of how individuals learn about the world. They differ in their source of knowledge; the rationalist uses reason (that is, the mind) whereas the empiricist uses experience. Constructivists believe that individuals create knowledge by acting upon (or thinking about) information they acquire through experience. Children of all ages have some understanding about the world. Their understanding guides them to interpret the information they receive. However, this information may also alter their understanding of the world. This active process continues throughout the individual's life. Several theorists (e.g., Jean Piaget, Lev. S. Vygotsky, and Jerome S. Bruner) developed constructivist views on the children's social and intellectual development.

Jean Piaget (1896–1980) explored how children of different ages resolve reasoning problems, communicate their dreams, make moral judgments, and conduct other mental activities. Piaget found that the children's thought processes develop through a series of stages that can be generalized to children in all cultures. Children find an appropriate way to adapt to their environment. They develop schemas or schemata to make sense of their world. They produce and alter schemes through *assimilation* and *accommodation*. In *assimilation*, children search their repertoire of schemes to solve problems. They analyze the situation to match the pattern of their repertoire of schemes and conform the environmental stimuli to their existing knowledge. Piaget assumes that: "To assimilate an object to a

TABLE 4.3. Stein's Developmental Sequence of the Feeling of Community

Sequence		Characteristics
Aptitude	**Potential**	The feeling of community is an innate potential that has to be consciously developed by training into skill and ability. It is innately so small that it must benefit from social understanding to develop. After becoming an ability, it may then acquire secondary dynamic characteristics of attitude and motivation.
Ability	**Behavioral**	Behavioral capacities include: making contact with others; relating to others in a useful way; and contributing to the common welfare. The ability to cooperate depends on the degree of the feeling of community.
	Intellectual	Intellectual capacities include: understanding others' point of view and needs; accepting common sense over private logic; recognizing the inter-dependency of people; appreciating the contributions of others; and reasoning with view of immediate and future social consequences.
	Emotional	Emotional capacities include: empathy for others (to see with their eyes, to hear with their ears, to feel with their hearts); feeling connected to others; and the ability to feel and express acceptance, liking, and love for others.
Style of Life	**Attitudinal**	Attitudinal capacities include: feeling at home on the earth; a sense of harmony with the universe; a deep identification with others; a letting go of a preoccupation with self; and a profound feeling of belonging and embeddedness in social evolution.
	Motivational	Motivational capacities include: sustaining an active, creative, and generous interest in the welfare of others; contributing significantly to the community; and making unconditional, ongoing, spontaneous, positive social effort. The feeling of community is not manifest as mere conformity; it implies a constant striving for improvement and correction toward an ideal community for all people. The feeling of community, as a value, can be adopted as the individual's primary meta-motivation. From an Adlerian viewpoint, genuine ethics are a result of a very high level of the feeling of community, and are a reflection of optimal mental health.
Early Development	**Mother**	The potential for contact and cooperation first develops between the child and mother. These capacities should be extended in ever widening social circles. She may mistakenly limit the child's interest to herself.
	Father	The father has the second chance for making a cooperative connection with the child and spreading it beyond the home. He may be able to enhance what the mother has started, or compensate for what she has been unable to accomplish.

TABLE 4.3. Stein's Developmental Sequence of the Feeling of Community (*Continued*)

Sequence		Characteristics
		Influential People and Social Adjustment
	Siblings	Brothers and sister have the third chance of stimulating a cooperative attitude and extending it to other children.
	Teachers	If the family members have not won the child's cooperation, teachers have the fourth and crucial opportunity to elicit this crucial quality. Many earlier mistakes made in the family can still be corrected in the school.
Later Development	**Friends**	Encouraging and supportive friends offer many opportunities for pursing interests and engaging in activities for mutual benefit. For some people, they may also provide an extended or substitute "family-like" network.
	Love/Sexual Partner	A mentally, emotionally, and physically intimate relationship can deeply enrich the feeling of community, both between the individuals involved, as well as between the couple and society.
	Work Associates	Meaningful work, with cooperative, encouraging, and creative associates, can validate the feeling of having made a valuable individual or team contribution.
	Spiritual Community	A spiritual community or practice may offer a feeling of belonging to a group, and sense of interconnectedness with all of life.
	Therapist	The therapist provides a safe and supportive relationship for the individual to make a trustworthy mental and emotional connection, stimulating the development of a mutually respectful cooperation. This experience must then be extended to others in that individual's life.
Adjustment	**Normal**	The feeling of community is the Adlerian barometer of mental health. It also provides a positive compensation for the normal inferiority feeling, by generating the knowledge of being genuinely valuable—which originates from contributing to the common welfare.
	Maladjustment	All forms of social failure and psychological disorder reveal a lack of a sufficient feeling of community. Problems are approached or avoided without adequate cooperation, and fictional goals of personal superiority are pursued, yielding imagined triumphs or defeats that have only private meaning and value.

Note: Henry T. Stein claims this Table is based on concepts originally developed by Heinz Ansbacher and that this is a work in progress.
Source: Stein, H. T. (2003). *Developmental sequence of the feeling of community*. San Francisco: Alfred Adler Institute of San Francisco and Northwestern Washington. Retrieved September 24, 2006, from http://ourworld. compuserve.com/homepages/hstein/dev-si.htm.

schema means conferring to that object one or several meanings" (Piaget, Jonckheere, & Mandelbrot, 1958, p. 59). Children will use *accommodation* when the pattern in the situations does not match the children's repertoire of schemes. Then they may not assimilate the incident or they may attempt to alter an existing scheme. Piaget (1963) states:

> New objects which present themselves to consciousness do not have their own qualities which can be isolated ... they are vague, nebulous, because in assimilable, and thus they create a discomfort from which there emerges sooner or later a new differentiation of the schemas of assimilation. (p. 141)

An instinctual balance, or *equilibrium,* develops between the assimilation and accommodation actions when the children's cognitive patterns evolve and interact with their environment. This *equilibrium* continues until new information initiates the process again. Adjusting to the environment is achieved through the assimilation and accommodation processes; therefore, within the children's biological-mental self the function of *organization* occurs to adequately combine all schemes that have pertinently conformed to each other. Piaget (1963) assumes that

> It is sufficiently well known that every intellectual operation is always related to all the others and that its own elements are controlled by the same law. Every schema is thus coordinated with all the other schemata and itself constitutes a totality with differentiated parts. Every act of intelligence presupposes a system of mutual implications and interconnected meanings. (p. 7)

Many perceive that Piaget's theory is a contrast to the theory of behaviorism. Children's play behavior represents Piaget's idea

TABLE 4.4. Piaget's Stages of Intellectual Development

Stage	Characteristics	Age
Sensorimotor	Children develop schemas based on sensory input and bodily motion.	Birth–$1\frac{1}{2}$ or 2 years
Preoperational	Children develop language and other symbolic representations. Intuitive thought is not systematic or sustained.	2–7 years
Concrete operational	Children deal with logical processes, can deal with only one form of classification at a time, logical thought requires actual physical objects or events.	7–11 years
Formal operational	Children reason logically; formulate and test hypotheses; think abstract.	11 years +

From Spodek, B., & Saracho, O. N. (1994). *Right from the start: Teaching children ages three to eight.* Boston: Allyn & Bacon.

TABLE 4.5. Vygotsky's Stages of Cultural Development

Stage I	Thinking in *unorganized congeries* or heaps. During this period the child puts things in groups (and may assign the group a label) on the basis of what are only chance links in the child's perception.
Stage II	Thinking in *complexes*. Individual objects are united in the child's mind not only by subjective impressions but also by bonds that actually exist among the objects. This is a step away from egocentric thinking and in the direction of objectivity. In a complex, the bonds between components are *concrete* and *factual* to some degree rather than abstract and logical. Five types of complexes succeed one another during this stage of thought.
Stage III	Thinking in *concepts*. On the threshold of this final major stage, we will pause and inspect two paths of thought and development—*synthesizing* and *analyzing*—that have converged to make conceptual thinking possible (Thomas, 2004, pp. 335-336).

of *equilibration*. When children play, they assimilate new information and accommodate to their intellectual frameworks. In this process, the children's knowledge systems resemble those of the adults, thus, becoming effective, competent, thinking grown-ups. Piaget identifies four major stages of cognitive development (See Table 4.4), in which children progress in a normal sequence and at their own developmental rate. Experiences and their own maturing abilities prompt this progress.

Piaget's theory suggests that to the degree that young children are intellectually competent, they process information and develop concepts, though in a way that is different from older children and adults. They construct knowledge through appropriate experiences; just talking to them is not enough.

Lev Semenovich Vygotsky (1896–1934) believed that children develop naturally as a result of maturation, while other forms of knowledge come from cultural transmission. Their thinking patterns are developed through their experiences in the culture in which they grow up. In addition, their advanced modes of thought (conceptual thinking) are verbally transmitted, which makes language essential to assess their thinking ability. That is, if they experience simplistic or "primitive" language, their thinking will be the same. In contrast, if they experience a language environment with varied and complex concepts, their thinking will be divergent and intricate, provided that their initial biological equipment (sense organic, central nervous system) is not handicapped. Vygotsky introduced three stages of cultural development (See Table 4.5), which are divided into substages (Thomas, 2004).

According to Vygotsky, children develop through their *zone of proximal development*, which is at the level they are able to function independently through a support system such as more mature thinkers.

Jerome Bruner's (1915–) primary theoretical framework indicates that learning is an active process in which learners use their present and past knowledge to construct new ideas or concepts. Learners use their cognitive structure to choose and process information and then develop hypotheses and make decisions. Their cognitive structure (i.e., schema, mental models) creates meaning and organization to the individuals' experiences, which helps them to "go beyond the information given."

As a structural theorist, Bruner assumes that information or knowledge is acquired through personal discovery. He shows how thought processes are subdivided into three distinct modes of reasoning. Bruner posits three modes of thought:

1. *Enactive mode.* Individuals use actions to stand for information (e.g., tying a shoe).
2. *Iconic mode*: Individuals use visual images to interpret information (e.g., thinking of someone's face).
3. *Symbolic mode*: Individuals use language.

Bruner proposes that cognition moves from an *enactive* to an *iconic* and finally to a *symbolic* mode of representation (See Table 4.6). Young infants interpret the world *enactively*. Children physically behave the way they think, which justifies the *enactive* mode of representation. Infants who clutch a rattle are communicating the thought that they want the rattle. Usually two- or three-year-olds are at the *iconic* mode. Children manifest an action through a sensory image, which may be visual in nature, auditory, tactile, or kinesthetic (Pylyshun, 2001). In this mode young children can have a mental "image" of a person who is absent, a previously performed action, or a situation that they have just witnessed. Five- or six-year-olds are usually at the *symbolic* mode. They try to convey experience. Language assists children to represent their experiences and helps them manipulate and change them. Infants learn language as a tool of thought and action in a combined mode (Bruner, 1983). Knowledge evolves through the same stages as representation in intellectual development, where they understand by doing, visualizing, and representing symbolically.

Later Bruner's (1986, 1990, 1996) theoretical framework included the social and cultural aspects of learning. His theoretical framework

TABLE 4.6. Bruner's Stages of Cognitive Development

Age	Stage	Characteristics
Infants	*enactive mode*	Infants interpret the world *enactively*. Children physically behave the way they think, which justifies the *enactive* mode of representation.
		Infants who clutch a rattle are communicating the thought that they want the rattle.
2 or 3 years	*iconic mode*	Children manifest an action through a sensory image, which may be visual in nature, auditory, tactile, or kinesthetic (Pyly-shun, 2001). In this mode young children can have a mental "image" of a person who is absent, a previously performed action, or a situation that they have just witnessed.
5 or 6 years	*symbolic mode*	Children try to convey experience. Language assists children to represent their experiences and helps them manipulate and change them.

is more in common with Vygotskian theory than with Piagetian Theory. Bruner believes that (1) young children need to make sense of the world, (2) mature thinkers need to assume an active role in assisting young children to develop their thinking, (3) learning influences development, and (4) intellectual development occurs within the cultural context of the child (Bruner, 1990).

Ecological Theory

In ecological theory the environment affects the children's lives and their development. This theory considers the whole child is an integrated organism that is affected by environmental elements. Development advances through small, supplementary quantities that sporadically increase to develop the personality through the integration of the children's repertoire of experiences. Since a new stimulus or experience adds a new ingredient to the children's knowledge, new meaningful experiences can modify the existing elements that contribute to the individuals' unique personality (Thomas, 2004). Urie Bronfenbrenner is the main proponent of ecological theory in child development.

Urie Bronfenbrenner (1917–2005) believed that the ecology of human development provides an understanding of how the active, growing human being relates to the environment. He examined the relationship between the children's immediate settings and those settings that are imposed. Bronfenbrenner explored the children's interpretations of their environment. Bronfenbrenner (1979) assumes that

1. The phenomenological (internally interpreted or experienced) environment dominates the real environment in guiding behavior.

2. It is folly to try to understand a child's action solely from the objective qualities of an environment without learning what those qualities mean for the child in that setting.

3. It is important to discover how the objects, people and events in the situation affect the child's motivations, and

4. It is essential to recognize the influence on behavior of "unreal" elements that arise from the child's imagination, fantasy, and idiosyncratic interpretations (pp. 24–25).

Bronfenbrenner's theory has had an impact in social policy. He has provided support to consider the home, school, community, and culture in the children's development.

THEORIES AND SOCIALIZATION

While the developmental theorists' concepts may overlap, they differ in the way that each theory relates to the various development areas. Several theories concentrate on all developmental areas, whereas others focus on only a narrow range of development (e.g., intellectual or socioemotional). They may also differ in their perception concerning the individuals' genetic makeup (nature) or may believe that the children's experiences (nurture) are essential in their development. Theorists, like Gesell, assume that nature influences the individuals' development; whereas a mediocre environment can restrict the individuals' predominant development. He believed that the individuals' environment has a minor influence on their development. Other theorists, like Bruner and Vygotsky, propose that the children's experiences contributes to a major degree to the individual's final development, particularly in relation to their cultural development. Many assume that both theories need to be considered. However, the family is the primary environmental influence, especially in the social context where children are raised. Developmental theories in conjunction with research describe the children's normal and average development, although many of them differ from the average. Norms provide a gauge on what to expect of the children; however, such early assessments must be individually altered for each individual child.

REFERENCES

Bronfenbrenner, U. (1979). *The ecology of human development: Experiments by nature and design.* Cambridge, MA: Harvard University Press.

Bruner, J. (1983). *Child's talk: Learning to use language.* New York: Norton.

Bruner, J. (1986). *Actual minds, possible worlds.* Cambridge, MA: Harvard University Press.

Bruner, J. (1990). *Acts of meaning.* Cambridge, MA: Harvard University Press.

Bruner, J. (1996). *The culture of education.* Cambridge, MA: Harvard University Press. Erikson, E. (1963). *Childhood and society.* New York: Norton.

Erikson, E. H. (1968). *Identity: Youth and crisis.* New York: Norton.

Erikson, E. (1982). *The life cycle completed: A review.* New York: Norton.

Piaget, J. (1963). *The origins of intelligence in children.* New York: Norton.

Piaget, J., Jonckheere, A., & Mandelbrot, B. (1958). *La lecture de l'expérience.* Études d'Epistemologie Génétique V. Paris: Presses Universitaires de France.

Pylyshun, Z. (2001). Is the imagery debate over? If so, what was it about? In E. Dupoux (Ed.), *Language, brain and cognitive development: Essays in honor of Jacques Mehler* (pp. 59–83). Cambridge, MA: MIT Press.

Savage, A. M., & Nicholl, S. W. (2003). *Faith, hope, and charity as character traits in Adler's individual psychology.* Lanham, MD: University Press of America.

Seligman, L. (2006). *Theories of counseling and psychotherapy: Systems, strategies, and skills.* Upper Saddle River, NJ: Prentice Hall.

Spodek, B., & Saracho, O. N. (1994). *Right from the start: Teaching children ages three to eight.* Boston: Allyn & Bacon.

Stein, H. T. (2003). *Developmental sequence of the feeling of community.* San Francisco: Alfred Adler Institute of San Francisco and Northwestern Washington. Retrieved September 24, 2006, from http://ourworld.compuserve.com/homepages/hstein/dev-si.htm.

Sullivan, H. S. (1953). *The interpersonal theory of psychiatry.* New York: Norton.

Thomas, R. M. (2004). *Comparing theories of development.* Belmont, CA: Wadsworth. CH01—17

The Sociology of Punishment and Punishment Today

by David Garland

1. THE PROBLEM OF PUNISHMENT TODAY

The aim of this book is simple. It sets out to provide a rounded sociological account of punishment in modern society, showing—at least in outline—how penal processes come to exist in their present form and with what kinds of consequences. To this end it employs the interpretative tools of social theory and the information and insights produced by historical studies, together with materials which are more properly penological.[1]

Such a straightforward project inevitably entails some presumptions which are not quite so straightforward. Most importantly, it presumes that juridical punishment is not the transparent and rather self-evident institution of crime control that it is commonly taken to be. Were this the case, a study of this kind would be rather unnecessary, there being little need to restate the obvious. But in fact punishment's role in modern society is not at all obvious or well known. Punishment today is a deeply problematic and barely understood aspect of social life, the rationale for which is by no means clear. That it is not always perceived as such is a consequence of the obscuring and reassuring effect of established institutions, rather than the transparent rationality of penal practices themselves.

Like all habitual patterns of social action, the structures of modern punishment have created a sense of their own inevitability and of the necessary rightness of the status quo. Our taken-for-granted ways of punishing have relieved us of the need for thinking deeply about punishment and what little thinking we are left to do is guided along certain narrowly formulated channels.[2] Thus we are led to discuss penal policy in ways which assume the current institutional framework, rather than question it—as when we consider how best to run prisons, organize probation, or enforce fines, rather than question why these measures are used in the first place. The institutions

---

1 My analyses draw primarily upon materials concerning Britain, the USA, and Canada. I do not, however, mean to imply that specific penal developments can always be explained in the same way in these different places, or that precisely the same penal policies and patterns of deployment are common to all of them.

2 On the question how institutions guide our thinking, see M. Douglas, *How Institutions Think* (Syracuse, NY, 1986), p. 69.

---

of punishment conveniently provide us with ready-made answers for the questions which crime in society would otherwise evoke. They tell us what criminality is and how it will be sanctioned, how much punishment is appropriate and what emotions can be expressed, who is entitled to punish and wherein lies their authority to do so. In consequence, these difficult and troublesome questions no longer arise. They are authoritatively settled, at least in principle, and only matters of detail need to be concluded—details which can be left to experts and administrators in specialist institutions set aside for that purpose.

Once a complex field of problems, needs, and conflicts is built over by an institutional framework in this way, these problematic and often unstable foundations disappear from view. In their place all that is immediately visible are the categories and forms of action which the established institution holds out to us. Through repeated use and respect for their authority, these instituted ways of doing things create their own 'regime of truth' which simultaneously shores up the institutional structure and closes off any fundamental questions which might undermine it. The penal system's very existence helps us to forget that other answers to these problems are possible: that institutions arc based upon convention rather than nature. For all these reasons, and for most of the twentieth century, the institutions of punishment have normally been surrounded by a sense of their own appropriateness and transparency. Questions about punishment became a matter for penologists—technical experts whose frame of reference was given by this institutional structure.

But institutions and their regimes arc not unshakeable nor beyond challenge, particularly where they fail to serve needs, contain conflicts, or answer troublesome questions in a way that is perceived as satisfactory. And, despite their institutional girding and a historical entrenchment stretching back to the early nineteenth century, a growing sense of doubt, dissatisfaction, and sheer puzzlement has now begun to emerge around our modern penal practices. The contemporary period is one in which pcnological optimism has given way to a persistent scepticism about the rationality and efficacy of modern penal institutions.[3] This shift of attitude began to emerge towards the end of the 1960s when rising crime rates, growing prison unrest, and a collapse of faith in the rehabilitative ideal combined to undermine confidence in 'penal progress' and the inevitability of 'penal reform'. The new era has been one of continuing crisis and disruption in a penal system which no longer takes seriously the rehabilitative values and ideologies upon which it was originally based. Within this context it is becoming the conventional wisdom of criminologists, penologists, and social scientists that contemporary methods—particularly that of imprisonment—appear increasingly to be 'irrational', 'dysfunctional', and downright counter-productive. Like the crime it is supposed to deal with, punishment is nowadays seen as a chronic social problem. It has become one of the most perplexing and perpetual 'crises' of modern social life, replete with intractable difficulties and disturbing results, and currently lacking any clear programme which could facilitate its reform.

---

3 Perhaps what is most in need of explanation is the persistence, since the Enlightenment, of the belief that punishment can work as a positive force for the good of the offender and for society, despite the recurring disappointments and sobering experiences of practitioners throughout this whole period. I will return to this question in ch. 8.

The most celebrated discussion of punishment's 'failure' is to be found in the work of Michel Foucault, who argued that penological failure has been a persistent—and indeed a 'functional'—characteristic of the modern prison ever since its inception. But the same presumption of failure appears in numerous other less avant-garde texts, including the work of the historian Lawrence Stone, one of Foucault's sternest critics. Stone takes it as simply uncontroversial to characterize twentieth-century prisons as 'vestigial institutions' which are 'even less useful for system maintenance than an appendix in an individual. According to this view, which is shared by many, twentieth-century prisons survive 'simply because they have taken on a quasi-independent life of their own, which enables them to survive the overwhelming evidence of their social dysfunction'.[4] And it is not just the prison that is problematic: the contemporary intuition that 'nothing works' extends with only slightly less force to probation, fines, and community corrections.

As explanations of punishment, Foucault's latent-functions approach and Stone's dead-weight-of-history suggestion raise more problems than they solve—as I will try to show in the chapters which follow. But the point of mentioning them here is to indicate the growing conviction among social scientists that the methods of modern punishment are neither obvious nor self-evidently rational; that, on the contrary, they stand in serious need of explication. Where once penal institutions appeared to offer a self-evident rationale, in the late twentieth century they increasingly come to seem less obviously appropriate. Their 'fit' with the social world and their grounding in the natural order of things begin to appear less and less convincing. It used to be that most criticism of punishment's failures and irrationalities was aimed at the past or at the soon-to-disappear present. Each critique was also, in its hope for penal reform, a kind of hymn to the future. Nowadays, punishment appears to lack a future—or at least a vision of one which might be different and preferable to that which currently prevails.[5]

Part of the problem is what Stone calls 'the overwhelming evidence of ... social dysfunction'—the by now well-known catalogue of punishment's inefficiencies (the failure of fines, probation, community corrections, and custodial measures alike substantially to reduce crime rates, the tendency of prison to create recidivists, the high social costs of penologically ineffective measures) and all the apparent irrationalities which seem to be the stock-in-trade of criminal justice. But these 'failures' can only partly explain why punishment seems increasingly problematic. In normal circumstances an established institution can finesse its failures. It can explain them away in terms which do not call into question the foundations of the organization—such as the need for more resources, minor reforms, better staff, more co-operation from other agencies, and so on. Most importantly, it can normally point to a future programme in which these problems will be better managed and the institution will reform itself. All social institutions have a margin of failure or ineffectiveness, but in

---

4 L. Stone, *The Past and the Present Revisited* (London, 1987), p. 10. On the 'failure' of punishments, see also S. Cohen, *Visions of Social Control* (Cambridge, 1985), p. 254, and D. Rothman, 'Prisons: The Failure Model', *Nation* (21 Dec. 1974), p. 647.

5 On the crisis of penal ideology, see A. E. Bottoms and R. H. Preston (eds.), *The Coming Penal Crisis* (Edinburgh, 1980), and F. Allen, *The Decline of the Rehabilitative Ideal* (New Haven, 1981).

normal circumstances this will be more or less tolerated without calling the institution itself into question. If the institution is meeting normal expectations and if its overall direction and basic legitimacy are unchallenged, then such failures are of no great consequence.

But in the case of modern punishments—whether custodial or non-custodial—a self-confidence in the established principles and an ability to redefine problems in institutional terms are currently lacking. Throughout the 1970s and 1980s the penal institutions of the United Kingdom, the United States of America, and many other Western nations have experienced a crisis of self-definition. In normal circumstances the administrators and employees of any penal system understand and justify their own actions within an established ideological framework—a working ideology. This official ideology is the set of categories, signs, and symbols through which punishment represents itself to itself and to others. Usually this ideology provides a highly developed rhetorical resource which can be used to give names, justifications, and a measure of coherence to the vast jumble of things that are done in the name of penal policy. Not the least of its uses is to supply the means to explain (or explain away) failures and to indicate the strategies which will, it is hoped, prevent their recurrence. For much of the present century, the term 'rehabilitation' was a key element of official ideology and institutional rhetoric. This all-inclusive sign provided a sense of purpose and justification for penal practice and made punishment appear meaningful for its various audiences. Today, however, this unifying and uplifting term is no longer the talismanic reference-point it once was. Following a sustained critique, the notion of rehabilitation has come to seem problematic at best, dangerous and unworkable at worst. In many jurisdictions the term—and the framework which it implies—has been struck from the official vocabulary. Elsewhere it is used cautiously and without confidence, in the absence of any effective substitute. Penal institutions have thus been deprived of the idiom, and indeed the mythology, around which modern punishment had anchored its self-definition.[6] For nearly two decades now those employed in prisons, probation, and penal administration have been engaged in an unsuccessful search to find a 'new philosophy' or a new 'rationale' for punishment. They have been forced to rethink what it is they do, and to reopen foundational questions about the justifications and purposes of penal sanctions, without so far having found a suitable set of terms upon which to rebuild an institutional identity.[7]

---

6 It is worth adding that the normalizing apparatus of enquiry, individualization, and classification which was developed in the treatment era has not been dismantled along with the abandonment of the ideal. On this, see Cohen, *Visions of Social Control.*

7 Numerous proposals for a new penal policy framework have emerged during the last two decades, the most important of them being the 'justice model' of sentencing, the 'humane containment' conception of imprisonment, and a conception of probation and community supervision as 'help' and 'support' rather than treatment. See N. Morris, *The Future of Imprisonment* (Chicago, 1974); A. von Hirsch, *Doing Justice* (New York, 1976); R. King and R. Morgan, *The Future of the Prison System* (Aldershot, 1980); and A. E. Bottoms and W. McWilliams, 'A Non-Treatment Paradigm for Probation Practice', *British Journal of Social Work*, 9 (1979), 159–202. Other proposals include 'selective incapacitation', a modified version of rehabilitation, and a 'minimalist' or even 'abolitionist' approach to criminal justice. See P. Greenwood, *Selective Incapacitation* (Santa Monica, 1982); F. T. Cullen and K. E. Gilbert, *Re-affirming Rehabilitation* (Cincinatti, 1982); N. Christie, *Limits to Pain* (Oxford, 1982), and H. Bianchi and R. van Swaaningen (eds.), *Abolitionism: Towards a Non-Repressive Approach to Crime* (Amsterdam, 1986).

If this were merely a matter of official rhetoric, or of the precise form which penal objectives should take, then we might expect a solution to be more readily available. Penal policy is, after all, a rich and flexible tradition which has always contained within itself a number of competing themes and elements, principles and counter-principles. Thus, over the last century and a half, its key terms have been developing and fluid rather than fixed, producing a series of descriptions—'moral reform', 'training', 'treatment', 'correction', 'rehabilitation', 'deterrence', 'incapacitation'—for what it is that penal sanctions do. But what seems to have come into question now, after the acknowledged failure of the most developed form of correctionalism, and in a period when Enlightenment social engineering has become deeply unfashionable, is a basic principle of modern punishment—namely the presumption that crime and deviance are social problems for which there can be a technical institutional solution. Indeed it is highly significant that the slogan which most marked this crisis of penal confidence was the phrase 'Nothing Works'—a statement which clearly conveys the instrumental means-to-an-end conception of punishment which marks the modern era.[8] Ever since the development of prisons in the early nineteenth century, and particularly since the emergence of a penological profession later in that century, there

has been an implicit claim—and eventually a public expectation—that the task of punishing and controlling deviants could be handled in a positive way by a technical apparatus. It seems to me that this basic claim has now been put in question.

The question that arises today is not one of institutional adjustment and reform. It is a more basic question which asks whether the social processes and ramifications of punishment can be contained within specialist institutions of any kind. This is, in a sense, a crisis of penological modernism. It is a scepticism about a penal project that is as old as the Enlightenment with its vision of punishment as one more means of engineering the good society, of organizing institutions so as to perfect mankind. After more than two centuries of rational optimism, even our 'experts' have begun to recognize the limits of social engineering and the dark side of social order. Our engineered world is facing its imperfections and is less optimistic, less confident. In the penal debates of the 1980s, we hear again, for the first time in almost two centuries, the re-emergence of basic moral and organizational questions. Lacking a new vocabulary, and dissatisfied with the modern institution's own terms, much of this discussion has looked back to the period immediately before the modern penal era. Contemporary proponents of 'the justice model' or of 'general deterrence' have revived the liberal discourse of eighteenth-century jurisprudence, raising basic questions about the right to punish, the limits on state power, the responsibility and dignity of the offender, the nature of criminality, the depiction of human nature, and so on. There have also been important attempts to reintroduce questions which had previously been silenced by institutional operations, such as the role of the victim, or the responsibilities

---

8 The slogan refers to the celebrated article by Martinson which surveyed the treatment research literature and reached a largely negative conclusion about the general efficacy of treatment programmes in penal settings. See R. Martinson, 'What Works?—Questions and Answers about Prison Reform', *The Public Interest*, 35 (1974). For a similarly negative evaluation of the British evidence, see S. R. Brody, 'The Effectiveness of Sentencing', *Home Office Research Unit Study*, 35 (London, 1976).

of the community in causing and preventing criminality. Notably too, there has been a re-emergence of moral arguments that claim that punitive (as opposed to correctional) measures can be a proper and defensible form of reaction to crime, a form of thinking which has been markedly absent from most twentieth-century penal discourse.

These newly revived forms of thinking about punishment are significant, not because they represent solutions to the current malaise, but because they indicate the extent of it. In returning to the consideration of basic moral and political questions, these discussions indicate the fading of our penal institutions' ability to naturalize their practices and depict the world in their terms. Questions about the meaning of punishment do not, these days, get immediately translated into the established terms of an institutional ideology. They are instead perceived as troublesome and unsettled. And of course in these circumstances, such questions begin to emerge with more and more frequency.

It is not, then, only social scientists who are nowadays led to doubt the grounding and rationale of modern modes of punishment. The very staff of the criminal justice institutions are themselves increasingly perplexed as to what they are about. Consequently, it is not an idle or an 'academic' question that is being pursued when we seek to understand the foundations, forms, and effects of penal measures as they exist today. It is, on the contrary, a pressing practical issue.

Like all books, then, this one is a product of its times and circumstances. The past two decades have been years in which we seem to have come up against the limits of a certain way of thinking and acting in the field of punishment. Like many others, I have been led to

reflect upon the roots of penal policy, and its social ramifications, instead of getting on with the job of improving and refining it. Indeed, at a time when penology was marked by sadly diminishing returns, this reflection upon fundamentals has been the abiding fascination of an otherwise narrow and unsettling field of study. The last 10 years or so have seen a sudden take-off in the number of studies in the history and sociology of punishment, no doubt because these forms of research are strongly drawn towards areas which appear currently to be problematic or undergoing transition. Indeed this new work on the foundations of punishment is in marked contrast to what went on before. In the mid-1950s, at the height of the correctional era in the USA, Donald Cressey asked why the sociology of punishment was such a neglected area of study—particularly, he might have added, given the landmark contributions of earlier writers such as Montesquieu, De Tocqueville and Durkheim.[9] Thirty years later and with the benefit of hindsight we can answer that in these years a technical penology, working within the institutions, was able to dominate the field and to limit the range of questions which appeared appropriate or worth while. It was a period of 'normal science', operating in circumstances where the axioms and problems had been authoritatively stated, and all that remained was to work out the details and fine-tune the institutional machinery. Now, however, when penologists have lost faith in the institutional project and have become critical and self-reflective, they are beginning once again to reassess the axioms upon which

---

9   D. R. Cressey, "Hypotheses in the Sociology of Punishment', *Sociology and Social Research*, 39 (1955), 394–400.

punishment is based. In this task, social theory and history prove more useful than penology, and increasingly these are the forms of enquiry which are being brought to bear.

Faced with the kinds of problems which I have described, one response would be to turn once again to the issue of justification and re-examine the normative arguments supplied by the philosophy of punishment. This, indeed, has been the course adopted by many writers in this field who feel that a careful reading of moral philosophy—usually of a liberal variety—can somehow supply the guidelines for a new and more acceptable programme of penal policy.[10] But in my view, there are reasons why such a project is both premature and misdirected. It seems to me that at present we lack a detailed appreciation of the nature of punishment, of its character as a social institution, and of its role in social life. The philosophies of punishment, at least in their traditional form, are based upon a rather idealized and one-dimensional image of punishment: an image which poses the problem of punishment as a variant of the classic liberal conundrum of how the state should relate to the individual.[11] But if, as I suspect, this image is an impoverished one, and fails to capture the full dimensions and complexities of punishment, then the solutions offered by philosophy are unlikely to match up to the problems of the institution. What is needed now is really a preliminary

to philosophy—a descriptive prolegomenon which sets out the social foundations of punishment, its characteristic modern forms, and its social significance. Only on this basis can philosophies be developed which adequately address the normative problems of this complex institution. Quite simply, we need to know what punishment is in order to think what it can and should be.

2. THE SOCIOLOGY OF PUNISHMENT

The present study is thus conceived as a work in the sociology of punishment or, more precisely, in the sociology of criminal law, criminal justice, and penal sanctioning.[12] Moving from the premiss that penal phenomena in modern society are problematic and badly understood, it seeks to explore the penal realm in all its different aspects, reopening basic questions about punishment's social foundations, seeking to chart its functions and its effects. Its ultimate aim is to uncover the structures of social action and the webs of cultural meaning within which modern punishment actually operates, thereby providing a proper descriptive basis for normative judgments about penal policy.

---

10   See e.g. von Hirsch, *Doing Justice* (New York, 1976) and P. Bean, *Punishment* (Oxford, 1981).

11   On the connections between the philosophy of punishment and the political philosophy of liberalism, see N. Lacey, *State Punishment* (London, 1988). On the deficiencies of the current philosophical approaches to punishment, see D. Garland, 'Philosophical Argument and Ideological Effect', *Contemporary Crises*, 7 (1983), 79–85.

12   Unfortunately we currently lack any widely used generic term which usefully describes the whole process of criminalizing and penalizing with which I intend to deal. In previous works I have adopted the term 'penality' to refer to the complex of laws, processes, discourses, and institutions which are involved in this sphere, and I will use it throughout the present study as a synonym for legal punishment in this broad sense. In some contemporary literature, the term 'social control' has come to be used in a similar way, see Cohen, *Visions of Social Control*, p. 3. I have, however, avoided this usage because 'social control' usually refers to a much wider range of practices, and also because, as we will see, I wish to argue that 'punishment' should not be thought of purely in terms of 'control'.

I take the sociology of punishment, broadly conceived, to be that body of thought which explores the relations between punishment and society, its purpose being to understand punishment as a social phenomenon and thus trace its role in social life. Being concerned with punishment and penal institutions, it shares its central subject-matter with 'penology', but is distinguishable from the latter by virtue of its wider parameters of study. Whereas penology situates itself within penal institutions and seeks to attain a knowledge of their internal 'penological' functioning (thoughout the nineteenth century 'penology' was a synonym for 'penitentiary science'), the sociology of punishment views the institutions from the outside, as it were, and seeks to understand their role as one distinctive set of social processes situated within a wider social network.

Writings which take this latter, sociological, form have existed since at least the mid-eighteenth century—emerging then, as now, at a time when the established institutions of punishment were coming under critical attack. In *The Spirit of the Laws*, Montesquieu pointed to the connections of structure and of belief which tied forms of punishing to forms of governing in a distinctive and revealing way: 'It would be an easy matter', he wrote, 'to prove that in all, or almost all, of the governments of Europe, punishments have increased or diminished in proportion as these governments favoured or discouraged liberty.'[13] From there he went on to sketch in outline the political and psychological dynamics which produce these connections, thus giving a sociological as well as a normative quality to his conclusion that 'the severity of punishment is fitter for despotic governments, whose principle is terror, than for a monarchy or republic, whose spring is honour and virtue'.[14] Almost a century later, Alexis de Tocqueville continued in this vein, though his study of the American penitentiary system suggested a more complex and ironic link between political liberalism and penal discipline. Pointing to an irony which would be rediscovered by subsequent writers such as Rothman and Foucault, he wrote in the 1830s that 'while society in the United States gives the example of the most extended liberty, the prisons of the same country offer the spectacle of the most complete despotism'.[15] In his subsequent study of *Democracy in America*, de Tocqueville would build upon this social insight afforded by punishment to show the subtle dialectic of freedom and restraint which operated within American society as a whole. These connecting insights, showing how punishment forms part of a wider culture, shaping and being shaped by it, have been the continuing hallmark of work of this kind. Indeed the issues posed by Montesquieu and de Tocqueville continue to be discussed and researched today.[16]

Despite these suggestive early works, however, the sociology of punishment has not become a well-developed area of social thought. With the partial exception of institutional studies of imprisonment, where a strong sociological research tradition has been founded,[17] the corpus of works is disparate

---

13 Baron de Montesquieu, *The Spirit of the Laws* (Edinburgh, 1762), p. 88.

14 Ibid.

15 G. de Beaumont and A. de Tocqueville, *On the Penitentiary System in the United States* (Philadelphia, 1833), p. 47.

16 See e.g. T. L. Dunn, *Democracy and Punishment: Disciplinary Origins of the United States* (Madison, 1987).

17 See D. Clemmer, *The Prison Community* (New York, 1940); R. Cloward *et al.*, *Theoretical Studies in Social Organisation of the Prison* (New York, 1960);

and uneven in quality, and lacks any settled research agenda which can command widespread assent and promote a sense of collective endeavour. Instead what one finds is a series of disjointed and unconnected studies, emanating from a diverse range of projects and intellectual traditions, and adopting quite different angles of approach to the study of punishment. Within this series of studies there are works of the highest intellectual calibre—like those of Émile Durkheim, Michel Foucault, or George Herbert Mead—and also other important studies by authors such as Rusche and Kirchheimer, Michael Ignatieff and Douglas Hay, all of which have provoked follow-up studies, criticism, and a fairly large secondary literature. But despite the fact that these studies all take punishment as their object and offer sociological explanations and characterizations of penal phenomena, they do not by any means form a coherent body of research. On the contrary, the sociology of punishment is presently constituted by a diverse variety of 'perspectives', each of which tends to develop its researches in virtual disregard of other ways of proceeding. In effect, the sociology of punishment is reinvented with each subsequent study, so that on each occasion we are presented with a new conception of the phenomena to be studied and the proper questions to be posed.

To some extent this clash of perspectives and absence of a settled paradigm is an endemic characteristic of all sociology, and has to do with the incorrigibly 'interpreted' nature of its object. But there are also a number of reasons why this situation seems particularly aggravated

in the sociology of punishment. In the first place, punishment—unlike other areas of social life such as religion, industry, or the family—has not been the site of intensive sociological enquiry, and has not been subjected to the rationalizing processes of discipline formation that modern scholarship normally entails. There are as yet no established textbooks or course descriptions which pattern the conduct of study in this field, or situate particular studies within an overarching discipline. Related to this is the fact that many of the leading studies in this area have been undertaken as aspects of a larger and different intellectual project, rather than as contributions to the sociology of punishment itself. For both Durkheim and Foucault, for example, punishment serves as a key with which to unlock a larger cultural text such as the nature of social solidarity or the disciplinary character of Western reason. Their concern has not been to help develop a comprehensive understanding of punishment—and although they do in fact contribute to such an understanding, this has been a by-product of their work rather than its central purpose. Few of the major authors in this field have conceived of themselves as partaking in a joint project or sharing a basic set of concerns and so there is little attempt to promote integration or synthesis. There has also been a tendency for different perspectives to be viewed—or to view themselves—as being in complete conflict with one another. This sense of incompatibility most often emerges where specific analyses of punishment are derived from global social theories—such as Marxism, or Durkheimian functionalism—which are, quite properly, viewed as being competing metaconceptions of society and its dynamics. Moreover, in the clash between one perspective and another, analytical differences often take on an ideological inflection as well—making

---

G. Sykes, *The Society of Captives* (Princeton, 1958); T. Morris and P. Morris, *Pentonville* (London, 1963); J. B. Jacobs, *Stateville: The Penitentiary in Mass Society* (Chicago, 1977); E. Goffman, *Asylums* (Garden City, NY, 1961).

communication between perspectives that much less likely.

To some extent these different approaches do indeed represent serious and unbridgeable disagreements about the character of the social world and the place of punishment within it. No amount of scholarly co-operation will efface the fact that sociology's objects are essentially contested and open to competing interpretations. But as things stand in the sociology of punishment, it is not at all clear where the key disagreements lie, or indeed to what extent different perspectives are in fact complementary rather than being in competition, at least at some levels of analysis. Two points are worth making in this respect—one about the nature of theory, and the other about levels of analysis.

It is, at present, possible to point to at least four distinctive theoretical perspectives within the sociology of punishment, three of them already established, and a fourth which is in the process of emerging. The Durkheimian tradition stresses punishment's moral and social-psychological roots as well as its putative solidarity-producing effects. Marxist studies highlight punishment's role in what it takes to be class-based processes of social and economic regulation. Michel Foucault's work has argued that disciplinary punishments operate as power—knowledge mechanisms within wider strategies of domination and subjectification, while the work of Norbert Elias has prompted writers such as Spierenburg to situate punishment within an analysis of changing sensibilities and cultural mentalities. None of these interpretative perspectives is absurd or without merit. They each make serious claims for our attention because they each have something important to say about their object of study. Moreover, as even this

brief characterization suggests, they are each concerned to bring into view different aspects of what turns out to be a rather complex set of penal phenomena. Each of them has a capacity to make visible particular aspects of a possibly complicated and many-sided reality and connect these aspects to wider social processes. Each mode of enquiry sets up a particular image of punishment, defining it in a particular way, highlighting some of the aspects, while inevitably obscuring or neglecting others.

If we treat these interpretations as representing a variety of perspectives—each one employing a different angle of approach and a shifting focus of attention—then there is no in-principle reason why they should not be brought together to help us understand a complex object in its various aspects and relations. However it is all too common for questions of interpretation—which are capable of multiple answers—to be understood as questions of ontology or of causal priority, in which case only a singular response will suffice. Once this occurs, and we assume that all theories are attempts to answer the questions 'what is the essential nature of punishment?' or 'what is *the* cause of punishment?' then we are always forced to choose between one or the other theoretical account. The result is an approach which tends to be needlessly reductionist and one-dimensional in its understanding.[18]

My point is simply that if we avoid this philosophical essentialism, then it is not clear that such choices are always necessary. Theories are conceptual means of interpreting and

---

18 As William Gass puts it, 'when we try to think philosophically about any human activity, we tend to single out one aspect as the explanatory center, crown it, and make every other element into a courtier, mistress, or servant'. W. Gass, 'Painting as an Art', *New York Review of Books*, 35: 15 (13 Oct. 1988), p. 48.

explicating information. They come into competition only when they offer alternative and incompatible explanations for the same data. Since one theory effectively supersedes another only when it explains the same range of data and problems more plausibly, it is by no means clear how the various theories of punishment stand in relation to each other. Indeed, in the sociology of punishment, theories have not been superseded so much as passed over in preference for other lines of questioning.

The point I wish to make about levels of analysis is rather similar. It is certainly the case that grand social theories such as those developed by Marx, Durkheim, or Elias give incompatible accounts of the central dynamics of social life. (Foucault's work is incompatible for the different reason that it denies the validity of theories pitched at this global level.) If it were the case that the analyses of punishment which derive from these various traditions were no more than miniaturizations of the larger global theories then all the incompatibilities would be reproduced at this more detailed level. But this in fact is not the case. Specific analyses which are launched from within a certain set of axioms will tend to ask distinctive questions, and focus upon particular aspects of the phenomenon under study, in accordance with the dictates of the general theory. But the findings produced in this way will not be mere reproductions of the global social theory—unless, of course, we are dealing with deductive dogmatics, in which case the theory is not being 'applied' but merely repeated.

Concrete spheres of social life, such as punishment, are never exact microcosms of the social structures depicted by general theory. Outside Leibnizian philosophy—in which every monadic element is an essential expression of the whole—each particular sector of society can be assumed to display its own peculiar mechanisms and dynamics. And so, in any process of theoretical interpretation which is open to empirical information, the concrete character of the phenomenon should help determine the analytical results as much as the set of axioms which launched the enquiry. This being the case, the specific findings of any theory brought to bear upon punishment may or may not be compatible with others produced from within a different interpretative perspective. The question of their relationship is always an empirical one, and is not settled in advance. Thus, for example, Marxist analyses may discover ways in which penal practice reinforces class divisions and ruling-class dominance, and Durkheimian studies may point to other elements of the penal process which appear to express sentiments or reinforce solidarities which are not class based. Unless one assumes that penal practice is all of a piece, with a single, unitary meaning—that it is all a matter of class, or all a matter of cross-class solidarity—there is no reason to reject either analysis out of hand. Instead what is required is a more subtle, in-depth analysis which examines how these two aspects seem to coexist within the complex set of practices which make up the penal realm. In the pages which follow, I will attempt to explore such issues and see to what extent a more comprehensive sociology can be constructed out of the specific interpretations which currently exist.

If, then, we are committed to a comprehensive examination of the structures and meanings of punishment in modern society, there appears to be no ready-to-hand general framework within the sociology of punishment which will allow us to pursue this enquiry. Instead we find a range of interpretative traditions, each one projecting a slightly different image of punishment and its connection with the rest of the social world, and each one bearing an as-yet-indeterminate relationship to the others. Given this situation, the best strategy appears to be one which is inclusive and open to synthesis, at least in the first instance. My intention is therefore to work through each of the existing theoretical traditions in turn, treating each tradition not as a rigid model or comprehensive account, but as a source of specific perspectives and partial interpretations. My method will be to identify and pursue the distinctive questions that each one poses and to examine what they have to say about the foundations, functions, and effects of punishment, and how this helps us understand punishment today. This will go beyond mere exposition, not least because much of the theory of punishment lies buried within detailed historical narratives, or else exists in a rudimentary form which needs to be worked up and refined. Moreover, I will frequently press arguments and lines of analysis beyond their original scope and sketch out new modes of interpretation wherever the established theories appear inadequate. The aim of this approach is to bring to light as many facets of punishment as possible, and also to bring the different interpretations into conversation with one another, so that their differences can be precisely specified and their complementary aspects can be shown as such. The outcome, it is hoped, will be a balanced synopsis of what the sociology of punishment has to offer, and a suggestion of how these ideas help us to understand the nature of punishment today.

The sociological accounts of punishment that we currently possess have each isolated and abstracted a particular aspect or facet of punishment and have provided powerful analyses based upon this. But although such interpretations can often be brilliantly illuminating and insightful, they are also prone to be partial and somewhat one-sided. One symptom of this is the tendency of historians of punishment, seeking to convey a rounded sense of the institution as it is operated at a particular time and place, to write *against* such theories, showing their monolithic interpretations to be incomplete at best, and completely untenable at worst. But the real point of their complaint is not that historians do not need theory. It is that theories which are too narrow in compass simply act as an obstacle to understanding and need to be replaced by better theories which will be more adequate to their task. A measure of abstraction is a necessary first step in the analysis of any complex phenomenon, and it is not unusual for a field of knowledge in its early stages of development to be characterized by competing abstractions and monocausal forms of explanation. But the ultimate objective of research must be to return to the concrete, to integrate and synthesize different abstractions in a way that simulates the overdetermination of real-world objects and approximates their complex wholeness. It seems to me that the sociology of punishment is now reaching that stage of maturity where it should be striving for integrated, pluralistic interpretations—interpretations which can come closer to accounting for the complexity and variegated detail which both historians and contemporary penologists repeatedly encounter.[19]

---

19 Such an endeavour will not settle, once and for all, interpretative disputes, but it ought to focus them more precisely and make them more productive. As Clifford Geertz says of cultural anthropology, it 'is a science whose progress is marked less by a perfection of consensus than by a refinement of debate. What gets better is the precision with which we vex each other.' C. Geertz, 'Thick Description: Toward an Interpretive

The present project then, is an attempt to extend and synthesize the range of interpretative material that currently forms the sociology of punishment, and to build up a more complete picture of how punishment might be understood in modern society. The writings of Foucault, Marx, Durkheim, or Elias excel in the tenacious, dogged pursuit of an explanatory theme—making a wilful attempt to drive a mode of thinking as far as it will go. As a means of discovery, or a way of producing new interpretative insight, this method can hardly be bettered, though, as we have seen, a kind of peripheral, contextual blindness is sometimes the price of this intensely focused vision. In the present study, however, different methods and values come to the fore. Its concern is to be balanced and perspicacious, synthesizing and comprehensive, and in so doing it will necessarily qualify the claims of these theorists, and suggest the limitations of their accounts. But it should perhaps be stressed that this book is not about the limitations of other theorists. It is about the constructive enterprise that their single-minded theorizing has made possible.

3. PUNISHMENT AS AN OBJECT OF STUDY

Having discussed the various interpretative stances adopted towards punishment, it is perhaps time to say something about punishment itself. The first point to note here is that 'punishment', despite this singular generic noun, is not a singular kind of entity. Indeed it seems likely that some of the variation of interpretative results which one finds in the sociology of punishment has to do with the nature of the thing analysed, rather than with the analytical process brought to bear upon it. We need to remind ourselves, again and again, that the phenomenon which we refer to, too simply, as 'punishment', is in fact a complex set of interlinked processes and institutions, rather than a uniform object or event. On close inspection, it becomes apparent that the different interpretative perspectives have tended to focus in upon quite different aspects or stages of this multifaceted process. Thus when Pashukanis discusses the ideological forms of the criminal law, Durkheim focuses upon condemnatory rituals, Foucault shifts attention to institutional routines, and Spierenburg points to the sensibilities involved, each of them is, in effect, moving back and forth between different phases of the penal process, rather than producing different interpretations of the same thing. Unfortunately though, such differences of focus have often been disguised by a lack of analytical specificity and by the failure of individual theorists to place their own work in the context of other interpretations. Given the synthesizing concerns of this study, it is important that it begins by discussing this question in some detail, and that in subsequent analyses it avoids this tendency to discuss 'punishment' as if it were all of a piece.

An observation made by Friedrich Nietzsche can serve to orient our discussion.

I would say that in a very late culture such as our present-day European culture the notion 'punishment' has not one but a great many meanings. The whole history of punishment and of its adaptation to the most various uses has finally crystallized into a kind of complex which it is difficult to break down and quite impossible to define.

Theory of Culture', in id. *The Interpretation of Cultures* (New York, 1973), p. 29.

... All terms which semiotically condense a whole process elude definition; only that which has no history can be defined.[20]

Punishment, then, is not reducible to a single meaning or a single purpose. It is not susceptible to a logical or formulaic definition (as some philosophers of punishment would have it) because it is a social institution embodying and 'condensing' a range of purposes and a stored-up depth of historical meaning. To understand 'punishment' at a particular time, as Nietzsche says, one has to explore its many dynamics and forces and build up a complex picture of the circuits of meaning and action within which it currently functions. This is precisely what the present study aims to do. But if such an investigation is to be undertaken, then clearly some parameters or co-ordinates of study have to be outlined—not as a substitute for empirical enquiry but as a guide to it. It is in this sense, and with this purpose, that I offer the following identification of my object of study.

Punishment is taken here to be the legal process whereby violators of the criminal law are condemned and sanctioned in accordance with specified legal categories and procedures. This process is itself complex and differentiated, being composed of the interlinked processes of law-making, conviction, sentencing, and the administration of penalties. It involves discursive frameworks of authority and condemnation, ritual procedures of imposing punishment, a repertoire of penal sanctions, institutions and agencies for the enforcement of sanctions and a rhetoric of symbols, figures, and images by means of which the penal process is represented to its various audiences. Two things should follow from this fact of internal differentiation. The first is that discussions of 'punishment' can have a whole range of possible referents which are all properly part of this institutional complex. The second is that the penal process is likely to exhibit internal conflicts and ambiguities, stemming from its fragmented character. As noted above, I have tried to capture this sense of internal complexity by proposing the generic term 'penality' to refer to the network of laws, processes, discourses, representations and institutions which make up the penal realm, and I will use this term as a more precise synonym for 'punishment' in its wider sense.

This focus upon the legal punishment of criminal law offenders means that although punishment also takes place outside the legal system—in schools, families, workplaces, military establishments, and so on—these forms of punitive practice will largely be left out of the present study. Punishment in some form or other is probably an intrinsic property of all settled forms of association and there is much to be learned from viewing punishment in these various social settings. Despite being derivative in a certain sense—in that all penal domains in modern society depend upon the delegation of authority from the sovereign legal order—these forms have their own specificity and are not mere imitations of state punishments. They will, however, be considered here only where their discussion can further our understanding of the legal order of punishment and not as a topic in themselves.[21] Nor will this study concentrate

---

20   F. Nietzsche, *The Genealogy of Morals* (New York, 1956), p. 212.

21   For an attempt to study punishment in a wider compass, looking at its use in areas other than the criminal law, see C. Harding and R. W. Ireland, *Punishment:*

upon the non-legal but often routine forms of punishment which occur in modern criminal justice—for example, the informal rituals of humiliation involved in some police work or the implicit penalties involved in the prosecution process—since my primary concern will be those punishments which are authorized by law.[22] This may appear to be a serious exclusion, since the informal actions of police, prosecutors, and state officials clearly play a large role in crime-control and constitute an important aspect of state power. However, my concern here is to understand legal punishment and its social foundations, not to chart the repertoire of deterrents that are in use, nor to trace all of the forms in which state power is exercised through the criminal justice apparatus.

The location of state punishment within a specifically legal order gives punishment certain distinctive characteristics which are not a feature of punishments in other social settings. For example, the sovereign claims of the law give legal punishments an obligatory, imperative, and ultimate nature which are unmet with elsewhere. Similarly, the forms of law, its categories, and principles are important in shaping penal discourses and procedures—as we will see when we discuss the work of Pashukanis in Chapter 5—though it should be stressed that penal institutions such as the prison are sometimes legally authorized to adopt procedures which fall far short of the normal juridical standards, for example, on due process in disciplinary hearings. Location

within a legal order, then, is one determinant of punishment's forms and functions, but is by no means the only determinant involved.

Although legal punishment is understood to have a variety of aims, its primary purpose is usually represented as being the instrumental one of reducing or containing rates of criminal behaviour. It is thus possible to conceive of punishment as being simply a means to a given end—to think of it as a legally approved method designed to facilitate the task of crime control. Nor is this an uncommon or particularly inadequate perception of punishment.

Crime control is indeed a determinant of penal practice and this ends—means conception is widely adopted both by penologists and by philosophers of punishment. This instrumental, punishment-as-crime-control conception has, however, been unattractive to sociologists of punishment. These sociologists have usually perceived a sense in which punishment's significance or social function runs beyond the narrow realm of crime control, and they consider such an instrumentalist conception to be an unjustified narrowing of the field of study. Indeed, in some instances, certain theorists have gone so far as to deny punishment's crime-control function altogether, arguing that penality is not well adapted to this particular end, and that therefore some other end must be posited to explain its character. The most celebrated instance of this is Émile Durkheim's declaration that 'if crime is not pathological then the purpose of punishment cannot be to cure it', but similar positions are adopted by writers such as Mead, Rusche and Kirchheimer, and, more recently, Michel Foucault. Each of these writers points to the 'failure' of punishment as a method of crime control and argues that it is badly adapted to

---

Rhetoric, Rule and Practice (London, 1989). Also A. Freiberg, 'Reconceptualizing Sanctions', *Criminology*, 25 (1987), 223-55.

22 See on this M. Feeley, *The Process is the Punishment* (Beverly Hills, 1979), and J. Skolnick, *Justice Without Trial* (New York, 1966).

this end, before going on to discuss alternative ways of understanding the phenomenon.

In a sense, this kind of approach is liberating for anyone who wishes to think about punishment, since it frees us from the need to think of punishment in 'penological' terms and opens up the question of penality's other social functions. There are, however, serious problems with such a position, despite its obvious attractions. For one thing, it continues to think of punishment as a means to an end: if not now the end of 'crime control' then some alternative telos, such as social solidarity (Durkheim) or political domination (Foucault). But this 'purposive' or teleological conception of a social institution makes for bad sociology. Not only is it quite possible, as Nietzsche points out, for a single, historically developed institution to condense a whole series of separate ends and purposes within its sphere of operation. It is also the case that institutions are never fully explicable purely in terms of their 'purposes'. Institutions like the prison, or the fine, or the guillotine, are social artefacts, embodying and regenerating wider cultural categories as well as being means to serve particular penological ends. Punishment is not wholly explicable in terms of its purposes because no social artefact can be explained in this way. Like architecture or diet or clothing or table manners, punishment has an instrumental purpose, but also a cultural style and an historical tradition, and a dependence upon 'institutional, technical and discursive conditions'.[23] If we are to understand such artefacts we have to think of them as social and cultural entities whose meanings can only be unravelled by careful analysis and detailed examination. As in all spheres of life, a specific need may call forth a technical response, but a whole process of historical and cultural production goes into the shaping of that 'technique'.

The need to control crime in its various forms, and to respond to the depredations of law-breakers, is thus only one of the factors which helps shape the institutions of penality. It is, no doubt, an important one, and it would make little sense, for example, to analyse US penal policy without bearing in mind the levels of crime experienced in the USA, and the social and political consequences which follow from this. But even if one could disentangle 'real' crime rates from the processes of policing, criminalizing, and punishing (through which we generate most of our knowledge of crime—and at least some of its actuality), it is clear enough that criminal conduct does not determine the kind of penal action that a society adopts. For one thing, it is not 'crime' or even criminological knowledge about crime which most affects policy decisions, but rather the ways in which 'the crime problem' is officially perceived and the political positions to which these perceptions give rise. For another, the specific forms of policing, trial, and punishment, the severity of sanctions and the frequency of their use, institutional regimes, and frameworks of condemnation are all fixed by social convention and tradition rather than by the contours of criminality. Thus to the extent that penal systems adapt their

---

23   The quotation is from P. Q. Hirst, *Law, Socialism and Democracy* (London, 1986), p. 152, where Hirst argues that ... means of punishment are *artefacts of social organization*, the products of definite institutional, technical and discursive conditions in the same way as other artefacts like technologies or built environments. Artefacts can be explained not by their individual "purpose" alone but by the ensemble of conditions under which such constructions or forms become possible.'

practices to the problems of crime control, they do so in ways which are heavily mediated by independent considerations such as cultural conventions, economic resources, institutional dynamics, and political arguments.[24]

Thinking of punishment as a social artefact serving a variety of purposes and premised upon an ensemble of social forces thus allows us to consider punishment in sociological terms without dismissing its penological purposes and effects. It avoids the absurdity of thinking about punishment as if it had nothing to do with crime, without falling into the trap of thinking of it solely in crime-control terms. We can thus accept that punishment is indeed oriented towards the control of crime—and so partly determined by that orientation—but insist that it has other determinants and other dynamics which have to be considered if punishment is to be fully understood.

Punishment, then, is a delimited legal process, but its existence and operation are dependent upon a wide array of other social forces and conditions. These conditioning circumstances take a variety of forms—some of which have been explicated by historical and sociological work in this field. Thus, for example, modern prisons presuppose definite architectural forms, security devices, disciplinary technologies, and developed regimes which organize time and space—as well as

the social means to finance, construct, and administer such complex organizations.[25] And as recent work has shown, specific forms of punishment are also dependent for their support upon less obvious social and historical circumstances including political discourses and specific forms of knowledge,[26] legal, moral, and cultural categories,[27] and specific patterns of psychic organization or sensibility.[28] Punishment may be a legal institution, administered by state functionaries, but it is necessarily grounded in wider patterns of knowing, feeling, and acting, and it depends upon these social roots and supports for its continuing legitimacy and operation. It is also grounded in history, for, like all social institutions, modern punishment is a historical outcome which is only imperfectly adapted to its current situation. It is a product of tradition as much as present policy: hence the need for a developmental as well as a functional perspective in the understanding of penal institutions. It is only by viewing punishment against the background of these wider forms of life and their history that we can begin to understand the informal logic which underpins penal practice. In consequence, we should be prepared to find that this 'logic' is the social logic of a complex institution built upon an ensemble of

---

24   For a discussion of research attempts to isolate the impact of crime rates upon penal policies, see W. Young, 'Influences Upon the Use of Imprisonment: A Review of the Literature', *The Howard Journal*, 25 (1986), 125–36. D. Downes, in his comparative study of penal policies in The Netherlands and England and Wales, shows that in a period when both countries experienced rising crime rates, England and Wales resorted to a policy of increased imprisonment while The Netherlands effected a substantial decarceration. D. Downes, *Contrasts in Tolerance* (Oxford, 1988).

25   See M. Foucault, *Discipline and Punish* (London, 1977); R. Evans, *The Fabrication of Virtue* (Cambridge, 1982); and G. Rusche and O. Kirchheimer, *Punishment and Social Structure* (New York, 1939, 1968).

26   Foucault, *Discipline and Punish*; D. Garland, *Punishment and Welfare* (Aldershot, 1985).

27   J. Langbein, *Torture and the Law of Proof* (Chicago, 1976);]. Bender, *Imagining the Penitentiary* (Chicago, 1987).

28   P. Spierenburg, *The Spectacle of Suffering* (Cambridge, 1984); D. Garland, 'The Punitive Mentality: Its Socio-Historical Development and Decline', *Contemporary Crises*, 10 (1986), 305-20.

conflicting and co-ordinating forces, rather than the purely instrumental logic of a technical means adapted to a given end.

The outline definition I have just provided, or something very like it, is the unstated point of departure for most sociological analyses of punishment. Different interpretative traditions take up different aspects of the phenomenon, and devote themselves to filling in the substantive content of one or other of the connections and relationships that I have sketched out in formal terms. My own discussion begins with the presumption that these various interpretations are not necessarily incompatible in every respect. Indeed, given the complexity of the social institution of penality, it is likely that what currently appear to be conflicts of interpretation may turn out to be more or less accurate characterizations of an institution which is itself 'conflicted'. By working through these various perspectives, measuring the worth of their arguments, and applying their interpretations to the contemporary scene, I intend to build up a more comprehensive and recognizable picture of the field of penality and its social supports. Wherever the existing interpretative perspectives fail to address aspects of punishment which I take to be important, I will endeavour to generate my own interpretations, drawing upon the work of other social theorists where necessary. Similarly, I will not feel constrained to discuss at length interpretative positions which appear in the literature but which I judge to be inadequate or inaccurate. My primary aim is to understand the reality of punishment, not to offer a full account of the literature which has grown up around it.

One final point should be made before embarking upon this enterprise. Much of the sociology of punishment proceeds as if the key questions always concerned the social and historical determinants of punishment, asking 'how are penal measures shaped by their social and historical context?' This, it seems to me, is only half the story. In the present book I will be concerned to emphasize the ways in which penality shapes its social environment as much as the reverse. Penal sanctions or institutions are not simply dependent variables at the end of some finite line of social causation. Like all social institutions, punishment interacts with its environment, forming part of the mutually constructing configuration of elements which make up the social world. All the classic sociological writings—from Durkheim to Foucault—are clear about this, and this dialectic will be emphasized throughout the present work. This, indeed, is one of the reasons why the sociological study of punishment is so potentially valuable. It tells us how we react to disorderly persons and threats to the social order—but also, and more importantly, it can reveal some of the ways in which personal and social order come to be constructed in the first place.

Criminal Justice As Social Control

by Joycelyn M. Pollock

WHAT YOU NEED TO KNOW

- Television presents a highly artificial perspective of crime, criminals, and the criminal justice system.
- Common law is the compilation of early decisions by magistrates in England. Common law is the basis of the legal system in the United States.
- Felonies are usually serious crimes punishable by more than a year in prison and misdemeanors are less serious crimes punishable by up to a year in jail (in most states).
- Police power is the power to make laws. The federal government's ability to create law is limited to the enumerated powers as stated in Article I of the Constitution. All other police power resides in the states.
- The "flow chart" of the criminal justice system starts with arrest and ends with release. Certain basic steps are common to all states.
- Expenditures for the criminal justice system have been increasing even

though there was a dramatic decline of crime in the 1990s through the early 2000s.
- An ideology is a body of doctrines or beliefs that guide an individual or group. Two ideologies relevant to criminal justice issues are the *crime control* and *due process* ideologies.

Blood, bloated corpses, high-speed chases, true-blue detectives, and evil criminals who revel in their wickedness are the images of crime on television. They are not reality. Criminal justice became one of the fastest growing majors on college campuses in the 1980s and 1990s. Since the *CSI* shows first appeared on television several years ago, a profession that had been arcane and "geeky" became the hottest new occupational interest. Forensic investigation majors have now been created in many universities to tap the huge market of interested students, many of whom may not realize that crime scene analysts typically have science degrees and if you didn't enjoy your high school biology or chemistry class, it may not be the profession for you. The definition of **forensic science** is "science that serves the

---

BOX 4.1 **WHAT ARE FORENSICS?**

"Forensic" is an adjective used to describe something as related to the legal system. A forensic pathologist is someone who conducts autopsies to determine cause of death; a forensic scientist uses a range of science to answer questions about crime; a forensic handwriting analyst is called upon to testify in forgery or fraud cases, and so on. You might remember that your high school debate class also might have used the word forensics, which has a second meaning of "the art or study of debate." This is because the root of the word comes from the Latin word forensis, meaning "forum." Legal cases were tried in front of a forum of citizens who decided guilt or innocence based on the skill of the orator who defended the guilty, thus the connection between the two uses of the word.

---

court"; in other words, *forensic* is an adjective that is used to describe something as related to the legal system. Some of the applications of the term are shown in Box 4.1.

Before the *CSI* shows, the television series *Law and Order* introduced countless viewers to the criminal justice system via the perspective of the police and prosecutors. Many viewers today know most of what they know about the criminal justice system through

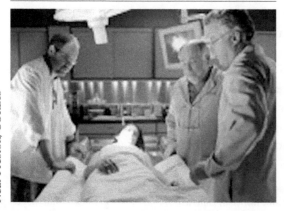

FIGURE 4.1 (L-R) Actors David Berman (as assistant coroner David Phillips), Robert David Hall (as coroner Al Robbins), and William Petersen (as Gil Grissom) examine a corpse in a scene from *CSI: Crime Scene Investigation*. *CSI: Crime Scene Investigation* and *Law & Order* have become so influential with viewers as imitations of life in the criminal justice system that some legal experts worry that they are distorting the expectations of actual jurors.

Neal Preston/CORBIS

these television series and others. This is not necessarily a new trend. In earlier decades, *Adam 12*, a series about two LAPD officers, depicted them reciting the *Miranda* warning to arrestees almost every week. Before long, we all knew that:

"You have the right to remain silent. If you give up that right, anything you say can and will be used against you in a court of law. You have the right to an attorney, and if you cannot afford one, one will be appointed to you." Viewers may not have known where the *Miranda* warnings came from, or when police needed to recite them, but they remembered the warning in the same way they did advertising jingles for chewing gum or coffee. Some officers ruefully admit that, in some ways, the most realistic police show was *Barney Miller*, a comedy/drama about New York City police detectives who dealt with a steady stream of strange and humorous victims and offenders, interspersed with mundane stories about the detectives' personal lives.

Television today would have us believe that crime scene investigators solve most crimes (*CSI* series), or that medical examiners solve the crimes (*Crossing Jordan*), prosecutors (*Shark*), or even that forensic anthropologists most often solve crimes (*Bones*). Of course,

---

BOX 4.2 **THE CSI EFFECT**

Lawyers and journalists have coined the term "CSI Effect" to describe the incredible effect this television show has had on criminal court trials and jury deliberation. What seems to be happening is that viewers confuse reality with television and expect that every criminal case should have the type of scientific evidence portrayed in the show. When prosecutors are unable to present DNA evidence, fingerprints from any type of material, findings from scent identifiers, and so on, jurors may acquit defendants, believing that if the evidence doesn't exist, the case must be weak. Defense attorneys also complain about the show's effect, arguing that jurors believe that scientific evidence is infallible and don't consider human error or technological glitches when such evidence is utilized by the prosecutor. Evidently, the show has even influenced criminals and some police say that criminals are more likely today to pour bleach around crime scenes in an attempt to destroy DNA and trace evidence.

Source: Willing, R. (2004). "CSI Effect Has Juries Wanting More Evidence." *USA Today*, August 5: B1.

most television dramas portray police detectives solving most crimes (i.e., *Law and Order*). In reality, the majority of crimes are cleared because of witnesses or citizens that point police to the offender.

What spurs our fascination with crime? Every decade of television has had its share of crime drama shows. Some of these are displayed in Box 4.3. In fact, crime dramas with either law enforcement or courtroom scenes seem to be the most common type of series other than medical dramas. Perhaps these professions are chosen because they are more likely to provide gripping tales of life and death. It is difficult to squeeze nail-biting drama out of a television show about accountants or teachers, for instance.

It is important to remember, however, that these television shows may color our perception of reality. For instance, when you ask someone what they think of when you say crime, they are probably going to say murder or rape or some violent crime; not a relatively low-dollar theft, which is much more common in reality. If you ask who they think of when you say criminal, they may think of

---

BOX 4.3 **TELEVISION CRIME DRAMAS**

1960s: Perry Mason, N.Y.P.D., Dragnet, Mannix, Felony Squad, Scales of Justice, Burke's Law, For the People

1970s: Adam 12, CHiPs, Barney Miller, Baretta, Columbo, Hawaii Five-O, Mod Squad, Quincy, M.E., Starsky & Hutch, Streets of San Francisco, Police Woman, Serpico, The D.A., The Guardians, Sword of Justice, The Blue Knight, McMillan and Wife, Owen Marshall, Counselor at Law, The Rookies, Police Story, McCloud, S.W.A.T.

1980s: Cagney & Lacey, Hill Street Blues, Miami Vice, Night Court, In the Heat of the Night, L.A. Law, Matlock, McClain's Law, Police Squad, Crime Story, Houston Knights, Mancuso, FBI, True Blue

1990s: Law and Order, N.Y.P.D. Blue, Homicide: Life in the Streets, The Commish, Profiler, High Incident, Murder One, NY Undercover, The Practice, Against the Law, Broken Badges, Equal Justice, Scene of the Crime, Street Justice, Undercover, Bodies of Evidence, Third Watch, Cold Case Squad, The Detectives, Walker, Texas Ranger, JAG, The Wright Verdicts, The Thin Blue Line, The Sentinel, Public Morals

the murderer or "gangbanger" portrayed on a popular television show, rather than the legions of petty offenders who pass through our courts every day. These perceptions have the power to influence our decision making and opinions about real issues. For instance, when habitual felon or "three strikes" laws are debated, most people believe that they apply only to seriously violent offenders, the type that they see on television generally. In reality, such laws often apply to property offenders, drug offenders, and others who voters are not necessarily thinking of when voting for such laws.

1. THE FUNCTION OF SOCIAL CONTROL

What is the function of the criminal justice system? You probably said "to punish wrongdoers" and that is partially correct. The underlying function of the system, however, is social control. There are other institutions of society that socialize us and control our behavior. Schools, churches, and neighborhood associations are examples of other institutions of social control. However, sometimes those institutions are unsuccessful in controlling a person's behavior and, when that happens, the criminal justice system steps in.

Every society needs to control the actions of citizens when they threaten the social order. One of the most well-known concepts in philosophy and the sociology of law is the **social contract**. This concept come out of the work of Thomas Hobbes (1588–1679), John Locke (1632–1704) and Jean-Jacques Rousseau (1712–1778).[1] According to Hobbes, before civilization, man lived in a "war of all against all" and life was not very pleasant. A more peaceful existence for everyone could only come about if every person agreed to give up the liberty to aggress against others in return

for society's protection against aggressors. Rousseau's "social contract" is the idea that citizens agree to abide by the law in return for the law's protection. Of course, it is not really the case that we all consciously agree to such a contract. Our agreement is implicit when we choose to accept the benefits of living within a society. Part of the idea of the social contract is that if we break the law, we have agreed to the consequences; specifically, prosecution and punishment.

The earliest tribal societies had leaders who mediated conflicts and handed down punishment. As society became more complex, layers of authority developed between the king/ruler and the populace, so that even as early as Hammurabi, "laws" were written down to be administered when offenses occurred. Gradually rudimentary court systems were created, and then, eventually, law enforcement emerged as a public agency (as opposed to private protection paid for by those who could afford it). The emergence of law and law enforcement is a very interesting historical process and one can see that it is part of the process of a community becoming "civilized."

2. THE AMERICAN LEGAL SYSTEM

Our legal system comes from English **common law.** Starting around the 1500s, magistrates appointed by the kings and queens of England handed down decisions regarding both civil disputes and criminal offenses. Over time, these decisions were written down to be used as guidance when similar cases were brought before that magistrate or others. The common law was the compilation of all those decisions. In the 1700s, William Blackstone, a famous English jurist, undertook the mammoth effort of

---

BOX 4.4 **THE CODE OF HAMMURABI**

Hammurabi was a ruler of Babylon. Hammurabi's reign [1795–1750 B.C.] is noted for many things, but one of the greatest is his celebrated code of law. It is not the earliest code of laws, but one of the most complete. It is also noteworthy in that this ruler made public the entire body of laws, arranged in orderly groups, so that the citizenry would know what was required of them. The code was carved upon a black stone monument, eight feet high, and clearly intended to be in public view. This noted stone was found in the year 1901, not in Babylon, but in a city in the Persian mountains. It consists of 282 laws. A few examples are offered below:

3. If any one bring an accusation of any crime before the elders, and does not prove what he has charged, he shall, if it be a capital offense charged, be put to death.

6. If any one steal the property of a temple or of the court, he shall be put to death, and also the one who receives the stolen thing from him shall be put to death.

8. If any one steal cattle or sheep, or an ass, or a pig or a goat, if it belong to a god or to the court, the thief shall pay thirty-fold therefore; if they belonged to a freed man of the king he shall pay tenfold; if the thief has nothing with which to pay he shall be put to death.

25. If fire break out in a house, and some one who comes to put it out cast his eye upon the property of the owner of the house, and take the property of the master of the house, he shall be thrown into that self-same fire.

132. If the "finger is pointed" at a man's wife about another man, but she is not caught sleeping with the other man, she shall jump into the river for her husband.

146. If a man take a wife and she give this man a maid-servant as wife and she bear him children, and then this maid assume equality with the wife: because she has borne him children her master shall not sell her for money, but he may keep her as a slave, reckoning her among the maid-servants.

195. If a son strike his father, his hands shall be hewn off.

196. If a man put out the eye of another man, his eye shall be put out.

197. If he break another man's bone, his bone shall be broken.

198. If he put out the eye of a freed man, or break the bone of a freed man, he shall pay one gold mina.

199. If he put out the eye of a man's slave, or break the bone of a man's slave, he shall pay one-half of its value.

---

organizing and identifying the principles of law that derived from these decisions. Blackstone's Law Commentaries collected the common laws together in one source for the first time.

After the American Revolution, the common law was still the pervading law of the land, but as states were created, many began to write their own **penal codes**, which are basically an organized list of laws of the state. You may have seen an Internet item that lists obscure and ridiculous old laws that supposedly still exist, such as no kissing in public or no shooting buffalos from a moving train. This is largely urban legend, because penal codes are periodically reviewed and rewritten by legislators, aided by the bar association of each state. On the other hand, it is an interesting exercise to become more familiar with the penal code of your own state and see some of the quirky, old, and/or ignored laws that do still exist.

EXERCISE: IN THE STATE OF ...

1. Go to **www.dumblaws.com/index.php.**
2. Look up the "dumb laws" listed for your state.
3. Check the link provided to read the original law or, when the link is not provided, obtain a copy of your state penal code. This is often available over the Internet. Use the Google or Yahoo search engines to find a link to your state's penal code. Try to find the law mentioned.

The exercise provided on page 7 is the first of many in this book designed to help you become more familiar with the criminal justice system of your own state. One of the challenges in writing a criminal justice text is that the criminal justice system and the laws of each state are slightly different. Thus, in each chapter, there is an exercise designed to help you become more familiar with your own state's criminal justice system. Today the Internet is an invaluable tool to quickly and conveniently discover most of this information. An important thing to remember, however, is that Web sites can be created by anyone. When researching criminal justice issues, it is best to look for official sites, such as state attorneys-general sites, federal sites such as the Bureau of Justice Statistics, and university sponsored sites. Of course, other sites can be used as well (such as the one identified in this exercise). However, be careful to double-check facts when using Web sites that are not affiliated with official sources.

Laws define the "do's and don'ts" of society. They can be broken down into felonies, misdemeanors, ordinances, and violations. **Felonies** are the most serious misbehaviors and are usually punishable by a year or more in prison. Most of the crimes you think of (murder, rape, assault) are felonies, although sometimes a crime might be either, such as larceny/theft, which may be a felony or a misdemeanor depending on the dollar amount of the theft. **Misdemeanors** are less serious (such as simple assault) and can be punished by up to a year in jail. It is possible that in your state misdemeanors must be committed in the presence of a police officer for them to be able to arrest the offender without an arrest warrant. In some states, when misdemeanors happen outside the presence of police, a victim must go to the prosecutor's office and file a complaint. The prosecutor will ask a magistrate to sign an arrest warrant if he or she decides there is probable cause. States usually further subdivide felonies and misdemeanors to classes or levels indicating their seriousness.

State legislatures have the power to create criminal laws. City ordinances (i.e., skating on the sidewalk), are created by city councils or the local political entity, and are usually punishable by fines. City code violations (i.e., keeping livestock within city limits) are also created by local political bodies and punished by fines.

Law enforcement exists at the state and local level to enforce these laws, although as you are probably aware, police officers and prosecutors have a great deal of discretion. Just because a law is broken does not necessarily mean there will be an arrest or prosecution. Typically, a state will have a state law enforcement agency (highway patrol) that enforces the state's highway laws, but can also be called in to help investigate local crime. There is usually a county-level law enforcement agency (county sheriff and deputies). Most of us are familiar with the city police officer, but there are also other types of law enforcement officers, depending on the state, such as constables, park or airport police departments, port authority police, transportation police, university police departments, and so on. These specialized police forces must be created by the state legislature. There are also different layers of courts that prosecute the laws. City ordinances and code violations are typically heard in municipal courts, while misdemeanors and felonies are heard in county and state courts. Every state has a court structure that allows for appeals, and the highest appellate court in the state is often called the state supreme court, not to be confused with the United States Supreme Court, the highest court in the country.

The federal criminal justice system parallels the state systems. Federal laws are passed by Congress and can be found in the United States Code. You can purchase a "compact" version that is only 700 pages! One thing to remember is that Article I of the United States Constitution specifically enumerates the powers held by the federal government. All other powers are held by states. The Tenth Amendment to the United States Constitution made this division of power clear by stating: *"The powers not delegated to the United States by the Constitution, nor prohibited by it to the States, are reserved to the States respectively, or to the people."* **Police power**, the authority to set and enforce most laws, lies with the states. The federal government's role in crime control has historically been strictly limited and must be derived from one of its other powers, i.e., the power to protect the borders or regulate interstate commerce.

> To look at the U.S. federal code, go to http://uscode.house.gov/

Despite the limitations created by the Constitution, we have a large number of federal laws that must be enforced by federal law enforcement agencies. We are most familiar with the FBI, but other federal agencies, such as the border patrol, customs, post office inspectors, and treasury agents, also investigate and enforce federal criminal laws.

As you know, the Department of Homeland Security was created after the terrorist attacks of September 11, 2001. The purpose of creating this department was to streamline and create better communication among the many federal law enforcement agencies that are involved with protecting the country from terrorist acts. Box 4.5 shows how the various agencies are linked into one large organization

> For information on DHS, see: http://www.dhs.gov/index.shtm

whose mission is to protect the country from terrorist threats.

It is important to note that federal laws and procedures have made a distinction between domestic crimes and international terrorism when allocating powers of investigation and prosecution to federal agencies. Typically, federal agencies, such as the FBI and CIA, have greater powers when investigating international offenders who are suspected of terrorism than when they are investigating "regular" crimes. Of course, there are often blurry lines between domestic crimes, such as bank robbery or smuggling drugs, and international terrorism. One of the most hotly contested elements of the USA PATRIOT Act was increased law

BOX 4.5 DEPARTMENT OF HOMELAND SECURITY

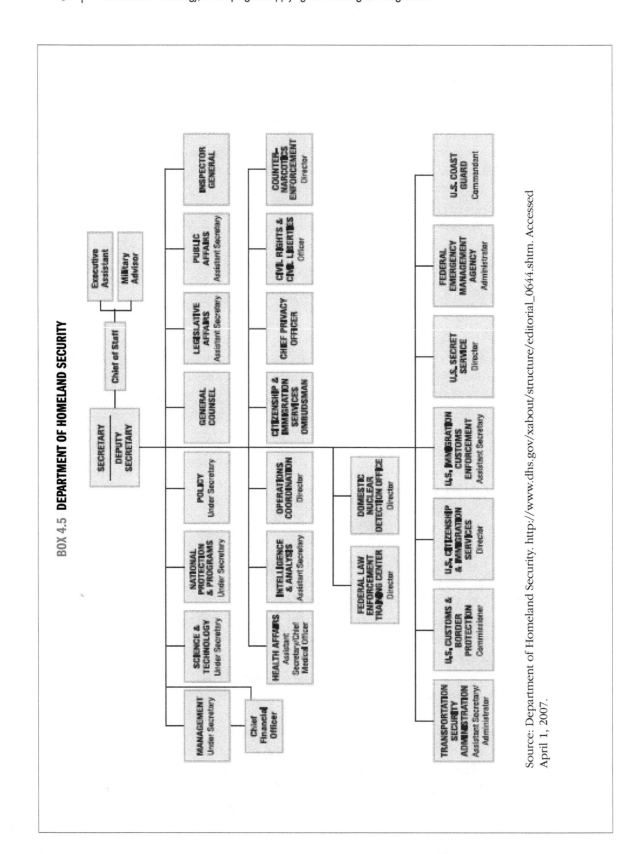

Source: Department of Homeland Security. http://www.dhs.gov/xabout/structure/editorial_0644.shtm. Accessed April 1, 2007.

enforcement powers in domestic investigations when there is reason to believe a connection to international terrorism exists. We will revisit the PATRIOT Act and law enforcement's role in protecting this nation from terrorism in Chapter 15.

3. FLOWCHART OF THE SYSTEM

In Box 4.6, a rough flowchart of a felony offender's experience going through the criminal justice system is presented. An individual may exit the system through:

- non-prosecution at any stage up to conviction;
- acquittal;
- successful completion of a pretrial diversion program;
- successful completion of probation;

- successful completion of parole;
- completion of jail or prison sentence.

The criminal justice system is typically divided into three subsystems: police, courts, and corrections. The use of these three subsystems has become a standard way to describe the system. Police take center stage up to arrest; their role is to investigate crimes, arrest the suspect, and gather evidence. Courts are obviously involved in the process of adjudication, which determines guilt or innocence and sets the amount of punishment for the guilty. Corrections takes over after sentencing. Of course, real life doesn't have such simple categories. Police investigate offenders who are on probation or parole. Pretrial adjudication programs often use probation officers to supervise clients who haven't been found guilty. Probationers who violate the conditions

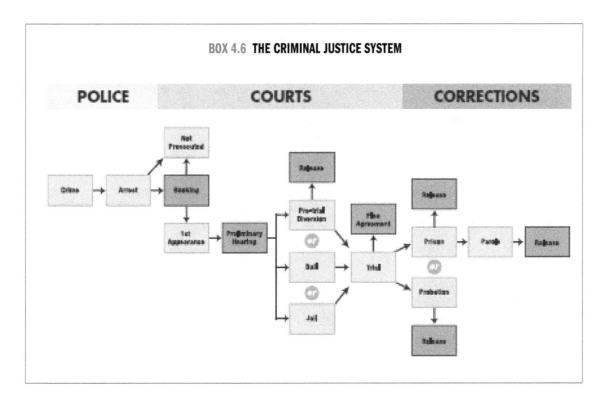

BOX 4.6 **THE CRIMINAL JUSTICE SYSTEM**

BOX 4.7 THE CRIMINAL JUSTICE PROCESS

Booking: is basically an administrative entry into jail. The suspect's fingerprints are taken, officers take his or her property, issue jail clothing, and sometimes, the suspect undergoes some form of health screening before being placed in the jail population.

First Appearance: is usually within the first 24 hours of arrest (and it must take place within a "reasonable" period after arrest). In this short hearing before a magistrate, the charges are read and the magistrate determines if there is sufficient probable cause for the arrest. The magistrate may also begin the process of determining if the suspect is indigent, in which case an attorney will be appointed.

Preliminary Hearing: is basically to determine whether there is sufficient evidence to go forward with a trial. Often the preliminary hearing is waived. In some states, the grand jury system completely takes the place of the preliminary hearing.

Grand Jury Hearing: is with a jury appointed by the administrative judge of a jurisdiction. This group hears the evidence presented by a prosecutor to determine if there is probable cause to go forward to trial. If they agree that there is, they issue an *indictment*. Not all states use the grand jury system.

Arraignment: is where the offender may plead guilt or innocence and, if indigent, have an attorney appointed if one has not been appointed yet.

Pretrial Diversion: may occur at any time before trial and after charges have been filed. Typically, the suspect must admit guilt and agree to conditions that range from work and restitution programs to community service.

Plea Bargaining: is an agreement between the defendant, represented by his or her attorney, and the prosecutor to plead guilty in exchange for a recommended sentence.

Pretrial Hearings: are when judges decide procedural issues relevant to the trial, such as the admission of evidence or change of venue.

Trials: may be "bench trials," which means that they are held only in front of a judge with no jury. If the defendant requests a jury trial, voir dire takes place before the jury is seated, which basically involves ensuring that jury members will be unbiased in their judgment.

Sentencing Hearing: is a separate proceeding, although appointed attorneys are required to continue to represent the offender through the sentencing hearing (and first appeal). There may be some time between the trial and the sentencing hearing in order for a presentence report to be written. While some states allow juries to sentence, others release the jury and have the judge do the sentencing.

Prison/Probation: is the basic sentencing decision in felony cases. Some states have strictly limited which crimes are eligible for a probation sentence; in other states, potentially any felon can be sentenced to probation.

Parole: comes *after* a prison sentence, while probation is *instead of* a prison sentence (in most cases). They are very similar in that both involve supervised release into the community.

---

of their probation may go back to court for a Motion to Revoke Probation hearing. Thus, it is important to understand what happens to the offender during the whole process from arrest through discharge from the system.

Once an offender is arrested, with or without an arrest warrant, the individual has started his or her entry into the "system." In Box 4.7, the steps of the system are described briefly. It is important to note that there are differences between the states in these steps.

We will more carefully explore the various steps taken in the criminal justice flowchart in a later chapter.

4. COSTS OF THE SYSTEM

The criminal justice system is an incredibly expensive operation. As Box 4.8 shows, the costs of the system have been increasing exponentially for the last 20 years and now reach 80 billion dollars just for state expenditures! States spend more for criminal justice than they do for education or health and human services. In fiscal year 2001, federal, state, and local governments spent more than $167 billion for police protection, corrections, and judicial and legal activities. It is estimated that criminal justice functions cost every person in the United States $600.00 per year.[2]

What is interesting about the huge increase in expenditures for criminal justice functions is that in the decade of the 1990s through the early 2000s, we experienced a dramatic decline in all types of crime. As we shall see shortly, some crime rates have declined to 30-year lows. The declining crime pattern was experienced across the country, in cities as well as small towns. We will discuss the crime decline in more detail in the next chapter.

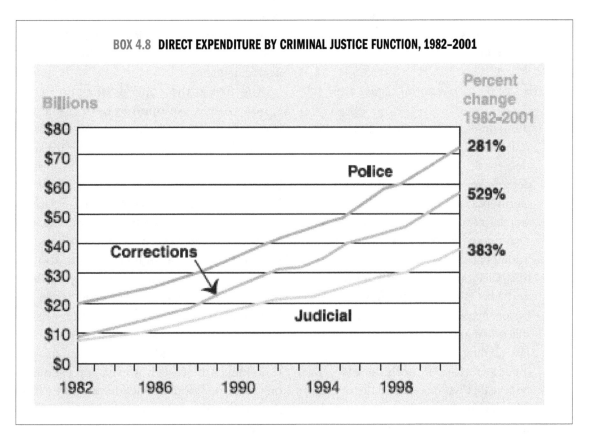

BOX 4.8 DIRECT EXPENDITURE BY CRIMINAL JUSTICE FUNCTION, 1982–2001

Source: Bureau of Justice Statistics, *Justice Expenditure and Employment Extracts*. Retrieved 2/15/07 from: http://www.ojp.usdoj.gov/bjs/glance/tables/exptyptab.htm.

5. MISSION AND GOALS OF THE SYSTEM

The basic mission of the criminal justice system is to prevent victimization by preventing criminal behavior. Each of the subsystems has its own specific, but complementary, goals to achieve this general mission. The goals of *law enforcement* are:

- to prevent crime by patrol;
- to educate the public on crime prevention; and
- to investigate crime and arrest those suspected of committing a crime.

The goals of the *court system* are to:

- determine guilt or innocence through due process; and
- determine a just sentence.

The goals of the *correctional system* are:

- punishment: we believe that criminals must be punished because they deserve it;
- deterrence: we believe that what we do to offenders will make others decide not to commit crime and also will encourage that offender not to commit additional crime;
- rehabilitation: we believe that programs and what is done to the offender in the system may create some internal change that will make him or her become more law-abiding;
- incapacitation: if nothing else, we believe that we should hold the offender in a manner that will prevent him or her from committing any crimes, at least for that period of time.

The important thing to remember is that basically each of the subsystems has the same overriding goal of crime prevention, but they seek to accomplish that goal in different ways. Most analyses and discussions of the criminal justice system utilize a **systems approach**, meaning that the various elements of police, courts, and corrections are viewed as working together as an integrated whole toward a single goal. In general, this is true, although the various subsystems sometimes have contradictory objectives. In fact, some police officers might say that the court system works "against" the police by letting offenders out as fast as police lock them up. Despite the sometimes contradictory objectives of the subsystems, a systems approach is helpful because it allows us to consider two major concepts that are relevant to our understanding of the criminal justice agencies.

The first is the concept of open versus closed systems. An **open system** is one that is permeable and responsive to outside influences. The criminal justice system, for instance, can be described as a fairly open system because it must and does respond to outside influences such as public opinion, legislative changes in the law, executive prioritizing, and so on. A **closed system** is one that does not respond to outside influences and, though the criminal justice system itself is open, there may be examples of certain agencies in the system that are closed. Historically, prisons were fairly closed systems that were outside of public scrutiny and fairly autonomous. This is no longer the case, however, and even prisons must respond to outside pressures from the public, prisoners' rights advocates, and the legislature.

The second concept is that of **homeostasis**—the idea that any system will adjust to changes by adapting in such a way to maintain "business as usual." This is important and can arguably explain why we are spending just as much money (actually more!) after a decade-long drop in crime as we did during the years with the highest crime rates. Systems theory argues that there is a tendency for systems to maintain a status quo. In criminal justice, we might point to the fact that rarely do we ever close prisons despite reduced crime rates, and rarely do changes in the law dramatically affect the courtroom work group's decision-making procedures. In general, the system responds to outside pressures by minor adjustments or reinterpretations that tend to allow a continuation of "business as usual." We will discuss these concepts in more detail in later chapters.

6. IDEOLOGIES IN CRIME AND JUSTICE

An **ideology** is a body of doctrines or beliefs that guide an individual or group. It is a way of organizing knowledge, in that we interpret things we see and hear in reference to our existing belief systems. In fact, we may even ignore information that doesn't fit our existing ideology and remember information that does. In 1968, Herbert Packer[3] described two models of law enforcement that are extremely helpful in understanding the issues and decisionmaking that occur in reference to the entire criminal justice system, not just law enforcement. In fact, what he termed *models* could also be called ideologies. Packer called his two models "*crime control*" and "*due process*."

In the **crime control ideology**, the basic belief is that controlling crime and punishing the criminal is more important than anything else, best expressed by a Supreme Court justice who argued that the criminal should not be set free because "the constable blundered." Some of the beliefs that are consistent with Herbert Packer's crime control ideology are:

- Reducing crime is the most important function of law enforcement.
- The failure of law enforcement means the breakdown of order.
- The criminal process guarantees social freedom.
- Efficiency is a top priority.
- The emphasis is on speed and finality.
- There is a presumption of guilt, once the suspect is in the system.

Packer's **due process ideology** supports controlling crime, but in this ideology, crime control is not the most important goal. The most important mission of the criminal justice system is the enforcement of law in a fair and just manner, as characterized by the comment: "It is better to let 10 guilty men go free than punish one innocent." Beliefs that are consistent with this ideology include:

- There is a possibility of error in the system.
- Prevention of mistakes is more important than efficiency.
- Protection of the process is as important as protection of innocents.
- The coercive power of the state is always subject to abuse.
- Every due process protection is there for a reason and should be strictly adhered to.

These basic ideologies are very pervasive in our thinking and opinions regarding criminal justice issues. You can see evidence of them in the television shows we discussed earlier, in politicians' statements, in television and radio talk show host's rantings, and in "letters to the editor" in the local newspaper. If one's ideology is purely "crime control," then some consistent beliefs would include:

- Criminals are the "enemy" and fundamentally different from "good" people.
- Police are the "army" that fights the enemy, using any means necessary to control, capture, and punish them.
- "Good" people accept and understand that police are in a "war" and must be allowed deference in their decisionmaking because they, not us, are the experts and only they "know the enemy."
- Due process protections, such as the *Miranda* warnings, exclusionary rule, and search warrants "hamstring" the police from doing their job.

On the other hand, if one has a basic ideology of due process, then other beliefs are more consistent, and might include:

- Criminals are not a distinct group; they also shop, pay taxes, have kids and parents, may be victims themselves, and often are one's next-door neighbor.
- Police have limited ability to affect crime rates one way or the other because crime is a complex social phenomenon and, in fact, the history of law enforcement originates in order maintenance, not crime control.
- Police, as "public servants," serve all people, and it is important to remember that suspects are not criminals until a court of law finds them so.

- The law is more important than catching criminals, so if police officers break the law to catch a criminal, then they become criminal themselves.

- Due process protections, such as the *Miranda* warnings, exclusionary rule and search warrants are an inherent element of the job of police; therefore, when they ignore, subvert, or skirt these protections, they are not doing their job.[4]

One's belief system influences how new information is received. For instance, the USA PATRIOT Act was lauded by those with a crime control ideology as a step in the right direction in that it allocated greater powers of search to law enforcement officers investigating terrorism. On the other hand, for some with a due process ideology, it was perceived as a direct attack on civil liberties and previous privacy protections enacted by Congress.

Of course, most of us do not have pure ideologies and so you might feel that you lie between these two, or, indeed, have a different overriding ideology entirely. The point of examining ideologies is simply that they sometimes obscure our understanding or acceptance of new information. There is a distinct possibility that your receptiveness to certain facts in this book, and every other book you read, is colored by your ideology. If, for instance, you don't believe something in this book is true, then you should go explore the facts, either by the footnote provided, or by your own research. The piece of information may be wrong, it may be out of date, or it may be that it simply doesn't fit your idea of the way things are, which is shaped by your ideology. Of course the writers of textbooks (including this one) have their own ideologies; therefore, their presentation of facts may be influenced by their own ideology. The goal of every textbook writer is to present a balanced view of the facts; however, facts are sometimes more complicated than we think and, although we may strive for objectivity, it is not always easy to do. One of the most difficult things, for instance, in writing research papers is to seek out all the facts and write a balanced review of the research, rather than use only those facts that fit the conclusion that you want to reach. At the end of this chapter is a short guide to writing a research paper. While there are more detailed instructions available in other sources, this short discussion may help you to identify and narrow a topic and organize the material in a logical and cogent manner.

7. CAREERS IN CRIMINAL JUSTICE

It is possible that you are reading this book because you are interested in a career in the field of criminal justice. One of the interesting features of the field is the wide variation in professions. Criminal justice encompasses drug counselors and border patrol agents, prison guards and public defenders. You've probably heard that "you'll never get rich" in this field, and that is true. Box 4.9 shows some low and high average salaries for certain selected professions associated with criminal justice.

Although there are no riches to be earned in this field, there are not that many professions that have such potential to change lives. Almost all the occupations and professions in this table (except for private security and private attorneys) are public servants. Public servants are individuals whose salary comes from the public purse; therefore, they have special duties to put the public's interest before

BOX 4.9 ANNUAL SALARIES

Position	Lowest $	Average $	Highest $
Police officer	26,910	45,210	68,880
Police chief	72,924-92,983		
Police sergeant	49,895-59, 454		
FBI (GS 10-13)	53,185-64,478		
Private detective	19,260	32,110	58,470
Security guards	14,390	20,320	33,270
Correctional officer	22,630	33,600	54,820
Probation officer	26,310	39,600	66,660
Attorney	94,930 (wide variation)		
Judges	29,920	93,070	141,750
Counselor	15,480	24,270	39,620

Source: Bureau of Labor Statistics. Retrieved 6/1/07 from: http://www.bls.gov/oco/.

their own. They have discretion and power over the lives of others, and therefore must be held to high standards of integrity and ethics. If public servants do not respect the law, then everyone is at risk and corruption inevitably follows. In the chapters that follow, we will examine in greater detail not only the offenders who pass through the criminal justice system, but also the women and men who are the agents of social control and the law.

8. CONCLUSION

In this chapter we learned some basic facts about the criminal justice system. Obviously the television shows that portray the system do not present completely accurate views of what happens in real life. We should be concerned that sometimes false perceptions influence decisions, such as what is described in the "CSI effect."

Criminal justice is basically an institution of social control. The powers invested in system actors come from the American Constitution, which places most "police powers" in the state. States pass laws, cities pass ordinances, and they all are enforced by law enforcement at the state and local level. The flowchart of the criminal justice system displays how an offender enters the system and how he or she can exit. We use systems theory to understand what we call the criminal justice system, but we must also recognize that the various subsystems may sometimes have contradictory objectives. Positions that are consistent with the ideologies of crime control or due process can be seen in the media. Ideologies are inevitable but they may prevent one from accepting facts that do not fit one's "view of the world." It is important to constantly challenge one's ideologies with facts as they develop. In the next chapter, we will further explore crime and how we measure it.

REVIEW QUESTIONS

1. What is common law?
2. What are the differences among felonies, misdemeanors, and violations?
3. What is police power? Who has the power to pass laws?
4. What powers were given specifically to the federal government?
5. Name and describe each of the steps of the flowchart of criminal justice.
6. How much do we spend on criminal justice agencies?
7. What has been the pattern of crime in the last decade?
8. What is systems theory and what are open and closed systems?
9. Explain the concept of homeostasis.
10. What is an ideology? Explain the crime control and due process ideologies.

VOCABULARY

closed system – does not respond to outside influences

common law – English magistrates' decisions regarding both civil disputes and criminal offenses; eventually they became a body of legal decisions that formed the basis of the American legal system

crime control ideology – the basic belief that controlling crime and punishing the criminal is the most important goal of the criminal justice system

due process ideology – the belief that the most important mission of the criminal justice system is the enforcement of law and protecting the rights of the individual

felonies – the most serious misbehaviors, usually punishable by a year or more in prison

forensic science – science that serves the court; in other words, *forensic* is an adjective that is used to describe something as related to the legal system

homeostasis – the idea that any system will adjust to changes by adapting in such a way as to maintain "business as usual"

ideology – a body of doctrines or beliefs that guide an individual or group; it is a way of organizing knowledge in that we interpret things we see and hear in reference to our existing ideologies

misdemeanors – less serious offenses (such as simple assault) that can be punished by up to a year in jail.

open system – one that is permeable and responsive to outside influences

penal codes – an organized list of laws of the state

police power – the authority to set and enforce most laws

social contract – a concept proposed by philosophers Hobbes, Locke, and Rousseau that explains that individuals give up the liberty to aggress against others in return for protection from being victimized themselves

systems approach – a type of analysis utilizing the definitions and characteristics of a system

FOR FURTHER READING

Bailey, Frankie and Donna Hale (1997). *Popular Culture, Crime and Justice*. Belmont, CA: Wadsworth/ITP.

Muraskin, Rosalyn and Shelly Domash (2006). *Crime and the Media: Headlines vs. Reality*. Upper Saddle River, NJ: Prentice Hall.

Packer, Herbert (1968). *The Limits of the Criminal Sanction*. Stanford, CA: Stanford University Press

Potter, Gary and Victor E. Kappeler (1998). *Constructing Crime: Perspectives in Making News and Social Problems*. Prospect Heights, IL: Waveland Press.

Rafter, Nicole (2000). *Shots in the Mirror: Crime Films and Society*. New York, NY: Oxford University Press.

Surette, Ray (1997). *Media, Crime, and Criminal Justice*, Second Edition. Belmont, CA: Wadsworth, ITP.

APPENDIX: WRITING A RESEARCH PAPER

You may be required to write a research paper; therefore this last section provides some guidance. Papers may range in length from 3 to 25 pages, so the comments below must be adjusted to fit the length of the paper assigned.

Choosing a topic. One of the most important steps in writing a good paper is choosing a topic. Luckily, in the field of criminal justice, there is a veritable wealth of topics to choose from that are interesting, current, and even controversial. You should try to discover a topic that is less typical; for instance, instead of the death penalty, you might do a cross-cultural comparison of the death penalty. If the paper is a small one, it is important to limit the topic. In fact, the easiest way to do that is to ask a research question: Do all states have the death penalty? Then three to five pages will be sufficient to describe states' laws and differences between the states. You will not need to do a whole history, presentation of legal issues, and methods of execution for such a topic title.

For possible topics, you can look in your textbook table of contents, scan the book itself or even read the local newspaper for current, topical issues. Some possible topics (assuming an average length paper) are:

The extent of the use of juvenile waivers to adult court

Changes in school discipline and use of school safety officers

Television and its link to violence

Drug use among teens – is it going up or down?

Gun control research–does it reduce crime?

The CSI effect on criminal prosecution

The effectiveness of community policing

Methods to improve ethical behavior in policing

Issues in the use of tasers: legal issues, misuse, effect

 on lethal force

The effectiveness of residential drug treatment versus

 out-patient treatment

The effectiveness of sex offender treatment

The need for gender-specific programming

Habeas Corpus and recent Supreme Court decisions

USA PATRIOT Act's effect on law enforcement

Illegal aliens' involvement in crime

Issues of female police officers: performance, sexual harassment The effect of domestic violence mandatory arrest policies

The causes of the crime decline of the 1990s

Community policing evaluations

These would all be too broad for paper lengths under 10 pages and so you would need to revise them. For instance, instead of looking at the effectiveness of drug or sex offender treatment in general, you might want to research one particular program or modality. Similarly, instead of a paper on habeas corpus in general, you may want to concentrate on two cases that deal with habeas corpus. The point is that you want to be able to present the issue or question and then comprehensively discuss it in the pages assigned.

Outline. The second step is to outline the paper, but if you don't know anything at all about your subject, you will need to do some research first. Today, the Internet makes research incredibly easy. You can use your library's online data search engine or, if you do not have access to one, you can use Google Scholar. Simply enter your topic and you will be able to access a number of academic journal articles on your subject. Remember that academic journals, not popular magazines, are usually required for research papers. Also, you may not be able to use "practitioner journals" such as *Corrections Today* or *Law Enforcement Digest*. Academic journals such as *Crime and Delinquency, Criminology, Justice Quarterly, Journal of Crime and Justice*, and *Prison Journal* are the most common sources for a research paper. Instructors seldom allow Wikipedia or other non-official Internet sources as acceptable bibliographic citations. Of course you should also actually go to your library

---

The Use of Probation Today

History

John Augustus, Boston shoemaker, 1841(reference, year)

Mission and Scope of Use

Probation in State X

State organization chart

Criticisms of Probation

Slap on the wrist? (reference, year)

Percent of people who are in favor of it (reference, year, page number)

Future of Probation

(remember that building?) and look for current books on your subject.

After finding several articles or books on your topic, read them and note the issues that are present in your topic. Certain themes, issues, or points, should become repetitive and these will form the basis of your outline. Start your outline with an introduction section that explains to the reader what the paper is about and a short description of the topic. This section should be no more than one page (or paragraph for short papers) but it must be on the first page, not come later. Then present the sub-topics in some logical order. For some topics, it may be a chronology; for others, it may be that you present positive points, then negative points. It is best to go from the general to the specific. Set your outline up in a document in bold font and perhaps in a larger font size. The advantage of word processing is that you can cut out sections and move them around if you need to as the paper develops. At this point, it is wise to check with your instructor to make sure that the outline fits the requirements of the assignment.

Enter Notes. The next step is to enter your research notes. You should never copy from your sources! Generally, research papers are too short to include quotes anyway so just resolve to write every word yourself. When you read the article, you should enter notes into the word document under the appropriate bold face heading with a reference. See the example below. Refrain from copying since when you begin to write, you will forget whether it is a quote or whether it is your sentence. Continue to enter in facts from the articles as you read them. Once all your references have been read and relevant facts entered, you can see where the gaps are in your outline. Then you need to either go find that information from new sources or rearrange your outline to eliminate those topics or issues. The general rule of thumb is that you should have the ratio of a reference per page assigned; which means that for a 10 page paper you need 10 references and so forth.

In the box provided, you see an outline for a paper on probation where some beginning notes are filled in. You must have complete reference citation for every fact entered as a note. Once your outline is filled in with notes, you can begin writing.

Write the paper. If the paper is long, it is important to provide subheadings. These can be the outline headings. You should always have an introductory paragraph or page that explains what the paper is about, and a conclusion paragraph or page that basically identifies the few key points you want the reader to remember. Do not introduce new information in the conclusion.

Referencing your sources is very important so as you take notes, make sure you have a system for identifying where they came from. It is important to reference with an author, year *and* a page number every time you use a number (i.e., the number in prison or the percent of people who recidivate). You must also reference with a page number when you use a direct quote. For all general information you may cite only to the author and year of the publication without a page number (but check with your instructor).

The most common reference citation style in criminal justice is the *modified* APA style. APA style manuals may be purchased and style sheets can be found on the Internet. Your instructor may provide a style sheet for you. Generally, the modified style puts the author's name, year and page number (if necessary) in parentheses in the text. For instance, if I entered a fact from my note above and I obtained the information from this textbook, it might read something like this:

1. The "father" of probation was John Augustus, a Boston shoemaker. He asked the court to release an offender arrested for public drunkenness into his custody in 1841 (Pollock 2007).

If I had used a direct quote or used a number from the source, I would need the page number as well.

John Augustus eventually helped supervise 267 offenders (Pollock 2007, 31) [or (Pollock, 2007: 31).]

There are many ways to cite, however, so find out whether there is a particular citation style that you are required to use. Regardless of which style you use, you must be consistent throughout the paper.

Write the conclusion. The last step in writing is providing a good conclusion paragraph. Typically, you do not insert any "editorializing" in the body of the paper, but it is sometimes acceptable to insert your own opinions and conclusions in the final section of the paper. After writing your paper, it is very important to check it for grammatical errors and omissions in citation. Make sure your references are complete and do not include any source as a reference that is not used in the text of the paper. In the checklist provided, you can see some of the most common writing problems. Make sure that you do not include them in your paper!

WRITING CHECKLIST

(These are the most common writing errors)

1. Is there a beginning paragraph that explains what the paper is going to do and a concluding paragraph that summarizes the content?
2. Is there proper citation *in the text*? Is there a cite after the source author's name? Follow the assigned style or be consistent in your use of any standard style of citation.
3. Is there a citation for every fact that is not general knowledge? Are there

citations *with page numbers* for direct quotes and any numbers or percents?

4. Are there any sentences copied from another source without quotes and/or without having a reference cite? Remember even changing a word in a sentence is still considered plagiarism.

5. Are there any paragraphs that are longer than about a fourth of a typed page? If so, break up into smaller paragraphs. Are paragraphs too short (less than three sentences)?

6. Are there any sentences that run on for more than three lines? If so, break up into two sentences.

7. Are there any Web pages used as references? If so, is the cite in the text the author's name (not the web address) and does the reference in back indicate the date you retrieved the Web site?

8. Are numbers spelled out in words if single digits and displayed as numerals in double digits and above? Also, if a sentence starts out with a number, it must be spelled out.

9. Are affect (think "influence") and effect (think "consequence") used correctly?

10. Are verb "strings" correct? ("they are running, walking, and singing;" or, "they ran, walked, and sang;" NOT: "they are running, walked and sing")

11. Are verbs consistently in past tense or present tense. He ran to the store and talked to the owner; NOT He is running to the store and talked to the owner.

12. Are female/male (adjectives) and men/women (nouns) used correctly?

13. Is there no more than one quote per page?

14. Are any quotes that are over three lines long indented and single spaced?

15. Are all noun/verbs in agreement, depending on whether they are plural or singular?

16. Are there any "I" statements? (Typically this is not appropriate in a research paper).

17. Are there any conclusory or opinion statements in the text? (Typically this is not appropriate in a research paper).

18. Is research referred to appropriately in the text? Typically, one writes: "Smith (1987) in his research on prisoners ..."; use of the title of the article or book is generally not appropriate.

19. Are law cases italicized or underlined with the citation provided?

20. If a secondary source is cited, is it appropriately referenced? (i.e., Smith, as cited in Jones, 1990: pgs).

21. Are *were* and *where* used correctly?

NOTES

1 See, Hobbes, T. (1651/1982). *Leviathan*. New York: Penguin Classics. See also Rousseau, J. (1762/1968). *The Social Contract*. New York: Penguin Classics.

2 Bureau of Justice Statistics. Retrieved 12/23/05 from ojp.usdoj.gov/bjs/glance/exptyp.htm.

3 Packer, H. (1968). *The Limits of the Criminal Sanction*. Stanford, CA: Stanford University Press.

4 Pollock, J. (2007). *Ethical Dilemmas and Decisions in Criminal Justice*, Fifth Edition. Belmont, CA: ITP/Wadsworth, pp. 190–191.

4 | Chapter Review

1. What is socialization? How does socialization influence our sense of self and our behavior?
2. How does power and authority (either formal or inferred) impact social conformity?
3. Discuss the concept of stigma. What impact does stigma and the assignment of deviant labels or identities have on individuals (including personally, within one-on-one interactions, or socially)?

CASE STUDY: OUR LIVES IN DIGITAL WORLDS AND NEW MEANS OF INTERACTION AND CONCEPTS OF IDENTITY AND SOCIAL PERFORMANCE

The online world and the development of social media (including options like "Second Life," etc.) have given us the opportunity to play out **"impression management"** (or, according to Erving Goffman, a sociologist, how we manage our social impression/identify in social settings and groups) in new and unique ways; it has in many cases given us the ability to create identities, roles, and status positions entirely different from those that we might occupy in face-to-face interaction and in real-life groups. Recently, National Public Radio (NPR) broadcasted a series of "Ted Talks" on

this very topic and the foundation of research that is being conducted on our identities both in digital and in-person spaces. You can access the broadcast here for February, 3, 2017:

http://www.npr.org/podcasts/510298/ted-radio-hour.

As with other exercises in this book, this broadcast may be influential in your own thought process as we continue to explore the influence and purpose of larger institutions (such as the media) and the influence that they can have in the establishment of identity.

DEVELOPING THE SOCIOLOGICAL IMAGINATION: FBI INDEX CRIMES

Recently a significant amount of research as well as media attention has been paid to what has been termed the "School to Prison Pipeline." It has been discussed in documentaries such as "Juvenile Justice in America" (2015) and the Oscar-nominated documentary *13th* (2015). The phrase refers to the increasing pattern of touch points students in U.S. society have with the criminal justice system during K-12 years specifically. The concept explores how such increasing interaction may unfairly target students of color or other minority groupings (including vulnerable groups such as those with disabilities), how these increasing interactions with law enforcement assist in assigning deviant labels and identities to young children that create criminal records for children (also termed "the criminalization of childhood" in some circles), and the impact of these interactions in creating the conditions that funnel children directly into the criminal justice system as adults. Many theorists and social scientists believe that the "school to prison pipeline" is a new form of social control, specifically the control of marginalized groups. Such theorists also propose that what is considered "criminal" can vary in society and not all behavior that is deviant may be considered a crime in need of punishment, particularly among children.

Measuring crime and criminal activity in a society is complex. For example, statistics only capture those crimes that are identified or prosecuted. The FBI Uniform Crime Report (available at https://ucr.fbi.gov/) provides local and national statistics for "**index crimes**" or the eight crimes the FBI combines to produce its annual crime index. These offenses include willful homicide, forcible rape, robbery, burglary, aggravated assault, larceny over $50, motor vehicle theft, and arson. Often these statistics are used to determine the relative safety of neighborhoods or the relative state of crime in a given area. Clearly, these measures do not report on various things that also might be considered crime or activity that might be harmful to individuals and society (such as "white collar crimes"); however, this is often what is measured and may influence our ideas on what is considered dangerous.

Review the types of crime discussed in the most recent "FBI Uniform Crime Report." What is the purpose (structural function) of reporting on these crimes specifically? What might be the controversy (conflict) in noting these specific crimes as areas of focus compared to other types of crime? Who in society is most likely to commit these types of crimes specifically? What are some types of crimes that are harmful to the individual and society that are not included in this report? How might our understanding (symbolic interaction) of what is considered "harmful" to society contribute to the stigmatization of certain groups in society as compared to other groups?

UNIT 2

Social Inequality

5 | Age, Race, Class, and the Institution of Work

CHAPTER SUMMARY

- This chapter explores the concept of social structure and how we, and others, navigate these structures as a means of accessing social power, prestige, and resources.

- This chapter looks at how social structures are made up of both social institutions and social interaction; therefore, social structures are those that are both institutionalized and experienced in interpersonal relationships.

- This chapter will challenge readers to think about the structures that individuals navigate and their impact on things like experiences within the institutions of education and work in the 21st Century.

PRELIMINARY QUESTIONS FOR READERS

- Think of the social class (or socioeconomic background) that you grew up with in your family of origin. How did this potentially abstract or possibly taken-for-granted standing, yet very real social structure, influence how your interacted with systems of education, work, or law? How did it impact how you thought of others or how others treated you?

- How does one's life experience differ based upon their access to social resources, power, or prestige? Think of a few examples and explain.

- What are some contemporary challenges in the institution of work? What are some challenges for you in balancing work, personal, and family life?

CHAPTER INTRODUCTION

Social Inequality: Social Differentiation and Social Stratification

According to Andersen and Taylor (2007), **social differentiation** is defined as the process by which different statuses develop in any group, organization, or society. Status differences can become organized into a hierarchical social system where various groups have different access to power, resources, and prestige. This is defined as **social stratification.** Although stratification systems vary in different countries, throughout history most societies have had some type of social stratification system whereby individuals and groups access the resources of that society.

The articles in this chapter provide examples of how the **social structures** (defined and explored in Chapter 2) of age, race, and gender and one's combination of these variables (referred to as **"intersectionality,"** also defined in Chapter 2) can impact how one navigates the social world, the institutions that he or she is a part of, his or her sense of self, and his or her place within the society and groups, and the social opportunities available to the individual. Different ages, class groups, racial and ethnic groupings, genders, and sexual and gender identities do currently and have had throughout history impacted differing access to social resources, prestige, and power in various societies and at various times.

AGE

The second article in this chapter explores **age** as the first hierarchical structure that places us in relationships of **power** (the ability to exercise control over other groups despite resistance) with others and within social groups.

SOCIAL CLASS

The United States operates within a class system. **Social class** can be defined as the division of individuals and groups according to the achieved or ascribed status position those individuals and groups have within a society. Most often social class can be used to describe an individual's socioeconomic status. One's class placement or socioeconomic status is not simply a label but also a social structure within which an individual operates and navigates and one that bears significant influence on one's access to social power, resources, and prestige. In fact, Max Weber (a German sociologist) discussed this influence in terms of one's "life chances" and ultimate life outcomes (including the ability to possess goods, have income, have access to certain jobs, and everyday quality of life).

Upper, middle, and lower class are labels that reflect the fact that we have, and operate within, a class system in the United States. The upper class may also be referred to as the "elites" in a society. The first article in this chapter, "Elites and Class Structures," discusses the concepts of class, the **"power elite"** model used within various social science disciplines, the differing opportunities based upon one's position in these groups, and how power may be replicated or sustained in a society over time. The middle class traditionally includes those with near median incomes (however, it is often difficult to define where middle class begins and ends); the lower middle class often includes lower-income workers; and the lower class is comprised primarily of those with the lowest income and who are the most under-resourced in society. Research suggests that those in the lower groupings are not only the those without access to resources but also often are those whom society has disadvantaged over the long-term (for example immigrant groups, the disabled, or those disproportionately impacted by economic trends that have created changes in the social institutions of work).

SOCIAL MOBILITY

Social mobility is the ability of individuals to move from one class to another class over time. Over the past 30–40 years, a significant amount of research has demonstrated that income inequality between classes has increased significantly, impacting opportunities for social mobility for many. Many economists and sociologists have attributed this phenomenon to a few significant factors: (1) industry reorganization (such as movement from manufacturing to service-based industries); (2) globalization; (3) the loss of union strength; (4) tax restructuring; and (5) corporate deregulation. This has resulted in wages that, for most workers, have not kept up with the rate of U.S. inflation. This has impacted social mobility in the United States specifically. Newer research suggests that, because of these factors, individuals are likely to either stay in the same class group as their parents or drop down a class standing (National Bureau of Economic Justice, 2016). The second article in this book explores the topic of globalization and its impact on production, social mobility, and social inequality.

POVERTY

Currently in the United States approximately 13.5% of the population is considered "poor" (U.S. Census, 2016). According to U.S. Census statistics, the poor in the United States are racially diverse, are diverse in age, and geographically reside in both urban and rural settings. The largest demographic grouping of the poor (or under resourced) in the U.S. and globally are women and children (commonly termed the **"Feminization of Poverty"**).

There is no single cause of poverty in a society and for many individuals and households. In fact, even many sociologists, economists, and other social scientists often disagree about the root causes of poverty. **The "Culture of Poverty" theory** communicates that the root causes of poverty lie within individual choices (otherwise "individual troubles" as C. Wright Mills would define it), including a lack of morals and initiative. Other social scientists view the root causes of poverty as structural and caused by factors and trends that impact institutions and as a result large proportions of the population. For example, statistically, poverty most often results from an unexpected expense or life event (such as divorce, illness, and unemployment) and issues such as national and state budget reductions, or economic restructuring, can also impact the numbers of those considered under-resourced in a society.

We can also study inequality between countries (or between those that have great wealth and those that have little, otherwise defined as **"global stratification."**) Stratification in this case has also intersected with race and world racial history. Many believe that this is fueled by **globalization** (or the process by which companies gain international influence). According to Anderson and Taylor (2007),

> The rich who dominate the world system are largely European with the addition of the U.S. and Japan. In these countries the population is largely white. In the poor countries of the world the population is largely people of color. As has been an established historical fact in world relations, exploitation of the human and natural resources of regions populated by people of color has characterized the history of Western Capitalism, with people of color historically being dominated by Western Imperialism and colonialism. In the new capitalist system, a new international division of labor has emerged that is not tied to a place but can employ cheap labor anywhere. Cheap labor is usually found in non-Western countries. The exploitation of cheap labor has created a poor and dependent workforce that is mostly people of color (pg. 212).

The fourth article in this chapter, "Race as Class" by Herbert J. Gans is a classic sociological reading in the study of class and racial inequities and explores the concept of race as a determinant of class standing and class standing as influencing racial classification partly (if not entirely) due to this history and the intersection of these variables throughout history.

RACE AND ETHNICITY
Distinguishing Between the Terminology

A **racial group** is a group that is categorized or labeled by society as a unique group based upon certain biological factors that group has in common (Schaeffer, 2009). One's racial category is an ascribed status, meaning that it is often a label assigned to an individual based upon his or her appearance. In contrast, an **ethnic group** is a group that may share ancestral origins but primarily has a common culture (such as a common language, religion, or way of life). It is possible for individuals to have very different racial and ethnic identifications. For example, an individual from Jamaica, although labeled by U.S. society as "black" may not consider himself "African-American" as defined in racial categorization, even though he may resonate with the experience and treatment of African-Americans in U.S. society.

RACIAL FORMATION

The terms and conditions by which a group becomes defined as a racial group have varied over time in the United States. The process by which a particular group becomes defined as a particular race is called **racial formation.** The process of classifying individuals according to race is thought to have first emerged in Europe in the 1800s. Most theorists agree that this was based off the idea that there were distinct differences among groups who appeared biologically different from one another. It is significant to note that while some still hold to this idea, others have argued that as a human species we are actually more alike biologically than we may be different from one another (Omi & Winant, 1994). Anthropology, for example, sees nuanced racial classifications and categories as entirely **socially constructed** (or created by society and often for the benefit of dominant groups) as, according to the discipline, there is only the "human race."

In the United States for a significant part of time, specific racial classification had two categories: white or non-white. This was primarily applied to distinguish between those of African-American descent and those who were not. Therefore, if a group was not African-American, it would often be classified as "white" (although there was often debate about which groups were considered to be closer to this label as compared to others). Clearly, there have been vast changes in racial categorization in the United States since this time. It has also not been a consistent or uniform process. Those groups labeled as "white," however, have been consistently given certain privileges in U.S. society. While this label may reference a specific skin color, it also contains much more than that, not just in the privileges granted to those groups who are a part of the label but also in status as this label also often reflects some shared ideas or characteristics that tend to represent the values of this historically dominant group (Omi & Winant, 1994).

CHOOSING ETHNIC IDENTITIES

Racial and ethnic identification is one that is heavily based in meaning for individuals when forming their personal identity. In "Ethnic Options" by Mary Waters (1990), the author makes the case that given the "melting pot" perception about American culture, individuals in U.S. society (more so than ever before) have a tremendous amount of flux and choice when determining the ethnic groups they choose to identify with (although this may not necessarily make a difference on the labels or classifications imposed upon them by society). In short, the book makes the argument that ethnic identity has as much to do with environment and experience as it does with biological attributes for individuals when forming their personal identity specifically. The racial stereotypes and expectations of society, however, can weigh heavily upon individuals in the formation of this identity and in such choices.

THE INSTITUTIONS OF EDUCATION AND WORK

Most social scientists consider the institution of education as an attempt to socialize individuals into the institution and processes of **work** (the systems by which individuals earn income and contribute their labor, or the organization of employment) in a given society. The institution of education serves the very important social function of socialization and social control as well as career or occupational training. Of course, the education that one receives in the

United States depending on what neighborhood the person lives in, for example, is not always equal in resources or quality.

A central debate within current education policy is to what extent the system of education is adequately preparing students for the workforce. This includes disparities due to socioeconomic status, compulsory testing, tracking systems (such as placing certain students in "gifted" programs instead of working as a classroom to achieve specific goals), and how cognitive and intellectual ability is measured. For example, some researchers suggest that intellectual quotient (IQ) and SAT or ACT testing measures (among other types of standardized testing) may not reflect the diversity in class, gender, and racial/ethnic differences. Many social scientists believe that the language and examples in such tests (and subsequently how these tests are then graded) tend to favor Caucasian and middle- to upper-class culture (Schaefer, 2009).

As education, and the quality of education one receives, directly impacts occupation, prestige, and, in many cases, class standing, many sociologists have studied how disparities in the quality of education in different areas of a society may also impact one's participation and contribution in the system of work (including what occupations may be available to an individual, for example). Sociologists have studied a variety of topics within the institution of work, including how inequality may be experienced and perpetuated depending on age, race, gender, familial status, number of children, and other characteristics and how this impacts ultimate life chances and opportunity. Other sociologists have looked at how larger economic trends can impact systems of work and, in turn, how those changes impact individual lives and the other institutions that are a part of that individual's life (for example, how do changes in the system of work impact the institution of family or one's sense of work/life balance). The third article in this chapter discusses some of these topics.

WORKS CITED

Andersen, M. L. & Taylor, H. F. (2007). *Sociology: The essentials*. 4th Edition. Belmont, CA: Thompson Wadsworth Press.

Omi, M. & Winant, H. (1994,). *Racial formation in the United States*. 2nd Edition. New York: Routledge.

Schaefer, R. (2009). *Race and ethnicity in the United States*. Upper Saddle River, NJ: Pearson Education.

Waters, M. (1990). *Ethnic options*. Berkeley and Los Angeles, CA: University of California Press.

Weber, M. (1978 [1922]). *Economy and society: An outline of interpretive sociology*. Berkeley, CA: University of California Press.

Elites and Classes

Mills and Bourdieu

by Michael Hartmann

The central reference point for all analyses which, whether explicitly or more implicitly, deal critically with the functionalist approach is the relationship between elites and classes. This applies for the two most prominent representatives of critical elite research, Mills with his "Power Elite" (Mills 1956 [1959]) and Bourdieu with his "Classe dominante" (Bourdieu 1979). They seek to explain elites with reference to their position vis-à-vis the other classes and strata of society. They challenge "pluralist" elite theories wherever these show critical weaknesses.

THE POWER ELITE (C. WRIGHT MILLS)

In *The Power Elite*[1], probably the best-known of his books, C. Wright Mills[2] early on gives the following general definition of elite: the "the power elite is composed of men whose positions enable them ... to make decisions having major consequences" (Mills 1959). In Mills' view the men of the elite are those at the head of the large economic, political, and military organizations, which he sees as the only organizations able to confer on them their great and, above all, durable power. These three sectors form the "real centers of power," and other sectors such as churches, universities, or the family are subordinate to them in that it is the former rather than the latter that determine the major developments in society. Decisions made in their highly centralized power apparatuses are increasingly interdependent and their structures are growingly interwoven, and intensive coordination is therefore unavoidable. In the end, the overlaps between the domains of power and the interdependence between them induce the powerful leaders of these three groups to "come together to form the power elite of America" (ibid.).

However, the power elite owes its rise and its stability not only to the intertwinement of the three sectors and the identity of their interests but also rests, as Mills succinctly puts it, "upon the similarity of origin and outlook and the social and political intermingling of the top circles from each of these dominant hierarchies" (ibid.). Although there is no aristocracy whose leading families decide on the distribution of top positions, most of the members of the power elite do come from the upper strata, that is, at least from families of academics or businesspeople. They have generally attended a university, frequently the famed private elite universities, their educational careers are similar in nature, and they are often marked by similar features such as religion or place of birth. Social origin alone, however, does not, for Mills, permit any final conclusions to be drawn with regard to the psychological and social ties that link the members of the power elite. It is also necessary to take a look at the recruitment and value standards valid within the various circles belonging to the power elite, since these provide—possibly even more than anything else—for the power elite's homogeneity. With the requirements placed on the leading men from the three sectors becoming increasingly similar, the training and selection of these men themselves finally serve to make them increasingly alike. Their manifold professional and personal contacts cement their common features even further, and it therefore can be said that nowhere in America is "there as great a 'class consciousness' as among the elite" (ibid).

Mills characterizes the upper class, that is, the "first families" in town and country as "a propertied class" which is distinguished from other sections of the population by its similar lifestyle, similar educational and professional careers, intensive contacts within the group, and a marked awareness of its own special position. These people live in the same exclusive areas, wear the same type of dress, attend clubs accessible only to their own circles, and generally tend to have close contacts with each other. Since many members are in positions of power, the close personal contacts and mutual trust and confidence naturally mean that problems are discussed in informal conversations. In this way their children effortlessly learn how important decisions are made. This in turn tends to blur the boundaries between personal matters and matters of interest to society as a whole. Social "'background' is one way

in which, on the basis of intimate association, the activities of an upper class may be tacitly co-ordinated" (ibid.). This is true at the local no less than at the national level. The tone is set by the upper echelons in the metropolises, and it is they who are at the top of the power and status hierarchy of the country as a whole.[3]

The conflict between "old and new wealth," ubiquitous and constant, is always resolved by the acceptance of the nouveau riche into the circle of the upper classes, though this may not always occur immediately, indeed sometimes not until the second generation. The renowned schools and universities in which the offspring of these circles are educated play, in Mills' view, an extremely important role here. At these institutions they learn to adopt common behavioral patterns, norms, and values, thus ensuring, more than any other institutions, the uniformity of the upper class and a blending of the "old" and "new" families. For Mills this is the "one clue to the national unity of the upper social classes in America today" (ibid.). All in all, the American upper class is, thanks to specifically American historical conditions (no aristocracy), "merely an enriched bourgeoisie;" access to this class is ultimately determined by money and not by the family tree (ibid.).

Mills argues that it is the owners of "large fortunes," the multimillionaires, who are at the top of this upper class; about three quarters of them come from rich families, and the fathers of roughly the same percentage of them are or were entrepreneurs. Wealth, then, is not only inherited but also shows a tendency "to monopolize new opportunities for getting 'great wealth'" (ibid.). Even so, unlike the past, multimillionaires no longer "reign alone on top of visible and simple hierarchies" but are increasingly bound up in the power hierarchies of large corporations, for today it is the large corporations, and not large fortunes, that are the source and basis of lasting wealth and power. In these organized centers of the owning class, then, rich families ally themselves with top executives, the administrators of their assets, either by combining the functions involved, through cooperation, or on the basis of common interests (ibid.). The men at the top of the large corporations who do not themselves come from the rich families at least have a similar social background, more than 70 percent of their fathers being entrepreneurs or academics, and only 10 percent of them workers or white-collar workers—in many cases already the second generation and in situations that remain relatively constant for decades (ibid.).

All these people profit from the prestige associated with leading positions in national corporations, since "members of society," both big-city and local, draw their standards of prestige from precisely these corporations (ibid.). The big-city upper class, "the upper 400," not having managed to become the "center of a national system of prestige," and celebrities from sports and entertainment being "ephemeral figures" without power of any stable sort, and since the elite is in need of "some sort of organization of enduring and stable prestige," much is to be said in favor of the business elite joining together with the political and military elites to form one single prestige system, sidelining show-business and sports stars (ibid.).

For Mills, the rise of the large corporations has, generally speaking, not only led to a concentration of power but also to greater inner cohesion among the owning class. Since most shares are held by multimillionaires and the chief executives of the major corporations, and in view of the reciprocal connections implied by posts on executive and supervisory boards, these persons have expanded their vision beyond the individual corporation to embrace the interests of large-scale industry as a whole and, ultimately, the interests of their entire class. Their decisions determine the course of the economy, employment rates, purchasing power, prices, and investment levels. It is not the "visible" politicians but "the chief executives who sit in the political directorate" who thus "hold the power and the means of defending the privileges of their corporate world." No power effectively can resist them (ibid.).[4]

At a later point Mills qualifies the impression he may have made with formulations of this kind. The political apparatus, he says, is not merely an "extension of the corporate world," the American government not "in any simple way … a committee of 'the ruling class.'" It is instead "a network of committees" whose members are also recruited from representatives of the political and military hierarchies (ibid.). Here Mills lodges a protest against any interpretation which would attribute political rule to the propertied class, and in particular against "the simple Marxian view" that sees in the "big economic man the real holder of power" (ibid.), and seeks to explain social developments simply as a reflection of the "will of the bourgeoisie" (ibid.). In a long footnote he makes his point even more clearly. It is here that he explains his reasons for using the term "power elite" instead of "ruling class." In his opinion the term "ruling class" is too fraught with connotations. Class is an economic term, rule a political concept. Thus the term "ruling class" implies a theory according to which an economic class exercises political rule. This simplified theory may or may not hold true for limited periods of time, but, Mills notes, he has no desire to drag this term into the concepts he employs, preferring instead to use more precise and generally valid concepts. Above all, he states, his aim is to counter the risk involved in the general usage of the term "ruling class," that is, the risk that the autonomy of the political elite might otherwise be underestimated. The representatives of all three sectors, business, politics, and the military, frequently have a considerable degree of autonomy in today's world and are obliged to make and enforce their most important decisions by seeking to forge alliances (ibid.).

However, Mills adds, the political elite has lost much of its influence in recent years, whereas the military elite has gained in influence, so that "the corporate rich and the high warlord, in their coinciding interests, rule." This mirrors the increased importance of both foreign and security policy and the fact that the economy "is at once a permanent-war economy and a private-corporation economy" (ibid.). The US military, which, because of the country's geographical situation and its traditional citizen-soldier system, was long without any particularly large role in society, has grown very substantially in importance as a result of the world-political situation and the destruction potential of today's weapons (ibid.). Not only does the military have increasingly close connections with industry, it has also become the largest sponsor and planner of research and science, in this way extending its influence into the education sector as well (ibid.).

The development of the political elite has gone the opposite way. It is above all two trends (in addition to the changes in foreign policy) that are seen here as responsible for its perceptible decline in importance. First, the replacement of the old, fading middle class consisting of farmers and self-employed persons by the new class of white-collar employees. These, however, lack the economic autonomy of the old middle class and are thus "powerless," whereas the old class held, for a time, an "independent base of power," grounded in personally owned property. Second, the organized working class, which appeared on the stage as a new political force in the 1930s, did not, contrary to initial impressions, develop into a "power-bloc independent of corporation and state." In fact, Mills goes on, this class soon lost some of its clout as a result of its increasing dependence on the machinery of government, and today it is involved only in small ways in the making of important decisions. Its leaders no longer have access to the national elite and are forced to be content with their role at the middle level of power (ibid).

All in all, Mills sums up, American society breaks down into three distinct segments. At the top, a genuine "elite of power" has developed, the middle levels consist of "a drifting set of stalemated, balancing forces" no longer able to forge links between the lower and the upper levels, and the lower level is politically fragmented and "growing increasingly powerless." It is at this level that a mass society has developed (ibid.). Mass society differs in four respects from classic public society. Instead of being actively formulated and discussed by individual citizens, opinions are passively absorbed from the mass media; there is virtually no room for deviant positions; the state controls the ways in which opinion is translated into action; and the mass now "has no autonomy from institutions" (ibid.). The reason why all this is possible is that people in mass society (above all in big cities) live in isolation from one another "sunk in their routines," uninterested in participating in public life (ibid.). Instead of viewing them in social contexts, they see their personal troubles and worries as disjointed, individual questions. There is a lack of political education and discussion. This all makes it possible to manipulate the mass. Thus "the idea of a mass society suggests the idea of an elite of power" (ibid.). The autonomous associations which in the past "[stood] between the various classes and the state" are losing their political effectiveness and being replaced by centralized organizations which, using all the means of power at their disposal, are taking "charge of the terrorized or—as the case may be—merely intimidated society of masses" (ibid.).

THE REPRODUCTION OF THE RULING CLASS (PIERRE BOURDIEU)

The analysis of the social elite or the "dominant or ruling class" likewise plays a central role in Pierre Bourdieu's[3] theory. Unlike Mills, however, Bourdieu is concerned less with the way in which the political system functions than with the mechanisms that reproduce the "dominant class." When asked by Loïc J.D. Wacquant in an interview conducted on the occasion of the publication of "La Noblesse d'État" about the reasons for the book, Bourdieu replied that he believed that "in advanced societies" it was not possible to investigate "the 'ruling class,' the 'elite,' the 'dominant class' … without elucidating the conditions under which they reproduce themselves" (Bourdieu 1993b).

Two propositions form the point of departure of Bourdieu's reflections:

Academic careers are largely dependent on the social background of school and university students.

The process of structural economic change forces the dominant faction of the ruling class—whose power extends to the business world—to radically alter its reproduction strategies, a shift that greatly increases the weight accorded to academic degrees in filling top positions.

With regard to the first point, Bourdieu sees discrepancies in academic success—which tend to differ as a function of parental background—as due primarily to the unequal endowment of families with economic and cultural capital. The acquisition of academic titles as an institutionalized and thus socially accepted form of cultural capital is dependent on the cultural capital of which a family is already in possession. Since cultural capital can only be accumulated personally, through "internalization," and is thus "fundamentally embodied" and lays claim to considerable personal time, primary socialization in the family appears to be either "a positive value (a gain in time, a head start) or a negative value (wasted time, and doubly so because more time must be spent correcting its effects)" (Bourdieu 1983). Cultural capital can be accumulated from earliest childhood on, without any loss of time or substance, only where the entire time invested in family upbringing is at the same time a period of accumulation (ibid.). Furthermore, availability of economic capital is not the only thing required for this internal family teaching/learning process—families, and as a rule mothers, have to be able to afford the time they need for the purpose—economic capital also improves the chances of such children to acquire a higher academic qualification by making it possible for them to postpone their entry into working life in favor of a protracted phase of education and training (ibid.). The more cultural and economic capital available to a family, the earlier the acquisition process can begin, the more effective it will later prove in school and university, and the longer it can be protracted (ibid.).

As regards the second point, Bourdieu sees the central impact of the process of structural change in the economy as a whole as well as in individual companies in the fact that traditional family businesses are increasingly being superseded by large corporations as well as in the growing differentiation, complexity, and bureaucratization of internal and external business relationships. Career trajectories within companies are generally depersonalized and rationalized, with the result that official academic titles have become far more important than ever before. A diploma from a "Grande école" "tends to become a necessary (but not sufficient) condition of access to positions of economic power"—and the larger the corporation, the more this applies (Bourdieu *et al.* 1973).[4] The dominant faction of the ruling class, whose power rests principally on the possession of economic capital, is forced to adapt its reproduction strategies to altered conditions. Whereas in the past executive positions inherited as family-owned companies were passed on to the next generation, today the focus is on acquiring exclusive academic titles. Part of the existing economic capital is transformed into institutionalized cultural capital with a view to securing the claims of offspring to top positions and power in corporations (ibid.). Even so, economic capital also retains its direct power beyond this process of transformation. It is, for example, far easier for the offspring of entrepreneurs to do without prestigious academic degrees (particularly those of the Grandes écoles) than it is for their rivals (ibid), and the incomes they earn with the same qualifications, Bourdieu continues, are also considerably higher, because

all this amounts to a "dissimulated form of appropriation of profit" (ibid).

In his later writings Bourdieu deepens his analysis of reproduction mechanisms in two distinct directions. First, he deals in greater detail with the role of the Grandes écoles in this process (Bourdieu 1996); and second, he looks more closely into the significance of habitus for these reproduction strategies. For Bourdieu, habitus is a key factor in this context in that it represents the internalization of "a determinate type of social and economic condition" (Bourdieu and Wacquant 1992) and it thus determines (as a rule unconsciously) the strategies that are pursued, or indeed can, generally, be pursued.

Bourdieu sees a person's habitus as mediating between this person's position in social space and his or her lifestyle. Habitus is a system of dispositions, a general, basic stance which determines a person's perception, feeling, thinking, behavior, and which, more than anything else, marks the boundaries drawn for every individual by his social origin and position. In an interview Bourdieu outlines these boundaries as follows: "A person who has, for example, a petty-bourgeois habitus, simply has, as Marx says, boundaries in his brain which he cannot cross. He for this reason finds certain things simply unthinkable, impossible" (Bourdieu 1992).

Anyone who has grown up in a working-class family, Bourdieu notes, will dress differently from someone whose father was a senior physician, he or she will like different food, enjoy different films and music, will be fond of different sports and leisure activities, have different reading and learning habits, speak a different language, have other career plans and a different circle of friends. The experiences, individual and collective, of the individual and his family and class will have become embodied in his habitus. While it is of course impossible that all members of a class should have precisely the same experiences in exactly the same order, the chances of their being confronted with situations typical for their class are far greater than they are for members of other classes (Bourdieu 1990). This is the basis of the class-specific habitus, which thus represents "embodied class" (Bourdieu 2004).

SUMMARY

The theoretical approaches of Mills and Bourdieu concur in two central points. Both agree that there is not a large number of interdependent sub-elites of generally equal standing, asserting instead that what we find is a single power elite or ruling class which, despite its internal differentiation (which both see), is marked by strong internal cohesion and dominated by the owning, or ruling, class, and above all by the faction of the dominant class that is endowed with economic capital. Mills and Bourdieu also both see the principal foundation of this cohesion in an identical or at least similar family and school socialization of members of the power elite or dominant class. They thus contradict the functionalist assumption that the meritocratic principle has opened access to the elite for all social groups. Furthermore, both Mills and Bourdieu, unlike most functionalist theorists, focus relatively sharply on the relationship between the power elite or dominant class and the other classes or strata of society as well as on the historical changes they have undergone. This can be seen particularly clearly in Mills' work, where he breaks down the position of US elites into various historical phases, especially in his analysis of the New Deal (Mills 1959), as well as in his depiction of the social conditions requisite to the rise of multimillionaires like Carnegie or Rockefeller (ibid.). Indeed, it can be said that comparisons between the different classes of society run through just about everything Bourdieu wrote. The differences between these classes are the factor that shapes both his early work on educational sociology and his later studies on habitus and power.

DISCUSSION QUESTIONS

1. What does Mills understand by the "power elite"?
2. How does Mills explain the relationship between the military, the political, and the business elite?
3. How does Mills characterize the mass society?
4. What is the difference between the two reproduction strategies of the "dominant faction of the ruling class in Bourdieu?
5. How does Bourdieu define the "habitus"?

NOTES

1 A summary of the most important results can be found in Mills' article in the *British Journal of Sociology* (Mills 1959).

2 C. Wright Mills (born in Waco, Texas in 1916, died in New York in 1962) was the son of an insurance representative. After studying at the Texas Agricultural and Mechanical College, the University

of Texas, and the University of Wisconsin, Mills held positions at the University of Maryland and Columbia University in New York. Politically, he was initially close to politics of the New Deal and later to the emerging New Left.

3 Pierre Bourdieu (born in Denguin, Béarn, France in 1930, died in Paris in 2002) was the son of a post office clerk. After studying at the renowned École Normale Supérieure (ENS) he worked at the University of Algiers, the Sorbonne in Paris, and the University of Lille, before being appointed in 1964 to a position at the prestigious École Pratique des Hautes Études (today École des Hautes Études en Sciences Sociales). In 1981 he was appointed professor of sociology at the Collège de France, France's most renowned scientific institution. Parallel to his scholarly work, Bourdieu was politically active on the side of the left.

4 In the above-mentioned interview with Wacquant, Bourdieu remarked that generally "in most of today's developed societies … the transmission of power—including economic power—is more and more dependent upon possession of educational credentials" (Bourdieu 1993b: 27).

BIBLIOGRAPHY

Bourdieu, P. (1974) "Avenir de classe et causalité du probable," in *Revue française de sociologie* 15: 9–42; Ger. "Klassenschicksal, individuelles Handeln und das Gesetz der Wahrscheinlichkeit," in P. Bourdieu, L. Boltanski, M. de Saint Martin and P. Maldidier (1981), *Über die Reproduktion sozialer Macht*, Frankfurt a.M.: EVA, pp. 169–226.

——— (1979) *La distinction, Critique sociale du jugement*, Paris: Éditions de Minuit: Engl. *Distinction. A Social Critique of the Judgement of Taste*, Cambridge, Mass.: Harvard University Press 2004 (original printing 1984/1986).

——— (1980) *Le sens pratique*, Paris: Éditions de Minuit; Engl. *The Logic of Practice*, Stanford: Stanford University Press 1990.

——— (1983) "Ökonomisches Kapital, kulturelles Kapital, soziales Kapital," in R. Kreckel (ed.) *Soziale Ungleichheiten. Soziale Welt*, Sonderband 2. Göttingen: Otto Schwartz & Co.: 183–98; Engl. "The (three) forms of capital," in J.G. Richardson (ed.), *Handbook of Theory and Research in the Sociology of Education*, New York & London: Greenwood Press 1986, pp. 241–58 (Reprint in A.H. Halsey, P. Brown and W.A. Stuart (eds), *Education, Culture, Economy, and Society*, Oxford: Oxford University Press 1997, pp. 46–58).

——— (1984) *Homo academicus*. Paris: Éditions de Minuit; Engl. *Homo academicus*, Cambridge: Polity Press 1988.

——— (1989a) *La noblesse d'Etat. Grandes écoles et esprit de corps*, Paris: Éditions de Minuit: Engl. *The State Nobility. Elite Schools in the Field of Power*, Cambridge: Polity Press 1996.

——— (1989b) *Satz und Gegensatz. Über die Verantwortung der Intellektuellen*, Berlin: Wagenbach Verlag.

——— (1992) "Die feinen Unterschiede," in M. Steinrücke (ed.), *Die verborgenen Mechanismen der Macht*, Hamburg: VSA-Verlag, pp. 31–47.

——— (1993a) *Soziologische Fragen*; Engl. *Sociology in Question*, London: Sage Publications.

——— (1993b) "From ruling class to the field of power," an interview with Pierre Bourdieu on "La Noblesse d'État," *Theory, Culture & Society* 10: 3, 19–44.

——— (1994) *Raisons pratiques. Sur la théorie de l'action*, Paris: Seuil; Engl. *Practical Reason: On The Theory of Action*, Cambridge: Polity Press 1998.

——— and Boltanski, L. (1975) "Le titre et le poste: rapports entre le système de reproduction," *Actes de la recherche en sciences sociales*, 2/3: 95–108; Ger. "Zum Verhältnis von Bildung und Beschäftigung," in P. Bourdieu, L. Boltanski, M. de

——— and Passeron, J.C. (1964) *Les héritiers. Les étudiants et la culture*, Paris: Éditions de Minuit, Engl. *The Inheritors. French Students and Their Relation to Culture*, Chicago: University of Chicago Press 1979.

——— and Saint Martin, M. de (1978) "Le patronat," *Actes de la recherche en sciences sociales*, 20/21: 2–82.

——— and Saint Martin, M. de (1982) "La sainte famille. L'épiscopat français dans la champ du pouvoir," *Actes de la recherche en sciences sociales* 44/45: 2–53.

——— and Saint Martin, M. de (1987) "Agrégation et ségrégation. Le champ des grandes écoles et le champ du pouvoir," *Actes de la recherche en sciences sociales* 69: 2–50.

———— and Wacquant, L.J.D. (1992) *Réponses pour une anthropologie réflexive*, Paris: Seuil; Engl. *An Invitation to Reflexive Sociology*, Chicago: University of Chicago Press.

———— Boltanski, L. and Saint Martin, M. de (1973) "Les stratégies de reconversion. Les classes sociales et le système d'enseignement," *Social Science Information* 12: 61–113, Engl. "Changes in social structure and changes in the demand for education," in S. Giner and M. Scotford-Archer (eds), *Contemporary Europe. Social Structures and Cultural Patterns*, London: Routledge and Kegan Paul 1977, pp. 197–227.

Mills, C.W (1959) *The Power Elite*, New York: OUP/Galaxy Books (original printing Oxford: Oxford University Press 1956).

Saint Martin, M. de (1993) *L'espace de la noblesse*, Paris: Éditions Métailié; Ger. *Der Adel. Soziologie eines Standes*, Constance: UVK 1993.

Age Matters

Age As a Basis of Inequality

by Toni Calasanti and Kate Slevin

AGE MATTERS

Feminist scholars have given little attention either to old women or to aging (Arber and Ginn 1991), despite Barbara McDonald's work in the women's movement in the 1980s and her plea that old age be recognized (McDonald 1983); despite the increases in absolute and relative numbers of those older than age sixty-five and the skewed sex ratio among old people in the United States; and despite the shifting age ratios in nations worldwide. The issues go ignored by most scholars, and one must ask why.

Feminists consider age but rarely old people or age relations. Most focus on young adult or middle-aged women and on girls. Some attend to Sontag's notion of the "double standard of aging," by which women suffer scorn and exclusion as they grow old—"a humiliating process of gradual sexual disqualification" (Sontag 1972: 102). But even studies of women "of a certain age" (Sontag 1972: 99) focus on middle age—a time when physical markers such as menopause, wrinkles, and the like

emerge and care work for old people begins to occupy women's time.

Feminist scholars recently have expressed more concern about *aging* (perhaps because more are aware of their own aging), but rarely do they study *old* people or examine age relations critically.[1] The scant scholarship on old age differs markedly from the passionate work on late middle age; it is "written from the outside, it is about *them*—the old—not us" (Twigg 2004: 64). Scholars employ others' data to document the disadvantages that women face in old age, such as low income, widowhood, and physical disability. But these accounts of the "problems of old women" (Gibson 1996) do not analyze age relations. For the most part, feminists have not talked to old women to explore their daily experiences; they have not attuned to the *advantages* old women might also have in relation to old men, such as stronger support networks (e.g., Barker, Morrow, and Mitteness 1998). They have not considered the intersections of inequalities with old age such that, for example, old black men are more likely to be poor than are old white women (Calasanti and Slevin 2001).

Feminists exclude old people both in their choice of research questions and in their theoretical approaches. They often write or say "older" rather than "old" to avoid the negativity of the latter. They may see old age as a social construction and take it as a sign of women's inequality that they are denigrated as "old" before men are, but we do not often question the stigma affixed to old age. We don't ask why it seems denigrating to label someone "old." Feminists have analyzed how terms related to girls and women, such as "sissy" and "girly," are used to put men and boys down and reinforce women's inferiority. Yet we have not considered the *age* relations that use these terms to keep old and young groups in their respective places.

The absence of a feminist critique of ageism and age relations furthers the oppression that old people face, especially those marginalized at the intersections of multiple hierarchies. For example, by accepting the cultural dictate to "age successfully" (e.g., Friedan 1993) that underlies the "new gerontology" (Holstein and Minkler 2003), feminists reinforce ageism. Developed by Rowe and Kahn, the notion of successful aging was meant to displace the view of old age as a time of disease and decline with a "vigorous emphasis on the potential for and indeed the likelihood of a healthy and engaged old age" (Holstein and Minkler 2003: 787). Successful aging requires maintenance of the activities popular among the middle-agers privileged with money and leisure time. Thus, staying fit, or at least appearing fit, is highly valued social capital. In this sense, successful aging means not aging, not being "old," or, at the very least, not looking old. The body has become central to identity and to aging, and the maintenance of its youthful appearance

has become a lifelong project that requires increasing levels of work.

Many of the age-resisting cultural practices are the purview of women. Successful aging assumes a "feminine" aspect in the ideal that the good elderly woman be healthy, slim, discreetly sexy, and independent (Ruddick 1999). Suffice it to say, our constructions of old age contain little that is positive. Fear of and disgust with growing old are widespread; people stigmatize it and associate it with personal failure, with "letting yourself go." Furthermore, class, gender, and racial biases embedded in these standards of middle age emphasize control over and choice about aging. We see advertising images of old people playing golf or tennis, traveling, sipping wine in front of sunsets, and strolling (or jogging) on the beaches of upscale resorts. Such pursuits, and the consumption depicted in ads for posh retirement communities, assume a sort of active lifestyle available only to a select group (McHugh 2000): men, whose race and class make them most likely to be able to afford it, and their spouses.

Cruikshank noted the "almost inescapable" judgment that old women's bodies are unattractive, but we know little about how old women endure this rejection (Cruikshank 2003: 147). Thus, though reporting on women who have aged "successfully" (e.g., Friedan 1993) might help negate ageist stereotypes of old women as useless or unhappy, it remains ageist in that it reinforces these standards of middle age. In light of the physical changes that occur as they age, then, many old people must develop strategies to preserve their "youthfulness" so that they will not be seen as old. As a result, old people and their bodies have become subject to a kind of discipline to activity. Those who are chronically impaired, or who prefer to be contemplative, are considered to be "problem" old people (Katz 2000; Holstein 1999; Holstein and Minkler 2003). Those who remain "active" are "not old"; those who are less active are "old" and thus less valuable.

This study of age relations also complicates theories of gender privilege. For instance, consumer capitalists can profit by the degradation of the status of men as they age. Katz (2001/2002) argued that the advertisements of the anti-aging industry present old men as potentially manly but in need of consumer regimens to remain so. Even old men who are white and rich are also generally retired and weakening, thus losing their institutional grips on the hegemonic ideals of manhood. Once out of the labor market and the realm of those considered sexually desirable by the young, old men find themselves second-class citizens. The men pictured in the anti-aging advertisements drive themselves into expensive and strenuous fun, translating the achievement orientations of the labor market into those of recreational consumption. Banned from the competition for salaries and promotions, they struggle for status by spending the wealth and strength they have to play as young men do in their attempt to appear as vigorous as possible.

Proponents of "agelessness" argue that being old is *all* a social construction (Andrews 1999)—based on how one thinks and acts. Thus we can avoid becoming old by simply not thinking and acting "old." To be sure, age categories are subjective, and all stages are constructions. Nevertheless, as Andrews (1999: 302) observed, "there is not much serious discussion about eliminating infancy, adolescence, or adulthood from the developmental landscape. It is only old age which comes under the scalpel." Whether our quest is to age successfully or to be ageless, this need to deny old age lies at the heart of ageism. We deny that

we are aging; and, when forced to confront the process, we treat it as ugly and tragic.

Age categories have real consequences, and bodies—old bodies—matter. They have a material reality along with their social interpretation (Laz 2003). Old people are *not*, in fact, just like middle-aged persons but only older. They are different. And as is the case with other forms of oppression, we must acknowledge and accept these differences, even see them as valuable. We must distinguish between age resistance and age denial (Twigg 2004: 63), and to do so, we must theorize the age relations that underlie the devaluation of old age.

AGE RELATIONS

Old age is a unique time of life and not simply an additive result of events occurring over the life course. Those who are perceived to be old are marginalized and lose power; they are subjected to violence (such as elder abuse) and to exploitation and cultural imperialism (Laws 1995). They suffer inequalities in distributions of authority, status, and money, and these inequalities are seen to be natural, and thus beyond dispute. Next, we briefly discuss how old people experience these inequalities.

LOSS OF POWER

Old people lose authority and autonomy. For instance, doctors treat old patients differently than younger clients, more often withholding information, services, and treatment of medical problems (Robb, Chen, and Haley 2002). On one hand, doctors often take the complaints of old people less seriously than younger clients, attributing them to "old age" (Quadagno 1999). On the other hand, old age has been *biomedicalized*—a process whereby the outcomes of social factors are defined as medical or personal problems to be alleviated by medical intervention. Old people lose their ability to make decisions about their bodies and undergo drug therapies rather than other curative treatments (Wilson 2000).

WORKPLACE ISSUES AND MARGINALIZATION

Ageism costs old people in the labor market both status and money. Although the attitudes and beliefs of employers are certainly implicated (e.g., Encel 1999), often ageism is more subtly incorporated into staffing and recruitment policies, career structures, and retirement policies (Bytheway 1995). The inability to earn money in later life means that most old people must rely on others—family or the state. And when we consider the economic dependence and security of old people, the oppressive nature of age relations become apparent. The fiscal policies and welfare retrenchment in many Western countries provide one lens on the discrimination faced by old people as they increasingly face cutbacks. As Wilson (2000: 9) noted, "Economic policies are often presented as rational and inevitable but, given the power structure of society, these so-called inevitable choices usually end up protecting younger age groups and resulting in unpleasant outcomes for those in later life (cuts in pensions or charges for health care)." Demographic projections about aging populations are often used to justify such changes, even though relevant evidence is often lacking. Furthermore, neither the public nor decision makers seem willing to consider counterevidence, such as cross-cultural comparisons that reveal little relationship between the percentage of social spending on old persons and their percentage within the overall population (Wilson 2000). Predictions of dire consequences attendant on an aging population are similarly unrelated. Indeed, with only 12.4 percent of its population age sixty-five years and older, the United States ranks thirty-seventh among countries with at least 10 percent of their population age sixty-five years and older, well below the almost 19 percent of the top three countries (Italy, Japan, and Greece) (Federal Interagency Forum on Aging Related Statistics 2004).

Decreases in income, erosion of pensions, and proposals to "reform" Social Security are not the only ways old people are marginalized when they leave the labor market. Laws (1995: 115) suggested that labor-market participation shapes identity—such that participation in waged labor "is a crucial element of citizenship, in the definition of social worthiness, and in the development of a subject's self-esteem." In conjunction with the sort of cultural denigration we describe next, the lack of labor-market participation encourages young people to see old people as "other" and not fully deserving of citizenship rights (Wilson 2000: 161). Such disenfranchisement may be informal (rather than based in laws), but it is real nonetheless (Laws 1995), as seen in the previous policy discussion.

WEALTH AND INCOME

In the contemporary United States, many people believe that old people hold vast economic resources—an assertion that is certainly counter to claims that old people lose status or money in later life. However, the greatest inequalities in terms of income and wealth exist among old people, such that many are quite poor. The small number of old people with tremendous wealth is offset by the vast majority who rely on Social Security to stay above the poverty line. In concrete terms, Social Security—whose monthly payments averaged $1,013 for men and $764 for women in 2003—provides more than half of all income received for two-thirds of old people in the United States; indeed it amounts to almost half of income for four-fifths. Even more, it composes 90 percent or more of all income for a full one-third of older people and 100 percent of income for more than one-fifth (22 percent).

The poverty threshold is higher for old people than the rest of the population. In 2003, an old person's income had to be below $8,825—compared to $9,573 for those younger than sixty-five—to be officially designated "poor" (DeNavas-Walt, Proctor, and Mills 2004). Notably, most of the public is unaware of this fact. Poverty thresholds are calculated based on estimates of costs for nutritionally adequate diets, and because of their slower metabolism, old people need fewer calories than younger people. Thus, old people are assumed to need less money than those younger than sixty-five, despite their high medical expenses. As a result, official statistics greatly underestimate the number of old persons who are poor.

CULTURAL DEVALUATION

Finally, old people are subject to a "cultural imperialism" exemplified by "the emphasis on youth and vitality that undermines the positive contributions of older people" (Laws 1995: 113). The reality that being old, in and of itself, is a position of low status is apparent in the burgeoning anti-aging industry (including the new field of "longevity medicine"), which is estimated to gross between $27 billion and $43 billion a year (with the expectation of a

rise to $64 billion by 2007), depending on how expansive a definition one uses (Mehlman, Binstock, Juengst, Ponsaran, and Whitehouse 2004; U.S. Senate Special Committee on Aging 2001; *Dateline NBC,* March 6, 2001). Besides ingesting nutritional supplements and testosterone or human growth hormones, increasing numbers of people spend hours at the gym, undergo cosmetic surgery, and use lotions, creams, and hair dyes to erase the physical markers of age. Such is the equation of old age with disease and physical and mental decline that visible signs of aging serve to justify limitation of the rights and authority of old people. Many view old age as a "natural" part of life with unavoidable decrements—an equation apparent in the medical doctors' treatment of symptoms as "just old age" rather than as signs of illness or injury that merit care. The equation of aging with a natural order justifies ageism.

Age relations differ from other power relations in that one's group membership shifts over time. As a result, one can experience both aspects of age relations—advantage and disadvantage—during a lifetime. Although other social locations can be malleable, such dramatic shifts in status remain uncommon. Few change racial or gender identities, but we all grow old or die first. Intersecting inequalities affect when this (becoming old) occurs, but the fact remains that where individuals stand in relation to old age *must* change (Calasanti and Slevin 2001).

The following sections provide just two examples of the ageism we discuss above, and how it intersects with gender relations. In the first instance, authors Kelly Joyce and Laura Mamo discuss further the process of biomedicalization that we noted above, pointing to some of the ways in which science and technology help to shape the meanings and experiences we attach to aging. Thus, in the present cultural context, aging bodies are increasingly seen to be "problems" that can be solved through the use of science and technology. Further, as they show in their discussion of sexuality, our understanding of how we should use technology and science to have "normal" bodies is shaped by gender as well. The second example, from the work of Julie Ann McMullin and Ellie D. Barger, is based on their study of unemployed older persons who are participating in programs developed to assist them find jobs. Here, we see that not only do workers over age forty-five face discrimination in employment, but that the kinds of barriers they confront are also conditioned by being a man or a woman.

Example 1:
Aging, Ageism, and Biomedicalization

Within biomedicine, the aged body is increasingly constructed as a set of age-related diseases as well as a site for continual restoration and improvement. Such conceptualizations of aging and aging bodies produce a market for potential scientific and technological interventions from treatments deemed to be lifesaving (cardiac implants, kidney dialysis) to therapies for prevention and risk reduction (Tamoxifen for breast cancer, prostate cancer screening) to technologies designed to improve lifestyle (cosmetic surgeries, baldness medications). In all, there is an urgency about the importance of technology and science to the meaning, interventions, and lived experiences of aging. Furthermore, these issues illustrate the extent to which scientific knowledge and its technical applications are central producers of the meaning of "normal" aging and the embodied, lived experiences of old age.

Intervening in aging processes, while perhaps debateable, is illustrative in medicine's current preoccupation with replacing, enhancing, and regenerating the body through practices such as hormone replacement therapy for menopause; prosthetic replacements for shoulders, knees, and hips; and new research into regenerative organs and limbs. A tension exists here between *being in* the body (a material, biophysiological state) and imagining or culturally constructing the limits, desires, and possibilities of the body. Aging, in this regard, is at best optional and at worst something (part biological, part cultural) to be individually negotiated and medically cured (Squier 2004).

Previous lines between health and illness are blurred. What was once healthy is today pre-symptomatic, at risk, and in need of anti-aging therapies. The creation, expansion, and redefinition of biomedical disease categories, such as Parkinson's, Alzheimer's, sexual dysfunction, and incontinence, and new biomedical risk categories, such as pre-diabetes and pre-cancer, are particularly relevant to feminist studies of aging in that these projects concomitantly produce the raced, gendered, and (anti)aging body. The search for biomarkers of difference in light of the Human Genome Diversity Project is one such example (Reardon 2005).

Pharmaceutical companies now compose an important part of biomedical practice. Called the era of "Big Pharma," the 1990s marked an increase in the presence and size of megapharmaceutical companies such as Pfizer Pharmaceuticals, Eli Lily, Merck Research Laboratories, and Bristol-Myers Squibb Company. These companies are among the most profitable industries in the United States, with average net returns that rank far above those of other American companies (Angell 2005). In 2000 and 2001, for example, the ten pharmaceutical companies in the Fortune 500 were leaders in the top two key measures of profitability, reporting "a profit of 17 cents for every dollar of revenue, compared with a Fortune 500 median of 3.1 cents per dollar of revenue and a return on assets of 14.1 percent, compared with a Fortune 500 median of 2.3 percent" (Pattison and Warren 2003: 1). This economic power, coupled with changes in direct-to-consumer advertising regulations, translates into pharmaceutical companies having enormous influence. As we demonstrate in the next section, pharmaceutical marketing redefines not only what it means to be healthy and sick but also what it means to be masculine and feminine, young and old.

One drug that helped redefine masculinity and femininity is Viagra. Several feminist scholars variously examine Viagra for the work it does to redefine gender (Fishman 2004; Loe 2004; Mamo and Fishman 2001; Marshall and Katz 2002; Potts 2000) yet few have explicitly argued that Viagra redefines aging masculinity and femininity using youthful assumptions about the body to do so. For example, feminist sociologist Meika Loe's (2004) work shows how urologists, scientific studies published in medical journals, the rise of Big Pharma, advertisements, and a large aging population all co-produced the disease "sexual dysfunction." More important, though, the rise of Viagra redefined "normal" sexuality so that men are expected to produce and maintain an erection on demand (Loe 2004: 19). As Loe (2004: 92) demonstrates, "Viagra can and is being used to enforce and perpetuate an ideal masculinity"—one that is impossible for many male bodies to attain. This redefinition of masculinity, as Loe convincingly argues,

simultaneously redefines femininity. Women, to accommodate their Viagra-infused partners, are now expected to be sexually active until death.

Loe's rich analysis successfully shows how the marketing and use of Viagra redefines gender and sexuality in troubling ways. However, her primary analytical focus is gender. Loe does provide an excellent chapter on senior female partners of Viagra users (see pp. 95–123) and briefly discusses the drug's relation to other anti-aging therapies such as Botox, the anti-wrinkle drug (see pp. 174–76), but a sustained discussion of ageism and aging male bodies is not Loe's central concern. While every book clearly cannot be inclusive of all issues, we contend that Viagra and other pharmaceuticals targeting sexual function are illustrative of a shift toward anti-aging therapies that reconfigure aging. For example, although the attainment of the always-erect penis is hard for many men to accomplish, it is especially difficult for aging men. Similarly, the redefinition of women's sexuality has a clear anti-aging tone as it excludes aging bodily processes and positions the young female body as the ideal. Moreover, the success of Viagra and other anti-aging interventions is related to the underlying ageism that permeates the United States. If aging bodies were perceived to be and constructed as part of routine, even "normal" social process, then such interventions would be harder to sell.

A feminist analysis of aging must continue to examine biomedicalization processes as social definitions of "normal" masculinity and femininity are increasing constructed on biomedical and corporate terrain. For example, menopause, potentially perceived as a normal part of aging, is currently positioned as an abnormality or pathology. As part of this cultural definition, a "normal" aging woman is expected to take actions, such as using hormone replacement therapy (now available in a "low dose" form in response to the Women's Health Initiative finding that the risks of taking hormone replacement therapy often outweigh the benefits), to avoid displaying bodily changes associated with aging. The ageism is clear here as well. Yet while feminist research on the medicalization of menopause is extensive (see, for example, Bell 1987; Lewis 1993; Lock 1993; and Martin 1989), few explicitly place ageism and age-relations at the center of analysis.[5] For example, Guillemin's (2000) research on menopause clinics studies how the understanding of menopause as hormone deficiency is generated and stabilized in interactions between clients and health care professionals. Menopause information seminars, diagnostic questionnaires, and the use of technologies such as bone densitometry all prime women to reframe their own initial perceptions of menopause into the medicalized model. While Guillemin clearly shows the importance of technoscience to the framing of menopause as pathology, she simultaneously neglects the role ageism plays in this reframing.

Medical constructions of heart disease, osteoporosis, colon cancer, and other illnesses all participate in and reshape cultural definitions of masculinity, femininity, and aging. In all, biomedicalization processes reconfigure aging bodies and their multiple identifications from the inside out by means of illness categories and their corresponding pharmaceutical and surgical interventions. At the same time, changes in advertising regulations make it easier for pharmaceutical companies to sell new ideas of "normal," ideas that seamlessly connect normalcy with youthfulness. Presented as an "ageless" body, what is actually being sold is an ideal, youthful body mutually shaped within ideals of femininity and masculinity. Viagra and hormone replacement therapy demonstrate that to stay feminine or masculine, consumers should "choose" to maintain the erect penises and perky breasts associated with teenage or twenty-something bodies.

Example 2:
Gendered Ageism/Age(ed) Sexism: The Case of Unemployed Older Workers

Since at least the 1970s, a considerable body of research and feminist scholarship has considered gender-based inequality and sexism in paid work. One of the key issues that emerged from this scholarship was a better understanding of how gender relations structure labor markets thereby placing women at a disadvantage relative to men. The story is now well-known. Labor markets are segregated such that women tend to be employed in less well-paid, devalued jobs that often involve nurturing or caregiving tasks. Sexism at work takes many forms and often restricts women's access to jobs and promotions. Sexual harassment remains pervasive in work environments, and double standards still exist, which make it difficult for women to negotiate and manage their work environments.

Relative to the structure of gender relations and the sexism that emerges as a result, very little is known about the mechanisms through which age relations are made manifest in paid-work environments. We know very little about whether older workers are discriminated against, whether they are harassed on the basis of their age, whether they are patronized or considered invisible. Although there is a general acknowledgment among feminist scholars that age is an important structural basis of inequality, very little research has considered whether and how intersections between age and gender relations influence inequality in labor markets. Indeed, most feminist research on the workplace has focused on the experiences of younger women and gender relations, thereby neglecting the workplace experiences of older women and the theoretical importance of age relations.

Within paid paid-labor markets, unemployed workers are among the most disadvantaged because they are in the uncertain and precarious position of needing to find work to earn a living and make ends meet. Older displaced workers are especially disadvantaged in this regard because, compared to younger displaced workers, they face longer spells of unemployment (Rowe and Nguyen 2003), are often rehired at lower wages or in part-time positions (McMullin and Marshall 2001), and have less time to financially recover from an unemployment spell before their retirement. Research on older displaced workers tends to be based on national statistical data and not on the experiences of the older workers. As a result we know little about the challenges that older workers face in their search for employment and how age and gender intersect in shaping their experiences.

Ageism in the Search for Paid Employment

Our data suggest that the job search experience and the meaning that respondents attribute to it are structured by age and gender relations. The most pervasive theme that emerged in our data was the belief that age influenced the job searches of the study participants in various ways. One woman described an experience where she was explicitly told that age entered into the hiring process:

> No one will tell you; no one will admit it. But I have a friend who owns his own company and he said, "If I interview three people, even though you have the experience, if I think I can get more years out of another one, I would hire another person." And you know, they don't have to say that, that's just the way it's done. (female, age sixty)

Another fifty-eight-year-old woman reflected on her struggle to find employment and recalled asking a manager who wrote a reference letter for her why she couldn't find a job. As she put it,

> I worked at a place for eleven and a half years. And, I did speak to the human resource person and she's given me, you know, a great reference. And I said, "What's wrong?" and she said, "It's age." … You know, I guess I don't think of myself in terms of being older yet.

The blunt response of the human resource professional simply linking age with not being able to get a job is telling. But also interesting is the respondent's denial of aging and being older. Similarly, another three quotations point to encounters at older-worker programs when three women first realized that their age might pose a barrier in the search for employment:

> I had a course … a specialized program for experienced workers they called it—for older workers. … It made me very much aware of what's going on out there. I was not realizing it. I never

realized that age was a factor. (female, age fifty-eight)

We saw a tape, a video about age barriers [at the older-worker program]. … This problem related to age, I didn't expect. (female, age sixty-one)

I watched a video at [name of older-worker program] that was about age discrimination. I found it so depressing that I had to leave in the middle of the video. I was so upset by it that it is hard for me to discuss it even now. … I would never want to see that again. … The longer it went on, the worse I felt I had to leave. (female, age fifty-three)

These illustrations point to the contradictions and identity struggles that some older workers face as they are being labeled "older" but do not "feel older" yet.

According to many of our informants, prospective employers would refer to older applicants using phrases such as "over-qualified" or "too experienced" rather than stating that a job applicant was too old. For example,

I went to two interviews there. They finally rejected me … I, as they put it, was "over-qualified." … But I couldn't get anyone to hire me. (male, age sixty-two)

There was one company I sent my résumé to. … I was kind of surprised that I didn't get an interview there and I sent an e-mail to the HR lady asking why and what happened. … Her e-mail seemed to indicate. … Her e-mail said "too experienced" and I just assumed she means—as meaning too old. (male, age forty-six)

In other cases, respondents were told that someone more "junior" was hired or that the organization was too "fast-paced" for them. Our informants recognized that these were simply euphemisms for being "too old" for the job, as indicated in the following quotes:

I got turned down for a job and I asked the temp agency who was responsible for getting the job [why I got turned down] because I wanted to know for sure … and the answer was, and I quote, "well they hired somebody more junior." So in other words, "junior" is a euphemism for "younger." Now I am not supposed to realize that. I am supposed to be too stupid to realize that. So obviously they realize that if they were to have said "we hired somebody younger" that's illegal, so now it seems like it is in vogue to say "more junior." Well, "junior" means younger doesn't it? So why shouldn't that be illegal too? (female, age fifty-three)

I can see the way they [employers] talk to me sometimes—kind of in a lingo here. 'Cause I can read the employers' lingo very well. … They tell me "the place is very fast-paced." … That's all a line of crap, as we know. … It's more or less saying "good-bye, I'm glad to have met you." Oh yeah. So I'm getting a bit tired of listening to that. (female, age forty-nine)

Hence, in efforts to avoid charges of ageism and age-based discrimination, employers seem to disguise their ageist hiring practices by rejecting older applicants with the use of more age-neutral terms.

GENDERED AGEISM:
THE EXPERIENCE FACTOR

The insidiousness of ageism in job search processes was further reflected by the view held by many of our study participants that employers would examine résumés and reject applicants based on the number of years spent in the labor force or the number of jobs held. The following three quotations are illustrative of the general view that years of experience are equated with age:

> They don't say anything, but you know when there is absolutely no reason why you shouldn't be considered—to just look at my résumé, they know how many years I've been in the business and they can sort of deduct that I'm not thirty-five or forty. (female, age sixty)
>
> You don't know if they're looking at your résumé and looking at … like figuring you got all that experience so obviously you got to be a certain age, right? (female, age fifty-three)
>
> As you can see by my résumé I have twenty-five years [experience] so you know I'm not thirty-five. (male, age fifty)

The relationship between age and paid-labor-market experience is, however, structured by gender. Indeed, equating age and experience reflects a gendered bias that assumes lifelong, full-time employment, which remains more typical of men's lives than of women's. Notably, the women in our sample tended to have less paid-work experience than did the men, mainly because of their responsibilities for raising children and their other gendered care activities. One fifty-three-year-old woman commented specifically on the erroneous assumption that "age and experience" are correlated. As she states,

> The assumption is that if you are older you have more experience. … The two concepts of age and experience go hand-in-hand. But it is not necessarily accurate because you can be older and have very little experience if you have done something else with your life or whatever or doing a career change or your life has gone some other direction. (female, age fifty-three)

One disadvantage that the older women in this study face is a result of the double-edged sword of domestic labor responsibilities. In the first place, women take years out of paid labor to care for children thereby limiting their paid-work experience. In the second place, domestic work is devalued and the skills associated with it are rendered useless and inapplicable in the realm of paid work. The devaluation of the skills associated with unpaid work made several women in the study fear the prospect of returning to paid employment. As one woman noted,

> If I really want to go back to full-time, probably I'd have to overcome my feeling that yes, I can do the job. … Still, there is a "but" that is coming out. It's not so much the confidence; I do have confidence to do my work, but to face the reality. … I started to feel scared. … It's a very, very scary thing, I tell you. … It's no longer the same as around thirty years ago. They look for a particular type of person. … So this is the first time I'm facing it. So it's really tough. (female, age sixty-one)

A fifty-six-year-old woman who decided to leave paid work as a pharmacist to stay home and raise her children explained the fear and struggles that she had with the idea of going back into pharmacy after being out of the field for so many years. She spoke with many of her friends and colleagues in the pharmaceutical industry about the possibility of going back to work, and this heightened her fears because her associates told her that much had changed in the industry since she left. This woman eventually got an offer to volunteer at a pharmacy. She struggled with this decision but eventually decided to take the job:

> I was probably too chicken to get a job. I guess really, I didn't feel confident that I could get a job in my field because I haven't been in it for so many years. I left it to raise my kids, and then when I wanted to go back to work I was too afraid. … It's funny actually. A lot of my friends around my age are already considering retiring—early. And here I am going back to work. (female, age fifty-six)

Hence, the combination of age-related norms about how old someone should be when they are looking for work and a gendered structure that makes women primarily responsible for the care of their children and families made it difficult for this woman to get a paid job. Instead, she took an unpaid job, which serves to reinforce the devaluation of her specific skills and women's skills more generally.

Notably, some of the men in our study indicated that their paid-work experience was a valuable asset in the job search process, particularly in a job interview. They suggested that being able to discuss their varied experience with potential employers was a technique that actively counteracted ageism in an interview setting. For example, one male participant described how in job interviews he would emphasize the value of his experience in past employment positions:

> There is also a lot to be said about the judgment that comes with experience. The ability to judge and the ability to make a decision. … The people they had there were very inexperienced. They couldn't make any decisions. I was able to make decisions and so I kept things moving. … I am used to decisions. That is why I think that someone like me—even though it was an unaccustomed situation for me—I was able to apply my past background. I jumped in, took over, and did what was necessary to get the thing moving again. And that is where someone like me ought to be appreciated. (male, age fifty-two)

Another male respondent explained how emphasizing his experience was a strategy he used in job interviews to reframe the meaning tied to age-related questions from potential employers:

> Depending on the questions [during a job interview], you know—"How old are you?"—rather than respond—"That's none of your business"—I would have said something like—"Well, I'm old enough to have twenty-five years of experience in this business," which gives them an age bracket and it doesn't affect

me. "As you can see by my résumé, I have twenty-five years [experience]." (male, age fifty)

Because many of the women in this study lacked paid-work experience, they did not have the one advantage that was associated with being an older worker that the men in the sample had.

DISCUSSION QUESTIONS

1. Why is old age under-studied by scholars? Why is this important?

2. What does it mean to "age successfully"? How is it shaped by gender, race, class and other inequalities?

3. In what ways do contemporary medical practice, science, and technology influence our ideas of "normal" aging? How do these vary by gender?

4. How are job search experiences shaped by age and gender relations?

NOTES

1 This holds regardless of whether the focus is on men or women. Even in those few instances where men's studies scholars adopt a life-course view, "the theoretical discourse on masculinities has concentrated on social practices of young to middle-aged men and, by default, marginalized the masculinities of elderly men" (Thompson 1994: 9).

REFERENCES

Andrews, M. (1999) "The Seductiveness of Agelessness," *Ageing and Society* 19:301–18.

Angell, M. (2005) *The Truth about the Drug Companies: How They Deceive Us and What We Can Do about It*. New York: Random House Trade Paperbacks.

Arber, S., and Ginn, J. (1991) *Gender and Later Life*. Thousand Oaks, CA: Sage.

Barker, J.C., Morrow, J., and Mitteness, L.S. (1998) "Gender, Informal Social Support Networks, and Elderly Urban African Americans," *Journal of Aging Studies* 12 (2): 199–222.

Bell, S. (1987) "Changing Ideas: The Medicalization of Menopause," *Social Science and Medicine* 24 (6): 535–42.

Bytheway, B. (1995) *Ageism*. Buckingham, UK: Open University Press.

Calasanti, T.M., and Slevin, K.F. (2001) *Gender, Social Inequalities, and Aging*. Walnut Creek, CA: AltaMira Press.

Cruikshank, M. (2003) *Learning to Be Old*. New York: Rowman and Littlefield.

DeNavas-Walt, C., Proctor, B.D., and Mills, R.J. (2004) "Income, Poverty, and Health Insurance Coverage in the United States: 2003," in *Current Population Reports, P60-226*. Washington, DC: U.S. Census Bureau, U.S. Government Printing Office.

Encel, S. (1999) "Age Discrimination in Employment in Australia," *Ageing International* 25:69–84.

Federal Interagency Forum on Aging Related Statistics. (2004) *Older Americans 2004: Key Indicators of Well-Being*. Washington, DC: U.S. Government Printing Office.

Fishman, J. (2004) "Manufacturing Desire: The Commodification of Female Sexual Dysfunction," *Social Studies of Science* 34 (2): 187–218.

Friedan, B. (1993) *The Fountain of Age*. New York: Simon and Schuster.

Gibson, D. (1996) "Broken Down by Age and Gender: 'The Problem of Old Women' Redefined," *Gender and Society* 10:433–48.

Guillemin, M. (2000) "Working Practices of the Menopause Clinic," *Science, Technology and Human Values* 25 (4): 449–71.

Holstein, M.B. (1999) "Women and Productive Aging: Troubling Implications," in *Critical Gerontology: Perspectives from Political and Moral Economy,* ed. M. Minkler and C.L. Estes, 359–73. Amityville, NY: Baywood.

Holstein, M.B., and Minkler, M. (2003) "Self, Society, and the New Gerontology, *The Gerontologist* 43 (6): 787–96.

Katz, S. (2000) "Busy Bodies: Activity, Aging, and the Management of Everyday Life," *Journal of Aging Studies* 14:135–52.

Katz, S. (2001/2002) "Growing Older without Aging? Positive Aging, Anti-ageism, and Anti-aging," *Generations* 25 (4): 27–32.

Laws, G. (1995) "Understanding Ageism: Lessons from Feminism and Postmodernism," *The Gerontologist* 35 (1): 112–18.

Laz, C. (2003) "Age Embodied," *Journal of Aging Studies* 17:503–19.

Lewis, J. (1993) "Feminism, Menopause, and Hormone Replacement Therapy," *Feminist Review* 43 (Spring): 38–56.

Lock, M. (1993) *Encounters with Aging: Mythologies of Menopause in Japan and North America.* Berkeley: University of California Press.

Loe, M. (2004) *The Rise of Viagra: How the Little Blue Pill Changed Sex in America.* New York: New York University Press.

Macdonald, B., and Rich, C. I cited the book exactly as it is, i.e., it is by Macdonald, with Rich (not and Rich) (1983) *Look Me in the Eye: Old Women, Aging and Ageism.* San Francisco: Spinsters, Ink.

Mamo, L., and Fishman, J. (2001) "Potency in All the Right Places: Viagra as a Gendered Technology of the Body," *Body & Society* 7 (4): 13–35.

Marshall, B., and Katz, S. (2002) "Forever Functional: Sexual Fitness and the Aging Male Body," *Body & Society* 8 (4): 43–70.

Martin, E. (1989) *The Woman in the Body: A Cultural Analysis of Reproduction.* Boston, MA: Beacon Press.

McHugh, K. (2000) "The 'Ageless Self'? Emplacement of Identities in Sun-Belt Retirement Communities," *Journal of Aging Studies* 14:103–15.

McMullin, J.A., and Marshall, V.W. (2001) "Ageism, Age Relations, and Garment Industry Work in Montreal," *The Gerontologist* 41:111–22.

Mehlman, M.J., Binstock, R.H., Juengst, E.T., Ponsaran, R.S., and Whitehouse, P.J. (2004) "Anti-aging Medicine: Can Consumers Be Better Protected?" *The Gerontologist* 44 (3): 304–10.

Pattison, N., and Warren, L. (2003) "2002 Drug Industry Profits: Hefty Pharmaceutical Company Margins Dwarf Other Industries," *Public Citizen's Congress Watch,* http://www.citizen.org/documents/Pharma_Reports/pdf.

Potts, A. (2000) "The Essence of the 'Hard On': Hege-monic Masculinity and the Cultural Construction of 'Erectile Dysfunction,' " *Men and Masculinities* 3 (1): 85–103.

Quadagno, J.S. (1999) *Aging and the Life Course.* Boston: McGraw-Hill.

Reardon, J. (2005) *Race to the Finish: Identity and Governance in an Age of Genomics.* Princeton, NJ: Princeton University Press.

Robb, C., Chen, H., and Haley, W.E. (2002) "Ageism in Mental Health Care: A Critical Review," *Journal of Clinical Geropsychology* 8 (1): 1–12.

Rowe, G., and Nguyen, H. (2003) "Older Workers and the Labour Market," *Perspectives on Labour and Income* (Spring).

Ruddick, S. (1999) "Virtues and Age," in *Mother Time: Women, Aging and Ethics,* ed. M.U. Walker, 45–60. Lanham, MD: Rowman and Littlefield.

Social Security Administration. (2004) *Fast Facts and Figures about Social Security, 2004.* Washington, DC: U.S. Government Printing Office.

Sontag, S. (1972) "The Double Standard of Aging," in *Saturday Review of the Society,* ed. M. Rainbolt and J. Fleetwood, 55:29–38. Reprinted in *On the Contrary: Essays by Men and Women,* Albany, NY: SUNY Press, 1983, 99–112.

Squier, S. (2004) *Liminal Lives: Imaging the Human at the Frontiers of Biomedicine.* Durham, NC: Duke University Press.

Twigg, J. (2004) "The Body, Gender, and Age: Feminist Insights in Social Gerontology," *Journal of Aging Studies* 18 (1): 59–73.

U.S. Senate Special Committee on Aging. (2001) *Swin-dlers, Hucksters and Snake Oil Salesman: Hype and Hope Marketing Anti-aging Products to Seniors* (Serial No. 107–14). Washington, DC: U.S. Government Printing Office.

Wilson, G. (2000) *Understanding Old Age.* Thousand Oaks, CA: Sage.

Contemporary Economic Sociology

Globalization, Production, Inequality

by Fran Tonkiss

Here we will examine how we might analyze social and economic inequalities 'after' class. We turn first to debates that trace social and economic divisions in advanced economies not along class lines but around a range of factors including economic insecurity and forms of social exclusion. The discussion goes on to set these issues of inequality and insecurity in a global context, focusing on the links between poverty, inequality and economic growth.

Recent approaches to economic inequality have seen a shift away from concepts of class—based on individuals' structural locations *within* an economic order—to notions of insecurity, as a condition where people have an uncertain or precarious relation to economic membership: that is, where they stand at least partly *outside* an economic order. Within European debates, this shift has been captured in the category of 'social exclusion', referring to the ways that economic and social marginality tend to overlap. In a US context, such arguments have been linked to theories of an impoverished 'underclass', a term used to denote the radical exclusion of vulnerable groups from the economic and social mainstream. In both cases, economic disparities

stem not only from people's relative incomes, nor from their position within relations of production and work, but from their access to formal economic participation and their levels of social and economic protection. The argument in this chapter is that current economic arrangements produce pronounced (if not entirely 'new') patterns of inequality, which continue to structure contemporary societies in quite systematic ways.

The latter part of the discussion takes up the issue of inequality in a global context. Here, lines of economic division are severe. The discussion focuses on large-scale analyses developed by researchers in major international agencies, examining the contentious relation between growth, poverty reduction and levels of inequality. The harsh disparities which characterize global economic relations can make theoretical and policy debates within advanced economies look almost trivial; however, the two parts of the discussion centre on common themes. The links between inequality, poverty and insecurity are critical to thinking about contemporary economic divisions in both national and international contexts. Degrees of inequality and of material deprivation vary sharply between the most and the least developed economies, but some of the key questions are the same. To what extent can poverty reduction be separated from decreasing inequality? Does it matter if the inequality gap widens so long as the poorest are protected? How does non-income poverty—exclusion, insecurity, incapacity—reinforce and reproduce economic and social divisions?

INEQUALITY 'AFTER' CLASS

The shift away from class that occurred within critical analysis from the 1980s was partly a response to changing forms of social and economic organization, but was also prompted by the claims of modes of inequality which sociology had been given to ignore or understate. An emphasis on class within social analysis had gone together with the relative neglect of inequality based on race or gender: racial or gender inequalities were frequently seen as secondary to class divisions, or appeared as effects of class structures. This conventional focus on class as the basis of social structure and the primary axis of social inequality has been roundly criticized for overlooking power relations which are not fundamentally about class, but rather centre on actual or ascribed identities of gender, race, culture, religion, or sexuality. Nancy Fraser (1995) has drawn a distinction in this respect between a 'social politics of equality', typically based on class, and a 'cultural politics of difference', associated with wider questions of identity. If class has been relegated from its primary analytic position, however, this does not mean that issues of economic inequality go away. Some of the most acute ways in which differences are socially marked, and personally and collectively experienced, are through economic

structures. In this sense, criticisms of class from the standpoint of race or gender do not simply signal a move away from economic to cultural concerns, or from questions of inequality to those of identity. Inequality is still reproduced economically, and a focus on divisions other than class in fact can show up more severe economic disparities. Racial and ethnic differences frequently have been marked by forms of economic discrimination, domination and exploitation that are more vicious than class divisions, and which cannot be explained by recourse to class categories. So too, 'gender has exhibited far more pronounced inequalities of power and material rewards as well as offering more extreme examples of exploitation and brutal coercion than those occurring between classes' (Waters 2000: 49).

The critique of class therefore does not mean that economic inequality is no longer of analytic interest; in fact it can direct attention to starker forms of economic power and injustice. Too often, however, approaches to economic inequality have been seen as captive to a narrow 'distributive paradigm' that is over-determined by class, and which simply neglects forms of injustice which are not principally economic in character. Such an argument underlies a broad shift within social and political thought away from problems of inequality and redistribution and towards issues of difference and recognition.

In Anthony Giddens' (2000) work on *The Third Way and its Critics* the author seeks to make the claim that reducing poverty should take priority over reducing inequality. Giddens contends that the politics of the left has always conceived equality in terms of 'equality of outcomes'—the attempt to even up economic disparities, particularly through state intervention into market processes. Such a conception lies behind policies to redress social and economic inequalities by way of redistribution, both through welfare transfers and by narrowing inequalities of income and wealth via taxation.

The move away from equality of outcome towards equality of opportunity has gone together with a growing policy focus on investments in human capital—through education, skills training, childcare provision, and so on—in contrast to the redistribution of economic capital. Such strategies see people's capacities, including their skills and credentials, as determining their life chances in market societies. The answer for governments, then, is to help people to develop these capacities. Social and economic outcomes might be shaped by the development of opportunities, rather than through direct interventions at the level of 'who gets what'. The distinction between equality of opportunity and equality of outcomes is therefore a distinction between enabling capacities and engineering consequences. Some of this, to be sure, is little more than semantics. Giddens might stress the difference between equalities of opportunity and of outcome, but in practice British government policy of the late 1990s and early 2000s sought to intervene at the level of 'outcomes' as well as fostering people's life chances. A commitment to reducing poverty in any reasonable time-frame cannot wait for the slow feed of social mobility through enhanced opportunities.

A major rationale for such an emphasis on equality of opportunity is the argument that non-income poverty is as critical to individual life chances as income poverty. In this extended sense, poverty is defined not solely on the basis of income, but in terms of a lack of basic capacities or capabilities—health, education and literacy, reasonable housing conditions,

safety—which allow individuals to participate in social membership and to make choices in respect of their own lives. We will revisit this approach to non-income poverty in thinking about global inequality; in the present context, it is linked with debates over social exclusion in advanced economies. The relation between poverty and social exclusion reproduces the distinction between economic outcomes and social opportunities which has characterized recent debates over inequality. While poverty is an economic category defined by material deprivation, exclusion refers to a broader sense of being shut out from full social and economic participation. It describes conditions of social deprivation which often overlap with, but are not simply identical to, economic disadvantage. This idea of social exclusion emerged from European policy debates of the 1980s, originating in France in particular, to refer to groups that stand in a marginal relation to core social and economic processes. In this way it does some of the same work as the notion of an 'underclass' in the United States, while aiming to avoid the latter's more negative connotations as well as its racial overtones.

Debates over the situation of an underclass in US society have been dogged by the conflation of economic, social and moral diagnoses. In an early work on the subject, Auletta (1982: xiii) noted that studies of poverty defined this excluded class in terms of '*behavioral*, as well as *income* deficiencies'. The sociologist Herbert Gans concurs, arguing that the characterization of an underclass was based less on structural economic locations than on cultural or behavioral ascriptions (1995). In this sense it re-hashes earlier debates over a 'culture of poverty' amongst low-income groups, based on the reproduction of certain patterns of behavior and social and economic norms. Oscar Lewis' original work on impoverished families in Mexico, Puerto Rico and New York analyzed specific cultures of poverty as adaptive strategies developed in contexts of systematic discrimination and structural economic disadvantage; however the concept proved amenable to later arguments that material deprivation in wealthy societies was somehow due to a cultural problem with the poor themselves (Lewis 1959, 1966, 1996).

European debates over social exclusion generally sought to avoid the kinds of moral association that hung around the idea of an underclass; nevertheless some common themes are apparent. Policies to combat social exclusion in Britain from the late 1990s, for example, included community development initiatives on housing estates, as well as projects to lower rates of truancy and teenage pregnancy. Each of these elements features in Gans' round-up of the behavioral definition of an underclass in the US. These problems of social exclusion, however, were represented in the British context principally as barriers to individual opportunity rather than in terms of behavioral failures. An emphasis on such factors as housing environments and exclusion from education is based on the premise that economic inequalities are not reproduced solely through differentials in income levels, nor does income alone determine individuals' life chances. Rather, economic divisions are cross-cut with social conditions in limiting opportunities and stunting capacities.

Such an approach to equality—based on reducing poverty, enhancing opportunity, and combating social exclusion—raises a number of critical issues. For one thing, it is not clear just how 'new' any of this is. Recent arguments for widening social inclusion can be seen to rework, without always acknowledging, older arguments for the role of welfare provision in securing basic social rights and extending social citizenship (see Marshall 1950; Titmuss 1968). In this sense, the politics of welfare is not only about economic protections but also about social membership.

While no-one, to be sure, would argue with the goal of reducing poverty, it is less clear that poverty reduction and social inclusion can be so neatly separated from the goal of decreasing inequality. There is an argument to be made that the maintenance—and in some cases, the deepening—of economic inequalities is incompatible with efforts to widen social inclusion (see Phillips 1999). In this view, it is not simply absolute poverty but relative inequalities that undermine social cohesion and divide social groups. In contexts of entrenched inequality, the danger is that the stably employed and relatively secure come to identify with the better-off, detaching their own concerns from those of the unemployed or insecure. Economic divisions are compounded by social distance and moral disengagement. An approach to equality based on promoting opportunities at the level of the individual, however, tends to side-step this broader question of the relation between social inclusion and reducing inequality.

STRUCTURES OF INEQUALITY

Arguments that class categories are no longer the most obvious or accurate way to think about patterns of inequality do not mean that economic divisions are no longer structured in systematic ways. A number of recent analyses stratify contemporary societies around broad economic cleavages, based not simply on economic class locations but also on conditions of insecurity and exclusion. In this way they take up the critique of class-based models of inequality, recognizing that economic divisions are not solely organized around relations of production and work. The models considered below depict current patterns of stratification via broad schemes based on income, security and inclusion: the figures are approximate, therefore, but the lines of inequality they trace are more compelling.

Lash and Urry (1994) retain a class model to typify the economic divisions that are characteristic of advanced capitalist economies. One of the key challenges to conventional models of class has been the expansion of the service economy, and the related growth of the middle classes. The authors see this as a substantive shift in capitalist social structures, but argue that post-industrial economies produce both a mass middle-class grouping and also marked patterns of impoverishment, insecurity and exclusion. This is in large part due to the polarized nature of contemporary service industries, which generate both high-grade and very low-grade (poorly paid, insecure, unprotected and 'junk') jobs. They set out a basic model of social stratification along the following lines:

1. The top stratum is the relatively small capitalist class of owners. The rich, as ever, are always with us.
2. The mass class in advanced capitalist societies is the middle stratum of professional, managerial, administrative and service workers.
3. The working class, defined in conventional terms by their productive labor, is becoming smaller and is increasingly economically insecure. They are especially vulnerable to manufacturing

downturns, downsizing, and the shift of productive jobs off-shore.
4. The bottom layer is occupied by a new lower class, defined by casual and insecure work (if any), social marginalization and poverty. This group tends to over-represent immigrant workers as well as women.

The interesting thing about this rather basic scheme is the depiction of a significant minority whose economic position is defined not by their work function but by their relative insecurity and exclusion from mainstream economic processes. Economic inequalities in this way are premised not only on relations of ownership and work, but on access to labor markets and security in work.

Indeed, Will Hutton (1995) sees insecurity as the central principle structuring contemporary economies. In his treatment of the 'thirty, thirty, forty society', Hutton jettisons the language of class to highlight patterns of relative economic security as the dividing line between different socioeconomic strata. Focusing on the British case, Hutton contends that the economy is broadly organized around:

1. Forty per cent who are stably employed and relatively secure: their work-places are most likely to be covered by trade union agreements, they are more likely to have company or personal pensions and to have savings.
2. Thirty per cent who are relatively insecure: their work is casualized, their jobs are more likely to be unprotected, they may lack savings or pensions.
3. Thirty per cent are marginalized or excluded: this includes the unemployed or under-employed, those whose work

is unprotected and low-paid, groups that live on state benefits or less.

Clearly this is a broad-brush depiction, and the figures are hit-or-miss. How the exact numbers carve up in such large-scale representations is less important than the lines of divisions these critics identify. In all cases, economic stratification does not simply follow income: rather, relative security becomes a key principle for understanding inequality. Structures of inequality are based on income and wealth but also on economic security, legal and welfare entitlement, and economic inclusion in society.

It is important to note, of course, that income and relative security will tend to overlap. Hutton points out that in increasingly flexible labor markets even very highly paid work can be insecure, but nonetheless the 'insecurity' of a freelance management consultant is not the same as that of casual cleaner. And while people's status within labor markets is crucial to their economic position, exclusion from the labor market altogether remains a primary source of inequality and insecurity.

While the framework of economic inclusion and exclusion, security and insecurity, can be applied to different international settings, the extremes of poverty and exclusion in the global system need to be considered in their own terms. It is to the question of global inequalities that the discussion now turns.

GLOBAL INEQUALITIES

The relation between poverty reduction and decreasing inequality is especially vexed in a global setting. In contexts of sheer deprivation and chronic hunger, reducing poverty is clearly the most immediate priority. It is less clear, however, how far poverty reduction can or should be linked with efforts to decrease inequality, both within and between nations. An important intervention in this debate is that made by the World Bank researchers Dollar and Kraay (2002), who emphasize the role of economic growth in poverty reduction. They contend that the recent period of globalization, dating from around 1980, has both promoted equality and decreased poverty. The authors track a long-term global trend towards greater inequality up to a peak in the 1970s; since 1980 growth has been more widely spread across the world economy; consequently the number of people living in absolute poverty has diminished. This is largely due to growth in China and India, which in 1980 included around one-third of the world's population but almost two-thirds of the world's poor.

For Dollar and Kraay economic growth is the key to taking people out of poverty, but to make a marked change to the global picture it is crucial that growth is not confined to those parts of the world that are already well-off. Poorer nations must have a share in economic growth, and the primary means to do this is through openness to international trade and investment. They are less interested, therefore, in nationalist or autarkic economic strategies than in the benefits to be gained from global integration. The authors argue that, during the period since 1980, the 'globalizers' amongst the less-developed countries have grown faster than 'non-globalizers' (and in many cases faster than developed economies). Those economies which have liberalized trade and attracted inward investment have seen the benefits in economic growth.

Such patterns are true not only for different national economies, but also for regions within national economies, as connected and 'disconnected' regions vary markedly in terms of growth. The problem of global inequality, then, is not so much that of growing inequality between the developed and the developing world, but of growing inequality within the developing world, based on varying access to global economic processes. Moreover, Dollar and Kraay argue that globalizing measures do not in themselves promote inequality; rather inequality within economies tends to reflect domestic policies on such matters as taxation, education, employment protection and welfare. It follows that ensuring the benefits of globalization—'spreading the wealth', as the authors put it—requires a policy mix which limits protectionist measures by rich nations, and promotes sound domestic governance in developing economies. Trade openness at the international level should be matched by policy interventions to narrow inequalities at the national level.

This analysis has been influential, but also controversial. Most simply it is seen as advocating a 'trickle-down' approach to economic growth—a criticism that does not exactly square with Dollar and Kraay's emphasis on the importance of domestic policy interventions in ensuring that economic benefits are spread. A more complex argument concerns the structural relation between poverty and inequality. How far can poverty reduction be separated from decreasing inequality? Should anti-poverty strategies centre on absolute poverty (the dollar a day measure) or relative poverty (degrees of inequality within societies)? There is evidence to suggest that more unequal economies do less well at translating economic growth into lower rates of poverty. The argument here is not simply a moral but an economic one: economic inequality can be seen not only as unjust

but as inefficient. Inequities in land ownership, in access to productive assets, income and market opportunities can impede economic growth and prospects for inward investment. Cornia and Kiiski (2001: 37) argue that high levels of inequality represent a barrier to growth in numerous developing and transitional economies. If reducing poverty and decreasing inequality do not always go together, moreover, increases in both poverty and inequality often do—as shown by mounting poverty and inequality in the former states of the Soviet Union (see Oxfam 2003; UNDP 1999: 3, 2003: 37–8).

Dollar and Kraay's case centers on a sustained downward turn in *global* inequality—that is, in the disparity between rich and poor nations. Inequality cuts, however, in different ways. The UNDP (2003: 39) asserts that 'in recent decades there has unquestionably been a widening gap between the incomes of the very richest and the very poorest'. In the early years of the twenty-first century, the richest 5 per cent of the global population commanded 114 times the income of the poorest 5 per cent, while the top 1 per cent had as much as the bottom 57 per cent. Alongside these inequities in income levels may be set the unequal share of economic activity between nations. Richer nations continue to enjoy the lion's share of overall wealth, trade, investment and technology. By the end of the twentieth century, the fifth of the global population in the wealthiest countries had 86 per cent of world GDP to the bottom fifth's 1 per cent share; furthermore, the world's richest nations had 74 per cent of the world's telephone connections (and 91 per cent of its Internet users), while the bottom fifth had only 1.5 per cent (all figures UNDP 1999: 3).

Moving from the level of global inequality to that of national inequality adds to this picture. Dollar and Kraay state that levels of inequality within nations tend to decrease only very slowly. Slow reductions in domestic inequality are one thing, however; growing inequality is another. Over the critical period identified by Dollar and Kraay, from 1980 to the end of the 1990s—when global inequality and absolute poverty figures were both reducing—inequality increased markedly *within* transitional economies in the former Soviet bloc, as well as in such advanced capitalist countries as Japan, Sweden, the United Kingdom, the United States, Canada and Australia (Cornia and Kiiski 2001; UNDP 1999: 3). Looking more closely at specific countries and regions tends to interrupt this steady narrative of widening growth, diminishing poverty and decreasing inequality.

During the 1980s just four nations saw downturns in their human development index—a measure of life expectancies, levels of health and education, and basic living standards—while in the 1990s 21 nations witnessed such reversals (UNDP 2003: 34). This was in large part due to the HIV/AIDS crisis, but in the most severely affected nations the effects of the epidemic were compounded by a lack of economic growth, growing debt and falling commodity prices. In a large comparative review using data from 73 countries, representing 80 per cent of world population and 91 per cent of world GDP, Cornia and Kiiski adjudge that inequality increased during the 1980s and 1990s in 48 of the sample nations, and fell in just 9 (Cornia and Kiiski 2001).

POVERTY, INEQUALITY, INSECURITY: CHALLENGES FOR HUMAN DEVELOPMENT

These trends provided the backdrop to the United Nations Millennium Declaration of September 2000, endorsed by 189 member states. The Declaration made a collective commitment to efforts to reduce poverty, improve health, support environmental sustainability, promote peace and protect human rights. It is highly debatable how far advances have been made on any of these fronts, but progress in reducing poverty at least is measurable. The 'road map' for realizing this declaration is detailed in the form of eight Millennium Development Goals, the first of which is a goal to halve by 2015 the number of people living under the global poverty line of $1 per day (UNDP 2003: 15). A few years in, however, international agencies were projecting that the chances of reaching that goal varied markedly between regions and across nations: East Asia, Southeast Asia and South Asia had the best regional prospects, Latin America and the Caribbean were unlikely to meet the target, while sub-Saharan Africa was extremely unlikely to achieve it (see ILO UNDP 2003; World Bank 2005). At the national level dozens of countries were identified as priority cases, 'perilously off track to meet the Goals' (UNDP 2003: 15).

The emphasis in these analyses is on the linkage between economic growth and poverty reduction. On the one hand, this relationship can be quite straightforward: economic growth can reduce poverty by directly increasing household incomes. However, this is not an automatic effect of growth: it is more likely 'that economic growth reduces income poverty most when initial income inequality is narrow' (UNDP 2003: 17), while people can only share in economic growth where they have access to land and other assets, jobs, markets and credit. On the other hand, economic growth can also indirectly reduce poverty by increasing public revenues and allowing governments to invest in education, health and infrastructure. Such measures all promote skills and productivity levels, but they also have an impact on non-economic poverty. Anti-poverty measures may relate both to the distribution of private goods, and to the definition, distribution and quality of public goods: those goods held in common or public ownership, from water and air to hospitals or roads. This is to draw out the connection between income poverty and a broader 'human poverty' which limits people's capacities to make decisions in their communities and about their own lives due to poor health, sub-standard living environments or lack of education—that is, the lack of basic social and economic capabilities (UNDP 2003: 27).

Such arguments are indebted to Amartya Sen's work on inequality (see especially Sen 1992, 1999). Sen's core argument is that conventional approaches to inequality have focused too heavily on the distribution of commodities and capital, rather than on the share of capabilities or chances. He contends that strategies of economic development should aim to promote human capacities and not simply redistribute goods. Such capacities include individual human capital—knowledge, skills, abilities—but also shared forms of technical and informational capital—technology, information, intellectual goods. More broadly, a stress on capabilities takes in levels of health and education, standards of housing and environmental quality, community development and civil rights.

Leading debates on global equality emphasize the links between reducing poverty, decreasing inequality, and promoting human capacities. The distinction between economic and other forms of justice is in this sense a false one. The UN Development Goals are articulated as social and economic rights, and therefore tied up with wider human rights instruments and objectives. Moreover, problems of poverty and inequality are understood not merely in terms of income poverty, but also in respect of different kinds of insecurity. While uncertainties in employment conditions, labor market prospects and financial support are very significant in this context, insecurity is not confined to these economic forms. Rather, this problem can be defined in a number of ways (UNDP 1999):

1. Financial volatility and economic insecurity, including the immediate and longer-term effects of financial crises and economic downturns.
2. Job and income insecurity, linked to restructuring and job losses as well as to more general effects of casualization.
3. Health insecurity: the most obvious case is that of HIV/AIDS, but globalization also means that other epidemics have the potential to travel faster and wider than in the past.
4. Cultural insecurity, the effects of which extend from the extremes of cultural genocide to monocultural policy-making and global trends towards homogenization in media and cultural goods and images.
5. Personal insecurity, linked to crime and victimizaton—including problems of organized crime, sexual violence and sex traffic, vigilante and gun crime.
6. Environmental insecurity, a gathering crisis seen in depleted stocks, threats to biodiversity, and climate change.

7. Political and community insecurity, seen in war, civil conflict, state persecution and poor governance.

In all of these domains—from fears over personal safety to environmental degradation and organized violence—the costs of insecurity tend to be borne by the poorest groups in society. Situations of insecurity and risk in this way overlap with conditions of poverty, serving to reinforce existing structures of social and economic inequality.

CONCLUSION

Debates over inequality 'after' class in advanced capitalist societies have turned on a series of distinctions between economic and other forms of equality; between reducing poverty and narrowing inequalities; between income differentials, insecurity and exclusion. Setting these arguments in a more global context, however, tends to dissolve such lines of distinction. Inequality, poverty and insecurity interact in complex but legible ways to reproduce deep disparities both between and within nations. Furthermore, social and economic rights— those implied by politics to reduce poverty, promote human welfare and narrow inequalities—can be seen as continuous with wider cultural, political and human rights. To adopt the familiar maxim, famines do not happen in functioning democracies. This may be a truism, but it points to the fact that the stakes involved in arguments over inequality are much higher at a global level than they are in the most developed economies. In the latter setting, hair-splitting over equalities of opportunity as opposed to outcomes can appear as another of the luxuries of the better-off. It is fair to say that arguments over inequality are generally fraught by competing definitions, measures, focal points, and prescriptions. Still, there are more fundamental questions at issue than disputes over methodology or analysis. Sen (2002) criticizes the idea that technical measures of (increasing or decreasing) inequality or of (increasing or decreasing) income are the acid-test of economic growth, or indeed of globalization. They are neither easily comparable nor do they tend to be conclusive. The more relevant assessment, for Sen, is not the measure of existing distributions of wealth, but an evaluation of their *fairness* in comparison to alternative arrangements. Taking up a notion of justice as fairness in a global context is to underline the premise—of some politics and all economic sociology—that economic processes ultimately cannot be isolated from the social contexts within which they operate. Technical measures of economic inequality offer conflicting accounts of what nevertheless are objective conditions, but these real conditions are instituted through policy, structured by relations of power, and legitimized, reproduced or challenged by social actors.

DISCUSSION QUESTIONS

1. What is one concept that Tonkiss argues could be more useful in the 21st century than class? Why is this concept more useful than class?

2. Describe "non-income poverty."

3. What is the relationship between inequality and poverty at the national level? At the global level?

REFERENCES

Auletta, K. (1982) *The Underclass*. New York: Random House.

Cornia, G. A. and Kiiski, S. (2001) 'Trends in income distribution in the post-World War Two period: evidence and interpretation', UN/Wider Discussion Paper 2001/89. United Nations University, World Institute for Development Economics Research, Helsinki. http://www.wider.unu.edu/publications.

Dollar, D. and Kraay, A. (2002) 'Spreading the wealth', *Foreign Affairs* 81/1: 120–33.

Fraser, N. (1995) 'From redistribution to recognition? Dilemmas of justice in a "post-socialist" age', *New Left Review* 212: 68–93.

Gans, H. T. (1995) *The War Against the Poor: The Underclass and Antipoverty Policy*. New York: Basic Books.

Giddens, A. (1981) *The Class Structure of the Advanced Societies* (second edition). London: Hutchinson.

Hutton, W. (1995) 'The thirty, thirty, forty society', in *The State We're In*. London: Jonathan Cape, 105–10.

Lash, S. and Urry, J. (1994) *Economies of Signs and Space*. London: Sage.

Lewis, O. (1959) *Five Families: Mexican Case Studies in the Culture of Poverty*. New York: Basic Books.

Lewis, O. (1966) *La Vida: A Puerto Rican Family in the Culture of Poverty—San Juan and New York*. New York: Random House.

Lewis, O. (1996) [1966] 'The culture of poverty', in R. T. Le Gates and F. Stout (eds) *The City Reader*. London and New York: Routledge, 218–24.

Marshall, T. H. (1950) *Citizenship and Social Class*. Cambridge: Cambridge University Press.

Oxfam (2003) 'Growth with equity is good for the poor', in F. Lechner and J. Boli (eds) *The Globalization Reader* (second edition). Oxford: Blackwell, 183–9.

Phillips, A. (1999) 'Does economic inequality matter?', in *Which Equalities Matter?* Cambridge: Polity, 44–73.

Sen, A. (1992) *Inequality Re-examined*. Oxford: Clarendon Press.

Sen, A. (1999) *Development as Freedom*. New York: Alfred A. Knopf.

Sen, A. (2002) 'How to judge globalism', *The American Prospect* 13/1: 2–6.

Titmuss, R. (1968) *Commitment to Welfare*. London: Allen and Unwin.

UNDP (1999) *Human Development Report 1999: Globalization with a Human Face*. New York: Oxford University Press.

UNDP (2003) *Human Development Report 2003: Millennium Development Goals—A Compact Among Nations to End Poverty*. New York: Oxford University Press.

Waters, M. (2000) 'Inequality after class', in K. Nash (ed.) *Readings in Contemporary Political Sociology*. Oxford: Blackwell, 43–62.

World Bank (2005) *Global Monitoring Report 2005*. Washington: World Bank.

Race As Class

by Herbert J. Gans

Herbert J. Gans is the author of many books, including Making Sense of America, *which reports some of his work on race and ethnicity. Why does the idea of race continue to exert so much influence in the United States? Because the skin colors and other physical features used to define race were selected precisely because they mirror the country's socioeconomic pecking order.*

Humans of all colors and shapes can make babies with each other. Consequently most biologists, who define races as subspecies that cannot interbreed, argue that scientifically there can be no human races. Nonetheless, lay people still see and distinguish between races. Thus, it is worth asking again why the lay notion of race continues to exist and to exert so much influence in human affairs.

Lay persons are not biologists, nor are they sociologists, who argue these days that race is a social construction arbitrary enough to be eliminated if "society" chose to do so. The laity operates with a very different definition of race. They see that humans vary, notably in skin color, the shape of the head, nose, and lips, and quality of hair, and they choose to define the variations as individual races.

More important, the lay public uses this definition of race to decide whether strangers (the so-called "other") are to be treated as superior, inferior, or equal. Race is even more useful for deciding quickly whether strangers might be threatening and thus should be excluded. Whites often consider dark-skinned strangers threatening until they prove otherwise, and none more than African Americans.

Scholars believe the color differences in human skins can be traced to climatic adaptation. They argue that the high levels of melanin in dark skin originally protected people living outside in hot, sunny climates, notably in Africa and South Asia, from skin cancer. Conversely, in cold climates, the low amount of melanin in light skins enabled the early humans to soak up vitamin D from a sun often hidden behind clouds. These color differences were reinforced by millennia of inbreeding when humans lived in small groups that were geographically and socially isolated. This inbreeding also produced variations in head and nose shapes and other facial features so that Northern Europeans look different from people from the Mediterranean area, such as Italians and, long ago, Jews. Likewise, East African faces differ from West African ones, and Chinese faces from Japanese ones. (Presumably the inbreeding and isolation also produced the DNA patterns that geneticists refer to in the latest scientific revival and redefinition of race.)

Geographic and social isolation ended long ago, however, and human population movements, intermarriage, and other occasions for mixing are eroding physical differences in bodily features. Skin color stopped being adaptive too after people found ways to protect themselves from the sun and could get their vitamin D from the grocery or vitamin store. Even so, enough color variety persists to justify America's perception of white, yellow, red, brown, and black races.

Never mind for the moment that the skin of "whites," as well as many East Asians and Latinos is actually pink; that Native Americans are not red; that most African Americans come in various shades of brown; and that really black skin is rare. Never mind either that color differences within each of these populations are as great as the differences between them, and that, as DNA testing makes quite clear, most people are of racially mixed origins even if they do not know it. But remember that this color palette was invented by whites. Nonwhite people would probably divide the range of skin colors quite differently.

Advocates of racial equality use these contradictions to fight against racism. However, the general public also has other priorities. As long as people can roughly agree about who looks "white," "yellow," or "black" and find that their notion of race works for their purposes, they ignore its inaccuracies, inconsistencies, and other deficiencies.

Note, however, that only some facial and bodily features are selected for the lay definition of race. Some, like the color of women's nipples or the shape of toes (and male navels) cannot serve because they are kept covered. Most other visible ones, like height, weight, hairlines, ear lobes, finger or hand sizes—and even skin texture—vary too randomly and frequently to be useful for categorizing and ranking people or judging strangers. After all, your own child is apt to have the same stubby fingers as a child of another skin color or, what is equally important, a child from a very different income level.

RACE, CLASS, AND STATUS

In fact, the skin colors and facial features commonly used to define race are selected precisely because, when arranged hierarchically, they resemble the country's class-and-status hierarchy. Thus, whites are on top of the socioeconomic pecking order as they are on top of the racial one, while variously shaded nonwhites are below them in socioeconomic position (class) and prestige (status).

The darkest people are for the most part at the bottom of the class-status hierarchy. This is no accident, and Americans have therefore always used race as a marker or indicator of both class and status. Sometimes they also use it to enforce class position, to keep some people "in their place." Indeed, these uses are a major reason for its persistence.

Of course, race functions as more than a class marker, and the correlation between race and the socioeconomic pecking order is far from statistically perfect: All races can be found at every level of that order. Still, the race-class correlation is strong enough to utilize race for the general ranking of others. It also becomes more useful for ranking dark-skinned people as white poverty declines so much that whiteness becomes equivalent to being middle or upper class.

The relation between race and class is unmistakable. For example, the 1998–2000 median household income of non-Hispanic whites was $45,500; of Hispanics (currently seen by many as a race) as well as Native Americans, $32,000; and of African Americans, $29,000. The poverty rates for these same groups were 7.8 percent among whites, 23.1 among Hispanics, 23.9 among blacks, and 25.9 among Native Americans. (Asians' median income was $52,600—which does much to explain why we see them as a model minority.)

True, race is not the only indicator used as a clue to socioeconomic status. Others exist and are useful because they can also be applied to ranking co-racials. They include language (itself a rough indicator of education), dress, and various kinds of taste, from given names to cultural preferences, among others.

American English has no widely known working-class dialect like the English Cockney, although "Brooklynese" is a rough equivalent, as is "black vernacular." Most blue-collar people dress differently at work from white-collar, professional, and managerial workers. Although contemporary American leisure-time dress no longer signifies the wearer's class, middle-income Americans do not usually wear Armani suits or French haute couture, and the people who do can spot the knockoffs bought by the less affluent.

Actually, the cultural differences in language, dress, and so forth that were socially most noticeable are declining. Consequently, race could become yet more useful as a status marker, since it is so easily noticed and so hard to hide or change. And in a society that likes to see itself as classless, race comes in very handy as a substitute.

> When the descendants of the European immigrants began to move up economically and socially, their skins apparently began to look lighter.

THE HISTORICAL BACKGROUND

Race became a marker of class and status almost with the first settling of the United States. The country's initial holders of cultural and political power were mostly WASPs (with a smattering of Dutch and Spanish in some parts of what later became the United States). They thus automatically assumed that their kind of whiteness marked the top of the class hierarchy. The bottom was assigned to the most powerless, who at first were Native Americans and slaves. However, even before the former had been virtually eradicated or pushed to the country's edges, the skin color and related facial features of the majority of colonial America's slaves had become the markers for the lowest class in the colonies.

Although dislike and fear of the dark are as old as the hills and found all over the world, the distinction between black and white skin became important in America only with slavery and was actually established only some decades after the first importation of black slaves. Originally, slave owners justified their enslavement of black Africans by their being heathens, not by their skin color.

In fact, early Southern plantation owners could have relied on white indentured servants to pick tobacco and cotton or purchased the white slaves that were available then, including the Slavs from whom the term *slave* is derived. They also had access to enslaved Native Americans. Blacks, however, were cheaper, more plentiful, more easily controlled, and physically more able to survive the intense heat and brutal working conditions of Southern plantations.

After slavery ended, blacks became farm laborers and sharecroppers, de facto indentured servants, really, and thus they remained at the bottom of the class hierarchy. When the pace of industrialization quickened, the country needed new sources of cheap labor. Northern industrialists, unable and unwilling to recruit southern African Americans, brought in very poor European immigrants, mostly peasants. Because these people were near the bottom of the class hierarchy, they were considered nonwhite and classified into races. Irish and Italian newcomers were sometimes even described as black (Italians as "guineas"), and the eastern and southern European immigrants were deemed "swarthy."

However, because skin color is socially constructed, it can also be reconstructed. Thus, when the descendants of the European immigrants began to move up economically and socially, their skins apparently began to look lighter to the whites who had come to America before them. When enough of these descendents became visibly middle class, their skin was seen as fully white. The biological skin color of the second and third generations had not changed, but it was socially blanched or whitened. The

Not quite white: early 20th-century immigrants.

process probably began in earnest just before the Great Depression and resumed after World War II. As the cultural and other differences of the original European immigrants disappeared, their descendants became known as white ethnics.

This pattern is now repeating itself among the peoples of the post-1965 immigration. Many of the new immigrants came with money and higher education, and descriptions of their skin color have been shaped by their class position. Unlike the poor Chinese who were imported in the 19th century to build the West and who were hated and feared by whites as a "yellow horde," today's affluent Asian newcomers do not seem to look yellow. In fact, they are already sometimes thought of as honorary whites, and later in the 21st century they may well turn into a new set of white ethnics. Poor East and Southeast Asians may not be so privileged, however, although they are too few to be called a "yellow horde."

Hispanics are today's equivalent of a "swarthy" race. However, the children and grandchildren of immigrants among them will probably undergo "whitening" as they become middle class. Poor Mexicans, particularly in the Southwest, are less likely to be whitened, however. (Recently a WASP Harvard professor came close to describing these Mexican immigrants as a brown horde.)

Meanwhile, black Hispanics from Puerto Rico, the Dominican Republic, and other Caribbean countries may continue to be perceived, treated, and mistreated as if they were African American. One result of that mistreatment is their low median household income of $35,000, which was just $1,000 more than that of non-Hispanic blacks but $4,000 below that of so-called white Hispanics.

Perhaps South Asians provide the best example of how race correlates with class and how it is affected by class position. Although the highly educated Indians and Sri Lankans who started coming to America after 1965 were often darker than African Americans, whites only noticed their economic success. They have rarely been seen as nonwhites, and are also often praised as a model minority.

Of course, even favorable color perceptions have not ended racial discrimination against newcomers, including model minorities and other affluent ones. When they become competitors for valued resources such as highly paid jobs, top schools, housing, and the like, they also become a threat to whites. California's Japanese-Americans still suffer from discrimination and prejudice four generations after their ancestors arrived here.

AFRICAN-AMERICAN EXCEPTIONALISM

The only population whose racial features are not automatically perceived differently with upward mobility are African Americans: Those who are affluent and well educated remain as visibly black to whites as before. Although a significant number of African Americans have become middle class since the civil rights legislation of the 1960s, they still suffer from far harsher and more pervasive discrimination and segregation than nonwhite immigrants of equivalent class position. This not only keeps whites and blacks apart but prevents blacks from moving toward equality with whites. In their case, race is used both as a marker of class and, by keeping blacks "in their place," an enforcer of class position and a brake on upward mobility.

In the white South of the past, African Americans were lynched for being "uppity." Today, the enforcement of class position is less deadly but, for example, the glass ceiling for professional and managerial African Americans is set lower than for Asian Americans, and on-the-job harassment remains routine.

Why African-American upward economic mobility is either blocked or, if allowed, not followed by public blanching of skin color remains a mystery. Many explanations have been proposed for the white exceptionalism with which African Americans are treated. The most common is "racism," an almost innate prejudice against people of different skin color that takes both personal and institutional forms. But this does not tell us why such prejudice toward African Americans remains stronger than that toward other nonwhites.

A second explanation is the previously mentioned white antipathy to blackness, with an allegedly primeval fear of darkness extrapolated into a primordial fear of dark-skinned people. But according to this explanation, dark-skinned immigrants such as South Asians should be treated much like African Americans.

A better explanation might focus on "Negroid" features. African as well as Caribbean immigrants with such features—for example, West Indians and Haitians—seem to be treated somewhat better than African Americans. But this remains true only for new immigrants; their children are generally treated like African Americans.

Alice Attie, "African American Children," http://aliceattie.com/photographs/harlem/. Copyright © by Alice Attie.

Two additional explanations are class-related. For generations, a majority or plurality of all African Americans were poor, and about a quarter still remain so. In addition, African Americans continue to commit a proportionally greater share of the street crime, especially street drug sales—often because legitimate job opportunities are scarce. African Americans are apparently also more often arrested without cause. As one result, poor African Americans are more often considered undeserving than are other poor people, although in some parts of America, poor Hispanics, especially those who are black, are similarly stigmatized.

The second class-based explanation proposes that white exceptionalist treatment of African Americans is a continuing effect of slavery: They are still perceived as ex-slaves. Many hateful stereotypes with which today's African Americans are demonized have changed little from those used to dehumanize the slaves. (Black Hispanics seem to be equally demonized, but then they were also slaves, if not on the North American continent.) Although slavery ended officially in 1864, ever since the end of Reconstruction subtle efforts to discourage African-American upward mobility have not abated, although these efforts are today much less pervasive or effective than earlier.

Some African Americans are now millionaires, but the gap in wealth between average African Americans and whites is much greater than the gap between incomes. The African-American middle class continues to grow, but many of its members barely have a toehold in it, and some are only a few paychecks away from a return to poverty. And the African-American poor still face the most formidable obstacles to upward mobility. Close to a majority of working-age African-American men are jobless or out of the labor force. Many

women, including single mothers, now work in the low-wage economy, but they must do without most of the support systems that help middle-class working mothers. Both federal and state governments have been punitive, even in recent Democratic administrations, and the Republicans have cut back nearly every antipoverty program they cannot abolish.

Daily life in a white-dominated society reminds many African Americans that they are perceived as inferiors, and these reminders are louder and more relentless for the poor, especially young men. Regularly suspected of being criminals, they must constantly prove that they are worthy of equal access to the American Dream. For generations, African Americans have watched immigrants pass them in the class hierarchy, and those who are poor must continue to compete with current immigrants for the lowest-paying jobs. If unskilled African Americans reject such jobs or fail to act as deferentially as immigrants, they justify the white belief that they are less deserving than immigrants. Blacks' resentment of such treatment gives whites additional evidence of their unworthiness, thereby justifying another cycle of efforts to keep them from moving up in class and status.

Such practices raise the suspicion that the white political economy and white Americans may, with the help of nonwhites who are not black, use African Americans to anchor the American class structure with a permanently lower-class population. In effect, America, or those making decisions in its name, could be seeking, not necessarily consciously, to establish an undercaste that cannot move out and up. Such undercastes exist in other societies: the gypsies of Eastern Europe, India's untouchables, "indigenous people" and "aborigines" in yet other places. But these are far poorer countries than the United States.

SOME IMPLICATIONS

The conventional wisdom and its accompanying morality treat racial prejudice, discrimination, and segregation as irrational social and individual evils that public policy can reduce but only changes in white behavior and values can eliminate. In fact, over the years, white prejudice as measured by attitude surveys has dramatically declined, far more dramatically than behavioral and institutional discrimination.

But what if discrimination and segregation are more than just a social evil? If they are used to keep African Americans down, then they also serve to eliminate or restrain competitors for valued or scarce resources, material and symbolic. Keeping African Americans from decent jobs and incomes as well as quality schools and housing makes more of these available to all the rest of the population. In that case, discrimination and segregation may decline significantly only if the rules of the competition change or if scarce resources, such as decent jobs, become plentiful enough to relax the competition, so that the African-American population can become as predominantly middle class as the white population. Then the stigmas, the stereotypes inherited from slavery, and the social and other arrangements that maintain segregation and discrimination could begin to lose their credibility. Perhaps "black" skin would eventually become as invisible as "yellow" skin is becoming.

THE MULTIRACIAL FUTURE

One trend that encourages upward mobility is the rapid increase in interracial marriage that began about a quarter century ago. As the children born to parents of different races also intermarry, more and more Americans will be multiracial, so that at some point far in the future the current quintet of skin colors will be irrelevant. About 40 percent of young Hispanics and two-thirds of young Asians now "marry out," but only about 10 percent of blacks now marry nonblacks—yet another instance of the exceptionalism that differentiates blacks.

Moreover, if race remains a class marker, new variations in skin color and in other visible bodily features will be taken to indicate class position. Thus, multiracials with "Negroid" characteristics could still find themselves disproportionately at the bottom of the class hierarchy. But what if at some point in the future everyone's skin color varied by only a few shades of brown? At that point, the dominant American classes might have to invent some new class markers.

If in some utopian future the class hierarchy disappears, people will probably stop judging differences in skin color and other features. Then lay Americans would probably agree with biologists that race does not exist. They might even insist that race does not need to exist.

RECOMMENDED RESOURCES

David Brion Davis. *Challenging the Boundaries of Slavery* (Harvard University Press, 2001). A historical account of the relation between race and slavery.

Joe R. Feagin and Melvin P. Sikes. *Living with Racism: The Black Middle-Class Experience* (Beacon, 1994). Documents continuing discrimination against middle- and upper-middle-class African Americans.

Barbara Jeanne Fields. "Slavery, Race and Ideology in the United States of America." *New Left Review* 181 (May/June 1990): 95–118. A provocative analysis of the relations between class and race.

Marvin Harris. "How Our Skins Got Their Color." In *Who We Are, Where We Came From, and Where We Are Going* (HarperCollins, 1989). An anthropologist explains the origins of different skin colors.

Jennifer Lee and Frank D. Bean. "Beyond Black and White: Remaking Race in America." *Contexts* (Summer 2003): 26–33. A concise analysis of changing perceptions and realities of race in America.

Are Jobs Enough for Economic Mobility?

by Roberta Iversen and Annie Armstrong

THE STORY

Twenty-five parents, their fifteen spouses or partners, and their sixty-six children in Philadelphia, Milwaukee, New Orleans, St. Louis, and Seattle let us share their lives from the late 1990s to mid-2003 to learn about low-income families and economic mobility. During this time we also talk with and observe at least one thousand auxiliaries associated with the families' mobility efforts. Through these contacts we learn that the families' attempts to move up economically through work both mesh and clash with the characteristics and conditions they encounter in workforce development programs and systems, firms, children's schools, and public policy.

The story begins with the families. Over the years, the families' infants enter child care and preschool, their preschool children progress to elementary school, their elementary-age children move up to middle school, their teenagers enter or complete high school, and new babies are born. The parents go to their children's basketball games, concerts, school conferences, and special education meetings. They go to the grocery, to the laundromat, to grandparents, to neighbors, to community centers, and to church. They tend to children with asthma, developmental delays, and school performance problems. They take children to doctors, go to doctors themselves, and worry about aging parents. The parents read to their children; the children read to their parents. The parents help with math homework and oversee school projects. They counsel children about conflicts with peers and give birthday parties.

At the same time the parents move up, down, and laterally in their jobs. Some take courses after work hours to try to upgrade their positions. Others wish they could. On the job they commune with coworkers, strive to get along with supervisors, and worry about how to make more money. They work overtime, get second or third jobs, and survive—at times relatively well and at other times barely—on sometimes-rising, sometimes-falling, but generally too-low wages. Many "do without" to provide enriching after-school or summer activities for their children and wish they could afford home computers and build assets and savings. Some make progress on these goals, but many do not no matter how hard they try. They make decisions they later question and mistakes they later rue about work, parenting, job training, and expenditures.

In many ways these families are like most other families in the United States, but they are different at the same time. In the richest large country in the world, they work full time year round, but they still do not earn enough to support their families. In this they are like one out of four other families in twenty-first-century America (Waldron, Roberts, & Reamer, 2004), most of whom work at full-time jobs that keep the country running but do not pay living wages.

Spending their childhoods and teen years in impoverished urban neighborhoods means that many of the parents receive too little education and have too few skills for today's jobs (Holzer, 1996). Most of their underfinanced, embattled urban schools yield poor-quality education, and their high school diplomas translate into eighth-grade reading level at best. These schools often fail to diagnose their learning disabilities or identify family problems that influence their dropping out of high school. Some complete their education in a foreign country, in one case a four-year college degree, to find that American firms do not recognize these accomplishments. Many seek vocational training in for-profit institutes that does not lead to a job and leaves them in debt. Policy prohibitions about debt then disqualify them from further education funding.

Other parents are immigrants and political refugees from war-torn countries who find that their new communities offer few acculturation or language services. This lack of services leaves them ill-equipped to navigate the dangers of low-level jobs, the medical system, and community programs for their children. Still other parents grow up in families who suffer from substance abuse, mental health problems, or domestic violence. Some struggle with bouts of depression themselves, which may result in alternating welfare and low-paid work. A few parents make serious mistakes in their youth or young adulthood, such as selling or taking drugs. Whether the cause is perceiving or experiencing few legitimate opportunities in the labor market or simply making wrong choices, they spend time in prison or rehabilitation facilities to compensate for these wrongs. Rehabilitation notwithstanding, felony incarceration may block or limit their access to housing subsidies, financial aid, and other opportunities that they need to move ahead.

At the same time, the parents, and indirectly their children, contend with a labor market that relies increasingly on contingent labor and with firms that offer inadequate wages and limited or too costly nonwage benefits, like health insurance. Despite the fact that the families contribute to the national well-being through production and taxes, they live in a country that denies subsidy assistance to many immigrants and refugees, disproportionately incarcerates African Americans and Hispanics, and puts time and allotment limits on transitional public assistance. Without adequate wages, benefits, and work supports, past history and current social and labor market conditions intersect to limit the families' economic mobility in a country that prides itself on meritocracy, a "second chance" after rehabilitation, and opportunity for all.

The story continues with the auxiliary contacts who further illustrate that economic mobility is highly complex. We learn this from instructors, administrators, and colleagues in the families' education and job training programs and institutions, often attending classes alongside the key parents[1] and following them as they navigate training, jobs, and family responsibilities. We learn this from neighbors, friends, extended family, faith leaders, human service workers, civic leaders, and policymakers in the families' neighborhoods and cities and observe how these varied community actors aid or constrain family economic mobility. We learn this from coworkers, managers, supervisors, CEOs, and labor leaders at the families' seventy-four firms as we accompany the parents through their work days and overnight shifts. We learn this from over 120 days spent with teachers, administrators, and students in the children's child-care facilities, preschools, and elementary and secondary schools, observing how children and faculty alike learn and simultaneously cope with impoverished and embattled environments.

The fact that these families identify labor market, education, and public policy institutions that do not but *could* facilitate mobility is a significant impetus for this book. In short, *Jobs Aren't Enough* argues that multiple social institutions influence contemporary economic mobility: in particular, the traditional institutions of the family and the labor market (firms) as they intersect with the institutions of education (public schools and workforce development) and public policy. As such this book is an exposé of *intersections*—their presence and more often their absence in the world of public beliefs about human and institutional behaviors and policy solutions to human and institutional problems that exist in the form of contained, unconnected silos. We focus here on intersections *between* the institution of the family and other social institutions as well as

on intersections *among* these institutions in different forms, intensities, and geographies.

We note at the outset that our research in New Orleans took place before Hurricane Katrina wreaked its havoc on the city and its surrounds. We address the particular implications of this disaster for the New Orleans families in the Afterword.

WHAT DO WE MEAN BY FAMILY, ECONOMIC MOBILITY, INSTITUTIONS, LOW INCOME, AND THE CONTEXT OF CAPITALISM?

First, we define family, economic mobility, institutions, and low income as used in this book. We then briefly discuss the economic system of capitalism as the context for the old mobility experiences of the families and institutions here and as the potential context for a new economic mobility.

FAMILY

Definitions and conceptualizations of "family" range from a strict view of biologically or adoptively related parents and children residing together to a constructionist view of whomever one considers "family" is family. In this book we tend toward the latter definition, privileging the way in which the respondents define their family constellation in their particular emotional, economic, spatial, and meaning-centered contexts. We also conceptualize family as "a social group, and social institution, with an identifiable structure based on positions and interactions among people who occupy those positions" (Gelles & Levine, 1999, p. 405). As such, families are agents of socialization and cultural reproduction: in effect, navigational vehicles for older and younger members alike. More broadly, we conceptualize all persons as "familied," meaning that every person's life holds others who are significant to them along the dimensions of structure and meaning that influence daily work, decisions, and social being.

ECONOMIC MOBILITY

By "economic mobility," which we call either mobility or economic mobility, we refer specifically to the phenomenon of moving forward financially through wage work. "Labor mobility" is the term commonly used in economics for how people move between jobs and occupations. "Social mobility" and "occupational mobility" are the terms commonly used in sociology (Breiger, 1990; Granovetter, 1995). We use the term economic mobility for several reasons. First, our concern is with the ability of low-earning parents to support their families through wage income, defined by the Census Bureau as "money income before taxes, exclusive of noncash benefits and employer-provided fringe benefits" (DeNavas-Walt, Proctor, & Mills, 2004, p. 1). For our purposes, social mobility is too closely aligned with social status, class, and systems of occupational ranking, and labor mobility focuses on individual workers, not on workers as parents or members of families. Second, economic mobility suggests an emphasis on the worker–family labor market interface and is thus more descriptive of our inquiry than is occupational mobility which addresses prestige criteria that are not relevant here. Economic mobility is also more consistent with the theoretical heritage of economic sociology which is the body of theory we draw upon and aim to extend.

Mobility has generally been viewed and explored as a microeconomic phenomenon; however we argue that mobility is both micro- and macroeconomic. In Weberian terms, we look at economically conditioned phenomena, those that partly—but only partly—can be explained through the influence of economic factors, and economically relevant phenomena, those that are not economic in themselves, but that influence economic phenomena (Weber, 1904/1949, p. 65). Historic examinations of "family" mobility focus on intergenerational patterns (Blau & Duncan, 1967), whereas more recent ones have begun to look at intragenerational patterns (Warren, Hauser, & Sheridan, 2002). Our focus on the family as a *generational institutional unit* affords exploration of the dynamic intersections within families as well as between families and other social institutions—intersections that have both intra- and intergenerational implications for economic mobility.

INSTITUTIONS

Although some might call the spheres of family, education, firms, and the state systems, we characterize them as social institutions. So doing we draw attention to the fact that institutions have structure. All involve aspects of authority and loyalty and are constituted and molded by policies and laws. All thus inherently intersect with one another, even if bureaucracies and funding streams do not acknowledge or attend to these intersections. In Brinton and Nee's (1998, p. 8) definition, institutions are "webs of interrelated rules and norms—formal and informal—that govern social relationships." In contrast, systems are contained entities that form a unity or organic whole in which the "relationships and interactions between elements explain the behavior of the whole" (Grint, 1991, p. 137). From a systems perspective, variation rests within rather than between, which tends to result in deterministic conceptions and atomistic silos. From a social institution perspective, variation occurs dynamically in the nexuses of the intersecting components.

LOW INCOME

In the United States, wage and salary earnings are the primary source of income for many families (McCall, 2000), particularly those like the ones in this book. However, definitions of "low income" vary and the term is often used synonymously with the term "working poor" (Gitterman, Howard, & Cotton, 2003). Briefly here, as we discuss this at length in Chapter 6, the most common metric used to define low income is 100 percent of the federal poverty level (FPL)—commonly called the poverty line, even though many scholars and policymakers view 200 percent of the poverty level as the minimum income that families need to meet their basic needs (Waldron, Roberts, & Reamer 2004). Others define low income more generously in terms of the median national income (Gitterman, Howard, & Cotton, 2003), which at $44,686 in 2004 dollars (Fronczek, 2005) is the equivalent of about 300% FPL. Still others assess income adequacy in terms of an alternative poverty metric such as the Self-Sufficiency Standard (Pearce, 2000, 2001; Wider Opportunities for Women, 2001, 2004).

We explicitly focus on wage income alone in the discussion of "low income" here, as the dominant metric to assess economic mobility and family well-being over the long run is what a parent can earn. Although transitional subsidies and wage supports mediate low incomes in the short run, we argue that earnings are ultimately the key to economic mobility. Accordingly, *Jobs Aren't Enough* uses what we consider to be a relatively conservative definition of low income—200 percent or less of the federal poverty level—a definition that, if anything, underreports the constraints that millions of working parents confront in their attempts to support their families through work.

For example, according to census analyses for 2004, thirty-seven million Americans live in families with incomes below 100 percent of the poverty level (Cadena & Sallee, 2005). In addition, the number of Americans with low incomes (below 200 percent FPL) increased by seven million between 2000 and 2003 (Ku, Broaddus, & Wachino, 2005), and by an additional 1.6 percent between 2003 and 2004 (Fronczek, 2005). In 2003 about 24.3 percent of Americans, essentially one in every four workers in the labor force, earned less than $9.04 an hour, which results in an annual income that just reaches 100 percent poverty for a family of four, even working full time year round (Mishel, Bernstein, & Allegretto, 2005). Especially pertinent to the families here, in 2002 more than one in four (27.4 percent) working parents with children in the United States was classified as low income by earning less than 200 percent of the federal poverty threshold (Waldron, Roberts, & Reamer, 2004). From another perspective, more than one in four children living with married parents is considered low income (Koball & Douglas-Hall, 2005). Thus from any vantage point, families with low incomes are widespread across the United States.

THE CONTEXT OF CAPITALISM

Although a review of the contested definitions and critiques of capitalist economic and social organization is beyond the purpose and scope of this book (see, e.g., Bowles & Gintis, 1987; Braverman, 1974; Edwards, 1979; Hart, 2005; Lafer, 2002; Wacquant, 2002), many consider capitalism to be the dominant way of organizing the economy, legally, politically, and socially in today's world (Swedberg, 2003, p. 54). As such, it forms part of the context for the families and other institutions here.

Common definitions of capitalism incorporate some variation of the theme that it constitutes an organization of economic interests that allows for the "pursuit of profit, and forever renewed profit" (Weber, 1904/1949). According to some, the commodification of and control over the labor process by employers under capitalism is the established route to such profit (Edwards, 1979; Marx, 1867/1978). On this view authority, exploitation and power hold sway and profit-making trumps other organizational aspects of firms such as investment in training and reciprocity relations. A contrasting approach to the general nature of capitalism is what Swedberg (2003, p. 57) calls "the economists' traditional definition of the economy as consisting of production, distribution, and exchange." Although all economies involve these three factors, capitalism is distinguished from other economic systems primarily by the fact that distribution is organized as exchange in the market rather than as reciprocity or redistribution. Presciently, in *Economy and Society* Weber (1922/1978) speaks not of a single capitalism but of capitalisms: rational (or modern) capitalism, political capitalism, and what can be termed traditional commercial capitalism. Leicht (2002) echoes this perspective almost a century later in his global perspective on "capitalisms" as do Hall and Soskice (2001) in their discussion of "varieties of capitalism," Esping-Anderson

(1990) in his configuration of "three worlds of welfare capitalism," Eisenstadt (1963/1993) in his identification of different "capitalist regimes," and Nee and Swedberg (2005) in their presentation of "the many forms and varieties" of contemporary capitalism.

Although some see capitalism as the cause of all labor market ills, we view capitalism as a social form that is historically based, nondeterministic, thus one in which practices and structures can be altered, at least at micro- and mesolevels of the labor market. Newman (2002, p. 1590) concludes similarly that "reformist struggles over government policies within capitalist states can change the fate of the poor for the better." Fundamentally, institutions are rule-governed social constructions (Nee, 2003); thus we argue, as does Miller (1999, 2003), that greater fairness and cooperation and increased economic mobility are possible through the reconstruction of contemporary labor and other social institutions, even in a market economy. In effect, social and economic relations are processes in perpetual construction and reconstruction, as Braverman (1974) suggests earlier and as Swedberg (2003, p. 63) underscores: "No single form of governance—including the market—is responsible for the way that a national economy works." As Bowles and Gintis (1987, p. xiii) hold, "The view that there is an ineluctable conflict between moral and material incentives, between cooperation and competition, or that one of these modes can operate effectively in the absence of the other, is a quaint and anachronistic aspect of our intellectual heritage. Finally, Heilbroner (1999, p. 320) argues that "Economic vision (here we might add economic sociology) ... could become the source of an awareness of ways by which a capitalist structure can broaden its motivations, increase its flexibility, and develop its social responsibility."

In this vein we are intrigued by the notion of an economic system in which *household and profit* matter (Weber, 1922/1978). Although Weber refers to large capitalist households of antiquity in his discussion, we argue that it may be worth reexamining this prioritization with an eye toward householding *and* profit making in contemporary firms. In this construction, household would not refer solely to consumption, as in Weber's formulation and in Aristotle's earlier one (Swedberg, 2005), but to taking joint responsibility for keeping the property (the firm) intact and for allocating profits equally to meet the interests of all the involved social actors. This reformulation is akin to Swedberg's (2003, p. 6) argument that because institutions are "durable amalgamations of interests *and* social relations," analysis of the capitalist economic system must take the interests of both individuals and corporate actors into account (Swedberg, 2004). Hart's (2005, p. xli) similar position is that "By creating a new, more inclusive brand of capitalism, one that incorporates previously excluded voices, concerns, and interests, the corporate sector could be the catalyst for a truly sustainable form of global development—and prosper in the process."

We hold that laws and policies currently upholding the modern economic order *can* be changed, prevailing political standpoints *can* be changed, and social perspectives in current ascendancy *can* be changed. As we discuss further in Chapter 8, however, all require significant change in what we refer to as the "public will."

PLAN OF THE BOOK

Jobs Aren't Enough is an ethnographic rendition of the experiences of families who are trying to transition from prior economic disadvantage to family-supporting wages through work. Their journeys and our previous work on occupational attainment and workforce development lead us in this initial chapter to question why and how economic mobility is still limited for so many in twenty-first-century America. The immediate context is the lived experience of low-income families trying to move up through work and the daily realities of how they and other social institutions (firms, workforce development, schools, and public policy) intersect to foster or obstruct their mobility goals.

The situation facing us and the families is thus. Scholarly and policy interest in urban poverty in the 1990s and early 2000s is primarily focused on welfare reform, particularly on the assessment of how different types of welfare-to-work programs move single mothers into the labor market, thereby lowering the rolls and costs of public assistance. Little notice is paid to the fact that increasing numbers of *two-parent working families* are poor (Annie E. Casey Foundation, 2001a, 2004). Even though rates of child poverty decrease slightly in the early 2000s, from 43 percent in 2000 to 40 percent in 2001 (Child Trends, 2003), two in five American children remain poor according to the most stringent measure of poverty—at or below 100 percent of the federal poverty line. Similar to other states, Wisconsin reports a 20 percent increase in child poverty between 2000 and 2003 (Dresser & Wright, 2004). Why is this occurring? Why are so many parents unable to support their families through work? This book as a whole implicates multiple intersecting social institutions in the persistent limits to family economic mobility.

The story continues in Chapter 2 with social theory because what the populace thinks, believes, and assumes about economic mobility forms the lattice for the relevant actors, social structures, and practices and policies in organizations and institutions.

FROM THE OLD TO THE NEW ECONOMIC MOBILITY

Chapter 2 first presents what we call the *old paradigm for economic mobility*. In this paradigm, jobs are the expected way for families to get ahead financially in the United States. Yet by the early 2000s over one in four parents works full time year round but does not earn enough to support his or her family. Explanations for this often split into two poles: the "it's their own fault" view and the "it's society's fault" view.

Holders of the "it's their own fault" view believe that opportunity, meritocracy, and initiative are realities in today's America, thus any deviation from the open terrain of mobility must be the person's fault. In effect these persons are viewed as atomistic, individually or personally responsible actors who are thus classified as the "nondeserving poor." Less extreme holders of the "own fault" view, especially those who remember the Great Depression or the civil rights period of the 1960s, may acknowledge—albeit hesitantly and carefully—that life events outside the control of individuals sometimes happen. The company goes out of business, the father becomes disabled from a work injury, or the mother leaves an abusive partner. These individuals are then classified as the "deserving poor," even though holders of this view still tend to believe that

atomistic, responsible actors can overcome these happenstances through initiative if they "just put their minds to it."

Holders of the "it's society's fault" view perceive seismic shifts in the socioeconomic landscape over the past several decades, such as shifts in the structure, practices, and geography of the labor market and firms; shifts in welfare and workforce development policy that curtail eligibility and skill training in favor of rapid job attachment; shifts in how the demography of contemporary workers matches the characteristics of contemporary firms—what we call a *life-stage mismatch* (Iversen, 2002)—and shifts that show increasing rates of child poverty in working households. The most extreme "society's fault" proponents believe that capitalism determines immobility; thus the economic chances of low-income working families cannot improve without radical reconstruction of the country's political economy. The more moderate "society's fault" proponents seek a middle ground between individual and societal responsibility, understanding that people sometimes make mistakes, wrong choices, or face structural conditions such as inadequate housing, poorly funded schools, inadequate wages, or discrimination that constrains or blocks their opportunity or initiative. More moderate proponents are also more likely to believe that the children of poor parents should not be made to suffer for a parent's limitations or for social structural constraints.

These are simplifications of the worldviews of the American populace to be sure, but they suggest the landscape of assumptions, beliefs, and theories that underlies the structure and practices of the contemporary institutions of social reproduction that are germane to economic mobility—the family, workforce development, firms, children's schools, and the state through its public policies. The voices in this book, all of whom inhabit these institutional spheres, show us how the old paradigm limits or precludes economic mobility for families without prior economic advantage.

These voices also point to the need for a *new paradigm for economic mobility* that we sketch out in Chapter 2, especially as firms and other institutions face the forces of globalization and restructuring, however great or small these forces actually are. To maintain our country's historic philosophical principles and economic productivity, we argue that concepts from economic sociology form the framework for a new paradigm that our ethnographic findings laminate. In effect, a new paradigm for economic mobility fosters foundational American principles that are obscured by geographic and political dispersion and by neoliberal reliance on the market to solve all ills and needs: principles of interdependence, fairness, equity, and real opportunity.

Understanding that economic mobility is a thoroughly relational process leads toward the establishment of genuine trust and reciprocity in the intersecting relationships among education and workforce development institutions, workers and firms, as well as among families, firms, and children's schools. Successful mobility outcomes thus require developing and extending social and cultural capital along with human capital, as the weak ties of social networks (Granovetter, 1973) and the sanctioned credentials that result from institutionalized cultural capital (Bourdieu, 2001) merge with human capital attainment to form a legitimizing signal for those who make mobility-influencing decisions about hiring, promotion, layoff, and termination.

Finally, understanding that economic mobility is increasingly dynamic and variable, and that choice and decision processes involve both cognitive and emotional components, leads toward the development of greater mutuality in the authority relations and practices of firms and other organizations. Power relations then become more horizontal than vertical, multiple voices are sought in the crafting of procedures and regulations, and responsibility becomes relational rather than individual.

BACKGROUNDS AND LOCATIONS OF THE PARENTS AND CHILDREN

This theoretical framework undergirds the remaining chapters in the book. Chapter 3 lays out the characteristics of the key parents that illustrate the confluence of old paradigm experiences and new paradigm needs. The parents contend with both personal and structural challenges and constraints to mobility, not the least of which is a vulnerability to symptoms of depression as they lose hard-won jobs and employer-paid health insurance during the economic downturn in 2001 and beyond. The parents utilize extant subsidies and work supports to augment inadequate wages and employ geographic strategies and community involvement to enhance their own and their children's well-being. These parents are found to be similar to millions of other low-income adults in the country today on a selection of demographic characteristics, extending the likelihood that their experiences and voices express widespread realities and sentiments. Chapter 3 also explores the role of "place" in economic mobility, concluding that although knowledge about place-based particularities is critical to the development of appropriate local policies and programs, state and national policies are the key to economic mobility writ large.

Chapter 4 leads us into the world of the children, illuminating the intersection of family history, developmental environments, violence and safety, and daily lives through the eyes and voices of the parents' preschool and school-age children and youth. Perhaps most important for intergenerational mobility, children of all ages cast a critical eye on the labor market based on how they experience their parents' work struggles. Although the children are grateful for the material benefits of their parents' new and better jobs, lessened family time, added family responsibilities, dangers and injuries to their mothers and fathers in the workplace, and mercurial job tenures seem to lead some children to express these concerns in the form of behavior and performance problems at school (details in Chapter 7) or through aggravated health conditions. Many children doubt that their merit will be rewarded with opportunity in the future as they see that trust, reciprocity, and mutuality are often lacking in the vital mobility spheres of firms and social policy.

The voices of the families and auxiliaries in the core analytical chapters of the book, Chapters 5 through 7, then show in depth how the institutions involved in economic mobility act and intersect.

WORKFORCE DEVELOPMENT PROGRAMS AND SYSTEMS

Chapter 5 takes us briefly through the history of federal education and job training legislation and programs, showing how they evolve from a human capital to a "work-first" focus. This evolution also entails a shift in nomenclature from "education and training" to "workforce development" which denotes a more systemic network orientation to employment and economic mobility.

Not fully successful yet in this goal at the federal level, local and regional workforce development networks, both in and external to the federal system, such as the one in which the key parents participate, are emerging. These new networks explicitly engage multiple organizations and institutions in a collaborative approach to both workforce and community economic development. Network partners often include but are not limited to workforce intermediaries, social and human service organizations, community colleges, vocational institutes, workforce policy boards, area businesses and firms, and state and local policymakers.

In effect, understanding that multiple institutions are integral to real opportunity for economic mobility leads toward the ways in which trust, power, reciprocity, and shared meanings can be used, horizontally and vertically, to craft and nurture dynamic and strategic partnerships among firms and other mobility-relevant social institutions. These partnerships aim to effectively span what Burt (1992, 2002) refers to in market relations as "structural holes," turning them into what we call *structured wholes* for the mobility of families and communities.

Countering earlier evaluation findings that education and job training programs "don't pay," conversion of workforce development networks into structured wholes constitutes the first bridge to economic opportunity for the families here. For sustained mobility, however, these networks need to be positioned to effect reciprocal changes in firms and public policy.

THE PARENTS' FIRMS

Despite good initial jobs in a wide array of industry sectors that result from the parents' workforce development programs, system reforms, and the tight economy of the late 1990s, Chapter 6 reveals that yesterday's firms seldom sustain or forward the mobility efforts of today's families. For the most part, the seventy-four firms in which the key parents work between 1998 and mid-2003 take the form of "autocratic family," "disengaged family," "fair-weather friend," or "roommate" rather than the more reciprocal form of "firm as partner" per the new mobility paradigm.

Chapters 3 and 5 show that work supports and skill training are important but not sufficient for economic mobility. Chapter 6 shows that wages, the adequacy of the wages, and how firms are organized and run profoundly affect the economic mobility of low-income families. Reportedly, these factors increasingly affect the mobility of managers and white collar workers as well (Cappelli, 1999; Osterman, 2005). While some view wage inadequacy as expectable in a capitalist political economy (Braverman, 1974; Edwards, 1979; Lafer, 2002), this chapter suggests that wage inadequacy results from choices about organizational conditions and relations that workers, firms, educators, and policymakers make according to old paradigm assumptions and myths, as other scholars see it in part (Miller, 1999, 2003; Nee, 2003; Newman, 2002; Swedberg, 2003). Turbulent global, national, and local conditions affecting the production capacities and profitability of contemporary firms, together with old paradigm forms of wage distribution, organizational structure, and relations, intersect in firms' and workers' responses to these external and internal challenges.

Despite turbulence, two in five of the families make substantial progress toward family-sustaining incomes—at least for a time. Still, three in five families do not, many of whose progress is buffeted by firm, economic, family, and policy disconnects. Although many parents change firms two or three times over the five years we know them, in line with the old paradigm view of advancement, few find that their hard work or persistence ensures mobility. For all the families, sustained mobility requires an intersecting network that consists of their firms, the economy, public policy, and their children's schools.

THE CHILDREN'S SCHOOLS

Children's schools influence children's mobility vertically (intergenerationally) through human capital attainment, but they also influence family mobility horizontally (intragenerationally) through their impact on parents' work. Chapter 7 details the dangers, material inadequacies, and tensions that children confront in their daily "work" at school that are likely to influence their future mobility. At the same time parents and schools both confront stumbling blocks to their respective goals because labor market and educational institutions frequently do not recognize the other's value. This chapter details two sets of intersecting but misaligned actors: first, children's schools, families, and firms; and second, children's schools, families, and public and school policies.

Further, because the institutional actors are organized and funded as silos, the communication and creative strategizing that could emerge from trusted, reciprocal relationships is philosophically and operationally absent. Parents make many sacrifices as they strive to meet their children's educational and developmental needs, often in the form of lost wages or lost jobs as a result of this fundamental misalignment. Inter- and intragenerational mobility are then constrained in turn. Only where multi-institutional alignments are created, fostered, and sustained can economic mobility for low-income families be widespread. What will it take to foster such alignment?

ENGAGING THE "PUBLIC WILL" TOWARD AN AGENDA FOR FAMILY ECONOMIC MOBILITY

During the ethnographic research and writing of this book, we expected to present a set of policy recommendations in Chapter 8. Instead we recognize that a wealth of program and policy strategies to move low-income families forward through work have been offered in recent years, yet most have not been funded or implemented, leaving one to ponder, where is the "public will"?

Accordingly, Chapter 8 expands upon the premise introduced in Chapter 2 that we (the people) *can* and *do* make choices about our own and others' well-being that keep low-income families relatively immobile but *could* help them be economically mobile. We articulate in this chapter how the philosophical and distributive principles that constitute a new view of mobility, such as trust and reciprocity, equity and equality, and above all, social relatedness can move toward institutional structure and form. We ultimately suggest reframing the notion of individual (personal) responsibility as "responsibility for persons" or "relational responsibility," an action that forces attention to the interdependence and mutuality of purpose

that can improve conditions for individuals, families and institutions alike in today's world. We conclude with a series of recommendations for action toward an agenda for family economic mobility.

Finally, we suggest that *Jobs Aren't Enough* can be read consecutively or selectively, through either engaging with the "whole story" or through focusing on chapters that amplify particular institutional and family characteristics and experiences. As with most stories however, we believe the coherence and richness of the book are cumulative. To enhance accessibility, we put several detailed documents in Appendices for those who wish to more deeply examine the research design and data.

Ultimately we hope that the book as a whole, as well as individual chapters, will be useful for educating students about the intersecting roles in economic mobility of stratification, poverty, education, workforce development, urban environments, gender, race and ethnicity, families, and institutions. We hope that policymakers and professionals will become more informed about the scope of the problems facing millions of American families that stem from an outdated view of mobility and be moved to remedy these through collaborative action. We hope that scholars in economic sociology and related fields will find this book a useful contribution toward further development of mobility theory. And finally we hope that all readers will find the families' stories compelling enough to consider new perspectives on mobility that can forward the country's foundational principles of interdependence, equity and real opportunity for all.

5 | Chapter Review

REVIEW QUESTIONS

1. What is a social structure? Provide one example of a tangible (observable or concrete) example of a social structure and then one that may be abstract.
2. How does social structure directly impact daily life for an individual and quality of life for that individual?
3. How do institutions reflect the dominant values of a culture and how are these values disseminated in a given society? How might this differ for individuals or groups based upon their socialization?

CASE STUDY: ARE JOBS ENOUGH FOR SOCIAL MOBILITY?

While we consider education (and subsequently work) as a means of social mobility, the final article in this chapter explores the various factors associated with social mobility and the various barriers that may be present, beyond simply education or job opportunities, that may impact class movement.

What are the barriers noted in the article that may influence social mobility? Are jobs enough for social mobility? What other social factors are influential in one's social class placement over time?

DEVELOPING THE SOCIOLOGICAL IMAGINATION
Understanding Institutional Discrimination and Its Residual Consequences

In Chapter 2's "Developing the Sociological Imagination" exercise, we briefly explored the concept of social structures and looked at how educational attainment may impact opportunity, where people live, and one's life chances. Continuing with this theme, this chapter's data exercise focuses on the concept of discrimination within society's institutions (specifically housing organization throughout U.S. history) and how this history may also impact where people live, what opportunity for advancement is therefore available, and how historic **institutional discrimination** may still be impacting social mobility and opportunity today for traditionally marginalized groups.

For this exercise, please read the following article (it also includes a film) on the history of housing development and residential segregation in the United States:

https://www.nytimes.com/2016/09/19/us/housing-bias-and-the-roots-of-segregation.html

Then go to the following link to look at how segregated your community is as compared to other areas of your state, region, and the United States:

http://www.remappingdebate.org/map-data-tool/mapping-and-analysis-new-data-documents-still-segregated-america-0

Select your zip code and another zip code that you are interested in and explore the concept of housing segregation in these two areas. Given what you have learned, how has history impacted these arrangements in your community? How might opportunities differ for different groups based upon these arrangements? From a sociological perspective, how does inequality that is experienced within institutions have the ability to impact individual lives? Using the example of residential segregation, how can institutions perpetuate inequality if these inequalities are not addressed?

6 | Gender, Sexuality, and the Family

CHAPTER SUMMARY

- This chapter introduces readers to the concept of gender, sexuality, and intimate partnership and the way in which sociologists go about studying these topics.

- The chapter also discusses the institution of family and changes that are currently being experienced in families.

- Readers are also asked to identify what might be influencing family arrangements in areas across the globe.

PRELIMINARY QUESTIONS FOR READERS

- What are common expectations with being male and female in your society? How is one's gender, as a social structure, experienced both within institutions and interpersonal relationships?

- Each person has a gender identity as well as a sexual identity. Think about the process that many have had to go through when "coming out." How might the "coming out" process represent how sexuality is socialized for individuals in a given society?

- Typically, intimate relationships form the basis for the start of what might be considered a family. Who do you consider part of your family? Are these individuals all related to you by blood or are others included in this definition for you?

CHAPTER INTRODUCTION
Defining Gender and Gender Identity

The term "**sex**" refers to one's biological identity, and **gender** can be referred to as the social or cultural expectations and behaviors associated with one's sex. **Gender roles** (or behavioral norms associated with one's sex) can vary significantly across different societies and cultures. For example, in different time periods and in varying parts of the world, in some societies women have been responsible for gathering food and completing various survival tasks, and men have had the primary responsibility for rearing children. Sociologists seek to understand how culture impacts one's sense of gender identity, particularly if one does not adhere to the social expectations associated with that gender identity. **Gender identity** can be defined as one's identification of one's self as a particular gender within the gender labels available within a society. It shapes our expectations of others and often the expectations we place upon ourselves. Our gender identity also may impact our abilities and interests, how we interact with others, how others interact with us, and our social behaviors in groups and within social institutions.

Most societies in the world are patriarchal societies, meaning that being male has a particular set of advantages, prestige, and access to social power. It also may mean that women are structurally disadvantaged as compared to men. The first article in this chapter explores what are perceived to be the origins of gender inequality and arranged gender hierarchies.

SEXUALITY

Just as one has a gender identity, individuals also have a **sexual identity** (or one's definition of one's sexual orientation). The second article in this chapter explores theories related to studying sexuality in society.

STUDYING COUPLING AND INTIMATE RELATIONSHIPS
What Is Romantic Love?

Romantic love is a term that is subject to thousands of varying definitions for both researchers and for those involved in romantic relationships. For example, one member of a couple may define love as giving (such as spending money), another may understand love as doing (such as making special meals or going on extravagant dates), or one may understand it as being (such as being emotionally supportive, participating in activities of mutual interest, or simply being physically intimate). While we likely consider all of these things as expressions of love, most of us internalize and demonstrate love through one or two of these means more so than the others. Some of these expressions of love can be influenced by our family of origin and how love was modeled. Therefore, given the diversity of experience, the way that we understand and give love is not always the way others may understand or demonstrate love.

HOW DO WE CHOOSE A PARTNER?

According to Myers (2002), social science research indicates that, in addition to sexual orientation and various aspects of personality, intimate partnerships are also influenced by:

- **Proximity:** We tend to form relationships with people who are geographically close to us, given some of the social obligations and expectations associated with an intimate partner relationships, forming a family, and raising a family.
- **Mere Exposure Effect:** Simply put, we tend to form relationships based upon exposure. We cannot have an intimate relationship with someone we do not have any awareness of.

- **Perceived Physical Attractiveness:** Different cultures have different ideas on the concept of beauty or what may be perceived as physically attractive qualities. As a result, our natural gravitation to others can sometimes be influenced by these cultural ideals.
- **Similarity:** A significant amount of research suggests that people tend to form intimate relationships with others who are like them and particularly, with others who understand similar social experiences (such as those in the same social class or among those with the same level of academic achievement).

WHAT DO WE EXPECT FROM AN INTIMATE RELATIONSHIP AND LONG-TERM PARTNER?

Technically, what we expect from intimate (or romantic) relationships is as varied as the people who form these relationships. We all enter into romantic relationships with ideas of what the relationship should be like and "what this person should do." This is often a result of our ideals, values, role models, and experiences. Expectations also tend to reflect, for many, what is socially acceptable within the type of relationship they are in. For example, it would likely seem unreasonable to expect that the person you went on a first date with would wash the dishes you used for breakfast. Perhaps this would not be the case in a relationship where one lives with another and where duties are shared and delegated. While understanding the differences in expectations that can occur across types of relationships, as

a culture, according to Myers (2002), there are some things that we do generally expect most intimate relationships (including marriage or life-long relationships) to include.

- **Loyalty:** While many couples have various rules as to sexual relations with relationships (such as monogamy or open marriages), typically most people in intimate relationships expect some degree of loyalty and commitment from the other, however this is defined by the couple.
- **Emotional Support:** Most people in intimate relationships also lean on the other for emotional support through the ups and downs of life. In fact, most people expect more of their

intimate partner in this regard than from other friends, family members, or acquaintances.

- **Delegation of Responsibilities:** Given that gender roles are changing more so than ever before, both partners in intimate relationships also lean on the other for financial support and assistance in accomplishing the tasks of raising children or the everyday business (such as bills, housework, etc.) of life together. While research suggests that women still do often carry the burden (more so than men) in heterosexual relationships for caring for the needs of children, an aging parent, cooking, and cleaning (no matter how much they are working outside of the home), more and more heterosexual women are expecting that their heterosexual partners participate equally and consistently in family responsibilities.

- **Security:** Intimate relationships also provide for many of us a sense of personal security—the security of acceptance, unconditional love, and companionship.

DEFINING THE FAMILY

In the social sciences, intimate partnership is often the basis for what is termed "the family." The **family** is considered one of the most (if not *the* most) important institutions within society. It is within this institution that we form our ideas of self, learn how to relate to one another, and where our deepest needs for intimacy, belonging, and connection are met. Our **family of origin** is the family we were born into. Our **family of procreation** is the family that we create.

The concept of what defines a family and who is considered part of a family is often subject to a variety of **social norms** (or culturally defined rules for behavior and, in this case, rules related to our interactions with one another). As a result, the definition of what is considered "a family" has varied over time, locations, and across different groups. This definition, however, carries with it important implications. For example, this definition in our country over time has determined who may marry whom and under what circumstances, who can benefit from public assistance within a group of relatives, and who can be covered under a certain health care policy (regardless of how dependent someone may be upon another).

Traditionally, the family has been defined as "a unit made up of two or more people who are related by blood, marriage, or adoption, and who live together, form an economic unit, and bear and raise children" (Benokraitis, 2002, p. 3). The problem for social scientists, however, is that this definition often excludes many other groups that also consider themselves families. In short, this traditional definition simply does not reflect the complexity and potential of family arrangements. A more modern definition then might be "an intimate environment in which two or more people (1) live together in a committed relationship; (2) the members see their identity as importantly attached to the group; (3) and the group shares close emotional ties and functions" (Benokraitis, 2002, p. 3).

FUNCTIONS OF THE FAMILY

Although family arrangements differ, most modern and historic families have fulfilled similar functions. According to Benokraitis (2002), families are expected to serve four major functions:

- **Legitimizing Sexual Activity:** Every society has formal and informal rules as to who it is appropriate to have sex with and when it is appropriate to engage in sexual activity. Marriage has served an important function in our society as it has been seen by some as a means of controlling sexual activity and procreation. In short, some have viewed the institution of marriage as a means of controlling the number of members in a society (or as a means of population control).
- **Socialization of Children:** Procreation is also an essential function of the family for society. In our society, although many couples do not have children, many do desire to have children. Once a couple has children, the family serves the important social function of socialization. Through socialization, children learn the language, knowledge, values, attitudes, and beliefs of their culture. In addition, children learn through socialization the interpersonal skills needed to function effectively in a society.
- **Emotional Support:** Families provide for the nurture, love, and emotional closeness that we need as individuals to feel happy and secure. Few other groups in society provide these intimate, vital functions for well-being.
- **Establishing a Member's Place in Society:** To a great extent, our position in society is defined by our family of origin. We are born into a certain social class, a certain racial or ethnic group, or into a certain religious affiliation. While we may change some of these memberships over time, our family of origin shapes our initial understanding of who we are, who we are not, and our roles in society. Some of our most fundamental beliefs about the roles of family members, differing racial groups, or the differences in socioeconomic status (and what these differences mean in terms of our position in a society) are learned from our family of origin.

THE CHANGING FAMILY

As you have likely observed, the roles, responsibilities, and obligations of members of the modern family are changing and have changed significantly in the last 50 years. According to Benokraitis (2002), in addition to changing roles and responsibilities, the picture of the modern family in the United States is also changing in other ways:

- **Demographic Changes:** As a country, people are having children later in life and having fewer children than in previous decades. As a result, the birth rate (the number of births to every 1,000 women) has been decreasing over time in the United States, Europe, Japan, and in many other modern societies.

- **Single Parents:** Single parents (primarily female heads of household) represent approximately 25% of all nuclear (immediate) families.
- **Marriage:** People in the United States (and in many European countries) are waiting until they are older to get married compared to previous decades. Despite this trend, the United States continues to have one of the highest rates of marriage in the industrialized world.
- **High Rates of Divorce and Remarriage:** Despite this high rate of divorce risk in the United States, as a country we also continue to have a high rate of remarriage. This high rate of remarriage is increasing the number of blended families in the United States.

Most social scientists see these changes as a result of:

- **Economic forces and trends:** It is no longer possible for many families to survive on one income in the United States; therefore, more women have entered the workforce. The realities and complexities of balancing work and family have impacted family responsibilities and the delegation of these responsibilities. This shift has challenged what many consider to be the traditional roles for men and women in a relationship.
- **Technological innovations,** such as birth control, have allowed many couples to participate more actively in family planning. Advances in fertility treatments have also made it possible for more women to bear children in their later years.
- **Popular culture and the media** can influence our values and perceptions about family and what is considered to be a traditional or nontraditional family. The media may also normalize various types of family arrangements.
- **Social movements** (namely the feminist movement in this example) not only influenced a woman's ability to participate in the workforce but also changed traditional perceptions about a woman's role to include areas of contribution beyond childbearing and child-rearing. This has meant that some women have delayed marriage to focus more on a career or other areas of individual interest.
- **Family laws and policies** and laws have also influenced the modern picture of the family and have influenced who can marry whom (marriage equality laws, for example) and how one can divorce (including how quickly one can divorce).

THREE PERSPECTIVES ON THE CHANGING FAMILY

The third article in this chapter focuses on the changes in the 21st-century family. According to Benokraitis (2002), some have seen these changes as a negative trend (or a sign that the institution of the family is deteriorating in our society), others see this as simply a modern reflection of family patterns that have existed for centuries, and others see the changes occurring in the contemporary family as beneficial for the institution itself. For example, some view the institution's resiliency in the face of great cultural change as a sign of the institution's enduring function for society. As each of these perspectives demonstrates, how we (and others in society) define whether or not such changes are positive or negative depend largely upon our worldview and our understanding of the function and purpose of the institution of family.

WORKS CITED

Andersen, M. L. and Taylor, H.F. (2007). *Sociology: The essentials*. 4th Edition. Belmont, CA: Thompson Wadsworth Press.

Benokraitis, N.V. (2002). *Marriages and families: Changes, choices, and constraints*. (4th Edition). Upper Saddle River, NJ: Prentice Hall.

Myers, D. (2002). *Social psychology*. 7th Edition. New York, New York: McGraw Hill.

Sharp, G. (2012). How do we define a family? *The Society Pages*. Retrieved from: https://thesocietypages.org/socimages/2012/12/26/how-do-we-define-a-family/.

On The Origins of Gender Inequality

by Joan Huber

The forager groups who represent 99 percent of human time on earth were relatively egalitarian, but 10,000 years ago the invention of the hoe and then the plow entailed a food surplus that led to warfare and a system of social stratification based on birth. The non-fit of reproduction with warfare let men monopolize both war and politics and consigned women to secondary status, but the reproductive constraints were poorly understood until the 1990s. Infants had been suckled at intervals of about fifteen minutes by day (less often at night) for two years, and at a lesser rate for at least two more until the invention of a safe substitute for human milk in the 1880s. The pattern evolved because frequent suckling precluded ovulation; the contraceptive effect maximized survival. If a forager mother gave birth before her older child could join the daily food search, the older one starved. A forager mother thus carried her youngest child everywhere and slept with it at night, for her low-fat milk sated its hunger only briefly. In the 1950s, demographers were still unaware of the contraceptive effect of prolonged lactation, but by the 1990s they agreed that prolonged breastfeeding was universal before the demographic transition. The invention of a safe alternative to human milk induced huge behavioral changes. Biggest and least recognized was the decrease to nearly zero in the number of three- to five-year-olds whose primary food was breast milk. Augmenting the fertility decline, the revolution in child feeding enabled women in modern economies to increase the range of their public activities by a substantial margin.

INTRODUCTION: TOOLS, FOOD, AND SOCIAL POWER

As humans must eat often or die, hunger is the chief determinant of social relationships (Goody 1976), and the tools used to produce food in a given ecological setting explain the distribution of power (Lenski 1970). A century of research in anthropology suggests that the Pleistocene foragers (who represent 99 percent of human time on earth) were more egalitarian than were the humans in all subsequent societies (Boehm 1999). After the use of tools to produce food led to social stratification based primarily on birth, the pace of social change rose. About 10,000 years ago, the hoe entailed permanent settlements, which attracted marauders, but 4,000 years ago the plow produced a much larger surplus that tempted rulers to seize as much as possible (Pryor 1985). Elites topped pyramidal social structures; peasants, serfs, and slaves were at the base (Lenski 1970).

Three universals prevailed in the cultures anthropologists studied: ideologies favoring

Joan Huber, "On the Origins of Gender Inequality," *Handbook on Evolution and Society: Toward an Evolutionary Social Science,* ed. Jonathan H. Turner, Richard Machalek, and Alexandra Maryanski, pp. 383–401. Copyright © 2015 by Taylor & Francis Group. Reprinted with permission.

men, male monopoly of political office, and female exclusion from prestige spheres (Quinn 1977: 183). As the non-fit of warfare and reproduction enabled men to monopolize war and politics (Collins et al. 1993), women were far more subordinated than were other primate females (Smuts 1985). Like all female apes, women had a cycle of pregnancy and lactation that was nearly continuous during all of their most vigorous years. The pattern evolved because it prevented ovulation (Howell 1979; Vallegia and Ellison 2003). When a woman gave birth before her older child could join the daily food search, the older child starved. Infants had been suckled at intervals of about fifteen minutes by day (less often at night) for two years and at a lesser rate for at least another two years (Xie 1990).

Yet if all women were absent from politics in plow societies, so were most men until the early modern period when inventions like the printing press enabled ordinary people to learn what was going on and to protest it. Women's claims for a voice first arose among the few who could read. Later, economic power migrated from elites to huge government and business entities that needed clerical workers. Such organizations inherently foster gender neutrality because their most basic need is for profits or votes (Jackson 1998). The demand for women workers that spurred women's career changes in the twentieth century was in fact an unplanned outcome of the increasing demand for educated workers (Oppenheimer 1973).

But why was the supply of women workers elastic enough to meet that demand? Where did mothers find the time to work away from home? Some reasons are well known: improved household tools and contraceptives. A third reason is barely recognized even today:

a profound revolution in child feeding. By the 1950s, infant formula began to replace human milk in the West (Stuart-Macadam 1995). The use of the bottle induced huge behavioral changes beginning with the decline in the number of women who breastfed at all. By far the biggest (and least noticed) change was the decrease to nearly zero in the number of three- to five-year-olds whose primary food had been human milk (Stuart-Macadam 1998:58). Also unnoticed is the decrease in the number of daily feeds whether by bottle or breast. Early in the 1900s, American infants were fed whenever they fussed. Now the clock determines the timing (Lawrence and Lawrence 1999). A pattern that marked our species from its beginnings vanished in a century. An explanation of how it came to be so must be based on research in evolutionary biology and anthropology (Hrdy 2011; Huber 2007).

EVOLUTIONARY ORIGINS OF HUMAN REPRODUCTION

In the mammal line, the evolutionary successes (many species, vigorous radiation) are rats, bats, and antelopes (Gould 1996: 63). Primates, small and unsuccessful mammals (Rowell 1972: 20), appeared 70 million years ago (MYA), attained a heyday 50 to 60 MYA, and then did little until our subspecies (*Homo sapiens sapiens*) produced food and peopled the earth (Lancaster 1975). With the greatest range in social organization of any vertebrate order, primates may be multi-male, monogamous, polyandrous, promiscuous, harem-like, or solitary (Janson 1992: 95). Long after the other great apes split off from our line, chimpanzees split off about 5 MYA; they and bonobos, our two equally closest relatives, split from each other 2 MYA (de Waal 2001: 2). In the hominid line, our species is the only one not yet extinct. Anatomically modern humans emerged in East and South Africa about 150,000 years ago (Turner and Maryanski 2005: 84).

In the 1960s and 1970s the savanna baboon became the model of the human ancestor (Altmann 1998). Emphasizing only the male, some accounts now read like cautionary tales lest women get uppity, yet the absence of women in the models generated a backlash. In the 1980s, research suggested that the infants most likely to survive were those born to the best gatherers and tool users; bipedalism enabled humans to carry food and offspring long distances (Tanner 1981: 268). Hunting large animals, a high-risk activity, likely became common only when supported by gathering (Zihlman 1978). Meat eating (like plant growth) varies with latitude: at the equator, 10 percent of the diet is meat; in the Arctic, 90 percent (Testart 1988).

A theory of human evolution must recognize that humans organize much larger societies than do other primates, whose low levels of sociality lead to weak ties (Maryanski and Turner 1992). It must also explain male bonding, as with chimpanzees; female bonding, as with bonobos; and the nuclear family, whose ties we share with neither species. Human social order revolves around reproductive units that do not exist in other primates (de Waal 2001: 6).

Natural selection is based on the tendency of living organisms to produce more off-spring than can survive. Survivors tend to be individuals whose variations best suit a local ecology (Gould 1996: 138). For example, skin color evolved to balance the need for ultraviolet radiation (UVR), which affects body chemicals needed to reproduce. At the equator, humans need a very dark skin to block out too much

UVR; at extreme latitudes, a very light skin to admit enough UVR (Jablonski 2006: 80). Human behavior is also affected by cultural change. New technologies can alter optimal responses to problems almost overnight. For example, Henry Ford paid workers five dollars a day so that they could buy the cars that gave teenagers a home away from home while rubber research to improve the ride led to a better condom. A series of remarkable inventions led to a churning of couple relationships that blurred the reciprocities that have long defined family life (Seltzer and Bianchi 2013).

All change, whether biological or cultural, involves trading costs. For example, some tubes in our aquatic ancestors that collected urine from the kidneys were hijacked 350 MYA to carry eggs and sperm to the watery world outside; sex can thus be linked with waste elimination (Potts and Short 1999:133). Language appeared when humans lived on the same continent; children learn sounds in the same order, p-m-a first (Ruhlen 1994:122). But the repositioning of larynx, tongue, and pharynx that permits speech also lets food fall into the larynx and cut off air. We are the only mammals who can choke while eating. No free lunch.

Two outcomes of natural selection, bipedal locomotion about 5 MYA and a bigger brain about 2 MYA, ensured that women carry their child everywhere during the child's most vigorous years. About 5 MYA when climate change reduced the carrying capacity of their niche, our ancestors left the trees, which induced changes in behavior, anatomy, and physiology (Trevathan 1987). Bipedalism required pelvic change lest walkers place their legs too far apart (like trying to walk fast in snowshoes). The male pelvis adjusted more easily than did the female one, which had to permit passage of the infant head during birth, a process that became even harder after the doubling in brain size that began 2 MYA. The prime mover for a bigger brain was likely a need for the social skills needed for life in the larger groups that better defended against predators (Falk 1997: 129). The cost of larger groups is that more persons compete for food. Some primates handle competitive tensions by mutual grooming, but complex human groups soon outgrew the capacity of grooming to preserve social order. Members of large groups would be scratching backs all day (Potts and Short 1999: 187). Language may have been the social glue that replaced grooming (Dunbar 1996: 79). Speech lets more people interact at the same time.

The pelvic changes needed for bipedalism coupled with the bigger brain that made birth more difficult for mother and infant made solitary birthing dangerous. Chimps and bonobos go off alone to give birth because the ratio of infant head to maternal pelvis is like that of yolk to white in a boiled egg—plenty of room. In humans, the infant head fills the pelvic cavity with only tiny slivers of space to spare. Human mothers and infants became more likely to survive the birth process with the help of an experienced woman. Even so, for most of human history, one birth in twenty ended in maternal death. In natural settings and in human populations lacking modern health care, women do not tend to outlive men. The female longevity advantage is of recent origin and occurs only in societies with modern medical resources. At about age eighty-five, male and female mortality rates converge (Crews 2003: 136, 107).

The contemporary strategy for birth emerged after the brain doubled in size. About 2 MYA, the hominid brain reached the biggest size that could be born to a mammal otherwise adapted to deliver an infant whose brain is half its adult size at birth (Trevathan 1987: 223). A bigger brain would preclude safe delivery. But natural selection neither enlarged the birth canal nor increased the total size of the adult female (as with gorillas). Instead, the birth occurred before the infant brain made the head too big for safe passage. At birth, the human brain is only 23 percent of its adult size. It attains 45 percent of adult size at seven months, while the chimpanzee brain is 45 percent of adult size at birth. Human females must invest far more time in child care than do any other female mammals (Lancaster 1985: 20).

Passage through the bony maternal pelvis is the hardest part of the birth process for the infant; its passage through the vagina is the most hazardous for the mother. Unless the flesh is cut to widen the opening, tearing of tissue from vagina to anus is common; unless the laceration is repaired, serious infection can occur (Trevathan 1987: 27). The rearrangement of the birth canal created the worst problem. In four-footed species like monkeys (and the probable human ancestor), the entrance and exit of the birth canal have their greatest breadth front to back; the infant head is also largest front to back. The infant emerges facing the front of its mother's body. She can guide it from the birth canal or it could crawl up to her nipples unassisted. Bipedalism unfortunately twisted the human birth canal in the middle so that the entrance is broadest side to side while the exit is broadest front to back. The widest breadths of entrance and exit are thus perpendicular to one another as are the relevant fetal dimensions: the head is largest front to back, but the infant's rigid shoulders are broadest side to side, not an example of intelligent design. The passage of the infant's broad, rigid shoulders through the mother's bony pelvis requires that the infant's chin be pressed against its throat instead of tilted backward. The coupling of this flexion with the restructured bony birth canal requires the infant to undergo a series of rotations to pass through the birth canal without hindrance. As a result of these rotations, the infant tends to be born facing away from its mother, which hinders her ability to reach down and clear a breathing passageway for it or to remove the cord from around its neck should it interfere with the infant's breathing or continued emergence. In most deliveries, if the mother tries to guide the infant from the birth canal, she risks pulling its head backward and damaging its nerves and muscles. This process transformed birth from a solitary to a social event (Trevathan 1999: 195). The human infant is in effect premature, more helpless, and far more work for the mother.

To the end of her reproductive period, a forager mother carried her youngest child everywhere for three or four years and slept with it at night to boot because her low-fat milk sated its hunger only briefly (Hrdy 1999). She gathered nuts and berries and killed small animals daily, all her children in tow, to teach them how to provide for themselves. By contrast, the offspring of nonhuman primates feed themselves and no one else. A sick or injured one can die of hunger or thirst. Relatives do not respond to its need for food (Lancaster 1991). Between 70 and 90 percent of these infants fail to reach adulthood, owing to malnutrition and diseases that follow weaning (Lancaster and Lancaster 1983). For nonhuman primates, as for most mammals, the juvenile phase is a selection funnel into which many enter but few emerge (Lancaster 1991). About half the infants born to foragers and horticulturists lived long enough to reproduce.

The long period of feeding juveniles and increasing the strength of adult male-female bonds was involved in the emergence of the human family: an adult female, an adult male, and their offspring. Turner and Maryanski (2005) argue that the origin is likely a result of neurological changes that enabled humans to develop organizational forms that were better knit than the weak ties of other ape adults. When humans could not take to the trees, weak ties threatened survival. Tightly knit groups can better fight off predators. Human adults became more organized. However, the ties between mother and infant remained much the same.

THE PHYSIOLOGY OF LACTATION

The physiology of lactation involves the mammary gland and the composition of the milk. UNICEF estimates that 97 percent of women can give milk (Jolly 1999: 330). According to Lawrence and Lawrence (1999), the mammary gland (medical name of the breast) undergoes three phases of growth: in the uterus, childhood, and the pubertal period. The adult female gland consists of a branching system of excretory ducts embedded in connective tissue. When a female is ten to twelve years old, the tree of ducts rapidly extends in a branching pattern. Alveolar buds form a year or two before the onset of menses. New buds sprout for several years, producing alveolar lobes. Female breasts enlarge to adult size at puberty. A nipple contains fifteen to twenty-five milk ducts, each of which opens into it. At birth, a sequence of events governed by hormonal action prepares the breast for lactation (Lawrence and Lawrence 1999). From forty to seventy-two hours after birth, a woman experiences milk coming in as a feeling of fullness, more quickly if she has borne a child earlier. The volume increases for two weeks, starting at less than 100 ml/day and rising to about 600 ml/day at ninety-six hours. Lactose, sodium chloride, and protein stabilize at twenty-four hours. The lactating glands adjust milk supply to demand. Reduction in the sucking stimulus reduces the hormone prolactin and milk synthesis. Variation in milk secretion is rapidly reflected in anatomic change in the mammary gland. In the absence of stimulation, mammary tissue regresses the first week after birth. Unless frequent suckling or use of a breast pump empties the lactating breast, milk production gradually ceases. The absence of suckling initiates the neuron-hormonal reflex to maintain prolactin secretion, and the ensuing engorgement of the breast causes diminished flow by compressing the blood vessels. Even women who never gave birth or breastfed can be induced to lactate (Lawrence and Lawrence 1999: 633). The process should begin several months before the infant's arrival. Lactation may occur in one to six weeks.

As the study of human milk is recent, scientists know less about its composition than one would expect. The milk of cows, goats, and sheep had long been studied owing to its economic importance; most of the research on human milk appeared after 1970 (Lawrence and Lawrence 1994: 91). Anthropologists rarely gathered detailed data on breastfeeding, which was and is very hard to study in the few populations that exercise no deliberate control over fertility (Panter-Brick 1992: 137). Composition and volume are hard to compare owing to different procedures to weigh and test, inconsistent extraction techniques, and variation in sampling time between feeds (Jelliffe and Jelliffe 1978). As studies rarely separate full and partial breastfeeding, averages tend to hide more than they reveal. Retrospective surveys of mothers who nursed their infants cost little but tend to yield unreliable data (Haaga 1988: 307). Interview data reveal low accord between timed data and the mother's memory of feeds (Vitzthum 1997: 247). Direct observation of suckling requires much time; few studies report such data (Ellison 1995: 316).

A question as simple as the volume of milk at a feeding must deal with several issues. The methods must be accurate, reproducible, non-invasive, and relatively easy to use at home, night or day; additionally, they must not interrupt the suckling. Milk composition constantly changes. The fat content increases toward the end of each feeding and rises from early morning to midday; earlier milk differs from later milk at the same feeding. Composition varies with stage of lactation, time of day, sampling time, and maternal nutrition. Pumped samples vary from those obtained by suckling and the content varies by method of pumping. Many of the earlier interpretations of milk content were in error as they were based on pooled samples from many donors at different times and stages of lactation. Maternal diet is a major concern in studies of milk content. Should it be poor, many of the nutrients in her milk will come from her body rather than her diet. The milk of a malnourished mother has about the same proportions of protein, fat, and carbohydrate as that of a well-nourished one, but a malnourished woman produces less milk.

Human milk evolved to meet the needs of infants who nurse on demand. The human brain at birth is relatively small. The infant's need for milk sugar is great because its brain can grow only if it gets large amounts of lactose (Small 1998: 185). Compared with the milk of other mammals, the mature milk of primates about three weeks after birth is dilute, very low in fat and protein, but high in lactose, all of which affect suckling frequency. Species that nurse less often must have milk with a much higher fat content. A mother rabbit returns only once a day to the concealed spot where she parked her offspring. Human milk is characteristic of a species that suckles its young almost continuously (Micozzi 1995: 357), a fact that was unknown to social scientists until the discovery of natural fertility.

Not long ago demographers thought that Malthus got it right: abstinence was the only certain contraceptive. Medical science saw the claim that breastfeeding prevented pregnancy as an old wives' tale because the biomedical nursing pattern had spaced feeds two to five hours apart, and the minimal suppression of ovarian function led physicians to doubt that lactation and fecundity were related (Vitzthum 1997: 244). Demographers were slow to see the significance of premodern child-spacing patterns, and economists were slower still (Page and Lesthaeghe 1981: ix). As recently as the 1950s, demographers were unaware of the effects of lactation on amenorrhea and infecundity (Hobcraft 1994: 413). Lorimer's (1954) influential UNESCO volume on human fertility discussed no effects, nor did Davis and Blake (1956) note any in a landmark paper listing all intermediate variables that affect fertility (Ellison 1995: 305).

In the 1950s Louis Henry defined natural fertility as the absence of deliberate control; a couple's behavior is neither bound to the number of children born nor modified when the number reaches the maximum a couple wants (Leridon and Menken 1977: 3). Giosa (1955) proposed that a major function of lactation might be its role as a natural birth spacer. In 1961, Henry (1961) suggested that lactation might be the primary determinant of natural fertility, and in the 1970s, data on Kalahari foragers revealed a lifetime average of five births (Howell 1979: 291). An international conference of world health groups later announced that breastfeeding was a safe and effective contraceptive (Ellison 1995: 305). Demographers now agree that natural fertility was nearly universal before the demographic transition that began in Western Europe (Wood 1990; Xie 1990). By the 1990s it was clear that the effects of breastfeeding on fertility vary among individuals and societies depending on the sucking stimulus, maternal diet, and secretion of hormones. Intensity interacts with availability of maternal energy to determine metabolic energy available for reproduction and duration of amenorrhea (Vallegia and Ellison 2003: 97).

Biologically, breastfeeding benefits both infant and mother. Infants receive ideal growth nutrients and maternal antibodies against diseases; mothers return more rapidly to their prepregnancy state and have lower rates of obesity later in life. By the 1990s, researchers noted an important new benefit for mothers: breastfeeding decreases the exposure of reproductive tissues to estrogenic hormones. The decline in frequency and duration of breastfeeding among Western women floods their bodies with hormones during a much larger part of the reproductive period; such women experience an average of 450 menstrual cycles over a lifetime versus 50 cycles for women who breastfeed often over a long period (see citations in Crews and Gerber 1994, p. 159, and Stuart-Macadam 1998, p. 57). Abundant calories and fats increase exposure to gonadal steroids by lowering the age of puberty. Women in modern societies carry a risk of malignancy ten to one hundred times greater than that of foragers. The rates of diseases linked to chronic hormone exposure are rising in both sexes: endometrial, colon, breast, and prostate cancer and coronary heart disease (Micozzi 1995; Whitten 1999: 211). The incidence of cancers likely reflects the profound ecological changes of modernization (Ellison 1999).

The biological and social costs of breast-feeding to the infant were and remain very low. The biological cost to the mother typically involves a breast infection that modern medicine can readily cure. By contrast, the social cost was very high when the cycle of pregnancy and lactation excluded her from all political and economic activities, and a study based on data from the National Longitudinal Survey of Youth indicates that it is still substantial (Rippeyoung and Noonan 2012). Economists long ignored the opportunity cost of maternal time (Butz 1977) though ordinary women seem to sense it. Historically, the costs tend to vary by time and place because "women's work" varies with the technology of food production in a given ecological setting, a topic I discuss after a comment on why we like certain foods.

THE ORIGINS OF HUMAN FOOD PREFERENCES

Constraints on human diets are a consequence of the interaction of ecology, technology, and social organization. Not long ago, social scientists (like Malthus) held that human inventions increased the food supply, which then spurred population growth. Then Danish economist Ester Boserup (1965) turned Malthus on his head. It was the increase in population size and subsequent need to feed more people that spurred inventions, not the other way around. Hungry people think of ways to produce more food (Cohen 1984: 1). However,

there are costs. Digging stick, hoe, and plow make land more productive only with greater input of human labor. People do not turn the soil, fodder animals, or collect manure unless they must (Netting 1993: 103). Technology is more a holding action than a liberating force (Cohen 1977: 285). In order to show how our ancestors coped with infant diet during the last 200,000 years, I first describe the primate diet that prevailed until hunger led foragers to domesticate plants and animals, and then discuss the effect of subsistence tools in given ecological settings on diets in societies based on hoe, herding, and plow technology.

The ancient primate diet consisted primarily of fruits; humans prefer food with similar nutrient and chemical content. According to Nesse and Williams (1994) and Whitten (1999), fruits are unique plants that evolved as sugary lures to give seeds a free ride in an animal gut to a distant germination site. Given fruits survived the selection process by attracting the animals most likely to disperse the seeds at the best time and place. Seeds are often quite poisonous because eating them too soon thwarts a plant's reproductive strategy. When the seeds are ready for a trip in a warm and moist gut to a good site for germination, all fruits signal the appropriate animal carriers that the flesh is sweet, soft, and succulent. When the bitter and astringent chemicals (like tannins) that are highly concentrated in unripe fruit decline, ripening is heralded by bright colors that make the fruit stand out against leaves. To make subtle judgments about ripeness, nutrient content, and plant defenses (which humans generally perceive as bitter), fruit eaters developed a nuanced sense of color, texture, and taste. Primates regained the color vision that had been lost owing to mammals' nocturnal origin, and became trichromatic, sensitive to those parts of the color spectrum that signal the changes in ripening fruit: yellow-orange, yellow, and blue-green. Most of the other animals are dichromatic. Ripening primate-dispersed fruits take on yellow-orange hues; bird-dispersed fruits assume red, blue, white, and purple colors.

Colonizing the globe and adapting to local ecosystems produced an array of diets, but we humans likely retained a perceptual basis for choosing food much like that of the foods relished by other apes. The short history of plant domestication makes it unlikely that our physiological ability to process food chemicals has diverged much from that of our ancestors. Foragers added seeds, roots, and tubers that they could more easily collect and store than the fruits of tropical hardwoods. Contemporary humans are more adapted to a forager diet than to diets that replaced it as our species spread over the globe. For example, scurvy, marked by swollen gums, livid skin spots, and prostration, arose among peoples who moved north and lost easy access to fresh fruit. It often afflicted British sailors on long voyages. They were cured by adding lime juice to their diet, which led to their being called "Limeys." Fruits rich in vitamin C were so important in the primate diet over such a long period that the biochemical machinery to make the vitamin degenerated in all humans and some apes (Nesse and Williams 1994: 130).

FROM FORAGING TO HOE AND HERDING

Hunter-gatherers had a level of social equality as high as any ever known (Chafetz 1984). Some inequality is unavoidable as each individual (save identical twins) has unique traits that help or challenge him or her in competing for material resources and social esteem. Warfare was rare among foragers. People were few in number, land was plentiful, and crowding minimal: one person to a square mile. Groups easily avoided one another in the search for food (Johnson and Earle 1987). As women's gathering yielded more calories on average than did men's hunting, the incentives for male control of sexuality were low, and casual sex and frequent divorce were common (Collins et al. 1993: 199). Storage was impossible, so there was no steady surplus of food. Each woman nursed only her own infant, for few women have milk enough for two. A woman carried her youngest child in a sling while she collected food. Foragers usually saw twins as bad luck because it was so hard to carry two. A mother might have to kill one or both (depending on the norms), usually by exposure. In very hard times, parents might have to expose an infant when there were too many mouths to feed.

Foragers had no alternatives to human milk as a food for young children. Foods of older children and adults were too tough and hard to chew and digest for those whose guts and teeth were too immature to process incompletely ripe fruit, nuts, insects, and small animals. After foragers learned to use fire, vegetable tubers and meats were cooked to soften them. Even so, they were hard for young children to digest. A mother's need to breastfeed was unquestioned. It was highly unlikely that another lactating woman would be available to serve as a wet nurse (Trevathan 1987: 32; Hrdy 1999: 402).

Societies based on the hoe or herding gave up on foraging when they could not cope with local resource failure. Searching for new ways to ensure a food supply, erstwhile foragers turned to a semi-sedentary mode based on use of the digging stick or hoe in areas of abundant rainfall. Where rainfall was scant or the terrain too rough to permit crops, they herded sheep, cattle, or goats. The two modes differ considerably, but the underlying technology is much the same, for animals and plants were domesticated at about the same time. The hoe or herding societies that succeeded forager bands increased the food supply, but the direct or indirect costs they incurred affected infant diet. For example, the higher the level of social inequality, the less likely it is that poor people get enough to eat. The efforts to restrict resources marked the beginnings of warfare (Johnson and Earle 1987: 58, 245). Biologists see most aggressive behavior as a response to environmental overcrowding (Wilson 1996: 84). Humans must solve the same ecological problems as other species if they are to produce children who live long enough to reproduce (Low, Clarke, and Lockridge 1992). Population pressure spurred the formation of local groups five to ten times larger than a typical family to act on issues concerning food storage and defense. A chief could organize a region if he could establish control over warfare, large-scale technology, central storage, and external trade. In kin-based tribal groups, kinship structure became an organization of coercion that upheld the property system (Collins et al. 1993: 199). The more often a society engaged in warfare, the more likely was social control to be vested in politico-military elites that excluded women.

A digging stick or metal-tipped hoe produces more food than does foraging, but it also requires more labor. According to Friedl (1975: 59ff), before planting crops in tropical forest or grassland savanna, men clear the land, which is often fallowed for as long as ten years and then cleared again to grow sweet potato, taro, yam, and banana in areas like the Pacific Islands and parts of West Africa or tapioca and cassava in tropical South America. East Africa and parts of North and South America produce cereal crops like millet and maize, and rice is grown in parts of South Asia. Domesticated animals like cattle or pigs become prestige objects in exchange as well as a source of meat and milk. Animals like cows, sheep, and goats provided alternatives to breastfeeding in the event of maternal death, but the new options were illusory because bovid milk has too little sugar to nourish a human infant's rapidly growing brain and too much fat to be digested properly.

Hoe cultures display the diversity of gender roles that became the basis for the relativist view of human behavior and belief held by Franz Boas and his students. Patterns of marriage and kinship tended to follow the division of labor, a crucial factor in the devising of reciprocal duties (Friedl 1975). After men cleared the land, both men and women planted and harvested crops, for a woman could do this while toting a nursling in a sling. Older children tended younger ones. Polygyny (a man has more than one wife at a time) increases productivity, for women did (and do) most of the work. Custom holds that a man can become rich only if he has many wives. A man often paid a bride-price to compensate a father for the loss of his daughter's services. The balance of the sexes was less skewed than might be expected because the death rate was high and women married early, men married late. By contrast, polyandry (a woman has more than one husband at a time) occurs only when food production is so difficult that it takes more than one man to support a woman and her children.

Men monopolized war. All adult males served as part-time warriors (Davie 1929: 30; Wright 1942: 84). Views of the few who studied war before the 1960s were widely accepted (Otterbein 1999: 796). Turney-High (1949) held that primitive war was more athletic contest than military exercise. By contrast, recent studies suggest that war was extremely bloody, and men, women, and children suffered great harm (LeBlanc 1999). War spawns sexual politics that typically involve segregation of men's and women's activities (Collins et al. 1993). As war and politics were inextricably intertwined, an extensive search noted that women were political actors in only a few societies in Africa and North America (Hobhouse, Wheeler, and Ginsberg 1930).

Herding societies appeared where tillage was difficult owing to mountainous terrain, a brief growing season, or low rainfall, as in Central Asia, Arabia, North Africa, parts of sub-Saharan Africa, and Europe (Lenski and Lenski 1978: 235). As many herders drank their animals' milk, many adults became able to digest lactose (milk sugar). Most humans lose that ability after weaning (Cavalli-Sforza 2000: 36). Moving livestock to seasonal pastures to convert grass into human food requires a nomadic lifestyle, but spatial mobility often leads to competition with agrarians over territory and disputes over water and stolen animals. The constant threat of conflict during migration stimulates the growth of centralized political authority, and the open grasslands where herders live pose few barriers to movement and political consolidation. A herding society may be as huge as the Asian empire of Ghenghis Khan, but a herding community may be only a little larger than a forager band, as a small unit can more easily maintain a herd in areas where scanty rainfall limits the food supply. About 3,000 years ago Asian herders acquired a huge advantage over the less mobile agrarians in the waves of conquest after they

learned to ride their horses; herders devastated Eurasian agrarian empires for more than 2,500 years. Sexual politics peaked when a military aristocracy rule disarmed peasants (Collins et al. 1993).

Anthropologists ignored women in pastoral societies until after the 1970s (Dyson-Hudson and Dyson-Hudson 1980). Gender stratification is perplexing as many herders also depend on the hoe or plow, tools that oppositely affect women's economic productivity. The collection of cross-cultural data on lactation is especially problematic in a mobile population that does not track chronological age (Wiley and Pike 1998). Most data on infant feeding date from the 1980s. Gray (1999: 167) notes that a typical Turkana mother suckles her infant on demand. Suckling lasted less than 2.5 minutes at 10- to 15-minute intervals by day. At night the infant slept at its mother's nipple. Mothers did not usually waken when the infant nursed. Only mothers of children nineteen months or older reported being away from the child more than thirty to sixty minutes.

PLOW SOCIETIES

Plow societies appeared in West Asia about 4,000 years ago. The first plows were made of wood. Techniques to smelt iron invented about 2,000 years later provided an iron blade. As iron is plentiful, plowshares proliferated and food production soared. Because large stores of food make a tempting target, warfare became widespread and has remained so ever since, thus illustrating a general rule of human organization: the larger the food supply, the greater the temptation to control its production and distribution (Lenski 1970). From its West Asian beginnings, plow technology spread to Europe, East Asia, and North Africa, wherever temperature and rainfall permitted the cultivation of grain crops. In sub-Saharan Africa the plow was rare because oxen, the best draft animals, can thrive neither in the humid zones of Central Africa nor in the West African coastal zones owing to the presence of the tse-tse fly, whose reproductive behavior in an extremely complex life cycle enables it to kill or severely weaken both cattle and humans (Shipton 1994: 357).

Domestication of various grains led to a proliferation of more digestible plant foods that needed much less chewing than did the foragers' roots and tubers. From an early age, an infant could swallow a mushy mix of grain and milk or water, but grain did not supply the nutrients of human milk. Moreover, a grain-based diet was highly dangerous for young children. Stored food is a good home for the disease pathogens that thrive in the warm climates of West Asia where the erstwhile foragers first settled. Most of the food adults ate was contaminated, and some of it was badly spoiled. Adults often developed immunity to many disease-producing organisms, but the immature infant gut, especially in the absence of the immune factors supplied by human milk, was highly vulnerable to pathogens that led to diarrhea and often to death from dehydration.

The most obvious effect of the plow was a vast increase in the Eurasian food supply. For the first time, continuous cultivation of a given area became possible by reducing weeds and turning the soil deeply enough to restore fertility. Use of the plow spurred the domestication of draft animals, and confining them in stalls to prevent their wandering off encouraged the collection of manure. Scattering manure over the fields increased food production, which led to the invention of writing, the better to track a much larger surplus. Early on, Moses became famous as a bureaucrat who watched over the pharaoh's granaries in the valley of the Nile.

Eurasian patterns of social stratification assumed the pyramidal form of feudalism: a ruling elite at the top; a slim layer of merchants, artisans, and craft workers; and at the bottom, a vast layer of peasants, serfs, and slaves. Use of the plow devastated the lives of ordinary people. A food surplus in the countryside coupled with the availability of iron weapons tempted elites to extract as much as possible from impoverished peasants (Goody 1976). The flatter and richer the land and the more food it could produce, the worse off were the men and women who did the work, much worse off than their forager ancestors (Lenski 1970).

With higher population density and settled agriculture, men did most of the heavy work involved in food production. Men monopolized the plow because the management of heavy draft animals in much larger fields was incompatible with the frequent suckling of an infant. With oxen a man could plow in a day an area far larger than a woman could till by hoe (Childe 1951: 100). When men monopolize food production, women become economic liabilities, in need of a dowry as a basis of support (Boserup 1970: 35). The less food women produce, the more they are valued only as mothers. Tropical Africa and Eurasia have different strategies of inheritance owing to the effect of the plow on the value of land coupled with women's low level of productivity (Goody 1976: 97). In the African hoe cultures south of the Sahara, land is plentiful and economic differences among families are minor. There is little pressure to provide an heir to an estate (Goody and Tambiah 1973: 22). Marriage has little effect on a daughter's economic position; all women, married or not, grow crops or do craft work.

The most significant effect of the plow on women's status was a result of the fact that its use made land the chief form of wealth. Individual land ownership gave rise to laws and customs that reflected elite men's monopoly on warfare and related politico-economic institutions. Rule and custom (primogeniture, for example) ensured that land could not be subdivided into pieces too small to support a family. The scarcer the land and the more intensively it was used, the greater the tendency to keep it in the nuclear family, the basic unit of human production and reproduction (Goody 1976: 97). Monogamy prevailed lest too many heirs claim a given property. As women served as transmitters of male property, concern with their sexual "purity" became acute. The larger a woman's endowment, the more her sexual behavior was controlled. In Catholic areas, canon law made divorce difficult or impossible. But monogamy constrained men less than it did women. The fact that men's out-of-wedlock children could inherit no property effectively reduced elite men's interest in controlling the behavior of other men.

Several customs attest the steep decline in women's status in Eurasia and North Africa (Huber and Spitze 1983). Women are in a bad fix when ecology and technology encourage ideologies that define a woman only as a mother because the lower the value of her labor, the less the restriction of her normal body functions affects food production. The plow thus tempted elite men to introduce the practice of depriving women of the use of part of their bodies. For example, in Western Europe, an elite husband could lock a chastity belt around his wife's private parts and carry away the key were he to go off on a crusade.

In the North African regions of plow use, such as Egypt, Ethiopia, Somalia, the Sudan, parts of Muslim West Africa, and Yemen, the practice of clitoridectomy is common (El Saadawi 1982: 33). Older women perform the operation on prepubertal girls. The purpose is to prevent sexual pleasure by cutting away part or all of the clitoral prepuce and tip, the entire clitoris, or the clitoris labia minora and part of the labia majora, scraping the two sides raw, then sewing them together save for a tiny opening to let urine or (later) menstrual blood drain, all of this without the use of any drugs to reduce pain or sanitary measures to reduce chances of serious infection. The consequences include chronic urinary infection and difficulties in childbirth and coitus. The custom still exists in parts of North Africa and among its migrants elsewhere, including the United States and Western Europe. It now affects about 140 million women worldwide (*Economist* 2012).

In India the practice of suttee among Hindu elites involved burning a widow alive on her husband's funeral pyre. The rationale was that it was her sins in a previous life that had caused her husband to die first (Stein 1978: 255). Some widows willingly climbed onto the pyre. Others did not. If a widow screamed and cried, her husband's male relatives would tie her down. The death of the wife gave control of the estate to the husband's brothers.

In China, foot-binding was widespread in the wheat-growing areas of the north (Levy 1966). Legend has it that the goal of the so-called lotus foot began when an emperor admired a dancer's feet and legs. The degree of maiming depended on the level of work a woman was expected to do. The bindings, first applied when the little girl was about three, were successively tightened. The pain was severe. Because the foot was made to be inches shorter, walking became nearly impossible. The practice was uncommon in the south because there the chief grain was rice, not wheat. Constant wading in the filthy water of the paddies often led to serious infection. The modern version of foot-binding is less painful. The stiletto heel creates a lotus-foot that makes walking difficult and running impossible but at least it can be taken off at night (Wikipedia 2014).

Yet the chastity belt seems mild compared with the effects of clitoridectomy, foot-binding, and suttee. Why were efforts to control women's sexual behavior so much more ferocious in Asia and North Africa than in Western Europe? Goody (1983) explains the relative mildness of the constraints on European women as an unexpected consequence of the measures the Catholic Church took to induce communicants to bequeath to it their wealth. Canon law reduced each person's number of close relatives (compared with Roman times, for example) by abolishing adoption and close-cousin marriage. Child-marriage was also banned and women often had the right to inherit land. The measures worked. About a third of French productive land was in church hands by the end of the seventh century. In German lands, northern France, and Italy, the church owned twice as much land in the ninth as in the eighth century.

INFANT FEEDING BEFORE MODERN MEDICINE

Settlements became permanent when humans learned how to tend plants to produce the food needed to support the activities that mark urban life. The upside of city life is the flourishing of the arts and the life of the mind. The downside is the effect of crowding on the disposal of human wastes; ubiquitous sewage threatened human health across all social classes. It was not so long ago that Queen Victoria's spouse was a victim of the "bad drains" in Buckingham Palace. Yet however hard urban life was for elites, it was much worse for ordinary folk (Cohen 1989). Nomad foragers had been as tall as the affluent today (Eaton, Eaton, and Konner 1999: 313). The suits of armor in contemporary museums suggest that the knights of old were surprisingly short. Peasants shrank even more on a diet that included far too much bread and not nearly enough meat, fruit, and vegetables. As Braudel (1979: 130) put it, the standard diet in early modern Europe was bread, more bread, and gruel. A diet bad for bones was also bad for teeth (Larsen 2000: 231). Nomad foods had required heavy-duty chewing, which increased the size of jaw muscle and bone. Grain-based foods need little chewing (and the sugar content hastens dental decay). With less use, jaw bone and muscle became smaller, while teeth, more under genetic control, stayed about the same size. However, the discrepancy in size between jaw and teeth gives rise to a degree of malocclusion that now provides a good living for orthodontists.

The level of social stratification induced by plow technology especially affected the infants of peasants and slave women. Any infant whose mother died lost the immune protection of maternal milk, but its chances improved markedly when its family was rich enough to hire a wet nurse, a woman paid to suckle a child not her own. When the wet nurse was also suckling her own child, as often happened, the huge drain on her system made it unlikely that she would have enough milk for two over a prolonged period, and her own child might starve (Wood 1994: 17, 204; Stini 1985: 203). Wealthy parents often bought the life of their own child with that of another (Fildes 1986). In Greek and Roman times slave women had often been used as wet nurses. By the medieval period, the practice was popular among upper-class Europeans. The proto-industrial period spread the demand for wet-nursing across a much wider segment of the class structure, according to European scholars' study of church and state archives; as no such sources are available in the new world, the study of wet-nursing in America is rare (Golden 2001: 3). The availability of wage work for women sharply raised the opportunity cost of prolonged suckling though the death rate of the wet nurses' own infants was very high (Fildes 1988: 193). When many wives worked in the burgeoning French silk industry, the parents shipped a majority of Lyonnais infants to nearby villages (Garden 1975: 122), and Parisian parents sent an even higher proportion of infants away. The death rate of these infants reduces optimism about the nature of our kind.

Hand-feeding of a grain-based pap in the event of maternal death or incapability goes back 4,000 years as indicated by the utensils found by archeologists (Fildes 1986: 262). In late medieval Iceland, the only infants who were fed human milk were those whose mothers were too poor to keep a cow (Hastrup 1985). However, Fildes (1986: 264) noted that in a cold climate with high standards of maternal care and cleanliness, the five-year survival rate of hand-fed and breastfed infants may have differed little because the post-weaning death rates were very high whatever the child's age at weaning.

Infant abandonment occurred when food was scarce. Europeans gave up infants in great number to the end of the Middle Ages (Boswell 1988: 428). Foundling hospitals emerged first in

Italy, then Spain, Portugal, and France from the 1200s to the 1600s and then in northern and central Europe in the 1700s. In proto-industrial Europe, whenever male wages were low, infant abandonment was associated with women's opportunities for wage work. In 1780, parents gave up perhaps 8,000 of the 30,000 infants born in Paris (Braudel 1979: 491). According to Kertzer (1993), abandonment rose sharply in Italy after the Catholic Church tightened its rules in response to the Reformation. The church banned all sexual relations outside marriage, but women paid the price. Limiting marriage to the formal ceremony undermined the traditional meaning of a man's promise of marriage, which long had sufficed to initiate sexual relations and was taken by the community as an obligation the man assumed to the woman and any child she bore. A rural woman working as an urban live-in servant was the most likely parent. Whether wet-nursed or fed by hand, few of these foundlings survived childhood (Kertzer 1993: 138).

The death rate of infants whose mothers did not suckle them was lowered only by the advent of modern sanitation (safe water and unspoiled food). At the outset of the Industrial Revolution, poor sanitation amid urban squalor had made human milk optimal for infant survival. Nineteenth-century documents report death rates of 80–90 percent for infants who were not breastfed (Preston and Haines 1991). In the rural "third world" (as in eighteenth-century London), 70 percent of infants died before their second birthday (Fildes 1986: 401). However, by 1910, discovery of the germ theory of disease in the 1880s made the bottle almost as safe as the breast in areas with modern sanitation (Huber 1990). It was safe water and food that induced the decline of gastrointestinal diseases, not medical treatment, for there were no therapeutic measures of value until about 1950 (McKeown 1976).

In both traditional and modern economies, breastfed infants suffer fewer ailments than do the bottle-fed, but so far as I have been able to discover, no evidence indicates that bottle-fed and breastfed children in modern settings differ significantly in the ability to live long enough to reproduce. Modern data are difficult to interpret because breast milk is often supplemented by formula and solid food in the infant's first year (Lawrence and Lawrence 1994: 28). Bottle-feeding clearly remains deadly where clean water is rare. For example, when poor women massively entered wage work in Northeast Brazil in the early 1940s, breastfeeding fell from 96 to 40 percent and kept falling despite extremely high infant death rates (Scheper-Hughes 1992: 317). Expansion of women's market opportunities persistently lowers the rate of breastfeeding (Da Vanzo 1988). In "third world" countries (as in industrializing Europe), mothers often seem to behave as if the opportunity cost of breastfeeding is very high, even when the effects of alternative modes of feeding on their infants' lives are both clear and severe.

Thus, late in the nineteenth century a mode of infant feeding that had evolved over millions of years began to erode as a result of discoveries spawned by modern medicine. Preference for bottle-feeding crossed all class and ethnic lines (Wolf 2001). Commercial firms and physicians took over the task of deciding what and when to feed infants. Mothers scheduled fewer feeds per day whether the mode was breast or bottle. Early on, educated mothers often saw breastfeeding as an outdated practice of immigrant women from poor countries. Later, such mothers were more likely to breastfeed than were less educated

women. However, all infants, whatever the mother's educational attainment, were fed substantially less often both day and night than were the infants of their species over the past 200,000 years.

When the women's movement reappeared in the early 1970s, the facts about prolonged lactation were not fully understood. Feminist research tended to focus on such areas as the effect of human milk on infant health, breastfeeding ideologies by race and class, and the social construction of the medical control of pregnancy and lactation. Some feminist theorists, convinced that human behavior is solely a cultural construction, still seem unaware that modern technology effectively altered the social consequences of an ancient biological constraint.

THE SOCIAL CONSEQUENCES OF PROLONGED LACTATION

As male domination has been universal in historical time, one might suspect that its origin was an innate male trait that was absent in females. Until recently, many scientific explanations did indeed ascribe the origin of male dominance to innate sex-linked psychological traits. As Udry (2000: 454) said, humans form social structures around gender because the sexes have different bio-influenced behavioral predispositions, and gendered social structure is a universal accommodation to this biological fact. By contrast, evolutionary biologists see human behavior as a result of a continuously interactive mix of genes with a given environment (Gottlieb 1998). As Maynard Smith (1989: 68) observed, human culture cannot be broken into trait clusters that can be counted and analyzed statistically; culture transcends biological constraints, as in cooking and the use of the wheel, tools, and spectacles. Below, after noting the sex differences in human physiology, I focus on the effects of culture on human behavior.

Physiological sex differences in humans are categorical or statistical. A categorical difference affects all or none of a given group. The only categorical differences in humans are those of reproduction: no man can bear a child or (until recently) provide the only food it could digest. Statistical differences occur in quantifiable degrees. Some of them evolved to permit infant birth or nourishment. For example, men's upper body strength is greater than women's owing to the requirements of breast-feeding. Men tend to be larger and stronger than women, though some women are larger and stronger than most men.

Although the male edge in size and strength is often used to explain why women took no part in warfare, Maccoby (1998) and Goldstein (2001) have shown that this view is invalid. Individual variation and overlap would have enabled a nontrivial minority of women to fight. Nor do testosterone levels explain male dominance (Mazur and Booth 1998). The only well-documented case of a female combat unit in a standing army was in West Africa, the 1700s to the 1900s (Goldstein 2001). They fought well but had to be celibate; if pregnant, they were killed (Herskovits 1938: 85).

The most likely origin of women's secondary status is the fact that any species whose females nursed their young on a battlefield would soon be extinct. This fact suggests two questions: When did warfare become common, and why did women's absence from the battlefield bar them from the politics of making and enforcing laws? The answers to both indicate the sweeping effects of culture

on human behavior. Anthropologists generally believe that warfare became common after the advent of hoe culture. For most of human time on earth, war was rare; crowding was minimal, one person to a square mile. After population pressure spawned groups five to ten times larger than a typical family to act on issues of food storage and defense, war became more common (Johnson and Earle 1987). When a chief institutionalized control over central storage, technology, external trade, and warfare, he could organize a region. Bronze weapons were used as early as 3000 BCE, iron weapons about 1500 BCE, and horses 1000 BCE. Metal weapons raised the efficiency and cost of war, and tended to restrict arms-bearing to elites (Andreski 1968: 38). The military was a key element in the formation of large-scale political institutions like complex chiefdoms and states (Earle 1997: 105). In Europe, metallurgy enabled politico-military elites to establish huge kingdoms whose eventual collapse led to feudalism (Bloch 1961). Lack of central control opened the door to robber hordes, for the protection and oppression of peasants fell to local landlords whose knights plundered the locals but protected them from the knightly thugs down the road. The European ruling class was a military one to the end of the old order in France (Keegan 1987: 4).

Women's absence from the battlefield precluded their presence in politics, for war and politics were intricately linked until the 1800s, as I soon note. Conquest always involved politics. Winners pacified losers in order to dun them for taxes, as when migrants from the Asian steppes overran Europe during the decline of Roman hegemony (Heather 1996). After conquest, we-they distinctions justified unequal relations between winners and losers.

The cycle of pregnancy and lactation alone would have excluded women from the process of pacification, but a masculine military ideology also played a part (Stiehm 1989; Enloe 1993). Collins et al. (1993) describe the tendency of all-male groups to become solidary around a masculine erotic identity. Sexual politics leads to separate male and female spheres, a dual status system, and the gendering of production. All-male groups still tend to harbor a sexually aggressive culture as in competitive athletics, gang violence, fraternity carousing, and military institutions.

Ethnocentrism stems from functional relations that reflect group interests. Long-term relationships of social inequality are marked by one pivotal factor: one group has a vested interest in preserving the distribution of resources that the relationship brings (Jackman 1994). The conflict of gender interests that begins with reproduction tends to spread into daily life. When ascribed statuses like sex and race are used as axes of social organization, the phenotypic markers and social warp and woof they provide makes for effective social control (Hechter 1987: 186). Male control of decision making enabled them to regulate marriage, inheritance, and property rights such that these institutions embody the self-interest of elite males. For nonelite males, service as warriors instills loyalty to comrades because it maximizes chances of survival on the battlefield. To offset the chances of early death, universal conscription was a carrot that offered full rights to all who served; the idea took root that only armed males had rights of full citizenship (Keegan 1996: 233). Military service infused the modern concept of citizenship from its beginnings (Kerber 1998: 236).

In plow regimes, political and military leadership were linked until inventions like that of the printing press in 1450 eventuated in nation-states with the means and will to require universal education. Military success has become a much less effective stepping stone to high office in the Western democracies. Separation of the entry tracks to leadership in war and politics was a result of new forms of governance made possible and (one hopes) inevitable by a rise in literacy that enabled a better-informed public to figure out what political leaders were really up to and, if needed, to raise enough commotion to encourage leaders to head in another direction. Political success is not based on size, strength, and aggressive proclivities. Larger and stronger males do not necessarily dominate shorter and weaker ones, nor do younger men dominate older ones. Political skills depend much more on other attributes. Human dominance derives from talents like competence, nurturance, flattery, and deception (Maccoby and Jacklin 1974: 274).

CONCLUSION

After the invention of agriculture, a nearly continuous period of pregnancy and lactation led to women's subordination worldwide. The virtual abandonment of the practice of natural fertility made possible by modern medicine after the 1880s has affected a wide variety of behaviors. During the twentieth century, reduced fertility and scheduled infant feeding have enabled many women to enter the public arena. Thus, modern women will likely press for greater social equality. Scientists will likely seek ways to avoid the exposure of human reproductive tissues to estrogenic hormones. And parents will likely try to compensate infants, born in effect three months early, for the loss of constant human contact and a food supply available on demand.

REFERENCES

Altmann, S. 1998. *Foraging for Survival: Yearling Baboons in Africa*. Chicago: University of Chicago Press.

Andreski, S. 1968. *Military Organization and Society*. Berkeley: University of California Press.

Bloch, M. 1961. *Feudal Society*. Chicago: University of Chicago Press.

Boehm, C. 1999. *Hierarchy in the Forest: The Evolution of Egalitarian Behavior*. Cambridge, MA: Harvard University Press.

Boserup, E. 1965. *The Conditions of Agricultural Growth*. Chicago: Aldine.

———. 1970. *Women's Role in Economic Development*. London: St. Martin's Press.

Boswell, J. 1988. *The Kindness of Strangers*. Harmondsworth, UK: Penguin.

Braudel, F. 1979. *The Structures of Everyday Life*. Edited and translated by S. Reynolds. New York: Harper and Row.

Butz, W. 1977. *Economic Aspects of Breastfeeding*. Santa Monica, CA: Rand.

Cavalli-Sforza, L. L. 2000. *Genes, Peoples, and Languages*. Translated by M. Seielsted. New York: North Point Press.

Chafetz, J. 1984. *Sex and Advantage*. Totowa, NJ: Rowman and Allenheld.

Childe, G. 1951. *Man Makes Himself*. New York: Mentor.

Cohen, M. 1977. *The Food Crisis in Prehistory*. New Haven, CT: Yale University Press.

———. 1984. "Introduction." In *Paleopathology and the Origins of Agriculture*, edited by M. Cohen and G. Armela-gos, 1–22. New York: Academic.

———. 1989. *Health and the Rise of Civilization*. New Haven, CT: Yale University Press.

Collins, R., J. Chafetz, R. Blumberg, S. Coltrane, and J. Turner. 1993. "Toward an Integrated Theory of Gender Stratification." *Sociological Perspectives* 36: 185–216.

Crews, D. 2003. *Human Senescence*. New York: Cambridge University Press.

Crews, D., and L. M. Gerber. 1994. "Chronic Degenerative Diseases and Agriculture." In *Biological Anthropology and Agriculture*, edited by D. Crews and R. M. Garruto, 154–181. New York: Oxford University Press.

Da Vanzo, J. 1988. "Infant Mortality and Socioeconomic Development." *Demography* 25: 581–595.

Davie, M. 1929. *The Evolution of War*. New Haven, CT: Yale University Press.

Davis, K., and J. Blake. 1956. "Social Structure and Fertility." *Economic Development and Cultural Change* 4: 211–235.

de Waal, F. 2001. "Bonobos and Human Social Evolution." In *Tree of Origin*, edited by F. de Waal, 1–17. Cambridge, MA: Harvard University Press.

Dunbar, R. 1996. *Gossip, Grooming, and the Evolution of Language*. Cambridge, MA: Harvard University Press.

Dyson-Hudson, R., and N. Dyson-Hudson. 1980. "Nomadic Pastoralists." *Annual Review of Anthropology* 9: 15–61.

Earle, T. 1997. *How Chiefs Come to Power*. Palo Alto, CA: Stanford University Press.

Eaton, B., S. B. Eaton, and M. Konner. 1999. "Paleolithic Nutrition Revisited." In *Evolutionary Medicine*, edited by W. Trevathan, E. O. Smith, and J. McKenna, 313–332. New York: Oxford University Press.

Economist. 2012. "Female Genital Mutilation." July 27–August 2, 52.

El Saadawi, N. 1982. *The Hidden Face of Eve: Women in the Arab World*. Boston: Beacon.

Ellison, P. 1995. "Breastfeeding, Fertility, and Maternal Condition." In *Breastfeeding: Biocultural Perspectives*, edited by P. Stuart-Macadam and K. Dettwyler, 305–345. New York: Aldine de Gruyter.

———. 1999. "Reproductive Ecology and Reproductive Cancers." In *Hormones, Health, and Behavior*, edited by C. Panter-Brick and C. Worthman, 184–209. New York: Cambridge University Press.

Enloe, C. 1993. *The Morning After*. Berkeley: University of California Press.

Falk, D. 1997. "Brain Evolution in Females: An Answer to Mr. Lovejoy." In *Women in Evolution*, edited by L. Hager, 114–136. London: Routledge.

Fildes, V. 1986. *Breasts, Bottles, and Babies*. Edinburgh: Edinburgh University Press.

———. 1988. *Wet Nursing: A History from Antiquity to the Present*. Oxford: Blackwell.

Friedl, E. 1975. *Women and Men: An Anthropologist's View*. New York: Holt, Rinehart and Winston.

Garden, M. 1975. *Lyon et les Lyonnais au XVIII Siécle*. Paris: Flammarion.

Giosa, R. 1955. "Incidence of Pregnancy during Lactation in 500 Cases." *American Journal of Obstetrics and Gynecology* 70: 162–174.

Golden, J. 2001. *A Social History of Wet Nursing in America*. Columbus: Ohio State University Press.

Goldstein, J. 2001. *War and Gender*. New York: Cambridge University Press.

Goody, J. 1976. *Production and Reproduction*. Cambridge: Cambridge University Press.

———. 1983. *The Development of Family and Marriage in Europe*. Cambridge: Cambridge University Press.

Goody, J., and S. Tambiah. 1973. *Bridewealth and Dowry*. Cambridge: Cambridge University Press.

Gottlieb, G. 1998. "Normally Occurring Environmental and Behavioral Influences on Gene Activity: From Central Dogma to Probabilistic Epigenesis." *Psychological Review* 105: 792–802.

Gould, S. J. 1996. *Full House*. New York: Harmony.

Gray, S. 1999. "Infant Care and Feeding." In *Turkana Herders of the Dry Savanna*, edited by M. Little and P. Leslie, 166–186. New York: Oxford University Press.

Haaga, J. 1988. "Reliability of Retrospective Survey Data." *Demography* 25: 307–314.

Hastrup, K. 1985. *Medieval Iceland*. Oxford: Clarendon.

Heather, P. 1996. *The Goths*. Cambridge: Blackwell.

Hechter, M. 1987. *Principles of Group Solidarity*. Berkeley: University of California Press.

Henry, L. 1961. "Some Data on Natural Fertility." *Eugenics Quarterly* 8: 81–91.

Herskovits, M. 1938. *Dahomey II*. New York: Northwestern University Press.

Hobcraft, J. 1994. "Why Can't Demographers and Physiologists Agree?" In *Human Reproductive Ecology*, edited by K. Campbell and J. Wood, 408–415. New York: New York Academy of Science.

Hobhouse, L., G. Wheeler, and M. Ginsberg. 1930. *Material Culture and Social Institutions of the Simpler Peoples*. London: Routledge and Kegan Paul.

Howell, N. 1979. *Demography of the Dobe !Kung*. New York: Academic.

Hrdy, S. B. 1999. *Mother Nature: A History of Mothers, Infants, and Natural Selection*. New York: Pantheon.

———. 2011. *Mothers and Others: The Evolutionary Origins of Mutual Understanding*. Cambridge, MA: Belknap Press of Harvard University Press.

Huber, J. 1990. "Macro-Micro Links in Gender Stratification." *American Sociological Review* 55: 1–10.

———. 2007. *On the Origins of Gender Inequality*. Boulder, CO: Paradigm Publishers.

Huber, J., and G. Spitze. 1983. *Gender Stratification: Children, Housework, and Jobs*. New York: Academic.

Jablonski, N. 2006. *Skin: A Natural History*. Berkeley: University of California Press.

Jackman, M. 1994. *The Velvet Glove*. Berkeley: University of California Press.

Jackson, R. M. 1998. *Destined for Equality*. Cambridge, MA: Harvard University Press.

Janson, C. 1992. "Evolutionary Ecology of Primate Social Structure." In *Evolutionary Ecology and Human Behavior*, edited by E. A. Smith and B. Winterhalder, 95–130. New York: Aldine de Gruyter.

Jelliffe, D., and P. Jelliffe. 1978. "Volume and Composition of Milk in Poorly Nourished Communities." *American Journal of Clinical Nutrition* 31: 492–515.

Johnson, A., and T. Earle. 1987. *The Evolution of Human Societies*. Palo Alto, CA: Stanford University Press.

Jolly, A. 1999. *Lucy's Legacy*. Cambridge, MA: Harvard University Press.

Keegan, J. 1987. *The Mask of Command*. London: Jonathan Cape.

———. 1996. *The Battle for History: Refighting World War II*. New York: Vintage.

Kerber, L. 1998. *No Constitutional Right to Be Ladies*. New York: Hill and Wang.

Kertzer, D. 1993. *Sacrificed for Honor*. Boston: Beacon.

Lancaster, J. 1975. *Primate Behavior and the Emergence of Human Culture*. New York: Holt, Rinehart and Winston.

———. 1985. "Evolutionary Perspectives on Sex Differences in the Higher Primates." In *Gender and the Life Course*, edited by A. Rossi, 3–27. New York: Aldine de Gruyter.

———. 1991. "A Feminist and Evolutionary Biologist Looks at Women." *Yearbook of Physical Anthropology* 34: 1–11.

Lancaster, J., and C. Lancaster. 1983. "Parental Investment: The Hominid Adaptation." In *How Humans Adapt*, edited by D. Ortner, 33–65. Washington, DC: Smithsonian.

Larsen, C. 2000. *Skeletons in Our Closet*. Princeton, NJ: Princeton University Press.

Lawrence, R., and R. Lawrence. 1994. *Breastfeeding*. 4th ed. St. Louis, MO: Mosby.

———. 1999. *Breastfeeding*. 5th ed. St. Louis, MO: Mosby.

LeBlanc, S. 1999. *Prehistoric War in the American Southwest*. Salt Lake City: University of Utah Press.

Lenski, G. 1970. *Human Societies*. New York: McGraw-Hill.

Lenski, G., and J. Lenski. 1978. *Human Societies*. 3rd ed. New York: McGraw-Hill.

Leridon, H., and J. Menken, eds. 1977. *Natural Fertility*. Liege, Belgium: Ordina.

Levy, H. 1966. *Chinese Footbinding*. New York: Walton Rawls.

Lorimer, F., ed. 1954. *Culture and Human Fertility*. Paris: UNESCO.

Low, B., A. Clarke, and K. Lockridge. 1992. "Toward an Ecological Demography." *Population and Development Review* 18: 1–31.

Maccoby, E. 1998. *The Two Sexes*. Cambridge, MA: Belknap Press of Harvard University Press.

Maccoby, E., and C. Jacklin. 1974. *The Psychology of Sex Differences*. Palo Alto, CA: Stanford University Press.

Maryanski, A., and J. Turner. 1992. *The Social Cage: Human Nature and the Evolution of Society*. Palo Alto, CA: Stanford University Press.

Maynard Smith, J. 1989. *Did Darwin Get It Right: Essays on Games, Sex, and Evolution*. New York: Chapman and Hall.

Mazur, A., and A. Booth. 1998. "Testosterone and Dominance in Men." *Behavioral and Brain Sciences* 21: 353–363.

McKeown, T. 1976. *The Role of Medicine*. London: Provincial Hospitals Trust.

Micozzi, M. 1995. "Breast Cancer, Reproductive Biology, and Breastfeeding." In *Breastfeeding: Biocultural Perspectives*, edited by P. Stuart-Macadam and K. Dettwyler, 347–384. New York: Aldine de Gruyter.

Nesse, R., and G. Williams. 1994. *Why We Get Sick*. New York: Vintage.

Netting, R. 1993. *Smallholders, Householders*. Palo Alto, CA: Stanford University Press.

Oppenheimer, V. K. 1973. "Demographic Influence on Female Employment and the Status of Women." *American Journal of Sociology* 78: 946–961.

Otterbein, K. 1999. "A History of Research on Warfare in Anthropology." *American Anthropologist* 101: 794–805.

Page, H., and R. Lesthaeghe. 1981. "Preface." In *Child-Spacing in Tropical Africa*, edited by H. Page and R. Lest haeghe, ix–x. London: Academic.

Panter-Brick, C. 1992. "Working Mothers in Rural Nepal." In *The Anthropology of Breastfeeding*, edited by V. Ma-her, 133–150. Oxford: Berg.

Potts, M., and R. Short. 1999. *Ever since Adam and Eve: The Evolution of Human Sexuality*. Cambridge: Cambridge University Press.

Preston, S., and M. Haines. 1991. *Fatal Years*. Princeton, NJ: Princeton University Press.

Pryor, F. 1985. "The Invention of the Plow." *Comparative Studies in History and Society* 27: 727–743.

Quinn, N. 1977. "Anthropological Studies of Women's Status." *Annual Review of Anthropology* 6: 181–225.

Rippeyoung, P., and M. Noonan. 2012. "Is Breastfeeding Truly Cost Free? Income Consequences of Breastfeeding." *American Sociological Review* 77: 244–267.

Rowell, T. 1972. *The Social Behavior of Monkeys*. New York: Penguin.

Ruhlen, M. 1994. *The Origin of Language*. New York: Wiley.

Scheper-Hughes, N. 1992. *Death without Weeping*. Berkeley: University of California Press.

Seltzer, J., and S. Bianchi. 2013. "Demographic Change and Parent-Child Relationships in Adulthood." *Annual Review of Sociology* 39: 275–290.

Shipton, P. 1994. "Land and Culture in Tropical Africa." *Annual Review of Anthropology* 23: 347–377.

Small, M. 1998. *Our Babies, Ourselves*. New York: Doubleday-Anchor.

Smuts, B. 1985. *Sex and Friendship in Baboons*. New York: Aldine de Gruyter.

Stein, D. 1978. "Suttee as a Normative Institution." *SIGNS* 4: 253–268.

Stiehm, J. 1989. *Arms and the Enlisted Woman*. Philadelphia: Temple University Press.

Stini, W. 1985. "Growth Rates and Sexual Dimorphism: An Evolutionary Perspective on Prehistoric Diets." In *The Analysis of Prehistoric Diets*, edited by R. Gilbert and J. Mielke, 191–226. Orlando, FL: Academic.

Stuart-Macadam, P. 1995. "Biocultural Perspectives on Breastfeeding." In *Breastfeeding*, edited by P. Stuart-Macadam and K. Dettwyler, 1–37. New York: Aldine de Gruyter.

———. 1998. "Iron Deficiency Anemia." In *Sex and Gender in Pathological Perspective*, edited by A. Grauer and P. Stuart-Macadam, 45–63. Cambridge: Cambridge University Press.

Tanner, N. M. 1981. *On Becoming Human*. Cambridge: Cambridge University Press.

Testart, A. 1988. "Major Problems in the Social Anthropology of Hunter-Gatherers." *Current Anthropology* 29: 1–31.

Trevathan, W. 1987. *Human Birth: An Evolutionary Perspective*. Hawthorne, NY: Aldine de Gruyter.

———. 1999. "Evolutionary Obstetrics." In *Evolutionary Medicine*, edited by W. Trevathan, E. O. Smith, and J. McKenna, 183–207. New York: Oxford University Press.

Turner, J., and A. Maryanski. 2005. *Incest: Origins of the Taboo*. Boulder, CO: Paradigm Publishers.

Turney-High, H. 1949. *Primitive War*. New York: Columbia University Press.

Udry, R. 2000. "Biological Limits of Gender Construction." *American Sociological Review* 65: 443–457.

Vallegia, C., and P. Ellison. 2003. "Energetics, Fecundity, and Human Life History." In *The Biodemography of Human Reproduction and Fertility*, edited by J. L. Rogers and H.-P. Kohler, 87–103. Boston: Kluwer.

Vitzthum, V. 1997. "Adaptation in Human Reproduction." In *The Evolving Female*, edited by A. Galloway, M. E. Morbeck, and A. Zihlman, 242–258. Princeton, NJ: Princeton University Press.

Whitten, P. 1999. "Diet, Hormones, and Health." In *Hormones, Health, and Behavior*, edited by C. Panter-Brick and C. Worthman, 210–243. Cambridge: Cambridge University Press.

Wikipedia. 2014. "Chinese Footbinding." Last modified September 22.

Wiley, A., and I. Pike. 1998. "An Alternative Way to Assess Early Mortality in Contemporary Populations." *American Journal of Physical Anthropology* 107: 315–330.

Wilson, E. O. 1996. *In Search of Nature*. Washington, DC: Island Press.

Wolf, J. 2001. *Public Health and the Decline of Breastfeeding*. Columbus: Ohio State University Press.

Wood, J. W. 1990. "Fertility in Anthropological Populations." *Annual Review of Anthropology* 19: 211–242.

———. 1994. *Dynamics of Human Reproduction: Biology, Biometry, Demography*. Hawthorne, NY: Aldine de Gruyter.

Wright, Q. 1942. *A Study of War*. Chicago: University of Chicago Press.

Xie, Y. 1990. "What Is Natural Fertility? The Remodeling of a Concept." *Population Index* 56: 656–663.

Zihlman, A. 1978. "Subsistence and Social Organization in Early Hominids." *SIGNS* 4: 4–9.

The New Sexuality Studies

Theoretical Perspectives

by Steven Seidman

What is the relationship between sex and society? Beginning with sexologists who propose a view of sex as fundamentally biological, I review various social approaches to understanding sexuality. I take for granted that there is a biological basis for human impulses, drives, and desires. However, it is social forces that fashion a biological reality into "sexuality." Individuals and groups give meaning to bodily sensations and feelings, make erotic acts into sexual identities, and create norms distinguishing between acceptable and unacceptable sexualities.

SEXOLOGY: THE SCIENCE OF SEXUALITY

Why do many of us in America and Europe view sexuality as natural? One reason is the development of a science of sexuality. In the late nineteenth and early twentieth centuries, there developed a science aimed at discovering the laws of sexuality. This science has come to be called sexology.

Who are the sexologists? Among the more famous are Richard von Krafft-Ebing, Havelock Ellis, and Magnus Hirschfeld. While few of us today have heard of these nineteenth century pioneers of sexology, many of us have heard of Alfred Kinsey or of Masters and Johnson. Sexologists have produced a body of knowledge that has influenced the way many of us think about sex, in part because their ideas have been stamped with the imprimatur of science.

What are the key ideas of sexology? First, sexology claims that humans are born with a sexual nature, and that sexuality is part of the biological makeup of all individuals. Second, sexology views sexuality as being at the core of what it means to be human: our sexual drive is no less basic than our need to eat or sleep. Sexuality is said to be basic to who we are. Third, sexuality is viewed as a powerful and driving force in our behavior. It influences all aspects of our lives, from the physical to the psychological. It motivates much of human behavior. Fourth, sexology states that the sexual instinct is, by nature, heterosexual. There is said to be a natural attraction between men and women. While few sexologists today believe that the chief purpose of sexuality is to procreate, they continue to think that heterosexuality is the natural and normal form of sexuality.

Sexologists aim to discover the laws of sexuality. Just as physics and biology distrust inherited ideas and test them in experiments, sexology has championed a vigorously scientific approach. Facts, not beliefs, are to guide this science. The truth of sexuality is to be discovered by means of the "case study" method. Like physicians or psychiatrists, sexologists use intensive interviews and observation to uncover the true nature of sexuality. The details of human sexual desires, fantasies, and practices are recorded for the purpose of revealing the laws of the sexual instinct. Sexologists develop elaborate classifications of sexual types and detail the range of normal and abnormal forms of sexuality.

Sexology has always had a social purpose. In the nineteenth and early twentieth centuries, some sexologists sought to expand tolerance for different forms of human sexuality by emphasizing that sexuality is natural. Other sexologists saw their work as a way to contribute to creating a healthy, fit population. Often this meant that sexology was aligned to a belief in racial purity and improvement. Some sexologists even discouraged the sexual intermingling of races.

As racist ideas lost favor during the twentieth century, sexology has often been allied to a mission of strengthening the institutions of marriage and the family. Sexologists have argued that sex is at the core of love and marriage, and that a stable happy marriage requires a mutually satisfying sexual relationship. Individuals should not be burdened by guilt; they must be sexually knowledgeable and skilled. Sexology has aimed to make sexually enlightened and skillful citizens who would marry and stay married, in part because of a mutually satisfying sex life.

While their writings are sometimes technical and often tedious, sexologists have shaped Western sexual culture. Their ideas about the naturalness of sexuality have been popularized by an army of sex advice writers. Many of us believe in the idea of a natural sexuality because of the sexologists.

FREUD: BETWEEN BIOLOGY AND SOCIOLOGY

Alongside sexology, the discipline of psychology has been the source of many of our ideas about sex. In particular, Freud, the founder of psychoanalysis, has been probably the single most influential thinker in shaping Western sexual culture.

Freud aimed to uncover the roots of human psychology in our sex drives. Freud accepted many of the ideas of the sexologists. He believed in the biological basis of sexuality and insisted that sexuality is at the root of many of our feelings and actions. Freud also thought that there is a normal course of sexual development and there are abnormal or perverse forms of sexuality. The defining feature of sexual abnormality was deviation from genital-centered, intercourse-oriented heterosexuality based on love and monogamy.

But Freud also disagreed with the sexologists. Whereas sexologists defined the sexual instinct as reproductive and naturally heterosexual, Freud argued that the sexual instinct is oriented to pleasure. Moreover, humans get pleasure not only from sexual intercourse, but also from kissing, touching, caressing, looking, and sometimes dominating and being dominated. Freud argued that the body has many erotic areas and there are many ways of experiencing sexual satisfaction. Accordingly, he held that nongenital pleasures are not necessarily abnormal. It is normal, for example, to enjoy the range of pleasures that are today called foreplay.

Viewing the sexual instinct as a drive for pleasure blurs the line between normal and abnormal. To most sexologists, any sexual expression that deviated from a heterosexual reproductive aim was abnormal. However, Freud allows for a wide range of normal sexual expression beyond heterosexual reproduction. Pursuing nonprocreative pleasures is not in itself abnormal; sex drives become abnormal only when they are fixated on one specific sex act or pleasure. For example, it is normal for individuals to feel pleasure from looking at someone or from kissing and touching. It is abnormal, though, when these pleasures replace heterosexual intercourse.

Freud was convinced that sex is at the core of the self. It is, he thought, the drive for erotic pleasure that places the individual in conflict with social norms of respectability and self-control. Sexuality is then a major focus of psychological and social conflict. The psychological character of the individual rests on how the sex drive is managed. Too much sexual expression leads to psychological and social instability. Excessive social control results in psychosexual frustration that brings personal unhappiness.

Freud adhered to a much deeper social understanding of sexuality than the sexologists. If the sexual instinct is somewhat flexible in its purpose, it is society that shapes its form and meaning. In particular, the family is the formative social environment shaping our psyches and sexualities. Our psychological and sexual selves take shape as we struggle with the conflict between a drive for sexual pleasure and the social expectation to be productive, responsible citizens.

FEMINISM: THE GENDER OF SEXUALITY

Feminists point out that all of us step into the world as men or women, regardless of the economic system. Our gender identity is not a superficial part of our lives, but shapes the personal and social aspects of our lives in important ways. Feminists view gender as a social identity and a set of norms that guide behavior. We are not born men or women but acquire these gender identities through a social process of learning and sometimes coercion. Feminists believe that our sexual desires, feelings, and preferences are imprinted by gender.

Feminists say that individuals acquire a sexual nature as they develop a gender identity. What exactly is the relationship between gender and sexuality?

In *The Reproduction of Mothering*, Nancy Chodorow argues that when women do the chief parenting work, gender patterns of sexual and individual development are different. For both boys and girls, the mother is often the primary source of love. However, girls sustain an intimacy with their mothers throughout their maturation; boys separate from their mothers at an early age in order to learn to be men. This difference shapes the psychosexual character of girls and boys.

The extended and intense intimacy between mothers and daughters results in girls developing a psyche that is relationship-oriented. Accordingly, girls tend to connect sex with intimacy and as a means of caring. They often approach sex more as a means of communication and intimacy than as a vehicle of erotic pleasure. Because boys typically break sharply from their mothers at an early age, and identify with their achievement-oriented fathers, they are more performance- and goal-oriented. Boys' sexuality tends to be more performance- and body-oriented. Boys can be intimate, but they will likely express sexual love in terms of the giving and receiving of erotic pleasure.

Chodorow's perspective is important because she holds that the family plays a crucial role in the making of the sexual self. Also, she says that boys and girls develop different sexual values and orientations.

Adrienne Rich also believes that gender dynamics creates sexual differences between men and women. She emphasizes the social creation of heterosexual men and women. In "Compulsive Heterosexuality and Lesbian Existence" she argues that we are all taught and coerced into adopting conventional gender identities. Why? Gender difference, Rich says, reinforces a society organized around the norm of heterosexuality. Shaping individuals into heterosexual men and women is a complex social process. Societies use positive inducements like economic rewards or a culture that romanticizes heterosexuality, but also resorts to ridicule, harassment, and violence to punish gender nonconformists and nonheterosexuals. The belief that heterosexuality is normal and natural plays a key role in creating heterosexual men and women. For example, many Europeans and Americans believe that there is a natural attraction between the sexes, that their bodies and minds "naturally" fit. Heterosexuality is then viewed as an extension of a natural order composed of two complementary sexes.

Catherine MacKinnon insists on the role of male dominance in shaping women's sexuality. She views sexuality as a product of men's power; sex is a means by which men control women. Indeed, it is the very basis of male domination. To the extent that men have the power to define what desires, feelings, and behaviors are sexual, they can define women's sexuality in a way that positions them as subordinate. For example, in male-dominated America, women's sexuality is supposed to be oriented to vaginal intercourse in marriage with the ultimate aim of procreation. This view defines women as heterosexual, or needing men, and as motivated to become wives and mothers, and therefore dependent on men.

Feminists like Rich and MacKinnon claim that the very essence of sexuality expresses men's wish for dominance. Every sexual desire and behavior in male-dominated societies is said to be related to gender dynamics, and either expresses men's dominance or women's resistance. From this perspective, feminists criticize the notion that women's sexual liberation is about claiming the right to pleasure or the freedom to do as one pleases, an approach that expresses men's view of sexual freedom. Instead, women's sexual liberation involves fashioning a sexual life that reflects their own needs, feelings, and desires. The point is not to liberate sexuality from social control, which could lead to more violence or unwanted pregnancy, but to claim the power to define one's own sexual desires and forge sexual-intimate lives.

Some feminists, like the anthropologist Gayle Rubin, have objected to the view that sexuality is a direct expression of gender politics. She argues that this perspective ignores considerable variation within women's and men's sexuality. Rubin believes that sexuality is connected to gender, yet also has its own dynamics.

In "Thinking Sex," Rubin makes the case that sex is fundamentally about erotic desires, fantasies, acts, identities, and politics—none of which are reducible to gender dynamics. She argues that all societies create sexual hierarchies that establish boundaries between good and bad or legitimate and illicit sexualities. Societies value specific desires, acts, and identities as normal, respectable, good, healthy, and moral; other forms of sexuality are classified as unhealthy, abnormal, sinful, and immoral. Society supports and privileges the "normal and good" forms of sexuality and aims to punish the "abnormal and bad" ones through law, violence, ridicule, or stigma. These sexual hierarchies create a series of outsider sexualites. This system of sexual regulation applies to both men and women. American society considers heterosexuality, monogamy, marriage, and reproductive sex to be considered good and normal; S/M (sadomasochism) and multiple-partner sex, commercial and public sex are defined and treated as bad. There are of course many sexualities that fall somewhere in between—for example, promiscuous heterosexuals or gays and lesbians in long-term monogamous relationships. It may be less socially acceptable for a woman to have multiple sex partners or to engage in S/M because of a gender order that associates femininity with purity and maternal feelings: still, these behaviors are disparaged by both men and women. Those who engage in such behaviors, regardless of gender, will be stigmatized and subject to a range of sanctions, from ridicule to criminalization. Rubin's point is simply that gender influences patterns of sexuality, but there is still a great deal about the organization and dynamics of sexuality that cannot be viewed solely through the lens of gender.

GAY AND LESBIAN STUDIES

Paralleling the rise of a gay movement, many advocates argued that some people are just born homosexual. If homosexuals have always existed, it is a natural status and therefore they should not be punished.

However, this view has been challenged by the new gay/lesbian studies. These new scholars assume that homosexual behavior is a natural part of the human condition, but the appearance of a homosexual identity is a rare historical event. When and why did a homosexual identity emerge, and how has the meaning of homosexuality changed historically?

Jonathan Katz argued that, between colonial times and the 1970s, homosexuality in the U.S. changed from indicating a behavior (sodomy), to an abnormal personality (the homosexual), and finally to an affirmative social identity (gay/lesbian). Carroll Smith-Rosenberg showed that Victorian women, whose lives were organized around domestic tasks, often formed close ties with each other that at times blurred the line between friendship and romance. These intimate bonds sometimes developed into romantic relationships that were celebrated as complementary to marriage. These "romantic friendships" were often romantic bonds which lasted a lifetime. Similarly, Lillian Faderman wrote the first history of lesbianism in the United States, in which she documents changes in the meaning of same-sex behavior and in the social organization of lesbianism. Both Smith-Rosenberg and Faderman make the provocative argument that tolerance for intimacy between women diminished in the first decades of the twentieth century. As women started to attend college, work outside the home, and demand equal rights, their close ties to one another were often viewed as threatening. These women were stigmatized as lesbians.

Building on this growing body of historical scholarship on sexuality, John D'Emilio offered the first detailed analysis of the rise of a homosexual identity and community in the United States. He analyzed the social forces that shaped homosexuality into an identity, community, and social movement. For example, D'Emilio argued that the Second World War played a key role in shaping an awareness of homosexuality and homosexual bonds. During the war, many soldiers were, for the first time, exposed to individuals who thought of themselves as homosexual. Moreover, the intense closeness among the men and women in the military encouraged homosexual experimentation. After the war, many of these men and women with homosexual feelings settled in New York, Chicago, San Francisco, and Los Angeles. It was in these cities that the first major gay and lesbian political organizations initially took shape in the 1950s.

Historians have continued to refine their conceptions of the sexual past. One significant revision is in George Chauncey's *Gay New York*. Whereas historians and sociologists had come to believe that the modern homosexual emerged in the early twentieth century and was immediately stuffed into the closet, Chauncey argues that, in working-class New York, individuals were not classified as either homosexual or heterosexual, but as either "normal men" or "fairies." The former were masculine men, while the latter were effeminate. In other words, the homosexual indicated a type of gender deviance. If you were a masculine man who had sex with effeminate men, you were not necessarily considered a homosexual. Gender expression, not sexual preference, defined being a homosexual. Moreover, rather than being isolated and closeted, an open public gay life flourished in bars, taverns, speakeasies, restaurants, ballrooms, and parks.

FOUCAULT: SEXUALITY AS A

SYSTEM OF SOCIAL CONTROL

Michel Foucault challenged the idea that sex was biological and natural. He proposed that it was the very idea or, in his terms, the discourse of sexuality that created what we know as sex. We are not born sexual, but learn to be sexual beings; this occurs only in societies that have created the idea of "sexuality."

But when did this idea of sexuality originate, and why? The birth of the science of sexuality in the nineteenth century was crucial. Scientists aimed to discover the hidden truth of human nature by uncovering the secrets of the sexual instinct. Sexologists charted the physiology and behavior of sexual desire, psychiatrists listened to their clients confess to a shadowy world of sexual fantasies, and demographers surveyed human fertility. But these researchers did not discover an uncharted territory of sex; they fashioned human pleasures, excitations, and acts into a new object of knowledge and social regulation: human sexuality. Foucault is not saying that the feelings and behaviors associated with the body were created by these discourses. Rather, these discourses compelled us to view these bodily experiences as expressions of human sexuality. The science of sexuality organized our diverse somatic experiences into a coherent, organized subject called sexuality.

Why did a discourse of sexuality appear and what was its social importance? Foucault thought that the modern state and other social institutions had good reasons to want to control people's sexuality. Between the seventeenth and nineteenth centuries in many European nations there were massive migrations to cities, a growing need for mass literacy and schooling, intense economic competition between nations, and the growing dependence of national power on economic prosperity. These developments created a strong political interest in gaining detailed and useful information about human bodies—how they reproduce, stay healthy, react to different external stimulation, and can be made more productive, efficient, and cooperative. For example, as cities became social and economic centers, governments and other institutions responsible for keeping order and for the care of the indigent sought information about migration patterns, fertility rates, nutrition, and health. This growing need to know and control bodies helped to create the idea of sexuality. To control sex is to exercise great control over the individual and whole populations. Sexuality is at the center of a modern system of social control.

Did Foucault give up the notion of sexual freedom? He wrote during a period of sexual rebellion. Sexual liberationists of all types declared that today we are more enlightened; the present is pregnant with possibilities for sexual freedom. Sexual liberation had two aspects. The first was a negative freedom—freedom from unnecessary control. Liberation also had a positive aspect—the right to express one's true sexual nature and identity.

Foucault agreed that expanding individual choice is a good thing. He supported the fight for gay rights. But gay rights is not liberation. It does not relieve individuals of horrific stigma and social discrimination. Also, the gay rights movement has reinforced a system that forces individuals to declare themselves either straight or gay, and reinforces the deviant status of bisexuality and other nonconventional sexualities. Moreover, a gay movement has its own ideal of how a gay person is supposed to look and act. In other words, the gay movement exercises control over its members, pressuring them to identify exclusively as gay and to act in ways that are recognized as gay.

If sexuality is today a system of social control, then ironically sexual liberation might involve freeing ourselves from the idea of sexuality. This would mean approaching our erotic desires and acts not as expressions of sexuality but as simply feelings and acts that give pleasure, create social ties, or are a source of cultural creativity. Foucault advocates a politics against sexuality—against a society that sexualizes selves, identities, and acts. Why would this be a good thing? By not assigning a moral meaning (either normal or abnormal) to adult, consensual sexual desires and behaviors, individuals would be subject to less social regulation. For example, instead of reversing the stigma of homosexuality by championing a normal gay identity, we could approach homosexuality as a desire and as a source of pleasure, new relationships and cultural expressions. Or, instead of celebrating the sexualization of the human body and all of its feelings and sensations, perhaps it is more liberating to desexualize pleasures, focus on nonsexual pleasures, learn to enjoy a wide range of sensual pleasures, and be free of controls that rely on notions of normality.

SEXUALITY AND SOCIAL LEARNING

Since the early decades of the twentieth century, sociologists have researched the role of religion, gender, class, race, and social values in shaping patterns of premarital, marital, and extramarital sex. In the 1960s and 1970s, Ira Reiss charted cultural and behavioral shifts among American youth as a sexual morality that associated sex exclusively with marriage transformed into one that permitted sex in a context of affection. Reiss believed that this cultural change was related to women's growing economic and social power. In this regard, he observed the decline of a double standard that permitted men to have sex outside of marriage, while labeling women who engaged in the same behavior as "bad girls."

Some sociologists have pressed for a full-blown sociology of sexuality. John Gagnon and William Simon proposed a "script" theory of sexuality. Instead of understanding humans as born sexual, they argued that sexuality is socially learned. In the course of growing up, society teaches us what feelings and desires count as sexual and what the appropriate "scripts" for sexual behavior are. Sexual scripts tell us with whom we're supposed to have sex (based on age, race, or class), where, when, and what it means when we do. Gagnon and Simon were in effect saying that sexuality is not an inborn property, but a product of social labeling.

The British sociologist, Ken Plummer, developed a labeling perspective on sex. In *Sexual Stigma*, he argued that individuals aren't born homosexual, but learn to be homosexual. An individual may feel desire or attraction to people of the same sex, but he or she must learn that these feelings are sexual and that they indicate a homosexual identity. People learn this in the course of interacting with both the straight and gay world. For example, a high-school student hearing derogatory comments about "fags" and "dykes" begins to associate homosexuality with a stigmatized identity. This same individual may eventually be exposed to a gay subculture, which champions a view of homosexuality as natural and good.

One of the pioneers of a sociological approach to sexuality was the British sociologist Jeffrey Weeks. He introduced the ideas of essentialism and constructionism. Essentialism is the notion that sexuality is a basic and essential part of being human. Constructionism states that sexuality is a product of social forces. Weeks proposed a strong view of the social character of sexuality: "First, we can no longer set 'sex' against 'society' as if they were separate domains. Secondly, there is a widespread recognition of the social variability of sexual forms, beliefs, ideologies, and behavior. Sexuality has … many histories. … Thirdly, we must learn to see that sexuality is something which society produces in complex ways. It is a result of diverse social practices that give meaning to human activities, to struggles between those who have power to define and regulate, and those who resist. Sexuality is not given, it is a product of negotiation, and struggle."

CONCLUSION

There has been a revolution in the way scholars think about sexuality. Until recently, scholars believed that humans were born with a sexual nature; the natural order created a series of sexual types: heterosexuals, homosexuals, masochists, pedophiles, and so on. A science of sexuality would reveal the nature of the sexual instinct. The idea of sexual normality would serve as the standard to judge and regulate sexual behavior.

Today, the leading edge of scholarship views sex as fundamentally social. We're born with bodies but it is society that determines which parts of the body and which pleasures and acts are sexual. And, the classification of sex acts into good and bad or acceptable and illicit is a product of social power; the dominant sexual norms express the dominant social groups. If we are supposed to grow up to be heterosexual, and if we are expected to link sex to love and marriage, this is because specific groups impose these social norms. Beliefs that there are natural and normal ways to be sexual are ideological. How we come to have such beliefs, and their personal and social consequences, are important questions for the study of sexuality. Indeed, the question of who gets to define what is sexual and which institutions are responsible for regulating our sexualities are key sociological and political questions in their own right.

DISCUSSION QUESTIONS

1. How would you define sexuality? What is the difference between sexuality and gender?

2. Do you agree that our ideas of sexuality come more from society and culture than biology? What are some commonly held views of sexuality—that is, what does our culture see as "normal" and "abnormal"? Can you trace where these views might come from?

REFERENCES

Butler, Judith, *Gender Trouble: Feminism and the Subversion of Identity* (New York: Routledge, 1990).

Chauncey, George, Gay *New York: Gender, Urban Culture, and the Making of the Gay Male World, 1890–1940* (New York: Basic Books, 1994).

Chodorow, Nancy, *The Reproduction of Mothering: Psychoanalysis and the Sociology of Gender* (Berkeley: University of California Press, 1978).

D'Emilio, John, *Sexual Politics, Sexual Communities: The Making of a Homosexual Minority in the United States, 1940–1970* (Chicago: University of Chicago Press. 1983).

Faderman, Lillian, *Odd Girls and Twilight Lovers: A History of Lesbian Life in Twentieth-Century America* (New York: Columbia University Press, 1991).

Foucault, Michel *The History of Sexuality. Vol 1: An Introduction* (New York: Vintage, 1980).

Gagnon, John and Simon, William, *Sexual Conduct: The Social Sources of Human Sexuality* (Chicago: Aldine, 1973).

Ned Katz, Jonathan, Gay, *American History* (New York: Crowell, 1976) and *Gay/Lesbian Almanac* (New York: Harper & Row, 1983).

MacKinnon, Catherine, *Towards a Feminist Theory of the State* (Cambridge, Mass.: Harvard University Press, 1989).

Plummer, Ken, *Sexual Stigma: An Interactionist Account* (London: Routledge & Kegan Paul, 1975).

Reiss, Ira, *Premarital Sexual Standards in America (*Glencoe, Ill.: Free Press, 1960) and The *Social Context of Premarital Sexual Permissiveness* (New York: Holt, Rinehart & Winston, 1967).

Rich, Adrienne, "Compulsory Heterosexuality and Lesbian Existence," *Signs 5* (1980).

Rubin, Gayle, "Thinking Sex: Notes for a Radical Theory of the Politics of Sexuality," in *Pleasure and Danger: Exploring Female Sexuality*, ed. Carole Vance (Boston: Routledge & Kegan Paul, 1984).

Smith-Rosenberg, Carroll, "The Female World of Love and Ritual," *Signs 1* (1975).

Weeks, Jeffrey, *Sexuality* (London: Tavistock, 1986), p. 26.

Understanding Diversity of Families in the 21st Century and Its Impact on the Work-Family Area of Study

Stephen R. Marks
University of Maine

Ian Wheeler-Nicholson (2000) recalls a childhood regularly punctuated by moves to a new town. It seemed that by every summer's end, family-life-as-usual would bring Ian to a new elementary school. He knew that any "new kid" was always at a disadvantage, especially one who was not rich, big, tough, nor athletic enough to seize control, and he had therefore learned to keep to himself so as not to attract attention. When one day his mother cryptically warned him not to tell anyone where his father is, just before he was to start yet another school, Ian's apprehensiveness rose higher than usual. That year he began to put things together. Another boy got called a "faggot" and beaten up for the crime of hanging out too much with girls and enjoying art. A girl was branded a "lesbo" because she was already developing breasts, and she was quite good at athletics. Ian's usual policy of smiling and saying nothing when people

talked to him was a much-needed protective cover. Through his relative silence, Ian recalls:

> I had stumbled on my mother's very own solution to the problem of leading a covert homosexual life. In later years, she would tell me that the main reason for our constant moves was that, in each place, eventually a nosy neighbor or co-worker would begin to suspect the truth about my mother or her partner. *My mother was always afraid of losing her job,* and there was the looming threat of violence. And so we became an itinerant family. (Wheeler-Nicholson, 2000, p. 111, italics added)

I offer this snippet of Ian's story because it defies the popular imagination, in which there resides an "average American family person" who must juggle the demands of spouse, children, job, friends, recreational interests, and so on. This mind's-eye family has found its way into family studies and other social sciences, and it has influenced studies of the work-family interface as well. It is the family referenced by the appeal to "family values," the family of political election rhetoric. Its adult members are married, White and heterosexual, and they have children living with them at home. Nowadays, the image of this traditional family has been updated: Instead of father working and mother at home, both partners have paid work, but one of them—the wife—works less than full-time in order to look after the children and take care of the home.

Ian's family, like millions of others, does not fit either the older or the updated versions of this traditional family image. Our typical models of the work-family interface are not fully adequate to the facts of daily life for people like Ian's mother and her partner Veronica. To be sure, like all workers and parents, these women had work schedules that fit the needs of their family either poorly or well, and the specific attributes of their jobs either promoted a better work-family balance or a worse one. But quite aside from these important job qualities, Ian's mother and Veronica were obviously struggling with a "stressor" that made a bigger impact on their work-family "interface" than any other, one that also spilled over onto Ian's life: As a lesbian couple raising a child, they were far too different from the "average American family" image, and that difference could have cost them their jobs and their family security.

WHAT IS FAMILY DIVERSITY?

This chapter highlights some features of family diversity in the 21st century. My focus is necessarily selective rather than a state-of-the-art treatment. Scholarship on family diversity has been mushrooming, and it is not possible in a single chapter to thoroughly survey the area (a recent book-length compendium may be found in Demo, Allen, & Fine, 2000).

In focusing on contemporary and emerging families as "diverse," I want to signal two different senses of the term "diversity." First, it points to the simple fact of variety. In this vein, we often spotlight the compositional variety of households—for example, two-parent families, single-parent families, "blended" families, extended families, couples (married or cohabiting), and people living alone (often networked with other households through kinship or "chosen" family). Beyond household composition, a focus on variety often seizes on the fact that different families are systematically linked to different life chances, depending on where the family is located on a society's most salient hierarchies—race-ethnicity, social class, gender, sexual orientation, and age. These hierarchies are often seen to "intersect" as a "matrix of domination" (Andersen & Collins, 1998), such that some families may enjoy double or triple privileges while others must struggle with multiple disadvantages. Of course, some individuals may be privileged in some categories and disadvantaged in others. For example, a wealthy lesbian African American couple may enjoy social class privileges, but they may run into multiple barriers not encountered by males, heterosexuals, and European Americans. In this chapter, I will consider a range of issues suggested both by the variety of household types and by the fact of differential location on society's major hierarchies.

A second meaning of the term "diversity" springs from the abiding sense that there is some "standard North American family" (Smith,

1993) or "average family," and that we ought to recognize points of difference from this standard or average. Ian's story (above) easily grabs our attention because it jolts us outside of this imagined standard. Here, my argument is that the "average family" is most accurately seen as an ideological trope that hides rather than reflects empirical diversity. White, middle-class, heterosexual families with children may be prominent because of their relative hegemony, but they are anything but average in the statistical sense, and they will become less and less so as the 21st century unfolds. Therefore, to break out of the "average family" image is to make more room in the center of our theory and research for those who had previously been relegated to the periphery as "minority groups." The minority status of these people is rapidly fading with their swelling populations, and it is incumbent on work and family scholars to see them clearly.

Plan of the Chapter

This chapter is organized into three major sections. The first section identifies five master trends that are shifting American families away from the traditional "average family" image. First, I consider the distribution of the population into various household types, taking particular notice of the historical decline of some types (e.g., households composed of two parents and at least one child) and the historical ascendancy of others (e.g., single-parent and single individual households). Second, I focus on the shifting racial-ethnic balance of the population, calling specific attention to the growing percentages of Hispanic and Asian Americans. Third, I consider how patterns of immigration are adding enormous complexity to how we reckon the racial-ethnic mix in this country. The fourth pattern is the decline of

heteronormativity. Here, I take special care to describe this process as something that not simply affects lesbians and gay men but also the inner workings of heterosexual households. Fifth, I consider the aging of the U.S. population and some of the challenges that this implies for families and for work-family scholars.

The second section is a consideration of how social class differences generate some of the most important factors of family diversity that bear on the work-family interface. In particular, I spotlight the importance of family income, differences in socialization patterns among the middle and working classes, and issues faced by some of the more vulnerable categories of the population—immigrants, low-income people, single parents, and lesbian and gay couples and families. In the third major section, I piggyback on some recent advances in the sociology of health to suggest how work and family scholars might focus more attention on patterns of prejudice and discrimination and their impact. Specifically, if we want a more fine-grained understanding of everyday obstacles within the lives of disadvantaged categories of the population, we will need to design our studies in ways that capture some of the unique stressors that these people encounter.

SOME PROCESSES OF SOCIETAL TRANSFORMATION

The Transformation of American Households

The first master trend concerns an increase in the percentages of Americans living in some types of households and a decrease of those living in other types. Single-parent households—both mother-child and father-child—are on the rise, as are households consisting of a single individual. Plainly, it is

TABLE 6.1 Households by Type—1970 and 2000

Year	Total Households	Married With Children	Married Without Children	One Person	Single Parent	Other Blood Relatives	Unmarried Couples: (Opposite Sex)
2000	104,705,000	24.1%	28.7%	25.5%	8.9 %	7.0%	4.5%
1970	63,401,000	40.3%	30.3%	17.1%	5.2%	5.5%	1.0%

Source: American Association for Single People. 2000 Census—AASP report.

now inaccurate to visualize an average household as a group consisting of a mother, a father, and one or more children. Table 6.1 shows the distribution of people across household categories, comparing 1970 with 2000 percentages. Consider that in the 2000 census, married couples living with one or more children comprised only 24% of all American households, down from 40% of the total in 1970. Put simply, less than one out of four households now fits the traditional family image, even less than the 26% of households occupied by a single person.

To be sure, an additional 29% of households in 2000 consisted of a married couple living alone. Many of the younger of these couples will eventually have children and will then join the ranks of those living in a traditional household, unless or until they separate or divorce. And many of the older couples have already raised children, who have since moved out to form their own households. These older couples (or some of them) at one point did live in a traditional nuclear family. It is no doubt true that the vast majority of American people have lived in a household with both their mother and father for at least a small portion of their lives, just as the vast majority have later formed new families consisting of a spouse and child or children, and so they too fit the traditional

image at least for a short period. In that sense, it is misleading to look at the distribution of households at only one point in time.

In another sense, however, the snapshot view of how people are distributed in households is a good way to gauge the full variety of needs that work-family scholars ought to address. People with dependent children have a different set of needs than people who live alone, as children's activities and school schedules in particular are a daily fact of parents' lives in ways that have no relevance for households with no dependent children. In turn, single-parent needs may also differ in important ways from those within two-parent households. For example, single parents may find their job options and work schedules far more constrained than do the adults within two-parent households, as the former must often take on the entire burden of coordinating with children's schedules.

The Racial-Ethnic Transformation

The second master trend is that White families have become a shrinking proportion of American families, as people of color (including self-identified Hispanics) comprise an increasingly larger percentage of the population. Table 6.2 draws on population projections for each of the five racial-ethnic groups tracked by the

TABLE 6.2 Percent of Total Population by Race—2000 and Projections for 2020 and 2050

	2000	2020	2050
Hispanic (of any race)	12.6	17.8	24.4
Asian	3.8	5.4	8.0
Black—Non-Hispanic	12.7	13.5	14.6
White—Non-Hispanic	69.4	61.3	50.1
All other races[1]	2.5	3.5	5.3

[1]Includes American Indian and Alaska Native, Native Hawaiian, Other Pacific Islander, and two or more races.
Source: U.S. Census Bureau, 2004, "U.S. Interim Projections by Age, Sex, Race, and Hispanic Origin."

census, focusing on the 2000 baseline and looking ahead to 2050.

The table shows with dramatic clarity the continuing racial-ethnic transformation that will shrink the proportion of non-Hispanic White people while the numbers of Asian Americans and Hispanic Americans will approximately double their year 2000 percentages. No one can know the full impact of this transformation, but perhaps a reasonable assumption is that if non-Hispanic Whites retain their lopsided share of American wealth, privilege, and power, racial-ethnic category will remain a central organizing component of American consciousness. And, as the White minority grows smaller, political pressures that challenge its hegemony will grow increasingly vehement.

Immigration Complicates the Categories

The third master trend is that immigration patterns are complicating the racial-ethnic transformation in at least two ways. First, unlike previous waves of immigration that brought predominantly White Europeans to our shores, the current wave consists largely of non-European Hispanics and people of color.

In 2002, Europeans comprised just 14% of the foreign-born U.S. population, while Hispanics comprised 52.2%, Asians 25.5%, and Carribeans 9.6% (Schmidley, 2003). Second, the increasing diversity within each overall category of the "new" immigrant—Asian, Black, and Hispanic—defies any easy generalizations that hold up across the category, as people from different nations of origin bring their different backgrounds and traditions to the new land.

Hispanics. I begin here with the regions and nations of origin that have been contributing the largest share of the Hispanic population in the United States. Table 6.3 shows Hispanic population estimates for 1990 and 2000, and it indicates the rate of growth in that time period, drawing on the Mumford Center's use of Current Population Report data to produce more detailed information about those Hispanics who were listed only as "Other Hispanics" in the 2000 census data collection procedures (see Logan, 2001b).

Most notable in Table 6.3 is the emergent shift toward "new Latinos" as the fastest-growing Hispanic groups. Although people of

TABLE 6.3 Hispanic Population Growth by Region and Selected Nations of Origin

	1990	2000	Increase
HISPANIC TOTAL	21,900,089	35,305,818	61%
Mexican	13,576,346	23,060,224	70%
Puerto Rican	2,705,979	3,640,460	35%
Cuban	1,067,416	1,315,346	23%
New Latino groups	3,019,780	6,153,989	104%
Dominican	537,120	1,121,257	109%
Central American	1,387,331	2,863,063	106%
South American	1,095,329	2,169,669	98%

Source: Adapted from Logan, J. L. (2001b). The new Latinos: Who they are, where they are. Lewis Mumford Center for Comparative Urban and Regional Research.

Mexican, Puerto Rican, and Cuban origin are still the largest Hispanic groups, new Latinos are now more numerous than Puerto Ricans and Cubans combined. Research on Hispanic families is still in its infancy. Most of it has focused on Mexicans, and even here, scholars have barely begun to document the probable variety that is out there. Nevertheless, some generalizations may be advanced, and I take them up in the section on social class.

Asians. As with Hispanics, the recent wave of Asian immigrants has diversified the category. Table 6.4, compiled by the Mumford Center (Logan, 2001a), indicates an overall population growth of Asian Americans of 69% between 1990 and 2000. People of Chinese or Filipino origin remain the largest contributors to the Asian population, but Indians have surged into third place, having increased at nearly twice the growth rate of Chinese or Filipinos in the 10-year period. Vietnamese have become the second fastest growing

category, having doubled their numbers over the same period.

Like Hispanics, Asian Americans from different nations of origin have fared differently in terms of their life chances in the United States. Although Asian American median household income suggests a relatively privileged standing, we will see that social class variations render the "model minority" image of Asians inadequate to capture the variety of Asian experience here.

Blacks. The overall rate of Black population growth has been far more moderate than that of either Hispanics or Asians, but immigration patterns are again creating some important diversification. Here, I follow current practice of distinguishing between African Americans (Blacks who were born here but claim a non-specific African heritage), Africans (recent immigrants principally from West or East Africa), and Afro-Caribbeans (e.g., Jamaicans and Haitians). The Mumford Center noted that

TABLE 6.4 Asian Population in the U.S., 1990 and 2000

Population	1990		2000		Population Growth
All Asians	7,273,662		12,275,972		69%
	Number	Percent	Number	Percent	
Chinese	1,645,472	22.6	2,734,841	22.3	66%
Filipinos	1,406,770	19.3	2,364,815	19.3	68%
Japanese	847,562	11.7	1,148,932	9.4	36%
Indians	815,447	11.2	1,899,599	15.5	133%
Koreans	798,849	11.0	1,228,427	10.0	54%
Vietnamese	614,547	8.4	1,223,736	10.0	99%
Other	1,145,015	15.7	1,306,330	13.5	14%

Source: Logan, J. L. (2001a). From many shores: Asians in Census 2000. Lewis Mumford Center for Comparative Urban and Regional Research, University at Albany, October 6, 2001.

between 1990 and 2000, recent arrivals from sub-Saharan Africa and from the Caribbean accounted for nearly 25% of the growth of the Black population (Logan & Deane, 2003). The report adds, "although not an often-recognized part of the American ethnic mosaic, both of these groups are emerging as large and fast-growing populations; Afro-Caribbeans now outnumber and are growing faster than such well-established ethnic minorities as Cubans and Koreans" (Logan & Deane, 2003). As with Hispanics and Asians, we will see that social class differences among the three major subcategories of Black people are considerable. These differences at times become politically explosive, as when the Black Republican candidate for a U.S. Senate seat in Illinois took issue in 2004 with the Black Democratic candidate's claim of an African American heritage (the latter has a Kenyan father and a White, American-born mother): "My ancestors toiled in slavery in this country," the Republican proclaimed; "my consciousness, who I am as a person, has been shaped by my struggle, deeply emotional and deeply painful, with the reality of that heritage" (Swams, 2004). Although the explicit focus here is on racial-ethnic identity claims, the implicit issue is opportunity for upward mobility through the social class system.

The Decline of Heteronormativity

The fourth master trend is that the foundations of heteronormativity are slowly eroding and will continue to do so as the century unfolds. Along with the demographic changes noted above, this is a social and cultural transformation that is generating a sea of change within family life. As noted by Oswald, Blume, and Marks (2005), heteronormativity is an ideological composite of several elements. It is, of course, a notion about "natural" versus unnatural sexuality, and as gay and lesbian families become more visible, their presence will increasingly challenge narrow images of what is natural. But heteronormativity is also a prescription for "normal" gender expression and family formation, and its impact affects heterosexual couples as well as gays and lesbians. At its core are two interrelated beliefs: First, males and females are held to be "opposite sexes" who are drawn together by natural forces of sexual attraction; and second, "natural" family patterns are held to spring from these attractions and to take shape in ways that simply reflect these differing (and opposite) gender sensibilities of men and women.

This heteronormative ideological system is being challenged on two fronts. First, a new wave of gay activism exploded across the American landscape late in 2003, triggered by decisions handed down by the Supreme Judicial Court in Massachusetts and culminating in 2004 in the first legally married lesbian and gay Americans in that state. In San Francisco, the spectacle of hundreds of gay and lesbian couples lining up outside City Hall to take their marriage vows (later invalidated by California's highest court) was a nightly phenomenon on network television news. Perhaps their sheer ordinariness was the biggest story. They seemed to be an utterly conventional cross-section of the American middle class—elderly, middle-aged, young, fresh-from-a-business-meeting or job at the bank, fat, thin, and attired in every imaginable style from staidly conservative to high fashion to punk.

Predictably, these developments have set off a new round of culture wars. Traditionalists have marshaled support for an amendment to the U.S. constitution that would define marriage as an arrangement solely between a man and a woman, and many state legislatures have recently made this definition the law of their respective states. Whatever the outcome, the fight for gay rights will not quietly go away. Even if the traditionalists ultimately prevail in limiting civil marriage to heterosexuals, they may have to accept strong same-sex domestic partnership provisions in exchange, and then the outcome may well be the same: Lesbian and gay couples will have found a recognized and protected place at the table of American families, a place that may no longer be threatened by the vagaries of unfriendly state laws.

The other challenge to heteronormativity is found squarely within heterosexual relationships. Until the last third of the 20th century, the notion of males and females as opposites had led to a rigid set of gender prescriptions. Males were seen as "instrumental" specialists who are good at such things as work and politics, while females excel at nurturing other people, particularly in the form of homemaking activities and family caregiving (Parsons, 1964). In the past 35 years, however, the rigidity of these prescriptions has been met with an ever-increasing set of challenges, and the genders have grown more and more alike. Men have been challenged to become more involved in housework and child care, and they have done so, albeit modestly (Coltrane, 2000). Women have fought for full participation in education, athletics, occupations, and politics, with a considerable degree of success. Labor force participation rates for U.S. women with an infant under age 1 have risen from 31% percent in 1976 to a high of 59% in 1998 (Downs, 2003). Since then, the rate has dropped slightly to 55% in 2000 and in 2002, but the year 2000 decline occurred only among White, married women over age 30 with some college education (O'Connell, 2001)—arguably the most economically privileged category of women in the United States.

For families, this convergence of the genders has generated some far-reaching changes that bear greatly on the emerging work-family interface. First, heterosexual women desiring marriage have delayed their first marriages: Age at first marriage averaged 21 in 1970, and by 2000 it rose to nearly 25. There is widespread consensus that this delay is part and parcel of the expanding educational and occupational opportunities for women. The National Center for Health Statistics reported that in this 30-year period, "the number of women completing college has nearly doubled and the number in the labor force has gone up by almost 40 percent" (Matthews & Hamilton, 2002). As women come to have attractive socioeconomic alternatives to marriage, there is no longer such a compelling economic urgency to marry, and women can afford to be more scrutinizing in their choice of a partner and in the timing of a union.

Second, if and when they do marry, women increasingly expect to have paid work until some time in their later mid-life or into their senior years, with only brief interruptions if any. It is now a commonplace assumption among most heterosexual married couples that two regular paychecks—his and hers—will be financially necessary to maintain their preferred level of income. The resulting pattern of daily couple life has made it more difficult to sustain the notion of the genders as opposites, especially when both partners have full-time jobs or careers. "Good partners" come to be seen as people who do their fair share of income-earning, housework, and (if the couple has children) child care, regardless of gender. Schwartz's *Peer Marriage* (1994)

may be seen as a postmodern primer for such couples—people oriented to gender sameness instead of oppositeness.

To be sure, vigorous forces of traditionalism will remain, as evidenced by the popularity of John Gray's books (e.g., 1992), which proclaim that men and women come from different planets. The General Social Survey is arguably the most representative sample of United States attitudes, and we can draw on some items in the 2002 survey (Davis & Smith, 2002) to illustrate the persistence of family traditionalism. Nearly 39% of Americans say they "agree" that "it is much better for everyone involved if the man is the achiever outside the home and the woman takes care of the home and family" (the other response choices are "disagree" and "neither agree nor disagree"). The same percentage agrees with the statement, "All in all, family life suffers when the woman has a full-time job." And a 1996 item asked which of "two types of relationships would the respondent prefer?: 1. A relationship where the man has the main responsibility for providing the household income and the woman has the main responsibility for taking care of the home and family, or 2. A relationship where the man and woman equally share responsibility for providing the household income and taking care of the home and family?" Nearly 30% chose the traditional family type (Davis & Smith, 1996).

The resulting "culture wars" between those who remain eager to create gendered domains of everyday life and those who see such differences as an anachronism will probably linger, but the GSS trends show that the more postmodern pattern is the ascendant one. If 39% of Americans still agree with the image of man-the-"achiever" and woman-the-homebody, this traditional preference is down dramatically from the 66% who agreed with the same item in 1977 (Davis & Smith, 2002). The fact is that as men and women's activities grow increasingly similar to each other, their overall sensibilities and their perceptions of what they need and what they want will more and more converge. Coltrane (1991) uncovered a tendency among active, role-sharing fathers to eschew friendships with other men who are not as involved as they are in child care. These men are more likely to compare themselves to women than to more traditional men, and at work they sometimes choose to hide their child-involvement from male coworkers who might judge them to be insufficiently career-motivated.

The children of these gender-convergent couples are likely to gravitate as adults to their parents' role-sharing pattern. Risman (1998) found that children from "fair families" fully absorb their parents' liberal gender ideology. Although they alter it in school, once they are exposed to their peers' creation of the genders as opposites, Risman suggested that as adults they are likely to revert to the postgendered pattern that was their initial family baseline.

As women and men who rear children together become more alike and less like opposites, and as their children eventually replicate what they have grown up with, the consequences for the work-family interface will be considerable. The pressure on workplaces to adapt not simply to the family needs of their female workers but also to those of their male workers will accelerate. As fathers continue their long, slow march toward greater family involvement, mothers will see less need to scale down their work involvement or to settle for lower pay. Neither men nor women will continue to tolerate the "motherhood wage penalty," which has persisted despite the fact that women now work longer into their pregnancies and return to work sooner after giving birth (Avellar & Smock, 2003).

The crux of the matter is that gender discrimination at work has long participated in the *creation* of gender difference by making it more valuable for men to prioritize work and for women to prioritize family, thus generating two different kinds of people. As men and women increasingly undo their differences at home, they will grow less tolerant of the forces that render them into opposites at work. Employers will then be forced to undo the motherhood wage penalty, and they will either become more family-friendly or they will lose their competitive edge when they recruit their employees.

The Graying of America

The final master trend is the aging of the American population. Table 6.5 shows the proportion of older people in U.S. Census data for 1970 and 2000, and it includes current projections for 2020 and 2050. The progression over these

TABLE 6.5 Percent of Older People in the U.S. Population—1970, 2000, 2020, and 2050

	1970	2000	2020	2050
Age 65 and over	9.8	12.4	16.3	20.7
Age 85 and over	0.7	1.5	2.2	5.0

Source: U.S. Census Bureau, 2004, U.S. Interim Projections by Age, Sex, Race, and Hispanic Origin.

four time points demonstrates a rather dramatic trend toward an aging population, culminating by mid-century in people age 65 or older comprising 20.7% of the population, up from 12.4% in the 2000 census. In absolute numbers, this will mean that more than 86 million of the projected 419 million total population of the United States will be older people. Moreover, additional projections provided by the U.S. Administration on Aging (AoA) suggest that these older people will have a considerably longer life expectancy. For example, a 65-year-old male in 2050 will be expected to live another 20.3 years, compared to the 15.5 more years he would have lived in 1995. And, an 85-year-old female who was projected in 1995 to live an additional 6.5 years would have a life expectancy of 9.4 years in 2050.

For work-family issues and for society as a whole, there are a number of consequences of this growing number of older Americans. Concerning paid work, the current trend of more elders (especially women) lengthening their stay in the labor force will no doubt accelerate, as longevity rates increase. The AoA (2003) reported that by 2005, 16% of women between age 65 and 74 will be in the labor force, an increase of 18% over the 1994 level. And 4.3% of women age 75 and higher will be in the labor force, an increase of 22% over the 1994 level. Looking forward, the American economy will be under pressure to accommodate this swelling population of elderly workers.

Concerning living arrangements, the vast majority of elders remain noninstitutionalized, and the AoA (2003) reported that in 2002 most of these people lived either in a separate household with their spouse (53.6%) or alone (30%). By gender, however, most men age 65 or older (73%) lived with a spouse, compared to only 41% of women, reflecting the fact that most husbands predecease their wives. The fact that elderly people typically live alone (with or without a spouse) should not suggest that they remain totally non-dependent. For elderly couples, wives will remain the primary caregivers of husbands who become ill or disabled, and given the increased labor force participation of elderly women, the stresses of balancing work with family needs may become considerable.

Of course, the other family caregiving resource for the elderly is their adult children, and a useful report compiled by the National Center on Caregiving (2003) notes that "the average caregiver is age 46, female, married and working outside the home ..." Many of these women are exemplars of what has been dubbed the "sandwich generation"—people who are dealing with their own dependent children while at the same time attending to the needs of aging parents. And whether sandwiched between two generations or not, fully 33% of women caring for their elders must cut back their work hours, pass up a promotion or new work opportunity (29%), and/or switch from full- to part-time (20%). Approximately one out of every six quit their jobs entirely (National Center on Caregiving, 2003). The resulting loss of income coupled with the time involved in elder care may give rise to considerable stress and worry, especially for single women and for women whose spouses or partners are doing very little of this care work. Caregiving, however, is not simply a stressor, as it may also be a powerful gratifier. Walker and Allen's (1991) study cautions against the caregiving-as-burden perspective, showing that for many of the adult daughters who provided regular care for their widowed mothers, the relationship provided far more gratifications than burdens, and this was so for both mothers and daughters. In any case, the challenge of working out these relationships will grow increasingly commonplace as the baby boom generation moves into its middle years, swelling the number of people sandwiched between two generations.

SOCIAL CLASS DIVISION

Accompanying the five master trends discussed in the previous section is a sixth one, more continuous with the past than a transformation of it: Social class differences among families of the 21st century will continue to result in some adults and their children having much better life chances than others. Indeed, the importance of the racial-ethnic transformation discussed in the previous section may inhere in the persistent social class disadvantages of the swelling populations of Hispanics and people of color. For example, what conclusion do we draw from the fact that while 27.3% of the nation's 72 million children in 2002 lived with a single parent, the number falls to 16.1% for White children while it rises to 48.3% for Black children (U.S. Census Bureau, 2003)? Below I will review several of the well-known advantages of a child growing up in a two-parent family, and I will argue that these benefits may have far more to do with social class advantages than with who resides in the household (e.g., one or two parents) or with what their racial-ethnic category is.

Social Class, Income, and the Work-Family Interface

Family income is a crude but widely accepted proxy for social class position, and I begin with some income variations among the overall racial-ethnic categories discussed earlier. Table 6.6 (DeNavas-Walt, Cleveland, & Webster, 2003)

TABLE 3.6 Real Median Household Income by Racial-Ethnic Category: 2002*

Asian alone	$50,604
White alone (not Hispanic)	$47,199
All races	$43,760
Hispanic Origin (of any race)	$35,447
Black alone	$31,408

*These "real" income averages include the cost and benefits of taxes, capital gains and losses, employer-provided health benefits, noncash transfers (e.g., food stamps), and annualized home equity.
Excluded from the table are the 2.4% of the population who indicated two or more races in the 2000 Census.
Source: U.S. Census Bureau, Current Population Survey, 2003 Annual Social and Economic Supplement.

shows the "real" median household income in 2002 for the four major racial ethnic categories.

The table shows clearly the considerable differences across racial-ethnic categories. Within category, however, there are important social class variations. Among Hispanics, all subcategories remain far behind the average U.S. median income, but Puerto Ricans "remain the most economically disadvantaged of all major Latino groups" (Baca Zinn & Wells, 2000, p. 257), while Cubans remain the most economically privileged. In addition, family patterns are not always the same among Latinos as they are for European Americans, and the work-family interface may therefore function differently for these two categories across the same social class. For example, studies of Mexicans have indicated that even within the middle class, kinship networks may remain more vigorous than among "Anglo" families. Baca Zinn and Wells (2000, p. 266) noted that "Mexican children are socialized into a context of 'thick' social relations," in contrast to the more isolated patterns of interaction within the European

American middle class, and that when the former enter the school system, they may be ill-equipped to deal with its more individualistic and competitive structures of relationships. As we will see later in this section, family-derived cultural capital may have a considerable impact on status attainment, as children move through school and enter the domain of work.

Asian subcategories are likewise associated with differential life chances. Among first- and second-generation Asian Americans in 1998–2000, the average Indian adult had the equivalent of a college education, compared to a high school education for the average Vietnamese (Logan, 2001a). Predictably, these differences in education carry over into other socioeconomic characteristics. The average personal income of Asian Indians in this period ($31,732) was twice the average Vietnamese ($15,758), and the 17.1% poverty rate of Vietnamese was nearly twice the rate (8.7%) for Indians (Logan, 2001).

Social class variations among Black subcategories are equally striking. While Table 3.6 showed that Blacks have by far the lowest overall economic standing, immigrants from Africa and from the Caribbean are far more advantaged than African Americans, and their median household income is considerably higher than Hispanics as well, although still much lower than either Asians or non-Hispanic Whites. Africans and Afro-Caribbeans have more years of education, much of which is typically acquired prior to their arrival here, and their unemployment and poverty rates are much lower than those of African Americans (see Logan & Deane, 2003).

The Special Vulnerability of Low-Income Immigrants

The National Immigration Law Center's (2004) "Facts about Immigrants" reported some useful social-class related information about the 30 million-plus U.S. immigrants, drawing on the Census as well as other sources. In 2000, approximately 11% of the population consisted of immigrants, who comprised some 15% of the total labor force. These people are economically vulnerable in disproportionate numbers. For example, "almost 43 percent of immigrants work at jobs paying less than $7.50 an hour, compared to 28 percent of all workers" (National Immigration Law Center, 2004). Fix, Zimmerman, and Passel (2001) noted that although immigrant employment rates benefited from the economic boom toward the end of the 1990s, the median wages of natives "rose more than 50 percent faster than immigrants."

Poverty rates are thus considerably higher for immigrant families than for natives. The Center for Immigration Studies (Camarota, 2001) reported that in 1999, "16.8 percent of immigrants compared to 11.2 percent of natives lived in poverty," but this rate jumps to 23.5 percent for the most recent wave of immigrants, those who entered in the 1990s. It follows that the native-born children of immigrant parents likewise have higher poverty rates than the children of native parents. Specifically, "among persons under age 21 living in poverty, 24.2 percent are the children of immigrants" (Camarota, 2001). As a consequence, these children are "more likely to [have no health insurance] (22 percent versus 10 percent); more likely to have no usual source of medical care (14 percent versus 4 percent); and more likely not to have a steady source of food (37 percent versus 27 percent)" (Capps, 2001). Of course, the situation is not indelibly fixed, as immigrant families tend to fare better with each successive generation. English fluency, coupled with high rates of intermarriage and the identification of oneself as a hyphenated American, suggest "a potential" for upward mobility (Frey, 1999).

Looking more closely at some elements of vulnerability for immigrant families, Sweatshop Watch (2004) pointed out that "the overwhelming majority of garment workers in the U.S. are immigrant women" and added that "the Department of Labor estimates that more than half of the country's 22,000 sewing shops violate minimum wage and overtime laws." In a 2001 interview, the author of *Sweatshop Warriors* (Louie, 2001) reported that "Latina/os represent 60 percent and Asians 35 percent of workers in all garment factories in the United States which the government classifies as sweatshops. Latina/os represent 53 percent and Asians 25 percent of workers in sweatshop restaurants. Eighty percent of farmworkers in the U.S. are of Mexican descent" (Multinational Monitor, 2001).

How Social Class Differences Affect Children

Although the 20% of U.S. children born to immigrants are especially vulnerable, social class origins are consequential for all children. The impact of social class has been explored by many work-family researchers. Some of these efforts have focused on how children are differentially prepared for educational achievement, depending on the social class position of the parents. The logic of explanation is that family resources—both money capital and cultural capital—provide the ticket to success at school, and this success (or lack of it) is the direct prelude to occupationally driven status attainment. Ample money resources place families in wealthy neighborhoods, which give children access to schools with well-paid teachers and abundant educational resources.

School achievement is then a springboard for recruitment into occupations.

Quantitative studies have linked parents' income (a proxy for social class) directly to greater levels of cognitive stimulation provided to their children—a prelude first to success at school and then at work. Votruba-Drzal (2003) found that additional increments of income have the biggest impact on cognitive stimulation within families that are at the lowest level of income—obviously the most vulnerable of all families. Cognitive stimulation was measured at the preschool level by such items as how often someone reads to the child and helps him or her learn the alphabet, and at the elementary school level by additional items such as taking the child to a museum or theater. In addition, Votruba-Drzal found that mothers' educational level was also positively related to cognitive stimulation in the home. She noted that because additional income may make it possible for a mother to purchase additional education for herself, perhaps thereby leading to still greater cognitive stimulation for her children, the effect of additional income may actually have been underestimated in the study. This is a consequence of including maternal education and family income simultaneously in the regression equations: "Any influence of income that is mediated by control variables [in this case, maternal education] ... will be attributed to the control variable itself and not income. In this respect, these analyses do not capture the totality of income's influence" (2003, p. 353).

Votruba-Drzal's findings partly replicate those of Entwisle and Alexander (2000) in their Beginning School Study in Baltimore. These researchers found several factors that contribute to educational advantage for the children in some families and disadvantage in others. Most important was a family's economic status, in keeping with Vortruba-Drzal's findings just cited. Also important were parents' expectations—both their opinions and their activities—concerning their children's school performance.

Social Class and Single-Parent Families

In the same Baltimore study, Entwisle and Alexander (2000, p. 333) also found that children in single-parent families fared worse when they started school than children in two-parent families. They added, however, that "children live in many kinds of [4]one-parent' homes," and they discovered that single mother-grandmother households gave children entering the first grade a considerable school advantage over those children who lived alone with a single mother. These children "had better work habits," "even a little better than those of the children in mother-father settings" (2000, p. 326).

The complexities of issues of poverty, single parenthood, and household composition become especially transparent in the Baltimore study. Children need adult encouragement and involvement to do well in school. When single mothers live alone with their children, poverty may drive these women into paid work for long hours each day, and the children may get less parental involvement. Add an involved grandparent to the family mix, however, and the children's education may benefit, even more so in some instances than if the child had been living in a two-parent family. The grandparent's influence on the child in some respects may become a proxy for the cognitive stimulation that added income and/or a second parent might otherwise have made possible. This situation is not at all uncommon. The Census Bureau reported that in 2002, more than 13% of all single-parented children had at least one grandparent living in their household

in addition to their parent. This figure understates the extent of grandparental influence, because some grandparents may not live in the same household as their children and grandchildren but may be near enough to provide an ongoing, even daily, influence on their grandchildren. In addition, Collins (2000) alerted us to the phenomenon of "othermothers"—networks of women who are not necessarily kin but who likewise may become an integral part of the lives of a mother's children.

In light of the variety of support systems that single parents may have access to, perhaps the recent governmental marriage-promotion campaign is well-intentioned but misguided. What children need for school achievement and for solid development in general is consistent adult encouragement, more so than they need fathers. If, along with mothers, fathers provide that encouragement, the child may indeed thrive. If someone else provides it instead, the child may thrive as well. What single mothers and single fathers need are real resources for themselves and their children: jobs that pay them a living wage, health care, child-care help, and good public services including schools and reliable transportation facilities.

Another look at the stresses on low-income families is a qualitative study by Dodson and Dickert (2004), again focusing mainly on single-mother households and the limited options that mothers in many such families have. The study also provides an understanding of the intergenerational transmission of social class, focusing on one pathway through which the lower end of the social stratification system may get reproduced. These researchers explored the involvement of daughters as "mini-moms" in low-income households. When women with young children must take low-wage jobs after being pushed off of welfare, they may not be able to afford day-care charges or have access to adult kin such as a grandmother who would serve as a caregiver. Under these circumstances, a mother's best option may be to depend on her oldest daughter to care for her much younger children while she is at work. The authors suggest that while these mini-moms may develop high levels of responsibility and parenting skills at a tender age, they sometimes do so at the expense of developing their education and job training. Without marketable skills and higher education, and with parenting skills being their most highly developed asset as they enter adulthood, early parenthood may then appear as their best option. The cycle of poverty is thus renewed intergenerationally. This is a remarkable account of how the lower end of the social stratification system gets reproduced through a family process in which parenting skills are cultivated and occupational skills (via education) are underplayed.

In this analysis, we can focus on the specific work-family pathway (mothers' hours at paid work spills over on daughters' school time and on other lost opportunities), but we might also recognize that the identified work-family spillover pattern is merely the midpoint of a more complex set of pathways. The starting point of the set—the independent variable—might be framed in any number of ways, and exactly what it is that "causes" this chain of circumstances is open to debate and creative interpretation. Garey and Arendell (2001) cautioned that "mother-blame"—holding mothers responsible for any and every child outcome that is held to be problematic—has a long legacy in social science. To move beyond it in this example, we need to consider the macro context that renders child-care solutions by "mini-moms" a rational choice for many low-income mothers. The causal pathway would then begin with political decisions that change the distribution of welfare, resulting in low-income mothers being forced into low-wage jobs with inflexible hours and poor benefits, all of which may result in young daughters being pressed into service as caregivers for their younger siblings while their mothers are at work.

Social Class and Work-to-Family Influences

Some social class-oriented approaches focus more directly on work-to-family influences, often adopting an implicit or explicit intergenerational transmission perspective. In large part due to the pioneering work of Kohn (1969; see also Kohn & Schooler, 1982), attention focused on how different jobs generate the personality tendencies that are required to perform them. In turn, job-driven personality tendencies then get transmitted to one's children via parenting "values."

Because middle-class jobs require different skills and proclivities than working-class jobs, parenting values accordingly vary by social class. Kohn found that middle-class professional jobs characterized by substantive complexity and by the requirement of independent thinking resulted in worker dispositions that were likewise oriented to complexity and to intellectual flexibility. These dispositions were then reenacted as values that guided childrearing. Working-class jobs with less substantive complexity and with a greater premium on conformity to the rigid requirements of supervisors will generate more compliant and obedient personalities, who will then adopt parenting values premised on the notion that children need to learn to conform to authority.

Kohn's line of analysis was extremely useful, as it got us thinking about how the specifics of job activities may generate spillover effects in the home sphere that vary by social class. In one of the best studies within this genre, Parcel and Menaghan (1994) found a positive relationship between the complexity of employed mothers' work and the quality of their home environments, the latter measured by such variables as intellectual stimulation and maternal warmth and responsiveness. The greater the job complexity and the opportunities for self-direction, the "higher" the home quality.

Menaghan's work stopped short of being a direct test of Kohn's thesis, because there is no attempt either to uncover the specific parenting values of these mothers or to uncover the extent to which these values are in fact transmitted to their children. Indeed, Kohn's thesis about social class and conformity was never offered as a theory of intergenerational transmission of different values for different social classes. That is, it is one thing to demonstrate that workers acquire certain parental values that vary by social class, in accordance with the substantive complexity of jobs. Kohn clearly established this link. It is another thing, however, to show that parents make specific efforts to transmit these values, or that their children actually wind up internalizing them. Kohn himself expressed some reservations about there being any appreciable similarity between the values of parents and the values of their children (see Kohn & Schooler, 1983, p. 309), and he makes no attempt to discover if children's levels of behavioral conformity or autonomy in some way follow from their parents' values for them.

Recent ethnographic work by Lareau (2003) launched an implicit challenge to the Kohn thesis at precisely its weakest link—the connection between what parents do at work and the values they actually teach their children at home. Kohn had assumed that having a middle-class job requiring autonomous thought and action would culminate in a process of cultivating the value of autonomy in their children. Lareau did find markedly different socialization patterns in middle-class families from those she observed in working-class and in poor families, but the differences did not entirely fit Kohn's assumed pattern. Indeed, it was the 9- and 10-year-olds from the working-class and poor families who appeared to be supreme exemplars of autonomy. Their parents reared them in accordance with a philosophy of "natural growth," which is oriented to "keeping children safe, enforcing discipline, and, when they deem it necessary, regulating their behavior in specific areas. Within these boundaries, working-class and poor children are allowed to grow and to thrive" (Lareau, 2003, pp. 66–67). They are given "an autonomous world, apart from adults, in which they are free to try out new experiences and develop important competencies. ... They learn how to manage their own time. They learn how to strategize" (p. 67).

In contrast, Lareau's middle-class parents embrace a philosophy of "concerted cultivation," through which children "are treated as a project to be developed" (p. 67). Here, children's pace of life is frenetic, exhausting, overscheduled, and overseen by the ever-watchful eyes of adults, who take their children from one adult-supervised activity to the next. The children rarely have significant portions of leisure time in which they are responsible for organizing their own activity, and when they do, they complain of being "bored"—something that Lareau never heard from children in working-class and poor families.

What middle-class children do learn, with the help of their carefully cultivated reasoning skills and their direct observations of their parents' constant interventions in institutions on their behalf, is that their own needs and interests are paramount. They emerge from their childhoods with the conviction that middle-class institutions ought to be responsive to them, and when they are not, one has every right to negotiate with them and the people who staff them so that they will better serve their individual needs. The contrast is clear: The children of working-class and poor parents learn a stance of constraint, as they navigate through the complex world of middle-class institutions beginning with the schools, and they channel their extensive autonomy-training into their free time. The middle-class children learn entitlement (see Marks, 2000, for an autobiographical narrative about the learning of entitlement). When they find their way into the world of work, they will come armed with the understanding that they will be treated as equals by any superordinates as well as by their peers. They will then apply their reasoning skills and their experience at using their agency to develop themselves *within* adult-run organizations and institutions and to consolidate their advantages, which they will once again transmit to their own children (see Cookson, Jr., & Persell, 1985, for an account of how upper-class families use elite boarding schools as central socializing agents that arrange and organize a still higher level of class advantage than Lareau's middle-class families secure for their children).

Here we have a remarkable treatment of family-to-work intergenerational transmission effects, all patterned by social class and fully illustrated through painstaking ethnographic detail. Lareau's explanatory framework is essentially a socialization argument. Parents from different social classes teach children different pathways through organizations and institutions, starting with the schools, and children's enactment of these differential approaches affect their success first at school and later in the domain of work. This is a social class-trumps-race approach, as Lareau is clear that the socialized outcomes within middle-class Black families in her sample bear a much greater resemblance to those in middle-class White families than to those in working-class and poor Black families.

Social Class and Lesbian and Gay Families

I end this section by exploring how social class affects lesbian and gay families, which have sometimes been heralded as modeling a more equitable approach to balancing work and family life. In Dunne's (1996, 2000a, 2000b) study of 60 lesbians in Britain, participants held fiercely to the importance of financial "co-independence" within an intimate relationship, and they credited their sexuality with being an important factor in making this possible. In the words of one respondent, "You almost have to be gay ... I couldn't hold down a marriage ... I couldn't run a house, a family and do the job that I do.... In the heterosexual relationships that I know, the man wants to be looked after, come home, dinner there" (Dunne, 2000a, p. 139). Dunne notes that while the majority of British heterosexual women do not earn enough income to keep them financially independent of their husbands or the State, fully 86% of her sample are in this empowering situation.

Dunne (2000a, 2000b) probes these issues further in a follow-up study of 37 lesbian couples living together with dependent children, most of whom were conceived through donor insemination and were still in their preschool years at the time of the interviews. Unlike heterosexual married birth mothers in Britain, who rarely contribute a substantial proportion of the family income, fully 50% of the lesbian birth mothers in this study earn at least half of the total household income. Respondents who managed to integrate employment identities with mothering identities did so in a variety of ways, such as taking turns being the primary earner or having both partners be half-time earners. In this way partners retain their financial co-independence without having to sacrifice their family time, and the couple can avoid the breadwinner-homemaker split experienced by most heterosexual married couples. Within some couples the higher-earning woman actually negotiated a reduction of hours and therefore pay, apparently willing to exchange a lowered standard of living for more child-care and family time.

Dunne offered a compelling vision of a more balanced work-family interface when both partners retain strong footholds in both domains, and in that respect, she demonstrated for lesbians the same egalitarian model that Schwartz (1994) and Risman (1998) demonstrated for "peer" and "postgender" heterosexual couples. Notice, however, that this accomplishment may be something of a social class privilege that cuts across whatever sexual orientation a couple has. Dunne conceded that her lesbian respondents tend to be "educationally and/or occupationally advantaged" (2000b, p. 14). Schwartz's (1994, p. 6) peer couples likewise appear to be highly educated, and the husbands in these marriages had jobs with "some flexibility and controllable hours." And Risman (1998) indicated that most couples in her "fair families" study were highly educated. All the husbands and most of the wives in Risman's sample had jobs in which working conditions were flexible, thereby providing

both partners the latitude to devote time to child-related activities—school, doctor appointments, or whatever.

Such family-friendly jobs are not available to most workers. Those who have them are likely to be highly educated professionals who have the power to negotiate more family-friendly work practices. Perhaps, then, Dunne makes too much of lesbians' freedom from the traditional gendered breadwinner/homemaker arrangement, and too little of the privileges that higher social class position confer on those who have them. Carrington's (1999) study of 52 lesbigay (his preferred designator) couples in the San Francisco Bay area is more alert to these variations of privilege. By closely tracking domesticity as a daily production process, encompassing feeding work, housework, kinwork, and consumption work, Carrington found little evidence among these 26 lesbian and 26 gay male couples of the domestic equality that is so heralded by lesbigay public ideology. Only 25% of his couples maintained a "rough parity" in their contribution to domestic work, and the biggest drivers of this accomplishment were jobs and money.

Carrington noted that wealthy lesbigay egalitarians were able to purchase a variety of their domestic needs from restaurants and from service workers at home, with the result that neither partner had an overload of domestic responsibilities. Other egalitarians were found among couples—both male and female—in which both partners worked in female-identified professions such as nursing, primary and secondary education, and social work. For these couples, the decisive factor was time as well as money. Their work-week rarely exceeded 40 hours, and although their paychecks were often modest, their jobs offered paid vacations, paid sick days and holidays, and a variety of other family-friendly practices. When both partners had this kind of job, they avoided the tendency of one partner becoming overwrought by career responsibilities and the other curtailing his or her job life in order to maintain the domestic front for both of them. When only one partner had this kind of job and the other had a more time-consuming position, the couple again gravitated to the split responsibilities that mirror the traditional heterosexual provider/homemaker split, even if both jobs were defined as full-time.

The majority of Carrington's families evolved into this kind of split, "encouraging the family member with the greatest economic opportunity to pursue paid work vigorously" (p. 188). The other partner then took on the lion's share of domesticity, either curtailing paid work obligations if total family income made that possible, or using the opportunities of flexible, family-friendly work schedules to maintain domesticity, often gravitating to this family role without having consciously chosen it.

As only five of Carrington's 52 lesbigay families had children residing with them, there was not enough of a subsample to look for distinguishing characteristics of such families. Had this kind of analysis been possible, perhaps Carrington, like Dunne, would have turned up a more evenly divided work-family balance than he did for most of his childless couples. If so, it could be that the lesbigay couples who opt for children are disproportionately found amongst those who already enjoy family-friendly jobs. The greater deliberateness required for lesbians to have children may extend into their planning for how they are going to manage child care together, and it is likely that their respective paid work requirements factor more consciously into their plans.

The fact remains, however, that in Carrington's sample, social class and the job-derived income that drives it means everything. Following Dizard and Gadlin's (1990) analysis of heterosexual families, Carrington argued that family and the domesticity that constitutes it is something that must get actively produced. When both partners lack the time and money resources that stem from social class privilege, the best that many couples can muster is a rather minimal production of family: "As resources accumulate, participants begin to think in familial terms about their lesbian-and gay-defined household lives. They have more resources required to create more elaborate domestic regimens, and more stable families" (1999, p. 111). Again, however, this elaboration is a perquisite of social class privilege that is not enjoyed by a majority of Americans, either heterosexual or gay.

PREJUDICE, DISCRIMINATION, AND THE WORK-FAMILY INTERFACE: A NEW RESEARCH PROGRAM

In this section I attempt to open a new line of inquiry, focusing on the impact of workplace prejudice and discrimination on individual and family well-being. This kind of analysis does not put attention on the impact of work hours, schedule fit, types of benefits, and other official job conditions that are specific to a given job. Obviously, job conditions matter, as they may have a powerful impact on individuals and their families, as Gerson and Jacobs (2001) have shown. Here, however, following previous analysis (Marks & Leslie, 2000), my concern is with some macrolevel structural variables that may cut across jobs and their attributes. Specifically, I focus on how membership in dominant versus nondominant social categories may differentially affect individuals' experiences and create ripple affects for their family processes. This difference by category is obviously true across jobs, as access to the "better" ones is restricted to relatively privileged social categories. But even within the same job and with the same benefits, doors may open for some people that are felt by others to be closed. People of color, women, people perceived to be gender deviants, lesbians and gay men, people who claim or are perceived as a nondominant ethnicity—these and other categorical differences may mark a person as "different" or "less than" at their workplace. Instead of being perceived solely in terms of their job performance, that performance may get refracted through the lens of their "difference," and then their treatment by their superordinates and by their coworkers may reflect that perceived difference.

Although this basic insight about categorical diversity may have profound implications for work-family studies on both theoretical and the methodological levels, these implications have yet to be seriously explored. Marks and Leslie (2000) suggested that in quantitative studies, the significance of social categories such as race may not be fully uncovered by simply sampling more than one racial-ethnic group, then dummy-coding the racial identification of the respondent, and finally running the hypotheses using race as either a control or a moderator variable. We argued that in addition to simple codes for racial category, researchers need to include more fine-grained measures of phenomena that are historically specific to the category. In the matter of race, for example, we need to conceptually specify the reasons why race might be important enough to influence other variables, and then operationalize these reasons in meaningful and creative ways. Given the legacy of racialized advantage and disadvantage in this country, variables that identify instances of prejudice and discrimination are obvious candidates for inclusion in our studies. Racial-ethnic identity salience—measured as a metric variable rather than using a dummy code—is another such candidate, especially given its potential for mollifying the impact of prejudice and discrimination.

Discrimination, Racial Category, and Racial Ethnic Identity

Turner (2003) recently noted that differences in exposure to social stress on the basis of different social statuses—race-ethnicity, gender, social class, and so on—may be far more important to variations in health outcomes than has typically been assumed. Although Turner's point will not come as much of a surprise to family scholars, who have long been alert to the impact of social stress on family-related outcomes, one major stressor that has not yet received much attention from family scholars is prejudice and discrimination. In a landmark paper, Kessler, Mickelson, and Williams (1999) drew on a national sample of 3,032 respondents between the ages of 25 and 74 to explore two kinds of discrimination: *major events*, which included specific instances of workplace discrimination (not being hired for a job, not being given a promotion, or having been fired from a job), and more routine, *day-to-day discrimination* (e.g., "people act as if you are inferior"; "people act as if you are not smart"). Respondents were also queried about the reasons for the perceived discrimination. Race-ethnicity, gender, appearance, and age were the most commonly reported reasons, while sexual orientation and several other reasons were also coded but less often cited (for an updated and extremely useful list of the scale items for major discrimination, day-to-day discrimination, and reasons why people think they received discriminatory treatment, see the appendix in Turner & Avison, 2003).

The results of this national survey were stunning. Fully 33.5% reported experiencing one or more major discrimination events, and 60.9% reported experiencing day-to-day discrimination. Non-Hispanic Whites perceived far less discrimination—both "major" and "day-to-day"—than either non-Hispanic Blacks or "others." And, the racialized disadvantage of identifying as non-Hispanic Black or some "other" race was further confirmed in the finding that these respondents reported with much greater frequency than Whites that their race was the reason for the discrimination. Although the link between perceived discrimination and mental health was inconsistently predicted by disadvantaged social status, the researchers concluded that "perceived discrimination needs to be treated much more seriously ... in future studies of stress and mental health" (p. 208).

These new strategies for measuring discriminatory treatment have great promise for enriching our approach to work-family scholarship, and it is well worth reviewing additional exemplars of epidemiological studies. These studies have perhaps overfocused on predicting depression, but because this research has grown increasingly sophisticated, work-family scholars might benefit from using it as a model, substituting more family-related outcomes for depression. Moreover, as Whitbeck, McMorris, Hoyt, Stubben, and LaFromboise (2002) have noted, depressive affect has been closely linked to a variety of childhood family phenomena,

such as having had a history of childhood neglect and/or sexual or physical abuse, and having had inconsistent parental discipline and limit setting.

In a California study of 3,012 Mexican origin respondents, Finch, Kolody, and Vega (2000) found "a clear, direct relationship between perceived discrimination and depressive symptomatology" (p. 309). Discrimination was measured by a three-item scale that asked respondents how often people dislike them, treat them unfairly, or treat friends unfairly because they are Mexican or of Mexican origin. In this study the perception of discrimination is unfortunately decontextualized, unlike the several work-related discrimination items in Kessler et al. (1999), and we are thus unable to determine where the perceived discrimination occurred. Presumably, a good deal of it occurred at a workplace, a point that work-family scholars would obviously seize upon in redesigning this study. The outcome measure—depression—is likewise of lesser interest to work-family scholars than other more family-relevant variables.

Whitbeck's et al. (2002) study of 287 American Indians is another impressive attempt to measure the impact of prejudice and discrimination as a stressor variable, and it draws on a creative measure of Indian identity to add complexity to the research design. In addition, it carefully links adult depressive symptoms to childhood family history variables. Prejudice and discrimination were measured by a 10 item scale with four response choices from "never" to "always." The items ask respondents if someone "said something derogatory ... because you are Native American"; if a store owner or sales clerk or other worker "treated you in a disrespectful way because you are Native American; if "someone ignored or excluded you from some activity because you were Native American," and so on (p. 414). The results are striking: Even with a variety of controls in the final model, "perceived discrimination was a powerful indicator of depressive symptoms among the American Indian adults" (p. 411). However, traditional identity-strengthening practices such as going to a powwow made it less likely that a person would have depressive symptoms. An interaction term revealed that those who had above-average levels of traditional Indian practices were most buffered from the impact of discrimination.

These central findings from Whitbeck et al. (2002) parallel later research by Sellers, Caldwell, Schmeelk-Cone, and Zimmerman (2003), who found that young African Americans for whom race was a highly central identity were relatively protected from the negative impact of perceived discrimination on psychological distress. They also parallel a recent study of Filipino Americans by Mossakowski (2003), who found that although perceived discrimination is associated with depressive symptoms, having a strong Filipino identity buffers that hazard. All three of these studies take racial/ethnic membership seriously, exploring both the vulnerabilities that result from being a subjugated group and the advantages that accrue to that group from identity-strengthening processes (For another attempt to assess the strength of racial/ethnic identity, but framed generically enough for researchers to use the scale for any and every racial/ethnic group, see Noh, Beiser, Kaspar, Hou, & Rummens, 1999). For purposes of work and family analyses, perhaps the most important drawback of the three studies cited here (along with Finch et al., 2000) is that most of their discrimination items remain decontextualized; there is little attempt to uncover the

domain (whether the workplace or some other locale) where the discrimination occurred.

Other recent research, drawing on an African American and European American sample in the Detroit area, was able to disentangle the contribution of poverty from the contribution of race, exploring variations in psychological distress and life satisfaction. Schulz et al. (2000) found that perceptions of "unfair treatment" and living below the poverty line were the critical independent variables that drove the variations in the outcomes they explored. The "unfair treatment" items are essentially versions of the "major" discrimination and "day-to-day" discrimination items used in Kessler, Mickelson, and Williams (1999), but in this study only three of the major discrimination items were used. Respondents were asked if they had ever been unfairly fired from a job or denied a promotion, not hired for a job for unfair reasons, or unfairly stopped or mistreated by the police. The findings of this study are complex, and they are outside the scope of our purposes for this volume. It is obvious, however, that two of the "unfair treatment" measures tap directly into instances of workplace discrimination in ways that ought to be of great interest to work-family scholars. Although the explored outcomes—psychological distress and life satisfaction—are of less import to us than more family-specific outcomes, this is a research model that is eminently adaptable to work-family studies.

As a final exemplar of recent epidemiological explorations of perceived discrimination and health and well-being, Forman's (2003) study of 1,199 African Americans is remarkable for its attention to both individual and institutional discrimination. Because its measures are exclusively oriented to workplace discrimination, it should be of particular interest to work and family researchers. Drawing on two different data sets, Forman explored the impact of "racial segmentation"—the perception that one's racial group is being targeted for a certain kind of job. For example, in the National Survey of Black Americans, respondents were asked two questions: (a) "In the place where you work, do Black people tend to get certain kinds of jobs?" and (b) "Is your job one that Black people tend to get more than whites?" (p. 338).

Forman's results indicated that "African Americans who perceive their current job to be a 'Black job' have lower levels of life satisfaction and higher levels of psychological distress than their counterparts who do not perceive their jobs in this light" (p. 345), and this linkage persisted even after controlling for reports of individual job discrimination and for other occupational characteristics. In addition, Forman found that this linkage was "particularly powerful for the African American middle class" (p. 345), in keeping with relative deprivation theory. That is, a paradox of the civil rights movement is that in its aftermath, although African Americans experienced an increase in available middle-class positions that were now open to them, levels of discontent often increased instead of lessened for people who entered these positions. This is because in comparison to the opportunities they perceive white workers to have, these "[Black jobs] afford minorities little opportunity to supervise production, to supervise largely white staffs, or to implement important organizational policies" (p. 334). African Americans are thus more prone to feel alienated despite the fact that their incomes may have risen.

Work and family researchers interested in family diversity should draw considerable inspiration from Forman's work and from the other exemplars cited here. It should be easy enough to link these discrimination measures to outcomes that are more central to our ongoing concerns. For example, to what extent does occupational discrimination erode a person's sense of work-family balance? How is a marriage affected by a person's perception of occupational discrimination—both the individual and the institutional variants of discrimination? Do married people who perceive discrimination keep their spouses insulated from the knowledge of that discrimination, and is there a gender difference in the likelihood of disclosure to the spouse? What are the consequences for the marital relationship of disclosure versus lack of disclosure, and are there different consequences by gender? In the face of discrimination at the workplace, who, if anyone, is more likely to withdraw from family relationships, and who, if anyone, is likely to draw closer to them in pursuit of some needed emotional sustenance? Are episodes of family violence more or less likely to occur in the aftermath of episodes of occupational discrimination? Does the strength of one's racial-ethnic identity in some way moderate the linkages between occupational discrimination and family relationship variables?

I offer the foregoing questions as mere "teases," hoping to inspire work and family scholars to launch new inquiries about the impact of social stratification in general and its consequences for occupational discrimination in particular. In turn, the possible linkages between occupational discrimination and family-specific phenomena are of course endless, limited only by the reach of our research imaginations.

In addition to more research on racial stratification and its impact, we need to expand our research on other forms of social stratification. Occupational discrimination may occur not only on the basis of race but also on the basis of gender, sexuality, age, social class, and so on, and may generate spillover effects for innumerable family-specific phenomena. Moreover, occupational discrimination is not the only conduit along which social stratification systems may make their impact on the work-family interface. We have seen in several different studies how racial-ethnic identity may serve as a buffer between occupational discrimination and mental health, but racial-ethnic and other identities that people bring with them to work may generate main effects as well as moderating effects.

Sexual Diversity at the Workplace

Consider, for example, the complex dynamics of lesbian and gay workers coming out at their workplace. Alan Bell (1995, p. 260) noted that as a gay man, in most of his jobs he has been "a minority of one":

> At about half these positions I've felt comfortable enough to disclose myself to the few co-workers I believed I could trust. But only in my current assignment, with the Los Angeles Department of City Planning, have I felt almost literally free— certainly not the same kind of freedom enjoyed by straights who live in a world designed for them—but a freedom nevertheless, the most amount of freedom I could imagine possible in an environment where heterosexuals are the majority.

In the Planning Department, Bell eventually discovered that three of his coworkers were also gay, a critical mass that made a difference. Hassan, fully "out" and ever-ready to widen the circle of knowers about him, was at times an inspiration—especially to Alex and Alan,

who initially were more given to reserve if not downright secretiveness. Hassan explained his open style as partly a political strategy: "If I act like a big flaming faggot, maybe other people won't feel as uncomfortable about being openly gay" (Bell, 1995, p. 266). Hassan, Alan, and Michael, all were instrumental in Alex coming out at work:

> Later, [Alex] said that each of us, in our own way, had been a role model for him. Michael had taught him how to dress and introduced him to the coolest [gay] clubs. I had counseled him about his career. Hassan had shown him how to be outrageously out. A role model himself these days, Alex volunteers for a community education program, visiting area high schools and junior colleges to speak to students about what it's like to be gay. (Bell, 1995, p. 266)

Bell's workplace evinces a quality of support for gay workers that is the opposite of a situation in which a stigmatized minority must contend with occupational discrimination. In sharp contrast, when Meagan Rosser (2000) approached her boss for some leave time to visit her mother's partner Charlotte, who was then dying of cancer, her boss's initial response was: "I don't know how I feel about this, Meagan. I mean, maybe if it was one of your *parents*...." Meagan protested that Charlotte *was* her parent, and although her boss relented, note the discriminatory hurdle Meagan had to jump over first. Consider how Bell and his gay coworkers are comparatively free to develop as keen of a sense of gay identity as they wish, with presumably salutary spillover effects on their families and relationships. Consider, too, the impact of these men on their heterosexually identified coworkers, who receive daily reminders that gay workers are merely workers like themselves, reminders that are perhaps shared in turn with their own family members. When lesbian and gay workers in Los Angeles organized on behalf of stronger domestic partnership provisions and better enforcement of nondiscrimination laws, Bell mentioned his involvement to some of his straight coworkers. Soon after, he was approached by two of them who wanted to join the fledgling organization, in solidarity with and support of their gay coworkers. Bell's workplace was clearly one that nurtured rather than stigmatized its minority members.

CONCLUSION

This is an age of increasing family diversity. It is a time when the institution of marriage—that venerated traditional cornerstone of family formation—is being stretched, scrutinized, debated, and fought about in the courts. It is a time when the racial-ethnic composition of the nation's families is undergoing a period of rapid transformation that will ultimately culminate in European Americans becoming a statistical minority. It is an age of globalization in which virtually nothing remains that is purely local. Work and family life is affected as much by events in the Middle East and within major multinational corporations as it is by local community developments. Under these circumstances, the best that we can do is to strain to be inclusive. Instead of bemoaning the loss of this or that traditional understanding of what a family is, our heritage is best served by going the extra mile to embrace the variety that is out there.

I end this essay by echoing the view put forth recently by Fineman (2004), who seeks to close up some of the distance between public responsibility and "private" lives. Fineman noted that domestic policies in this country have always been too narrowly legalistic. If the state defines you as a legitimate family, it will offer you some subsidies, and then only if you default in your "private" capacity to meet your own and your family's needs. Fineman argued that it is caregiving relationship, not sexual affiliation, which should be the focal point of public policy. This view implies an end to all discrimination based on sexual orientation as well as an eagerness to recognize and support all the families within which people live, including those that stretch across more than one household. In order to create the smoothest integration between work and family life, we need domestic partner benefits at least as much as we need marriage. And we need living wages, national health care, and guaranteed family and medical leave when necessary, all organized around caregiving relationships rather than around narrow definitions of "the" family.

REFERENCES

Administration on Aging. (2003). A profile of Older Americans: 2003. U.S. Department of Health and Human Services. http://research.aarp.org/general/profile_2003.pdf.

American Association for Single People, (retrieved August 14, 2004). 2000 Census—AASP report. http://www.unmarriedamerica.org/Census%202000/households-type-trends-family%20diversity.htm.

Andersen, M., & Collins, P. H. (Eds.). (1998). *Race, class, and gender: An anthology* (3rd ed.). Belmont, CA: Wadsworth.

Avellar, S., & Smock, P. J. (2003). Has the price of motherhood declined over time? A cross-cohort comparison of the motherhood wage penalty. *Journal of Marriage and Family, 65,* 597–607.

Baca Zinn, M., & Wells, B. (2000). Diversity within Latino families: New lessons for family social science. In D. H. Demo, K. R. Allen, & M. A. Fine (Eds.), *Handbook of family diversity* (pp. 252–273). New York: Oxford University Press.

Bell, A. (1995). Alex, Hassan, and Michael. In J. Preston (Ed., with M. Lowenthal), *Friends and lovers: Gay men write about the families they create me* (pp. 293–303). Berkeley: University of California Press.

Camarota, S. A. (2001). Immigrants in the United States—2000: A snapshot of America's foreign-born population. Center for Immigration Studies, http://www.cis.org/articles/2001/backl01.pdf.

Carrington, C. (1999). *No place like home: Relationships and family life among lesbians and gay men.* Chicago: University of Chicago Press.

Capps, R. (2001). Hardship among children of immigrants: Findings from the 1999 National Survey of America's Families. Urban Institute. http://www.urban.org/UploadedPDF/anf_b29.pdf.

Collins, P. H. (2000). *Black feminist thought: Knowledge, consciousness, and the politics of empowerment* (2nd ed.). New York: Routledge.

Coltrane, S. (1991). Social networks and men's family roles. *Mens Studies Review, 8,* 8–15.

Coltrane, S. (2000). Research on household labor: Modeling and measuring the social embeddedness of routine family work. *Journal of Marriage and the Family, 62,* 1208–1233.

Cookson, P. W., & Persell, C. H. (1985). *Preparing for power: America's elite boarding schools.* New York: Basic Books.

Davis, J. A., & Smith, T. W. (2002, 1996, 1977). *General social surveys, 2002, 1996, 1977.* Principal investigator, J. A. Davis; Director and Co-principal investigator, T. W. Smith; Co-principal investigator, P. V. Marsden, NORC ed. Chicago: National Opinion Research Center, producer, 2002, Storrs, CT. The Roper Center for Public Opinion Research, University of Connecticut, distributor.

Demo, D. H., Allen, K. R., & Fine, M. A. (Eds.). (2000). *Handbook of family diversity.* New York: Oxford University Press.

DeNavas-Walt, C., Cleveland, R., & Webster, B. H., Jr. (2003). Income in the United States: 2002. U.S. Census Bureau, Current Population Reports, P 60–221, Washington, DC: U.S. Government Printing Office.

Dizard, J., & Gadlin, H. (1990). *The minimal family.* Amherst: University of Massachusetts Press.

Dodson, L., & Dickert, G. (2004). Girls' family labor in low-income households: A decade of qualitative research. *Journal of Marriage and the Family, 66,* 318–332.

Downs, B. (2003). Fertility of American women: June 2002. U.S. Census Bureau: Current Population Reports.

Dunne, G. A. (1996). *Lesbian lifestyles: Women's work and the politics of sexuality.* Toronto: University of Toronto Press.

Dunne, G. A. (2000a). Lesbians as authentic workers? Institutional heterosexuality and the reproduction of gender inequalities. *Sexualities, 3,* 133–148.

Dunne, G. A. (2000b). Opting into motherhood: Lesbians blurring the the boundaries and transforming the meaning of motherhood. *Gender & Society, 14,* 11–35.

Entwisle, D. R., & Alexander, K. L. (2000). Diversity in family structure: Effects on schooling. In D. H. Demo, K. R. Allen, & M. A. Fine (Eds.), *Handbook of family diversity* (pp. 316–337). New York: Oxford University Press.

Finch, B. K., Kolody, B. K., & Vega, W. A. (2000). Perceived discrimination and depression among Mexican-origin adults in California. *Journal of Health and Social Behavior, 41,* 295–313.

Fineman, M. A. (2004). The autonomy myth: A theory of dependency. New York: New Press.

Fix, M., Zimmerman, W., & Passel, J. S. (2001). The integration of immigrant families in the U.S. Washington, DC: The Urban Institute. http://www.urban.org/UploadedPDF/immig_integration.pdf.

Forman, T. A. (2003). The social psychological costs of racial segmentation in the workplace: A study of African Americans' well-being. *Journal of Health and Social Behavior, 44,* 332–352.

Frey, W. H. (1999). The United States population: Where the new immigrants are. *Electronic Journal of the U.S. Information Agency,* Vol. 4, No. 2. http://usinfo.state.gov/joumals/itsv/0699/ijse/toc.htm.

Garey, A. I., & Arendell, T. (2001). Children, work, and family: Some thoughts on "mother-blame." In R. Hertz & N. L. Marshall (Eds.), *Working families:*

The transformation of the American home (pp. 293–303). Berkeley: University of California Press.

Gerson, K., & Jacobs, J. A. (2001). Changing the structure and culture of work: Work and family conflict, work flexibility, and gender equity in the modem workplace. In R. Hertz & N. L. Marshall (Eds.), *Working families: The transformation of the American home* (pp. 207–226). Berkeley: University of California Press.

Gray, J. (1992). *Men are from Mars, women are from Venus: A practical guide for improving communication and getting what you want in your relationships.* New York: HarperCollins.

Kessler, R. C., Mickelson, K. D., & Williams, D. R. (1999). The prevalence, distribution, and mental health correlates of perceived discrimination in the United States. *Journal of Health and Social Behavior, 40,* 208–230.

Kohn, M. L. (1969). *Class and conformity: A study in values.* Homewood, IL: Dorsey.

Kohn, M. L., & Schooler, C. (1982). Job conditions and personality: A longitudinal assessment of their reciprocal effects. *American Journal of Sociology, 87,* 1257–1284.

Kohn, M. L., & Schooler, C. (1983). Work and personality: An inquiry into the impact of social stratification. Norwood, NJ: Ablex.

Lareau, A. (2003). Unequal childhoods: Class, race, and family life. Berkeley: University of California Press.

Logan, J. L. (2001a). From many shores: Asians in Census 2000. Lewis Mumford Center for Comparative Urban and Regional Research. http://mumfordl.dyndns.org/cen2000/AsianPop/Asian-Report/AsianDownload.pdf.

Logan, J. L. (2001b). The new Latinos: Who they are, where they are. University at Albany: Lewis Mumford Center for Comparative Urban and Regional Research. http://www.hccwpa.org/Census_and_Data/HCC_New_Latino2.htm.

Logan, J. L., & Deane, G. (2003). Black diversity in metropolitan America. University at Albany: Lewis Mumford Center for Comparative Urban and Regional Research. http://mumfordl.dyndns.org/cen2000/BlackWhite/BlackDiversityReport/black-diversityO 1.htm.

Louie, Miriam Ching Yoon. (2001). *Sweatshop warriors: Immigrant women workers take on the global factory.* Cambridge, MA: South End Press.

Marks, S. R. (2000). Teasing out the lessons of the 1960s: Family diversity and family privilege. *Journal of Marriage and the Family, 62,* 609–622.

Marks, S. R., & Leslie, L. A. (2000). Family diversity and intersecting categories: Toward a richer approach to multiple roles. In D. H. Demo, K. R. Allen, & M. A. Fine (Eds.), *Handbook of family diversity* (pp. 402–423). New York: Oxford University Press.

Matthews, T. J., & Hamilton, B. E. (2002). Mean age of mother, 1970–2000. National Vital Statistics Reports, V. 51 no. 1. Hyattsville, MD: National Center for Health Statistics, 2002.

Mossakowski, K. N. (2003). Coping with perceived discrimination: Does ethnic identity protect mental health? *Journal of Health and Social Behavior, 44,* 318–331.

Multinational Monitor. (2001). Migrating from exploitation to dignity: Immigrant women workers and the struggle for justice. Volume 22, Number 10, retrieved September 16, 2004. http://multinationalmonitor.org/mm2001/01october/octO 1 interviewlouie.html.

National Center on Caregiving. (2003). Women and caregiving: Facts and figures, http://www.caregiver.org/caregiver/jsp/content_node.jsp?nodeid=892.

National Immigration Law Center. (July 2004). Facts about immigrants, http://www.nilc.org/immspbs/research/pbimmfacts_0704.pdf.

Noh, S., Beiser, M., Kaspar, V., Hou, F., & Rummens, J. (1999). Perceived racial discrimination, depression, and coping: A study of Southeast Asian refugees in Canada. *Journal of Health and Social Behavior, 40,* 193–207.

O'Connell, M. (2001). Labor force participation for mothers with infants declines for first time, Census Bureau reports. www.census.gov/Press-Release/www/releases/archives/fertility/000329.html.

Oswald, R. F., Blume, L. B., & Marks, S. R. (2005). Decentering heteronormativity: A model for family studies. In V. L. Bengston, A. C. Acock, K. R. Allen, P. Dilworth Anderson, & D. M. Klein (Eds.), *Sourcebook of family theory and research* (pp. 143–154). Thousand Oaks, CA: Sage Publications.

Parcel, T. L., & Menaghan, E. G. (1994). *Parents' jobs and children s lives.* New York: DeGruyter.

Parsons, T. (1964). *Social structure and personality.* New York: Macmillan.

Risman, B. (1998). *Gender vertigo.* New Haven: Yale University Press.

Rosser, M. (2000). Charlotte. In N. Howey & E. Samuels (Eds.), *Out of the ordinary: Essays on growing up with gay, lesbian, and transgender parents* (pp. 151–162). New York: St. Martin's Press.

Schmidley, D. (2003). *The foreign-born population in the United States: March, 2002.* Current Population Reports P20–539, U.S. Census Bureau, Washington, DC. http://www.census.gov/prod/2003pubs/p20–539.pdf.

Schulz, A., Williams, D., Israel, B., Becker, A., Parker, E., James, S. A., & Jackson, J. (2000). Unfair treatment, neighborhood effects, and mental health in the Detroit metropolitan area. *Journal of Health ancl Social Behavior, 41,* 314–332.

Schwartz, P. (1994). *Peer marriage: How love between equals really works.* New York: Free Press.

Sellers, R. M., Caldwell, C. H., Schmeelk-Cone, K. H., & Zimmerman, M. A. (2003). Racial identity, racial discrimination, perceived stress, and psychological distress among African American young adults. *Journal of Health and Social Behavior, 43,* 302–317.

Smith, D. (1993). The standard North American family: SNAF as an ideological code. *Journal of Family Issues, 14,* 50–65.

Swams, R. L. (retrieved August 29, 2004). "African-American" becomes a term for debate. *New York Times.*

Sweatshop Watch, (retrieved September 16, 2004). The garment industry. Oakland, CA. http://swatch.igc.org/swatch/industry/.

Turner, R. J. (2003). The pursuit of socially modifiable contingencies in mental health. *Journal of Health and Social Behavior, 44,* 1–17.

Turner, R. J., & Avison, W. R. (2003). Status variations in stress exposure: Implications for the interpretation of research on race, socioeconomic status, and gender. *Journal of Health and Social Behavior, 44,* 488–505.

U.S. Census Bureau. (2000). *Population projections of the United States by age, sex, race, Hispanic origin, and nativity: 1999 to 2100.* Population Projections Program, Population Division, Washington, DC.

U.S. Census Bureau. (June 12, 2003). Children's living arrangements and characteristics: March 2002. Population Division, Fertility & Family Statistics Branch. www.census.gov/population/socdemo/hh-fam/cps2002/tabC4-all.pdf.

U.S. Census Bureau. (2004). U.S. interim projections by age, sex, race, and Hispanic origin, www.census.gov/ipc/www/usinterimproj/.

Votruba-Drzal, E. (2003). Income changes and cognitive stimulation in young children's home learning environments. *Journal of Marriage and Family, 65,* 341–355.

Walker, A. J., & Allen, K. R. (1991). Relationships between caregiving daughters and their elderly mothers. *The Gerontologist, 31,* 389–396.

Wheeler-Nicholson, I. (2000). Smile and say nothing. In N. Howey & E. Samuels (Eds.), Out *of the ordinary: Essays on growing up with gay, lesbian, and transgender parents* (pp. 103–112). New York: St. Martin's Press.

Whitbeck, L. B., McMorris, B. J., Hoyt, D. R., Stubben, J. D., & LaFromboise, T. (2002). Perceived discrimination, traditional practices, and depressive symptoms among American Indians in the upper Midwest. *Journal of Health and Social Behavior, 43,* 400–418.

6 | Chapter Review

1. How could gender be perceived as a social construct? What changes have we seen over time or over cultural divides that might point to the socially constructed nature of masculinity and femininity?
2. According to various social science theories, sexuality may be considered a fluid process, with different potential options over the course of a lifetime. Using the article provided, how could sexual identity be considered, while a biological process, also a social process?
3. What are some of the most significant changes occurring within the institution of family? How has this influenced, or can this influence, social definitions and understandings of this institution over time?

CASE STUDY: THE CHANGING DEFINITION OF FAMILY AND CHANGING ROLES AND RELATIONSHIPS WITHIN FAMILIES

In 2012, the Russell Sage Foundation released the findings of a study (conducted since 2006) that asked a rather large sampling frame in the United States about how each individual understood and defined the term "family." "Overall, the authors found that definitions of the family in the U.S. were becoming more inclusive. Presumably, this trend has continued and even accelerated since the 2006 survey, given how attitudes have shifted on a number of issues involving gay and lesbian rights in the past few years" (Sharp, 2012). Presumably this trend toward inclusiveness has also likely increased since 2012, particularly given the Supreme Court overturn of the Defense of Marriage Act (DOMA) in 2013 and the 2015 Supreme Court ruling identifying the constitutional right of gay and lesbians to marry. A summary of the study can be found at:

https://thesocietypages.org/socimages/2012/12/26/how-do-we-define-a-family/

Read about some of the role and responsibility changes occurring within modern nuclear families in the U.S. at:

https://www.americanprogress.org/issues/women/reports/2009/10/16/6789/the-shriver-report

Based upon the articles in this chapter and at the links above, what is influencing changes in how society may view or define the institution of family and what roles and responsibilities are assigned to members of families?

DEVELOPING THE SOCIOLOGICAL IMAGINATION
International Attitudes Toward Changing Gender Roles

For this exercise, you will be asked to explore international attitudes toward changing gender roles and roles within families utilizing the international social survey available at:

https://dbk.gesis.org/dbksearch/sdesc2.asp?no=2620&db=e&doi=10.4232/1.2620

You will first be asked to create a login. Once you have done so go to the "Data" tab and download the specific set of gender data available and described at the link above. Download the dataset in the format that is most conducive to your operating system. For those on university campuses, this would likely be SPSS (.sav) datasets. For those in need of tutorials on how to use SPSS, there are various available online and step-by-step videos on how to use the SPSS system on YouTube. Once you have downloaded the dataset within your preferred system, explore two countries and their attitudes towards three specific questions asked within this dataset. You may choose the questions that you explore. What are the differences in attitudes between these two countries? What social factors may be contributing to these differences in attitudes?

UNIT 3

Social Change & Applying Sociology

7 | Demography and Social Change

CHAPTER SUMMARY

- This chapter introduces readers to the study of population, globalization, and urbanization.

- This chapter also introduces readers to the components involved with social change.

- The institution of religion is utilized as an example of how institutions may respond to otherwise promote or resist social changes.

PRELIMINARY QUESTIONS FOR READERS

- What is the historical significance of studying population and urbanization for sociologists?

- What do you believe are the components necessary for social change?

- How might religion as an institution be a force or resistance to changes in a society?

CHAPTER INTRODUCTION
Demography and Types of Demographic Data

Demography is the study of a population's characteristics, including the study of a society's diversity, birth rates, death rates, and migration trends. The first article in this chapter explores the process of studying population and urbanization. Demographers throughout history have focused on at least three specific variables that measure the growth and composition of a society. However, demographers have looked at additional population characteristics data as well (marriage rates, urbanization, gender, race, and class statistics, for example). These three specific variables include (1) **Birth rates**: specifically the number of babies born each year for every 1,000 members of the population. This term reflects the fertility of a population which is live births per number of women in the population; (2) **Death Rates:** specifically the number of deaths each year per 1,000 people or the number of deaths divided by the population; and (3) **Migration:** the number of individuals coming in or leaving a country. These population characteristics can often provide a great deal of insight into the needs or changing elements of a society.

As discussed briefly in the first article, many demographers refer to "population pyramids" to look at the size and composition of a society at any given time. Not only can demographers refer to current population pyramid graphs, but they can also look at projected population pyramids that can predict population growth and composition. The most typical population pyramids consist of the number of males per 100 females, or the number of males divided by the number of females multiplied by 100 (sex-ratio pyramids) and those that represent the age and gender structure of society (age-sex pyramids). Countries with a high birth rate tend to have a high proportion of women in their childbearing years. This chapter's data exercises give readers the opportunity to explore and analyze population pyramids.

SOCIAL CHANGE

According to Anderson and Taylor (2007), as societies grow, they also change, and they generally become more modern. **Modernization,** according to Anderson and Taylor (2007), is the process of social and cultural change, often initiated by industrialization, that can be followed by increased social differentiation among other potential outcomes. **Social change** is the modification of social elements over time (such as social institutions, methods of social interaction, stratification systems, and a society's popular culture). The following have been noted as some of the major causes of social change around the world (Anderson & Taylor, 2007):

- **Political Revolution** is the overthrow of a state, government, or the total transformation of social institutions (for example, a political coup).
- **Cultural diffusion** is the transmission of cultural elements from one society or cultural group to another.
- **Inequality**, such as wealth or resource distribution, can encourage advocacy and social movements.

- **Technological Innovation**. For example, the emergence of the Internet impacted how we relate to one another, made work across the globe much faster and easier, and created networks for individuals to share thoughts and mobilize for change.
- **Demographic Changes**, such as population and correlated cultural changes, can occur as a result of increased diversity.
- **War and Terrorism**.
- **Social movements**. Social movements are led by groups that come together to promote or resist social change.

Although collective behavior can appear to be spontaneous (i.e., fashion trends), it typically communicates changes and debates that are happening with social institutions or social structures.

Globalization has relied upon modernization and the conditions available in urban spaces to thrive (such as a center of commerce). The second article in this chapter explores how globalization (defined in Chapter 5) has impacted social changes in gender relationships and the institution of work around the world.

WORKS CITED

Andersen, M. L., and Taylor, H. F. (2007). *Sociology: The essentials*. 4th Edition. Belmont, CA: Thompson Wadsworth Press.

Demography and World Population Growth

by David D. Kemp

POPULATION ECOLOGY

A population is a group of individuals, usually of the same species, occupying a specific area. In the case of the human species the area involved is effectively the entire earth, but human population distribution is uneven. Although humans have developed a remarkable ability to adapt to different environmental conditions and to manipulate environments to meet their ends, some regions remain largely unpopulated. Empty spaces such as those in the Arctic and Antarctic, the deserts of Africa and Asia and the mountainous regions of all the continents, for example, are not unaffected by human activities, but in population numbers they contrast sharply with adjacent more populous regions.

Carrying Capacity

In these parts of the earth thinly populated by humans, the population of other species tends to be low also, reflecting the limited resources available to support life. In ecological terms, the carrying capacity of these areas is low. This

concept, linking population numbers with the availability of natural resources, originated in ecology, but it is now considered too simplistic for many ecological situations. It continues to be used in conservation ecology and ecological economics, however, and in consideration of relationships between society and the environment (Turner II and Keys 2002). Carrying capacity is a measure of the maximum number of organisms that can be supported in a particular environment, and under natural conditions it represents a theoretical equilibrium state within a dynamic system. If the species in an area are below carrying capacity, for example, populations will tend to increase until some form of balance is reached with the resources available. If the carrying capacity is exceeded, because of the rapid growth in the number of organisms in the ecosystem, for example, there will be insufficient resources to support the excess population, and numbers will decline until equilibrium between the resource base and the population is re-established. Typically, the population fluctuates above

FIGURE 7.1 The relationship between population growth and the carrying capacity of the environment

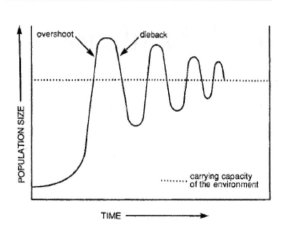

and below the level of the carrying capacity before it eventually approaches equilibrium again (Figure 7.1). If provided with an adequate supply of food, animal populations will increase rapidly. If the food supply is then restricted, or if the demand for food exceeds the capacity of the environment to provide it, the population will decline rapidly again. Such cycles are not uncommon in animal communities. Laboratory and field studies have shown that population growth follows a specific pattern in most cases. Growth may start off slowly, but quickly becomes exponential. This period of rapid growth will continue as long as the population is allowed to develop in an optimal environment with unlimited resources. If environmental restrictions are introduced, the exponential growth will be brought to an end. In laboratory experiments, restrictions may include the reduction in the area available for expansion or a reduction in the amount of food available. Such restrictions may also be seen in real life, where, for example, expansion is restricted by natural features in the landscape, or where drought, floods or other natural disasters diminish the food supply. The

resulting increase in the death rate may be augmented by outbreaks of disease caused by malnourishment and overcrowding, while growing dissension within the population, as competition for scarce resources grows, may also lead to increased mortality. As these dynamics are resolved, the population will eventually stabilize, indicating that the carrying capacity of the environment has been reached and population and environmental resources are again in balance.

The carrying capacity of a specific environment is not static. It will vary with the resources available. In areas with marked seasons, for example, the carrying capacity will vary between summer and winter, being much lower in the winter when food resources are not readily available. This does not mean that all individuals in excess of the winter carrying capacity will die off. In most cases they will migrate to areas where there is sufficient food to support them. The mass migration of birds from northern Europe to Africa and subarctic North America to Central and South America is an annual response to reduced carrying capacity during the northern winter. Variations in carrying capacity also occur as the result of longer-term environmental change. In the past this was usually associated with natural physical change in the environment—variations in climate, for example—but more recently, human interference has become a major contributor to change. Natural resource extraction, habitat changes associated with forestry or agriculture and the growth of urbanization all reduce the carrying capacity of the environment for nonhuman species. In contrast, agricultural activities or waste disposal in a particular environment can increase the food supply and raise the carrying capacity for insect species or small mammals such as mice and rats, causing their populations to increase.

The utility of the carrying capacity concept in ecological studies has been questioned, particularly for environments that are not in equilibrium (Middleton 1999), and it receives less attention in ecology than it once did. In contrast, it has contributed significantly to studies of society–environment relationships at various times in the second half of the twentieth century and even before that in the eighteenth century, through the ideas of Thomas Malthus, which linked food supply and population growth (see Box 4.4, Thomas Malthus). The Club of Rome report, called *Limits to Growth*, published in the early 1970s (Meadows *et al.* 1972), was essentially an exercise in relating population growth to carrying capacity, through such elements as resource use, industrial output, food supply and pollution. More recently, the success of sustainable development as a means of providing, among other things, a more equitable distribution of resources requires that economic growth and technological development bring about increases in carrying capacity as they have done in the past.

By transferring resources from one region to another, or by applying technology to increase resource availability, humans have artificially increased the carrying capacity of many areas, to the extent that in some of the more populous parts of the world the human population easily exceeds the natural carrying capacity of the land. Effective as such developments may be, any restriction in the supply of these resources, or a rapid increase in population beyond the availability of additional resources, would set in train the processes that naturally bring population into line with the carrying capacity of the environment. Regular bouts of famine in sub-Saharan Africa

associated with drought have indicated the reality of that situation over the past several decades. Although the concept of carrying capacity is usually applied at the ecosystem or regional level, there is also a theoretical carrying capacity for the earth as a whole, applied to the maximum human population that it may support. A realistic value is probably impossible to estimate, since factors other than resource availability—acceptable quality of life, for example—will help to decide what the final carrying capacity will be.

The concept of carrying capacity is applied in a number of socio-economic contexts. In agriculture, for example, the carrying capacity of an area will determine the number of grazing animals it will support, or, when applied to recreational land use, it represents the number of people and types of activity that can be accommodated without environmental disruption. Human interference frequently causes the carrying capacity of an area to be exceeded. Introducing extra grazing animals on rangeland or allowing too many people to use a recreational area will eventually lead to the deterioration of the environment.

The complexity of the relationship between resources and populations, particularly human populations, ensures that issues associated with the concept of carrying capacity will be subject to much debate. On the one hand, the earth is a closed material system, its resources are ultimately finite, and it would seem reasonable to suggest that somewhere in the future there will be an upper limit to the numbers they can support. On the other, human ingenuity has done much to extend and improve resource availability and continues to do so with considerable success (see Chapter 5). The extent to which this ongoing increase in the earth's carrying capacity can continue or whether there is an ultimate limit to population are questions that cannot yet be answered, however, but finding the answers will require further consideration of the nature, causes and effects of population change.

R-Strategists And K-Strategists

Organisms such as insects and small mammals can respond rapidly to conditions that favour them, because of their reproductive strategy. They are called R-strategists, characterized by small size and relatively short life spans during which they mature quickly to produce large numbers of offspring. They do little to support these offspring, but depend upon quantity rather than quality for the survival of the species. Numbers fluctuate wildly. Efficient reproduction allows the population to grow rapidly as long as the conditions are favourable. If these conditions change—food supply is curtailed, for example—the population will crash and remain low until conditions improve again.

In contrast, humans belong to a group of organisms that have a completely different reproductive strategy. These are the so-called K-strategists, organisms that are usually large, have relatively long lives and produce only a limited number of offspring. They invest considerable time and energy providing for the survival of these offspring, so that they in turn can reproduce and ensure the continuation of the species. Along with humans and other primates, larger mammals such as deer, lions, bears and elephants are all K-strategists. They do not respond to change as rapidly as r-strategists, but neither do their numbers rise and fall as wildly. Because of their time commitment to their offspring, they survive best under stable environmental conditions.

Although the human species cannot compete in terms of total numbers and reproductive capacity with organisms such as bacteria or insects, whose body size is small and whose reproductive cycles are short, humans are the most numerous of all the mammals. Only the rat comes close to matching human population totals. Among the higher primates—gibbons, chimpanzees, orangutans and gorillas—the human position is even more supreme, its numbers exceeding the sum total of all other species of primates.

THE EARTH'S HUMAN POPULATION

Spectacular as that situation may appear, the end result would be even more so if human beings reproduced at full capacity. With a gestation period (the length of time between conception and birth) of nine months and a reproductive span of about thirty years, it is technically possible for a woman to give birth to about thirty children. This is a measure of the fecundity, or maximum productive capacity, of a population. Given the time required for physical recovery and for nursing the child, such a high number is unlikely to be achieved, although totals in the high teens and low twenties have been recorded. It has been estimated that, under ideal living conditions, the maximum number of births that might be expected is between fifteen and seventeen (Molnar and Molnar 2000). Fortunately, the number of children actually born to a couple is generally far less than that.

Fertility

The actual number of live births is a measure of the fertility of a population. This can be expressed in a number of ways (Table 7.1). The general fertility rate (GFR) is a measure of

TABLE 7.1 REPRESENTATION OF FERTILITY AND MORTALITY IN A POPULATION

Crude birth rate (CBR) Annual number of live births per thousand persons in a population

Crude death rate (CDR) Annual number of deaths per thousand persons **in a population**

Rate of natural increase (RNI) The difference between the CBR and CDR, usually expressed as a percentage

General fertility rate (GFR) The total number of births per thousand women within an age range of fifteen to forty-nine in a population

Age-specific fertility rate (ASFR) The total number of births per thousand women measured at five-year intervals within the age range of fifteen to forty-nine

Total fertility rate (TFR) An estimate of the average number of children born to a woman during her lifetime

Replacement fertility rate (RFR) A TFR of 2.1

the total number of births per thousand women within the age range of fifteen to forty-nine. Within that age range, an age-specific fertility rate (ASFR) can be calculated using five-year intervals. Typically, highest fertility occurs in the twenty to twenty-nine age group. One commonly used expression of fertility is the total fertility rate (TFR), which is an estimate of the average number of children that would be born to each woman in a population during her childbearing years, based on birth rates among all women in the same age group in the population (Hornby and Jones 1993). In the early 1990s, for example, the TFR ranged from 6.0 in Asia to 1.7 in Europe, with a worldwide average of 3.2. By 1998 the world TFR had fallen to 2.9 and according to UN Population Division estimates, between 2000 and 2005 the TFR will range from 4.91 in Africa to 1.38 in Europe, with a world average of 2.69 (UNPD 2002). A TFR of 2.1 is called the replacement fertility rate, since it represents the number of children required to replace the parents. The extra 0.1 is required to allow for children who die in

infancy and therefore produce no offspring. All these numbers are well below the maximum productive capacity or fecundity of a population, and that was so even when the earth's human population was growing much more rapidly than it is now. Although the earth's human population has grown rapidly over the past two centuries, without the continued difference between fertility and fecundity the rate of change would have been even greater.

Mortality

The birth rate of a population is only one element in population change. It might be considered the input element. At the other end of the system is the death rate or mortality rate. Together, birth rate and death rate allow the natural change in the population to be calculated. If the birth rate is greater the change will be positive and the population will grow. In contrast, a death rate higher than the birth rate will produce a declining population.

Death rates tend to fluctuate more than birth rates, with one bad natural disaster often having spectacular effects. For example, in the fourteenth century, the 'Black Death' in Europe left some 20 million dead and another attack in the seventeenth century had a death toll of 10 million. In England, between 35 per cent and 40 per cent of the population died when the Black Death struck in 1348 and 1349, and the population continued to decline for a hundred years after that, before beginning to recover in the latter part of the fifteenth century (Hatcher 1996). The HIV/AIDS epidemic killed 2.4 million people in Africa in 2002 and has the potential to cause millions more deaths in the next decade (UNAIDS/WHO 2002) (see Box 7.1, HIV/AIDS). Smaller-scale disasters involving disease, drought, famine, typhoons and hurricanes may have significant effects on

BOX 7.1 **HIV/AIDS**

Acquired immune deficiency syndrome, or AIDS, is an incurable disease caused by the human immunodeficiency virus (HIV). The virus suppresses the immune system, leaving the victim open to a variety of deadly respiratory infections and rare forms of cancer. It is transmitted through sexual activity and intravenous drug use, and in the twenty years since 1981, when it was first recognized, some 27 million people have died as a result of the infection. An estimated 42 million people are living with HIV, but the latency period for the virus is between seven and ten years, during which time there are no outward signs of AIDS. At that stage it can be detected only by blood tests, and many poorer nations lack the resources required for large-scale testing. Thus the numbers probably underestimate the reality of the situation. There is currently no cure for AIDS, and although the symptoms can be treated using an array of drugs, the costs of such treatment are high.

The distribution of those infected by HIV is very uneven (Figure 7.2). More than 85 per cent of the victims are in the developing world, with the nations of sub-Saharan Africa, where some 29.4 million are living with HIV, by far the worst affected. In several countries in southern Africa at least one in five adults is HIV-positive. In South Africa the rate rose to almost 25 per cent in 2000, while in Botswana, where the prevalence rate is 36 per cent, the epidemic appears out of control. Only in Uganda has there been any success in turning the epidemic round. There, a concentrated effort has reduced a rate of 14 per cent in the early 1990s to 8 per cent in 2000.

Elsewhere in the world, the numbers infected by HIV are less, ranging from 15,000 in Australia and New Zealand and about 500,000 in North Africa and the Middle East to 1.9 million in Latin America and the Caribbean, 1.0 million in Eastern Europe and Central Asia and 1.5 million in the other industrialized nations. The region causing most concern outside Africa is Asia. This, the most populous region in the world, has more than 6 million people infected with HIV/AIDS, and the potential for a rapid rise in that number is high, particularly in India, where 3.7 million people are already living with the virus, and in China, where existing rates of infection are low, but are rising steeply.

The demographic impact of such conditions is already apparent in some areas. In southern Africa in the late 1980s, for example, the life expectancy was fifty-eight years. That represented some thirty years of improvement, but it is expected that by 2010 life expectancy will have fallen again to about forty-five years, mainly as a result of the AIDS epidemic. Death rates are rising across the region, and in nations with high levels of HIV/AIDS infection, such as Zimbabwe, Botswana and Namibia, increasing mortality will soon equal or surpass the high fertility rates to create zero population growth. Behind such figures are devastating socio-economic impacts. Hidden are the orphaned children, 12.1 million in southern Africa alone, the decline in family income as breadwinners become too ill to work, and the overall physical and mental strain imposed on women.

The effects spread across society to disrupt and even reverse social and economic development. As more personnel are infected, the work force declines or becomes less efficient, costs rise and productivity is driven down. No sector of the population is spared. Businessmen and educators succumb, as do members of the armed forces or workers in mining, transport and manufacturing industries. The economic effects are already being felt in Africa and parts of Asia and will only become worse. Health costs are rising. Although drugs have been developed to mitigate the effects of the opportunistic infections that strike HIV/AIDS victims, they are costly, which puts them out of reach of those in the developing world who need them. There is no cure for the disease, and the numbers requiring some form of medical care will continue to increase until education and prevention become sufficiently effective that the level of infection is reduced. Despite the ominous trend in the number and rate of infections through the 1980s and 1990s, politicians in some countries denied the existence of a problem, delaying an appropriate response and condemning thousands to infection and premature death. In contrast, countries such as Uganda and Brazil have shown that aggressive intervention, involving both education and prevention, can stabilize or reduce the rate of infection, but that too comes at a cost, a cost that cannot be met by many developing nations without outside aid.

BOX 7.1 **HIV/AIDS** (*Continued*)

The world has faced nothing like the HIV/AIDS epidemic since the influenza epidemic of the early twentieth century or even the Black Death of the fourteenth century. Advances in medical knowledge and expertise should allow this most recent threat to be fought more effectively, but the economic, political and social dynamics of the issue mean that success will be possible only with the increased commitment of money and resources to the problem, put in place and managed through global co-operation. Without that, the world faces a crisis that will lead to the curbing or even reversal of socio-economic development, a growing gap between rich and poor nations and a serious threat of social and political instability.

For More Information See:

Brown, L.R., Gardner, G. and Halweil, B. (1999) *Beyond Malthus*, New York/London: Norton.

UNAIDS (2001) *Together We Can*, Geneva: Joint UN Programme on HIV/AIDS.

WHO (2003) *AIDS Epidemic Update: December 2002*, viewed at http://www.who.int.hiv.pub.epidemiology/epi2002/en/ (accessed 16 June 2003).

FIGURE 7.2 The global distribution and impact of HIV/AIDS

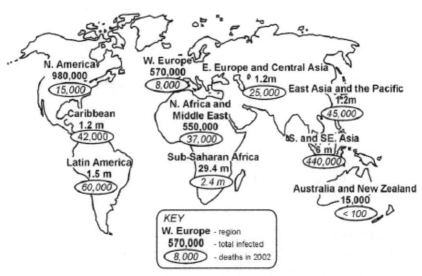

INTERNATIONAL HIV/AIDS SITUATION - 2002

People living with HIV/AIDS - 42 m

New infections 2002 - 5 m

Deaths due to HIV/AIDS 2002 - 3.1 m

Total deaths since outbreak began - 27 m

Source: Unaids/Who, *AIDS Epidemic Update*, Geneva: Joint UN Programme on HIV/AIDS and World Health Organization (2002).

local or regional populations. Famine associated with climate variability in northern Europe in the 1690s brought about the deaths of about 20 per cent of the population of Finland (Jutikkala 1956) and perhaps 10 per cent of the population of Scotland (Anderson 1996a). The infamous Irish potato famine of the mid-nineteenth century brought about the loss of more than 800,000 lives in the five-year period between 1846 and 1851, creating the momentum for an overall reduction in population that has never been replaced (Cousens 1960). More recently, in China between 1958 and 1961 as many as 20 million people died in a famine caused by a combination of drought and government mismanagement of the agricultural system (Jowett 1990), and drought and famine caused the deaths of hundreds of thousands of people in sub-Saharan Africa in the 1960s, 1970s and 1980s.

Although human activity exacerbated some of these natural disasters, humans most commonly contribute to increased death rates through war. The death toll in World War I, for example, was 10 million and in World War II, 50 million (Keegan 2000). Since the latter ended in 1945 there have been some 150 conflicts, in which up to 20 million lives have been lost (Otok 1989). In all wars up to the end of World War I, the main casualties were among the combatants. Since then, civilians have provided a higher proportion of casualties as a result of total guerrilla wars and civil wars that flared up in the second half of the twentieth century. Because of the nature of war, most of the dead are in the young adult male group. In World War I, for example, more than half of the 700,000 casualties in the British armed forces were twenty to twenty-nine-year-old males, and within that group a disproportionately high percentage of those killed

were officers (Winter 1977). The 300,000 fatalities in the French army between August and November 1914 included deaths among the young men in the twenty to thirty age range that were ten times the normal mortality for that group (Keegan 2000). Although these men were in their prime reproductive years and their loss created socio-cultural changes that might have been expected to influence population dynamics—disrupted marriage patterns, for example—the overall impact on total population was ultimately relatively small. Dips in death rate curves and the uneven distribution of males and females in diagrams of the population structure are common for all the major belligerent nations, but the increase in fertility that immediately followed the war more than offset the decline in numbers caused by the deaths. A similar pattern occurred after World War II, creating the so-called 'post-war baby boom' (Figure 7.3).

Natural Increase

Birth rates and death rates are commonly expressed as a rate per thousand rather than in total numbers, allowing for ease of comparison between countries and regions. The number of live births per thousand of the population in a given year is the crude birth rate (CBR) while the number of deaths per thousand of the population in a given year is the crude death rate (CDR). A comparison of the CBR and the CDR provides the rate of natural increase (RNI) in the population, usually expressed as a percentage. Nigeria in 1998, for example, with a CBR of 45 and a CDR of 15 had an RNI of 3 per cent. In comparison, the RNI in the United Kingdom was only 0.2 per cent and in both Russia and Ukraine, where the death rate exceeded the birth rate, the RNI was negative (Figure 7.4). The RNI of a nation or region can

FIGURE 7.3 The effects of war on population structure. The example of Russia

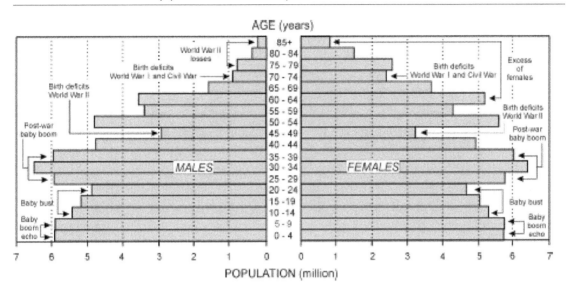

Source: based on data from the US Census Bureau International Data Base. Viewed at http://www.census.gov/ipc/www/idbpyr.html (accessed 2 July 2003).

FIGURE 7.4 The rate of natural increase (RNI) in the population of selected countries

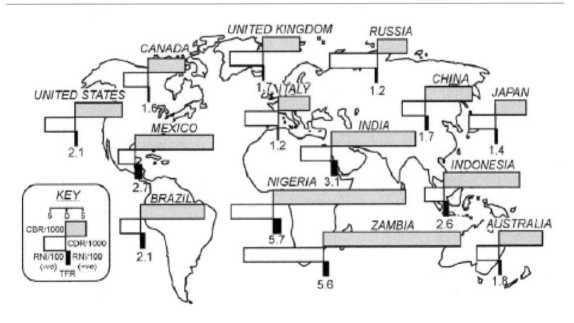

Source: UN Population Division, *World Population Prospects 1950–2050 (The 2000 Revision)*, New York: United Nations (2001).

be used to project the future size of its population in much the same way as an interest rate is used to calculate compound interest for a savings account. Just as the principal, to be included in subsequent calculations, the number of births estimated using the RNI for one year is added to the population base to be included in the calculations in succeeding years. Using that approach, population totals can be projected several years into the future, although longer-term projections are likely to be less accurate because of changes in the RNI with time, and need to be revised regularly. Using the same approach, the RNI can be used to calculate the time needed for a population to double in size. For most purposes, doubling time can be estimated by dividing the number 70 by the RNI of the population. In Nigeria, for example, where the RNI is 3.0 per cent, the population will double in only twenty-three years, whereas in the United Kingdom, with an RNI of 0.2 per cent, doubling time is 350 years. For the world as a whole at the current rate of natural increase, the doubling time is close to fifty years. Useful as such figures are for comparative purposes, they have to be treated with caution, since rates of natural increase can change quite rapidly owing to variations in birth and death rates.

Migration

The relatively simple relationship between births and deaths is modified by a third element in the equation. That element is migration. In terms of world population totals, migration may seem comparatively unimportant, since it only brings about a redistribution of population; it does not change it. On a local and regional scale, however, migration will augment or decrease the rate of natural change. Migrants tend to be young people still within their childbearing years. Thus any children they have are a loss to the population of the country they left and a gain for the country to which they have moved. Traditionally, in modern times, certain regions have been areas of emigration—outflow of population—whereas others have been areas of immigration—inflow of population (Figure 7.5). In the nineteenth and early twentieth centuries, European countries were the main source of emigrants, with 44 million leaving for North America, Australasia and other destinations such as South Africa and South America between 1821 and 1915 (Devine 1999). Although Italy, Germany, Spain and Portugal provided more total immigrants, in terms of emigration *per capita*, Scotland, Ireland and Norway led the way for most of the nineteenth and early twentieth centuries (Devine 1999). Between 1900 and 1910, 15,000 people per year left Finland, mainly for North America, while at the same time emigration from eastern and southern Europe to North America grew and continued strong up to the First World War. Although migration has been a common characteristic of human history, the scale of the migrations of the nineteenth and early twentieth centuries was unparalleled and initiated the worldwide expansion of European culture. Between the wars and in the 1950s emigration from Europe continued at varying rates, but in more recent years the Indian sub-continent, Southeast Asia and the Caribbean have become areas of major out-migration.

The destinations of these millions of migrants varied with time. In the 1840s and in the early twentieth century Canada was popular with emigrants from Britain. In the 1850s, 1860s and 1870s, Australia and New Zealand were seen as attractive destinations,

FIGURE 7.5 Global migration flows in the nineteenth and twentieth centuries

but the major draw for most emigrants from Europe was the United States. For half the emigrants from Scotland between 1853 and 1914, for example, the United States was the preferred destination, reached either directly or via Canada (Devine 1999). At the end of the twentieth century, all these areas remained popular destinations, but the sources of immigrants had changed dramatically. Between 1991 and 2001, for example, over 1.8 million immigrants entered Canada. Of these, less than 50,000 came from Britain. European countries still provided nearly 200,000, but by far the greatest number of immigrants, slightly over 1 million, came from Asia (Statistics Canada 2003). For Australia, well into the second half of the twentieth century, Europe, particularly Britain and Ireland, remained the main source

of immigrants, but by the late 1980s, Asia was providing more immigrants than Europe (Hugo 2001). Similar changes took place in the United States, where, in 1890, 86 per cent of the immigrants were from Europe. Little more than a century later, in 2000, only 14 per cent of the immigrants were from Europe, with 32 per cent from Asia and by far the largest number, 47 per cent, from Latin America, with Mexico at 23 per cent the main source in that region (MPI 2003).

Migration from Europe continues, but some of the countries that were the main sources of emigration in the nineteenth and early twentieth centuries are now experiencing immigration from the developing world. Britain, for example, became the destination of choice for many emigrants from former colonies in the Indian subcontinent, West Indies and Africa, while France experienced a steady flow of immigrants from its former territories in northern, western and central Africa. According to the UN Population Division (2001), that pattern is likely to continue and perhaps accelerate in the near future, as the populations of the nations in Europe, plus Japan and the Republic of Korea, begin to decline. All have below-replacement fertility, which unchanged would bring about significant declines in population over the next fifty years. In Italy, the population of 57 million in 2000 would decline to 41 million by the middle of the century and in Japan it would fall from 127 to 105 million in the same time period. Compounding these declines is an increase in the age of the population. With fewer births and an increase in longevity, the proportion of older people in a population increases; the size of the working-age population declines and the imbalance in the age distribution of the population creates significant socio-economic stress. It is this imbalance, rather than the decline in total numbers, that is problematic. In all these nations, society has developed in such a way that older members of the population are supported by the activities of the working-age group. As the numbers in that group decline and the post-retirement population grows, maintaining an adequate level of support may no longer be possible. In the absence of any major increase in fertility, the UN Population Division has suggested that replacement migration could provide a solution to the problems of declining and aging populations. The numbers involved would be large. For the members of the European Union, for example, migration at a rate of 13 million per year from 2000 to 2050 would be required to maintain the current size of the working-age population. Such numbers are well beyond past experience and would require the reconsideration of existing criteria for international immigration. Even in countries such as the United States, Canada and Australia, which have traditionally been the destinations for most of the world's migrants, the total fertility rates are close to or below replacement values, and the role of replacement migration needs to be considered in setting future population policies in these areas also. Thus, although the difference between birth rates and death rates will continue to determine the total world population, migration will have an increasingly important part to play in establishing the local, regional and national structure and nature of that population.

Zero Population Growth

The change in a population is determined by the interplay of these three elements—birth rate, death rate and migration. The population of a country will grow if, over a period of time, the number of births plus the number of immigrants exceeds the number of deaths plus the number of emigrants. If deaths plus emigrants exceed births plus immigrants, then the population will decline. If both are equal, zero population growth (ZPG) is said to exist. ZPG is sometimes confused with replacement reproduction, in which each family consists of only sufficient children to replace the parents. If adhered to, that situation would eventually produce ZPG, but it would not be immediate because of the time lag involved as age groups move through the system. As long as the numbers entering the reproductive sector of the population exceed those leaving it, the population will continue to grow, even with a birth rate at the replacement level (see Box 7.2, Population structure). To reach ZPG more

BOX 7.2 **POPULATION STRUCTURE**

Raw population totals tell nothing about the structure of the group of individuals that they represent. They provide no information on the age and gender of the group, or the proportion of males and females, children and adults that it contains, yet these elements have an important influence on the current and future socio-economic impacts of the population. To illustrate and investigate these aspects of population structure, demographers have devised the population pyramid or age–sex diagram. A pyramid represents the male and female members of the population in five-year age groupings or cohorts arranged along either side of a central vertical axis. The horizontal axis indicates the percentage of males or females in each cohort. Since the numbers in any population tend to decline with age, the diagram takes on the appearance of a pyramid (Figure 7.6). The exact shape of the pyramid shows the historical development of the population structure, and indicates the potential for future change.

Those countries currently experiencing rapid population growth, such as the developing nations of Africa, have a population pyramid with a wide base and a narrow apex, indicating a high proportion of individuals in the younger age groups. Perhaps as much as 35 per cent of the population will be under fifteen years old, foreshadowing continued growth as they move into the reproductive sector (fifteen to forty-nine years). If no action is taken, fertility increases and the base of the pyramid widens further. Reduced infant mortality also helps to maintain the broad base. The introduction of family planning programmes in some of these nations has begun to reduce the percentage of children in the youngest cohorts, but as long as the number of people entering the reproductive sector exceeds those leaving it, the population will continue to increase.

The developed nations had similar population structures as recently as the beginning of the twentieth century, but since then significant changes have taken place and their population pyramids differ considerably from those of the developing nations. As a result of the combination of reduced fertility and reduced mortality, the base of the pyramid in a developed nation is narrower—on average, only 19 per cent of the population is less than fifteen years old—and the upper section is wider, giving the pyramid a shape that is columnar rather than triangular. Within this general shape there are variations associated with such events as war, migration, the 'baby boom' and a variety of socio-economic events, which impacted on different nations in different ways (Figure 4.2). Developed nations such the United States, Canada and Australia continue to grow slowly because of immigration, but many of the nations in Europe are experiencing either zero growth or are declining. In their pyramids, this is evident from the very narrow bases, the slowing of the flow through the reproductive sector and the increasing numbers in the post-reproductive sector.

An important element in population growth, reflected in population pyramids, is the time lag involved. Any change at the base of the pyramid will be felt over a considerable period of time as the individuals in that age group progress through the system. The 'baby boom' generation born between 1946 and 1964, for example, forms an obvious bulge in the pyramids of most developed nations. Despite the reduced fertility of that group, it produced a 'baby boom echo' as it moved through the productive sector because of its sheer size. As it continues through into the post-reproductive sector the number of births will decline, narrowing the base of the pyramid, while the increase in the upper age groups will create a pyramid that appears top-heavy.

All these changes have socio-economic impacts and although the time lag involved allows the impact to be predicted, it also means that any significant change at a specific level in the pyramid can ripple through the system for many years.

For more information see:

Miller, G.T. (2000) *Sustaining the Earth* (4th edn), Pacific Grove CA: Brooks Cole.

Molnar, S. and Molnar, I.M. (2000) *Environmental Change and Human Survival*, Upper Saddle River NJ: Prentice Hall.

FIGURE 7.6 Population pyramids characteristics of specific stages in the demographic transition

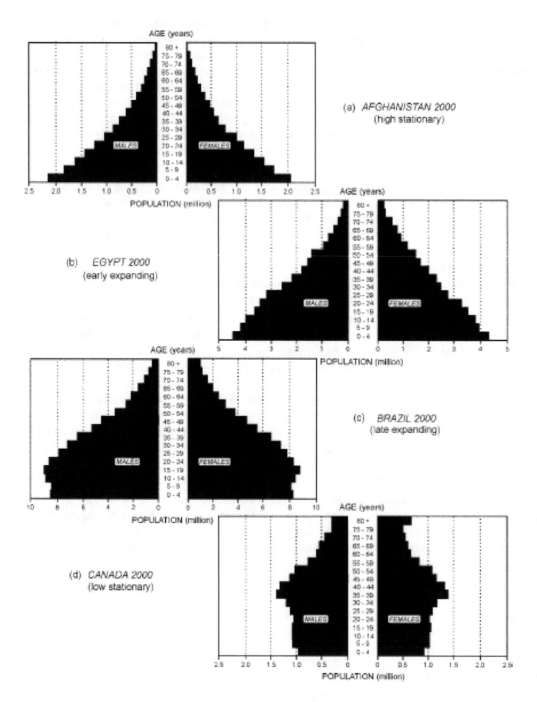

Source: based on data from the US Census Bureau International Data Base. Viewed at http://www.census.gov/ipcs/www/idbpyr.html (accessed 2 July 2003).

rapidly, the reproduction rate would have to be reduced significantly below the 2.1 children per family normally considered to be the replacement reproduction rate. Despite this, there are nations in the developed world that have already reached or even surpassed the conditions associated with ZPG.

STAGES OF WORLD POPULATION GROWTH

The pattern of world population growth is complex, but it has not been haphazard. It can be represented by a general model, which compares birth rate, death rate and the resulting population change. The model suggests that world population has gone through a series of sequential stages delineated as follows: (1) high stationary, (2) early expanding, (3) late expanding, (4) low stationary, (5) declining (Figure 7.7). This model of population dynamics, referred to as the 'demographic transition', was based on the European experience of population change during and following the industrial revolution (Molnar and Molnar

2000). Originally derived from the relationship between population and economic change, the different stages have been recognized in other areas where the European pattern of development has been introduced. Differences in timing within and between regions have to be considered, and the factors that have brought about progress through the various stages of the transition also vary with time and place. Although nineteenth-century technology in Europe and twentieth-century technology applied in the developing world were quite different, for example, both brought about the decline in mortality characteristic of the second stage of the transition. As with all models, the demographic transition model is a simplified representation of a complex phenomenon, but despite its origins it is sufficiently flexible that it can be used to chart stages in worldwide population growth. In addition, passage through each of these stages is associated with socio-economic and (sometimes) cultural change and with the evolution of the relationship between society and environment.

FIGURE 7.7 The demographic transition model

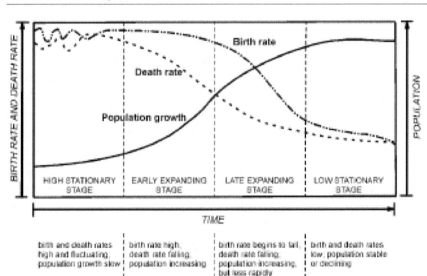

HIGH STATIONARY STAGE

For most of the human existence on earth, the entire world must have been in this phase. High birth rates of as much as 30–40 per thousand per year were countered by similarly high death rates, total population therefore remained low and growth was close to zero. Populations lived at or near subsistence levels, with numbers fluctuating significantly in the short term, much as animal populations fluctuate, and for many of the same reasons. The tendency to population growth in good times was offset by frequent natural events such as famines, epidemics, floods, droughts and climate fluctuations, which, given its low level of technology, society had no means of mitigating. The fossil records from prehistoric times and even early documentary material suggest that, during the high stationary phase, the length of an average generation was very short, with only the rare individual surviving to pass through a full reproductive cycle into old age. Despite this, over the longer term, fertility was sufficiently high to compensate for the high mortality rates and allow the human species to survive.

Few, if any, countries remain in this high stationary phase in the modern world, mainly because of the worldwide spread of technology, which has helped to reduce the death rate and allowed the birth rate to remain high. Countries such as Afghanistan, with a crude birth rate of 49 per thousand and a crude death rate of 22 per thousand between 1990 and 1995 (UNPD 2001), are not long out of this phase, and any increase in the death rate would push them back into it. The rising death rate associated with the HIV/AIDS epidemic in some African countries may have the same effect there (see Box 4.1, HIV/AIDS). However, most developing countries have moved well

into the next phase of the model over the past several decades.

Early Expanding Stage

This period is characterized by a continuation of high fertility (perhaps even increasing fertility), but with a lowering of the previously high mortality rates. Birth rates of 40+ per thousand per year, combined with death rates of 20–5 per thousand per year are quite typical, and the difference between these figures produces large net increases in population. The maximum rate reached when this phase was well established in Britain, for example, was 1.6 per cent per annum (Hornby and Jones 1993). Such a situation may well have existed in the original agricultural hearths such as Egypt and Mesopotamia, following the discovery of agriculture. These areas were small, however, and their overall effect on world population was limited. The pattern was first identified much later in Europe, where nations gradually moved into the early expanding phase some time in the mid to late eighteenth century, with progress in agriculture providing the initial impetus. The increase in the quantity and quality of the food supply, made possible by the new agricultural techniques introduced at that time, improved nutrition at all levels of society. People were healthier, longevity increased and infant mortality declined significantly. At about the same time the first effects of the industrial revolution were being felt. Although the conditions associated with the establishment of the world's first urban/industrial society were often more likely to increase mortality than to reduce it, ultimately better sanitation, improved housing and an increase in medical knowledge contributed to a decline in death rates, which, coupled with continuing high birth rates, produced the population increase associated with the early expanding phase. Such generalizations hide local and regional variations. In Britain, for example, there was a distinct increase in fertility at the beginning of this stage. This may also have been due to the improvement in the general health of the population, but some researchers have identified more frequent and earlier marriage, associated with economic growth, as responsible for the increase (Hornby and Jones 1993). In France, both birth rate and death rate declined, and in Germany both remained high. Despite these differences, however, entry into this phase of the demographic transition increased the population of Western Europe from 60–4 million in 1750 to almost 116 million in 1850 (Anderson 1996a).

An examination of crude birth rates and death rates shows that there are a number of nations in Africa and Asia that currently fit the characteristics of the early expanding phase. Ethiopia, for example, has a crude birth rate of 46 and a crude death rate of 21 and in Nigeria the equivalent values are 45 and 15. Pakistan, with birth and death rates of 39 and 11 respectively, and Kenya, with 33 and 13, appear to have recently passed through the early expanding phase. Although the patterns are similar, the causes of expansion in the twentieth century were different from those in Europe in the eighteenth and nineteenth centuries. Improvements in agriculture helped to reduce the death rate but it was little influenced by industrial development, and the major contribution to declining mortality was often from health improvements introduced from the developed nations. Another difference from the European experience was the total population involved. In the eighteenth century European populations were small as the demographic transition began and the

rate of natural increase never exceeded 2 per cent. In Asia, Africa and parts of Latin America, many of the nations already had large populations when they entered the early expanding phase. Combined with rates of natural increase that regularly exceeded 3 per cent, this produced significant additions to their populations.

Late Expanding Stage

Birth rates decline in this phase, but death rates decline even more and a net population increase continues to be registered. Birth rates range typically from 30 to 35 per thousand per year, with death rates less than 20 and often lower than 15 per thousand per year. Britain moved into this phase towards the end of the nineteenth century and remained there until about 1920, during which time the rate of natural increase of the population fell from about 1.4 per cent to about 0.8 per cent (Woods 1996). By that time also, most other Western European nations had moved into the late expanding phase and the pattern was repeated in North America and Australia. The fall in the birth rate seems to have been associated with the continuing industrialization of the economy and the urban patterns of living that accompanied it, but the exact causes remain unclear. The rate fell initially among those in the business or professional classes, perhaps reflecting a reduced need for large families in the new economy, but by the 1920s and 1930s all classes were exhibiting reduced fertility (see, for example, Devine 1999). More attention to, and a wider knowledge of, birth control or family planning may also have contributed to the decline, although only in the later stages of this phase. In reality, there are no clear and definitive reasons for the falling birth rate, but as the late expanding phase progressed family size declined in all the industrialized nations. At the same time, the overcrowding, squalor and disease that had been a feature of many of the new industrial towns and cities of the early and mid-nineteenth century, and had led to increased mortality in some urban centres, were being tempered by modern sanitation and public health services (Woods 1996). The net result was a significant decline in the death rate, particularly among young children. In Scotland, for example, the infant mortality rate declined from 150 per thousand live births in 1850 to 109 per thousand immediately before World War I (Devine 1999). The equivalent figures in England and Wales were 140 per thousand live births in 1880 falling to 95 per thousand in 1916 (Anderson 1996b) with a further decline to 77 per thousand by 1920. In France and Germany the infant mortality rate had declined to 90 per thousand live births by 1920 and in the United States the rate at that time was 85 (Molnar and Molnar 2000).

Many developing nations, such as Kenya in Africa, India and Indonesia in Asia and Brazil and Mexico in Latin America, now have crude birth and death rates that fit this category. Although the pattern appears similar, their present state is not directly comparable with the situation in Europe in the late nineteenth and early twentieth centuries. Industrialization has taken place in parts of India, Brazil and Mexico, for example, but in other areas the change has come without it. Similarly, urbanization is proceeding rapidly in developing nations, but without the planning that characterized at least the later stages of European and North American urbanization (see Box 7.3, Urbanization). Much of the change has come about as a result of the introduction of improved health care and its impact on the death rate. Sharply reduced mortality and a declining but still relatively high fertility rate have produced increases of between 1.5 per cent and 2.5 per cent. With the higher populations generated during passage through the early expanding phase this has ensured that net growth continues to be high in these nations.

Low Stationary Stage

The low stationary category is marked by birth and death rates that are both low and roughly equal. By the 1930s, most of the countries in western, northern and central Europe, along with the United States, Canada, Australia and New Zealand, were in this stage. Fertility continued the decline begun in the previous phase until the crude birth rate began to stabilize at or below about 15 per thousand per year. With continued improvements in health services and living conditions, the death rate also declined to similar levels and the net growth in population slowed down significantly, to rates below 1 per cent per annum and sometimes less than 0.5 per cent. While mortality has probably reached its lowest possible level in most of these areas, changing socio-economic conditions have contributed to considerable fluctuations in fertility. Later marriage and the postponement of the birth of the first child contributed to the decline in fertility, as did the introduction of the contraceptive pill in the 1960s. In contrast, the post-war 'baby boom' produced a significant increase in fertility in the 1940s and 1950s and an echo from that boom has been felt in the 1980s and 1990s.

Significantly, only two or three nations in all of Asia, Africa or Latin America have ever attained the low stationary category. Japan moved into that category in the mid-1950s with the beginning of a rapid decline in fertility,

BOX 7.3 **URBANIZATION**

At the beginning of the twenty-first century some 47 per cent of the world's population is living in towns and cities, and the United Nations estimates that by 2030 more than 60 per cent will be urban dwellers. In these three decades, the world's urban population will grow at double the rate of the population as a whole, with the main increase—averaging more than 2 per cent per year—occurring in the cities of the developing nations, where the urban population will grow from 40 per cent of the total in 2000 to 56 per cent by 2030. Combined with very low levels of growth in rural areas—less than 0.1 per cent per annum—this will have a significant impact on the distribution of population in these nations. Urbanization will proceed at a slower pace in the developed world, but the process is already well advanced there, and by 2030 84 per cent of the population will be living in urban areas.

The rate of change and the absolute numbers involved vary from continent to continent, but the overwhelming growth in the developing world is evident. Of the nineteen cities with a population of 10 million or more in 2000, for example, fifteen are in developing nations and, according to United Nations' estimates, by 2015, twenty-three cities will have populations in excess of 10 million, with nineteen being in developing nations (Figure 4.8). Although such cities do illustrate what increased urbanization means in absolute numbers, most of the growth in urban population will take place in communities of less than 1 million. Cities of that size in the developing world will account for 45 per cent of the total urban growth between 2000 and 2015, whereas similar cities in the developed nations will provide only 3 per cent. Compared with the developing nations of Africa and Asia, areas in Europe and North America will continue to have a higher proportion of their population living in urban areas, but it is expected that by 2010 more than half the world's population will be urbanized, with Asia alone having 2.6 billion urban dwellers.

HISTORY OF URBANIZATION

The current level of urbanization and its ongoing spectacular growth is very much a modern phenomenon, but urbanization itself has a long history that can be traced back to the very beginnings of civilization. Although the early civilizations, which grew up in the valleys of the Nile, the Tigris and Euphrates and the Indus, owed their existence to the development of agriculture, they evolved into societies that built the world's first cities, some 6000 years ago. Cities such as Memphis, Babylon and Mohenjo Daro were the forerunners of Athens and Sparta in Greece and of the city-states of Italy, from ancient Rome to Florence and Venice, which flourished during the Renaissance. Elsewhere, from China to Central and South America, urban settlements developed where local conditions could support a concentrated population. Although their inhabitants numbered tens of thousands, perhaps hundreds of thousands in a few cases, these cities were the exception until at least the eighteenth century in Europe, and much later elsewhere. Most of the world's population lived a rural existence or inhabited small towns that had grown to have populations of a few thousand because they were administrative centres, market towns or ports.

Modern urbanization grew in step with the industrialization that began in England in the mid-eighteenth century. At that time London was the largest city in the country, with a population of about 800,000, but no other city had more than 100,000. The industrial revolution created towns and cities where none had been before and caused existing urban centres to double or triple in size in only a few decades. The combination of coal and iron led to the development of heavy industry, producing the raw materials for the manufacture of steam engines, locomotives, ships, bridges and the ancillary items such as rails, wheels, girders and boilers associated with them. The textile industry followed, leaving its cottage industry roots to become a factory industry. It moved in from small towns and rural areas to take advantage of the level of mechanization possible in the cities and attracted by the availability of both a work force and a market in the growing urban population. An expanding network of railways allowed cities to spread and incorporate adjacent settlements, until in some areas individual towns flowed together with no obvious boundary between them. This occurred initially in

BOX 7.3 **URBANIZATION** (*Continued*)

the English Midlands and central Scotland, but soon spread to areas with similar attributes, such as the Ruhr valley in Germany and the Pittsburgh area in the United States. These were the first urban/industrial conurbations.

The initial growth in the cities came about as the result of the movement of workers from agriculture to industry. Both push and pull mechanisms were involved. The growing number of jobs available in the new cities, and generally higher wages, pulled workers from the adjacent rural areas and also the small towns serving these areas. The push from the country to the town came about as a result of a rural population that had grown with the improvements in agriculture, but was being displaced as mechanization began to reduce the need for human labour. The flow of rural–urban migrants was mainly of young people who through high fertility rates contributed to the growth of the cities by natural increase. The contribution from natural increase would have been greater but for the limits set by poor sanitation, inadequate housing, pollution and malnutrition, which remained part of the urban scene until the twentieth century, and raised urban mortality rates.

When the first census was held in Britain in 1801, the country was still predominantly rural, with only 34 per cent of the population living in urban areas. By the middle of the century, in 1851, the swing to urban living was well established, with 54 per cent of the population living in towns and cities by then. At the beginning of the twentieth century, the urban population made up some 78 per cent of the total, and by its end more than 90 per cent. Similar trends were followed in most of industrialized Europe, where urbanization levels now range from 85 per cent to 95 per cent. In North America slightly more than three-quarters of the population live in towns and cities, while in Australia and New Zealand the level is about 85 per cent.

URBANIZATION IN THE TWENTIETH CENTURY

Hidden within these figures are significant changes in regional and national urban patterns. The second half of the twentieth century saw the geographical spread of many cities through suburban residential development. Started originally with streetcars (trams) and suburban railways, it reached its peak with the widespread adoption of the automobile as the preferred form of commuter transport, particularly in North America. Running parallel to this and contributing to the spread was a decline in population in urban core areas, as those who could, sought the advantages of clean air, open space and the other amenities available in the suburbs. The subsequent decline and decay of the urban core areas has been reversed somewhat by gentrification and the building of high-rise condominiums for those unwilling to face the daily aggravation of traffic jams and ever lengthening commuting times.

As the cities have spread, in some areas they have created conurbations that are immensely large in terms of both population totals and geographical extent (Figure 6.5). The first of these was recognized in 1961 and named Megalopolis. It consisted of a continuous stretch of urban development extending from Boston to Washington DC along the eastern seaboard of the United States. A similar, if slightly less intense, corridor now runs through the American mid-west, from Pittsburgh to Chicago (Chipitts) and, in California, the development between San Francisco and San Diego (Sansan) has many of the attributes of a megalopolis. The pattern is repeated on a smaller scale in Europe, along the lower Rhine and Ruhr in Germany and in England in the London– Liverpool corridor. The largest urban conglomeration in the world is in Japan, where the Tokaido megalopolis, stretching between Tokyo and Osaka along the south coast of Honshu, is home to more than 50 million people.

BOX 7.3 **URBANIZATION** (*Continued*)

URBANIZATION IN THE DEVELOPING WORLD

Modern urbanization in the developing world is unlike the earlier growth of towns and cities in that it is driven not by industrialization but by natural growth and migration from rural areas. Industrial activities, such as textile and clothing manufacture or the production and assembly of small appliances for markets in the developed nations, are present in many of the cities, but they are often highly automated or mechanized and do not have a high demand for labour. Rather than a pull from industry, migration to urban areas is driven by a push from the countryside, where the available land is no longer able to support the rapidly growing population. Under these circumstances, there is often no real alternative but to move into the city. Such a move may not bring with it any improvement in opportunities, and many migrants end up living in poverty in the squatter settlements that are part of all major cities in the developing world. Sited on the periphery of the cities, they provide a sharp contrast to the affluent residential suburbs that surround major cities in the developed world. The cities differ in their core areas also. Cities in the developing world lack the transport net that allowed the movement from core to periphery in the industrial cities, and as a result their central cores are more densely populated. Urban infrastructure put in place when the cities were much smaller can no longer cope with modern population pressures. Housing is generally inadequate, the provision of services such as water supply and sanitation is difficult and organized waste disposal often non-existent. With the potential for disease that all this brings, and with a diet that is usually less nutritious than that in the surrounding rural areas, the urban poor in the developing world face a life of poverty, pollution, malnourishment and ill health that can only get worse as the world's urban population continues to rise.

For more information see:

Brown, L.R., Gardner, G. and Halweil, B. (1999) *Beyond Malthus*, New York/London: Norton.

Hartshorn, T.A. (1992) *Interpreting the City: an Urban Geography* (2nd edn), New York: Wiley.

UN Population Division (2002) *World Urbanization Prospects: The 2001 Revision*, viewed at http://www.un.org/esa/population/publications/wup2001/WUP2001_CH1.pdf (accessed 16 June 2003).

---

which brought births below replacement level by 1973 (Retherford *et al.* 1996). The decline came about as a result of major social and economic changes following World War II and was encouraged by a government concerned about serious population pressure on the nation's resources. The increased use of contraception and the legalization of abortion had a direct impact on the birth rate, as did changes in Japanese society, which led to major educational and employment gains by women. Together, over less than three decades, these measures cut the crude birth rate by half, which along with continued declines in the death rate brought Japan into line with other industrialized countries in Europe and North America (Molnar and Molnar 2000).

Much smaller than Japan in both area and total population, Singapore in the 1950s and 1960s had a birth rate of 30–45 per thousand per year coupled with a death rate that had declined below 10 per thousand per year by 1960. This gave a natural increase of about 3 per cent per annum and caused severe population pressure on housing, social services and employment. Government-sponsored family planning programmes introduced in the mid-1960s to deal with these concerns were so

FIGURE 7.8 Projected annual population growth in the world's megacities (population over 10 million)

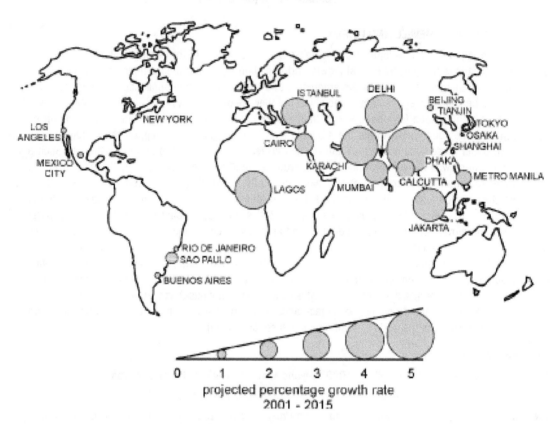

projected percentage growth rate
2001 - 2015

Source: based on data in UN Population Division, *World Urbanization Prospects* (2001). Viewed at http://www.un.org/esa/population/pubsarchive/urbanization/urbanization.pdf

effective that, by the mid-1970s, the rate of growth was halved. The object of the family planning programmes had been to create a stable population, characteristic of the low stationary phase, but the combination of contraception and abortion, together with a variety of socio-economic improvements and changes in lifestyle happening at the same time, drove birth rates below replacement levels. This raised the fear that the population was drifting into decline and the government was forced to relax some aspects of its family planning programmes (Hornby and Jones 1993).

China, with crude birth and death rates of 17 per thousand and 7 per thousand per year respectively, is technically in the low stationary phase. As with Japan and Singapore this was achieved through the widespread and aggressive use of family planning. So effective were the programmes that in the early 1990s fertility in China fell below replacement levels (Yi 1996). Even with the relative stability of the low stationary phase of the demographic transition, however, the sheer size of the population of China means the addition of some 10 million people to the population every year, and that situation will continue until there is a significant decline in the number within the reproductive sector of the population.

Declining Stage

The traditional demographic transition model had only four phases, but in some nations a fifth phase—one in which the population actually declines—might be considered. In the declining phase, an excess of deaths over births causes the total population of a country to decrease. Sometimes it may be brought on by a high death rate, as in Ireland during the potato famine, or an extremely low birth rate can be a contributing factor, as was the case in Europe in the period between the world wars. In China, between 1958 and 1961, rising death rates and falling birth rates combined to halt a rapidly growing population and send it into decline. Several European nations have moved in and out of this category over the past sixty to seventy years, including Britain, Germany and France. In France deaths exceeded births for ten years between 1936 and 1946, and the situation was a constant source of concern to politicians there and elsewhere. A similar situation prevailed in Eastern Europe in the 1990s, mainly as a result of falling birth rates, and in Russia a falling birth rate plus a rising death rate has caused a serious decline in the population, perhaps by as much as 0.5 per cent per year (Figure 4.2) (Becker and Hemley 1998). In the past, such declines have been turned round with a significant increase in birth rates. In Europe, for example, the dire predictions from the 1930s were confounded by the post-war 'baby boom'. Such a response seems less likely in the twenty-first century, because of the aging of the population in these areas, and it may be that if numbers are to be maintained nations in decline will have to consider replacement

migration as a solution to a declining and aging population (UNPD 2001).

THE DEMOGRAPHIC TRANSITION AND THE ENVIRONMENT

As the world's population proceeded through the stages of the demographic transition the relationship between people and their environment changed also. When most of the world was in the high stationary phase, numbers were small and the level of technology was extremely low. As a result, stress on the environment was limited. Demand was for renewable resources, such as water, wood, and plant and animal products. Any damage to the environment, by fire or over-hunting, for example, was quite easily repaired by the environment's built-in recovery processes.

The falling death rate characteristic of the early expanding phase of the demographic transition, probably first experienced some 5000–7000 years ago in the original agricultural hearths (Figure 1.4), owed much to the improved nutrition made possible by developments in agriculture. The available food surpluses also permitted the growth of permanent settlements, with strong central government, a definite division of labour and a need for transport and communication systems. Some of these settlements grew into cities inhabited by tens of thousands of people and in the process the environment was changed. A previously unknown built environment appeared in the landscape; crops replaced natural vegetation; domesticated animals outnumbered the native species; the aquatic environment was altered to allow irrigation. Important as these developments were, the numbers and areas involved were small in world terms and the environmental impact was quite limited. The first signs of future problems were already visible, however. Natural resources such as the soil came under particular stress and in the first agriculturally based societies in Mesopotamia and Central America problems of soil erosion and nutrient depletion were not unknown.

When Britain and Western Europe entered this phase, the impacts of the agricultural revolution were followed by those of the industrial revolution. The demand for renewable resources such as water and wood continued to grow at a rate that exceeded the ability of the environment to recover. In addition, the increasing use of non-renewable resources such as coal and iron created a level of stress in the environment previously unknown. The mining, processing and use of these products changed the landscape, and polluted the air and water. Threats to the environment came not only from the rapidly increasing number of people, but also from the urban/industrial society that they adopted. The atmosphere in most urban areas deteriorated rapidly, becoming filled with smog, while the local rivers, lakes and streams were polluted by the sewage generated by thousands of people living in the growing cities. As such conditions gradually spread around the world along with industrialization and the migration of Europeans, stress on the environment began to be universal.

Environmental disruption accompanied the growth in population in the late expanding phase and even into the low stationary phase when the rate of growth declined. Although the rate of growth in countries now in the low stationary phase is similar to that in the high stationary phase, the total population numbers are much higher. The relatively simple relationship between society and environment that existed in the earlier phase has also long gone. The needs of an affluent, technologically advanced society place such great demands on the environment that even the stabilization of the population cannot guarantee a decline in environmental deterioration.

Differences in Environmental Impacts in the Developed and Developing Worlds

Additional complications are introduced because not all of the world's regions have passed through the various stages of the demographic transition at the same time and at the same rate. Industrialized nations already in the low stationary or even declining phase, for example, disrupt the environment of nations in earlier phases as they search for and exploit new sources of raw materials not available to them within their own borders (Smith 2000). The developing nations currently in the early or late expanding phases of the transition have not experienced the industrialization, the technological development or the production and consumption patterns that characterized these stages in the developed world. Despite this, population growth rates well in excess of the highest rates ever experienced in Europe in the eighteenth and nineteenth centuries, plus the adoption of industrial and agricultural technology, often under pressure from the developed nations, have ensured that environmental stress is high in the developing world. This is particularly true of renewable resources such as soil, water and forests. Declining soil fertility and soil erosion reduce the ability of the land to produce food, while fragmentation of land holdings and the spread of urbanization take land out of production and increase pressure on the remaining soil resources. New land is then brought into production to offset this, often at the expense of other resources. Harrison (1992) has estimated, for example, that population pressure in the developing countries between 1973 and 1988 led to the clearing of more than 1.1 billion km² of forest to meet the demand for additional farmland. The same pressures have forced agricultural settlements to creep up hillsides in countries such as Indonesia, the Philippines and Nepal or to expand into semi-arid lands in the Sudano-Sahelian region of Africa, in China, India and Mexico (United Nations 1994). In both of these circumstances, a common result is environmental degradation associated with the loss of soil fertility and soil erosion.

The environment also comes under threat through the growing demand for the fuel-wood that supplies the bulk of the household energy in most of the developing world. Although wood is a renewable resource, it remains so only if the amount harvested is less than that replenished through growth. That point has passed in many areas and the stock of growing wood is depleting rapidly (Myers 1994). The removal of trees from slopes encourages soil erosion, and in areas where fuel-wood is no longer available the burning of animal dung or crop waste causes a reduction in organic matter returned to the soil, which lowers its fertility and leaves it open to erosion.

Directly linked with the rapidly growing population in developing nations is urbanization (see Box 4.3, Urbanization). It is not like the urbanization that accompanied the industrialization of Europe in the eighteenth and nineteenth centuries, but it creates similar environmental deterioration. Lack of zoning regulations or lack of enforcement allows the growth of small industry, with its accompanying noise and air pollution, adjacent to residential property. The use of open fires for cooking, burning coal and biomass fuels, contributes

particulate matter to the urban atmosphere up to levels that are several times the World Health Organization (WHO) limits. As a result, respiratory disease is common, reaching serious levels in many cities in China, and is particularly high in Calcutta and Mexico City. Noxious exhaust fumes from rising levels of car, bus and truck traffic in the cities of the developing world add to the mix. Even indoors the inhabitants are not safe. Emissions from open-hearth fires or cooking stoves with inadequate ventilation create a major health hazard, especially for women (United Nations 1994).

Urbanization also places great stress on water resources. The water supply is seldom sufficient to meet the needs of the rapidly expanding urban areas and that which is available is often contaminated. The absence of sewage collection and disposal systems in the cities of the developing world contributes to serious deterioration in the aquatic environment, which then feeds back through contaminated drinking water, to expose the population to regular outbreaks of waterborne enteric diseases. Other waste, such as municipal garbage, is seldom collected, while the indiscriminate dumping of refuse can lead to groundwater contamination and provide a breeding ground for vermin and a variety of pathogens (Falkenmark 1994).

There is abundant evidence to support the claim that population pressures in the developing world make less contribution to global environmental deterioration than increased affluence and technological development in the industrialized nations (see, for example, Ehrlich and Ehrlich 1991; Miller 1994; Smith 2000). However, reality is not as simple as that. Much as technology and economic development have contributed to environmental problems, they have also been used to reduce acid precipitation, ozone depletion and water pollution; the rapid population growth among the developing nations has not been addressed in the same way, if it has been addressed at all, and continues to have an immediate and serious impact on the environment. Where technology or resource planning has been introduced, however, the result has been a much reduced impact. In the Sahel, for example, Mortimore (1989) has suggested that high population densities may not be out of place in areas where proposed soil and water conservation schemes are labour-intensive, and in the Machakos district of Kenya rapid population growth in the second half of the twentieth century was accompanied by environmental improvement as a result of the introduction of erosion control and more appropriate agricultural practices (Tiffen *et al.* 1994). Such studies indicate that population growth does not always lead to environmental deterioration, but these examples tend to be the exception, and the search for a more appropriate balance between population and environment continues.

Stabilization of the population might help, but that has already taken place in the developed world and cannot be accomplished easily in nations continuing to grow rapidly. Even if the population in the developing nations could be moved into the low stationary phase it does not follow that environmental deterioration would cease. Experience in the developed world suggests that stabilization is accompanied by improved economic conditions, which in turn create problems for the environment through the increased demand for resources. According to the Worldwatch Institute this degree of stabilization is unlikely to occur, and if it does it will be as a result of regression into the high stationary phase

rather than progression into the low stationary phase. Many developing nations are already suffering from such 'demographic fatigue' in dealing with the effects of a rapidly growing population that their capacity to respond to crises such as drought, famine and disease is very limited. In Africa, for example, the AIDs crisis is spiralling out of control and set to overwhelm more than a dozen nations in the south and central part of the continent alone (see Box 4.1, HIV/AIDS). Under such conditions, population stabilization will be accomplished by a rising death rate rather than a falling birth rate (Brown *et al.* 1999). With the subsequent deterioration in the economic and social infrastructure, the means, and even the will, to deal with environmental issues could be lost, with disastrous consequences.

In short, while there appears to be a simple relationship between environment and population in the early stages of the demographic transition, progression through the transition brings increasing complexity. Direct population pressure on the environment is enhanced by socio-economic and technological change. Stabilization of population alone is insufficient to control environmental deterioration and any progress is likely to require the direct application of appropriate technology.

WORLD POPULATION GROWTH AND TRENDS

Prior to the mid-eighteenth century, the earth's human population remained in the high stationary stage of the demographic transition. As a result, with an average growth rate of less than 0.1 per cent, world population changed little, reaching perhaps 500–800 million immediately prior to the industrial revolution. With the rapid expansion that followed it passed the 2 billion mark sometime in the late 1920s and

FIGURE 7.9 World population growth during the last millennium, AD 1000–2000

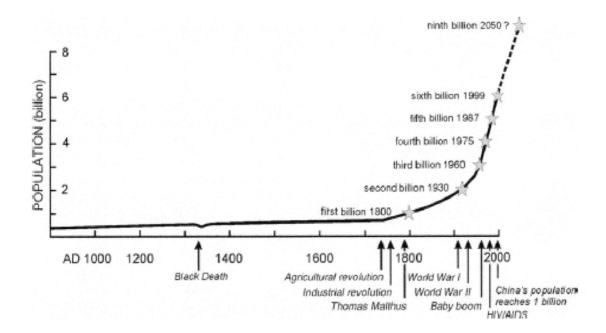

by the beginning of the twenty-first century stood at about 6 billion (Hornby and Jones 1993; UNPD 2001) (Figure 7.9).

The initial expansion took place in Britain, but quickly spread along with industrialization into Europe and North America. These areas moved through the early expanding phase into the late expanding phase and by the 1920s and 1930s most were in or approaching the low stationary category. Population in the world as a whole continued to grow rapidly, however. The advanced industrial nations, through commerce and colonial expansion, had created conditions in other parts of the world which were to lead to phenomenal growth, largely through the reduction of the death rate. Because of the rapidity of the change, that situation created considerable alarm in the developed world. In the eighteenth and nineteenth centuries the reduction in the death rate came about gradually, and its impact on

population growth was buffered somewhat by factors that tended at the same time to reduce the birth rate—a rising standard of living and industrialization, for example—which made children no longer an economic asset. In addition, the rapid growth in Britain and Western Europe was offset by emigration.

The differences are well illustrated by the following examples. In Britain the death rate took seventy years to decline from 22 to 12 per thousand per year. In Japan that same reduction took twenty-seven years, in Mexico about twenty years and in Sri Lanka less than ten years, all following World War II and mainly as a result of better nutrition and health care. Combined with a high birth rate, this produced population growth averaging 3 per cent per annum in all these nations, or about twice the highest rate ever experienced in Britain. With figures such as these, it is scarcely surprising that by the 1960s and 1970s concern about

FIGURE 7.10 Predictions of world population growth

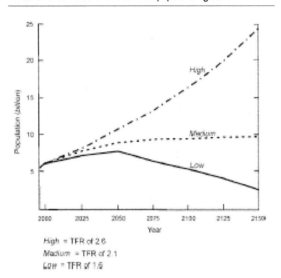

High = TFR of 2.6
Medium = TFR of 2.1
Low = TFR of 1.6

Source: UN Population Division, *World Population Prospects 1950– 2050 (The 2000 Revision)*, New York: United Nations (2001).

future population growth and its impact on resource use and the environment were high (Hornby and Jones 1993).

The rate of growth of the world's population peaked at 2 per cent per annum in the late 1960s, after which it began to fall, in response to declining birth rates, to reach 1.3 per cent per annum in 1998 (UNPD 2001). Total population continued to rise, however, because the reduced rate of growth was offset by the impact of the large number of young people of reproductive age in the system. This momentum will continue as long as the number of people entering the reproductive sector exceeds the number leaving it (see Box 4.2, Population structure). In world terms, this means that even if reproductive rates are brought down to replacement levels (TFR = 2.1) immediately, population will continue to grow beyond 10 billion before stabilizing, perhaps sometime in the mid-twenty-second century (Shenstone

1997). The annual population increase peaked in 1987 with the addition of 87 million children to the world total. By the first half of the 1990s that number had declined to 81 million annually, and the United Nations has estimated that between 1995 and 2000 the annual increase averaged 79 million. Even with a continuing decline in growth rate, it is projected—based on a TFR of 2.1—that between 2010 and 2015 the annual increase in population will be 73 million and by 2050 less than 36 million (UNPD 2001). The net result would be the addition of 2.8 billion people to the world population in the first half of the twenty-first century.

Although it is clear that a significant increase in population should be expected, the totals remain speculative. Past predictions for individual countries and for the world have been consistently wrong. In Britain, for example, it was estimated that, at the rates prevailing in the early 1930s, the population, which stood at 46 million in 1931, would fall below 40 million by 1961 and within a hundred years to 5 million (Branson and Heinemann 1973). The population of Britain in 2000 was actually close to 59 million. More recent predictions have tended to be on the high side and have required regular reassessment. Despite improved reporting and sophisticated analysis, for example, the United Nations reduced its projections of world population totals twice in the 1990s. In an attempt to deal with such variability, the United Nations provides population projections in high, medium and low variants (Figure 4.10). The high variant assumes a TFR of 2.6, which would produce a world population of 10.7 billion by 2050; the medium projection, based on a replacement TFR of 2.1, is of 8.9 billion by 2050; the low variant assumes a TFR of 1.6 and projects a population of 7.3 billion by 2050. The medium variant is the projection most commonly used for planning purposes (UNPD 2001).

Population Growth and Resources

Whatever the ultimate rate of growth, and however long it takes for the world's population to stabilize, it is widely agreed that the population increase in the developing world presents the greatest challenge. It is expected that 98 per cent of the growth between 1999 and 2015 will take place in developing nations. These are nations that are already facing serious—perhaps insurmountable—economic, social and environmental problems. Some may already be approaching the carrying capacity of the land they occupy; others face problems of sustainability if nothing is done to slow the rate of growth. A reduction in the population growth should also lead to a reduction in pressure on food supply and other resources, while encouraging the development that would allow the low growth rates to be maintained. However, many of the countries involved are already so fatigued, socially and economically, in dealing with the implications of rapid growth that any recovery will be slow and any development so far into the future that before it is achieved many will have succumbed to famine, resource depletion, uncontrollable political instability and economic decline (Brown *et al.* 1999).

Alarming as such developments may seem, the concepts they represent are not new. As early as 1798 an English clergyman called Thomas Malthus pointed out that population grows not arithmetically but geometrically, like compound interest in a bank account (see Box 4.4, Thomas Malthus). On the other hand, food production can increase only in arithmetical progression, so that population growth would eventually outstrip food

production, and famine, disease, pestilence and war would follow.

Shortly after Malthus published his ideas they were apparently confounded. The opening up of new land in the Americas, Australasia and South Africa, coupled with the introduction of new agricultural techniques, allowed food production to keep up with population increases, and in some cases to outdistance it. In places, however, the truth of the Malthusian predictions was all too clear—as in the case of the potato famine in Ireland, where the logistical problems of replacing the lost potato crop, coupled with political unwillingness to try, contributed to the death of several hundred thousand people. Migration from Europe also helped the situation by reducing the number of mouths to be fed at home and providing the labour by which new land around the world could be brought into production. These areas with small populations, but large food-producing capacity, then began to export food to the more populous and developed countries in Europe. All in all, during the nineteenth and early twentieth centuries, food production increased at more than arithmetical progression, contrary to the Malthusian formula. The application of technology to agriculture plus successful research and development improved production from plants and animals, allowing food production to be maintained at levels sufficiently high to meet the needs of the world's current population. Unfortunately, the availability of food varies from one part of the world to another and famines similar to those predicted by Malthus continue to occur. Whatever the historical experience, it remains true that there is a fundamental difference between the maximum rates of population growth and the maximum rates of growth of food production. Despite continuing success in

BOX 7.4 **THOMAS MALTHUS (1766–1834)**

Thomas Robert Malthus, an English clergyman and economist, was one of the first to address the problems associated with a rapidly growing population. In 1798 he published a short book entitled *An Essay on the Principles of Population as it Affects the Future Improvement of Society,* in which he set out his concerns and conclusions about the changes he saw taking place at the time. The impact of the original small volume was significant and it grew through a series of revisions between 1803 and 1872 as Malthus developed his ideas further and responded to his critics. Central to the essay was the discrepancy likely to arise between a growing population and its food supply. He recognized that whereas population growth tended to follow a geometric progression (1, 2, 4, 8, 16, 32, 64 ...), the growth in food production, on which the population depended, was arithmetic (1, 2, 3, 4, 5, 6, 7 ...) and concluded that population growth would ultimately exceed the available food supply. At that stage, famine, disease and warfare would reduce the population until it was once again within the bounds of available sustenance. As an alternative, Malthus suggested, the practice of 'moral restraint'—abstinence and delayed marriage—could reduce population growth to manageable rates. Although this seemed preferable to poverty, vice and misery, Malthus had little confidence that the population would exercise the necessary restraint and foresaw that the more drastic events would provide the main checks on population growth.

These theories were of interest outside the social, political and economic fields from which they were developed. In reality they dealt with patterns common among animal populations, which tend to expand and contract in concert with their food supply. Malthus saw the human animal as no different from other animals in that respect. This annoyed his fellow clergymen, but it caught the interest of natural scientists, and the most famous of them all, Charles Darwin, acknowledged Malthus's influence on the development of his ideas on natural selection.

On the other side of the world, in China, Huang (or Hung) Liang-chi (1744–1809) had come to the same conclusion at about the same time. Huang was a scholar and intellectual who had been sentenced to death for criticizing the emperor, but had the sentence reduced to exile. He recognized the rapid population growth in China at the time and noted that the means of subsistence could not be expected to match it. Like Malthus he noted the impact of natural checks on the growth of population, which he identified as flood, drought, plague and pestilence, but he also recognized that in the long run they were quite ineffective, since population would begin to increase again once the natural checks had run their course.

In China, the cycle of population increase and decline associated with the inability of the food supply to match the growth of the population continued for some 200 years after Huang's recognition of the problem. In Europe, on the other hand, the Malthusian predictions did not come to pass. The opening up of new lands for European migration and improved agricultural technology kept the natural checks at bay, and the development of birth control and other family planning techniques took the place of 'moral restraint'. Continuing high productivity levels in the twentieth century, coupled with a significant reduction in fertility in the developed nations, seemed to show that Mallthus's fears were unfounded. In the latter half of the century, however, rapidly expanding populations in the developing world, unable to produce enough food for their own survival, are again experiencing starvation, disease and war. For some these represent the main natural checks on population growth foreseen by Malthus, but modern socio-economic and technological conditions are quite different from those in the eighteenth century and the relationship between population and food supply is much more complex.

For more information see:

Dupaquier, J., Fauve-Chamoux, A. and Grebenik, E. (eds) (1983) *Malthus Past and Present, London/*New York: Academic Press.

Ehrlich, P.R. and Ehrlich, A.H. (1990) *The Population Explosion*, New York: Simon and Schuster.

meeting the needs of a growing world population, there are fears that the present level cannot be maintained indefinitely (Molnar and Molnar 2000). It is possible that Malthus was not wrong—only premature.

The human species faces a dilemma in all of this. On one hand, it needs to ensure its survival and on the other it needs to ensure that success in multiplying its numbers does not strain the resources or irreparably damage the environment on which it depends. Successful breeding leads to pressure on resources, and there are neo-Malthusians who see this pressure at a maximum already. If nothing is done to bring down the current rate of increase, society will find itself living in a world exposed to disastrous miseries and Malthusian predictions may yet come to pass (Brown *et al.* 1999). Aware of the serious implications of such a scenario, many nations have introduced policies that mandate some form of population planning and control.

Population Planning And Control

In theory, the reduction in the rate of population growth can be accomplished relatively easily. Since population growth is directly related to the difference between birth and death rates, a combination of reduced birth rate and increased death rate would be most effective. Many primitive societies are said to have practised some form of death control such as infanticide or the abandonment of older people when times were hard, but at present any attempt to increase death rates would be looked on with horror. Thus it is birth control, in its broadest sense, that has to bear the burden of reducing population.

FIGURE 7.11 Individual and societal influences in family size

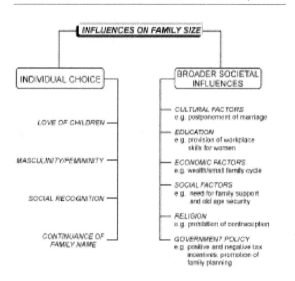

Birth control

Effective birth control methods have been available since at least the second half of the nineteenth century, but until then—and even since then in many areas—almost the only birth control methods practised were indirect, usually cultural or social in nature. Often they came about not by deliberate choice, but as a by-product of some physical, cultural or economic activity. Breast-feeding is recognized as providing some protection from conception, for example. Any number of taboos and customs surround sexual behaviour and create a considerable gap between fertility and fecundity. Although these cultural or social methods of population control are less efficient than mechanical or chemical methods, they do work. Even during Victorian and Edwardian times in Britain, when families of fifteen and even twenty were not unknown, the actual number of births was always far below the maximum reproductive capacity of the population.

The range of cultural or social elements that contribute to birth control is wide and includes societal fashions, family decisions, economic position in society, education and employment opportunities (Figure 7.11). In all this, the role of women became increasingly important. Societal fashions, for example, influence marriage customs, which in turn can decide whether a woman's first child arrives early in her childbearing years or is postponed until long after puberty. The latter situation has become more and more common in developed nations, where it is not unusual for women to give birth to their first child after the age of thirty. In some countries—China, for example—the postponement of marriage has become official government policy and, combined with effective birth control, does seem to help to reduce the rate of population growth. Economic conditions that encourage or require women to become part of the labour force also lead to a reduction in the birth rate. In Eastern Europe, for example, following a brief 'baby boom' after World War II, the birth rate declined steadily into the 1980s as the number of women in the work force increased (Hornby and Jones 1993). Elsewhere also, an economic need for women to be in paid employment, combined with other factors such as the growing number of women entering higher education and a subsequent desire to use that education, led couples to postpone starting a family, a decision that made a major contribution to the decline in fertility in the developed nations in the 1970s and 1980s. By providing women with the skills to participate more fully in the workplace, education has had a significant role in population control in the developed world and there is strong evidence that improving access to education for women at all levels—elementary to post-secondary— is one of the best ways to slow population growth. This appears to be particularly true in many parts of the developing world, where women have traditionally received much less formal schooling than their male counterparts. Educated women are more likely to be employed outside the home and to marry later, which leads them to have fewer children. It has been estimated that up to 60 per cent of the decline in fertility in parts of Latin America is due to higher levels of education for young women (ICPQL 1996).

Biological, chemical and mechanical methods of birth control

Modern societal conditions, such as those involving economics and education, which contribute to family planning are indirect and would not work without various direct forms of biological, mechanical and chemical birth control. Biological methods range from total or periodic abstinence to prolonged breast-feeding and include abortion. Although not a method of contraception, since its aim is to put an end to the results of conception rather than prevent it, abortion has been widely used to reduce birth rates, particularly in countries where safer and less invasive methods have not been available. Such was the case in many countries in Eastern Europe, where modern contraceptives were not readily available until the 1980s. It has been estimated, for example, that in Hungary in the 1950s as many as 150,000 illegal abortions occurred annually. With legalization, the number rose to 207,000 in 1969, only falling again in the 1980s—to less than 80,000—as modern contraceptive methods became available (Hornby and Jones 1993). In China, despite a high level of contraceptive use, almost 54 million abortions were carried out between 1980 and 1984, largely as a result of pressure to have all second and subsequent pregnancies terminated in support of the government's one-child policy (Jowett 1990). Effective as abortion appears to be, it has serious implications for the health of the women involved, particularly when the procedure is carried out illegally. Illegal abortions, which account for some 20 million of the 45 million to 50 million operations performed annually, are often unsafe. Most occur in the developing world, where the death rate is estimated at one for every 250 abortions (ICPQL 1996). Abortion is not an appropriate substitute for modern methods of contraception, but it is likely to continue at relatively high levels in some areas until a combination of economics, education and changing social attitudes allow it to be replaced.

Most of the success in birth control can be attributed to the widespread use of mechanical and chemical methods of contraception. Those providing a physical barrier to conception—condoms and diaphragms, for example—have been available since at least the 1930s, but their overall impact on fertility is difficult to measure and may well have been small (Anderson 1996b). A major advance in contraceptive technology occurred with the introduction of the contraceptive pill in 1963. Its effectiveness and ease of use made it instantly popular, and in developed nations its impact is evident in fertility patterns between about 1964 and 1980 (Murphy 1993). In Britain, for example, the beginning of a twenty-year decline in fertility in the late 1960s is seen as largely attributable to the introduction of the contraceptive pill, with slight reverses in the decline in 1970 and after 1977 being associated with concern over health hazards arising from its long-term use (Murphy 1993; Hornby and Jones 1993). New approaches to contraception continue to be explored. In the past, the emphasis has been on improving effectiveness and ease of use,

but more recently, with the growing concern over the spread of the AIDS epidemic (see Box 4.1, HIV/AIDS), health agencies have been promoting the use of condoms, which have the ability to prevent conception as well as slow the spread of the HIV virus.

The most commonly used methods of mechanical and chemical contraception are 94 to 98 per cent effective. They are only effective, however, if they are used. According to UN surveys, 58 per cent of married women of reproductive age (i.e. fifteen to forty-nine) use some form of contraception, 42 per cent do not (UNPD 1999). The level of contraceptive prevalence is spread unevenly across the world (Table 7.2). As might be expected, it is highest among the developed nations. All have prevalence rates in excess of 50 per cent

TABLE 7.2 LEVELS OF CONTRACEPTIVE USE IN SELECTED AREAS (%)

Country	%
World	58
Less developed nations	55
Africa	20
Asia (except Japan)	60
Latin America and Caribbean 66 Oceania	29
More developed nations	70
Japan	59
North America	71
Europe	72
Australia and New Zealand	76

Source: based on data in UNPD (United Nations Population Division) *World Contraceptive Use 1998,* New York: United Nations (1999).

and almost three-quarters have rates of 70 per cent or more. In contrast, values in the developing world range from close to 83 per cent in China—the highest in the world—to as low as 1 per cent in Guinea and Mauritania in Africa. More than half of the nations in Africa have prevalence rates less than 20 per cent; in Latin America and the Caribbean the average is 49 per cent, but in some countries—Haiti and Bolivia, for example—rates continue to be below 20 per cent; in Asia, Thailand and Indonesia, with prevalence rates of 72 per cent and 52 per cent respectively, have successful population stabilization policies, but in India, which may soon surpass China in total population, the rate remains at only 41 per cent. Even in those countries where contraceptive use is low, it does not follow that this reflects the choice of the population. The United Nations recognizes the existence of an 'unmet need' for contraception in many developing nations, particularly those in sub-Saharan Africa (UNPD 1999). Although the necessity to supply that need may be recognized most of the nations involved are unable to set up and finance the appropriate programmes without international aid. Assistance is already provided by the developed nations through a fund created at the 1993 International Conference on Population and Development and was projected to amount to US$5.7 billion by 2000. That figure was not reached. Until it is, countries such as those in sub-Saharan Africa will continue to have an unmet need for contraception and will suffer the consequences of total fertility rates as high as 6.1 and annual growth rates close to 3 per cent (Shenstone 1997; ICPQL 1996).

Direct State Participation in Population Planning

Although decisions on birth control take place ultimately at the family or individual level, the overall management of population growth is a complex and dynamic matter, which is unlikely to be successful without government participation at the national or even international level. The days when a large and growing population was seen as an indication of a nation's success or prestige are long gone. Most governments are now involved at some level in the management of population growth. The approach may be relatively benign, through advertising, propaganda and the provision of family planning materials, for example, or more aggressive, as in China, where the one-child policy placed a direct limit on family size, or in India, where forced female sterilization was common in the 1970s (Jowett 1990; Jacobson 1991). Various forms of negative reinforcement or coercion through social and economic disincentives are also common. These range from penalties for marrying too young to increased hospital costs for second or third children. Families with more than the recommended number of children may also suffer discrimination in the form of reduced tax relief or restricted access to education. Such approaches appear to have been successful in China (Cheng 1991) and in Singapore (Hornby and Jones 1993), for example, but it is not always possible to determine how much of the reduction in fertility is due to direct planning and how much happened as a result of other factors. In Singapore, the family planning initiatives were introduced at a time when social and economic conditions were improving, and that may have contributed to the success of the programmes. A similar combination of family planning and economic change occurred in Japan (Retherford *et al*.

1996) beginning in the 1950s and producing results comparable to those in Singapore.

Family Size

It is not surprising that socio-economic change should have such an impact on population growth. Even before direct family planning was available in the late nineteenth and early twentieth centuries, birth rates had begun to fall in the European industrialized nations, but the desire for, or acceptance of, smaller families is a more recent phenomenon. In the past, and in some nations at present, larger families were seen to provide certain benefits. Even children younger than ten years old can contribute to the overall family income, for example, and in pre-industrial Europe young boys and girls routinely worked on farms and in mines. Later they were employed in the textile and other manufacturing industries. In the absence of help from the state, children were insurance against neglect and poverty in old age, and in the days before improved health care a large family was one way of increasing the odds that at least a few of the children would survive to provide some form of parental care. The provision of child labour and family support of the elderly continues to be important in some parts of the developing world. That will tend to slow the trend towards smaller families, but in much of the world, including many developing nations, it has become apparent that social and economic factors combine to generate a situation in which a certain lifestyle can be maintained only if the family remains small. In general, whatever the society, middle and upper-level socio-economic groups tend to have smaller families, while lower socio-economic groups have larger families. With fewer mouths to feed and bodies to clothe, well-to-do families become wealthier. Children receive the benefits of a good education and have a better chance of finding good employment when they grow up. A positive cycle develops. Small families promote wealth and wealth promotes small families. From this it might be argued that an overall improvement in economic conditions would be the best contraceptive. Unfortunately, the world cannot wait that long. Customs and habits do not change overnight. Even with effective, conventional family planning methods change is slow, especially in the developing world, where the present numbers are so high that the time lag in population reduction may be several decades long.

Barriers to Population Planning

Although the benefits of a rational population policy incorporating family planning are becoming increasingly clear, cultural, economic, religious and political barriers remain in some areas. In rural communities in the developing world, where children are important for family support and old-age security, fertility continues to be high. These are often also the areas in which participation in education is low, particularly for women, and the well established relationship between rising education levels and falling fertility does not come into play (ICPQL 1996). Elsewhere, moral or religious pressure may be brought to bear in such a way that increased births will result. The attitude of the Roman Catholic Church towards population control has aroused considerable controversy. The Church has argued the morality of birth control for many years, and prohibition of most methods continues in place. The doctrines of the Church are being eroded at the local and national level, however, as individuals decide perhaps that it is less morally wrong to practise artificial methods of birth control than it is to bring children into the world to face a life of misery, poverty and disease. Questions of morality also arise in the diversion of funding to armaments in India, Pakistan and some nations in sub-Saharan Africa. Social programmes, such as education and health, suffer and family planning programmes are neglected. To be effective, any population policy must do more than provide the physical necessities of modern family planning. It must also be aware of, and address, the cultural, economic educational and religious issues that have the potential to set obstacles in the way of achieving the stabilization of the population.

Approaches Towards Asolution

Although population growth has slowed and steadied in many parts of the world, it will continue to be high in some areas for many years to come. The greatest impacts will be local or regional, but because of the nature of modern economics and politics the effects will be felt worldwide. Stabilization of the world's population can be successful only through international co-operation, with those nations that have achieved it, and have resources available, helping those that are having difficulty coping with the economic and social consequences of a rapidly growing population. That help may take the form of direct monetary aid to provide access to family planning for a larger proportion of the population, but it must also include consideration of other factors known to be related to population growth. The Brundtland Commission in 1987 recognized, for example, that the sustainable development that it promoted would not be successful without the integration of population policies and socio-economic development programmes (Starke 1990). The International Conference on Population and Development, held in Cairo in

1994, supported that approach, but also identified the improvement of reproductive health and the empowerment of women as important elements in any population policy (Shenstone 1997), while the Independent Commission on Population and the Quality of Life included education and counselling in a list of elements needed to provide an appropriate level and quality of population planning (ICPQL 1996).

SUMMARY AND CONCLUSION

The consideration of population is essential to the understanding of modern environmental issues. In the past, the relationship that human beings had with the environment differed little from that of other animals. Small numbers and primitive technology, which restricted access to resources, limited the progress that society was able to achieve, but at the same time the impact on the environment was minimal. Exponential population growth combined with major advances in technology that increased the demand for resources has radically changed that situation, particularly over the last three centuries, and the environment has suffered serious damage. The relationship between population growth and environmental deterioration is not a simple one—the countries of the developed world continue to exert major pressure on environmental resources, for example, even after their total populations have stabilized or, in some cases, declined. The developing nations, technologically much less advanced, are less demanding of resources, but even a population with limited needs can have a significant impact on the environment if the numbers are sufficiently large, and in the developing world the numbers are large enough to have created demands on land and water resources that cannot easily be met. Serious water and air pollution, which matches or surpasses that common in the industrial nations from the early nineteenth to the late twentieth centuries, is also in large part a function of the rapidly growing population.

Although there is no agreement on what an ideal population for the earth as a whole or a specific country might have to be to achieve a balance between population and environmental resources, by the last three decades of the twentieth century it was widely accepted that the world's population was growing too rapidly and the rate would have to be curtailed. Since then, the United Nations, international aid organizations and environmental groups have encouraged the development of population planning programmes, and government-sponsored or controlled programmes are now common. There is some indication that the rate of growth has peaked, but given the time-lag associated with population change it will be some time before the world population

stabilizes. Even when this happens environmental problems will remain until some balance can be reached between what the population wants from the environment and what the environment is able to provide.

At the regional or national level no one solution to the present problems will apply to all situations and no solution will be immediate. Variations in time and effectiveness have to be expected. Variations take place because population deals with people—not just numbers—and people respond to a variety of stimuli, and not always in logical ways. There may be no one approach that suits all situations, but if no resolution is achieved then the checks and balances which severely impacted the population of Ireland in the 1840s, the Sahel in the 1960s and 1970s, Ethiopia in the 1980s and perhaps Afghanistan and North Korea in the early twenty-first century may well come into play with increasing regularity as the century progresses.

SUGGESTED READING

Hunter, L.M. (2000) *The Environmental Implications of Population Dynamics*, Santa Monica CA: Rand Corporation. Deals with the complexity of relationship between population growth and environmental change, considering problems such as the ongoing rapid population growth in the developing world and over-consumption in developed nations.

McCullough, C. (2000) *Morgan's Run*, New York: Simon and Schuster. A well researched novel of forced immigration—the First (convict) Fleet to Australia in the eighteenth century. Provides a particularly interesting account of the response of the convicts to the different environment in Australia, particularly on Norfolk Island.

Scott, S. and Duncan, C. (2001) *Biology of Plagues: Evidence from Historical Populations*, Cambridge: Cambridge University Press. Challenges the traditional explanation of the Black Death as being the result of bubonic plague—a bacterial disease—and suggests that it was caused by a viral haemorrhagic

disease such as ebola. Makes an interesting comparison with Zeigler's account.

Ziegler, P. (1998) *The Black Death*, Godalming: Bramley Books (originally published 1969). An account of the devastating impact of the Black Death on the population of Europe and its ongoing social and economic impacts.

QUESTIONS FOR REVISION AND FURTHER STUDY

1. Debate the proposition that 'The growth in resource consumption, particularly as a result of increased affluence in the developed world, represents a much more serious crisis for the world than the current growth in population.'

2. Using population data available in United Nations publications or on the World Wide Web (see, for example, the US Census Bureau, International Data Base at http://www.census.gov/ipc/www/idbsum.html), draw two population pyramids, similar to those in the 'Population structure' box, one representing the age/gender distribution in a developing country and one showing the age/gender distribution in a developed nation. How do the two pyramids differ? What does their shape tell you about future population growth in these countries?

3. Examine the role of migration in the country in which you live. Does it create net emigration (out-migration) or net immigration (in-migration)? Were the migration patterns the same 100 years ago? If not, what caused them to change between then and now? Do you think the patterns are likely to change again in the future?

Globalization and Social Change

Economic Integration, New Divisions of Labor, and Gender Relations

by Diane Perrons

The deepening of market relations across the globe affects the lives of almost everyone, albeit in different ways. With the increasing convergence of economic, social and political systems, and their integration through financial markets, multinational firms, supra national institutions and commodity chains[1], events in one location can have widespread repercussions and the fortunes of people in different areas become inextricably interconnected. Financial crises in one part of the globe quickly spread to others and impact on their real economies; for example, the financial crisis in South East Asia in the 1990s led to job losses in North East England. Likewise, in the Philippines the ensuing public expenditure cuts, in addition to those associated with earlier rounds of structural adjustment, created an excess supply of highly qualified people, some of whom migrated to high income countries to become care and domestic workers and so fill gaps created by the feminisation of employment there.

Globalization is both a cause and consequence of the deepening of market relations across the globe. The new international division of labour that came into existence in the 1970s, as corporations decentralized parts of manufacturing has now been extended to high and low paid services and perishable agricultural commodities, to take advantage of different time and climate zones as well as lower cost labour. Further interconnections are established as people move in search of work and a better life and, in contrast to the past, even long distance migrations can be transitory. Both these developments have been facilitated by continued improvements in information and communication technologies and have contributed to the feminization of employment.

Globalisation and Social Change explores these connections by drawing on in depth studies of female employment in agribusiness, electronics, care and sex work, as well as studies of the decline of male employment in traditional industrial sectors. The vignettes of people and places attempt to illuminate how the growing interconnections between people and places shape human lives in different locations throughout the world. This extract focuses in particular on one of these illustrations—care work—and emphasises the human side of globalization in the context of an increasingly interconnected world.

CONTEXT, ISSUES AND QUESTIONS

As the majority of the workforce in these new sectors are women there have been changes in gender roles, responsibilities and relations. One key question is what form does the feminization of employment take. Second, will this feminization lead to greater gender equality or even the 'end of patriarchy' as suggested by Manuel Castells (1997). Alternatively is the extent of change limited by the new and more precarious forms of employment associated with the neoliberal economic agenda and the continuing, profoundly gendered social context within which it takes place? The material in this extract pays particular attention to the likely implications arising from the feminisation of employment for gender relations.

The Feminization of Employment

Everywhere women's labour force participation rate is lower than men's, but with the exception of West Africa and South Asia the feminization of paid employment in recent decades is undeniable. Employment feminization was especially rapid during the 1980s and early 1990s and has increased the 'share of women in wage employment in the non-agricultural sector', one of the indicators used to calculate progress towards Millennium Development Goal 3, to 'Promote Gender Equality and Empower Women' [2]. On this measure, women have achieved parity (a figure of between 45–55%) primarily in Western Europe, other high income countries, Eastern Europe and Latin America. This measure is designed to reflect the more empowering effect of paid work in the non-agricultural sector where women are more likely to receive wages directly and less likely to be regarded as family helpers. However, it fails to take into account the nature of contemporary employment; in particular women's overrepresentation in the informal sector which has been expanding rapidly (Chant and Pedwell 2008).

Gender Relations and Households

Households are generally understood as units of shared residence and or shared resources and through which daily and intergenerational reproduction takes place. While household structures are permeable and household relations vary cross culturally, men have traditionally played the provider role, while women have specialised in caring, more or less universally. These differentiated roles have never been absolute and the boundaries between them are fuzzy but the feminization of employment has challenged the male provider role, in two ways. First, because women are acquiring incomes in their own right and second, because the male ability to act as sole provider has been challenged by contemporary 'feminized' forms of employment that offer new forms of work, lower incomes and a lower degree of security.

In high income countries, the displacement of heavy industry by lighter assembly work has affected men's sense of masculinity in a similar way as the displacement of cattle keeping in Kenya by a more settled form of farming, 'Shamba work' (Jackson 2001). In both cases the new work was associated with women and considered demeaning. Thus work has embedded gender ascriptions, which though neither permanent nor uniform across cultures and countries, affects self image or identity.

Changing gender relations is not necessarily a zero-sum game in which men are inevitably the losers. While transitional generations of men may have a sense of loss and women a sense of gain, these changes often become normalised and traditional gender relations can be reborn inside new employment forms and indeed men can reinvent their sense of self-worth and masculinity within the domestic sphere. Moreover, in some instances women also collude in sustaining the more traditional masculine self-image so that unequal gender relations in some ways endure quite significant changes in material conditions. This is not to say that important changes have not taken place. Many women have been empowered by receiving direct incomes, but the illustrations of the implications of new employment forms associated with globalization suggest that so far it would be premature to suggest that the end of patriarchy is on the immediate horizon. In this extract attention is given to the processes generating the global care chain and the ensuing implications for gender relations.

THE GLOBAL CARE CHAIN

One of the characteristics of the new global economy is that some workers are highly paid but time starved and this generates demand for a wide range of marketised services including cleaning, catering and caring, which are low paid and in which typically women are overrepresented. For highly paid professional people, work is rarely physically demanding, it takes place in congenial surroundings and for some may be preferable to domestic work, childcare or even leisure.

Indeed some employers provide a range of concierge services or 'lifestyle fixers' to enhance the workplace and facilitate long working hours, as the human resource manager at Microsoft explains:

"If you want to keep staff then you have to look after them," says Hilda Barrett, group human resources manager at Microsoft. "That's why we try and create a campus atmosphere at our office. We have top quality, gourmet food always available and in the evenings we even run cookery classes. Oh yes, and you also get Waitrose Direct, a grocery shopping service. Who wants to waste their spare time pushing a supermarket trolley?"

Extract from Work Unlimited—Anita Chaudhuri
Guardian Wednesday August 30, 2000.

It is not clear how many employers provide services of this kind, and to what proportion of employees they are available. They are clearly a bonus or perk for employees and can easily be withdrawn if circumstances change. In South East England a new media company withdrew its breakfast service in the downturn of 2001, while a major investment bank in the City of London provided all of the services identified in the quotation from Microsoft plus an emergency crèche to enable their employees to continue working if their usual arrangements failed. Some employers are beginning to appreciate that they will have to be more flexible if they are to retain highly qualified women in senior positions given the contemporary unequal gender division of domestic labour. Nevertheless, so far this flexibility takes place within very narrow confines. Employees referred to the firm that provided an emergency crèche, as 'understanding' because they accepted that mothers with young children might work a 10, rather than a 12 or 13, hour day in the office and be allowed them to complete work at home. Rather as in the case of firms allowing mothers breast-feeding breaks during the 10–12 hour working day, this seems to be more of a necessary concession, than an active promotion of work life balance. In both cases there seems to have been a reconciliation of life to work rather than vice versa.

Demand for marketed services, domestic, childcare workers and nannies is growing to facilitate long working hours, and more simply as a consequence of women working away from home, given the context of an unchanged domestic division of labour between women and men. Rather than leading to higher pay, however, this expansion has led to the development of global care chains, similar to commodity chains but depending directly on the movement of people, overwhelmingly women, which has changed the gender balance of contemporary migration flows.

Arlie Hochschild (2000), drawing on Rhacel Parreñas's research, refers to the case of 'Vicky Diaz' from the Philippines, a college-educated, former teacher and travel agent and mother of five who earns 400 US dollars a week working as a nanny for the two-year-old son of a wealthy Los Angeles family, while paying her own family's live-in worker in the Philippines 40 dollars a week. Vicky is a specific instance of the global care chain, which in general consists of:

> 'A series of personnel links between people across the globe based on the paid or unpaid work of caring. Usually women make up these chains, though

it's possible that some chains are made up of both women and men, or, in rare cases, made up just of men. Such care chains may be local, national or global. Global care chains … usually start in a poor country and end in a rich one. But some such chains start in poor countries, and move from rural to urban areas within that same poor country. Or they start in one poor country and extend to another slightly less poor country and then link one place to another within the latter country. Chains also vary in the number of links—some have one, others two or three—and each link varies in its connective strength. One common form of such a chain is: (1) an older daughter from a poor family who cares for her siblings while (2) her mother works as a nanny caring for the children of a migrating nanny who, in turn, (3) cares for the child of a family in a rich country (Hochschild 2000:131).

Thus, rather than value being unequally appropriated at different stages in the chain, as in a conventional commodity or value chain, care chains take a directly hierarchical form on the basis of gender, race and generation as poorer people, generally women from poorer regions of the world, care for the children and elderly relatives of people in richer regions. In other words, 'mothering is passed down the race/class/nation hierarchy, as each woman becomes a provider and hires a 'wife" (Hochschild: 2000: 137). Care chains are typically racialized as Caucasian workers are generally paid more than Asians and Asians more than those of African descent. In Rome, the Filipinas are paid more than Cape Verdeans (Tacoli 1999), and in Canada, Filipinas are 'housekeepers' and have to combine housework with childcare while Europeans are more likely to be 'nannies' and only required to care for children, even though the Filipina may be a university graduate and the European a qualified nursery nurse with fewer years of education (Pratt 1999). Thus, uneven development within the context of globalization, together with the undervaluation or nonrecognition of qualifications from poorer countries, can create a spatial dislocation by social class, as the following Filipina graduate interviewed in Rachel Parreñas's study commented:

'When my employer gave me the bucket for cleaning, I did not know where I had to start. Of course we are not so rich in the Philippines, *but we had maids*. I did not know how to start cleaning, and my feelings were of self pity. I kept on thinking that I just came to the United States to be a maid.' (my emphasis Parreñas 2001:150).

MIGRATION: AN INDIVIDUAL SOLUTION TO A STRUCTURAL PROBLEM?

Caring is sometimes a relatively easy way of gaining entry to richer countries. People do care work while qualifying for a Green Card in the USA before moving on to other forms of employment. Similarly in Canada, after two years as a live-in caregiver, people can apply for full citizenship, which would enable them to send for their families as well as take up other forms of employment. Thus, while the global care chain remains in place, individuals do not necessarily remain in fixed positions; care work can facilitate migration and be a stepping-stone to other activities. Nevertheless,

in the meantime care workers can be exposed to all the hazards associated with individualized forms of employment; in particular, indeterminate working hours, low wages and in some instances, sexual abuse. Even in countries where they exist, employment regulations do not always apply to live in caregivers and even when they do, may be difficult to effect, as workers may be unaware of them, unwilling to do anything that could prejudice their chance of permanent citizenship, or in some cases prefer the higher short-term incomes associated with unregistered work, for example the illegal Filipina care workers in Italy (Tacoli 1999).

Care chains are in some ways an inevitable consequence of globalization in the context of uneven capitalist development, unequal gender relations and reductions in state expenditure. As women move into paid employment outside the home, gaps arise in care and reproductive work that are filled by lower paid women internally and, when this supply is exhausted, from elsewhere. As with other forms of economic migration it is an individual solution to a structural problem and does little to redress the inequalities that generate the movements, except through migrant remittances. These remittances are a vital source of hard currency to many countries and form a significant component of GDP: for example 10% in the Philippines and 16.7% in Jamaica (IMO 2006; Sassen 2003). Indeed remittances have been institutionalized to the extent that to facilitate transfers between Hong Kong where many Filipinas work as maids and the Philippines ATMs have been established on street corners and 7-eleven convenience stores. So while migration is an individual solution to structural inequality, it has become institutionalized as some states rely on remittances to resolve their economic problems, especially debt and have developed formal labour export programmes to sustain such developments.

Structural inequalities between countries can explain the broad directions of migration, and the specific links between countries can be explained by the size and nature of the development gap, geographical proximity and cultural and historical ties. Thus there are major movements of people from Sri Lanka and the Philippines to the oil rich states in the Middle East, and richer countries in the Far East, such as Japan and Singapore; from South to North America, and from Eastern to Western Europe, in addition to patterns that follow former colonial relations. However, neither uneven development nor geographical or cultural proximity can explain individual migration decisions or the gendered nature of the care chain.

Individual migration decisions rest on how personal circumstances and preferences intersect with the wider economic and social context, that is on push and pull factors. In general, migrants are among the more highly skilled in their countries of origin but find themselves in the lower echelons of the societies to which they move, and this pattern exists in care work. The Filipinas who migrate to Rome, for example, are rarely the poorest. Rather they people who have experienced a sudden deterioration in personal finances, due to the death of a partner or loss of a middle-class job owing to public expenditure cuts, (often linked to structural adjustment policies), but who seek to maintain their living standard, in particular their children's education. The case of Vicky Diaz, referred to above is exemplary in this respect. Before working in the US, she had worked illegally in Taiwan as a housekeeper, factory worker and janitor. She was happy with the income but felt insecure

owing to her illegal status so she returned to the Philippines, but only stayed 3 months before using her savings from Taiwan to pay $8000 to use another woman's passport to go to the US. In the last nine years she has only spent three months with her family. She is currently trying to legalize her position so that she can reunify her family in the United States. Parreñas comments that:

> 'Vicky claims that she works outside of the Philippines so that her family does not become destitute, it is actually more accurate to say that Vicki works in Los Angeles to sustain a comfortable middle class life for her family in the Philippines' (Parreñas 2001:88).

The relative scale of different motivations is unknown but migration also takes place to escape from low incomes, oppression at home, in countries where divorce is not permitted, or, simply for adventure and to see the world, especially where local opportunities are limited (Tacoli 1999). Individual motivations are complex and varied. However, this does not mean that the undervaluation of this form of work, the conditions experienced by care workers and indeed its hierarchical and racialized nature should be overlooked. Migrants also experience emotional trauma from leaving their own families behind (Parreñas 2001 and 2005). Potentially, these anxieties and tensions can be eased by contemporary technologies, as Carla, a South African nurse working in Brighton and Hove while leaving her children, aged 2 and 8 with her mother in the Eastern Cape, explained:

'I always leave the computer on, I have to—I am a mother; there might be an email—they might need me.'

This could be construed as a form of 'virtual mothering,' which seems inherently contradictory but nevertheless gives a sense of closeness, especially in the case of older children that would have been missing in the past. Carla went on to say that her own mother was more of a mother to her children even before she came to the UK as she had been a union activist and often away from home. Carla was fortunate in the sense that her earnings were sufficient for her children to visit at Christmas and in the summer. The examples of Carla and Vicki both indicate that it is important not to victimize people who are simply making choices to make a better life for themselves and their children, albeit within constraints outside their control. In this sense globalization has expanded the range of choices for some people, although equally may have created the circumstances that that made these rather desperate choices necessary. The diversity of individual decision making can never be fully captured in theory, but there are common trends which derive from the structured economic and gendered inequalities in which these individual choices are made.

Gendering of Care Work

Globalization and uneven development cannot, however, explain the gendered nature of the care chain, the existence of which also undermines the suggestion that the feminization of employment is associated with the end of patriarchy. Buying childcare and domestic work may liberate some women from these traditional responsibilities, but these tasks are generally only transferred to other women, thus effectively leaving the gender distribution of roles unchanged. There is a redistribution of care work between women but little is done to revalue care or to bring about a more lateral sharing of care between women and men, although this may happen to some degree as women's absence from the home forces men to play a greater role irrespective of their preferences. The extent to which men engage in domestic and caring work has only recently been measured in national time use budget surveys and the limited quantifiable data that exists suggest that men's contribution remains low. Qualitative studies have similarly not found any major change, though it is possible that men's contribution may be understated, due to the lower frequency, but greater duration of household tasks performed by men (Jackson 2001) and because men may be reluctant to reveal the extent of this work, as it conflicts with prevailing conceptions of masculinity.

In market societies there is an inherent tendency for care work and personal services to be underpaid as they are highly labour intensive. Care is also a composite good, having a custodial aspect, making sure that no harm comes to the individuals being cared for, and a nurturing aspect; the emotional and psychological needs of the cared for (Folbre and Nelson 2000). Thus measuring the quality and effects of care work is inherently difficult owing to this composite character, its individualized performance, the fact that the cared for may be unable to effectively express their preferences and because the outcomes are associated with 'positive social externalities', i.e., good quality care leads to benefits for society as a whole. These factors together with the way that caring work is seen to be a natural talent of womanhood rather than a material competency or skill help to explain why wages are well below average. Where carework is fragmented in individual homes, small nurseries or care homes, low pay is sustained by the difficulty of establishing collective bargaining or exercising industrial power, and, perhaps as importantly, the way that the humane empathies of care workers are relied upon to prevent them from utilizing their potential power. This is not to suggest that industrial action never takes place. In 2002 in South East England many care home, childcare workers and learning support assistants protested against low public sector pay and the strength of their feeling led to headlines in the national newspaper, as Paul Kelso reported:

'A mums' army marched on Brighton town hall yesterday in support of the council workers' strike. Several hundred classroom assistants, social workers, carers, librarians, housing officers and street cleaners, most of them women attending their first union rally gathered to highlight the problems they say low pay is bringing to the outwardly affluent resort' (Kelso 2002:5).

Even though this action led to a pay increase, the new wage was equal to only 43% of current average hourly earnings for all adults (40% of the male, 49% of the female and 65% of the part time average), indicating the enduring relative low social value of care work. Thus even amongst organised care workers, wages are barely above the legal minimum, so outside these protected environments conditions are likely to be worse. If, however, workers endure very basic living conditions and low levels of personal consumption while working, allowing some money to be remitted, the purchasing power in the countries of origin is far greater, which explains why this migration take place, and why professional workers in poorer countries are prepared to work as domestics in the richer countries of the world. However, these movements do little to redress the structural inequalities between countries, which have been aggravated by some of the policies enforced on low and medium income countries by global institutions.

In its present form the marketization of care services is likely to both reinforce and to some extent undermine gender divisions. Feminization of employment does not automatically undermine patriarchalism but rather is associated with continuing divisions between women and men over the domestic division of labour and widening differentials between women as richer households buy childcare and domestic services, which is supplied largely by low-paid women workers. A more radical solution would be to encourage a greater sharing of roles between women and men. As Hochschild (2000: 144) has argued, 'if fathers shared the care of children, world-wide, care would be spread laterally instead of being passed down a social class ladder.' To affect greater gender equity a re-division of responsibilities between women and men would be required. An alternative possibility, provided that attention was also given to the terms and conditions of employment, would be for the state to play a greater role in meeting the care deficit. At present the level of state assistance varies between countries, being high for example in more social democratic countries such as the Nordic states. In the neo-liberal USA and UK, however, it could be argued that the state too has become a 'deadbeat dad' (Ehrenrich and Hochschild 2003:9) and made little or no provisions for the much higher proportion of working parents.

Obtaining equality in the workplace is unlikely while the question of providing adequate caring remains unresolved. Furthermore, as long as either individual or collective care is disproportionately supplied by low-paid female labour, then class and ethnic divisions between women will increase and gender inequity will remain. To resolve these issues it is therefore necessary to link workplace equity and child-care provision within the broader question of overall daily and generational social reproduction. There is a wealth of evidence to suggest that neither paid nor caring work is equated solely with negative utility. Qualitative analyses of mothers in paid work, ranging from high powered managers to assembly line workers, suggest that going to work can be a 'rest', a means of socialization and maintaining self-esteem, even where the conditions of paid work are extremely hazardous. Similarly caring for people can sometimes be similar to leisure. Whether watching football, walking in the park or sitting on the beach with a young child, is work, care, or leisure, depends largely on the relationships between the people involved, rather than on what is actually taking place. This point is clearly appreciated by paid domestic workers who point out that employers often like to treat them as one of the family in some respects, but not others. Strong emotional ties can be established between carers and the children they care for, which highlights the difficult and complex nature of care work, but these emotional ties can also be a form of exploitation, with undetermined working hours and low wages.

More generally, the lack of clear boundaries between work, care and leisure suggests that people's time could be more evenly spread between these activities, something that might also occur if care work was given higher monetary rewards. Hochschild (2000) argues that there is a cultural embrace for the idea of sharing parenting more between parents in the United States but a lag in implementation and the same could be said of the UK, where an increasing proportion of mothers are in paid employment, but this is often part time and fitted in around caring responsibilities. Similar accommodations are simply not expected of men and so where women do play a greater role in the labour market, the caring tasks are in general combined with paid work or transferred to the market and carried out by lower paid women, some of whom may be part of the global care chain.

IMPACT OF EMPLOYMENT ON GENDER RELATIONS—END OF THE FAMILY, END OF PATRIARCHY?

One of the common themes emerging from the qualitative experiential accounts of women's increased participation in the paid work, is that despite exploitation, it provides a sense of freedom, a space and time where they can be themselves and some enjoyment from socializing with other women. Paid employment is also found to raise self-confidence, self esteem and respect from other people in their household, so overall women are to some degree empowered by independent incomes. Fruit pickers, retail, electronic, textile and care workers and even some of the sex workers share these sentiments. Manuel Castells (1997) goes further by suggesting that the feminization of employment, together with new reproductive technologies, the feminist movement and the global culture in which ideas quickly spread, poses a challenge to patriarchalism. According to Castells (1997: 134–5):

'Patriarchalism is a founding structure of all contemporary societies. It is characterised by the institutionally enforced authority of males over females and their children in the family unit. … The patriarchal family, the cornerstone of patriarchalism, is being challenged in this end of the millennium by the inseparably related processes of the transformation of women's work and the transformation of women's consciousness.'

He goes on to say that

'if the patriarchal family crumbles, the whole system of patriarchalism, gradually but surely, and the whole of our lives, will be transformed. This is a scary perspective, and not only for men (Castells 1997:136).

Castells (1997) argues that although the feminization of employment places an 'unbearable burden on women's lives' as the paid work is generally added on to their other roles it increases women's bargaining power relative to men and undermines their role as sole or main provider. He emphasizes that he is only identifying and illustrating tendencies but a wide range of qualitative studies supports his ideas, in this respect. For example, a manager at a textile factory in Bangladesh observes that

'Girls in my factory marry several times because if there is any trouble with the husband, they think they can survive on their own, they need not stay. They walk out and simply get married again' (textile factory manager reported in Kabeer 1995).

Employment in the electronics factories in Malaysia also allowed single women greater freedom, even in the 1970s. Grossman (1979) comments that given the severe working and living conditions she was about to ask the women why they worked there but then:

After casting a sidelong glance at the men at the next table, Tuti shot the rest of us a conspiratorial smile, eyes twinkling. I stared straight into the coffee I was stirring, pulling the Malay words together in my mind to ask why they had come to work in this factory. Suddenly I laughed to myself, realizing that part of the answer was right there at this coffee stand at 11 'o'clock at night. … They come for the money, of course but also for the freedom. They talk of freedom to go out late at night, to have a boyfriend, to wear blue jeans, high heels and make up. Implicitly they contrast this freedom with the sheltered regulated lives they would lead with their families in Malay villages and small towns. They revel in their escape from the watchful eyes of fathers and brothers (Grossman 1979: 13).

More recent studies have focused on men's reactions to these changes, and similar associations have been found between the expansion in the number of women receiving independent incomes and men's loss of self-esteem. In Sylvia Chant's interviews with low-income men in 1997 in Guanacaste, Costa Rica, Martín, a 30-year-old bricklayer commented, 'A woman who has her own money loses affection for her husband. Many marriages have been ruined because of this' and similarly Luís, a waiter argued that a man who cannot provide for his wife and children loses self esteem and that his social image 'isn't worth anything' (Chant 2001: 211). Similarly in Sri Lanka husbands of migrant maids are stigmatized for being unable to fulfil traditional gender roles.

Entry into paid work alone does not automatically bring about change. Many women are made to hand over their earnings to their husbands or families and men can also adjust to the changing circumstances by investing new arrangements with a revised, but nonetheless important, self-image. Javier Pineda (2001) reports on Cali, Colombia, where male employment had declined and women had been offered the chance to be involved in a micro-credit scheme financed by WWB.[3] While women owned the new activities, several men explained how, nonetheless there was a complementary division of tasks, as Ramón argued:

> It is very easy to get adapted to the work because we have to divide the work. I took production and she does management. Why? Because for a good worker is very difficult to manage and produce at the same time, because it does not pay. Then she is at the front of the business and I am at the front of production (Ramón a respondent in Pineda 2001: 81).

Other men described this same division of labour as women doing the 'light' work while men did the 'heavy' work, thereby maintaining self-image through retaining stereotypical gender divisions in the new context. This division might reasonably be referred to as mental and manual labour, but if it was it would imply a reversal of the gender hierarchy. The fact that it is not described in this way suggests that existing unequal gender relations have a resilience or durability that can withstand changing forms of employment, thus work is not only a bearer of gender relations (Elson 1999) but something through which unequal gender relations can be reborn.

Cooperative Conflict Model of Household Relations

More formally, these issues have been theorized in the cooperative conflict model (Sen 1990; Kabeer 1995), which explores intra-household bargaining and the criteria for breakdown. At the micro level, despite growing individualization and the 'crisis' of the family, most societies continue to be organized around households, which are institutions based on relatively long-term commitments and through which individuals obtain their survival needs and within which children are born and raised. Households take different forms in different societies, their boundaries can be permeable, and their composition can change over time. Within households there are generally different possible divisions of labour between members, especially relating to the amount and timing of paid and unpaid work in order to meet their survival needs or lifestyle preferences. The cooperative conflict model perspective considers how households arrive at their choices.[4]

Households rest on implicit contracts relating to the claims and obligations that household members can legitimately make on each other. When there are different possible divisions of labour, individual households members are likely to benefit to different degrees depending on the choices made, which is why there is conflict as well as cooperation, so final choices are arrived at through bargaining. This can be done in a very implicit and sometimes non-conscious way. Their relative fall back positions, that is the level of utility or well being they would experience if the cooperation broke down, influences the bargaining position or power of the different household members. Those with stronger fall back positions, that is those less dependent on the cooperative arrangement, have more power to affect the outcome. The influences on the fall back positions are profoundly gendered and generally and especially in the past, have 'coalesce (d) in favour of men as a category' (Kabeer 2000:29). The reason is largely because market/public work, in which men are overrepresented, is perceived to be more important than home/private work, and thus men are perceived to make more significant contributions to the household and correspondingly merit a greater say in how household resources are allocated. Even with the growing feminization of employment, men's market work is generally paid more than women's market work. Effectively this model would support Castells's (1997) claims and that of the textile manager in Bangladesh quoted above, that paid work increases the fall back position of women and makes them less dependent on the survival of the household and correspondingly increases their likelihood of breaking the implicit contract. Given the continuing unequal division of domestic labour and childcare, generally women remain within the household and it is men who leave or are even asked to leave, as their contributions fall, and their presence becomes less essential, giving rise to the increase in female-headed households observed throughout the world.

The impact of the feminization of employment can, however, be overstated. It is important to recognize that not all women are able to keep the income they earn; contemporary paid work is often flexible and insecure; vertical and horizontal segregation remain and women are concentrated in lower positions and lower paying sectors, so the relationship between paid work and the strength of the fall back position is also gendered. Further, many women are entering the paid labour force just at the moment when the terms and conditions of employment have deteriorated and when men's employment and incomes are in decline, making more than one earned income a condition for survival or to maintain customary lifestyles. In the Mexican maquiladoras, for example, wages paid have been found to be lower than those paid in industries arising from the previous import substitution strategy. Thus whereas in the past, men would earn a family wage, allowing the traditional gender division of labour, in the new context more than one income is necessary. Women and men therefore negotiate together to organize their working times, for example, offsetting night and day shifts to cover their childcare responsibilities, or draw upon other generally female younger relatives to live with them to help care for children, while continuing their own education (Cravey 1997). These circumstances, combined with the increasing trend towards having to pay for public services such as health and education, as well as the pervasive and insistent global marketing of consumer goods, means that women's incomes are generally fully absorbed even where they have control over them, making this control more of an added responsibility than an opportunity to exercise individual discretion and empowerment.

Household situations vary. They exist within local, regional and national and now global settings all of which may shape social norms and the nature of bargaining within individual households. That is in addition to patriarchal or unequal gender relations within the household, the economic, social and cultural context is characterized by widening spatial inequalities, as Diane Elson (1999) argues:

'There is a paradox at the heart of contemporary restructuring as far as many women are concerned. On the one hand, their bargaining power in relation to the men in their households, their communities, their networks, and the organizations of their civil society, may often (though not, as we have argued, inevitably) be increasing as a result of their greater participation in labour markets. But at the same time their, their households, their communities, their networks, the organization of their civil society are more and more at the mercy of global market forces that are out of control' (Elson 1999:618).

In particular, the global context heightens competition and the way that corporations have responded to this through chains of subcontracting has increased the insecurity of paid employment. Furthermore, despite the evident gains from paid work for women as individuals, two key problems remain which limit women's bargaining position in the household and correspondingly the extent to which it is possible to argue that patriarchy is challenged by the feminization of employment. First of all, structures remain that limit the range of paid work that women do, for example, their presence in high level jobs, partly but not

exclusively determined by their continuing responsibility for organizing, managing and carrying out a disproportionate share of reproductive, domestic and care work together with working hours that deny these responsibilities. Second, the kinds of jobs in which women are disproportionately represented are on average paid less than those where men are overrepresented, reflecting in part the low social value given to certain forms of work, especially care, simply because women do them, i.e. pay norms themselves embody gender inequality. Third, even when the income generating capacities of women and men have been reversed, that is where women are the sole earners in a dual person heterosexual household, despite the loss of role as provider, men are still able to retain a dominant position by redefining their masculinity (Perrons 2004, Ch.5).

CONCLUSION

This extract has examined the effect of globalization on people's lives, in particular the way that there has been a geographical expansion of capitalist social relations of production as a whole range of activities, from agribusiness to care work, have become integrated on a global scale. It has put some substance to the idea that people in different places are increasingly interconnected through their work and explored the idea that the feminization of employment will profoundly alter gender relations. While changes have taken place, and many women feel more empowered as a consequence of independent incomes, the impact on gender equality is more limited. One reason for this is because of the new circumstances in which paid work is carried out and another, because unequal gender relations seem to be resilient to material change and reappear in new ways with new forms of employment.

DISCUSSION QUESTIONS

1. What do you know about the origins of the goods and services you purchase and the conditions under which they are produced or supplied?

2. Will the feminization of employment lead to greater gender equality or the 'end of patriarchy' as has suggested by Manuel Castells (1997).

3. How well does the cooperative conflict model represent the negotiation of gender relations within the household?

4. To what extent is the transformative potential of the feminization of employment constrained by the new and more precarious forms of employment and the continuing, profoundly gendered social context within which it takes place?

5. Do men inevitably lose from the feminization of employment?

NOTES

1. Global value or commodity chains describe the complex interconnections between the different stages of a commodity's life from direct production through to final sale. The connections are often between a major firm and complex tiers of subcontractors across the globe. The amount of value produced and retained at each stage is assessed.

2. This is Millennium Indicator 11, the other three indicators under Millennium Goal 3 are the ratio of girls to boys in primary sector and tertiary education; ratio of literate women to men 15–24 years old and the proportion of seats held by women in parliament.

3. WWB—is Women's World Banking, a financial NGO.

4. The cooperative conflict household bargaining model was developed in part to redress the individualism associated with traditional neoclassical economics. Unorthodox economic household allocation models decision-making is assumed to take place on the basis of atomistically determined individual tastes and preferences and final preferences determined by a benevolent dictator who acts on the basis of maximizing overall household utility.

REFERENCES

Castells, M. (1997) *The Power of Identity* Oxford: Blackwell.

Chant, S. (2001) 'Families on the verge of Breakdown? Views on Contemporary Trends in Family Life in Gunacaste, Costa Rica' in C. Jackson (ed) *Men at Work. Labour, Masculinities Development*, London: Frank Cass.

Chant, S. and Pedwell, C. (2008) *Women, gender and informal economy: an assessment of ILO research and suggested ways forward. An overview of ILO research on women gender and the informal economy*, Geneva: International Labour Organization.

Chaudhuri, A. (2000) Work Unlimited—*The Guardian* August 30.

Cravey, A. (1997) 'The Politics of Reproduction: Households in the Mexican Industrial Transition', *Economic Geography,* 73 (2):166–186.

Ehrenrich, B. and Hochschild, A. (2003) *Global Women,* London: Granta BooksElson, D (1999) 'Labour markets as gendered institutions: equality, efficiency and empowerment issues,' *World Development* 27 (3): 611–27.

Folbre, N and Nelson, J. (2000) For Love or Money—Or both? *Journal of Economic Perspectives* 14 (4): 123–140.

Grossman, R. (1979) 'Women's place in the integrated circuit,' Southeast Asia Chronicle—pacific Research SRC 66 (9) No. 5.

Hochschild, A. (2000) 'Global care chains and emotional surplus value', in W. Hutton and A. Giddens (eds) *On the edge. Living with global capitalism,* London: Jonathan Cape.

International Migration Outlook (2006) International migration remittances and their role in development http://www.oecd.org/dataoecd/61/46/38840502.pdf.

Jackson, C. (ed) (2001) *Men at Work. Labour, Masculinities, Development* London: Frank Cass.

Kabeer, N. (1995) Necessary, sufficient or irrelevant? : women, wages and intra-household power relations in urban Bangladesh, IDS Discussion paper no. 25 Sussex : Institute of Development Studies.

Kabeer, N. (2000) *The power to choose: Bangladeshi women and labour market decisions in London and Dhaka*, London: Verso.

Parreñes, R. (2001) *Servants of Globalization Women, Migration and Domestic Work*, California: Stanford University Press.

Parreñas, R. (2005) Children of Global Migration, Transnational Families and Gendered Worlds, California: Stanford University Press.

Perrons, D (2004) *Globalization and Social Change. People and Places in a Divided World*, London: Routledge.

Pineda, J. (2001) Partners in Women-headed Households: Emerging Masculinites? In C. Jackson (ed) *Men at Work. Labour, Masculinities, Development*, London: Frank Cass.

Sassen, S. (2003) Global cities and survival circuits, in B. Ehrenrich and A. Hochschild (eds) *Global Women,* London: Granta.

Sen, A. (1990) 'Gender and cooperative conflicts', in I. Tinker (ed.) *Persistent inequalities, women and world development*, Oxford: Oxford University Press.

Tacoli, C. (1999) 'International migration and the restructuring of gender asymmetries: continuity and change among Filipino migrants in Rome,' *International Migration Review* 33 (Fall): 658–659.

Religion and Social Change

by Charles H. Lippy and Eric Tranby

IN THIS CHAPTER

In this chapter, we focus on the complex relationship between religion and broader social changes. We first focus on how and why religion works as a conservative force in society that favors the status quo. We then turn to the conditions under which religion becomes a force for progressive social change, examining the assets of religion that make it a powerful force for social change of any kind, when and how religious groups start or join social movements, and when social movements mobilize religious resources and rhetoric to motivate participation and engagement. We conclude by discussing religious violence, particularly the link between fundamentalism and religious terrorism, as well as delving more deeply into the phenomenon of modern fundamentalism.

MAIN TOPICS COVERED

- Religion has a varied and complex relationship with social change. The form of the relationship depends on whether individuals, groups, or a whole society are involved and also on the historical period when it develops.

- Religion often acts as a conservative force in society, favoring keeping things the old way.

- Religious believers have used their faith as the basis for challenging inequality and advocating for progressive social change.

- Sociologists of religion have developed theories to explain what attributes of religion make it a powerful force for social change.

- Modern religious violence is frequently tied to religious fundamentalism, itself a contested phenomenon with multiple definitions and characteristics.

- When religious violence is used by religious fundamentalists, it takes the form of theater and is meant to place religion at the center of political and private life.

- Religious terrorism is distinct from secular terrorism, and religious fundamentalism does not usually lead to violence, especially in democratic societies.

RELIGION AND SOCIAL CHANGE: A COMPLICATED RELATIONSHIP

Religion has varied and complex relationships with social change, and its effects depend on the individual, group, society, and broader historical period under examination. In this chapter we will explore three ways in which religion can be a force for social change and the conditions under which it operates in each of these three ways. First, religion can be inherently conservative in favoring the established status quo because religious beliefs and practices help to maintain the political and economic power structure of society. Second, religion can be an agent of progressive social change because religious beliefs and practices provide the motivation and resources to dismantle oppressive and discriminatory political and economic power structures. Third, religion can be a force for division and violence in modern society by fostering fundamentalism and intolerance.

Religion continues to have a large public role in the modern world, even if religious authority is, in general, declining. In other words, we assume that religion is not just a private entity that operates within its own sphere or simply provides meaning to individuals' lives. It does these things, but it also plays a role in supporting or resisting broader social change and popular social movements, which is the focus of this chapter. In previous chapters, we focused on other aspects of the public roles of religion, including the relationship between religion and political behavior (Chapter 9) and the ways in which religion is transmitted (Chapter 8). We also described how religion shapes gender norms and roles (Chapter 10) and racial stereotypes (Chapter 12). In Chapter 19, we explore how religion shapes attitudes regarding national identity and belonging.

RELIGION AS A CONSERVATIVE FORCE

Historically, sociologists of religion and other religious scholars have considered religion to be an inherently conservative force in society, where conservative means aiming to keep society from changing, and thus to "conserve" society. In other words, religious belief and practice help to support and maintain the political, economic, and cultural structures of society. However, the strength of this relationship is weaker in contemporary American life than it has been previously.

In classical theory and research, this conservatism usually takes the form of justifying the actions of the religious, political, and economic elite. Think back, for example, to Marx's statement that "religion is an opiate" because it blinds people to the broader inequalities in society. It is easy to see why this has historically been the case because, like any other institution, religious institutions are dependent upon the favor of those in power. In particular, state-sponsored or mandated religions are unlikely to speak out against the status quo because they usually depend on their tax exempt status, a form of government support, in order to survive financially. Illustrating these doctrines are divine right theologies developed by various cultures that argue the leader of the culture or the civil government has been ordained by God(s) or is a representative of God(s) on earth as a way to justify power. In the contemporary US, many religious institutions work within the political process to achieve their aims rather than believing in the divine right of our elected leaders, as described in Chapter 9.

More recently, analysts claim that religion supports the status quo through its lack of opposition to inequalities in society. For example, many Protestant thinkers teach that inequalities in wealth and poverty and other

---

BOX 7.1 THEODICIES OF SUFFERING AND DOMINANCE

According to Max Weber, a theodicy is a system of belief that helps to explain human suffering, inequalities, sickness, and other negative aspects of human life and society. Theodicies help to explain the gap between what we believe should happen and what actually does happen, more commonly referred to as the questions of "why bad things happen to good people." There are multiple types of theodicies, but two dominate:

-   Suffering theodicies are the religious beliefs that help the lower segments of society come to terms with their position and what they can do to gain redemption.

-   Dominance theodicies are the religious beliefs that help the upper segments of society come to terms with their position and any ethical obligations because of it.

---

types of power differential are part of the natural order and will always be part of society. There are also teachings, codified in the public mind by books like *The Secret* by Rhonda Byrne and the emphasis on the Prosperity Gospel in some evangelical denominations described in Chapter 5, that moral, ethical, or proper behavior results in greater life success, including material success. An implication or indirectly stated part of these theologies is that not being successful in life, particularly being poor, is a direct result of immoral behavior. The idea of the relationship between religion, power, and inequality was formalized by Max Weber in his concept of theodicy, or systems of belief that help to explain human suffering, inequality, or other negative aspects of human life and society. Theodicies, when powerful, make it unlikely that religious leaders or believers will actively work to overcome inequality in their society because these inequalities are explained in religious terms.

RELIGION AS A FORCE FOR PROGRESSIVE SOCIAL CHANGE

Although religion is usually considered to be a conservative force in society, there are numerous examples where religious believers, leaders, and institutions have used their faith as the basis for challenging existing power structures and inequalities and starting or joining large-scale progressive social movements. Examples of movements in the US that have received support from religions, particularly Protestants of various stripes, include the anti-slavery movement, the temperance movement, and the labor movement in the nineteenth and early twentieth centuries. The role of religious institutions in the civil rights movement, anti-colonialism movements, anti-war movements, the feminist movement, the pro-life movement, and the movement for or opposition to equal rights for alternative sexualities is the subject of much discussion in Part II and Part III of this book. Religious institutions have also been invested in ongoing local movements to combat poverty or hunger, as discussed in Chapter 12, and environmental action. Not all popular movements use religious justification, and some religious groups have opposed or tried to suppress such social movements. For example, Chapter 11 discussed the ways in which religion was used both to justify and to oppose slavery by different stakeholders.

Research on social movements has largely ignored religion for two primary reasons. First, many social movements researchers assume that society is becoming more secular over time and therefore do not consider religion an important area of study. Second, others believe that religion does not influence participation in social movements because they assume that religion largely exists to provide individuals with meaning and create social solidarity. However, sociologists of religion have explored a number of issues related to religion and social movements. These include what attributes or characteristics religion has that make it a powerful force for social change, when religious groups will start or join social movements, and when social movements will mobilize religious resources and rhetoric to motivate participation and engagement.

Christian Smith, in his book *Disruptive Religion*, systematically categorizes all the possible assets (attributes and characteristics) that religion has to mobilize, promote, and assist social movements. Smith places religious assets for social movements in six main categories: transcendent motivation, organizational resources,

---

BOX 7.2 RELIGIOUS ASSETS FOR SOCIAL MOVEMENTS

Christian Smith, in his book *Disruptive Religion*, systematically categorizes all the possible assets that religion has that are significant for social movement activism. Smith places religious assets for social movements in six main categories:

- Transcendent motivation
  - legitimation for protest rooted in the sacred
  - moral imperatives
  - motivating icons, rituals, or other forms
  - altruistic ideologies and practices.
- Organizational assets
  - trained and experienced leadership
  - financial resources
  - communication channels
  - authority structures.
- Shared identity
  - common purpose among strangers
  - large-scale identifying structures.
- Social and geographic positioning
  - geographic and regional dispersion
  - social diffusion across social boundaries.
- Privileged legitimacy
  - respect for religious leaders
  - freedom of religion.
- Institutional self-interest.

shared identity, social and geographic positioning, privileged legitimacy, and institutional self-interest. *Transcendent motivation* allows social movements to be rooted in the sacred and define the main goal of the movement as preserving moral imperatives such as love, justice, freedom, and equity. Religion, then, supplies the social movement with icons, rituals, songs, and testimonies of faith in order to motivate members towards social action. For example, the hymn "We Shall Overcome" is indelibly linked with the civil rights movement due to its frequent use by protesters. It demands that members are self-disciplined, altruistic, and ready to sacrifice themselves for a greater good, all for the sake of their faith. The extended and long-term focus of many evangelical groups and individuals on abortion illustrates the dedication that religion can encourage in members. This dedication, however, can also lead to extremist acts, which we discuss later in this chapter.

Religious institutions have substantive *organizational resources* because religions have trained and capable leaders readily available as well as financial support from member donations and pre-existing networks of communication for recruits. Believers in the same religion have a *shared identity*, which provides a basis for strangers to unite towards a common purpose and can serve as a foundation for several groups or congregations of people to come together to advocate for a common purpose or goal. Religious institutions, because they are often spread across a region or the whole country, have optimal *social and geographic positioning* in that movements can unite over large distances rather than only in one location. Religion also has the unique ability to cut across social class, occupational, racial, ethnic, and national lines.

Additionally, religious officials are often taken more seriously than politicians, social radicals, or others, and religion has more autonomy in the US than many other institutions due to our religious freedoms (the basis for which is described in Chapter 9) giving religion *privileged legitimacy*. The civil rights movement is the quintessential example of each of these assets. As described in Chapter 11, Black Protestant churches served as an organizational and logistical base for the movement, especially in its early days, and these meetings could not legally be interfered with by the civil authorities. The leaders of the movement used religious motivation to appeal to mainline Protestants and Catholics in many parts of the country, in addition to African Americans.

Finally, religion can aid social movements in order to preserve *institutional self-interest* when the state encroaches in areas that religion used to control. For a very recent example, see the controversy among Catholic leaders over the Obama administration's decision in 2012 to require the health care plans of religious organizations to cover contraception for female employees.

While religious groups have tremendous assets and ability to give to social movements, the conditions have to be right before they will start or join social movements. For example, Protestants only began to back the antislavery and temperance movements in large numbers when many preachers began to call on Protestants to engage in personal transformation and public confessions to absolve the special sins of the nation. Additionally, religious groups generally only start or join social movements when a feature or change in society is perceived to be a threat to deeply held religious beliefs or when participation in a social movement is portrayed by the leaders of the social movement as a struggle between good and evil. For example, social movements related to gender, sexuality, poverty, hunger, slavery, war, or the pro-life movement generate a great deal of religious interest because these issues have been a central focus of much religious teaching. On the other hand, environmental activism, anti-globalization, and the labor movement have far less religious support because there are fewer core religious teachings on them. This is slowly changing, however, with the 2011 release of a documentary and lecture in the evangelical Protestant media called *Resisting the Green Dragon*. The backers of this media enterprise developed it in direct opposition to the environmental movement. They believe that the environmental movement is turning into a religion among some young people and, therefore, is a threat to the power of religion.

Religious leaders profoundly affect the likelihood of denominations or particular congregations to start or join social movements. For example, when the governing structure of the denomination or congregation is very hierarchical, as in the Catholic church, members will be far more likely to join social movements if those at the top of the hierarchy advocate participation. Members of more democratically structured congregations or denominations are less likely to listen to those at the top of the hierarchy, but are more likely to join if their clergy advocates for it or if the member personally feels it is important. The age, race, and gender of the religious leader also matter. For example, research reviewed in Chapter 10 shows that female leaders are more likely to take positions that advocate for social movement protest. In addition, younger leaders, leaders who are a racial minority, and those from or in an urban setting are more

likely to lead the congregation to participate in social movements.

Secular social movements often try to mobilize religious resources and rhetoric by building coalitions with congregations or religious individuals. It is no surprise that leaders of secular social movements would attempt to do this, given the powerful assets of religion described by Smith, but this mobilization only works under a certain set of circumstances. First, when the majority of those in the movement share a religion, or have closely related religions, the movement will try to draw on religious resources and rhetoric. This is especially likely to be true when the movement is targeted at a dominant structure with a different religion. Second, secular social movements are likely to draw on religion when religious beliefs or leaders are at odds with the status quo or otherwise sympathetic to the movement. These two points are illustrated by the pro-life movement, which unites evangelicals and fundamentalists against what they perceive to be secular political and social forces favoring abortion. Third, secular social movements may attempt to mobilize social movements when alternative organizational structures and political access is not available. For example, Mary Patillo-McCoy and other researchers have found that the African American church continues to be heavily involved in social justice movements and features a more encompassing ministry than white denominations because African Americans are still unable to fully participate in the economic, social, and political life of the country.

Attempts to mobilize religious support into broader social movements can be very powerful in initiating social change. However, there is a limit to this role. Differences in religious beliefs can be an obstacle to mobilizing groups for change, as can differences in race/ethnicity,

---

BOX 7.3 EXAMPLES OF FUNDAMENTALIST GROUPS

Beginning in the 1970s, fundamentalist groups emerged in many of the world's major religions. Below are examples of some fundamentalist groups. The Christian fundamentalist groups active in the US are described in Chapters 2 and 10.

- Christian fundamentalist groups:
    - the Moral Majority
    - the Christian Coalition
    - fundamentalist LDS movements.
- Islamic fundamentalist groups:
    - Islamic theocracy in Iran
    - Hamas and Hezbollah
    - the Muslim Brotherhood.
- Buddhist fundamentalist groups:
    - Nichiren Buddhism
    - the New Kadampa Tradition and the Dorje Shugden.
- Hindu fundamentalist groups:
    - Hindutva and Hindu Nationalism.
- Jewish fundamentalist groups
    - Haredi (ultra-Orthodox Judaism).

---

sexuality, or gender. For example, rather than uniting around views of same-sex relationships, mainline Protestant congregations and individual congregations carve out "niches" for themselves in regards to sexuality, with some being more welcoming and others less so. These congregational niches let members be with those who share the same assumptions about these moral debates. Additionally, official Catholic Church policy endorses very traditional roles; however, it has also (inadvertently) provided spaces, such as social justice organizations, academic institutions, liturgy groups, and parishes with no priest, that have allowed the feminist movement to flourish. Disagreements about appropriate strategies and tactics for action between secular and religious leaders are common and can lead to rifts in

social movements. See, for example, the split between the Christian leaders of the civil rights movement, who favored non-violent action, and the secular and Nation of Islam leaders of the Black Nationalist movement, who favored more radical action.

RELIGION AS A FORCE FOR FOSTERING FUNDAMENTALISM AND VIOLENCE

Violence motivated by religion is an old and pervasive issue. For example, in 2011, more than fifty people died each day around the world in attacks motivated in part by religion. Religious violence occurs across religious groups, within religious groups, and as acts of religious terrorism. Because religion functions, in part, to define boundaries around social groups, as detailed in

---

BOX 7.4 WHAT IS FUNDAMENTALISM?

Scholars have wrestled with trying to define fundamentalism precisely. Here are some of their attempts:

- Martin Riesebrodt (1990): "an urban movement directed primarily against dissolution of personalistic, patriarchal notions of order and social relations and their replacement by depersonalized principles."
- Gabriel A. Almond (2003): "a discernible pattern of religious militancy by which self-styled 'true believers' attempt to arrest the erosion of religious identity, fortify the borders of the religious community, and create viable alternatives to secular institutions and behaviors."

Chapter 1, some level of religious violence is likely to be inevitable, especially for groups that define themselves explicitly in opposition to the outside world. There are numerous historical and contemporary examples of religious violence, such as the Crusades, the Thirty Years' War, and the conflict in Northern Ireland. The focus of this chapter is on modern religious violence, usually terrorism, which has been a focus of American religious, social, and political life since the terrorist attacks on New York and Washington DC on September 11, 2001. Terrorism is often tied to religious fundamentalism. In this context, religious fundamentalism refers to the transnational, transcultural version of evangelical fundamentalism described in Chapter 2 and Chapter 5.

In the 1970s and 1980s, fundamentalist movements emerged, or re-emerged, in most of the world's major religions nearly simultaneously. Examples include the Christian Coalition in the US, Hamas and Hezbollah in Palestine, and Hindutva in India. Michael Emerson and David Hartman, in their review of the sociological literature on fundamentalism, state that sociologists were unprepared for this emergence. This means that religious fundamentalism is a recent area of focus in the sociology of religion. As a result, there is much we still do not know about the reasons for the global emergence of fundamentalism when it did or how best to measure it.

Even defining fundamentalism is a contentious issue, but there is consensus that fundamentalism is a contextual phenomenon and cannot be defined without understanding the social reality that surrounds it. In particular, fundamentalism cannot be understood apart from modernity nor exist outside of modernity, a notion described in Chapter 2. Most simply, fundamentalism can be defined as the rejection of some aspects of modernity on religious grounds. Fundamentalists, then, define themselves in opposition to modern society and attempt to stop what they believe is the destruction of values, social ties, and meaning caused by modernity. On the other hand, from a modernist viewpoint, fundamentalists are religious reactionaries attempting to restore oppression, patriarchy, and intolerance.

A number of researchers have tried to define the characteristics of fundamentalist groups and movements. Martin Riesebrodt compares the fundamentalist movements in the US, as described in Chapter 5, and the rise of the Shi'ite fundamentalist movement in Iran, culminating in the rise of a theocracy. He finds similarities in terms of the ideological characteristics of the two movements. Both movements reacted to what they perceived

---

BOX 7.5 CHARACTERISTICS OF FUNDAMENTALIST GROUPS

Riesebrodt and Almond, Appleby, and Sivan compare fundamentalist groups across countries. They identify several ideological and organizational characteristics that fundamentalist groups have in common.

- Ideological characteristics:
  - reaction to the marginalization of religion
  - statutory ethical monism
  - selective and dualistic worldview
  - millennialism and messianism
  - patriarchal moralism.
- Organizational characteristics:
  - select, chosen membership
  - sharp ideological or physical boundaries
  - authoritarian organizational structure
  - behavioral requirements.

---

to be the *marginalization of religion* in their society. Using these similarities, Riesebrodt characterized fundamentalism as having an organic social ethic based on *statutory ethical monism*. This means that the only source of morality in fundamentalism movements is the one revealed by God and contained in the holy texts of divine law; other notions of morality are rejected. Fundamentalists believe that their ethical and moral rules are universal in that they apply to all people in all times and cultures and regulate all situations and spheres of life. Thus, fundamentalism is religious republicanism, which is the attempt to realize divine law, the adherence to one's own religious roots, and the rejection of non-religious influence in all spheres of life. Religious republicanism, then, had a *selective and dualistic worldview* in that it divides the world into two opposing viewpoints: God and Satan. Riesebrodt also identifies *millennialism and messianism* as characteristics of fundamentalist movements. In other words, fundamentalists believe that

they herald the coming end of the world in which there will be a victory over evil and true believers will be ushered into the spiritual realm by a savior or messiah.

Riesebrodt also identified other similarities in the two movements. For example, both featured *patriarchal moralism* such that female bodies were seen as seducers of men and women's appropriate role within society is as mothers and housekeepers. Fundamentalist groups in both countries also rejected organized welfare, instead focusing on the moral and voluntary obligation of the rich to give to the poor.

Almond, Appleby, and Sivan compare eighteen fundamentalist movements throughout the world. They find similar ideological characteristics among them, as did Riesebrodt, but also outline some common structural or organizational characteristics of these movements. They find that fundamentalist movements have a *select, chosen membership* in which members believe that they are divinely called to the group. They also find that fundamentalist groups draw *sharp ideological or physical boundaries* to separate themselves from sinful society and achieve high levels of group solidarity and cohesion. Third, fundamentalist movements usually have an *authoritarian organizational structure* led by a charismatic leader or leadership. Finally, fundamentalist groups usually have elaborate *behavioral requirements* in order to create a powerful, conforming dimension among followers. Such behavior includes distinctive music, rules for dress, and censorship of reading materials. Given this set of characteristics, Christianity, Judaism, and Islam are more likely than other religions to have strong fundamentalist movements, although they do exist across religions.

In the US, fundamentalism seemed to disappear from the religious scene in the 1920s, as described in Chapter 5. However, the historian Joel Carpenter presents a convincing case that fundamentalists didn't disappear completely, but instead retreated from the public arena. They formed a vast network of agencies that linked them together, including publishing houses like Scripture Press and independent Bible schools and colleges such as the Practical Bible Training School and Bob Jones University. Within these networks, US fundamentalists eschewed politics and most of the trappings of society as polluted by sin and otherwise tainted. They were content to remain apart so long as American culture maintained a veneer of Christian religiosity: to give some examples, the addition of "under God" to the Pledge of Allegiance, placing "In God We Trust" on all coins and currency (described in Chapter 4), the fact that children in public schools across the nation engaged in prayer before the start of the school day, and public school assemblies often began with reading a passage from the Bible. However, the 1960s and ensuing decades brought about challenges to this Christian veneer, with the Supreme Court decisions forbidding devotional prayer, Bible reading in public schools, and *Roe v. Wade* (described in Chapter 5 and 9), increasing religious pluralism (the focus of Chapters 18 and 19), and decreasing religious affiliation (the focus of Chapter 16). These changes spurred fundamentalists to action, with major fundamentalist leaders, such a Jerry Falwell and Pat Robertson, establishing powerful organizations meant to influence public life.

Fundamentalist movements are of interest to sociologists of religion because, in part, they are thought to lead to religious violence and religious terrorism. Mark Juergensmeyer's volume on religious terrorism is the seminal sociological volume on the topic. He first demonstrates that most fundamentalist groups are not violent, although some are, and that not all religiously based violence is carried out by fundamentalists, although religious terrorism is. He then argues that fundamentalism can turn to violence because it provides the ideology, motivation, and organizational structure for individuals to commit violent acts.

Religious violence takes a particular form when committed by fundamentalists. Religious terrorism is used as a theatrical form of violence; in other words, it is as a symbolic act. It uses images of a cosmic war between good and evil or martyrdom and is performed to dramatize a cause. Religious violence is meant to place religion at the center of political and private life and oppose the secularization of society. By looking at terrorism through the lens of the theater, Juergensmeyer examines the stage where terrorist attacks occur, the symbolic meaning behind the target of the violence, the time or date when the "performance" is done, and how the audience perceives the event. For example, the terrorist attacks on September 11, 2001, targeted the World Trade Center, a symbol of American economic power, the Pentagon, a symbol of American military power, and (unsuccessfully) either the US Capitol building or the White House, the seat of American political power. The attackers chose that day because the weather would be clear, ensuring a maximum number of people would see the attacks. The stated motivation of the attackers was to end the US presence in Saudi Arabia, end the American support of Israel, and to end US sanctions against Iraq. Osama Bin Laden declared a holy war and the killing of American civilians until such aims were met. A key element of this type of violence is that it is unlikely to end due to compromise on the part of fundamentalists because it is based on absolutist moral values and seen as morally justified. The long nature of the "war on terror" illustrates the duration of these conflicts.

Because religious terrorism is a form of theater, there are differences between religious terrorism and secular terrorism. Religious terrorism draws from religion in ways that provide divine motives or duties, is more likely to target civilian populations, and uses violence as an end in and of itself, with limited or incoherent political goals. Again, the September 11 attacks are an excellent example of these characteristics. Secular terrorism, on the other hand, tends to draw from feelings of oppression or exclusion as a justification for action, to target government or military targets, and to have coherent or explicitly political, social, or economic goals. For example, the Oklahoma City bombing was an attack on a federal office building in Oklahoma City, OK, by Timothy McVeigh in 1995. The attacks were motivated by a desire to retaliate against the Federal Bureau of Investigation, the Bureau of Alcohol, Tobacco, Firearms, and Explosives, and the Drug Enforcement Agency. The building was specifically selected to maximize casualties among these agencies and minimize casualties among nongovernmental employees.

Sociologists of religion have also explored why fundamentalism leads to violence in some cases but not in others. This research finds that violent religious groups are more likely to arise in places where the state tries to regulate or suppress religious freedom. For example, Islamic terrorist groups are largely active in countries in the Middle East and Southeast Asia, which are often heavily security oriented with little religious or civic freedom. On the other hand, violent religious groups occur far more rarely in democratic societies because fundamentalist groups work through political avenues. Religious terrorism is particularly rare in the US because many fundamentalist groups work through the political system, instead of trying to overthrow that system.

By way of review, we discussed three potential relationships between religion and social change. We first discussed the default position of many sociologists of religion, namely that religion works as a conservative force in society that supports societal elites or otherwise favors the status quo. Next, we discussed historical examples of and conditions under which religion becomes a force for resisting or even overthrowing the status quo. Finally, we discussed religious violence and the link between fundamentalism and religious terrorism. It is worth noting that all of the topics in this chapter indirectly involve the government. As discussed in Chapter 9, the most common way in which religious groups try to instigate social change in democratic societies is through the electoral and policy process.

KEY POINTS YOU NEED TO KNOW

- Religion can either stop social change, act as a force for progressive social change, or be a source of fundamentalism and violence.
- Religion can act as a conservative force in society that helps to support and maintain the political, economic, and cultural structure of society.
- Religious believers, leaders, and institutions have also used their faith as the basis for starting or joining large-scale progressive social movements.
- Religious institutions have numerous attributes and assets that are significant for social movement activism, particularly transcendent motivation.
- Religious groups will start or join social movements when religious leaders and believers are personally invested in the social change.
- Secular social movements will mobilize religious resources and rhetoric by building coalitions with congregations or religious individuals in com munities.
- Modern religious terrorism is tied to religious fundamentalism.
- Fundamentalism can be defined as the rejection of some aspects of modernity on religious grounds.
- Religious violence takes the form of theater in which violence is committed as a symbolic act. This makes religious terrorism distinct from secular terrorism.

DISCUSSION QUESTIONS

1. How do religious groups support the status quo and act as a conservative force on social change?
2. What do religious institutions and believers have to contribute to social movements?
3. Why do religious institutions, leaders, and believers support some social movements and not others?
4. What are some limits on religious participation in secular social movements?
5. What is religious fundamentalism? Why is defining it difficult?
6. What are the key ideological characteristics of religious fundamentalism?
7. In what ways is religious terrorism an act of theater?
8. How is religious terrorism different from secular terrorism?
9. Why do some fundamentalist groups turn to violence and others do not?

FURTHER READING

Almond, G.A., Appleby R.S., and Sivan E. (2003) *Strong Religion: The Rise of Fundamentalisms around the World,* Chicago: University of Chicago Press.

Casanova, J. (1994) *Public Religions in the Modern World*, Chicago: University of Chicago Press.

Emerson, M.O. and Hartman, D. (2006) "The Rise of Religious Fundamentalism," *Annual Review of Sociology*, 32: 127–44.

Hoffman, B. (2001) "'Holy Terror': The Implications of Terrorism Motivated by a Religious Imperative," *Studies in Conflict and Terrorism*, 18: 271–84.

Juergensmeyer, M. (2000) *Terror in the Mind of God: The Global Rise of Religious Violence*, Los Angeles: University of California Press.

Katzenstein, M.F. (1998) *Faithful and Fearless: Moving Feminist Protest inside the Church and Military*, Princeton, NJ: Princeton University Press.

Moon, D. (2004) *God, Sex and Politics*, Chicago: University of Chicago Press.

Pattillo-McCoy, M. (1998) "Church Culture as a Strategy of Action," *American Sociological Review*, 63: 767–84.

Peterson, R.A. and Demerath, N.J., III (1942) "Introduction," in L. Pope, *Millhands and Preachers*, New Haven: Yale University Press, xvii–1.

Riesebrodt, M. (1993) *Pious Passion: The Emergence of Modern Fundamentalism in the United States and Iran*, Berkeley: University of California Press.

Robinson, L.W. (1987) "When Will Revolutionary Movements Use Religion?", in T. Robbins and R. Robertson (eds.), *Church-State Relations: Tensions and Transitions*, New Brunswick, NJ: Transaction Books, 53–63.

Smith, C. (ed.) (1996) *Disruptive Religion: The Force of Faith in Social Movement Activism*, New York: Routledge.

Wellman, J.K. and Tokuno, K. (2004) "Is Religious Violence Inevitable?" *Journal for the Scientific Study of Religion*, 43: 291–96.

Wilde, M. (2004) "How Culture Mattered at Vatican II: Collegiality Trumps Authority in the Council's Social Movement Organizations," *American Sociological Review*, 69: 576–602.

Young, M.P. (2002) "Confessional Protest: The Religious Birth of U.S. National Social Movements," *American Sociological Review*, 67: 660–88.

Zald, M.N. and McCarthy, J.D. (1987) "Religious Groups as Crucibles of Social Movements," in M.N. Zald and J.D. McCarthy (eds.), *Social Movements in an Organizational Society*, New Brunswick, NJ: Transaction Books, 67–96.

7 | Chapter Review

REVIEW QUESTIONS

1. Thinking back to the origins of sociology, why is the study of population and urbanization significant to the discipline? How might a study of population and urbanization inform us of how we are changing as a society?
2. What are the primary components of social change?
3. How might social movements and movements within institutions (such as religion) promote or incite conflict within social or cultural change?
4. How might the concept of globalization influence international attitudes toward changing gender roles as you explored in the "Developing the Sociological Imagination" exercise in Chapter 6?

CASE STUDY: INSTITUTIONS AS ENCOURAGING OR CONTENDING SOCIAL CHANGES

Sociologists approach **religion** both as an institution that serves particular functions in society as well as a social institution that holds great meaning and value for some individuals. It can provide community and belonging. Religion can also be seen as an institution that can both produce social conflict and promote social justice in any given society. For example, religious communities in many societies may resist certain social changes if they conflict with long held, and historic, religious beliefs.

Religious institutions, however, as seen in the U.S. civil rights movement in the 1960s, can also play a fundamental role in creating social change designed to address disparity and inequality. The final article in this chapter explores these concepts and the role that religion as an institution has had in various points in social change in the United States.

What role has religion had in U.S. social change historically? What current issues does the institution of religion have significant

381

influence within? It has been shown that as societies become more modern, they might rely less on religious institutions. Why? And why might this point to how such an institution might react to such social changes? How *might the study of this particular institution and its role in the process of social change also be applied to understand, in general, how various social institutions impact or resist social advancements?*

DEVELOPING THE SOCIOLOGICAL IMAGINATION
Population Pyramids and Population Projections

In 4–5 paragraphs, analyze the 2015 population pyramid of Iraq available at:

https://www.census.gov/population/international/data/idb/region.php?N=%20Results%20&T=12&A=separate&RT=0&Y=2015&R=-1&C=IZ

What challenges are being faced by this country that might provide insight when looking at the chart below? What context does age and gender provide? What can you likely predict about the future of Iraq if things continue as expressed in this chart? What would sociological theory say about the relative "development" or "demographic stage" of Iraq at this time?

Applied, Clinical, and Public Sociology

CHAPTER SUMMARY

- This chapter explores the definitions of applied, clinical, and public sociology.

- This chapter also explores the role of sociologists in areas of social, political, and professional life.

- Finally, this chapter asks readers to assess the value of the discipline in their own lives and areas of influence.

PRELIMINARY QUESTIONS FOR READERS

- What value might sociology have for understanding social problems and in proposing solutions for social problems?

- What might be the social or political challenges a sociologist might encounter when attempting to apply the "sociological imagination" in issues of social or economic importance in a public space or a social institution?

CHAPTER INTRODUCTION
Sociology in the Applied, Clinical, and Public Realms

While the history of sociology has long been applied (particularly in historical social movements related to the issues of class, race, gender, and sexuality or other areas of social inequality), the terminology utilized to discuss such involvement has been one that has continually been evolving (DuBois & Wright, 2008). The first article in this chapter explores the definitions of applied, clinical, and public sociology and the current states of these practical and growing possibilities. For example, many universities across the globe now offer degrees in applied or clinical sociology.

AUTHOR'S REFLECTIONS ON THE FUTURE OF SOCIOLOGY

Over the past several decades, there has been significant academic and social discourse on the purpose, benefits, and functions of higher education. A system that was once accessible only to the elite now, partly as a result of its inclusion as part of Franklin D. Roosevelt's "social contract," has become an irreplaceable institution in many communities and social life to the extent that a college education in the last 30 years has become one of the most significant factors in individual and family social mobility (Neelsen, 1975). Of course, the importance of this institution extends beyond just human achievement and for the benefit of the communities in which people live, and important arguments have been made as to universities' overall benefit to society. While much of the discourse has centered on the shift in this institution aligning with industry or adopting business models for revenue generation, important cases have been made on the importance of student engagement in communities and the preparation that this service and engagement can have in the development of student preparation for the workforce and in contributing to society over the long term (Hodges, 2004).

At the same time, many disciplines (particularly those that may be more philosophical in nature) have been under pressure to make content relevant and "useful" to industry (or applicable in the "real world"), particularly in the face of federal and state budget cuts where funding for programs often comes directly from student enrollment numbers (Neelsen, 1975).

This shift has had a particular impact on the social sciences, where many degree programs have pivoted to focus more on public scholarship and applied work as a core degree component (Albert, 2003). For many programs, this has focused on organizational problem solving, research methodology, and individual or group applications (such as clinical work). Part of this process has also included involving students in applied work within the community.

Given these trends, I believe that the future of the discipline of sociology, particularly within higher education, is applied and clinical, and the higher education community would be best served by teaching and providing students with opportunities to engage in meaningful applied research and clinical work. For example, ethnographies (the scientific description of the customs of individual peoples and cultures) are becoming increasingly sought after by companies that are interested in understanding working conditions, culture, and understanding employee morale. These are studies that sociologists and other social scientists are well suited (if not best suited) to perform.

In addition, this book has focused on the value that developing the sociological imagination has for individuals, groups, and in public spaces, particularly in addressing social problems. The value and insight that the discipline offers to industry, policy, politics, government, and nongovernmental programs is unmatched in any other current discipline. The discipline's focus on diversity, understanding social structures, and interpreting and understanding social meanings has powerful applications for social service, health, and community, as well as economic development.

Communities are the places in which we work and live. Of course, as a global community, we are more intertwined and interconnected than ever before. We owe it to ourselves and others, as part of our local and global spaces, to develop and apply the sociological imagination for the good of all and so that our communities and societies are able to make full use of the talents and resources each citizen can contribute to society.

WORKS CITED

Albert, M. (March, 2003). Universities and the market economy: The differential impact on knowledge production in sociology and economics. *Higher Education*, 45(2), pp. 147–182.

Du Bois, W. and Wright, D. (2008). *Applying sociology: Making a better world*. White Plains, NY: Pearson.

Hodges Persell, C. and Wenglinsky, H. (Apr. 2004) For profit post-secondary education and civic engagement. *Higher Education*, 47(3), pp. 337–359.

Neelsen, J. P. (Feb., 1975) Education and social mobility. *Comparative Education Review*, 19(1), pp. 129–143.

Including Sociological Practice

A Global Perspective and the U.S. Case

by Jan Marie Fritz, Ph.D., C.C.S.[1]
University of Cincinnati

INTRODUCTION

This volume examines the shape of sociology. This includes looking at the number and kind of specializations that have developed within the field; the relation between the specializations and the core of the discipline; and the strength of the discipline in terms of unique contributions to knowledge and to quality of life in nation-states and globally.

To contribute to this discussion, this chapter focuses on one specialization—sociological practice—and particularly on developments in the United States, a country that has a century-old tradition of sociological practice (Fritz, 1985; Perlstadt, 2007). Sociological practice is first defined and then there is a discussion of the history and current situation of this subfield. The core of this article is about the development of sociological practice in the United States and the relation of sociological practice to sociology during that time.

DEFINING SOCIOLOGICAL PRACTICE

Sociological practice—intervention and/or practical research—may or may not be part of a general definition of sociology. If sociological practice is an expected part of sociology, there might not be a need for an additional term or terms to describe practice. In countries where practice activities are not something that all or most sociologists could be involved in, there could be a need for a term or terms to cover practice and the different kinds of practice. For example, in Italy there is discussion of "professional sociology" and "clinical sociology" while "sociotechnics"[2] emerged in Poland.

In the United States, sociological practice is an umbrella term that covers *clinical sociology*, *applied sociology* and *engaged public sociology* (e.g., Fritz, 2008; Association for Applied and Clinical Sociology, 2010; American Sociological Association Section on Sociological Practice and Public Sociology).[3] While the terms are, at times, defined differently,[4] the general definitions provided here should ground the discussion that follows.

Clinical sociology is a creative, humanistic and multidisciplinary specialization that seeks to improve the quality of people's lives (e.g., Fritz, 1985; Gargano, 2008:154; Fritz, 2008:1). Clinical sociologists (Fritz, 2008:1):

work with client systems to assess situations and avoid, reduce or eliminate problems through a combination of analysis and intervention. *Clinical analysis* is the critical assessment of beliefs, policies, or practices, with an interest in improving the situation. *Intervention* is based on continuing analysis; it is the creation of new systems as well as the change of existing systems and can include a focus on prevention or promotion (e.g., preventing environmental racism or promoting community sustainability).

Clinical sociologists are employed, for instance, as managers, consultants, organizational development specialists, mediators, policymakers and therapists. While research (particularly needs assessment and evaluation) may be part of their work, these functions also may be carried out by others.

Applied sociology refers to research for practical purposes. According to Britt (2000:168), it is "policy-oriented (and) action-directed." Harry Perlstadt (2007:342) has noted that applied sociology, "in its broadest sense,... encompasses evaluation research, needs assessment, market research, social indicators and demographics" in many areas such as medicine, business and education. Like others describing the field, Britt (2000:168) has indicated that applied sociology is not "oriented toward those who have a concern for the advancement of sociological knowledge. "Instead, it is:

oriented more toward those who are making decisions, developing or monitoring programs, or concerned about the accountability of those who are making decisions and developing programs.

Public sociology, according to Michael Burawoy (2007:28), "brings sociology into a conversation with publics, understood as people who are themselves in conversation." As examples of public sociologists, Burawoy mentions those whose works are "read beyond the academy, and... become a vehicle of public discussion about the nature of (the) society." Burawoy includes as public sociologists those who write for the opinion pages for newspapers and the activists who work, for example, for community-based movements concerned with labor, women or neighborhood issues. *Engaged public sociology*—with a focus in areas such as public policy development, human rights intervention and/or community development—fits with what has been described above as clinical sociology and is included under the label of sociological practice.

Some general points about the three approaches are noted here: the *different approaches may be combined* in a practitioner's work though most practitioners will favor one of the terms to describe her/his practice; practitioners have *different audiences*—clients and/or the public—in comparison to those sociologists who primarily or only speak to each other and students (those who are scholar-practitioners [5] usually have both audiences); practitioners and scholar-practitioners have an *orientation toward usefulness* (rather than mainly or only generating sociological knowledge); and there is an understanding that *practical problems foster the development and reformulation of theory and method.* Clinical sociology is usually explicitly defined as *multidisciplinary* in preparation and delivery (Fritz, 1985:xix); applied sociology (Perlstadt, 2007) and an engaged public sociology often are multidisciplinary, particularly in terms of theory, research methods and/or skills, but this may not be mentioned as part of the definition.

THE HISTORY OF SOCIOLOGICAL PRACTICE: A GLOBAL PERSPECTIVE

Sociological practice is as old as the field of sociology, and its roots are found in many parts of the world. Clinical sociology and engaged public sociology, for instance, can be traced back to the fourteenth-century work of the Arab scholar and statesperson Abd-al-Rahman ibn Khaldun (1332–1406) (Lee, 1979:488; Fritz, 1985). Ibn Khaldun (1958; Lee, 1979) provided numerous clinical observations based on his varied work experiences such as secretary of state to the ruler of Morocco and chief judge of Egypt.

Auguste Comte (1798–1857), Émile Durkheim (1858–1917), and Karl Marx (1818–1883) are frequently identified as precursors to or initial figures in the development of sociological practice (e.g., Gouldner, 1956; Fritz, 2008). Comte, the French scholar who coined the term *sociology*, believed that the scientific study of societies would provide the basis for social action. Perlstadt (2007:342–343) notes Comte's "translational role" between basic research and "activists/interventionists." Émile Durkheim's work on the relation between levels of influence (e.g., social in relation to individual factors) led Alvin Gouldner (1965) to write that "more than any other classical sociologist (Durkheim) used a clinical model." Karl Marx, as Alfred McClung Lee noted in 1979, brought to his written work "the grasp of human affairs only possible through extensive involvement in praxis …, social action,… agitation, and … social organization."

Sociological practice has developed in a number of countries including France and Italy (Fritz, 2008). French is the language of many of the current international clinical sociology conferences, and many publications clearly linked to clinical sociology have appeared in Quebec, Canada, and France (e.g., Gaulejac, Hanique and Roche, 2007; Rheaume, 2008). The French clinical sociologists emphasize clinical analysis and frequently focus on the relationship between psychology and sociology. They have a solid international network and have done an excellent job of attracting psychologists and professionals in other fields to their network. There is an extensive publication record including the writing of the Van Bockstaeles and their colleagues (1963), Enriquez (1997); Enriquez, Houle, Rhéaume, and Sévigny, R. (1993), Gaulejac and Roy (1993), Sevigny (1996) and Gaulejac, Hanique and Roche (2007).

During the last twenty years, Italians have hosted sociological practice conferences and workshops, offered a graduate program in clinical sociology, established associations of clinical sociologists and professional sociologists, and published clinical sociology books and articles. Among the publications are ones by Tosi and Battisti (1995), Luison (1998), and Corsale (2008).

Sociological practice also is found in other parts of the world. Of particular interest would be developments in the Netherlands (Schultz et al., 1993), China (Li, 1999), Greece (e.g., Rigas and Papadaki, 2008), Brazil (Takeuti and Niewiadomski, 2008), Mexico (e.g., Taracena, 2008), Japan (Noguchi, 2008), and Malaysia (e.g., Wan, 2006). Mexico, Brazil, France, Canada, Italy, the United States, and Greece are among those countries that have hosted international sociological practice conferences.

The international development of sociological practice is supported primarily by three organizations. The International Sociological Association is home to the clinical sociology division (RC46) that was organized in 1982 at the ISA World Congress in Mexico City and also to the division on sociotechnics/sociological practice (RC26). Other major influences are the clinical sociology section of the Association internationale des Sociologues de la Langue française (International Association of French Language Sociologists) and the clinical sociology division of the l'Association française de sociologie (the French Sociology Association). All these groups hold conferences and encourage publication. The clinical sociology division of the ISA, for example, has co-sponsored a book about teaching clinical sociology (Fritz, 2006) and is developing a book about effective community intervention.

It is clear that a global interest in sociological practice has emerged. While there is a common core (e.g., conceptual framework, acceptance of a wide range of theories and research methods), there are differences. In some countries, for instance, clinical sociologists are more interested in providing analyses to policymakers and the public (e.g., France) than in undertaking intervention (e.g., the U.S.) and there can be differences in their areas of focus.[6] In some countries or areas of practice, practitioners may introduce themselves as *sociological* practitioners, clinical *sociologists*, public *sociologists*, or applied *sociologists*, while in other settings, the labels used by practitioners may be connected to the work they do (e.g., analyst, consultant, policy research) rather than

to the discipline of sociology. Finally, it should be mentioned that while scholar-practitioners in certain areas of the world (e.g., the United States, French Canada, and France) have had important roles in the development of sociological practice, there are now many other national and regional influences that will help shape the future of this global specialization.

THE HISTORY AND CONTRIBUTIONS OF SOCIOLOGICAL PRACTICE IN THE UNITED STATES

There is no excellent publication[7] about the history of global sociological practice. As Roger Straus (2002:16) has lamented, the "historic role of sociology in developing applied social research methods remains largely unknown and unacknowledged" and "sociological practice (has) become, literally, an underground tradition within our discipline." That has been true globally and is often the case even within a country. The United States is one of the countries where the threads of the national history have been detailed to some extent (e.g., Bulmer,1992; Fritz, 1985, 1991; Lazarsfeld and Reitz with Pasanella, 1975). Because the history for the United States is long (more than a century), a good deal of material is available about this important history and yet sociological practice is still not fully integrated in the discipline, this chapter focuses on the United States.

Sociological practice, in the United States, began in the late 1800s and early 1900s (Fritz, 1985). This period included the Progressive Era (mid-1890s through 1916), a time of reform as well as the emergence of corporate capitalism. At the turn of the twentieth century, there were social problems that led to public protests and the development of reform organizations. It is not surprising that many of the early sociologists were scholar-practitioners or practitioners who were interested in reducing or resolving the problems that faced their communities.

Words that referred to sociological practice appeared in presentations, publications, and course titles beginning some 100 years ago (Fritz, 1985, Perlstadt, 2007). The roots of American sociological practice have been traced to the 1883 publication of Lester Ward's *Dynamic Sociology: or Applied Social Science* (Britt, 2000:168), Albion Small's 1896 "Scholarship and Social Agitation" (Fritz, 2007:353), and to many others connected to the "practical sociology" of the early 1900s (Krause, 2007:369).

The first known use of the words "clinical sociology" was in the late 1920s and early 1930s. The words appeared in course titles at the University of Chicago, documents written by a medical school dean at Yale who wanted to have physicians trained in what he called clinical sociology, and a 1931 journal article, "Clinical Sociology," by Louis Wirth that appeared in the *American Journal of Sociology*) (Fritz, 2007). Public sociology is a more recent concept and the term may have first been proposed by Herbert Gans (1989:7) in his 1988 presidential address to the American Sociological Association.[8] The roots of engaged public sociology are in the same traditions as mentioned for applied sociology and clinical sociology.

The history of sociological practice in the United States has been chronicled by scholar-practitioners in articles and important books (e.g., Blasi's 2005 *Diverse Histories of American Sociology*, Bryant and Peck's 2007 *21st Century Sociology*). A chapter by Breslau (2007:59) in Calhoun's 2007 centennial book on the history of American sociology, for instance, notes that

in the late 1800s and early 1900s, surveys of sociology teachers in the United States showed "that practitioners and teachers of practical sociology were by far more numerous than the general sociologists, who were found in a small number of elite universities." Breslau (2007: 59, 61) concluded that "all indications are that it was the demand for instruction in practical matters, rather than a demand for academic research, that drove the growth of the discipline in those decades" but also wrote that the founding of professional social work and public administration led to "the loss of (sociology's) applied wing and its role as the credentialing discipline for practical sociologists…"

If the early 1900s has been characterized as a period in which many sociologists were focused on social problems, the periods that followed 1920 are seen as ones that focused on the development of empirical sociology and included the "growth of a more applied orientation" (Bulmer, 1992:318). Bulmer (1992:319) details reasons for the growth of applied sociology, which include the scientific development of sociology, increasing importance of philanthropic organizations, impact of social science on policymaking at the national level, and interest of government in social science.

Perlstadt (2007) also has detailed the many contributions of applied sociologists in the late 1800s and early 1900s. These include ones by Lester Ward (for most of his career a paleontologist with the US Geological Survey and who "brought the term applied sociology into the discipline"); Florence Kelley, the "activist researcher," who with Jane Addams and others, developed the groundbreaking "The Hull-House Maps and Papers"; and the Sociology Department that was established within the Ford Motor Company. In discussing later periods, Perlstadt (2007:348) also writes about the initial interest in "social engineering" (and then the disinterest because of Soviet five-year plans and political developments in Germany) and the "substantial boost"—federal funding—that applied sociology received because of World War II and then the War on Poverty.

Doug McAdam (2007:423-4) discusses the 1950s through 1980s in the United States as a period in which there was "devaluation" of practical work by "mainstream" sociologists. He writes:

> If the modal sociologist of the 1950s and early 1960s was a progressive social engineer seeking solutions to society's problems, (her/his) counterpart, circa 1980, was an 'outsider' far removed from the mainstream institutions and practical policy questions that had been the focus of so much scholarship in the postwar period.

McAdam continues by noting that there was a dramatic decline in both the "*status and visibility*" of practical work during that 30-year period.

CONTEMPORARY SOCIOLOGICAL PRACTICE IN THE UNITED STATES: SOME CONSIDERATIONS

In the last forty years, there have been many interesting developments in the sociological practice specialization in the United States. These include theoretical and methodological contributions that connect academic/basic and practical interests (Perlstadt, 2007), a very developed literature for teaching sociological practice,[9] workshops that support practice, the development of certification and accreditation practices, and numerous publications in many different areas of application. This section will focus on a few of the accomplishments and concerns: the development of professional associations, a certification process for individuals, an accreditation process for programs, and the level of the sociology programs that include a focus on sociological practice.

Support for practice activity in the United States now comes primarily from two professional groups. These are the Association for Applied and Clinical Sociology (AACS) and the section on Sociological Practice and Public Sociology,[10] part of the American Sociological Association. The names of both groups changed over the years to include new directions and combine constituencies. The predecessor groups of AACS—the Clinical Sociology Association, which became the Sociological Practice Association and the Society for Applied Sociology—were particularly influential in the development of practice particularly in terms of sponsoring publications and developing credentialing processes for individuals and programs.

One particularly unusual aspect of sociological practice in the United States is that the Association for Applied and Clinical Sociology offers a certification process for individual practitioners.[11] The Ph.D. certification process was first offered by a predecessor organization in 1983 and certification was first awarded in 1984. Certification at the master's level was available in 1986. The current process involves the submission of a portfolio, letters of assessment, university transcripts and documents that verify applied or clinical practice. If an applicant's portfolio and application documents are approved, the applicant will be invited to give a peer-reviewed demonstration.

The Association for Applied and Clinical Sociology's predecessor organizations also put in place the Commission on Applied and Clinical Sociology. The Commission is a free-standing organization that came into existence in 1995. It currently accredits undergraduate and master's programs (full programs as well as tracks or concentrations) in sociological practice, clinical sociology, applied sociology, and public sociology.[12] While accreditation is not essential, the accreditation standards help programs develop, promote, and support quality sociological education and practice.[13]

The accreditation standards require the specification of learning outcomes and help programs look at how they integrate sociological theory, knowledge, methods, skills, professional orientation, and ethics. The accredited programs currently are all in the United States but the Commission was contacted by a university department in another country that developed its practice programs based on the Commission's standards. The department asked about the possibility of applying for accreditation and the Commission, after it completed a site visit, agreed to consider an application.

One indicator of the acceptance of sociological practice in the field of sociology is the level of the programs that have sociological practice options. If there are practice programs or concentrations, they usually are found at the undergraduate and master's levels. At both levels, the enrolled students may want degrees that will help them get work after graduation or increase their standing with their current employers. The master's programs usually offer more courses in the area of specialization.

Education at the master's level in the United States is the fastest growing area of graduate education (Snyder et al, 2008). Some of these students are enrolled in 5-year or combined bachelor's/master's programs. In sociology departments, the master's programs sometimes have two tracks—one for students who are interested in getting a Ph.D and one for students who will take positions as practitioners.

According to the 2008 draft report of the American Sociological Association's Task Force on the Master's Degree in Professional Sociology, the most common graduate degree in sociology in the United States is the master's degree[14] and, in the case of sociology, this degree "often represents the face of sociology to the public." The report also notes "the phenomenal rise in Master's education nationwide and across disciplines" which "suggests a significant demand in the workplace for the skills associated with Master's degrees." About 49 percent of the social science graduates are expected to go on to graduate school within 10 years and about 2/3 of these students will enroll in master's programs (Nevell and Chen, 2007; Redd, 2007). These students may—or may not—choose to enroll in a sociology program.

At the doctoral level, observers have noticed some interesting trends. McAdam (2007), for instance, writes that the situation "may be changing, but it is still the case that the most applied subfields are virtually absent from the highest-ranked sociology departments" and that this is particularly interesting as all this has happened while the "baby boom cohorts, attracted by the 'relevance' of sociology" entered the field.

The Task Force on the Master's Degree in Professional Sociology (American Sociological Association, 2008) wrote that some faculty members have indicated that they have noticed a trend at the doctoral level regarding practice. The Task Force indicated that several professors reported that there were students who are interested in applied research, but they connect this interest to their specialties (e.g., criminology or environmental sociology) rather than to an applied sociology specialization. The professors think this situation is different than some years ago when students might have been interested, for instance, in a specialization in health sociology AND in applied sociology rather than just choosing the first option. If this is a trend, questions will have to be raised about whether standard courses and traineeships are adequately preparing these students for applied or clinical work and what this might mean for the future of the specialization in sociological practice.

CONCLUSION

Even in a country where the history of sociological practice is long and historically has involved many of the influential people in the field, the specialization has still not been embraced by the discipline and become a focal area or a combined concentration (e.g., environment and sociological practice) in our doctoral programs. Sometimes when the history of sociology is discussed, the early scholar-practitioners (some of whom were very important figures in the history of the discipline) are not even linked to the current specialization in sociological practice or to the long tradition of practice. This unfortunate reading of the situation has contributed to the fact that sociological practice, and particularly clinical sociology, are seen by some sociologists as something that is unusual and new rather than a continuing interest within the field. It also means that our doctoral students—many of whom will become professors—may have little exposure to sociological practice.

Incorporating sociological practice throughout sociology programs encourages faculty and students to combine substantive knowledge, critical thinking, and creative problem-solving with specific skills. A program does not have to give up an emphasis on theory and basic research to add sociological practice; these additional skills are added value for the students, faculty members, program and, community.

It would be interesting to examine and compare the development of sociological practice in other political, economic, and cultural settings. Doing so would be a step in writing that missing "rounded historical account" (Bulmer, 1992) of global sociological practice.

REFERENCES

American Sociological Association. (2010). Mission Statement. Retrieved January 10, 2010, from http://www.asanet.org/sections/SPSS.cfm.

American Sociological Association Task Force on the Professional Master's Degree (2008). Draft (August 15) of *Thinking about the Master's Degree in Sociology: Academic, Applied, Professional and Everything in Between*. Washington, D.C.: American Sociological Association.

Association for Applied and Clinical Sociology. (2010). What is applied and clinical sociology? Retreived January 10, 2010, from http://www.aacsnet.org/wp/?page_id=59.

Breslau, Daniel (2007). The American Spencerians: Theorizing a new science. In Craig Calhoun (Ed.), *Sociology in America: A History* (pp. 39–62). Chicago and London: University of Chicago Press.

Britt, David (2000). Applied Sociology. In Edgar F. Borgatta and Rhonda J.V. Montgomery (Eds.) *Encyclopedia of Sociology* (pp. 168–171). Second edition. Volume 1. New York: Macmillan Reference USA.

Bryant, C.G. (1995). *Practical Sociology: Post-empiricism and the Reconstruction of Theory and Application.* Cambridge: Polity.

Bulmer, Martin. (1987). The growth of applied sociology after 1945: The prewar establishment of the postwar infrastructure. In Halliday, T.C., and M. Janowitz (Eds.), *Sociology and Its Publics.* Chicago: University of Chicago Press.

Burawoy, Michael (2007) For public sociology. In Dan Clawson, Robert Zussman, Joya Misra, Naomi Gerstel, Randall Stokes, Douglas Anderton and Michael Burawoy (Eds.), *Public Sociology: Fifteen Eminent Sociologists Debate Politics and the Profession in the Twenty-First Century* (pp. 23–65). Berkeley: University of California Press.

Calhoun, Craig (Ed.) (2007). *Sociology in America: A History.* An American Sociological Association centennial publication. Chicago and London: University of Chicago Press.

Clawson, Dan, Robert Zussman, Joya Misra, Naomi Gerstel, Randall Stokes, Douglas Anderton and Michael Burawoy (Eds) (2007) *Public Sociology: Fifteen Eminent Sociologists Debate Politics and the Profession in the Twenty-First Century.* Berkeley: University of California Press.

Commission on Applied and Clinical Sociology (2008). http://www.sociologycommission.org. Accessed on August 7.

Corsale, Massimo (Ed.) (2008). Monographic section on health and illness problems faced by clinical sociologists. *International Revue of Sociology* 18(3), 415–517.

Donoghue, Frank (2008). *The Last Professors: The Corporate University and the Fate of the Humanities.* New York: Fordham University Press.

Du Bois, William & Wright, R. D. (Eds.). (2001). *Applying Sociology: Making a Better World.* Boston: Allyn and Bacon.

Enriquez, E. (1997). L'approche clinique: genèse et développement en France et en Europe de l'Ouest [The clinical approach: genesis and development in Western Europe]. *International Sociology*, 12, 151–164.

Enriquez, E., Houle, G., Rhéaume, J., and Sévigny, R. (1993). L'analyse clinique dans les sciences humaines [Clinical Analysis in Human Sciences]. Montreal: Éditions Saint-Martin.

Fritz, Jan. Marie. (1985). *The Clinical Sociology Handbook.* New York: Garland.

Fritz, Jan Marie. (1991) The emergence of American clinical sociology. In H. Rebach and J. Bruhn (Eds.), *Handbook of Clinical Sociology* (pp. 17–32). New York: Plenum.

Fritz, Jan Marie and Elizabeth J. Clark (1993). The assessment and change of policies and behavior: A comparison of two social science approaches. In K. Mesman Schultz, J.T.A. Koster, F.L. Leeuw, B.M.J. Wolters (Eds.), *Between Sociology and Sociological Practice: Essays on Social Policy Research*, (pp. 82–89). Nijmegen: Institute for Applied Social Sciences.

Fritz, Jan Marie (Ed.) (2006). *The Clinical Sociology Resource Book.* Sixth edition. Washington, D.C.: American Sociological Association Teaching Resources Center.

Fritz, Jan Marie (2007). Clinical sociology. In Clifton D. Bryant and Dennis L. Peck (Eds.), *21st Century Sociology: A Reference Handbook* (pp. 353–359). Volume 2. Thousand Oaks, London, and New Delhi: Sage.

Fritz, Jan Marie (Ed.) (2008). *International Clinical Sociology.* New York: Springer.

Gans, Herbert J. 1989. Sociology in America: The discipline and the public American Sociological Association, 1988 presidential address. *American Sociological Review* 51, 1–16.

Gargano, Giuseppe. (2008). On the origins of clinical sociology in France: Some milestones. In Jan Marie Fritz (Ed.), *International Clinical Sociology* (pp. 54–71). New York: Springer.

Gaulejac, Vincent de. (2008). On the origins of clinical sociology in France: Some milestones. In Jan Marie Fritz (Ed.) *International Clinical Sociology* (pp. 54–71). New York: Springer.

Gaulejac, Vincent de, Fabienne Hanique and Pierre Roche (2007). La sociologie clinique: Enjeux théoriques et methodologiques [Clinical sociology]. Ramonville Saint-Agne: Eres.

Gaulejac, Vincent de, and Roy, Shirley (Eds.). (1993). Sociologie clinique [Clinical sociology]. Paris: Desclée de Brouwer.

Gouldner, A.W. (1957) Theoretical requirements of the applied social sciences, *American Sociological Review*, 22, 92–102.

Halliday, T.C., and Janowitz, M. (1987). *Sociology and Its Publics.* Chicago: University of Chicago Press.

Horowitz, Irving Louis, (Ed.). (1967). *The Rise and Fall of Project Camelot: Studies in the Relationship*

Between Social Science and Practical Politics. Cambridge: The MIT Press.

Ibn Khaldun, Abd-al-Rahman. (1958). The Muqaddimah—An introduction to history. Translated by Franz Rosenthal. New York: Bollingen Foundation.

Krause, Jerry. (2007). Sociological practice. In Clifton D. Bryant and Dennis L. Peck (Eds.). *21st Century Sociology Reference Handbook,* (pp. 369–378). Volume 2. Thousand Oaks, London, and New Delhi, India: Sage.

Larson, Calvin J. (1993). *Pure and Applied Sociological Theory.* Fort Worth: Harcourt Brace Jovanovich.

Lazarsfeld, P. F., and Reitz, J.G. (1975). *An Introduction to Applied Sociology.* New York, Oxford: Elsevier.

Lee, A. M. (1979). The services of clinical sociology. *American Behavioral Scientist.* 22(4), 487–511.

Lehnerer, Melodye (2003). *Careers in Clinical Sociology.* Washington, D.C.: American Sociological Association.

Li, De. (1999). Reconstructing Chinese sociology: A quest for an applied science. *Sociological Practice: A Journal of Clinical and Applied Research,* 1(4), 273–284.

Luison, L. (ed.). (1998). Introduzione alla Sociologia Clinica: Teorie, Metodi e Tecniche di Intervento [Introduction to Clinical Sociology—Theory, Methods and Intervention Techniques]. Milan: FrancoAngeli.

McAdam, Doug (2007). From relevance to irrelevance: The curious impact of the sixties on public sociology. In Craig Calhoun (Ed.), *Sociology in America: A History,* (pp. 411–426). Chicago and London: The Chicago University Press.

Nevill, Stephanie C. and Xianglei Chen. (2007). *The path through graduate school: A longitudinal examination 10 years after Bachelor's Degree* (NCES 2007-162). US Department of Education Statistics. Retrieved August 7, 2008 from http://nces.ed.gov/programs/digest/d05/tables/dti5_293.asp.

Noguchi, Yuji. (2008). Clinical sociology in Japan. In Jan Marie Fritz (Ed.), *International Clinical Sociology,* (pp. 72–81). New York: Springer.

Perlstadt, Harry (1998). Accreditation of sociology programs: A bridge to a broader audience. *Canadian Journal of Sociology, 23*(1), 195–207.

Perlstadt, Harry (2006). Applied Sociology. Chapter 39. In C.D. Bryant and D.L. Peck (Eds.) *Handbook of 21st Century Sociology. Vol. 2.* Thousand Oaks, CA: Sage Publications.

Perlstadt, Harry (2007). Applied Sociology In Clifton D. Bryant and Dennis L. Peck (Eds.), *21st Century Sociology Reference Handbook,* (pp. 342–352). Volume 2. Thousand Oaks, London, and New Delhi, India: Sage.

Podgorecki, A. (1979). Definition and scope of sociotechnics. In A. Podgorecki and M. Los (Eds.), *Multi-dimensional Sociology.* (pp. 273–289). London: Routledge & Kegan Paul.

Rebach, Howard M. and Bruhn, John G. (Eds.) (1991). *Handbook of Clinical Sociology.* New York: Plenum.

Redd, Kenneth E. (2007) *Graduate Enrollment and Degrees: 1996 to 2006.* Washington, D.C.: Council of Graduate Schools.

Rheaume, Jacques (1997). The project of clinical sociology in Quebec. *International Sociology,* 12, pp. 165–174.

Rheaume, Jacques (2008). 'Clinical Sociology in Quebec: When Europe Meets America' In Jan Marie Fritz (Ed.), *International Clinical Sociology,* pp. 36–53. New York: Springer.

Rigas, Anastasia-Valentine, and Papadaki, Adriani. (2008). Psychosocial interventions and the rehabilitation of drug users in Greece. In Jan Marie Fritz (Ed.), *International Clinical Sociology,* (pp. 115–134). New York: Springer.

Schultz, K.M., Koster, J.T.A., Leeuw, F.L., and Wolters, B.M.J. (Eds.) (1993). Between Sociology and Sociological Practice: Essays on social policy research: Liber Amicorum dedicated to Mark van de Vall. Nijmegen: Institute for Appllied Social Sciences.

Sévigny, R. (1996). The clinical approach in the social sciences. *International Sociology,* 12, 135–150.

Sévigny, R., Rheaume, J., Houle, G., and Enriquez, E. (1993). *L'Analyse Clinique dans les Sciences Humaines* [Clinical Analysis in the Human Sciences]. Montreal: Éditions Saint-Martin.

Small, Albion W. (1896) "Scholarship and Social Agitation." *The American Journal of Sociology,* 1(5):564–582.

Snyder, Thomas D., Sally A. Dillow and Charlene M. Hoffman (2008). *Digest of Education Statistics 2007* (NCES 2008-022) National Center for Education Statistics, Institute of Education Sciences, US Department of Education. Washington, D.C.: US Government Printing Office. Available at www.edpubs.org. Accessed August 7, 2008.

Spalter-Roth, Roberta (2008). Sociologists in applied, research, and policy settings: Satisfaction outside the professoriate. Presentation at the International Sociological Association Forum for RC46 Clinical Sociology. Barcelona, Spain. September.

Straus, Roger A., (Ed.). (2004) *Using Sociology: An Introduction from the Applied and Clinical Perspectives*. Third edition. Dixon Hills, N.Y.: General Hall.

Straus, R. A. (1999). Using Sociology: An Introduction from the Applied and Clinical Perspectives (3rd ed.). New York: Rowman and Littlefield.

Sullivan, Thomas J. (1992). *Applied Sociology: Research and Critical Thinking*. New York: MacMillan.

Takeuti, Norma Missae, and Christophe Niewiadomski. (2009). Reinvencoes do sujeito social: Teorias e praticas biograficas [Reinvention of the Social Subject]. Porto Alegre, Brazil: Sulina.

Timasheff, Nicholas S. and George A. Theodorson. (1976). *Sociological Theory, Its Nature and Growth*. New York: Random House.

Tosi, M., and Battisti, F. (Eds.). (1995). *Sociologia clinica e sistemi socio-sanitari: Dalle premesse epistemologiche allo studio di casi e interventi* [Clinical Sociology and Public Health Systems]. Milan: Franco Angeli.

Van Bockstaele, J., Van Bockstaele, M., Barrot, C., and Magny, C. (1963). *Travaux de sociologie clinique* [Clinical Sociology Work]. L'Année Sociologique. Paris: Presses Universitaires de France.

Wan, A. H. (2004). *The Crowning of Sociology: The Genesis of Clinical Sociology*. Unpublished manuscript.

Wirth, L. (1931). Clinical sociology. *American Journal of Sociology*, 37, 49–66.

Zetterberg, H.L. (1962). *Social Theory and Social Practice*. New York: Bedminster Press.

NOTES

1   The author has had the opportunity to visit many academic institutions around the world. She also is a consultant for academic departments for the Department Resources Group of the American Sociological Association and a member of a commission that accredits sociological practice programs. In the latter role, she has had the opportunity to make national and international site visits.

2   Adam Podgorecki (1979), a founder of the Polish school of sociotechnics, defined it in the following way: "Sociotechnics (social engineering) may be defined as the theory of efficient social action, or more concretely, applied social science, the task of which is to inform the potential practitioner in what manner to see effective ways and means to realize intended social aims, provided there is a given accepted system of values as well as a usable set of verified propositions describing and explaining human behavior" (Fritz and Clark, 1993).

3   Sullivan (1992:19), in his book about applied sociology, wrote that "three spheres taken together (applied researcher, consultants, sociological clinician) constitute what is called sociological practice."

4   Some applied sociologists substitute the term applied sociology for the term sociological practice.

5   Scholar-practitioners are those who are both scholars (frequently with university positions) and undertake some kind of practice (e.g., clinical or applied work).

6   Clinical sociologists in Japan, for instance, have focused on the health sector (Noguchi, 2008).

7   There is no "rounded historical account" as Martin Bulmer (1992) would put it.

8   Gans (1989, p. 7) described public sociologists as "empirical researchers, analysts or theorists like the rest of us, although often their work is particularly thoughtful, imaginative or original in some respect." He also said they "have to be academics or practitioners, there currently being no free-lance writing market to provide a living for even one sociologist."

9   The American Sociological Association (ASA) has many resources for practice programs and courses including *The Clinical Sociology Resource Book* (sixth edition) (Fritz, 2006); *Careers in Clinical Sociology* (Lehnerer, 2003) and curriculum books about applied sociology and sociological practice. The ASA also provides helpful research (e.g., Spalter-Roth's 2008 survey of 600 practitioners).

10   Information about the division can be found on the website of the American Sociological Association: http://www.asanet.org/sections/SPSS.cfm.

11 Complete application information is provided on the Association's website: http://www.aacsnet.org

12 An applicant program has to complete a self-study and host a site visit. The Commission is always interested in hearing from sociology programs that want to learn more about the standards or have questions about the process.

13 Successful sociological practice programs at all levels are not just those with sufficient financial resources. Other factors that have been found to be important include: program culture (e.g., intellectually challenging, a supportive atmosphere, tenure/promotion standards encourage or are supportive of practice, commitment of faculty, embrace diversity), creative leadership; active learning experiences (e.g., studios, internships, traineeships, community-based/participatory research), and direct connection to the job market (American Sociological Association, 2008).

14 Master's degrees account for 90 percent of all graduate degrees awarded in the United States (Council of Graduate Schools, 2005).

The Sociologist and the Public Sphere

by Immanuel Wallerstein

The debate about the proper role of the sociologist or any other variety of scientist/scholar/intellectual in the public sphere is perpetual, repeatedly insistent, and totally unresolved. Political authorities are never happy if intellectuals offer them reasoned resistance and are seldom happy if intellectuals decline to support them in what they consider fundamental issues of value and policy. Intellectuals are never happy if they are pressed by public authorities or anyone else to espouse positions that are not theirs and are seldom happy if public authorities do not take cognizance of what intellectuals consider to be important findings or evaluations that they make or could make. And there are always organizational structures (religious structures, revolutionary movements, defenders of abstract rights) that insist that their values take precedence over those of public authorities and that therefore intellectuals who agree with them, or are members or supporters of these structures, ought to challenge public authorities when the values of these organizations are impaired in some way or are unfulfilled.

It is a minefield to find one's way amid these conflicting pressures. Some intellectuals have resolved the issue by avowing allegiances and operating in function of them—whether it is allegiance to a state or to a movement or to a church. Others have resolved this issue by trying to effectuate a radical separation of what they do as intellectuals/scientists/scholars (the search for scientific/scholarly truth) and the uses public authorities or their opponents make of the knowledge claims of the intellectuals. The shorthand name of this latter position is "value neutrality."

The two classic explications of these positions, familiar to most sociologists, are those of Max Weber and Antonio Gramsci. Weber, operating in an intellectual milieu (Wilhelmine Germany) in which the dominant academic figures of the universities espoused a position of fundamental support for the German state, resisted this position by making a claim for the virtue of value neutrality as the underpinning of sound scholarship. Gramsci, operating in an intellectual milieu (early-twentieth-century Italy) in which, in his view, intellectuals used the cover of value neutrality to support the liberal, bourgeois state, made the claim that one should be an "organic intellectual," that is, one who puts talents at the service of the social movement opposing the liberal state.

The problem with being an organic intellectual, whether committed to a social movement or to the state or to any other organization, is that those who are in leadership positions in the public arena tend in the long run to be pragmatists who pursue intermediate objectives and who therefore often change, are obliged to change, their short-range political positions. And the organic intellectual who is committed to supporting a given organization is called upon to follow the swings of position at the expense of intellectual consistency or even honesty. This is a good part of what explains the frequency with which such organic intellectuals become disillusioned and break intellectually and politically with the groups to whose support and direction they have been committed.

The alternative classical position is equally discomforting for the honest intellectual. The problem with espousing value neutrality is that it is intrinsically impossible to keep one's values from entering one's scientific/scholarly work. These values enter automatically at so many levels: at the level of the fundamental epistemology with which one approaches one's work; at the level of the choice of the objects of research; at the level of the choice of relevant evidence; at the level of the interpretation of the findings; at the level of the presentation of the findings. And all this becomes even worse in the frequent instances in which there are overt attempts to constrain the intellectual/scientist/scholar by those who control the material conditions of existence or the funding of research, which thereby accentuates the scientist's/scholar's dependence on presumed values. Weber himself understood this dilemma and therefore the limitations of value neutrality quite well, although this is less true of most of those who cite him as an authority on this question.

So, if it is almost impossible to be honest in the position of an organic intellectual and it is equally almost impossible to be honest in the claim of being value-neutral, what possible position is available to the intellectual in relation to the public realm? I should like to outline what seems to me the only reasonable stance. I believe the scientist/scholar has three functions that can never be evaded. They are linked functions, and sequential, but nonetheless each function involves a quite different task. The first function is that of seeking the most plausible analysis of the issues being investigated, both in detail and in their total context. I call this the intellectual function. The second function is that of evaluating the moral implications of the realities being investigated and effectuating a substantively rational choice.[1] I call this the moral function. And the third function is to analyze the best way of effectuating a realization of the moral good as the intellectual has analyzed it. I call this the political function.

I have said that scientists/scholars can never evade performing all three functions, however much they claim they can do so, and are doing so. This is the trap of the false claim of value neutrality, which asserts that the scientist/scholar is capable of isolating (and should perform only) the intellectual task and allow others (or oneself at other moments of time) to perform the moral and political tasks. In making this claim, one is burying (and thereby denying) the implicit moral and political choices that are in fact being made. But hiding them (from others and from oneself) does not mean that they are not being made. It simply means that it becomes much more difficult openly to discuss these choices and therefore to discuss the implications these choices have for the validity of the intellectual work being done or not being done.

Whereas espousing value neutrality seems to emphasize the intellectual task at the expense of the other two, it is not true that the organic intellectual is doing the opposite and being holistic. In fact, the organic intellectual is simply privileging the political task and hiding the fact that the intellectual and moral choices are being tacitly made, but once again hidden from view, and therefore one cannot openly discuss them, nor evaluate the degree to which the political choices are affecting the validity of the intellectual and moral choices.

How can one openly and sensibly engage in all three tasks? I have said they are sequential. I believe that the starting point is and has to be the intellectual task—the attempt to throw light upon, to analyze, the social reality under investigation. This is neither a micro nor a macro choice. This is neither a quantitative nor a qualitative choice. Micro/macro and quantitative/qualitative are simply dimensions of possible methodological tools that require ad hoc decisions as to their utility and validity in light of the issues under analysis and the data that are reasonably available or can be constructed to do the research. What is crucial is that all such analyses, whatever their immediate objective, be placed in the appropriate large-scale spatial context and the long-term temporal context (not merely the past but the relevant future) that is appropriate for the analysis.[2]

The intellectual analyses are no doubt always affected by one's moral predilections and one's political preferences. And whenever these predilections are not self-evident, the scholar/scientist should feel under the intellectual/moral/political obligation to make these presuppositions clear. Nonetheless, intellectual analyses have their own logic and therefore

their own relative autonomy. They are offered in the public sphere to the criticism of one and all and have to be reasonably robust, defensible logically, and historically plausible. They are to be sure always tentative and open to revision, but that does not mean that they are incapable of being taken as sound and momentarily true, meaning that the results may be employed by others in their subsequent analyses as presumptively correct and as evidence that reinforces the analyses of subsequent scientists/scholars.

Advocates of value neutrality would probably assent to this last paragraph but then say that this is where the responsibility of the intellectual stops. But it seems to me obvious that it never stops there. Anything that foresees a trend line foresees situations in which there are choices to be made. And the intellectual cannot afford to neglect not merely to indicate the likelihood and nature of such choices but also to indicate the moral implications of making one choice rather than another. The intellectual can do this only by invoking the sense of, appreciation of, the "good" (and not merely of the "true"). The scientist/scholar can argue that this is not her or his function, but then what is happening is that the reading of the implications of these choices is left to others and the intellectual analyst has merely acceded in advance to their evaluations and recommendations. The intellectual has not thereby avoided making the choices but has simply done so passively rather than actively. The intellectual remains responsible for the moral evaluations that are passively made as a result of the analyses.

Of course, there is the question of the basis on which we are to make our moral choices. This is not an intellectual question, in the sense that empirical analyses or theoretical syntheses lead one inevitably to particular moral choices. Moral choices are the outcome of one's moral philosophy (or, if you prefer, one's religious beliefs). And as we are all aware, there is a wide range of avowed moral philosophies. We can discuss them with each other, debate them, but we can never arrive at a decision which is in some analytic sense the true one (even if many, if not most, people are convinced that the one they hold is the only possible correct choice).

Nonetheless, moral choices are neither random nor accidental. They are the result of our moral education and our reflection. And the world is better off if there is inter-active reflection on the fundamental issues under debate. Here intellectuals/scholars/scientists can play a useful role, by clarifying the assumptions about reality that are hidden in the moral philosophies, and subjecting these assumptions about reality to standard scholarly/scientific analysis to see how plausible they are. In doing this, intellectuals may, at least, root out false debates and narrow the divergences about moral issues to what are really differing moral options. This will not end debate, even fierce debate, but it may make it somewhat more reasonable and therefore somewhat more amenable to possible social (that is, historical) compromises.

Nor does the game stop there. Once the intellectual has opted for the good—whether actively or passively—the next question is how one can arrive at the good. This is what we mean by a political task. The good is not a self-realization; it is the outcome of human choices. And the most superficial look at human history tells us that our collective choices have not always been for what we ourselves would define as the good. This is surely true for what lies ahead. Political choices are always being made. And once again the intellectual who has made the analysis and then perhaps indicated the moral choice among the real alternatives is deceiving him- or herself and the world in claiming that these choices are somehow not the responsibility of the analyst. As with the moral function, avoiding the assumption of responsibility for the political function is opting nonetheless for a political choice, but doing so passively and, one might add, surreptitiously. The political function is still being performed.

Political choices are, as anyone who has ever been active politically over long periods of time knows, by no means self-evident. We are all always puzzling why political choices that seem to us not merely desirable but in our view ones that should have been appealing to large majorities of the population are somehow not made. We cannot understand how bad choices continue to prevail. Here, too, the intellectual/scholar/scientist can play a useful political role. He or she can use the analyst's skills to attempt to answer the puzzles and thereby to help in the political process by pointing to alternative strategies and tactics that are more promising in realizing the good, as he or she has defined it in considering the moral options.

It is not necessarily that the intellectual/scholar/scientist is a better political analyst than the full-time politician/activist. It is that he or she may have a bit more psychological distance from the previous strategies/tactics employed, a bit less involvement of ego in maintaining the failing policies of the past, and therefore a slightly more "objective" analysis. In any case, political decisions are seldom individual ones. They are made by groups (whether self-defined or latent), and the group loses nothing (and potentially gains much) if the intellectual/

scholar/scientist adds his or her analyses to the public debate.

So, here we have it: the inescapable succession of tasks for the intellectual/scientist/scholar and the clear distinction nonetheless among the three tasks. None of them can be subordinated to the others. All are always being done, whether actively or passively. And doing them actively has the benefit of honesty and of permitting open debate about substantive rationality.

Notice two things about the successive tasks, as I have outlined them. They are not a prescription for particular modes of analysis, particular moral preferences, or particular political strategies or objectives. They remain the role of the intellectual/scientist/scholar no matter what views he or she holds. The tasks are there but will be performed differently whether one is, in the conventional sense, of the left, center, or right, however these terms be defined; whether one's morality is religious or secular; whether one's intellectual analyses are based on methodological individualism or world-systems analysis, or indeed anything else.

The second thing to notice is the meaning therefore of public sociology. I am not enamored of the term. It has the flavor of something special, a sub-branch of sociology, something one does part of the time alongside whatever else one does. I am trying to make the case that all sociologists—living, dead, or yet to be born—are, and cannot be other than, public sociologists. The only distinction is between those who are willing to avow the mantle and those who are not. And, in general, openness in science/scholarship is far more productive of useful results than engaging in work with hidden premises and preferences. We can never come close to a more universal universalism, a more plausible historical social science, a more reasonable accommodation of multiple readings of the good, and therefore ultimately a democratic political system if there is not greater openness in our public discussion. And in this activity, intellectuals/scientists/scholars cannot be, should not be, the laggards.

NOTES

1   *Substantive rationality* is, of course, Weber's term. However, for English users, it must be noted that this is a bad translation of the original German *Rationalität materiell*. Weber was referring to the ancient distinction of Greek philosophy between the formal and the material. Weber, in effect, and in detail if one reads him carefully, was asking us to take seriously the relevance to our own work of material as well as of formal rationality.

2   I refer the reader to my views of how this might best be done as outlined in Immanuel Wallerstein, *World-Systems Analysis: An Introduction,* Durham, NC: Duke University Press, 2004.

8 | Chapter Review

REVIEW QUESTIONS

1. What is the difference between applied, clinical, and public sociology?
2. According to the second article provided, what are the debates about the sociologist and his or her contribution to life outside of the university?
3. According to the articles, what is the future of the discipline of sociology?

CASE STUDY: THE SOCIOLOGIST AND THE PUBLIC SPHERE

Each chapter in this text has contained a case study and data exercise to assist in building your sociological imagination. Each of these concepts presented in the book's chapters has been applied to the analysis of social life and social problems. This chapter's case study article, "The Sociologist and the Public Sphere," is more of a philosophical exercise—one that asks questions about what role a sociologist *should or could* have in public spheres. While there is a general understanding among social scientists that sociology can be beneficial when applied, the details of how involved or how welcome such information is in various areas of public life has been debated over time. This article explores some of these questions and may be influential in your own thought process as to the potential incorporation of the discipline into everyday life and in commerce, industry, policy, government, and academia.

DEVELOPING THE SOCIOLOGICAL IMAGINATION
Applying Sociological Frameworks to a Study of Personal Identity

For this week's exercise in both an effort to not only apply sociology to the public spheres and the discussion of social problems but also to our own lives, please answer the following questions. These questions are intended to guide readers in how groups, structures, and networks have impacted reader's lives thus far and how an understanding of sociological concepts can benefit all of our futures.

What are the groups that have had the most influence on your socialization thus far? How has this impacted the understanding of yourself, your world, and your overall worldview?

We all have a unique set of social advantages and disadvantages. For example, your ethnicity or class standing may provide you with certain advantages in the society in which you live. Discuss your own unique set of both advantages and disadvantages. How might someone with a particular set *of advantages use them to assist those who experience disadvantage?*

Within your particular area of study or career, how might applying sociology or sociological principles or otherwise thinking sociologically benefit that area of study or area of work? For example, if you work with families, how might a sociological understanding of family dynamics benefit this work?

With what was discussed in this book, what stood out to you as most relevant to your own life course? How did (or does) this assist in understanding your past or present? How might this assist in defining your future as an individual as a member of society and as a member of various groups?

BRINGING IT ALL TOGETHER
Book Summation Exercise

Think of a social institution that has prominence in your life (whether that is the institution of family, education, work, or another of your choosing) and answer the following questions. This exercise follows the subheadings found in the second article in the first chapter, "How to Think Sociologically," and under the subheading "Thinking Sociologically."

What has been the historical purpose of this institution? What has been its social purpose? How has it created or otherwise supported social organization or social order?

What are some larger realities (challenges, etc.) that the institution itself may be facing within society or popular culture?

How do individual actions within this institution impact the institution itself? How does the institution impact individuals?

How is this institution experienced differently by different groups in society (i.e. different class groups, different race or ethnic groups, different genders, and so forth)?

What are some challenges or benefits of the institution that you experience? How might this be influenced by the larger social or cultural environment expectations surrounding this institution and its purpose for society?

What are some tangible examples of what this institution provides for society, and what are some latent (or unintended) consequences of this institution for society or the individual?

Printed in the USA
CPSIA information can be obtained
at www.ICGtesting.com
LVHW060426220823
755870LV00004B/27